FOURTH EDITION

REAL ESTATE
APPRAISAL
PRINCIPLES & PROCEDURES
2nd Printing

Walt Huber
Glendale Community College

Levin P. Messick, IFAC
Fullerton College
President, AC Appraisers, Inc.

William Pivar
Professor Emeritus

COPYRIGHT 2001, 2004, 2005, 2006, 2011, 2013 – 4th Edition, 2nd Printing
Educational Textbook Company, Inc.
P. O. Box 3597
Covina, California 91722
(626) 339-7733
FAX (626) 332-4744
etctextbooks.com

Library of Congress Cataloging-in-Publication Data

Huber, Walt - 1941
Real Estate Appraisal – Principles and Procedures / Walt Huber, Levin P. Messick, IFAC,
William Pivar

Summary: Covers all material required of college real estate appraisal classes. Very clear
and simple language, easy-to-read format with photographs, charts and cases. Includes
glossary and index.

1. Real property – Valuation.
2. Dwellings – Valuation.

Includes Index

HD 1387. H547 2001
333.33'82 - dc21

ISBN: **(10) 0-916772-76-4**
       (13) 978-0-916772-76-5

This publication is designed to provide accurate and authoritative information in regard
to the subject matter covered. It is sold with the understanding that the publisher is not
engaged in rendering appraisal, legal, accounting, or other professional services. If legal
advice or other expert assistance is required, the services of a competent professional
person should be sought.

Preface

REAL ESTATE APPRAISAL PRINCIPLES AND PROCEDURES, **by** Walt Huber, Levin P. Messick, IFAC, and William Pivar, is designed for students who wish to pursue real estate appraisal as a career. However, it is also written with other real estate professionals in mind. After all, what is real estate appraisal, but the application of economic theory to real estate to determine property value. Real estate brokers, salespersons, and loan officers can benefit from understanding why one property is worth more than another. In the field of real estate, competence is often judged by one's superior knowledge. A client's confidence is crucial in this business, and the more skill you possess, the better you are able to serve his or her needs.

Walter Huber and William Pivar are real estate professionals, each with over thirty years of college-level real estate instruction under his belt. They have authored over thirty textbooks between them. Their many years of experience as full-time professors have given them a unique perspective on students' strengths and weaknesses. Levin P. Messick of Fullerton College is a respected college appraisal instructor with over twenty-seven years experience as an independent fee appraiser, and the president of AC Appraisals, Inc., of Fullerton, California. He has graciously lent his knowledge and expertise to this endeavor, helping create this exceptional textbook.

Combining their knowledge and expertise, the authors have collaborated to write a text utilizing a time-saving format that simplifies, organizes, and highlights vital information. This method practically ensures the reader will be better able to grasp concepts, review material, and ultimately pass tests with ease. In addition to detailed outlines at the beginning of each chapter, the outline format is followed throughout the text, which makes looking up material a breeze.

We owe a special debt to Jack C. Flynn for his help with this newest edition of the textbook. Jack is an instructor of appraisal at Glendale Community College and has been teaching and practicing real estate for over 40 years. He owns the successful appraisal and real estate business, Anchor Pacific Company in San Marino California. He holds a life certificate with the Appraisal Institute, Senior Member of the American Society of Appraisers (ASA), National Association of Realtors® (NAR), Appraisal Division (GAA), and Certified General by the state of California.

We would also like to extend our thanks to the Appraisal Foundation for allowing us to provide brief quotes from USPAP, as well as the National Association of Independent Fee Appraisers for allowing us to print their codes of ethics. We also appreciate the firm of Marshall and Swift, the leader in residential and commercial building cost data, for giving us permission to reproduce many of their graphics. Day One, Bradford Technologies, Forms and Worms, and FREA were all most generous in providing us with the appraisal forms you will find in this book (endorsement not implied).

What's New in This Edition

We constantly strive to bring the Appraisal and Real Estate Student up to date.

Our tradition is to surpass, not just maintain, the reputation for excellence that this *Real Estate Appraisal (Principles and Procedures), 4th edition,* book has established in the appraisal, real estate, and educational community.

Updating the material in this book, which includes adding one of the most sweeping changes to affect the "appraisal loan industry" in decades—the **Uniform Appraisal Dataset (UAD)**—required by Fannie Mae and Freddie Mac (numbered forms that can only be filed electronically), is paramount to achieving our goal. Fannie Mae and Freddie Mac have taken the initiative to establish uniform forms and to standardize definitions and responses in the appraisal report. Translated, this means the most commonly used appraisal forms required to standardized language [definitions, numbers, and text boxes (type in)], signed and submitted electronically to the lenders on approved forms. This information is provided in its entirety in our **Appendix 5**.

Our interpretations of these new requirements *(in brackets [ ] and italics)* are inserted frequently throughout the book, where the authors believe it improves the student's understanding.

This UAD Edition has, at press time, the latest version of the UAD adopted by the secondary market. Keep in mind that the UAD is subject to change. Also, the Appraisal Foundation has expressed reservations that the current version could lead to misleading appraisals. Appraisers need to insure that their appraisals are first and foremost USPAP compliant. Your authors would also like to point out that not all appraisals are for loan purposes. In the final analysis, USPAP notes that the appraiser is required to ensure that sufficient information is added, in the form of an addendum, to any form report to keep it from misleading the client.

Note: A burgundy-framed box indicates that the material is from Appendix 5 (UAD).

USPAP and The UAD

Some users and readers of appraisal reports (such as borrowers) may not understand some of the standardized responses and abbreviations mandated by the UAD. Will appraisal reports completed using the UAD abbreviations conform to the USPAP?

Yes. Appraisers can include the UAD definitions and abbreviations from the Field-Specific Standardization Requirements as an addendum to the appraisal report so that users and readers of appraisal reports will be able to understand the UAD required standardized responses and definitions. Fannie Mae and Freddie Mac anticipate that most software vendors will facilitate this process by creating standard addenda for appraisers to include in the appraisal report. Appraisers remain responsible for ensuring compliance with USPAP requirements. When appropriate, an appraiser must supplement the information provided in any appraisal report form being used in order to comply with the appraisal reporting requirements of USPAP.

Acknowledgements

We would be remiss in our duties not to acknowledge the exceptional contributions of Colleen Taber, editor, Rick Lee, prepress editor and layout, as well as the creative talents of Philip Dockter, art director, Melinda Winters, cover art designer, and Troy Stacey, cover design.

We are grateful for the contributions made by appraiser Edward S. Stahl, Professor Emeritus, Solano College; Donna Grogan, CPM, El Camino College; William Nunally, Sacramento City College; Kim Tyler, Shasta College; Jim Michaelsen, Santa Rosa Junior College; Nick Zoumbos, Riverside College and Crafton Hills College; Joe Newton, Bakersfield College; the late Fred Martinez and Allan Nutall, City College of San Francisco; Martin Welc, Saddleback College; Elliot Dixon, East Los Angeles College; Frank Pangborn, Irvine Valley College; and Charles Ellis, Occidental College.

Our authors, although seasoned veterans themselves, welcome strategy advice from comrades in the trenches. We would like to thank the following professors for the time and effort they contributed with suggestions, critiques, and general input on the text:

John Aust, Ph.D, Santiago Canyon College
Carol A. Jensen, City College San Francisco
Steve Costello, CMDC (FNC Company), National Comparable Data Specialist
Ed Culbertson, Ph.D, Professor of Real Estate, MiraCosta College
Thomas Felde, Felde Publications
Jim Glickman, MAI, Sacramento City College
Wes Green, American River College
Donald Holman, Instructor, El Camino College
David Kemp, R.E. Instructor, Certified General Appraiser, Palomar College
Patrick McKinney, Instructor, Southwestern College
Marvin N. Nadler, West Los Angeles College, and U.C.L.A. Extension
D. Brian Shumway, Real Estate Appraisal Instructor, Mt. San Jacinto College
John Wallace, MAI, CCIM, San Diego Mesa College
Lloyd D. Werner, IFAS, DAC, Portland Community College

We thank the following appraisers and real estate professionals for their suggestions and contributions toward improving our textbook.

Rick Arellano, Appraiser
Assistant Professor Computer Applications
and Office Technology
Ohlone College
Fremont, CA

Sharon Bertolucci
Half Moon Bay, CA

Larry Bivens
AC Appraisals, Inc.
Fullerton, CA

Paul D. Bowen
Valuation and Environmental Consultant
Puyallup, WA

Michael R. Cartwright, CMA, ASA, RPG
Mineral Business Appraisal
Reno, NV

Elizabeth Champagne, MAI
CB Richard Ellis
San Francisco, CA

Donald Choice, MAI
San Diego, CA

Dennis Corrigan, CPA, CIA, E.E.
Xavier College
Chicago, IL

Steven G. Coull, IFAS, DAC
Canadian National Association
of Real Estate Appraisers
Qualicum Beach, BC

Tim Cullen
Tim Cullen Real Estate Appraisers
San Diego, CA

Denis DeSaix
Mike Baz
Metrocal Appraisal
Livermore, CA

Michael W. Dreier
Cabrillo College
Santa Cruz, CA

Frank Fanelli, ASA
Manager Real Estate Division
City of Oakland California
Oakland, CA

Paul Ganley
Arizona/California License
Scottsdale, AZ

Marge Haley
Martha Nolan
Laura Reeves
Lisa Cohen
San Mateo Assessor's Office
San Mateo, CA

Guy Hall
AC Appraisals, Inc.
Fullerton, CA

Michael Hamilton
Albuquerque, NM

George H. Harrison, Ph.D.
President
The Columbia Institute
San Antonio, TX

Amber Hatter
Ohlone College
Fremont, CA

Glen M. Higdon
Real Estate & Manufactured Home
Antioch, CA

Lori L. Horn, SRA
Burlingame, CA

Sanford T. Jones, III and Sanford T. Jones, IV
AC Appraisals, Inc.
Fullerton, CA

James Kaysen, WCGA
Kaysen Realty Valuation Company
Grafton, WI

Milan Krajci, Ph.D.
San Francisco, CA

Michael Layne
Fullerton, CA

Ric Love
Del Norte Appraisal Associates
Crescent City, CA

Betty J. Lowery
Irvine, CA

Arlette Lyons, GRI
Professor of Real Estate
Mt. San Antonio College
Walnut, CA

William Madia
Deena Coakley
Steven M. Bigel
KMB Appraisal Services, LTD
Crestwood, IL

Linda L. Manning
Residential, Industrial, Commercial, Land
Walnut Creek, CA

Calixto R. Manriquez, Inc.
San Jose, CA

Jeremy McCarty, SRA
Electronic Appraisal Solutions
Roseville, CA

Richard McCauley & Associates
Fresno, CA

George S. McLeod, IFAS
Houston, TX

Pete Mueller
Mueller Appraisal
Toledo, OH

Raul Nepomuceno
Union City, CA

John Norberg
Appraisal Research Corporation
San Jose State University
San Jose, CA

Stephen O'Leary
Lansing Community College
Lansing, MI

Robert D. Rodriguez
Timothy Glaser
Mighty Appraisal
West Hills, CA

Linda Serra
Glendale College
Glendale, CA

Margaret Singleton, MAI, SRA, ASA
San Diego, CA

Douglas G. Smith IFAS
Appraisal Services
Butte, MT

Crawford M. Spens
Longview, WA

Richard Stephan
Professor of Real Estate
Mt. San Antonio College
Walnut, CA

Ann Susko, IFA
Valleywide Appraisal Services
Phoenix, AZ

Larry Tack, IFA
Salinas, CA

Mike Tognotti
Location Cubed
San Mateo, CA

Dr. Dan J. Tosh, Ph.D., SCREA
P. O. Box 1287
Brentwood, CA

Sidney S. Uyetake, SRA
Uyetake, Uyetake & Associates Inc.
Honolulu, HI

T. Hugh Windsor, PCA
Stockton, CA

L.P. Woodard, Jr.
Placentia, CA

Mike Woods
Pam Woods
Factory Built Financial
Temecula, CA

R. H. Woodworth, IFAS
Highline Community College
Woodworth & Associates
Olympia, WA

Mary Ann Zamel
Professor of Real Estate
Mt. San Antonio College
Walnut, CA

Leonel Bello
City College of San Francisco

James Taylor
Long Beach City College

Barry A. Cleverdon
Sierra College

Mel Taylor
Los Angeles Trade-Tech College

Jeff Baker
Mt. San Antonio College

Faz Elahi
West Los Angeles College

Steve Sodergren
Antelope Valley College

Leslie Bellamy
Loa Angeles Southwest College

Table of Contents

Chapter 3:   The Appraisal Process   69

Chapter 5:   Data Collection and Analysis   143

Chapter 8: Cost Approach to Value   *257*

Real Estate Appraisal

Chapter 9: Sales Comparison Approach to Value 283

I. MARKET THEORY OF VALUE (p. 285)
II. REAL ESTATE MARKETS (p. 286)
   A. Description of Improvements (URAR) (p. 287)
III. COMPARABLE SALES (p. 292)
IV. STEPS IN THE SALES COMPARISON APPROACH (p. 292)
   A. Data Collection (p. 293)
   B. Verification of Data (p. 293)
   C. Selecting Units of Comparison (p. 295)
   D. Analysis and Adjustment of Comparable Prices (p. 296)
   E. Reconciliation of Comparable Value Indicators (p. 297)
V. THE ADJUSTMENT PROCESS (p. 297)
   A. Elements of Comparison (p. 298)
VI. ADJUSTMENT TECHNIQUES (p. 311)
   A. Paired Data Analysis (p. 312)
   B. Relative Comparison Analysis (p. 315)
   C. Analysis of Price Per Square Foot (p. 316)
VII. CALCULATION OF PERCENTAGE ADJUSTMENTS (p. 316)
VIII. SEQUENCE OF ADJUSTMENTS (p. 318)
IX. RECONCILIATION (p. 319)
X. CHAPTER SUMMARY (p. 322)
XI. CHAPTER QUIZ (p. 324)

Chapter 10: Income Approach to Value   329

I. USE OF THE INCOME APPROACH (p. 331)
II. INVESTOR'S PERCEPTION OF VALUE (p. 331)
   A. Rate of Return (p. 332)
   B. Competing Investment Opportunities (p. 334)
III. INCOME CAPITALIZATION (p. 334)
   A. Direct Capitalization (p. 335)
   B. Income Estimation (p. 336)
   C. Multipliers and Capitalization Rates (p. 340)
   D. Calculating Value by Direct Capitalization (p. 344)
   E. Yield Capitalization (p. 347)
IV. DISCOUNTING (p. 347)
   A. Compounding (p. 348)
   B. Annuities (p. 349)
   C. Yield Rates (p. 349)
V. CHAPTER SUMMARY (p. 352)
VI. CHAPTER QUIZ (p. 355)

xiv

Chapter 14: The Appraisal Profession   445

Chapter 15: Financial Institutions and Regulations   479

Editor's Note:

As the Uniform Standards of Professional Appraisal Practice (USPAP) are revised every two years, the references to USPAP in this text may become outdated. The reader is encouraged to obtain the latest edition of USPAP from the Appraisal Foundation's subscription service.

NEW!
Appendix 5 (UAD)
Appraisal Loan Standards

Social Media is Changing the Real Estate Appraisal Market

Meet Sassy, our Social Networking Butterfly®. She's there to remind you that using social networking sites should be an integral part of your business marketing strategy as a real estate appraiser. Most real estate professionals and appraisers are now using the Internet, smart phones, and social networking sites.

"Sassy's world of mobile connectivity today has impacted every aspect of real estate buying, selling, leasing, and appraisal, allowing us to improve our success for sellers, buyers, owners, and tenants." – Walt Huber

The website **appraiserforum.com** is a social networking site built specifically for appraisers in the industry. It offers a variety of forums for discussion, including appraisal education, appraisal review, commercial/industrial appraisals, Fannie Mae, Freddie Mac, USPAP, and the list goes on and on. There is also a form for members of the public to ask general appraisal questions.

Through appraisal social networking sites, you can access appraiser webinars, continuing education sites, and commercial software sites. In addition, social networking speeds up our advertising turn-around time. We no longer have to wait 3-5 days for an ad to appear in the classified section of the newspaper and then wait another day before responses start coming in. With a few clicks on your home computer or smart phone, you may get immediate results with virtually no downtime in the placing of the ad or the responses to that ad!

Not only can placing ads on sites save you time, but also money! For the time being anyway, many social networking sites are free, unlike expensive newspaper ads. The world of real estate is changing!

Although the authors do not endorse any particular websites, the following are some popular social networking sites:

Facebook is one of the most popular social networking sites being utilized by real estate professionals. It's a user-friendly, user-generated site that allows you to create a profile, join or start groups, and add applications to enhance your page. In addition to your personal profile, where you can include photos, interests, status updates, and more, you can also create groups and fan pages to connect with others who share a common cause or interest. (**Note:** Facebook rules prohibit the combining of social and business sites.)

YouTube is one of the essential networking sites now being used by real estate professionals. Virtual tours of properties can be taken by video phone and posted on YouTube in a matter of minutes. It's easy to use, inexpensive, and offers access to available properties to a universal audience, including local and international prospects.

LinkedIn is a business-oriented site mainly used for "professionals networking"—with a sort of "resume" posting appeal. When you join, you create a profile that summarizes your professional expertise and accomplishments. You then invite others from your sphere of influence to connect with you through the site. Your network consists of your connections, your connections' connections, and their connections (a "gated-access" approach).

Craigslist is a mostly free site where you can post properties for sale or for lease, or your services as a professional broker/salesperson or appraiser. It is quickly replacing the newspaper as the place to advertise real estate! It's easy to use and, with the exception of brokered apartments in New York City, costs nothing, and gets immediate responses to posts – no downtime!

Yellowpages.com is just what it sounds like—an online version of the yellow pages, but with exposure to millions of viewers unlike the paper version!

Twitter, another "hot" social networking site, is a micro-blogging site that allows users to post and read short messages (140 characters max) called "tweets." You can customize your profile with a company profile and photo, and Twitter provides some great applications, such as "**TweetLister**," that automatically posts a listing whenever it becomes available. The immediacy, far-reaching exposure, and no-cost factors make social networking sites like this an increasing substitution for traditional forms of marketing, like direct mail and newspaper advertising.

Popular appraisal-specific sites (no endorsement implied) include the following:

appraiserswatercooler.com
The Appraiser's Watercooler

appraisalword.com
Appraisal Word

appraisalscoop.com
Appraisal Scoop

appraisalpress.com/news/articles/reaching_new_clients_through_social_networking_sites/
Appraisal Press

Chapter 1
Introduction

KEY WORDS AND TERMS

Ad Valorem Taxes
Advisory Opinions
Appraisal
Appraisal Foundation
Appraisal Practice
Bundle of Rights
Consulting
Easement
Eminent Domain
Encumbrances
Escheat
Fee Simple
Fixtures
Improvement
Intended Use
Intended Users

Leasehold Estate
Lien
Life Estate
Personal Property
Police Power
Private Restrictions
Real Property
Review
Scope of Work
Special Assessment
Standard of Value
Trade Fixture
Uniform Appraisal Dataset (UAD)
Uniform Standards of Professional
    Appraisal Practice (USPAP)

LEARNING OBJECTIVES

In order to fill their vital role, appraisers must have a solid understanding of the nature of real estate and real property rights.

After completing this chapter, you should be able to:

1. define the terms "appraisal," "consulting," and "review" as they apply to appraisal practice;

2. describe the kinds of services that appraisers perform, and list some common uses of appraisals;

CHAPTER OUTLINE

3. define the terms "real estate" and "real property" as they are used in appraisal practice;
4. describe the various components of real estate, and explain how real estate is distinguished from personal property;
5. list the major types of real property interests, and describe their characteristics; and
6. describe the three powers of government that limit private property rights.

I. Why Appraisal Is Important

The appraisal of real estate is a vital function in our society. Appraisals are utilized in hundreds of different ways in both government and the private sector. The importance of the appraiser's role is reflected in the standards of professionalism established by the industry itself, as well as increasing government regulation of appraisal practices.

In the United States, more families own their own homes than in any other nation in the world. Ownership is a prime goal of families and is likely to represent the largest single purchase of their lives. However, our society is mobile, with employment changes as well as family and income changes resulting in relocation. The result is that the average homeowner requires a valuation and sale and a valuation and purchase several times within their lives.

In the stock market, we deal with homogeneous shares. Since shares are equal and there is a central organized marketplace, at any given time an exact price buyers are willing to pay and sellers are willing to sell can be determined.

Real estate, unlike shares of stock, is not homogeneous. Every property has differences from other properties. Even identical new structures are sited on different lots. In addition, real estate marketplaces are local in nature so property values vary geographically.

Appraisal gives order to the real estate and mortgage markets. Estimates based on appraisal principles and judgment of appraisers are relied upon by lenders, buyers, and sellers in their decision-making process.

II. Definition of Appraisal

APPRAISAL: (noun) The act of developing an opinion of value: an opinion of value (see page 585 for full USPAP definition).

An appraisal must be numerically expressed as a specific amount, as a range of numbers, or as a relationship (e.g., not more than, not less than) to a previous value opinion or numerical benchmark (e.g. assessed value, collateral value).

A. OPINION

The two key words in this definition are "opinion" and "value." An appraisal is an opinion because it relies significantly on the appraiser's professional judgment and experience.

Anyone may estimate, but only professionals render opinions. A person who is offered goods or services and declines to make a purchase at the offered price has made an estimate of value and possibly decided that the price is too high. This estimate, however, is often arrived at based on feelings or "gut instinct" as it is often called.

Appraisal utilizes an orderly process. An **ORDERLY PROCESS** *is a logical series of steps that are taken in order to ensure a reliable result.* This orderly process begins with the education and knowledge required of an appraiser. All fifty states and the federal government have minimum educational and experience requirements for the licensing of real estate appraisers. This helps to insure a higher level of competency on the part of the appraiser. In addition, various appraisal organizations have appraisal designation programs to add to and refine this competency. In valuing properties, professionals utilize the Appraisal Process, consisting of a series of steps (covered in Chapter 3). Additionally, appraisers are required to adhere to the Uniform Standards of Professional Appraisal Practice (USPAP). This helps ensure that data collection and reporting is carried out in an orderly fashion that is both useful and understandable by the appraiser's clients. The standards also require high uniform standards of competency and ethics on the part of practitioners. Adherence to the orderly process not only helps to maintain this level of competency, but also to ensure clients of the reliability of the professional appraiser's opinion of value.

B. VALUE

VALUE: The monetary relationship between properties and those who buy, sell, or use those properties (see page 585 for full USPAP definition).

Value expresses an economic concept. As such, it is never a fact but always an opinion of the worth of a property at a given time in accordance with a specific definition of value. In appraisal practice, value must always be qualified-for example, market value, liquidation value, or investment value.

We will see in Chapter 2 that market forces determine value. An appraiser's opinion is what he or she believes the value to be.

C. APPRAISAL – ART OR SCIENCE?

While the theory and techniques used in appraisal have a scientific basis, their application more closely resembles an art. This is because an appraiser must use his or her judgment when considering factors that are subjective. Subjective factors can include design, location, anticipated changes in use, or expected economic changes in the marketplace, to name just a few. Large differences in the value of a single property appraised by several appraisers can often be attributed to a misapplication of theory or process or of mathematical errors. Large value differences can also occur when appraisers offer their services in market areas and with property types with which they are unfamiliar or unqualified to appraise. A mistake of this nature is a reflection on the judgment of the appraiser. For some, good judgment is only developed from long experience, and for others never at all. An appraisal mentor of one of the authors claims that a good appraisal has ten parts. Five of the parts are: honesty, experience, theory, knowledge, and proper process. The other five parts are good old-fashioned common sense (judgment).

D. APPRAISAL PRACTICE

APPRAISAL PRACTICE: Valuation services performed by an individual acting as an appraiser, including but not limited to appraisal, appraisal review, or appraisal consulting (see page 585 for full USPAP definition).

Appraisal practice is provided only by appraisers, while valuation services are provided by a variety of professionals and others. The terms appraisal, appraisal review, and appraisal consulting are intentionally generic and are not mutually exclusive. For example, an opinion of value may be required as part of an appraisal review and is required as a component of the analysis in an appraisal consulting assignment. The use of other nomenclature for an appraisal, appraisal review, or appraisal consulting assignment (e.g., analysis counseling, evaluation, study, submission, or valuation) does not exempt an appraiser from adherence to the Uniform Standards of Appraisal Practice.

E. CONSULTING

CONSULTANTS often provide services to clients that deal with marketability and development analysis, land use, and investment analysis. This work may or may not require the appraiser/consultant to render value judgments (see page 585 for full USPAP definition)

An appraisal consulting assignment involves an opinion of value but does not have an appraisal or an appraisal review as its primary purpose.

The Uniform Standards of Professional Appraisal Practice (USPAP) are very clear that the appraiser/consultant must not advocate (champion) the client's interest. For this reason, the appraiser/consultant must label all of his/her work as a consultation. This is because the appraiser/ consultant is acting as an advisor for a specific client. The advice that is good for a specific client's interests might not be good advice for others.

F. REVIEW

Another type of work performed by some appraisers is appraisal review.

APPRAISAL REVIEW: The act or process of developing and communicating an opinion about the quality of another appraiser's work that was performed as part of an appraisal, appraisal review, or appraisal consulting assignment (see page 585 for full USPAP definition).

The subject of an appraisal review assignment may be all or part of a report, workfile, or a combination of these.

III. History of Appraisal

The roots of the modern real estate appraisal industry in the United States can be traced back to "Black Monday," the start of the Great Depression in 1929. Prior to that time, appraisal was not viewed as a separate occupation. Few people specialized in appraisal practice, and those who did often lacked a good understanding of value theories. Commonly accepted standards and guidelines for the appraisal process were virtually non-existent.

In 1929, the first nationally-recognized standards for appraisal practice were published by the Appraisal Division of the National Association of Real Estate Boards (now known as the National Association of Realtors®). The Appraisal Division became the American Institute of Real Estate Appraisers in 1932. The Society of Residential Appraisers, one of the oldest professional appraisal associations in the U.S., was also founded at about the same time. In 1990, this organization merged with the American Institute of Real Estate Appraisers to form the Appraisal Institute.

 appraisalinstitute.org

Over the course of the next 50 years, the demand for professional appraisal services grew. But even though appraisers were then better educated in the tools of their trade, there was still very little regulation of the appraisal industry, and no uniform standards for appraiser qualification or appraisal practice.

The *GARN-ST. GERMAIN DEPOSITORY INSTITUTIONS ACT* *removed many regulator restraints from the savings and loan industry.* Abusive practices led to high risk loans, losses, and a government bailout of failed savings and loan institutions.

Because of the belief that unrealistic appraisals were a significant factor in the failure of many lending institutions, the *FINANCIAL INSTITUTIONS REFORM, RECOVERY, AND ENFORCEMENT ACT (FIRREA)* *requires state licensing and certification for appraisers, and established the requirement for nationwide competency standards and Uniform Standards of Practice for Professional Appraisers.*

A. APPRAISAL FOUNDATION

In response to FIRREA, some of the larger appraisal organizations in the country jointly founded the **APPRAISAL FOUNDATION,** *to set standards for appraisals and appraiser qualification for both licensing and certification.*

Licensing and certification authority was given to the states, to be overseen by the Appraisal Foundation Under Title XI of FIRREA.

 appraisalfoundation.org

Licensing and certification was given to the Appraisal Foundation under section 103 of FIRREA (Title XI). State regulatory agencies are monitored by the Appraisal Subcommittee, which is also responsible for monitoring the actions of the Appraisal Foundation and the Federal financial institutions regulatory agencies.

While states are allowed to set forth their own standards for appraisal licensing and certification, they must conform with those appraisal standards set forth by the Appraiser Qualifications Board of the Appraisal Foundation.

The standards of the Appraisal Foundation apply to "federally related transactions."

FEDERALLY RELATED TRANSACTIONS *are transactions involving a federal agency or regulatory agency.* The original definition of Federally Related Transactions was contained in FIRREA (TITLE XI, section 1121) and is as follows:

> The term "federally related transaction" means any real estate-related financial transaction which:
>
> (A) A federal financial institutions regulatory agency or the Resolution Trust Corporation engages in, contracts for or regulates; and
>
> (B) Requires the services of an appraiser.

This new law did nothing to stop excesses in the lending industry. Unsafe lending practices would lead to the collapse of the financial markets in 2008. This collapse led to the adoption of the SAFE Act, the HVCC, Appraisal Management Companies, and finally the passage of the Financial Reform Act. (See *Residential Appraisal and Report Writing*, by Huber and Messick, for more details.)

Exempt from the requirements of a licensed or certified appraiser are residential transactions of $250,000 or less and nonresidential transactions of $1 million or less.

IV. Purposes and Uses of Appraisals

The potential uses of land are influenced by geographic, legal, social, and economic considerations. These considerations form the background against which appraisal activities are conducted.

A. STANDARDS OF APPRAISAL

The Appraisal Standards Board of the Appraisal Foundation has developed Uniform Standards of Professional Appraisal Practice (USPAP). Applicable standards will be referenced throughout this text.

Title XI, Section 1110 of FIRREA states:

Each federal financial institution's regulator agency and the Resolution Trust Corporation shall prescribe appropriate standards for the performance of real estate appraisals in connection with federally related transactions under the jurisdiction of each such agency or instrumentality. These rules shall require at a minimum:
(1) that real estate appraisals be performed in accordance with generally accepted standards as evidenced by the appraisal standards promulgated by the Appraisal Standards Board of the Appraisal Foundation; and
(2) that such appraisals shall be written appraisals. Each such agency or instrumentality may require compliance with additional standards if it makes a determination that such additional standards are required in order to properly carry out its statutory responsibilities.

B. STATEMENTS

The Appraisal Foundation has adopted Statements which are considered an integral part of the Standards of Professional Appraisal Practice. These Statements illustrate how the requirements of the standards are to be applied in various situations.

C. ADVISORY OPINIONS

Advisory Opinions are issued by the Appraisal Standards Board.

These opinions do not establish new standards. Their purpose is to illustrate the applicability of standards to specific situations. (They are not legal opinions.)

D. INTENDED USE, INTENDED USERS, AND STANDARD OF VALUE (PURPOSE)

Formerly, in appraisal practice the terms "purpose and use" of an appraisal were used. As in any living profession, the descriptive language of the profession changes over time. The word "purpose" has been replaced by the term "standard of value" in an attempt to reduce the confusion many people experienced in drawing a distinction between the terms "purpose and use."

STANDARD OF VALUE refers to the type of value information that the client wants the appraiser to supply. In other words, is the client looking for market value, insurance value, tax value, value in use, investment value, etc? (Value will be discussed at length in Chapter 2.)

INTENDED USE refers to what the client plans to do with the appraisal. Some intended uses might be: providing a loan, determining value for condemnation purposes, determining a property's value to settle an estate, and determining how much to insure a building for, to name just a few.

INTENDED USERS refers to the client or clients. Is there more than one reader of the report? Will others, aside from just the client, be relying on the information presented in the report?

As might be imagined, the answers to these questions set the level of research and development as well as the depth and complexity of the report that will be generated. *Appraisers refer to the development and reporting process, based on these factors, as the SCOPE OF WORK* (see Chapter 12).

The following is a list of possible intended users and intended uses of an appraisal. It is not all inclusive, but is intended to give the student an idea of the bewildering array of uses for which clients seek to use appraisals. As can be easily seen, an appraisal for one intended user and intended use may not work for some other intended user or intended use.

Appraisals are used by and for:

1. sellers to set asking prices and evaluate offers;
2. buyers to determine offering prices;
3. lenders to evaluate security for loans;

4. insurance companies and their clients to determine the amounts of insurance coverage;

5. builders and developers to assess project feasibility;

6. landlords to set rent rates and lease terms;

7. government agencies to set just compensation for property condemnations;

8. taxing authorities and taxpayers to determine the amounts due for property, income, estate and gift taxes;

9. land use planners to help guide decisions in regard to zoning and other public land use restrictions;

10. businesses to evaluate investment opportunities, comply with financial regulations, and assist in mergers or stock offerings;

11. parties in legal proceedings to provide evidence for their claims;

12. parties in marriage dissolution;
(In Santa Monica, California, a divorce settlement was based on an appraisal that resulted in one spouse receiving the rent-controlled apartment and the other spouse receiving the BMW.)

13. courts and executors to determine distribution of estates and division of property;

14. parties involved in trades to balance out the relative values;

15. listing agents to realistically propose listing prices;

16. owners in their estate planning so they can decide on distribution and avoid taxes by keeping their estates below the estate tax limit through gifts to prospective heirs while alive; and

17. partners in partnership dissolution.

E. CAREER OPPORTUNITIES

Most appraisers are employed in one of two basic categories. *STAFF APPRAISERS are employed by a business, government agency, or other organization, to perform appraisal services that relate to the employer's operations.* For example, a staff appraiser may be an employee of an insurance company, and perform appraisals related to the company's insurance business.

In contrast, *INDEPENDENT FEE APPRAISERS are either self-employed or work for companies whose primary business is to provide appraisal services to others.* They may perform appraisals for many different clients. Independent fee appraisers (or the appraisal companies that employ them) normally charge a separate fee for each appraisal assignment. Staff appraisers, on the other hand, are compensated in the form of hourly wages or salary.

naifa.com
(National Association of Independent Fee Appraisers)

Some of the most important employers of appraisers include:

1. independent fee appraisal companies;
2. federal, state, and local government agencies concerned with taxation, and use, land or property management, construction, or loan guarantees;
3. financial institutions such as banks, credit unions, mortgage companies, and savings and loan associations;
4. insurance companies;
5. real estate developers;
6. large corporations with significant real estate assets;
7. Real Estate Investment Trusts, to evaluate property to be purchased; and
8. franchisors to evaluate lease values.

F. REAL ESTATE

Earlier in this chapter, we saw that the purpose of most appraisals is to estimate a defined type of value for a particular interest in a particular property as of a specified date. Obviously, the concept of property is of vital importance in the appraisal process. In general, property can be defined as anything that can be owned. Appraisers estimate the value of many different sorts of property, including such things as land, buildings, businesses, artwork, and antiques. For the purposes of this book, however, we are concerned only with the appraisal of real estate.

1. Definitions of Real Estate

In appraisal practice, the term real estate has a very specific meaning. The Uniform Standards of Professional Appraisal Practice defines *REAL ESTATE* as *"an identified parcel or tract of land, including improvements, if any."* For appraisal purposes, a parcel or tract of land is identified by its formal legal description, which precisely locates the boundaries of the parcel. (Legal descriptions are discussed in detail in Chapter 4.)

In theory, a parcel of land consists of an inverted pyramid, with its peak at the center of the earth and its sides extending through the surface boundaries of the parcel and out into space (see **Figure 1-1**). So *OWNERSHIP OF LAND includes ownership of the sub-surface below and the airspace above, as well as ownership of the surface of the land.* Things that occur naturally on or in the land, such as minerals, vegetation, or bodies of water, are often considered part of the land as well.

The second component of real estate, in addition to land, is improvements. An *IMPROVEMENT is something that is added to the land by human effort such as utilities, buildings, or landscaping.* It is something that was not originally part of the real estate, but has become so by virtue of being attached to the land or closely associated with it in some way. Improvements are often referred to as fixtures, because they are usually affixed to the land (or to other fixtures on the land such as buildings) in a relatively permanent fashion.

Figure 1-1

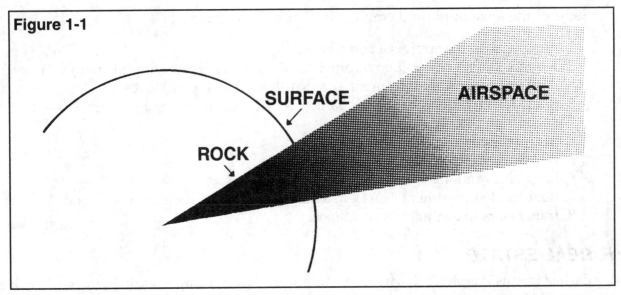

A *FIXTURE is an item, which was formerly personal property, that has become real property* (see **Figure 1-2**).

Figure 1-2   Test to Determine if an Item is a Fixture:

M 1. Method of attachment (How easily removable or permanently attached?)
A 2. Adaptability (Is the item attached by plumbing or plaster or just plugged in?)
R 3. Relationship of the parties (A landlord's purchase doesn't leave with the tenant.)
I 4. Intention (Personal property should not be permanently attached.)
A 5. Agreement (Any item can be personal property if agreed to in writing.)

In the textbook, we sometimes place an acronym in front of a word to help you remember! MARIA represents the first letter of each numbered sentence.

Case/Example: A stack of lumber sitting in a garage is not an improvement. But lumber in a fence on the property becomes attached to the land and constitutes an improvement or fixture that is part of the real estate.

V. Distinguishing Real Estate from Personal Property

Real estate, or real property, is distinguished from **PERSONAL PROPERTY**, *which is property that is not real estate.*

In most real estate appraisals, the value of personal property items is excluded from the estimated real estate value. So an appraiser must be able to distinguish between items that are part of the real estate, and items that are personal property. While most items fall squarely into one category or the other, the distinction between real estate and personal property is not always easy to make.

A. METHOD OF ATTACHMENT

The legal tests for determining whether an item is real estate or personal property vary some what from state to state, but they all tend to address the same basic issues. A key consideration is the method of attachment of the item to the real estate. Movable items are usually personal property; immovable items are usually real estate.

The harder it is to remove something from the land, the more likely it is to be considered real estate, and vice versa.

Case/Example: A manufactured home that is mounted on wheels and connected to temporary utility hookups is likely to be viewed as personal property. But the same manufactured home, if attached to a permanent foundation in the same location, would probably be considered part of the real estate.

B. ADAPTABILITY

A second consideration in distinguishing real estate from personal property is the adaptability of the item to the real estate. In other words, items are more likely to be part of the real estate if they are specifically designed to function as part of it.

Case/Example: The keys to a house are normally considered part of the real estate, because their function is so closely tied to the particular property. Their adaptability makes them part of the real estate even though they are not physically attached to it in any way.

C. RELATIONSHIP OF THE PARTIES

The relationship of the parties and which one put in the personal property fixture can determine who has the claim on the real estate.

For example, if a lender repossessed a property and installed an air conditioner, the courts would probably determine that their purpose was to repair the property and planned to include it in the sale.

D. INTENTION OF THE INTERESTED PARTIES

The third major factor that affects classification of items as real estate or personal property is the intention of the interested parties. In the sale of a house, for example, the buyer and seller may agree that a certain antique light fixture is not part of the real estate, and will be removed and taken away by the seller.

E. AGREEMENT OF THE PARTIES

The ownership of the fixtures can be determined from their expressed agreement, (as in the case of the light fixture above), or by the surrounding circumstances. For example, tenants often install fixtures in rented properties, with the intention of removing them at the conclusion of the lease. In the absence of any agreement to the contrary, such tenant-installed items are usually considered the personal property of the tenant, even if attached.

While intention of the parties is the most important test of a fixture where the question is "Does it belong to the buyer or the seller?", for lenders and borrowers it is "Is the item part of the real estate so as to be covered by the loan?"

If NOT specifically covered in the loan agreement, a court could determine that the items are personal property, although the lender assumed otherwise.

In some cases, appraisers included property in their appraisals which were later determined to be personal property. The defaulting borrowers removed the property, leaving inadequate security for the lenders.

Assume an appraiser was to appraise a parcel of land on which there was a manufactured home. The inclusion of the manufactured home value in the appraisal could leave the lender with little security if it is later determined that the manufactured home did not qualify as real property. State law governs the classification of manufactured homes. Generally, they must be on permanent foundations and subject to real estate taxation rather than license fees to be regarded as real property.

An appraiser should protect lenders and buyers by pointing out any gray area as to the property so that it would be indicated in the loan agreement or purchase contract of the parties that items were to be regarded as personal or real property.

F. TRADE FIXTURES

Fixtures that are installed by a tenant in connection with the operation of a business on the leased property are known as TRADE FIXTURES. It is commonly accepted that such fixtures remain the personal property of the tenant (unless specifically agreed otherwise), and may be removed by the tenant when the lease expires. The tenant is, however, responsible for repairing any damage caused to the real estate by removing the items.

VI. Real Property

The terms real estate and real property are often used interchangeably. *REAL ESTATE is the physical land and improvements, while REAL PROPERTY is "the interests, benefits, and rights inherent in the ownership of real estate."* These include the land, anything permanently attached or affixed to the land, anything incidental or appurtenant to the land, and anything immovable by law. The value that is estimated in a real estate appraisal is always the value of a specific, defined real property interest.

A. BUNDLE OF RIGHTS

Real property ownership is often described as a "bundle of rights" that pertains to a parcel of real estate.

Ownership is like a bundle of sticks, each stick is a right.

A bundle of rights may have lots of sticks (rights) or just one stick (right); it is not how many sticks you have but what is the value of each stick (right). The *BUNDLE OF OWNERSHIP RIGHTS includes the right to "use," "enjoy," "exclude others" and "occupy" the property, to "sell" it or "lease" it, to "encumber" it (as by a mortgage lien, for example) and to "dispose" of it by the use of a will.*

The ownership rights to a particular parcel may include appurtenant rights as well. An *APPURTENANCE is something that goes along with the ownership of land.*

Common examples of appurtenances include such things as easements and riparian water rights.

Case/Example: A property that does not have direct access to a public street will usually have an easement for right-of-way across some adjacent parcel. The right to use the right-of-way for access is part of the bundle of ownership rights that goes with ownership of the property.

Because real estate appraisals are always concerned with a defined real property interest, appraisers must have a good understanding of the characteristics of the different types of interests. **Figure 1-3** lists some of the most common interests in real property. As you can see from this list, one of the most important features of a real property interest is whether or not it entitles the holder to possession of the real estate. *POSSESSORY INTERESTS are called estates, while* **NON-POSSESSORY INTERESTS** *are known as encumbrances.*

B. ESTATES

An *ESTATE is a real property interest that includes the exclusive right to occupy and use the real estate (the right to possession).* In an estate, the right to possession may exist in the present, or it may be a future right. For example, an owner who leases her property gives up the right of possession to the tenant for the term of the lease. However, the owner still has an estate, because she is entitled to regain possession when the lease expires at some future time.

1. Freehold Estates (Fee Simple and Life)

Estates are further subdivided according to whether or not they include title to the property. *An estate that includes title is a* **FREEHOLD ESTATE**, *while an estate that includes possession without title is a* **LEASEHOLD ESTATE**.

Figure 1-3

Types of Real Property

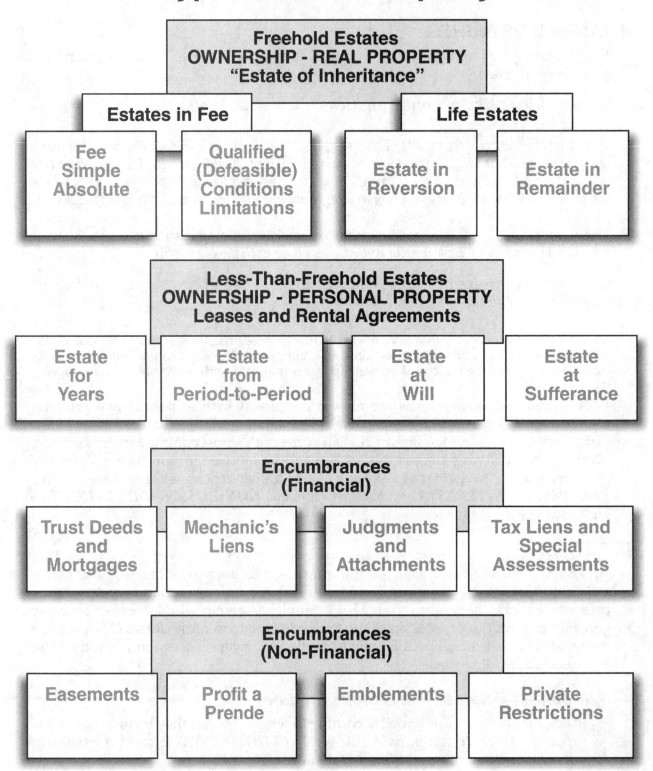

Freehold Estates
OWNERSHIP - REAL PROPERTY
"Estate of Inheritance"

Estates in Fee

Fee
Simple
Absolute

Qualified
(Defeasible)
Conditions
Limitations

Life Estates

Estate in
Reversion

Estate in
Remainder

Less-Than-Freehold Estates
OWNERSHIP - PERSONAL PROPERTY
Leases and Rental Agreements

Estate
for
Years

Estate
from
Period-to-Period

Estate
at
Will

Estate
at
Sufferance

Encumbrances
(Financial)

Trust Deeds
and
Mortgages

Mechanic's
Liens

Judgments
and
Attachments

Tax Liens and
Special
Assessments

Encumbrances
(Non-Financial)

Easements

Profit a
Prende

Emblements

Private
Restrictions

The most common freehold estate is the fee simple, often referred to as simply the "fee." The *FEE SIMPLE is the most complete and comprehensive form of real property interest; it includes the entire bundle of rights.* It is also the most commonly appraised interest in residential real estate appraisals.

A second type of freehold estate is the life estate. A *LIFE ESTATE is similar to the fee simple, except that it terminates automatically upon someone's death, either the death of the person holding the life estate (the life tenant), or the death of some other person designated as the measuring life.* The person who is designated to receive title to the property after the end of the life estate has an estate in reversion or an estate in remainder. *The party (grantor) granting a life estate is said to hold an ESTATE IN REVERSION. If an owner granting a life estate names another person to receive title upon the death of the current life estate holder, that other person claims an ESTATE IN REMAINDER.* Life estates are a relatively rare form of real property.

The value of a life estate would be affected by the benefits the property offers and the life expectancy of the holder of the life estate. Similarly, the value of reversionary or remainder interests would be based on the property value and the life expectancy of the holder of the life estate.

In some major cities, apartments that have been converted to condominiums have tenants who cannot be evicted because of rent control. The units are nevertheless appraised and sold at values which consider the life expectancy of the tenant in possession.

2. Leasehold Estates (Tenancy For Years and Periodic)

A tenant or lessee under a lease has a real property interest called a leasehold estate. The rights that accompany a leasehold estate are determined by the terms of the lease agreement. The most important of these rights is the exclusive right to use and occupy the leased real estate for the specified lease term, but the lease agreement may give the lessee other rights with respect to the property as well. For example, the lease may specify that the lessee is entitled to transfer or sublease his interest to a third party.

Leases are classified according to how and when they are terminated.

A lease that terminates on a specific date (such as a lease for six months or one year) creates a TENANCY FOR YEARS. A lease that automatically renews itself until one of the parties takes action to terminate it (such as a month-to-month lease) creates a PERIODIC TENANCY.

If a tenant remains in possession of the leased property after the termination of a tenancy for years or periodic tenancy, the result is a tenancy at will or a tenancy at sufferance. In a *TENANCY AT WILL, the landlord agrees to let the tenant remain in possession for an indefinite period of time, usually until agreement can be reached on the terms of a new lease.* In a **TENANCY AT SUFFERANCE**, *the tenant is remaining in possession without the express consent of the landlord.* Either of these two tenancies can be terminated by either party at any time.

The value of a leasehold interest can be important in division of interests such as in estates, partnership dissolution and when marriages end. In addition, when property is taken by eminent domain, the tenant might be entitled to compensation for his or her leasehold interest.

In some areas of the country there are a great many homes built on leased land, such as Indian leases. The appraiser should consider the term remaining on the lease, the likelihood of renewal and lease conditions in the appraisal of the leasehold interests.

C. ENCUMBRANCES

The second major category of real property interests is encumbrances. *ENCUMBRANCES are interests that do not include the exclusive right to use and occupy real estate; in other words, they are non-possessory interests.* Encumbrances may be financial interests such as mortgages, or non-financial interests such as easements.

1. Financial Encumbrances

Financial encumbrances are commonly known as "liens" or "security interests."

A *LIEN is an interest that is held by a creditor. It gives the creditor the right to sell the debtor's real estate and use the proceeds of the sale to pay off the debt, in the event that the debtor does not pay the debt according to its terms. The forced sale of property to satisfy a debt is referred to as* **FORECLOSURE**.

Liens can be classified as either "voluntary" or "involuntary," and also as either "general" or "specific."

A *VOLUNTARY LIEN is a security interest that is created voluntarily by the debtor.* Mortgages and deeds of trust that are used to secure loans are common examples of voluntary liens.

INVOLUNTARY LIENS arise through the operation of law. They include such liens as tax liens, judgment liens, and construction liens.

A *GENERAL LIEN is a lien that affects all of the real estate owned by the debtor.* Judgment liens are usually general liens, since they apply to any property that the judgment debtor owns. *SPECIFIC LIENS, on the other hand, apply only to a particular property or group of properties.* Voluntary liens (such as mortgages) are usually specific liens, since they usually specify the particular property or properties that will serve as security for the mortgage debt. Some types of involuntary liens (such as property tax liens or construction liens) are also specific to a particular property.

2. Non-Financial Encumbrances

Unlike financial encumbrances, non-financial encumbrances affect the use of real estate.

The three most common forms of non-possessory use rights are easements, profits, and private restrictions.

a. Easements

An *EASEMENT is a non-exclusive right to use someone else's property for a particular purpose. A property that is subject to an easement is known as a SERVIENT (BURDENED) TENEMENT*.

Case/Example: If your neighbor has a right-of-way easement across your property for purposes of access, your property is the servient tenement. *Your neighbor's benefited property would be called the DOMINANT TENEMENT*.

In the example above, the **RIGHT-OF-WAY** *is a servient tenement, because it benefits a particular parcel of real estate (the dominant tenement)*. Because the easement is for the benefit of the real estate, it is a right that is appurtenant to ownership of the benefited parcel. If the property was sold, the easement right would pass to the new owner along with the rest of the ownership rights in the property.

In contrast to appurtenant easements, *EASEMENTS IN GROSS do not benefit a particular parcel of real estate; they benefit individuals or organizations*. An easement that is granted to a utility company for installation and maintenance of utility lines is a common example of an easement in gross.

An abstract of title, preliminary title insurance policy, or property profile would show easements of record which might not be evident from a physical inspection.

Case/Example: An underground utility or the future right to place transmission lines over a property would not be evident from physical inspection. Conversely, prescriptive easement rights would not be a matter of record but would likely be discovered by physical inspection of the property.

b. Profit a Prendre

A *PROFIT A PRENDRE is a right to take something from the property such as crops, fruit, gravel, timber, or minerals*. It is a negative encumbrance that diminishes the value of the property.

A profit a prendre differs from an easement, which is merely the right to use, in that it confers on another the right to take something from the property.

A profit a prendre is also different than a lease for minerals or oil and gas in that there are NO royalties paid to the landowner.

c. Emblement

An *EMBLEMENT is the "one time" right of a tenant to harvest a crop that he/she had planted prior to a sale of the property.* That right extends only to the first crop after the sale. It does not diminish the value of the property. An emblement should not be confused with a profit a prendre, which is an "on-going" right to grow and harvest a crop.

d. Private Restrictions

Some of the most common non-financial encumbrances for residential real estate are *PRIVATE RESTRICTIONS, also known as private deed restrictions or covenants, conditions, and restrictions (CC&Rs).* These restrictions are created by deed, usually at the time when a subdivision is created. The subdivision developer creates the restrictions, and includes them in the deeds that transfer ownership of each of the subdivision lots to their individual owners.

Private restrictions are a form of land use regulation, similar to zoning.

They can cover a wide range of subjects, including building sizes and styles, fence heights, landscaping, parking, and even what sort of pets may be kept on the property.

The big difference between private restrictions and zoning is that private restrictions are NOT enforced by the government.

They must be enforced by the private landowners in the subdivision to which they apply, usually through some sort of homeowners' association.

VII. Government Restrictions of Property Rights

Earlier in this chapter, we saw that the fee simple interest in real estate is the most complete and comprehensive form of real property interest. But even though the fee simple owner has the full bundle of ownership rights, his or her control of the real estate is not absolute.

All private ownership rights are subject to the legitimate powers of government, including the powers of eminent domain, taxation, police power and escheat.

A. EMINENT DOMAIN

EMINENT DOMAIN is the power of government to take private property for public use, provided that just compensation is paid to the private property owner for the taking. If a government agency cannot acquire needed property through a voluntary sale by the owner, it may use the power of eminent domain to file a condemnation lawsuit, forcing the owner to give up the property in return for just compensation.

Condemnation lawsuits commonly require the services of appraisers to give expert testimony regarding the fair value of the condemned property.

B. TAXATION

Ownership of real estate is subject to taxation in the form of general property taxes and special assessments. General property taxes are usually assessed on an annual basis, and they apply to all properties that are not exempted by law. Because they are based on the value of the real estate, they are often referred to as *AD VALOREM TAXES, which is Latin for "according to value."* General property taxes are levied by the individual states, each of which has its own separate laws governing tax rates, assessments, exemptions and other details.

SPECIAL ASSESSMENTS are taxes that are levied against particular properties in order to cover the cost of some public improvements that benefit those properties. The properties that are subject to the assessments comprise a special assessment district, or local improvement district. Properties outside the district are not subject to the special assessment tax.

Unlike general property taxes, special assessments are a one-time tax.

They expire once sufficient tax revenue has been collected to pay for the improvements.

C. POLICE POWER

The third power of government that influences real estate ownership is the police power. *POLICE POWER is the power of government to make and enforce regulations for the protection of the public health, safety, and welfare.* This broad power is exercised in many forms, and it frequently has significant effects on property values. It is the basis for land use regulations such as community planning ordinances and zoning laws, and also for building codes, subdivision development regulations, and environmental protection legislation.

D. ESCHEAT

The fourth government power is escheat. *ESCHEAT is the power to have property revert to the state if the owner dies without heirs or a will (INTESTATE).* Heirs are relatives and may inherit without a will.

A will allows personal property to be given to a legatee and real property to a devisee. Those so named in a will do NOT have to be related to the person making the will.

VIII. Uniform Appraisal Dataset (UAD) Overview

The goal of this book is to announce the new Federal appraisal loan standards called "Datasets." More specifically, the Uniform Appraisal Dataset Specification (UAD) is found in Appendix 5. See **Figure 1-4** for the Fannie Mae explanation.

The first four appendices include forms that use those standards, i.e., standardized language established by Fannie Mae and Freddie Mac for definitions, numbers, and typed-in text boxes by using information from the Dataset.

Our other Appendices are:

Appendix 1: Uniform Residential Appraisal Report (URAR)
Appendix 2: Individual Condominium Unit Appraisal Report
Appendix 3: Exterior-Only Inspection Individual Condominium Unit Appraisal Report
Appendix 4: Exterior-Only Inspection Residential Appraisal Report
Appendix 5: Uniform Appraisal Dataset Specification (UAD)

In this new 4th Edition, we introduce this new Fannie and Freddie information specifications as follows:

Note: Any time we reference Appendix 5, we will put it in a burgundy-framed box so that you know it illustrates the new UAD information.

Figure 1-4

Doing Business with Us

Uniform Appraisal Dataset (UAD) Overview[*]

February 18, 2011

To improve the quality and consistency of appraisal data on loans delivered to the government-sponsored enterprises (GSEs), Fannie Mae and Freddie Mac, at the direction of the Federal Housing Finance Agency (FHFA), have developed the Uniform Appraisal Dataset (UAD), which defines all fields required for an appraisal submission for specific appraisal forms and standardizes definitions and responses for a key subset of fields.

The GSEs are also developing the Uniform Collateral Data Portal (UCDP), which is a single portal for the electronic submission of appraisal data. Lenders will be required to use UCDP to deliver electronic appraisal data that conforms to the UAD before the delivery date of the mortgage loan to Fannie Mae or Freddie Mac. This requirement applies to all conventional mortgage loans for which an appraisal report is required.

The UAD standardizes certain data points to support consistent appraisal reporting, regardless of geographic location of the property or any localized reporting conventions, by addressing vague or disparate data currently included on some appraisal reports, such as:

- Variations in formatting numbers, dates, and measures
- Inconsistent terminology for identical information (such as waterfront vs. oceanfront)
- Inconsistent use of descriptions (for example, quality of construction is sometimes reported in absolute terms such as "brick" and sometimes in relative terms, such as "average")

To address these inconsistencies, the UAD standardization includes:

- Standardized formats for fields that include dates, values, etc.
- Allowable values from a list of choices provided for certain fields
- Standardized abbreviations to allow more information to fit on the printed appraisal forms
- Standardized ratings and definitions for the "Condition" and "Quality" of the property and "Updated/Remodeled" status

Through the UAD and UCDP, lenders will have a GSE-consistent approach and understanding of appraisal definitions and requirements and a common submission portal for submitting appraisal data. This critical appraisal data standardization effort will:

- Provide lenders with greater confidence in loan quality by offering enhanced appraisal data quality and integrity regarding the collateral valuation of their loans.
- Create efficiency and consistency in appraisal reviews by offering appraisers and lenders an improved view and understanding of the GSE appraisal data requirements.
- Support processes to manage and mitigate valuation risk by resolving inconsistencies with appraisal data, including formatting, terminology, and use of descriptions.

---

[*] This communication relates to the Uniform Mortgage Data Program, an effort undertaken jointly by Fannie Mae and Freddie Mac at the direction of their regulator, the Federal Housing Finance Agency.

2.18.2011   Page 1 of 5

The GSEs are not changing the look of the existing appraisal forms, but some fields on the forms are being leveraged to include additional information. Appraisal software forms providers will incorporate the UAD requirements into their appraisal report form software. Appraisers are encouraged to update their forms software and receive training to be ready to support these changes next year. Appraisal report form providers expect to have their software updated to incorporate the UAD by the second quarter of 2011. Appraisers should contact their form software provider for more information on their implementation plans.

UAD Specification

Fannie Mae and Freddie Mac have published the full business and technical implementation details needed to adopt the UAD. The UAD Specification documents are available on the GSEs' respective Web sites to help lenders, appraisers, and other industry organizations develop their business and technical implementation plans.

UAD Specification: Business Documentation

For Lenders

To help lenders understand the UAD business requirements, the GSEs are providing the following document:

- **Field-Specific Standardization Requirements**: This document provides a list of standardized definitions and responses for a key subset of fields on the four UAD appraisal report forms, which are defined later in this document. Each form field is labeled as one of the following:

  - **Requirement:** UCDP will validate the data and will return an error message if the data does not conform to the defined reporting format. In the initial implementation of UCDP, error messages will appear as warnings; in the future, they will transition to fatal errors.

  - **Instruction:** UCDP will not verify the reporting format, but the data must be transmitted if populated by the appraiser.

As lenders prepare to adopt the UAD, Fannie Mae and Freddie Mac recommend that they thoroughly review the Field-Specific Standardization Requirements to determine if any process changes are required in their underwriting and property valuation areas to meet the UAD requirements.

UAD Technical Specification

For Appraisal Software/Forms Vendors, Appraisal Management Companies, and High-Volume Lenders

The UAD Technical Specification leverages the Mortgage Industry Standards Maintenance Organization's (MISMO®) Property Valuation Response Version 2.6 Schema Errata 1. The GSEs have added proprietary extensions. The UAD Technical Specification also uses the flexible and widely used XML file format to provide the technical framework for the UAD.

The UAD Technical Specification, including the Introduction and its six supporting appendices, provides the actionable technical documentation needed to translate the data entered on the appraisal report forms into the format required for submission via UCDP. Appraisal software form providers, lenders, and other organizations such as appraisal management companies (AMCs) that will be extracting the data from the appraisal report forms electronically should carefully review the following documents:

- **Uniform Appraisal Dataset Technical Specification Introduction**

  The UAD Specification Introduction provides an overview and framework for development of the appraisal XML file format using the MISMO Property Valuation Response Version 2.6 Schema Errata 1 with proprietary GSE extensions.

- **Appendix A and Appendix B: GSE Appraisal Forms Mapping**

  These documents illustrate how the appraisal data is supported within the corresponding appraisal XML file by providing field-level data mapping instructions for the four UAD appraisal report forms. Instructions for each field include identifying if the data point will be:

  - **Required:** Data points that must be included in all appraisal XML files delivered to either GSE.

  - **Conditionally Required:** Data points that must be included in all appraisal XML files delivered to either GSE when a defined business condition exists.

  - **Transmit:** Data points that must be supported and included in all appraisal XML files delivered to either GSE if the data point is populated by the appraiser.

  Appendix A is a PDF version and is the true and preserved source of the UAD. Technology systems must support all of the data points defined in Appendix A. Appendix B is a Microsoft Excel version and provides industry participants with a flexible format for viewing and sorting the appraisal data in a spreadsheet.

- **Appendix C: Appraisal Forms with Numbered Fields**

  The GSEs have numbered the data fields in the four UAD appraisal report forms so every field label has a corresponding form reference number. Appendix C provides a standardized appraisal form template containing the field label and corresponding form reference number for the four UAD appraisal forms.

- **Appendix D: Field-Specific Standardization Requirements**

  This document provides a list of standardized definitions and responses for a key subset of fields on the four UAD appraisal report forms.

- **Appendix E: PDF Rendering and Parsing Instructions**

  This document provides instructions for rendering a PDF and parsing appraisal form fields populated by more than one data value.

- **Appendix F: Property Information Valuation Response v2.6 GSE Extension Schema Errata 1:**

  This document provides the GSE XML schema and is best viewed in XML Editor Software.

UAD Effective Date

For appraisals with an effective date (date of inspection is the effective date of the appraisal) on or after September 1, 2011, the following four appraisal report forms, collectively referred to as the "four UAD forms," must be completed in compliance with the UAD for conventional mortgage loans sold to Fannie Mae or Freddie Mac:

- Uniform Residential Appraisal Report (Fannie Mae Form 1004/Freddie Mac Form 70)

- Individual Condominium Unit Appraisal Report (Fannie Mae Form 1073/Freddie Mac Form 465)

- Exterior-Only Inspection Individual Condominium Unit Appraisal Report (Fannie Mae Form 1075/Freddie Mac Form 466)

- Exterior-Only Inspection Residential Appraisal Report (Fannie Mae/Freddie Mac Form 2055)

Data Delivery Requirements and Effective Date

UCDP is the common data portal through which lenders will submit electronic appraisal reports for delivery to Fannie Mae or Freddie Mac. For all conventional mortgage loans delivered to Fannie Mae or Freddie Mac on or after March 19, 2012, the following eight appraisal report forms must be submitted through the UCDP if a) the loan application is dated on or after December 1, 2011, and b) an appraisal report is required. The appraisal report must be submitted through the UCDP before the delivery date of the mortgage loan to Fannie Mae and/or Freddie Mac and must include all exhibits, addenda, and photographs. UCDP will be available in June 2011.

UAD Forms

- Uniform Residential Appraisal Report (Fannie Mae Form 1004/Freddie Mac Form 70)
- Individual Condominium Unit Appraisal Report (Fannie Mae Form 1073/Freddie Mac Form 465)
- Exterior-Only Inspection Individual Condominium Unit Appraisal Report (Fannie Mae Form 1075/Freddie Mac Form 466)
- Exterior-Only Inspection Residential Appraisal Report (Fannie Mae/Freddie Mac Form 2055)

Non-UAD Forms (Forms not required to include the UAD standardization and/or mapping)

- Manufactured Home Appraisal Report (Fannie Mae Form 1004C/Freddie Mac Form 70B)
- Small Residential Income Property Appraisal Report (Fannie Mae Form 1025/Freddie Mac Form 72)
- Individual Cooperative Interest Appraisal Report (Fannie Mae Form 2090)
- Exterior-Only Inspection Individual Cooperative Interest Appraisal Report (Fannie Mae Form 2095)

Various XML formats will be supported in UCDP. The following list includes the XML formats that will be supported in UCDP for the four UAD forms:

- MISMO 2.6 Errata 1 GSE Extended format (preferred format)
- ACI format
- AI Ready format

The following list includes the XML formats that will be supported in UCDP for the non-UAD forms:

- MISMO 2.6 Errata 1 format
- MISMO 2.6 Errata 1 GSE Extended format
- ACI format
- AI Ready format

Either an XML data stream with an embedded first-generation PDF file or a first-generation PDF file must be submitted to UCDP. PDF files must include all appraisal exhibits, addenda, and photographs, and, for loans sold to Fannie Mae, the Fannie Mae Form 1004MC. If the appraisal is only available in a PDF format, without the corresponding XML data, a conversion tool will be available in UCDP for a fee (offered by the vendor supporting UCDP).

The GSEs may expand the UAD and the standardized responses to the other residential appraisal forms at a later date. However, for selected fields captured in the four UAD forms, some appraisal form providers may elect to update those fields on the remaining non-UAD forms, if applicable, but they are not required to do so.

Support and Training

The GSEs will provide a full range of job aids, training opportunities, and other resources to assist lenders in implementing the UAD requirements. These tools will help lenders understand how to incorporate the UAD into their business processes.

To aid appraisers in adopting the new data standards, the GSEs are working with appraisal trade associations to distribute appraiser-specific information, training, and job aids.

Additional Information

Fannie Mae and Freddie Mac are providing identical information in the UAD Overview documents. For additional information:

- Visit eFannieMae.com for the full UAD Specification and updated FAQs.
- Contact your Fannie Mae customer account team.

A. Possessory interests (estates) have the exclusive right to use and occupy the real estate, either now or at some time in the future.

1. Freehold estates include the fee simple, which is the most complete form of real property interest, and the life estate.

2. Leasehold estates have the right of possession, but not title. They are created by lease agreements. The most common leasehold estates are the tenancy for years (term lease) and the periodic tenancy (periodic lease).

B. Non-possessory interests are referred to as encumbrances. They may be financial or non-financial in nature.

1. Financial encumbrances (liens or security interests) give the right to sell the property to satisfy a debt. The sale is accomplished through foreclosure. Liens may be general or specific, voluntary or involuntary.

2. Easements give a non-exclusive right to use someone else's property for a particular purpose. Easements that benefit a parcel of land are said to be appurtenant to that land. Easements that do not benefit land are called easements in gross.

3. A profit a prendre gives the right to take something from the land of another.

4. Private restrictions are common in subdivision developments, and may cover a wide range of land use considerations.

C. Private property interests are limited by the powers of government.

1. Eminent domain is the power to take private land for public use, with payment of just compensation. If necessary, this power is exercised through the legal process of condemnation.

2. States have the power to impose taxes on real estate. General real estate taxes apply to all non-exempt property, and are assessed regularly on the basis of property values. Special assessments apply only to properties that benefit from some public improvement, and are levied only to the extent necessary to cover the cost of the improvement.

3. Police power is the power of government to make laws for the public health, safety, and welfare. Planning and zoning, building codes, subdivision development regulations and environmental protection laws are examples of police power regulations.

4. Escheat is the power to have property revert to the state if the owner dies leaving no will or qualified heirs.

IV. For loan appraisals, use the Uniform Appraisal Dataset (UAD) described here and in Appendix 5.

X. CHAPTER QUIZ

1. According to the USPAP, appraisal practice includes:

    a. appraisal only.
    b. appraisal, review, and consulting.
    c. all work performed by an appraiser.
    d. none of the above.

2. The organization that is responsible for national qualification standards for appraisal certification, and for the Uniform Standards of Professional Appraisal Practice, is the:

    a. Appraisal Institute.
    b. Appraisal Foundation.
    c. Federal Appraisal Council.
    d. Federal National Mortgage Association.

3. According to the USPAP, real estate includes:

    a. land only.
    b. land and improvements.
    c. land, improvements, and encumbrances.
    d. land, improvements, and trade fixtures.

4. An estate that includes possession without title is:

    a. the fee simple.
    b. the leasehold.
    c. the leased fee.
    d. none of the above.

5. The power of government to regulate for the public health, safety, and welfare is known as:

    a. the police power.
    b. the power of eminent domain.
    c. states' rights.
    d. sovereignty.

6. A possessory estate that includes title to the real estate is a(n):

    a. freehold estate.
    b. easement estate.
    c. leasehold estate.
    d. tenancy estate.

7. A mortgage lien is an example of a lien that is:

a. general and voluntary.
b. general and involuntary.
c. specific and voluntary.
d. specific and involuntary.

8. The term "ad valorem" refers to:

a. the calculation of just compensation for eminent domain purposes.
b. the effect on property value that results from location in a special improvement district.
c. the manner in which general property taxes are assessed, according to value.
d. the general nature of judgment liens.

9. An easement granted to a utility company for the purpose of installing and maintaining utility lines for a residence is an example of:

a. an appurtenant easement.
b. a dominant easement.
c. a servient easement.
d. an easement in gross.

10. The estimation of a defined value for a specific real property interest in a specific parcel of real estate, as of a specific date, is:

a. valuation.
b. the definition of an appraisal.
c. the use of an appraisal.
d. the practice of appraisal.

ANSWERS: 1. c; 2. b; 3. b; 4. b; 5. d; 6. a; 7. c; 8. c; 9. d; 10. a

Chapter 2
Understanding Value

KEY WORDS AND TERMS

Anticipation
Assessed Value
Balance
Capital
Change
Competition
Conformity
Consistent Use
Contribution
Coordination
Cost
Diminishing Returns
Environmental Hazards
Environmental Restrictions
Gentrification
Going Concern (Value)
Government (Intervention)
Highest and Best Use
Increasing Returns
Insurable Value
Investment Value
Labor
Land
Liquidation Value
Location

Marginal (Productivity)
Market
Market Value
Plottage
Principles of Value
Production
Progression
Rate of Return
Real Estate Cycle
Regression
Replacement Cost
Reproduction Cost
Scarcity
Substitution
Supply and Demand
Surplus Productivity
Topography
Transferability
Utility
Vacancy Factor
Value
Value In Use
View
Zoning

CHAPTER OUTLINE

LEARNING OBJECTIVES

The appraiser's job is to engage in an "orderly process" that will lead to a valid opinion of value.

In order to accomplish this it is necessary to have a good understanding of the meaning of value, how it is created, and the forces that affect it. After completing this chapter, you should:

1. be able to define value and identify its characteristics;

2. be able to distinguish between value, price, and cost;

3. understand the concept of agents of production, balance, surplus productivity, marginal productivity, contribution, increasing and decreasing returns, highest and best use, consistent use and conformity, as well as their application to real estate appraisal;

4. be able to define the most frequently used Standards of Value and their characteristics (market value, use value, investment value, liquidation value, assessed value, and insurable value); and

5. understand the ways in which social, economic, governmental, and environmental factors influence real estate values.

I. What Is Value?

In its simplest form, the term value means the relative worth of a thing, expressed in terms of some other thing. Value is normally expressed in terms of an accepted medium of exchange, such as money. Thus, a common definition of **VALUE** is *"the monetary worth of property, goods or services to buyers and sellers."*

Value is the relative worth of a thing expressed as money.

Value is, of course related to benefits. Value then is "the present worth of future benefits" expressed in monetary terms.

The concept of value seems simple on its face, but it has been (and continues to be) the subject of a great deal of study. Today's concepts of value have evolved over centuries, and the principles of value that are used by today's appraisers took many years to become widely accepted in the real estate industry. As we try to understand those principles of value, it is important to note that they are all dependent on one another. In the end, the theory of value must be viewed as a unified whole.

In this chapter, we will first examine the characteristics of value, and discuss the distinction between the terms value, price, and cost. We will then explore the economic principles that help describe how value is created in the marketplace, and look at some of the rules used by appraisers when applying those economic principles. Finally, we will examine the many factors that can influence value, for better or for worse, in the market.

II. Four Characteristics of Value

Modern economic theory holds that value is not intrinsic; in other words, the value of something is not inherent in the thing itself, but is created by certain external forces and circumstances. *The circumstances under which value is created are known as the FOUR CHARACTERISTICS OF VALUE.*

The four characteristics of value are:

1. utility;
2. scarcity;
3. transferability; and
4. effective demand.

A. UTILITY

For something to have value, it must first have utility, *UTILITY means it must be able to satisfy some want or need of potential buyers*. Real estate has utility for a wide range of purposes, such as a site for permanent structures (homes, offices, factories, etc.), producing agricultural and mineral products and recreation.

Case/Example: A building lot in a residential subdivision has utility because it is suitable for the construction of a home.

B. SCARCITY

The second characteristic of value is scarcity. Even if a thing has utility, it will not have value if it is overabundant. The classic example of this is air: it is certainly very useful for breathing, but is so abundant as to have no value. *SCARCITY is a key element of the theory that value is dependent on supply and demand*. At some point, when supply far outstrips demand, value becomes negligible.

Case/Example: Waterfront property is valued more than non-waterfront property because of its scarcity. If every home in a community had water frontage, then waterfront property would not be scarce, and it would not command a premium price.

C. TRANSFERABILITY

In addition to utility and scarcity, value depends on transferability. *TRANSFERABILITY is the ability to will, lease, give, or sell a property*. If ownership cannot be transferred from a seller to a buyer, value cannot exist. Because value, by definition, presumes an exchange (be it real or theoretical), transferability is essential.

Case/Example: Congress has dedicated certain lands as national parks, to be held forever for the enjoyment of the public. These lands cannot be bought or sold, so they do not have "value" in the economic sense of the term. This fact is evident from the common description of our parks as "priceless" national treasures.

D. EFFECTIVE DEMAND

The fourth characteristic, effective demand, refers to the combination of desire and purchasing power. For something to have value, purchasers must desire to own it. *DESIRE is distinct from utility: a certain pair of shoes may be perfectly useful, but may not be desired if they are out of style*. However, desire alone does not equal effective demand.

Desire must be combined with **PURCHASING POWER**, *the ability to pay for the item*. Purchasing power is measured in terms of economic conditions such as inflation, unemployment, and wage scales, and has a tremendous impact on real estate values.

Case/Example: Real estate in a town with strong employment at high wages has value because there is effective demand for it. It is desirable because of its proximity to good jobs, and the jobs themselves generate the purchasing power needed to create value.

III. Value Distinguished from Price and Cost

The terms value, price, and cost are often used interchangeably in everyday conversation, but they have distinct meanings for appraisal purposes. *VALUE refers to what a piece of property is theoretically worth under certain circumstances.* **PRICE**, *on the other hand, refers to the actual amount paid by a particular buyer to a particular seller in an actual transaction*. Value is a concept; price is a fact.

> *Price is the "amount paid" for something in the past. Cost is the "total expenditures" for labor, materials and services. Value is the "expected price" under a specific set of assumptions.*

Case/Example: A purchaser buys a house for $100,000. The sale includes seller financing with a below-market interest rate. $100,000 is the price. The value of the house is probably less than $100,000, because part of what the buyer is paying for is the favorable interest rate. In any event, an appraiser could not determine the value solely on the basis of the price.

The term cost is used most often to refer to the production of an item, as opposed to price and value which refer to an exchange. In the context of real estate, *COST is the sum of money required to develop and/or build improvements on the land*.

Case/Example: A homeowner pays $20,000 to install an outdoor swimming pool. The home is located in an area with a cold climate, where the weather is suitable for swimming only 8 weeks out of the year. $20,000 is the cost of the improvement. Its value is likely to be much less, since the improvement has such limited utility.

There are many different types of costs.

A. DIRECT AND INDIRECT COSTS

Costs are sometimes categorized as direct and indirect costs. *DIRECT COSTS refer to the costs of labor and materials used to build an improvement. INDIRECT COSTS refer to the other costs that are incurred in the construction process.* Examples of indirect costs include contractor's overhead, architectural fees, financing costs (interest), and permit fees.

B. DEVELOPMENT COST AND CONSTRUCTION COST

Appraisers also distinguish between development cost and construction cost.

DEVELOPMENT COST refers to the cost to create a project, such as a housing development. CONSTRUCTION COST is the cost to build an improvement, such as a house. Development cost may include construction costs for the individual improvements that are a part of the development, such as all the houses in the development.

Case/Example: The following costs are associated with the creation of a single-family residential property:

$30,000 raw land cost
$12,000 site utilities, clearing, grading, etc.
$ 7,000 architectural fees
$80,000 construction costs for house
$ 4,000 construction loan interest

The construction cost for the residence is $80,000. The development cost for the project is the total of all the costs, or $133,000 for this unit.

The development time is important since it affects the period a developer's capital is tied up as well as the direct cost of interest on borrowed capital. Some developers consider the holding cost of invested capital as an expense because the capital could have been earning interest elsewhere if it were not tied up in the project.

Development cost refers to the cost to "create a project." Construction cost is the cost "to build" an improvement.

C. REPLACEMENT COST AND REPRODUCTION COST

For appraisal purposes, an important distinction is drawn between the terms replacement cost and reproduction cost. The *REPLACEMENT COST of a building is the cost to create a substitute building of equivalent function and utility, using current methods, materials, and techniques. REPRODUCTION COST is the cost to create an exact replica of the building, using the same design, materials, and construction methods as the original.* The distinction between replacement cost and reproduction cost will be explained in detail in Chapter 8.

Replacement cost is the cost to create a substitute building of "equivalent function." Reproduction cost is the cost to create an "exact replica" of the building, so that it looks identical.

IV. Principles of Appraisal (Economic Value)

Appraisal is based on economic principles of value. They are often referred to as: appraisal principles, principles of value, economic principles or just principles.

We have seen that value requires utility, scarcity, transferability, and effective demand. We have also discovered that value is a concept, as opposed to price and cost which are established facts. Next we will turn our attention to the way that value is created in the market, through the principles of value.

The **PRINCIPLES OF VALUE** *are a series of statements or rules; together they describe the way value is created in the real estate market.* Principles of value can also be called appraisal principles, economic principles, and in this textbook, "principle(s)." These principles are widely accepted by the real estate industry and serve as a guide to estimating value (see **Figure 2-1**).

Figure 2-1

Principles of Value

Supply and Demand	Contribution
Substitution	Increasing and Decreasing Returns
Competition	Highest and Best Use
Change	
Anticipation	Consistent Use
Balance	Conformity, Progression, and Regression
Surplus Productivity	

Underlying each principle of value is the concept of markets. Broadly speaking, the term *MARKET refers to buyers and sellers interacting to exchange property*. Markets can be defined in a number of different ways, but typically a market is defined in terms of a particular type of product or service that is bought and sold for money (or exchanged for other assets) within a particular geographical area. In real estate, we speak of the market for a particular type of property (single-family homes, residential building lots, high rise apartments, vacation condominiums, etc.) in a particular location, district, or region.

Case/Example: The definition of a market can be very specific, such as the market for "single-story ranch-style homes between $150,000-$180,000, located within 5 miles of the city center." Or a market can be broadly categorized, as in the market for "income-producing properties in the western United States," or simply "the United States real estate market."

No matter how a market is defined, it always refers to the actions of buyers and sellers in the exchange of ownership.

A. PRINCIPLE OF SUPPLY AND DEMAND

One of the most basic principles of value is that of supply and demand. *SUPPLY refers to the amount of some type of property being offered for sale in a given market at a given price. DEMAND is the amount of that same type of property that buyers want to purchase at that same price.* The *PRINCIPLE OF SUPPLY AND DEMAND states that the value of the property in a competitive market is determined by the relative levels of supply and demand.* Property does not have an inherent or intrinsic value; rather, it is worth more when demand exceeds supply, and worth less when supply exceeds demand.

The principle of supply and demand is constantly at work in the residential real estate market. When demand for housing in a community is on the rise, two things can happen. If vacant land is available for new construction, home builders become more active, increasing the supply of housing to meet the increased demand. On the other hand, if supply cannot be increased because the area is already built up, prices will rise as more and more buyers compete for the limited supply of housing. When demand for housing is in decline, the normal result is a drop in both prices and new construction activity.

Case/Example: Many people have recently discovered that Montana is a wonderful place to build a vacation home. This has created an increase in demand for what was previously considered mere range land. As predicted by the law of supply and demand, the price of such land has skyrocketed as a result of the surge in demand.

The supply side also affects real estate values. *OVERBUILDING results when too many competing housing contractors saturate a market, depressing prices.* Conversely, a new zoning law that prevents new housing from being developed on vacant land (thus limiting the supply) can cause the values of existing properties to rise.

Case/Example: During an economic boom, builders rushed to erect dozens of new office towers and complexes, anticipating an increase in demand for office space. But the economy cooled, and the expected demand did not materialize. Because of the resulting oversupply, many of the new buildings went vacant, and office rents (and values) plummeted in the frantic competition to attract tenants.

Appraisers must be well informed of the supply of and demand for properties in their area of expertise. Equally important, they must be aware of the actions of the many forces that cause supply and demand to change over time in the marketplace.

The rule of supply and demand is the fundamental principle of value. When we examine the workings of the market, we can see that the rule of supply and demand operates because of certain fundamental characteristics of markets. The principles of substitution, competition, change, and anticipation describe these fundamental characteristics.

B. PRINCIPLE OF SUBSTITUTION

According to the principle of *SUBSTITUTION*, *the value of a property cannot exceed the value of equivalent substitute properties that are available in the market.* In other words, reasonable buyers will compare similar properties in the market, and choose the least expensive one that meets their requirements.

Case/Example: Similar units in a condominium complex are selling for about $145,000. An owner who needs to make a quick sale might list her condo for $140,000. The lower price would make her condo more likely to sell than the comparable but higher priced units.

The principle of substitution is applied by appraisers in each of the three approaches to estimating value (which will be described in detail in subsequent chapters). The appraiser compares the prices of substitute existing properties in the **sales comparison approach**, compares the cost to build a new substitute property in the **cost approach** and compares the cost to acquire a substitute income investment in the **income approach**.

In applying the principle of substitution, the appraiser must be keenly aware of what constitutes "equivalent" substitute property in the particular market.

Case/Example: Two houses may be physically identical, but may not be equivalent because they are in different neighborhoods. Homes in the same neighborhood with the same number of rooms and square footage may not be equivalent because they vary in the quality of construction.

By studying the actions of the market, the appraiser can discern those characteristics that are deemed "equivalent" by the market, and those that are not.

C. PRINCIPLE OF COMPETITION

The rule of supply and demand operates because of competition in the market. *COMPETITION occurs when supply and demand are out of balance.* When supply is greater than demand, sellers must compete for buyers. Conversely, buyers are in competition when demand exceeds supply. Competition tends to bring supply and demand back into balance. When buyers compete, prices rise, which stimulates supply and reduces demand. When sellers compete, prices fall, which stimulates demand and dampens supply.

Case/Example: If there is an oversupply of housing, sellers may be forced to reduce prices to attract buyers. Price reductions improve the marketability of a competing property by virtue of the principle of substitution. Theoretically, continued price reductions will either stimulate more demand by increasing the purchasing power of buyers, or reduce supply as sellers take their properties off the market to wait for better times. It is the competition between buyers that drives the price reductions and restores the balance of supply and demand.

Competition can also correct an excess of demand as well as supply. When buyers must compete, prices are driven up, which has the effect of reducing demand. Increasing prices decreases the purchasing power of buyers. Increasing prices also increases the supply as more sellers enter the market to take advantage of the higher selling prices.

Appraisers must be aware of the competitive status of the real estate market, and also be alert for signs of excess competition, which can have a negative effect on value. Excess competition is essentially an overreaction or overcorrection by the market, brought on by the lure of excess profit. Seeking to take advantage of this profit, sellers and builders bring so much new property to the market that supply outstrips demand, and values decline.

D. PRINCIPLE OF CHANGE

It is a fact of life that things change. The **PRINCIPLE OF CHANGE** *recognizes that the forces of supply and demand are in constant flux.* It states that supply and demand fluctuate in response to changes in social, economic, and other conditions that influence value. This is the fundamental reason for the requirement that appraisers estimate value as of a specific date.

The law of change states: change always takes place even if it is imperceptible.

The principle of change is especially important in regard to the sales comparison approach (the most commonly used of the three methods) to value. Yesterday's selling price does not necessarily indicate today's value. As the appraiser examines equivalent properties (called comparable properties) to estimate the value of the property being appraised, the appraiser must take into account market conditions in effect when the comparable properties sold, and make adjustments for any changes in the market between the sale dates of the comparables and the appraisal date. Thus, the more recently the comparable property sold, the more reliable it is as an indicator of value.

Case/Example: An appraiser identifies three properties that are comparable to the subject property and located in the same neighborhood. The first comparable sold three months ago for $185,000. Subsequently, the county announced plans to build a medium security prison near the neighborhood. The second and third comparables sold after this announcement, for $172,000 and $174,000. The appraiser must adjust the value of the first comparable to reflect the change in the market resulting from the anticipated prison construction.

Change in real estate is often described in terms of the real estate cycle.

The **REAL ESTATE CYCLE** *is a pattern in changing values.* The first stage of the cycle is the **DEVELOPMENT STAGE**, *when values increase as raw land is improved. This is followed by a stage of relative stability in value, called **MATURITY**,* and then a stage of *progressive* **DECLINE**. The cycle may then be repeated, substituting the initial development stage with a period of renewal, modernization and increasing demand known as revitalization (see **Figure 2-2**).

Figure 2-2 REAL PROPERTY LIFE CYCLE (AGE CYCLE)

MATURITY (Values Stable)

DEVELOPMENT (Values Increase)

DECLINE (Values Decrease)

Case/Example: In a new subdivision, property values tend to increase as raw land is developed into homesites and homes (development stage). Once the subdivision development is completed, values will normally remain fairly stable for some period of time (maturity stage). Eventually, though, the homes will begin to deteriorate with age, and their value may also suffer from competition with newer, more modern developments in the surrounding area (decline stage). If homes in the neighborhood are then renovated or replaced with newer structures (revitalization stage), values will once again rise, starting a new cycle.

The phenomenon of gentrification is an example of revitalization. *GENTRIFICATION occurs when properties in a lower class neighborhood are purchased and renovated or rehabilitated by more affluent (middle and upper-class) buyers.*

The Georgetown area of Washington, D.C. is an example of an area which was once regarded with disdain, and now is a sought-after and prestigious area. Most gentrification has taken place in major city areas, close to the city centers, where structures have desirable architectural features.

E. PRINCIPLE OF ANTICIPATION

The principle of anticipation is related to the principle of change. The *PRINCIPLE OF ANTICIPATION states that value is affected by the expectations of buyers regarding the future benefits to be gained from property ownership.* Specifically, value is affected by buyers' anticipation of the utility of owning property, and of the gain (or loss) to be realized on reselling the property.

Case/Example: Expectations of a slump in economic activity would tend to depress property values, while anticipation of a large employer relocating into town would tend to have the opposite effect.

F. PRINCIPLE OF BALANCE

The *PRINCIPLE OF BALANCE states that production (the rate of return) is maximized when the four agents of production are in balance.* The value of an individual property that is overimproved or underimproved, suffers because the agents of production are not in balance. Too much or too little capital, labor and coordination have been invested in relation to the land.

Case/Example: A certain building lot costs $20,000. If improved with a 1,000 square foot home costing $50 per square foot to build, it would sell for $77,000. This is a profit of $7,000, a 10% return on the investment of $70,000 ($20,000 for the land, plus $50,000 for the home). If the lot were improved with a 2,000 square foot home, again at $50 per square foot cost, it would sell for $130,000, a profit of $10,000 and a return of about 8.3%. In this case, the larger home would represent an overimprovement, an imbalance among the agents of production. Because even though the amount of profit on the larger home is greater in terms of dollar amount, it is less in terms of a percentage rate of return: 8.3% as opposed to 10%.

The principle of balance can be applied to neighborhoods, or districts, as well as to individual properties. Overdevelopment of office space in a city, for example, decreases the value of all office space in the city. Prices and rents will be depressed until the market is able to absorb the oversupply. In this case, too much labor, capital and coordination has been invested in office space, relative to the demand for it. The agents of production are out of balance, and values suffer as a result.

1. Point of Diminishing Returns

The point at which the agents of production are in balance is referred to as the POINT OF DIMINISHING RETURNS. When the point of diminishing returns is reached, additional expenditures for capital, labor, or management fail to increase productivity (or value) enough to offset their costs. The point of diminishing returns is explained in more detail below in the section on the Principle of Increasing and Decreasing Returns.

G. PRINCIPLE OF SURPLUS PRODUCTIVITY

SURPLUS PRODUCTIVITY is a way of measuring the value of land that has been improved. It is assumed that the productivity (net income) that is attributable to the agents of capital, labor, and coordination is equivalent to their costs. In other words, when the cost of capital, labor, and coordination is deducted from the total net income for a property, the remaining income (called the surplus productivity) can be attributed to the land. Thus, the surplus productivity indicates the value of the land. (This concept forms the basis of residual techniques for estimating land value, which are discussed in Chapter 6.)

Case/Example: A property has net income of $10,000 per year. If the cost of labor, capital and management for the property is $8,000 per year, the remaining net income of $2,000 is attributed to the value of the land.

H. PRINCIPLE OF CONTRIBUTION

The value of an individual component of a property is measured according to the principle of contribution. The **PRINCIPLE OF CONTRIBUTION** *states that the value of a component, regardless of its cost, is equal to the amount of value it adds to the property as a whole (or the amount by which its absence decreases the value of the property as a whole). This amount of value is referred to as the component's **MARGINAL PRODUCTIVITY**. The actual cost of the component is called its **MARGINAL COST**.*

Case/Example: By installing new siding on a house, the owner increased the value of the house by $5,000. $5,000 represents the value of the siding, its marginal productivity. This is true regardless of the cost of the siding (its marginal cost), which may have been more or less than $5,000. If the siding cost less than $5,000, it added more value than it cost. If the siding cost more than $5,000, it added less value than it cost (and perhaps should not have been added at all).

This principle is particularly useful to the sales comparison approach to value. It is used to help answer questions such as: What is the difference in value between a lot that is 100 feet deep and one that is 120 feet deep? How does the absence of a garage affect the value of a house? How much is value increased by adding an extra bathroom or bedroom? Instead of relying on simple cost estimates, the principle of contribution directs the appraiser to analyze the market values of those various components to answer similar types of questions.

Case/Example: In a neighborhood of similar residential properties, homes with two bathrooms sell for $140,000, while three-bath homes sell for $145,000. In this case, the contribution to value made by a third bathroom, its marginal productivity, would be $5,000. When adjusting the value of a comparable property to account for a difference in number of baths, the appraiser would base the adjustment on the $5,000 difference in value as determined by the market. This indication of market value would be given more weight in the appraisal than the actual cost of adding a third bath.

I. PRINCIPLE OF INCREASING AND DECREASING RETURNS

The principle of increasing and decreasing returns is quite similar to the principle of contribution. Assume that the amount of one or more of the agents of production (land, for example) remains fixed. *As the amount invested in the other agent(s) is incrementally increased, the rate of return on the investment will first increase at a progressively higher rate. This is called INCREASING RETURNS. This rate will continue to increase, but at a progressively lower rate, and will finally begin to decrease, at this point, the rate of return is called DIMINISHING RETURNS*.

Case/Example: A builder intends to develop a lot with a single-family residence, at a construction cost of $60 per square foot. By analyzing the local housing market, the builder estimates the likely sales price of the residence, based on various potential square footages. The following chart shows the effect of increased size of the house on the builders overall rate of return (profit).

Figure 2-3 is a distribution that illustrates the principle of increasing and decreasing returns.

V. Effect of Use on Real Estate Value

Our discussion of the economic theory of value has covered the rule of supply and demand, markets and market principles, and the use of production as a measure of value. We will conclude this discussion with a look at the interaction between the way real estate is used and its value.

A. HIGHEST AND BEST USE PRINCIPLE

The principle of highest and best use is crucial to valuing real estate. The *HIGHEST AND BEST USE principle states that the value of property is determined by the most profitable use to which the property may reasonably (and legally) be put*. Thus, to determine market value for a property, the appraiser must first analyze its highest and best use.

Note that highest and best use must be a "legal" use.

This means that the use must be allowed under the applicable zoning restrictions, or that a variance could easily be obtained for the use. When analyzing highest and best use, the appraiser must be aware of what uses are permitted by the zoning laws.

Figure 2-3

Principle of Increasing and Decreasing Returns

The value added by each additional 100 square feet

Size in Sq. Ft.	Estimated Sales Price	Marginal Productivity of Additional 100 Sq. Ft.	Marginal Cost of Additional 100 Sq. Ft.	Marginal Return on Additional 100 Sq. Ft.	Overall Rate of Return
#1,500	$94,500	n/a	n/a	n/a	5%
#1,600	$101,800	$7,300	$6,000	$1,300	6%
#1,700	$110,200	$8,400	$6,000	$2,400	8%
#1,800	$119,900	$9,700	$6,000	$3,700	11%
#1,900	$128,800	$8,900	$6,000	$2,900	13%
#2,000	$136,800	$8,000	$6,000	$2,000	14%
#2,100	$143,600	$6,800	$6,000	$800	14%
#2,200	$149,200	$5,600	$6,000	<$400>	13%
#2,300	$153,200	$4,000	$6,000	<$2,000>	11%

The amount of value added by each additional 100 square feet (the marginal productivity) varies depending on the size of the residence, whereas the cost of each additional 100 square feet (marginal cost) remains constant. At sizes up to 2,100 square feet, increasing the size of the house will increase the builder's rate of return. Above 2,100 square feet, however, the rate of return begins to decline. The chart above shows the effect of increasing size on the builder's overall rate of return.

Through highest and best use analysis, an appraiser identifies the use conclusion upon which the final value estimate is based.

When analyzing improved real estate for its highest and best use, the appraiser draws a distinction between the actual highest and best use, and the highest and best use that would apply if the property were vacant (i.e., unimproved). The fact that the highest and best use of the property, if vacant, would be something other than the current use does not necessarily mean that the property's current use is not its highest and best use. That would only be the case if the value of the land in a vacant state (for some other use) exceeded its value as currently developed, as illustrated by the following examples.

Case/Example: A property is improved with a single-family residence. The appraiser estimates that the value of the land for its current use is $50,000 and the value of the residence is $70,000. In evaluating highest and best use, the appraiser determines that if vacant, the highest and best use of the land would be multi-family residential, for which purpose the land is estimated to be worth $80,000. In this situation, the highest and best use of the land is its current use, since the current total value of the land and improvements ($50,000 + 70,000 = $120,000) exceeds the value of the land alone for a different use.

Case/Example: Suppose we have the same circumstances as in the previous example, but the residence is run-down and estimated to be worth only $20,000. Thus, the total value of land and improvements for its current use is $70,000. In this case, the appraiser could well determine that the highest and best use of the land was for multi-family residential use, assuming the cost of removing the existing improvements was less than $10,000 ($80,000 value if vacant for new use less $70,000 value as improved for current use).

There are two functions in analyzing the highest and best use of the property as improved. The first function is the same as that of highest and best use of land as though vacant—to help identify comparable properties. Comparable improved properties should have the same or similar highest and best uses as the subject property.

The second function of highest and best use of the property as improved is to decide whether improvements should be demolished, renovated, or retained in their present condition.

B. CONSISTENT USE PRINCIPLE

The principle of consistent use relates to the appraisal of improved property.

CONSISTENT USE requires both the land and the improvements to be valued for the same use, even if they are being valued separately. It is improper to value the land for one use and the improvements for a different use.

Case/Example: The appraiser could not, in the two preceding examples, value the improvements for their current single-family residential use and value the land for multi-family residential use. The land and the improvements must be valued consistently, either both for single-family use or both for multi-family use.

C. CONFORMITY, PROGRESSION, AND REGRESSION PRINCIPLES

According to the *PRINCIPLE OF CONFORMITY, property values are enhanced when the uses of surrounding properties conform to the use of the subject property.* This is the rationale behind zoning regulations, which seek to group compatible uses together and to separate incompatible uses.

In practice, the principle of conformity is influenced by local perceptions of the kind of conformity that is desirable. Variation in architectural styles, for example, may be viewed favorably in one context, and unfavorably in another. A mix of commercial and residential uses in an urban setting could have a positive effect on values, where the same mix of uses in a suburban setting could have a negative effect. In applying the principle of conformity, the appraiser needs a sound appreciation for local customs and standards.

Note that the racial or ethnic composition of an area is NOT a consideration when applying the principle of conformity. The appraiser should NEVER consider the presence or lack of ethnic diversity in an area to be an indicator of value. NOT only has time proven that ethnic composition does not affect value, but to assume that it does would run afoul of anti-discrimination laws.

Progression and regression are terms used to describe the effect on value when a property does not conform to the level of improvement of surrounding properties. *When a property that is much more luxurious than surrounding properties suffers a decline in value, it is called REGRESSION. By the same token, a modest home in an area of more expensive houses would see a relative increase in value called PROGRESSION.*

VI. Production as a Measure of Value

We have seen that value is determined by the forces of supply and demand, in markets that operate according to the principles of substitution, competition, change, and anticipation. Now we will examine another concept that is also very important to an understanding of value: production.

In economic theory, *PRODUCTION refers to the creation of wealth.* Production is the ability to create wealth that can be used to measure the value of land and its improvements. As we shall see, the concept of production has many applications in the appraisal process.

A. AGENTS OF PRODUCTION PRINCIPLE

The *FOUR AGENTS OF PRODUCTION are:*

1. *CAPITAL (financial resources),*

2. *LAND (natural resources),*

3. *LABOR (employment), and*

4. *COORDINATION (management or entrepreneurship).*

These agents can work individually or in concert with each other, to generate a return in the form of income or profit. *It is the RATE OF RETURN (OR PROFIT), in relationship to the amount of resources invested, that is the measure of production and value.*

Case/Example: In a real estate development, investors provide capital, the developer provides management (coordination), and construction crews provide labor. These three agents of production are combined with the fourth agent, land, to create something of value, such as a housing development.

The economic system based on the principles of private property ownership and personal rights, known as **CAPITALISM***, was expounded by Adam Smith in his 1776 book,* Wealth of Nations*, in which he set forth the idea that value should be the combination of the four agents of production.*

For land, an owner should be entitled to rent, for labor there should be wages, and for capital there should be interest. Management should receive profit appropriate to the risk.

As an example of the capitalistic theory in action, assume a property can be purchased for $100,000. The builder wishes to build a home on the property. The builder estimates total lot preparation construction and landscaping costs at $190,000 and that the project will take nine months from land purchase to completion with an additional three months to sell the property. The builder estimates the interest he will have to pay at 10 percent and that he should also receive 10 percent on his own cash investment. He estimates that this total interest and return on capital should come to $28,000, before anticipated sale of the property.

Because of possible changes in the economy, delays and other costs, he feels that he should receive a profit of 22 percent if he is willing to take the risk.

Total costs:

Land:	$100,000
Improvements:	$190,000
Interest:	$28,000
Profit:	$69,960
Price:	**$387,960**

Therefore, the builder could conclude that $387,960 would be a fair price for the home to be built. Market forces, however, could result in a higher possible price or a lower price that could even result in a loss.

VII. Types of Value

There are several types of value. In carrying out the **orderly process** of appraisal, it is vital to distinguish among the different types of value, and to identify the **Standard of Value** that the appraiser will be estimating. This is a critical part of the process and the appraisal must contain a definition of the Standard of Value that is being estimated. The various types of value that may be estimated in real estate appraisals include investment value, value in use, liquidation value, insurance value, assessment value, going concern value, and market value (see **Figure 2-4**).

Figure 2-4

Some Common Types of Value

INSURANCE VALUE	EASEMENT VALUE
CAPITALIZED VALUE	INTERIM VALUE
MORTGAGE LOAN VALUE	BOOK VALUE
RENTAL VALUE	REPLACEMENT VALUE
LEASE VALUE	ANNUITY VALUE
SCRAP VALUE	ASSESSED VALUE
JUNK VALUE	INHERITANCE VALUE
COURT VALUE	CASH VALUE
SQUARE FOOT VALUE	DEPRECIATED VALUE
FRONT FOOT VALUE	LISTING VALUE

A. MARKET VALUE

The type of value that is most often estimated in real estate appraisals is market value. Market value is sometimes referred to as exchange value or value in exchange. It is the value of property as determined by the open market. The Federal Register, V55, No. 251, December 31, 1990, Washington, D.C., offers the following definition:

"The most probable price which a property should bring in a competitive and open market under all conditions requisite to a fair sale, the buyer and seller each acting prudently and knowledgeably, and assuming the price is not affected by undue stimulus. Implicit in this definition is the consummation of a sale as of a specified date and the passing of title from seller to buyer under conditions whereby:

1. *the buyer and seller are typically motivated;*

2. *both parties are well informed or well advised, and acting in what they consider their best interests;*

3. *a reasonable time is allowed for exposure in the open market;*

4. *payment is made in terms of cash in United States dollars or in terms of financial arrangements comparable thereto; and*

5. *the price represents the normal consideration for the property sold unaffected by special or creative financing or sales concessions granted by anyone associated with the sale."*

This definition of market value is a standard part of any form report used by lenders.

In other words, *MARKET VALUE refers to the amount of cash (or cash equivalent) that is most likely to be paid for a property on a given date in a fair and reasonable open market transaction.* For a market transaction to be fair and reasonable, several conditions must apply:

1. Both the buyer and seller must be typically well informed as to the conditions of the market and the subject property.

2. Both the buyer and seller must be acting reasonably, in their own self-interest, and without undue duress.

3. The property must be exposed to the market for a reasonable period of time.

4. No extraordinary circumstances, such as liberal financing or concessions, are involved.

When these four factors are present, the transaction is said to be an "arm's length transaction."

1. Market Value in Non-Cash Equivalent Transactions

As a practical matter, very few real estate transactions are "all cash" in today's market. When the financing for a transaction is comparable to the typical financing available in the market, it is considered the equivalent of cash. However, if the financing includes concessions that are not typical in the market (such as a below-market interest rate in a seller-financed transaction), the non-cash equivalent terms must be identified by the appraiser in the appraisal report, and their affect on value must be taken into account.

2. Other Definitions of Market Value

The term market value has been in use for many years, and has been subject to varying interpretations by economists, judges, and legislatures. As a result, market value does not necessarily mean the same thing in all situations. For example, state laws pertaining to condemnation (the taking of private property for a public purpose) and tax assessment frequently include definitions of market value. When performing an appraisal for purposes governed by state law, the appraiser should use the law's definition of market value.

B. PRICE

Market value is what a property should bring at sale, but price is entirely different. The *PRICE is the amount actually paid for a property.* While price could be equivalent to market value, it could also be greater or less than market value. A great deal of differentialism from market value could be the result of a number of factors or combination of factors such as:

1. an uninformed seller who did not know the market value;
2. an uninformed buyer who did not know the market value;
3. a seller who had to sell immediately;

appraiser clearly understand the investment requirements of the particular investor. Because the goals of the individual investor may have a significant effect on the value estimate, investment value is inherently subjective in nature. By comparison, market value is said to represent a more "objective" standard.

Case/Example: An investor has purchased five of the six parcels it needs in order to develop a planned office complex. In addition, the investor has already spent thousands of dollars on development studies and preliminary planning for the complex. Because of its unique circumstances, this investor may be willing to pay a premium to acquire the sixth parcel that it needs for the development. If the owner (seller) of the parcel is aware of the developer's situation, the owner may hold out for an offer of greater than market value for the property.

E. LIQUIDATION VALUE

Liquidation value is not a form of market value. The primary distinction is that *LIQUIDATION VALUE assumes that the property must be sold in a limited period of time, which rarely constitutes "reasonable" exposure to the market.* Liquidation value is typically estimated in the context of a financial institution that is considering foreclosure on a property.

F. ASSESSED VALUE

ASSESSED VALUE is set by state taxing authorities for the purpose of assessing ad valorem property taxes (annual property taxes that are based on the value of the property, the proceeds of which are used to support general government services). To determine assessed value, the appraiser must first estimate market value (as defined by the tax law), then apply a percentage (called the assessment ratio) as specified under the assessment statute.

Assessed Value = Market Value x Assessment Ratio

Case/Example: One state may specify that property is to be assessed at 100% of market value, while another assesses property at 10% of market value. A $100,000 property would be assessed at $100,000 in the first state (100% x $100,000), and at $10,000 in the second state (10% x $100,000).

Some legislators like to peg assessments at less than market value because they feel lower assessments will result in a lesser number of tax appeals and taxpayer dissatisfaction. Actually, the taxpayers pay the same since lower assessments mean higher tax rates to bring in the required revenue.

In some states, assessed value is based on price paid, and in a few states, there is a limit on annual increases in assessed valuation. Assessed value tends to lag behind market value. In many areas, property is not assessed annually, although an overall factor may be added to increase tax revenue.

G. INSURABLE VALUE

INSURABLE VALUE is defined by the terms of a particular insurance policy. It refers to the value of property for purposes of reimbursement under policy.

An appraiser might be asked to determine reproduction or replacement cost. Reproduction cost would be the cost to replace the structure as built, while replacement cost is the cost to replace the structure with one of similar desirability and utility.

H. GOING CONCERN VALUE

GOING CONCERN VALUE is the total value of a proven, ongoing business operation, which includes real property that is an integral part of the operation. Going concern value is normally inapplicable to residential real estate. However, it could apply to a new apartment project which has completed its lease-up period with 100 percent occupancy on attractive terms. Such a property would be more valuable than a newly completed project that has yet to start its lease-up phase.

VIII. Forces Affecting Value

Value is determined by the forces of supply and demand in the marketplace. In turn, the forces of supply and demand are influenced by a broad range of external factors. The factors that affect supply and demand, and consequently value, are frequently broken down into four general categories:

1. Social
2. Economic
3. Political
4. Environmental (Physical)

In actual practice, the various influences are interwoven, but the distinctions remain useful for purposes of discussion and analysis.

A. SOCIAL FACTORS

SOCIAL FACTORS are the numbers, characteristics, lifestyles, standards, and preferences of the people in a particular market that constitute the social forces influencing value in that market. Real estate values are affected by changes in population, which may be due to changes in birth or death rates, or to migration into or out of an area. Demand for different types of properties is related to the age distribution of the population, the numbers of households of various sizes and compositions, and attitudes towards architectural style and utility. Social preferences with respect to recreational activities, education, and cultural amenities also drive the forces of supply and demand for real estate.

1. Prestige

For various reasons, certain areas have desirability greater than would be indicated by physical, economic and political factors. As an example, an area where prominent persons lived might be considered highly desirable.

2. Recreation

Property close to or having access to desirable recreational activities such as golf or tennis might have enhanced value.

3. Culture

Property in communities offering good libraries, museums, live theater, music, etc., might have enhanced value over properties lacking their amenities.

4. Family Orientation

An area regarded as family friendly with highly regarded schools, children's activities, etc., would generally result in enhanced valuation.

5. Homeowner Restrictions

Restrictive covenants of homeowner associations can enhance or detract from value.

The social characteristics of a market can be stable or volatile, but are always subject to the principle of change. The appraiser can stay informed about social forces in the market by studying census data and other statistical information collected by national, state, and local governments, as well as demographic studies published by business organizations, scholars, and other sources.

In considering social factors within an appraisal, the appraiser may not consider race, ethnicity, sex, sexual orientation, and religious belief to have an effect, either positve or negative, on value. The appraiser must have no bias with respect to any parties involved in the transaction. Your authors often point out to their classes that the job description is <u>Real Estate</u> Appraiser—not people appraiser!

B. ECONOMIC FACTORS

The *ECONOMIC FACTORS that most strongly affect real estate values relate to the availability and cost of money for real estate lending, construction, and investment, and the purchasing power of buyers in the real estate market.* Money markets are influenced by relatively broad forces, such as the international investment climate, currency exchange rates, savings rates, inflation rates, national fiscal policy, and government borrowing.

Purchasing power tends to react to more localized influences, such as local wage and unemployment rates, the strength and diversity of the local economic base, and local construction costs and costs of living. But these local influences are often themselves affected by larger scale economic forces. Unemployment, for example, is often more closely tied to a particular industry than to a particular locality. It becomes a local force in areas that are dependent on the particular industry, but its causes are likely to be national or international.

We have broken down economic related factors into the following significant categories.

1. The Local Economy

The state of the local economy as to growth, employment, and wages will affect both residential and commercial values within an area.

Case/Example: Communities dependent on oil and gas exploration for employment have undergone cycles of boom and bust in recent decades. When oil prices are high, employment in the oil industry is also high, and property values rise in these communities. Conversely, property values have been devastated when oil prices declined, causing business failures and high unemployment among those in the industry.

2. Interest Rates

While short-term interest rates will effect expansion and contraction of business inventories, long-term rates effect construction of residential and commercial property.

As interest rates drop, homes become affordable for more people, raising demand for existing housing as well as new construction.

3. Rents

High rents encourage home ownership and all types of new construction, while low rents discourage ownership and construction.

4. Vacancy Factors

Prior overbuilding might result in a high vacancy factor that would be reflected in lower income and lower valuations for commercial property. High vacancy factors in residential rentals often mean lower rents or rent concessions, which result in a lower net income and a lower property evaluation.

5. Plottage

The possibility that an economic site can be combined with a contiguous site, where the combined value would be greater than the separate site values, would be a positive influence on value (plottage increment).

6. Parking

The availability of adequate on-site and/or off-site parking will affect value for both commercial and residential property.

7. Corner Influence

Commercial property located on a corner is generally regarded as being more valuable than property in the center of a block. In fact, the closer to the corner, the greater the value. The reason being that the corner property is more likely to be noticed by foot and vehicular traffic and corners provide greater signage and/or window exposure. Property at a stop light is even more valuable as it is more likely to be noticed.

Residential corner lots have more traffic, more noise and less privacy.

C. POLITICAL FACTORS

There is an increasing trend for governmental forces to attempt to mitigate or direct economic forces, to the point where it is often difficult to distinguish between the two. Examples include such things as monetary and trade policies, taxes and tax exemptions, and government regulation of the financial market. In fact, few economic forces are without some government influence. When analyzing the effect of economic factors on real estate value, the appraiser must bear in mind the effects of government actions in the economic arena.

Political or governmental factors result from direct and indirect government influence and intervention.

Political factors include the following.

1. Taxes

High tax areas might result in lower valuations but lower tax areas might result in greater demand and higher property evaluations.

2. Zoning

The zoning of a property can materially affect value as it determines the use to which a property can be put. Zoning which allows a shopping center is likely to result in a valuation many times higher than if the parcel were zoned for single-family dwellings.

The proportion of property zoned for a particular use will also affect value. If too much land in an area were zoned for office use, the result would likely be a lower per square foot value for such land than if not enough land had been set aside for such use.

3. Rent Control

Controls that limit rent to less than the market forces will limit value. The severity of the rent control ordinance will effect the reduction as to value.

4. Growth Limitations

Moratoriums on new construction, limitation on the number of building permits being issued and high development fees limit new construction. The effect is generally higher rents and higher values for existing structures and lower evaluations for undeveloped land.

5. Environmental Restrictions

Environmental restrictions include restrictions against development because of such things as endangered species, prohibitions on filling in wet lands, and requirements to create or maintain greenbelts.

Environmental legislation is a growing area of government influence with a major impact on real estate values.

Case/Example: Environmental restrictions may increase the cost of housing development by requiring developers to mitigate adverse environmental affects of construction or to set aside land for open space. Government policy regarding harvest of timber from national and state lands affects the cost of lumber for construction.

6. Building and Health Codes

Like zoning, building and health codes are based on the police power of the state to protect the health, safety, and welfare of citizens. Requirements of codes are often outdated and can add additional expense to development.

D. ENVIRONMENTAL (PHYSICAL) FACTORS

ENVIRONMENTAL (PHYSICAL) FACTORS are those aspects of the physical environment, whether natural or man-made, that influence value.

There are a number of specific physical factors which influence value, including the following.

1. Location

It is now rather a trite saying, but it is true, "The three most important factors influencing value are location, location, location."

The location in relation to desired amenities and to developed and natural assets affect value.

2. Climate

Temperature, wind, rain, and snow all affect the desirability of areas for recreation and quality of life, which, in turn, influences value.

3. Water

The availability of a sufficient and affordable supply of quality water plays a significant role in expansion and relocation of industries, as well as residential development.

4. Transportation

The availability of adequate highways, rail, and airports, as well as public transportation, all affect value.

Case/Example: A new freeway is built that allows commuters from a small town to reach jobs in the city in half the time it used to take. Suddenly, it is practical for those with jobs in the city to live in the town, and property values go up.

The condition and size of streets, the amount of traffic, as well as ingress and egress, will affect value as to specific properties.

5. View

View is a significant factor and, in some areas, a water view can more than double the value of a property when compared to similar properties lacking such a view.

6. Soil

Soil that can support a structure would generally be more valuable than locations requiring a great deal of work to make the site ready for development.

Case/Example: Recent discoveries in earthquake-prone areas have determined that some soils that otherwise test as stable and suitable for construction can liquefy during an earthquake. This condition can cause foundation failure and building collapse, particularly in multiple-story buildings. Soils testing can now determine this condition. As may be imagined, parcels with soil that exhibits this condition have diminished value.

7. Size and Shape

All other things being equal, a larger site is more valuable than a smaller site, but value is not necessarily proportionate to size. As an example, a residential lot 80 feet wide by 300 feet deep would not be three times as valuable as a lot 80 feet wide by 100 feet deep.

A regular shaped lot with reasonable width and depth is generally more valuable on a square foot basis than an irregular shaped lot, such as a triangle.

8. Exposure

Residential property where the morning sun lights up the kitchen and dining areas and where the patio enjoys a sunset view are likely to be more valuable than similar properties lacking these amenities.

9. Environmental Hazards

The presences of any negative environmental problem like contaminated soil, asbestos building products or even a chemical plant in the area could adversely effect value.

10. Topography

Flat or rolling land with good drainage would be more valuable than land prone to flood or with steep slopes that would limit development or increase costs.

IX. CHAPTER SUMMARY

I. The Concept of Value.

A. Value is "the monetary worth of property, goods, services, etc."

B. Value is not intrinsic; a thing's value depends on utility, scarcity, transferability, and effective demand (desire plus purchasing power).

C. Value is not the same as price. Price refers to an actual transaction, whereas value is a concept.

D. Value is not the same as cost. Cost refers to the expenditures necessary to build or create a property, whereas value (and price) refer to the exchange of property.

 1. Replacement cost is the cost to create a substitute of equal utility; reproduction cost is the cost to create an exact replica.

II. Economic Theory of Value.

A. A market is the interactions between buyers and sellers with regard to the exchange of property.

B. The relative levels of supply and demand determine the value of property in a competitive market.

 1. Values go up when demand exceeds supply, and go down when supply exceeds demand.

 2. The value of a property cannot exceed the price of a substitute property of comparable utility.

 3. If a property's income is less than its opportunity cost, a reasonable investor will not purchase it.

 4. When supply and demand are out of balance, competition increases. Competition tends to bring supply and demand back into balance.

C. The forces of supply and demand are constantly subject to change.

 1. Appraisers must estimate value as of a specified date.

 2. Value is dependent on the expectation of future benefits to be realized from property ownership.

 3. Change is manifested in the real estate cycle, with value fluctuating as the cycle proceeds from development, to maturity, to decline and then revitalization.

III. Production as a Measure of Value.

    A. Wealth is created by the four agents of production: capital, land, labor, and coordination.

    B. Value of a particular property, or of all properties in a particular market, is optimized when the agents of production are in balance. The point where the agents of production are in balance is the point of diminishing returns.

    C. Surplus productivity is attributed to the land. It is what is left of the property's net income after deducting the costs of capital, labor and coordination.

    D. The value of a component of a property is its marginal productivity, the amount by which its presence increases the value of the property as a whole.

    E. Incremental increases in the investment of an agent of production in a property will first cause the rate of return to increase, but will eventually reach a point (the point of diminishing returns) where the return begins to decrease.

IV. The Effect of Use on Real Estate Value.

    A. Property should be valued for its highest and best use, which is any reasonable and legal use that will yield the most profit.

        1. Highest and best use depends on the nature and value of a property's improvements. The highest and best use of a property if vacant is not necessarily its highest and best use as currently improved.

    B. Both land and improvements must be appraised for the same (consistent) use.

    C. A property's value is enhanced when the uses of surrounding properties conform to the use of the subject property.

V. Types of Value.

    A. Appraisal reports must define the Standard of Value that is being appraised.

    B. Market value is determined by the market in an arm's length transaction.

        1. Buyer and seller must be reasonably informed as to the conditions of the market and the property.

        2. Buyer and seller must be acting reasonably, for self-interest, and without duress.

        3. The property must be exposed to the market for a reasonable period of time.

        4. Market value may vary depending on its specific definition. Whether a particular definition is applicable depends on the circumstances of the appraisal.

5. Market value must be adjusted to take into account financing terms that are not equivalent to cash, and any other concessions that are not typical of the market.

C. Value in use is the value of property for a specific purpose only, as opposed to its highest and best use.

D. Investment value is the value to a particular investor, as opposed to value to the market.

E. Liquidation value is what a property would bring with limited exposure to the market, as in a foreclosure sale.

F. Assessed value is market value multiplied by the applicable assessment ratio.

G. Insurable value is value for purposes of reimbursement under an insurance policy.

H. Going concern value is the value of an ongoing business that includes real property as an integral part of its operations.

VI. Factors Affecting Value.

A. Value is affected by social, economic, governmental, and environmental influences.

B. Social influences are such factors as demographics and social standards.

C. Economic influences affect real estate values by affecting the cost of capital and the purchasing power of buyers and investors.

D. Government influences include the many laws and regulations that affect value, such as zoning, taxes, environmental laws, financial regulations, and building codes.

E. Environmental influences on value include land characteristics, climate, infrastructure and location.

X. CHAPTER QUIZ

1. Market value is sometimes referred to as:

   a. value in use.
   b. value in exchange.
   c. investment value.
   d. none of the above.

2. Which of the following is NOT a characteristic of value?

   a. Utility
   b. Scarcity
   c. Demand
   d. Cost

3. Effective demand consists of:

   a. desire and purchasing power.
   b. utility and scarcity.
   c. supply and purchasing power.
   d. none of the above.

4. According to the principle of substitution:

   a. appraisers should substitute the sales price of comparable properties for the value of the subject property.
   b. all other factors being equal, a buyer will choose the less expensive of two comparable properties.
   c. lots of the same size in the same neighborhood are equivalent in value.
   d. all of the above.

5. Surplus productivity is attributed to:

   a. capital.
   b. land.
   c. labor.
   d. coordination.

6. The point where increased investment in the agents of production no longer results in increased profit is known as the point of:

   a. no return.
   b. marginal productivity.
   c. surplus productivity.
   d. diminishing returns.

7. Which approach is the principle of substitution most commonly associated with?

    a. Sales comparison approach

    b. Cost approach

    c. Income approach

    d. All of the above

8. The principle of highest and best use holds that:

    a. improved property should always be appraised for its current use.

    b. the land should always be appraised for its highest and best use, even if the improvements are appraised for some other use.

    c. the market views the value of property in light of all possible legal uses.

    d. commercial use is inherently more valuable than residential use.

9. The cost to create an exact replica of an improvement is referred to as:

    a. replacement cost.

    b. substitution cost.

    c. insurable value.

    d. reproduction cost.

10. The principle of supply and demand states that prices will tend to increase when:

    a. supply exceeds demand.

    b. demand exceeds supply.

    c. supply and demand are in balance.

    d. competition increases.

ANSWERS: 1. b; 2. d; 3. a; 4. b; 5. b; 6. d; 7. d; 8. c; 9. d; 10. b

Chapter 3
The Appraisal Process

KEY WORDS AND TERMS

Appraisal Process
Assumptions
Cost Approach
Define the Problem
Effective Date of Appraisal
Freehold Interest
General Data
Gross Multiplier
Income Approach
Limiting Conditions

Narrative Report
Oral Report
Reconciliation
Sales Comparison Approach
Scope of Appraisal
Site Valuation
Standard of Value
Valuation Date
Uniform Appraisal Dataset (UAD)

LEARNING OBJECTIVES

After completing this chapter, you should be able to:

1. identify each of the steps in the appraisal process;

2. define the purpose, use, and scope of an appraisal, and understand the differences between them;

3. understand the difference between the effective date of an appraisal (the valuation date) and the date of the appraisal report;

4. identify the pieces of information that are essential to defining an appraisal problem and understand why each one is necessary;

5. understand the significance of assumptions and limiting conditions in an appraisal report;

6. understand the procedures for preliminary analysis of an appraisal problem;

7. understand the differences between general and specific data, and how each is used in an appraisal;

CHAPTER OUTLINE

8. understand the distinction between primary data and secondary data;

9. define the meaning of the term "site" as it applies to real estate appraisal;

10. identify the reasons for the separate valuation of the site and site improvements;

11. identify the three approaches to value;

12. understand the significance of the reconciliation process; and

13. identify types of appraisal reports, and explain their major differences.

I. The Eight Steps of the Appraisal Process

*The orderly process utilized by appraisers to obtain a reliable and competent opinion of value is commonly called the **APPRAISAL PROCESS**.* The series of steps that make up the appraisal process have been refined over many years.

This chapter will present an overview of the steps in the appraisal process. The first two steps, defining the appraisal problem, and determining what resources are necessary to solve it, will be discussed in detail in this chapter. The remaining steps in the process will be described briefly here, and then examined in greater detail in later chapters.

USPAP requires an appraiser to understand and employ recognized methods and techniques. Standard 1 of the most current edition of USPAP states:

In developing a real property appraisal, an appraiser must identify the problem to be solved and the scope of work necessary to solve the problem, and correctly complete research and analysis necessary to produce a credible appraisal.

Thus, it is essential to understand and follow these steps of the appraisal process in order to arrive at a legitimate value estimate:

The Appraisal Process

1. Define the appraisal problem.
2. Preliminary analysis. (Determine the necessary and available resources required to solve the problem.)
3. Collect, verify, and analyze the necessary data.
4. Determine the property's highest and best use.
5. Estimate the value of the site.
6. Apply the three approaches to value.
7. Reconcile the various value indicators to reach a final value estimate.
8. Prepare and deliver an appropriate appraisal report.

It is worth noting that in the past, many appraisal textbooks and references have treated Steps 2 and 3 as a single step, or have ignored Step 2 entirely. The trend, however, is to recognize that preliminary analysis is an important and unique part of the appraisal process.

Although we will discuss the steps in the appraisal process in the same order in which they are listed, this does not mean that the appraiser must always complete each step before going on to the next one. As a practical matter, the various steps in the appraisal process often overlap. Data collection, for example, may begin even before the appraisal problem is fully defined, and data analysis may occur throughout the entire appraisal process. **Figure 3-1** is an illustrated flow chart of the appraisal process.

Figure 3-1

Defining the Appraisal Problem

WHAT

Identification of real estate
Identification of real property interest
Identification of Standard of Value

WHY

Intended use
Intended users

WHEN

Effective date of appraisal
Date of appraisal report

HOW

Scope of the appraisal
Assumptions
Limiting conditions

The steps in the appraisal process should NOT be seen as isolated tasks, but rather as components that make up the unified process of "valuation."

II. Step 1: Defining Appraisal Problem

The appraisal process begins by defining the appraisal problem.

This step has two important considerations. First, the appraiser must know why the client is hiring the appraiser (what the client wants to know). Second, and equally important, the appraiser must understand the terms and conditions of the appraisal assignment (how it will be carried out).

DEFINING THE APPRAISAL PROBLEM *means answering some basic questions about the particular appraisal assignment.*

   1. **What** is to be appraised?
   2. **When** is it to be appraised?
   3. **Why** is it to be appraised?
   4. **How** is it to be appraised?

A. WHAT IS TO BE APPRAISED?

To determine what is to be appraised, the appraiser must identify three things:

   1. the real estate that is the subject of the appraisal;
   2. the real property interest that is the subject of the appraisal; and
   3. the Standard of Value, clearly defined, that is desired by the client.

The reader of an appraisal must have no doubt about what is being appraised.

1. Identification of the Real Estate

Real estate is commonly identified by means of a street address or a building name. But in official documents, such as deeds or mortgages, real estate is identified by means of its legal description. The reason for this is that legal descriptions are the most accurate way to identify real estate; they leave the least room for ambiguity or confusion. A person reading a legal description can determine exactly what real estate is being referred to. Since an appraisal report is an important document relating to real estate, appraisals also identify real estate by means of legal descriptions. The appraisal may, and often does, include the name or common address of the property, but should always include the legal description as well.

Case/Example: All of the following descriptions refer to the same piece of real estate. An appraisal might include all three descriptions, but should always include the legal description.

Building Name:	The Smith Tower, an office building
Common Address:	1024 Western Avenue, Seattle, Washington
Legal Description:	Lot 17, Division 3, Pierce Addition, City of Seattle, County of King, as recorded in King County, Washington

The legal description of the real estate is often provided by the appraiser's client. The appraiser can obtain (or verify) the legal description by consulting a copy of the property owner's deed. A copy of the deed can usually be obtained from the client, the property owner or manager, the real estate broker, or from the local county records office. Unless otherwise agreed to between the appraiser and the client, the appraiser should not accept responsibility for the accuracy of the legal description, since this is beyond the training and expertise of most appraisers.

There are three major categories of legal descriptions:

1. Metes and Bounds System;
2. Rectangular or Government Survey System; and
3. Lot, Block, and Tract System.

These are discussed in detail in Chapter 4.

The following section from the Uniform Residential Appraisal Report (**Figure** 3-2) is entitled "Subject" and describes the property by requiring specific details.

Figure 3-2

Subject Section - URAR

Uniform Residential Appraisal Report   File # 3   4   4a

The purpose of this summary appraisal report is to provide the lender/client with an accurate, and adequately supported, opinion of the market value of the subject property.

Property Address 6	City 7	State 8 Zip Code 9	
Borrower 10	Owner of Public Record 11	County 12	
Legal Description 13			
Assessor's Parcel # 14	Tax Year 15	R.E. Taxes $ 16	
Neighborhood Name 17	Map Reference 18	Census Tract 19	
Occupant [20] Owner [21] Tenant [22] Vacant	Special Assessments $ 23	[24] PUD HOA $ 25 [26] per year [27] per month	
Property Rights Appraised [28] Fee Simple [29] Leasehold [30] Other (describe) 31			
Assignment Type [32] Purchase Transaction [33] Refinance Transaction [34] Other (describe) 35			
Lender/Client 36	Address 37		
Is the subject property currently offered for sale or has it been offered for sale in the twelve months prior to the effective date of this appraisal? [38] Yes [39] No			
Report data source(s) used, offering price(s), and date(s). e-2; 40			

Note: Information contained in *[brackets]* refers to the author's interpretation of the UAD specifications, and while some of the text is exact, much of it may be edited. Always refer to the **Fannie Mae and Freddie Mac Uniform Appraisal Dataset (UAD) Specification** online or in **Appendix 5** of this textbook for further details.

Property Address: In some rural areas a fire number is sued. If there is no address assigned as is often the case with new construction, then enter N/A or "To Follow." *[The appraiser must enter an address that conforms to the United States Postal Service (USPS) address standards in Publication 28 – Postal Addressing Standards (pub28) – for complete addresses. Address standards can be found at USPS.gov. The subject address must be populated consistently throughout the form.]*

City: For a rural area, township and a county could be used.

State: State abbreviation. *[2-letter USPS abbreviation.]*

Zip Code: *[5-digit ZIP Code or ZIP+4 code (either with or without the dash).]*

Borrower: May or may not be current owner.

Owner of Public Record: Full name as appears on record.

County: : *[Name of the county in which the subject property is located. If not located in any county, enter the name of the local municipality or district in which the property is located.]*

Legal Description: The appraiser can get this information from a tax roll, deed, or abstract of title.

> **Practical Tip:** Because of space limitations, long legal descriptions may have to be included as an addendum to the report.

Assessor's Parcel #: *[Same format as taxing agency including all spaces and dashes as applicable. If no parcel number is available, enter 'None' ... separate multiple parcel numbers with a semicolon.]*

Tax Year: *[Enter the tax year. If it spans two calendar years, enter the first year only.]*

Real Estate Taxes: Dollar amount for current year. *[Currency, whole dollars only.]*

Neighborhood Name: *[Enter a neighborhood name. It may be a name recognized by the municipality in which the property is sited, such as a subdivision name. If not applicable, enter the common name used by residents.]*

Map Reference: Use the atlas or guide common to your area, including edition used.

> **Practical Tip:** You should provide a written reference in the report as to which guide and what edition was used.

Census Tract: This information is available from online service providers.

Occupant: *[Check the appropriate (only one) box to indicate if the property is occupied by the owner, tenant, or vacant as of effective date of appraisal. If there is an accessory unit, check the status of the main unit.]*

Always use an "X" to mark the boxes, rather than a check mark!

Special Assessments: These consist of one-time charges for things such as lighting, street repairs, etc. *[Must be expressed as an annual or annualized amount. For more than one, enter the annualized sum of all special assessments. If none, enter the numeral zero (0). Currency, whole dollars only.]*

PUD: *[If Planned Unit Development (PUD) box is checked, select 'Yes' or 'No' to the question, "Is the developer/builder in control of the Homeowners' Association (HOA)?" located in the PUD Information section.]*

HOA: *[Enter all applicable homeowners' association (HOA) fees associated with the subject property. In checkbox, indicate if the amount is payable per year or per month. Only one selection is permitted. If the amount is paid on a different frequency (e.g., bi-monthly or semi-annually), it must be normalized as either per year or per month for reporting.]* (See **Appendix 5** for more details.)

> **Note:** *[For appraisals of condominium units, the amount of any applicable condominium association fees must be included in the HOA fees section.]*

Property Rights Appraised. "Other" might consist of leased fee or life estate properties.

Assignment Type: *[Indicate the transaction type for the assignment – Purchase, Refinance, or Other. Only one selection is permitted. If 'Other' is selected, a description must be provided.]*

Lender/ Client: The appraiser must enter the name of the lender. Any applicable AMC name should only be entered in the Appraiser Certification Section.

Listing Information Generally, this information is contained in multiple listing service databases. *[Is the subject property currently offered for sale or has it been offered for sale in the 12 months prior to the effective date of this appraisal? Report data source(s) used, offering price(s), and date(s). If the "No" box is checked, the data source(s) used must be provided. If the answer is "Yes," then Days on Market (DOM), Offering Price(s), Offering Date(s), and Data Source(s) used must be provided.]*

> **Note:** The details of this requirement are very specific and lengthy. Please refer to the **Field-Specific Standardization Requirements** in **Appendix 5** of this textbook.

Report Data Sources: Name all sources of data used in the report.

a. Personal Property (Sometimes Included)

Not all appraisals are done for lenders, so in some cases, items of personal property need to be included in the appraisal. For example, a buyer might include some equipment or furnishings in the terms of sale. If the appraiser is valuing the personal item it must be included in an addendum to the report.

b. Repairs and New Construction

Identifying the real estate also involves identifying any repairs, improvements or new construction that are to be completed. Any repairs the appraiser assumes will take place must be identified and clearly specified in the appraisal report as influencing the estimate of value. In the case of new construction, adequate plans and specifications must exist to allow the appraiser to form a reasonable opinion of he value of the new improvements.

2. Identification of Real Property Interest

Real estate is more than just the physical land and buildings; it is also the rights that go with the land.

a. Ownership Rights

A valuation of real property includes both physical real estate and rights that one or more individuals, partnerships, or corporations may have or contemplate having in the ownership or use of land and improvements.

In addition to the identity of the subject real estate, the appraiser also must know what real property rights the client wants to have appraised. (For more information regarding real property rights, refer back to Chapter 1.)

You will note that the Subject Section of the URAR (Figure 3-2) includes the property rights being appraised.

Most appraisals estimate the value of the complete ownership rights, known as the fee simple. But appraisers may also estimate the value of partial freehold interests (such as a one-half partnership interest), or leasehold interests.

Obviously, the fee simple value of a property will not be the same as the value of a partial or limited interest. So it is vital to identify the real property interest that is the subject of the appraisal. (For a more detailed discussion of appraising partial or limited interests, see Chapter 13.)

Real property rights that may be appraised: fee simple ownership, leasehold interest, mineral or other subsurface rights, water rights, air rights, rights of co-owner (partner, spouse or co-tenant), easement rights, etc.

The appraiser must know what rights outside the property transfer with the property. A property might include rights in a common ownership of amenities such as a community pool, golf club membership, water rights and even easements. Appurtenant rights and interests that transfer with real estate can significantly effect value. Appurtenant easement rights over land of others generally enhances value.

An appurtenant easement allowing beach or docking privileges would significantly enhance the value of water related residential property. A negative easement prohibiting another from blocking a favorable view would also be a plus factor as to value, which should be considered by the appraiser.

b. Restrictions

In addition to knowing what property rights the client wants to have appraised, the appraiser must also identify any rights and restrictions that apply to the subject property. The property may include irrigation rights, for example, or the right to use an easement across adjoining property. On the other hand, property rights may be restricted by such things as zoning ordinances, public and private easements, rights-of-way, and private deed restrictions. The rights and restrictions that apply to the property may enhance or detract from its value.

Case/Example: Property A and Property B are similar in all respects, except that Property A is crossed by a public right-of-way. Because the right-of-way limits the use of Property A, it may have a lower value than Property B.

c. Property Taxes

Property taxes are a form of restriction on property rights. The appraiser must identify the taxes that apply to the subject property and analyze their affect on value. Property that is subject to a higher rate of taxation than other comparable properties, for example, may be less valuable.

In the case of legal descriptions, the appraiser can identify many of the rights and restrictions that apply to a property by consulting the deed.

Additional information can be found in a title abstract or title insurance policy. Information regarding zoning restrictions is available as a matter of public record from local zoning or planning offices. Similarly, property tax information may be obtained from local tax authorities.

3. The Standard of Value

Next the appraiser must determine the Standard of Value. The **STANDARD OF VALUE** *refers to the type of value the client expects the appraiser to provide.* Does the client want investment value, insurable value, value in use, or market value? Whichever type of value the client is requesting must be clearly defined in the appraisal report. (For more information on types and definitions of value, refer back to Chapter 2.)

In order to collect the proper information and to prepare a report that will be useful to the client, the appraiser and the client must agree on the Standard of Value that is to be utilized.

Case/Example: A lender hires an appraiser to determine the value of a property, because the lender wishes to know whether or not it should approve a borrower's loan for the purchase of the property. In this case the Standard of Value would be market value. The intended use would be for an approved loan and the intended user(s) would be the lender and those to whom the lender might assign the loan (FHLMC, FNMA, VA, and FHA).

FHLMC/FNMA (Fannie Mae/Freddie Mac), America's largest secondary lenders, define *MARKET VALUE as "the most probable price which a property should bring in a competitive and open market under all conditions requisite to fair sale, the buyer and seller, each acting prudently, knowledgeably, and assuming the price is NOT affected by undue stimulus."*

B. WHEN IS IT TO BE APPRAISED?

The appraiser must identify the effective date (or valuation date) of the appraisal, and also the time frame in which the client requires the appraisal report.

1. Effective Date of the Appraisal (Valuation Date)

Value estimates are always made as of a specific date, which is called the EFFECTIVE DATE OF THE APPRAISAL. This is because value typically changes over time. Market conditions, as well as the physical condition of the property, are subject to constant change, and both of these factors affect value.

Case/Example: A residential property is appraised at $120,000 as of June 1. On June 2, the house is completely destroyed by a tornado, substantially reducing the value of the property. But the value estimate contained in the appraisal is still valid, because it was made as of a specific date, prior to the catastrophe. (The appraisal may also have included an assumption clause, stating that the value estimate was based on the assumption that the described improvements were in good repair.)

The Reconciliation Section of the URAR (see Figure 3-4) makes it clear that, for the uniform report, the market value is based on the date of the appraiser's inspection.

a. Value as of the Current Date

In most cases, the client will want to know the value as of the current date. Occasionally, the appraiser may be asked to estimate value as of a past or future date.

Chapter 3

b. Appraisal of Past Values

Appraisals of past values are possible if adequate data (comparable sales, etc.) exist for the period of time in question. Such data are, in fact, often available, provided the valuation date is not too far in the past, so the process of estimating past value is normally not much different than the appraisal of current value.

"Appraisals of past value" are most often required in connection with legal proceedings, such as divorce settlements or tax audits.

Case/Example: The 2005 property taxes for a particular property are based on the assessed value of the property as of January 1, 2005. The property owner is informed of the assessed value in August, 2005. In order to challenge the assessment, the owner may need to obtain an appraisal of the property as of January 1, 2005, the date of the assessment. An appraiser may make such a past value estimate, provided that adequate data are available for the time in question.

c. Appraisal of Future Value

Unlike appraisals of past value, appraisals of future value are always speculative (theoretical) because it is impossible to predict future market conditions.

Data for the future does not exist and must be assumed. An appraisal of this type often requires the appraiser to rely on **Extraordinary Assumptions** and **Hypothetical Conditions**.

An *EXTRAORDINARY ASSUMPTION is an assumption that is related to a specific assignment.* If it is found to be false it would alter the value opinion of the appraiser. A *HYPOTHETICAL CONDITION is one that is contrary to what actually exists but is supposed for the purpose of the individual assignment.*

Case/Example: An investor asks an appraiser to determine what the value five years from now of a hundred unit apartment building will be. The apartment building has not yet been built although plans and specifications for it exist and the investor currently owns the land on which it will be built. In this case, the building is a hypothetical condition of the assignment (it doesn't actually exist). The analysis of future conditions, such as market conditions, demographic changes, and economic trends, are based on extraordinary assumptions.

The appraiser must clearly document all extraordinary assumptions and hypothetical conditions in the report.

An appraisal of future value is normally used in a business context to help someone to decide whether or not to make a particular investment or whether or not to proceed with a particular project or development.

2. Date of Appraisal Report

The appraisal report date, as opposed to the valuation date, does not directly effect the value estimate. It is simply the date on which the appraisal report is issued.

In defining an appraisal problem, the report date is important for two reasons. First, the client needs to know that the appraisal will be issued in time to be of some use in the client's decision making process, and the appraiser needs to feel confident that the appraisal can be competently prepared within that time frame. Second, the report date shows whether the property is being valued as of the past, present, or future.

Even in the case of an appraisal for current value, the valuation date and report date will NOT necessarily be identical.

The report date may be the same as the valuation date, or it may be a somewhat later date. The difference is due to the time that is required to analyze the data and prepare the report. The *VALUATION DATE is the date as of which value is estimated, commonly the date that the appraiser inspects the subject property.* The *REPORT DATE is the date the appraiser completes and signs the report.*

C. WHY IS IT TO BE APPRAISED?

To proceed with the appraisal assignment, the appraiser must know why the client wants the appraisal; that is, what the appraisal will be used for. This is important because appraisals are used to help the client make a particular decision. For example, lenders use appraisals to help decide whether to make a loan for a given amount; buyers and sellers use appraisals to help decide whether to buy or sell a property for a given price.

If a client or other person makes a decision based on an appraisal and that decision turns out to be a costly mistake, the injured person may try to hold the appraiser liable for the damage caused by the decision.

To limit potential liability, the appraiser should clearly specify that the value estimate is valid only for its intended use by the client, and is not valid for any other use or any other user.

Case/Example: In an appraisal for property tax assessment purposes, the appraiser estimated a value that was $10,000 less than the true value of the property. If local property taxes are 1.5% of assessed value, then the consequences of the appraiser's error are a loss of tax revenue equal to 1.5% of $10,000, or $150. But if a home buyer were to rely on the same appraisal, the buyer's potential loss would be the full $10,000. By limiting the validity of the appraisal to the use for which it was intended, the appraiser avoids potentially devastating liability.

1. The Intended Use of the Appraisal

The intended use of the appraisal can also have some effect on the appraisal process. If an appraisal is part of a borrower's loan application, for example, the lender is probably most concerned with the potential resale value of the property. Therefore, the appraiser may place greater emphasis on the sales comparison approach to value. On the other hand, the appraiser may tend to give more weight to the income approach to value if the client will be using the appraisal as part of an investment decision. By knowing how the appraisal will be used, the appraiser can make these kinds of judgment calls more competently.

Paragraph 21 of the **Appraiser's Certification**, from Freddie Mac Form 70 (Fannie Mae Form 1004, March 2005), limits the use of the report by limiting distribution without consent to anyone other than the borrower, mortgagee, mortgage insurer, successors in interest, etc. In other words the appraiser must provide consent before anyone without a direct need to know can receive access to the report.

D. HOW IS IT BEING VALUED?

Before proceeding with the appraisal, the appraiser and client should agree on the scope of the appraisal, and on the assumptions and other limiting conditions that apply to it.

1. Scope of the Appraisal

The *SCOPE OF THE APPRAISAL is the amount of research and report development that will be required to produce an appraisal result that is reliable and easily understood by the intended users.* The scope of work is determined by the Standard of Value required, the intended use of the appraisal, and the number of intended users.

Case/Example: A lender requests an appraisal for market value on a single-family residence. The appraisal will be used to determine if the value of the property has increased sufficiently to remove the borrower's private mortgage insurance payments. Both the lender and the appraiser were involved in the appraisal for the original loan. In this case, the scope of work is limited and a less expensive "drive-by" appraisal may well suffice.

Case/Example: A group of investors are considering the purchase of a 100-unit apartment building. They want to know both the market value and the value in use. Members of the investment group who will receive the report(s) include a doctor, a criminal defense lawyer, a mortgage banker, a plumber, and a widowed school teacher with three small children. Obviously the standards of value requested, the intended use, and most particularly the varying levels of sophistication of the intended users will require an extremely clear and detailed report.

The appraiser determines the scope of the appraisal. The appraiser's determination of the scope of work is based on the value standard, the intended use, and the intended users. The appraiser must also conform to USPAP and all federal and state law. It is the appraiser's responsibility to provide the client with what they really need rather than what they may want.

Most residential appraisals are carried out on the Uniform Residential Appraisal Report form. A copy of the URAR may be found in its entirety in Chapter 12.

2. Assumptions

Virtually all appraisal reports contain a section on assumptions and other limiting conditions. *ASSUMPTIONS are facts that the appraiser assumes are true, but does not independently verify.*

Case/Example: The appraisal may assume that title to the subject property is good and marketable, that the use of the subject property is in accordance with applicable zoning laws, and that there are no hidden conditions that affect the value of the property. However, the appraiser may not independently verify these facts.

Customarily, the appraisal report will state the basic assumptions on which the value estimate is based, and then specifically identify any exceptions to those assumptions.

Case/Example: An appraisal may state that it is based on the assumption that title to the property is free and clear of any liens and encumbrances. However, the appraiser may specifically note that the property is subject to a utility easement, and take this fact into consideration in arriving at a value estimate.

3. Limiting Conditions

Limiting conditions are similar to assumptions. In fact, assumptions may be viewed as simply one type of limiting condition. From the appraiser's point of view, the distinction between assumptions and limiting conditions is of little concern, and many times they are both listed in the same section of the appraisal report.

A *LIMITING CONDITION is a statement or explanation that limits the application of the conclusions contained in the report.* Some of the main limiting conditions of an appraisal have been discussed above: the identity of the real estate and real property interest, the purpose and use of the appraisal, and the effective date of the appraisal. These are all limiting conditions because they specify (limit) exactly what conclusions may be drawn from the appraisal.

Case/Example: Among the many limiting conditions that may be found in appraisals are statements to the effect that:
1. the sole purpose of the appraisal is to estimate value;
2. the appraisal does not constitute a survey;
3. the appraisal does not constitute a legal opinion regarding title or other legal matters;

4. the appraisal does not constitute an engineering report or property inspection report;
5. the appraisal is made under conditions of uncertainty and is based on a limited amount of data; and
6. the appraisal is made with certain assumptions regarding the needs and expertise of the client.

Assumptions and limiting conditions have three primary purposes. First, they assist the client and other readers of the appraisal report to understand its meaning, and second to help them avoid drawing unwarranted conclusions from reading the report. This is an increasingly important issue, since federal law now requires lenders to provide copies of appraisal reports to their borrowers in many situations. A lender may understand the assumptions and limitations of an appraisal report without having them spelled out, but an unsophisticated borrower is not likely to have the same level of understanding.

Case/Example: John applies for a loan from ABC Bank to purchase a house. ABC Bank gives John a copy of the appraisal report that was made in connection with John's loan application. John may assume that the appraiser has verified the boundaries of the property and the condition of the title, and found them to be okay, but this is not normally the case in an appraisal. By clearly stating (in the limiting conditions) that the appraisal does not constitute a survey or a legal opinion of the condition of the title, the appraisal report can prevent John from assuming that the boundaries and title to the property are okay.

The third purpose of assumptions and limiting conditions is to limit the liability of the appraiser.

This is not to say that limiting conditions can be used as an excuse for an incompetent appraisal; they can't. But limiting conditions can and do limit the circumstances under which an appraiser may be held liable for the results of any actions that are taken based on an appraisal report. For example (as mentioned in the discussion of use of the appraisal), the appraisal may state that its conclusions are valid only for the particular client, and only for the use stated in the report.

In March of 2005, Fannie Mae and Freddie Mac made major changes to the Statement of Assumptions and Limiting Conditions and the Appraiser's Certification, both in language, meaning, and content. The old Form 439 has been retired and the greatly expanded wording of the new document is now part of the six pages of the 2005 Uniform Residential Appraisal Report (see **Figure 3-3**).

The introduction at the top of the page notes that the form is not to be used for condominiums, co-operatives, and manufactured homes for Fannie Mae appraisals. Fannie Mae has developed separate forms for these types of residential properties. The introduction also notes that no modifications, additions, or deletions may be made to the scope of work, the intended use, the intended user, definition of market value, the limiting conditions, and certifications. It is stated that additional certifications may be made to comply with the law or conform to an appraiser's

Figure 3-3

2

Uniform Residential Appraisal Report

File # 3   4   4a

This report form is designed to report an appraisal of a one-unit property or a one-unit property with an accessory unit; including a unit in a planned unit development (PUD). This report form is not designed to report an appraisal of a manufactured home or a unit in a condominium or cooperative project.

This appraisal report is subject to the following scope of work, intended use, intended user, definition of market value, statement of assumptions and limiting conditions, and certifications. Modifications, additions, or deletions to the intended use, intended user, definition of market value, or assumptions and limiting conditions are not permitted. The appraiser may expand the scope of work to include any additional research or analysis necessary based on the complexity of this appraisal assignment. Modifications or deletions to the certifications are also not permitted. However, additional certifications that do not constitute material alterations to this appraisal report, such as those required by law or those related to the appraiser's continuing education or membership in an appraisal organization, are permitted.

SCOPE OF WORK: The scope of work for this appraisal is defined by the complexity of this appraisal assignment and the reporting requirements of this appraisal report form, including the following definition of market value, statement of assumptions and limiting conditions, and certifications. The appraiser must, at a minimum: (1) perform a complete visual inspection of the interior and exterior areas of the subject property, (2) inspect the neighborhood, (3) inspect each of the comparable sales from at least the street, (4) research, verify, and analyze data from reliable public and/or private sources, and (5) report his or her analysis, opinions, and conclusions in this appraisal report.

INTENDED USE: The intended use of this appraisal report is for the lender/client to evaluate the property that is the subject of this appraisal for a mortgage finance transaction.

INTENDED USER: The intended user of this appraisal report is the lender/client.

DEFINITION OF MARKET VALUE: The most probable price which a property should bring in a competitive and open market under all conditions requisite to a fair sale, the buyer and seller, each acting prudently, knowledgeably and assuming the price is not affected by undue stimulus. Implicit in this definition is the consummation of a sale as of a specified date and the passing of title from seller to buyer under conditions whereby: (1) buyer and seller are typically motivated; (2) both parties are well informed or well advised, and each acting in what he or she considers his or her own best interest; (3) a reasonable time is allowed for exposure in the open market; (4) payment is made in terms of cash in U. S. dollars or in terms of financial arrangements comparable thereto; and (5) the price represents the normal consideration for the property sold unaffected by special or creative financing or sales concessions* granted by anyone associated with the sale.

*Adjustments to the comparables must be made for special or creative financing or sales concessions. No adjustments are necessary for those costs which are normally paid by sellers as a result of tradition or law in a market area; these costs are readily identifiable since the seller pays these costs in virtually all sales transactions. Special or creative financing adjustments can be made to the comparable property by comparisons to financing terms offered by a third party institutional lender that is not already involved in the property or transaction. Any adjustment should not be calculated on a mechanical dollar for dollar cost of the financing or concession but the dollar amount of any adjustment should approximate the market's reaction to the financing or concessions based on the appraiser's judgment.

STATEMENT OF ASSUMPTIONS AND LIMITING CONDITIONS: The appraiser's certification in this report is subject to the following assumptions and limiting conditions:

1. The appraiser will not be responsible for matters of a legal nature that affect either the property being appraised or the title to it, except for information that he or she became aware of during the research involved in performing this appraisal. The appraiser assumes that the title is good and marketable and will not render any opinions about the title.

2. The appraiser has provided a sketch in this appraisal report to show the approximate dimensions of the improvements. The sketch is included only to assist the reader in visualizing the property and understanding the appraiser's determination of its size.

3. The appraiser has examined the available flood maps that are provided by the Federal Emergency Management Agency (or other data sources) and has noted in this appraisal report whether any portion of the subject site is located in an identified Special Flood Hazard Area. Because the appraiser is not a surveyor, he or she makes no guarantees, express or implied, regarding this determination.

4. The appraiser will not give testimony or appear in court because he or she made an appraisal of the property in question, unless specific arrangements to do so have been made beforehand, or as otherwise required by law.

5. The appraiser has noted in this appraisal report any adverse conditions (such as needed repairs, deterioration, the presence of hazardous wastes, toxic substances, etc.) observed during the inspection of the subject property or that he or she became aware of during the research involved in performing this appraisal. Unless otherwise stated in this appraisal report, the appraiser has no knowledge of any hidden or unapparent physical deficiencies or adverse conditions of the property (such as, but not limited to, needed repairs, deterioration, the presence of hazardous wastes, toxic substances, adverse environmental conditions, etc.) that would make the property less valuable, and has assumed that there are no such conditions and makes no guarantees or warranties, express or implied. The appraiser will not be responsible for any such conditions that do exist or for any engineering or testing that might be required to discover whether such conditions exist. Because the appraiser is not an expert in the field of environmental hazards, this appraisal report must not be considered as an environmental assessment of the property.

6. The appraiser has based his or her appraisal report and valuation conclusion for an appraisal that is subject to satisfactory completion, repairs, or alterations on the assumption that the completion, repairs, or alterations of the subject property will be performed in a professional manner.

Freddie Mac Form 70 March 2005   226   *UAD Version 9/2011*   Page 4 of 6   Fannie Mae Form 1004 March 2005

Uniform Residential Appraisal Report

File # 3   4   4a

APPRAISER'S CERTIFICATION: The Appraiser certifies and agrees that:

1. I have, at a minimum, developed and reported this appraisal in accordance with the scope of work requirements stated in this appraisal report.

2. I performed a complete visual inspection of the interior and exterior areas of the subject property. I reported the condition of the improvements in factual, specific terms. I identified and reported the physical deficiencies that could affect the livability, soundness, or structural integrity of the property.

3. I performed this appraisal in accordance with the requirements of the Uniform Standards of Professional Appraisal Practice that were adopted and promulgated by the Appraisal Standards Board of The Appraisal Foundation and that were in place at the time this appraisal report was prepared.

4. I developed my opinion of the market value of the real property that is the subject of this report based on the sales comparison approach to value. I have adequate comparable market data to develop a reliable sales comparison approach for this appraisal assignment. I further certify that I considered the cost and income approaches to value but did not develop them, unless otherwise indicated in this report.

5. I researched, verified, analyzed, and reported on any current agreement for sale for the subject property, any offering for sale of the subject property in the twelve months prior to the effective date of this appraisal, and the prior sales of the subject property for a minimum of three years prior to the effective date of this appraisal, unless otherwise indicated in this report.

6. I researched, verified, analyzed, and reported on the prior sales of the comparable sales for a minimum of one year prior to the date of sale of the comparable sale, unless otherwise indicated in this report.

7. I selected and used comparable sales that are locationally, physically, and functionally the most similar to the subject property.

8. I have not used comparable sales that were the result of combining a land sale with the contract purchase price of a home that has been built or will be built on the land.

9. I have reported adjustments to the comparable sales that reflect the market's reaction to the differences between the subject property and the comparable sales.

10. I verified, from a disinterested source, all information in this report that was provided by parties who have a financial interest in the sale or financing of the subject property.

11. I have knowledge and experience in appraising this type of property in this market area.

12. I am aware of, and have access to, the necessary and appropriate public and private data sources, such as multiple listing services, tax assessment records, public land records and other such data sources for the area in which the property is located.

13. I obtained the information, estimates, and opinions furnished by other parties and expressed in this appraisal report from reliable sources that I believe to be true and correct.

14. I have taken into consideration the factors that have an impact on value with respect to the subject neighborhood, subject property, and the proximity of the subject property to adverse influences in the development of my opinion of market value. I have noted in this appraisal report any adverse conditions (such as, but not limited to, needed repairs, deterioration, the presence of hazardous wastes, toxic substances, adverse environmental conditions, etc.) observed during the inspection of the subject property or that I became aware of during the research involved in performing this appraisal. I have considered these adverse conditions in my analysis of the property value, and have reported on the effect of the conditions on the value and marketability of the subject property.

15. I have not knowingly withheld any significant information from this appraisal report and, to the best of my knowledge, all statements and information in this appraisal report are true and correct.

16. I stated in this appraisal report my own personal, unbiased, and professional analysis, opinions, and conclusions, which are subject only to the assumptions and limiting conditions in this appraisal report.

17. I have no present or prospective interest in the property that is the subject of this report, and I have no present or prospective personal interest or bias with respect to the participants in the transaction. I did not base, either partially or completely, my analysis and/or opinion of market value in this appraisal report on the race, color, religion, sex, age, marital status, handicap, familial status, or national origin of either the prospective owners or occupants of the subject property or of the present owners or occupants of the properties in the vicinity of the subject property or on any other basis prohibited by law.

18. My employment and/or compensation for performing this appraisal or any future or anticipated appraisals was not conditioned on any agreement or understanding, written or otherwise, that I would report (or present analysis supporting) a predetermined specific value, a predetermined minimum value, a range or direction in value, a value that favors the cause of any party, or the attainment of a specific result or occurrence of a specific subsequent event (such as approval of a pending mortgage loan application).

19. I personally prepared all conclusions and opinions about the real estate that were set forth in this appraisal report. If I relied on significant real property appraisal assistance from any individual or individuals in the performance of this appraisal or the preparation of this appraisal report, I have named such individual(s) and disclosed the specific tasks performed in this appraisal report. I certify that any individual so named is qualified to perform the tasks. I have not authorized anyone to make a change to any item in this appraisal report; therefore, any change made to this appraisal is unauthorized and I will take no responsibility for it.

20. I identified the lender/client in this appraisal report who is the individual, organization, or agent for the organization that ordered and will receive this appraisal report.

Uniform Residential Appraisal Report

File # 3   4   4a

21. The lender/client may disclose or distribute this appraisal report to: the borrower; another lender at the request of the borrower; the mortgagee or its successors and assigns; mortgage insurers; government sponsored enterprises; other secondary market participants; data collection or reporting services; professional appraisal organizations; any department, agency, or instrumentality of the United States; and any state, the District of Columbia, or other jurisdictions; without having to obtain the appraiser's or supervisory appraiser's (if applicable) consent. Such consent must be obtained before this appraisal report may be disclosed or distributed to any other party (including, but not limited to, the public through advertising, public relations, news, sales, or other media).

22. I am aware that any disclosure or distribution of this appraisal report by me or the lender/client may be subject to certain laws and regulations. Further, I am also subject to the provisions of the Uniform Standards of Professional Appraisal Practice that pertain to disclosure or distribution by me.

23. The borrower, another lender at the request of the borrower, the mortgagee or its successors and assigns, mortgage insurers, government sponsored enterprises, and other secondary market participants may rely on this appraisal report as part of any mortgage finance transaction that involves any one or more of these parties.

24. If this appraisal report was transmitted as an "electronic record" containing my "electronic signature," as those terms are defined in applicable federal and/or state laws (excluding audio and video recordings), or a facsimile transmission of this appraisal report containing a copy or representation of my signature, the appraisal report shall be as effective, enforceable and valid as if a paper version of this appraisal report were delivered containing my original hand written signature.

25. Any intentional or negligent misrepresentation(s) contained in this appraisal report may result in civil liability and/or criminal penalties including, but not limited to, fine or imprisonment or both under the provisions of Title 18, United States Code, Section 1001, et seq., or similar state laws.

SUPERVISORY APPRAISER'S CERTIFICATION: The Supervisory Appraiser certifies and agrees that:

1. I directly supervised the appraiser for this appraisal assignment, have read the appraisal report, and agree with the appraiser's analysis, opinions, statements, conclusions, and the appraiser's certification.

2. I accept full responsibility for the contents of this appraisal report including, but not limited to, the appraiser's analysis, opinions, statements, conclusions, and the appraiser's certification.

3. The appraiser identified in this appraisal report is either a sub-contractor or an employee of the supervisory appraiser (or the appraisal firm), is qualified to perform this appraisal, and is acceptable to perform this appraisal under the applicable state law.

4. This appraisal report complies with the Uniform Standards of Professional Appraisal Practice that were adopted and promulgated by the Appraisal Standards Board of The Appraisal Foundation and that were in place at the time this appraisal report was prepared.

5. If this appraisal report was transmitted as an "electronic record" containing my "electronic signature," as those terms are defined in applicable federal and/or state laws (excluding audio and video recordings), or a facsimile transmission of this appraisal report containing a copy or representation of my signature, the appraisal report shall be as effective, enforceable and valid as if a paper version of this appraisal report were delivered containing my original hand written signature.

Signature_____

Name 5 _____

Company Name 6 _____

Company Address 7_____

                  8a, 8b 8c _____

Telephone Number 9_____

Email Address 10_____

Date of Signature and Report 11 _____

Effective Date of Appraisal 12 _____

State Certification # 13_____

or State License # 14_____

or Other (describe) 15 _____ State # 16 _____

State 17 _____

Expiration Date of Certification or License 18 _____

ADDRESS OF PROPERTY APPRAISED

19 _____

20a, 20b, 20c _____

APPRAISED VALUE OF SUBJECT PROPERTY $ 21 _____

LENDER/CLIENT

Name 22 _____

Company Name 23 _____

Company Address 24_____

        _____

Email Address 26_____

SUPERVISORY APPRAISER (ONLY IF REQUIRED)

Signature_____

Name 27_____

Company Name 28 _____

Company Address 29_____

                  30a, 30b 30c _____

Telephone Number 31 _____

Email Address 32 _____

Date of Signature 33 _____

State Certification # 34_____

or State License # 35 _____

State 36 _____

Expiration Date of Certification or License 37 _____

SUBJECT PROPERTY

- **38** Did not inspect subject property
- **39** Did inspect exterior of subject property from street
  Date of Inspection 40 _____
- **41** Did inspect interior and exterior of subject property
  Date of Inspection 42 _____

COMPARABLE SALES

- **43** Did not inspect exterior of comparable sales from street
- **44** Did inspect exterior of comparable sales from street
  Date of Inspection 45 _____

---

membership requirements in an appraisal organization. As a result, the Limiting Conditions and Certification form seems to be suited for Fannie Mae's and Freddie Mac's lending purposes alone.

Scope of Work: The form defines the minimum acceptable scope of work requirements that are satisfactory to Fannie Mae. The appraiser is permitted to expand the scope of work for a complex appraisal.

Intended Use: This form may be used for a mortgage finance transaction only.

Intended User: The lender/client as named in the report. Per USPAP all intended user(s) must be named by name or by type.

Definition of Market Value: This is the same as noted elsewhere in the text.

Statement of Assumptions and Limiting Conditions:

Paragraph 1. This provides that legal title is not a concern to the appraiser. The appraiser assumes that the title is marketable.

Paragraph 2. Notes that the sketch provided in the report is approximate only. It is not a survey.

Paragraph 3. While the appraiser has looked at the FEMA flood maps, there is no guarantee on the part of the appraiser regarding the accuracy of the maps. Once again, the appraiser is not a surveyor.

Paragraph 4. The appraiser will only testify or go to court if arrangements are made in advance to do so.

Paragraph 5. While the appraiser has noted apparent adverse conditions discovered during his/her research and inspection, unless stated, the appraiser has no knowledge of any hidden and unapparent adverse conditions and has assumed there are none. The appraiser is not a building inspector, engineer, or an environmentalist.

Paragraph 6. The appraiser assumes that work in progress or subject to completion will be completed in a professional manner (the old form used the term "workmanlike manner").

The prior **Statement of Limiting Conditions** contained ten paragraphs. As may be seen, the current document has only six. Several paragraphs have been removed to the certification. In the old document, one of the paragraphs required the appraiser to estimate the value of the land to its highest and best use and the improvements to their contributory value when doing the cost approach. These separate values were not to be used in any other appraisal and were invalid if so used. This paragraph seems to have been overlooked in the new document. When doing a cost approach to value, it might be a good idea to make this statement in an addendum to clarify to the reader not to attempt to use the separate values out of context.

The Appraiser's Certification: The new document consists of twenty-five paragraphs rather than the nine contained in the old document. The current USPAP certifications appear to be contained within the new document but the wording differs from that contained within the USPAP document. Fannie Mae appears to have added new elements unilaterally to the Appraiser's Certification simply because they feel that they can do so. Several of these new certifications were developed to make appraisers aware of certain lending and valuation practices that are unacceptable to Fannie Mae. In addition, there are several address appraisal competency issues. The most controversial of these new certifications are paragraphs 21-23. These will be discussed in more detail in the authors' explanations of the new certifications in the paragraphs that follow:

Paragraph 1. The appraiser followed the Scope of Work.

Paragraph 2. The appraiser viewed both the interior and exterior of the subject property.

Paragraph 3. The appraiser followed the current USPAP requirements.

Paragraph 4. The appraiser only utilized the sales comparison approach. He/she is to consider the cost and income approaches, but does not have to include them in the report.

Paragraph 5. The appraiser noted all listings of the subject property within the past 12 months and all sales of the subject property within the past 3 years.

Paragraph 6. The appraiser noted all prior sales of the comparables for the past 12 months.

Paragraph 7. The appraiser utilized the most similar comparable sales.

Paragraph 8. The appraiser is not supposed to add up the cost of the land and the improvements from two separate contracts and call it market value. Such "put together" sales are not considered "arm's length" transactions.

Paragraph 9. Adjustments must be based on market reactions.

Paragraph 10. All information provided by anyone with an interest in the property must be verified by parties that are "arm's length."

Paragraph 11. The appraiser certifies that he/she has both geographic competency and the necessary competency to appraise the property type.

Paragraph 12. The appraiser is aware of and able to obtain all necessary data to perform a credible report.

Paragraph 13. Any data provided by others that is utilized in the report is believed to be reliable and correct.

Paragraph 14. If any adverse conditions were either seen by or made aware of to the appraiser, they have been listed in the report and their effect on value has been analyzed.

Paragraph 15. The appraiser has not knowingly withheld information and the statements and information contained in the report are true and correct to the best of the appraiser's knowledge.

Paragraph 16. The appraiser is not biased. The analyses and conclusions are the appraiser's and are limited only by the assumptions and limiting conditions contained in the report.

Paragraph 17. The appraiser has no current or future interest in the property being appraised. Further, the appraiser has no bias as to race, religion, color, sex, marital status, handicap, familial status, or national origin of any of the parties involved.

Paragraph 18. No predetermined values. No predetermined results.

Paragraph 19. The appraiser did his/her own work. Anyone who helped in a professional manner is named and what he/she did is listed. No one is allowed to make any changes in the appraiser's work and any such changes are unauthorized.

Paragraph 20. The lender/client is identified in the report. The lender/client is the individual, organization, or agent for the organization that ordered and will receive the report.

Paragraph 21. The lender/client may disclose or distribute the report to: the borrower; another lender designated by the borrower; the mortgagee and its successors and assigns; mortgage insurers; government sponsored enterprises; other secondary market participants; and any data collection agency; any government agency both state and federal. The appraiser's consent is not required for any of this. The only people from whom the appraiser may withhold disclosure of the report are members of the news media.

Note: This language has changes from the old document that are very important. In the new document, this paragraph definitely appears to make the borrower an intended user. It may also be argued that the borrower is now a client as well, able to force the lender to distribute the report to another lender for a loan or additional loans. It remains to be seen what effect this wording will have on appraisers' errors and omissions insurance policies or if the expanded disclosure will violate some federal or state privacy and nondisclosure laws.

Paragraph 22. Warns the appraiser that he/she may not distribute the report except as noted in USPAP. Also note that the lender/client may be subject to certain distribution laws, as well.

Paragraph 23. The borrower, another lender at the request of the borrower, and all the entities mentioned in paragraph 21, may rely on the report for any mortgage loan transaction.

Note: The appraiser is limited by USPAP to distributing the report only to the client. Paragraphs 21 and 23 appear to have empowered the borrowers, making them intended users and clients. Indeed, the borrower controls the distribution of the report to other lenders and the borrower is now included in the list of those who may "Rely" on the report for <u>any</u> mortgage finance purposes! This language appears to force the appraiser into a fiduciary obligation to the borrower as well as the lender.

Paragraph 24. States that a report with either an "electronic signature" from a computer or a facsimile signature from a fax machine is the same as an "original ink signature" from an appraiser. In other words, any copy of a report made by anyone (not just the appraiser) is as good as an original.

Paragraph 25. No intentional or negligent misrepresentations are allowed by federal law.

Supervisory Appraiser's Certification: If there is a supervisory appraiser involved, the last five paragraphs require him/her to supervise, and agree with the conclusions of the report. In addition, the supervisor assumes full responsibility for the report, certifies that the employee or sub-contractor who performed the appraisal is qualified to do so, the report complies with the current USPAP, and that an electronic computer copy or a fax is as good as an original.

As a final comment on the document, your authors must note that the wording of the certification raises serious questions about breach of public trust, unauthorized disclosure of borrower's confidential information by lenders, violation of non-disclosure laws in certain states, the fiduciary obligations of appraisers in certain states, the status of a borrower as an intended user/client, and the free distribution of the appraiser's intellectual capital (his/her analyses and conclusions) without his/her knowledge, to anyone desiring to use and reuse them for any purpose, with no compensation to the appraiser, and possible increased liability for such additional use.

This Statement of Limiting Conditions and Appraiser's Certification is really only applicable to Fannie Mae/Freddie Mac Appraisals. Fannie Mae states in the document that no changes, deletions, or additions to the certification may be made and, if made, will not be accepted by Fannie Mae.

The Appraisal Standards Board of the Appraisal Foundation has noted in a Frequently Asked Questions Bulletin (FAQ) issued in July of 2005 that they have no comment on Fannie Mae policies but that appraisers are required by USPAP to supplement inadequate appraisal forms.

"An appraiser __must__ supplement a report form, when necessary, to insure that any intended user of the appraisal is not misled and that the report complies with the applicable content requirements set forth in the Standards Rules."

E. DEFINING THE APPRAISAL PROBLEM IN THE APPRAISAL REPORT

While defining the appraisal problem is the first step in the appraisal process, the information that is gathered for this purpose must also be included in the final appraisal report.

The following discussion of Appraisal Process Steps 2 through 8 is only a summary. Each of these last seven steps will be explored in depth in later chapters.

III. Step 2: Preliminary Analysis

The next step of the appraisal process, preliminary analysis, involves five steps:

1. Identifying the data necessary to solve the appraisal problem.
2. Identifying the sources of those data.
3. Determining resources available.
4. Creating a plan or schedule for the appraisal assignment.
5. Fee proposal and contract.

In many cases, the preliminary analysis begins even before the appraisal problem is fully defined, and both the problem definition and the preliminary analysis overlap with Step 3 in the appraisal process, collecting the data.

Case/Example: A client contacts an appraiser to ask about getting her property appraised. The client wants to know the current market value of her property so she can decide whether to sell it. The client gives the appraiser the property's address and a brief description of the property. At this point, the appraisal problem is not yet completely defined, but the appraiser has already begun collecting data (the location and physical characteristics of the subject property), and may have begun a preliminary analysis of the appraisal assignment by mentally reviewing his or her knowledge of comparable properties.

Preliminary analysis can begin as soon as the appraiser has obtained certain minimum information regarding the appraisal assignment: the identification of the real estate and real property rights to be appraised, the valuation date, the standard of value and use of the appraisal, and some basic information concerning the subject property, such as its location and general description. All of this information is often available at the initial meeting between the appraiser and client, so preliminary analysis may begin even before the client and appraiser enter a contractual agreement to proceed.

A. IDENTIFYING THE NECESSARY DATA

Data may be classified as either *GENERAL DATA (pertaining to real estate values in general)* or *SPECIFIC DATA (pertaining to a particular property);* and general data may be further classified as broad market trend data or more localized competitive supply and demand data. Data is also categorized as primary or secondary, depending on whether it is generated directly by the appraiser or obtained from published sources. (See Chapter 5 for more details.)

"General Data": data about the market in general
"Specific Data": data about specific properties
"Primary Data": data generated by the appraiser (or other experts)
"Secondary Data": data generated by others (published sources)

B. IDENTIFYING THE SOURCES OF DATA

Appraisers use data from many different sources. In many cases, a large part of the data necessary for an appraisal will already be in the appraiser's files. For example, the appraiser may maintain files containing regional, city, and neighborhood data for the area in which the appraiser customarily practices, as well as data regarding local construction costs.

C. PRELIMINARY ANALYSIS

In the *PRELIMINARY ANALYSIS PHASE, the appraiser will identify the relevant data that is already in the appraiser's possession, and that which is not. In the case of information* that the appraiser needs but does not already have, the appraiser will then identify the potential sources for such information. Some common sources of additional information include personal inspection by the appraiser, interviews with owners, brokers, lenders, and public officials, and reviews of statistical data published by government agencies, trade groups, and other research organizations. (Sources of information for appraisal data are discussed in more detail in Chapter 5.)

D. CREATING A PLAN

The third element of the preliminary analysis step is planning or scheduling the work that will be necessary for completing the appraisal assignment. If the assignment is routine, and especially if all the work will be done personally by the appraiser, the work plan may be nothing more than a mental review of the steps that must be taken.

For more complex assignments, or appraisals that require the work of experts or assistants other than the appraiser, a written schedule is useful to plan the work flow and insure timely completion of the appraisal.

E. FEE PROPOSAL AND CONTRACT

A number of lenders make the determination of how much they will pay for an appraisal, leaving the appraisers to decide if they can afford to do the work under the fee conditions. Other clients require the quote of a fee or fee range in advance of any commitment to an appraisal assignment.

While many appraisals are made based on a telephone call, more comprehensive appraisals on commercial property are more likely to be based on a contract signed by the client and the appraiser.

The fee an appraiser may charge depends on his or her reputation. No matter what the fee may be, competent work is a requirement of the job. It is unethical for the fee to be a percentage of the value.

IV. Step 3: Collecting, Verifying, and Analyzing the Data

Selecting and gathering data is one of the primary activities in the appraisal process.

Without data, the appraiser has no basis for a value estimate.

The amount and type of data that must be collected will vary depending on the particular appraisal assignment, but in every case, it is the appraiser's judgment that determines the relevant data.

Case/Example: When appraising a home in 2004, an appraiser was able to gather data on several similar homes that had recently sold in the same neighborhood. But when the appraiser was asked to appraise the same home in 2006, she found that market activity had declined significantly in the neighborhood, and there were no recent comparable sales to rely upon. In this case, the appraiser would have to look for comparable sales outside the subject neighborhood, relying on her judgment and knowledge of the market to identify the most comparable properties.

All of the data collected by the appraiser must be verified in one form or another.

Verification may take the form of a personal inspection, as when the appraiser verifies the dimensions of the subject property by physical measurement. Or it may mean cross-checking information, such as interviewing the owner of a comparable property to verify the terms of the sale.

The method of verifying information depends on the nature of the data and the scope of the appraisal.

The appraiser should verify all data to the extent reasonably possible within the scope of the appraisal.

Case/Example: The appraiser normally verifies building dimensions of the subject property by personally measuring the improvements. This is considered reasonable because the size of the subject property may have a significant impact on its value, and the measurement process does not involve any great expense. In the case of comparable properties, however, verification of building size is usually accomplished by visual inspection only, without actual measurements being taken. In this case, the visual inspection should pick up any major discrepancies in building size data; smaller size differences are not as great a concern for comparable properties, since more than one comparable is relied on in the appraisal.

While data must be verified in terms of its accuracy, it must also be assessed in terms of its relevance to the appraisal assignment at hand. Both of these factors are said to influence the reliability of the data as it is used in the appraisal. All data used in an appraisal must meet these two tests of reliability:

1. the appraiser must have a reasonable basis for believing the data is accurate; and
2. the data must be relevant in some form as an indicator of the value of the subject property.

Data analysis occurs throughout the appraisal process. As data is selected and collected, it is analyzed for its accuracy and relevance (reliability).

The data then serves as the basis for the analysis of highest and best use, and the valuation of the subject in the three approaches to value. And in the reconciliation step, the appraiser will again thoroughly review all of the data relied upon to reach the value estimate. (Data collecting, verifying and analysis will be covered in detail in Chapter 5.)

V. Step 4: Highest and Best Use Analysis

As discussed in Chapter 2, property is normally appraised at its highest and best use, the use that results in the greatest return on the investment. For improved property, highest and best use is analyzed both for the property as improved, and for the property as vacant. *HIGHEST AND BEST USE ANALYSIS is important when land and improvements must be valued separately (as in the cost approach to value).* A highest and best use analysis also indicates whether any existing improvements are contributing to the value of the land, or should be removed to permit some more profitable use.

VI. Step 5: Valuing the Site

A *SITE VALUATION is an estimate of the value of a property, excluding the value of any existing or proposed improvements.* In the case of unimproved property, site valuation is the same as appraising the property "as is." For improved property, site valuation means appraising the property as if vacant. If a structure would have to be removed from a site because it fails to contribute to value, then the cost of removal should be deducted from the separate value assigned to the land in order to arrive at an opinion of the property's "as is" market value.

The term "site" refers to a parcel of land that has been improved by clearing, grading, and providing access and utilities.

> *A "site" is land that has been prepared for some use, typically for the construction of some type of building.*

The term "site improvements" can be confusing, because not all site improvements are considered part of the land for appraisal purposes. Site improvements that are valued as part of the land, such as clearing and grading, are sometimes referred to as improvements *"OFF" THE SITE (OFF-SITE). Contrast these to site improvements, such as buildings and landscaping, that are called improvements "ON" THE SITE (ON-SITE) and are valued separately from the land.*

A. REASONS FOR SEPARATE SITE VALUATION

There are three reasons why a separate site valuation may be necessary.

First, site valuation is an integral part of analyzing highest and best use. By definition, analysis of the highest and best use of a property as if vacant implies a separate site valuation.

The second reason for a separate site valuation is to obtain data for certain valuation techniques. In particular, the cost approach to value and the building residual technique of income capitalization both require a separate estimate of site value. If either of these techniques is used in an appraisal, a separate site valuation is necessary. (The cost approach to value is covered in detail in Chapter 8. The building residual technique is discussed in Chapter 10.)

A separate valuation of site and improvements may also be required by law, particularly in appraisals for property tax assessment and condemnation purposes. In these cases, a separate site evaluation is required by the scope of the appraisal assignment itself. (Site valuation is covered in detail in Chapter 6.)

VII. Step 6: Applying the Three Approaches to Value

Having collected data, analyzed highest and best use, and evaluated the site, the appraiser is ready to apply the three approaches to value. These are the sales comparison approach, the cost approach, and the income approach. Each of these approaches results in an indication of value, also called a value indicator. The appraiser will then reconcile these value indicators in Step 7, reconciliation.

A. COST APPROACH

The **COST APPROACH** *assumes that the value of improved property is indicated by the value of the site, plus the cost (new) to construct the improvements, less any depreciation that the improvements have suffered.* **DEPRECIATION** *is the difference in value between the cost (new) of the improvements and their current value, regardless of the reasons for the difference.* The cost approach can be expressed by the formula:

Property Value of Site (by Cost Approach)
  = Reproduction Cost of Improvements
  - Depreciation from all Causes
  + Land Value (determined separately)

As noted earlier in this chapter, the cost approach requires a separate valuation of the site. The appraiser then estimates what it would cost to replace any existing structures, and adds this amount to the site value. The cost of replacing the structures is estimated as of the date of valuation.

Finally, the appraiser estimates the difference in value between the existing improvements and the cost of replacing them (depreciation), and deducts this amount to arrive at the final value indicator. This does not mean that the appraiser simply subtracts the current value of the improvements from their cost; if the current value of the improvements were known, there would be no reason to calculate depreciation in the first place. Rather, the appraiser must estimate the effect on value of separate items, such as physical deterioration of the improvements, or a loss in value due to an out-dated design. Estimating accrued depreciation is often the most difficult part of applying the cost approach to value, especially for older improvements or improvements that do not conform to the highest and best use of the land as if vacant. (The cost approach to valuation will be covered in detail in Chapter 8.)

B. SALES COMPARISON APPROACH

The sales comparison approach to value is also known as the market approach or market data approach. Under the *SALES COMPARISON APPROACH, the value of the subject property is indicated by the values (sale prices) of similar properties in the market.* These similar properties are referred to as comparables. The two keys to effective use of the sales comparison approach are:

1. identifying similar properties that are truly "comparable" to the subject property; and
2. making the proper adjustments to the sales prices of the comparable properties to account for any differences between the subject property and the comparables.

The considerations in identifying legitimate comparables were discussed earlier in this chapter. It is relatively rare, however, to find two properties that are so comparable that there is no difference in their values. For this reason, the adjustment process is central to the sales comparison approach. In the adjustment process, the sales price of the comparable property is adjusted (up or down) to reflect aspects of the comparable property that are viewed as less valuable or more valuable in comparison to the subject property.

Case/Example: An appraiser identifies a comparable property that is similar to the subject property in all respects, except the subject property has only one bath, while the comparable has two. The comparable property sold recently for $145,000. Current market data indicates that an extra bath adds $5,000 to the values of homes similar to these. So the appraiser would subtract the value of the more desirable feature (the extra bath) from the price of the comparable, to arrive at an indicated value of $140,000 for the subject property.

The sales comparison approach may be summarized by the formula:

Subject Value = Comparable Sales Price +/- Adjustments

(The sales comparison approach to valuation will be covered in detail in Chapter 9.)

C. INCOME APPROACH

The third approach to value is the income approach. This *INCOME APPROACH assumes that the value of property is indicated by the amount of income that the property can generate: the greater the income, the greater the value.*

The income approach may use net income or gross income.

Typically, residential appraisers utilize the gross rent multiplier to determine value by the income approach. *In this approach, the monthly income from each comparable rental sale is divided into its sale price to determine a GROSS RENT MULTIPLIER.* The appraiser then selects a multiplier from the range thus determined and multiplies it by the subject's gross monthly income (say, $1,525 in this case) to determine a value by the income approach.

This process would be carried out for each rental sales comparable (six comparables in this case). From the above process, a range of multipliers would result.

Case/Example: 132, 133, 135, 135, 135, 140

From the above example, we can see that **135** is the most likely multiplier. Thus:

$1,525 Subject Monthly Rent x 135 = $206,000 (rounded) Value by Income Approach.

(The income approach to valuation is covered in detail in Chapter 10.)

VIII. Step 7: Reconciling the Value Indicators

Each of the three approaches to value results in a separate indication of value for the subject property. In general, the greater the similarity among the three value indicators, the more reliable they are. However, it is very rare for all three value indicators to be identical. When the value indicators are not identical, the appraiser must somehow forge the value indicators into one estimate of value. This process is called reconciliation. *RECONCILIATION is the process of analyzing the appraisal problem, selecting the most appropriate method of the three, and giving it the most weight in determining the final estimate of value.*

> *Reconciliation is the easiest process when the value indicators are very similar.*

In that case, it is usually safe to assume that the value of the property lies somewhere between the lowest value indicator and the highest.

Case/Example: An appraiser arrives at the following value indicators:

Cost Approach: $150,000
Market Approach: $145,200
Income Approach: $144,500

Since the value indicators are reasonably similar to each other, the value of the property is probably somewhere between $144,500 (the lowest indicator) and $150,000 (the highest indicator).

However, the process of reconciliation is not a simple averaging of the three value indicators. In fact, there is no set formula at all for reconciling the values. The process relies entirely on the judgment and ability of the appraiser to arrive at the most reliable estimate of value.

A primary consideration in the reconciliation process is the relative reliability of the three value indicators, especially when there is a wide disparity between the three indicators. For this reason, the reconciliation process requires a thorough review of the complete appraisal process. The appraiser must review the reliability of the data, the logic and analysis applied to the data, and the resulting value indicators.

Figure 3-4 is taken from the "Reconciliation" section of the Uniform Residential Appraisal Report. It shows if the appraisal is being made "as is" or "subject to" completion of work.

Figure 3-4

Reconciliation Section - URAR

Indicated Value by: Sales Comparison Approach $ 125 Cost Approach (if developed) $ 126 Income Approach (if developed) $ 127	
128	

This appraisal is made 129 "as is" 130 subject to completion per plans and specifications on the basis of a hypothetical condition that the improvements have been completed 131 subject to the following repairs or alterations on the basis of a hypothetical condition that the repairs or alterations have been completed, or 132 subject to the following required inspection based on the extraordinary assumption that the condition or deficiency does not require alteration or repair: 133

Based on a complete visual inspection of the interior and exterior areas of the subject property, defined scope of work, statement of assumptions and limiting conditions, and appraiser's certification, my (our) opinion of the market value, as defined, of the real property that is the subject of this report is
$ 134 , as of 135 , which is the date of inspection and the effective date of this appraisal.

In addition to reviewing and considering the reliability of the various value indicators, the appraiser will also consider the use of the appraisal. For example, all things being equal, more weight may be placed on the value indicated by the income approach in the case of an appraisal that will be used by an investor who is looking for income property. On the other hand, if the appraisal is being used to help the owner-occupant purchaser qualify for a home loan, the sales comparison data approach may be considered the most reliable. (Reconciliation and final value estimation will be covered in detail in Chapter 11.)

IX. Step 8: Reporting the Value Estimate

The final step in the appraisal process is the preparation of the appraisal report.

A. THE THREE BASIC APPRAISAL REPORTS

According to Standard 2 of USPAP, there are three types of appraisal reports:

1. **Self-contained Appraisal Report** – describes information in detail. It is typically found in a narrative form.
2. **Summary Appraisal Report** – summarizes sufficient information to be understood by the client. It is typically found in a form report.
3. **Restricted Use Appraisal Report** – states information and is restricted to the use of one client.

All of these reports may be either oral or in writing. Reports for federally-related loan transactions must be in writing. The Uniform Standards of Professional Appraisal Practice do not dictate the form or format of either type of report.

Reports can either be in narrative, in a form report, or an oral report.

Note: Form reports provided by lenders (including Fannie and Freddie) are not always compliant with USPAP. The appraiser is cautioned that he or she is required to supplement a form report with an addendum when necessary to ensure compliance with USPAP.

1. Narrative Report

A *NARRATIVE REPORT is the most detailed form of appraisal report.* It describes the data analyzed by the appraiser, the conclusions drawn, and the reasoning behind the stated conclusions.

2. Form Report

The *FORM REPORT is probably the most commonly used type of report for residential appraisals.* Form reports are used by many lenders and government agencies. The form report typically presents the data used by the appraiser and the appraiser's conclusions. There is a limited amount of space on the form for discussing the reasoning behind the appraiser's conclusions; if necessary, the appraiser should use an addendum to provide additional information needed in order to understand the appraiser's value conclusions.

All appraisal forms submitted to Fannie Mae and Freddie Mac must now be completed and turned in electronically (see efanniemae.com).

Note: Form reports provided by lenders (including Fannie and Freddie) are not always compliant with USPAP. The appraiser is cautioned that he or she is required to supplement a form report when necessary to ensure compliance with USPAP.

3. Oral Report

An *ORAL REPORT, as the term implies, is delivered to the client orally rather than in writing.* The amount of detail contained in an oral report will depend on the circumstances and the needs of the client.

B. ESSENTIAL ELEMENTS OF THE APPRAISAL REPORT

It is important to note that regardless of the form of the appraisal report, the appraiser should always keep good detailed records of the data, analysis, and conclusions that form the basis of the appraisal. Also, even the simplest appraisal report should contain the following elements:

1. identification of the subject real estate;
2. identification of the real property rights appraised;
3. the purpose of the appraisal;
4. the definition of value used in the appraisal;
5. the effective date of the appraisal, and date of the report;
6. a description of the scope of the appraisal; and
7. any assumptions and limiting conditions that affect the appraisal.

Appraisal reports will be covered in detail in Chapter 12.

Note: For appraisal reports prepared using the Uniform Appraisal Dataset (UAD) specification, the PDF must be noted with the UAD version that was utilized in the preparation. E.g., the following notation "UAD Version 9/2011" must appear at the bottom of each page in the bottom margin with placement to the left of the page number:

Freddie Mac Form 70 March 2005	226 *UAD Version 9/2011* Page 1 of 6	Fannie Mae Form 1004 March 2005

X. CHAPTER SUMMARY

I. The appraisal process consists of 8 steps that guide the appraiser to a competent estimate of value.

II. Step 1 – Defining the Appraisal Problem.

  A. Appraiser must know what the client wants, and the terms and conditions of the appraisal assignment.

  B. What is to be appraised?

    1. Identity of the real estate is established by the legal description.

      a. The appraiser must identify and consider any personal property that is included in the appraisal, as well as any repairs and improvements that will be made to the property.

2. The real property rights to be appraised will affect the value estimate. Most appraisals are concerned with the fee simple interest, but appraisals may be made for limited or partial interests as well.

3. The appraiser must consider all the rights that benefit the property, as well as all restrictions that may affect value.

4. The purpose of the appraisal is the type of value to be estimated. The value should always be defined.

C. When is it to be appraised?

1. Appraisals estimate value as of a specified date: the valuation date or effective date of the appraisal.

2. The valuation date may or may not be the same as the appraisal report date. Appraisals are sometimes made for past or future values, as well as current values.

D. Why is it to be appraised?

1. The use of the appraisal will affect the appraiser's selection of data, and also the appraiser's judgments in the reconciliation phase of the appraisal.

2. Knowing the use of the appraisal also allows the appraiser to limit liability arising from the appraisal.

E. How is it being valued?

1. The scope of the appraisal is the extent to which the appraiser will collect, verify and report data. Scope may vary depending on the nature of the appraisal assignment, and may affect the cost of the appraisal (the appraisal fee).

2. Assumptions and limiting conditions are stated in order to help readers of appraisal reports to understand the significance of the data and conclusions presented in the report. This is especially important when the reader is relatively unsophisticated, and likely to draw unwarranted conclusions from the report.

3. Assumptions and limiting conditions also protect the appraiser by limiting liability.

F. USPAP requires that the elements identified in defining the appraisal problem be included in the appraisal report.

III. Step 2 – Preliminary Analysis.

A. The appraiser must identify the data that will be necessary to complete the appraisal report.

1. General data relates to the market in general. Specific data relates to a particular property. Competitive supply and demand data is information about the future supply of and demand for competitive properties in the marketplace.

2. Primary data is collected directly by the appraiser. Secondary data is collected from published sources.

3. Data is used in appraisal to identify: market trends, probable future supply and demand of competitive properties, and characteristics of the subject property and comparables.

B. A property is comparable if it is physically similar to the subject property, appeals to the same kinds of buyers, is located in the same market area, and is sold within a limited period of time from the effective date of the appraisal.

C. The appraiser must identify the sources from which the necessary data can be obtained.

D. The appraiser then prepares a work schedule for the appraisal assignment (either mentally or on paper).

IV. Step 3 – Collecting the Data.

A. The accuracy of data used in an appraisal must be verified, either by personal inspection or by cross-checking between sources.

B. All data used in an appraisal should be relevant to the value of the subject property.

V. Step 4 – Analyzing Highest and Best Use.

A. All appraisals must consider highest and best use.

B. For improved property, the appraiser must analyze highest and best use of the property as improved, and also of the property as if vacant.

VI. Step 5 – Valuing the Site.

A. A site is land that has been prepared for use or construction, as by clearing, grading, and provision of access and utilities.

B. Site valuation may be necessary for highest and best use analysis, for application of certain appraisal techniques, and/or by virtue of the scope of the appraisal.

VII. Step 6 – Applying the Three Approaches to Value.

A. The sales comparison approach (market data approach) indicates value by analyzing the sales of similar (comparable) properties.

1. The more similar the comparables are to the subject property, the more reliable they are as indicators of value.

2. Sales prices of comparables must be adjusted to account for any differences between the comparables and the subject property, including physical differences, changes in market conditions, and differences in the terms of sale.

B. The cost approach indicates value by estimating the value of the land separately, then adding the estimated cost (new) of the improvements, and then subtracting depreciation that the improvements have suffered.

1. The older the improvements, the more difficult it becomes to estimate depreciation, and the less reliable is the value indication given by the cost approach.

C. The income approach uses a gross rent multiplier for residential properties.

VIII. Step 7 – Reconciling the Value Indicators.

A. The appraiser must reconcile any differences between the values indicated by the three approaches to value.

B. Reconciliation involves analysis of the reliability of the value indicators, and application of the appraiser's judgment as to the most reliable estimate of value.

IX. Step 8 – Reporting the Value Estimate.

A. The narrative report is the most detailed type of appraisal report. It sets out the data relied on by the appraiser, and explains the analysis of the data and the reasoning that led to the appraisers final estimate of value.

B. Form reports include much of the data that supports the appraiser's conclusion, but may not include complete explanations of the appraiser's reasoning. Form reports are used by many lenders, insurers and government agencies.

C. Appraisal reports are sometimes given orally, generally in courtroom settings.

D. Regardless of the form of an appraisal report, it must contain the elements required by USPAP.

XI. CHAPTER QUIZ

1. The effective date of an appraisal is:

    a. the date of the appraisal report.

    b. the date the appraiser accepts the appraisal assignment.

    c. the date as of which value is estimated.

    d. the date on which the appraiser inspects the subject property.

2. The standard of value refers to:

    a. the kind of value the client wants to know.

    b. the amount of appraisal fee.

    c. the dollar amount of the opinion of value.

    d. none of the above.

3. In defining an appraisal problem, it is important to identify:

    a. the use of the appraisal.

    b. the standard of value.

    c. the intended uses.

    d. all of the above.

4. In defining an appraisal problem, it is important to identify:

    a. the use of the appraisal.

    b. the purpose of the appraisal.

    c. the scope of the appraisal.

    d. all of the above.

5. An appraiser may analyze sales of comparable properties in the:

    a. sales comparison approach.

    b. cost approach.

    c. income approach.

    d. all of the above.

6. Which of the following is NOT a part of defining an appraisal problem?

    a. Identifying the real estate

    b. Identifying the real property interest

    c. Identifying the sources of data

    d. Agreeing on the limiting conditions

7. In an appraisal report, real estate is identified by means of its legal description because:

    a. it is the most commonly accepted way to do it.

    b. it is required by law in all cases.

    c. it is the most accurate way to describe the real estate.

    d. it helps prevent unauthorized persons from understanding the appraisal report.

8. The assumptions and limiting conditions stated in an appraisal report are for the benefit of:

   a. the appraiser.
   b. the client.
   c. third parties.
   d. all of the above.

9. Which of the following would NOT be considered specific data?

   a. The location of a property
   b. Evidence of population shifts in a neighborhood
   c. The size of a lot
   d. The terms and conditions of a sale

10. A site may be valued separately from its improvements:

   a. to provide data for certain valuation techniques.
   b. because it is required by the scope of the appraisal.
   c. as part of the highest and best use analysis.
   d. all of the above.

ANSWERS: 1. c; 2. a; 3. d; 4. d; 5. d; 6. c; 7. c; 8. d; 9. b; 10. d

Chapter 4
Property Description and Appraisal Math

KEY WORDS AND TERMS

Annuity
Artificial Markers
Baseline
Bench Mark
Direct Capitalization
Discounting
Compound Interest
Correction Line
Future Value
Geodetic Survey System
Guide Meridian
Government Lots
Interest Formula
Legal Description
Lot, Block, and Tract System
Mean
Median

Meridian
Metes and Bounds System
Mode
Natural Monument
Point of Beginning
Present Value
Range
Range Lines
Reciprocal
Rectangular Survey System
Reference Point (Monument)
Sections
Standard Deviation
Standard Parallels
Townships
True Point of Beginning

LEARNING OBJECTIVES

After completing this chapter, you should be able to:

1. name the three major systems of land description used in the United States, and explain how land is described under each system;

2. calculate the area and volume of complex figures;

3. solve problems involving percentages, interest, capitalization rates, and income multipliers; and

4. use a financial calculator or table to solve problems involving discounting and annuities.

Chapter 4

I. Property Description

The orderly process of creating boundaries for land ownership and describing them is referred to as a legal description. The land within the boundaries is often referred to as a "parcel, lot, plot, or tract." These terms may refer to all types of improved or unimproved land.

A **PARCEL** *of land generally refers to any piece of land that may be identified by a legal description in one ownership.* Thus, every parcel of real estate is unique.

Although an appraiser is not a surveyor, he or she should be able to read and understand a "legal" description of real estate, since most appraisals require a legal description in order to adequately identify the subject property. Appraisers must also be comfortable applying a variety of different mathematical techniques and formulas that are used in the valuation process.

In everyday life, real estate is normally identified by its street address, for example "111 Main Street" or "1517 Park Avenue." Some properties may also be known by a common name, such as "Empire State Building," or "South Fork Ranch." These methods of property description are suitable for many purposes, but they are of little use when it comes to determining the exact boundaries of a parcel of real estate.

A street address or a descriptive name are informal descriptions. They are NOT considered to be legal descriptions.

Therefore, the appraiser should use what is called a legal description of the subject property. A **LEGAL DESCRIPTION** *of property is one that is adequate to identify the property's exact boundaries.*

In most cases, a property's legal description is given to the appraiser by the appraisal client. It is not the appraiser's responsibility to verify the accuracy of the description or to survey the property. However, an appraiser should be able to recognize whether the description meets the local standards, and he or she should also be able to identify the real estate that is described in the legal description.

There are three methods of legal description commonly used in the United States:

1. The Metes and Bounds System
2. The Rectangular (U.S. Government) Survey System
3. The Lot, Block, and Tract System

Different areas of the country use different systems or combinations of systems, depending on local law and custom. Appraisers should have a basic understanding of each of the three major systems of land description.

II. Metes and Bounds System

The metes and bounds system is the oldest of the three methods of legal description. It also tends to be the most complicated. This **METES AND BOUNDS SYSTEM** *is the method of identifying (describing) property in relation to its boundaries, distances, and angles from a given starting point*. It gives directions and distances that could be followed by a surveyor to trace the boundaries of the property.

There are three basic elements in a metes and bounds description:

1. Reference Points;
2. Courses; and
3. Distances.

A. REFERENCE POINTS

A **REFERENCE POINT** *(sometimes called a monument) is an identifiable, fixed position from which measurements may be taken*. A common example of a reference point is a fixed survey marker that has been permanently set in the ground. Artificial landmarks such as metal stakes are also used as reference points in metes and bounds descriptions.

"Artificial markers" are man made. "Natural monuments" would be natural objects such as trees or rocks.

All metes and bounds descriptions begin at a reference point that serves to locate the property with respect to adjoining surveys in the area. *This initial reference point is known as the* **POINT OF BEGINNING (POB). BOUNDS** *describe the point of beginning, which is also the point (or reference point) of return, and all intermediate points*. The term "point of beginning" can sometimes be confusing, since it can be used to refer to a stone monument as the place to start (see **Figure 4-1**).

A metes and bounds description of this property would start by identifying the true point of beginning, in reference to the stone monument located 2804' south of the true point of beginning. These different points are the initial reference point for the description, and the point at which the description of the actual property boundaries begins. Sometimes these two points coincide, but often they do not.

To distinguish between the initial reference point of the description and the first point on the actual property boundary, the latter is sometimes referred to as the **TRUE POINT OF BEGINNING**. Figure 4-1 shows the relationship between the point of beginning, which is the initial reference point for the description, and the true point of beginning, which is the point at which the description of the actual boundaries of the property begins.

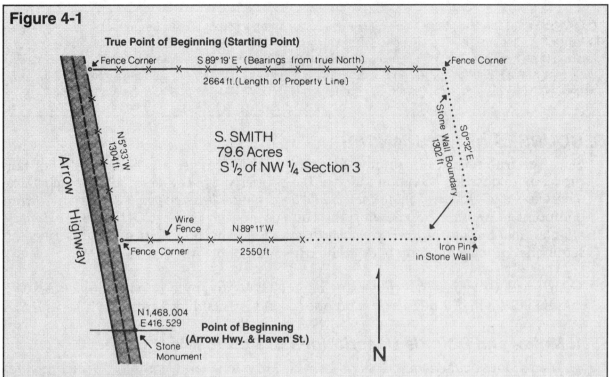

Figure 4-1

PLACE OF START

Essentially, the description is a set of instructions that would enable someone to walk around the boundaries of the property. Each instruction corresponds to one boundary of the property; it tells which direction to go to follow the boundary (the course), and how far to go before changing to another direction (the distance).

Example: A typical instruction or "call" in a metes and bounds description might read: "South 89 degrees 19 minutes East, 2664 feet". This tells the reader to proceed on a course that is 89º 19' to the East of true north, for a distance of 2664 feet.

A course in a metes and bounds description may be stated in one of two ways. If the course is precisely along one of the four cardinal directions, it is usually stated as simply North, South, East or West. All other courses are stated in terms of their quadrant (northeast, northwest, southeast, or southwest) and their angle in relation to a line running north and south.

Northwesterly and northeasterly courses are stated in terms of the angle from north; southwesterly and southeasterly courses are stated in terms of the angle from south. The angle is given in terms of degrees, minutes, and seconds. (In angular measurements, a degree (º) is equal to 1/360th of a full circle; a minute (') is equal to 1/60th of a degree; and a second (") is equal to 1/60th of a minute or 1/360th of a degree.) The size of the angle is written in between the two cardinal directions that form the boundaries of the quadrant.

Example: A southeasterly course that forms an angle of 89º 19' E degrees from true north would be stated as South 89 degrees 19 minutes East, or S 89º 19' E. The angle is written between the two cardinal directions that identify the quadrant.

Case/Example: Starting at the stone monument at the intersection of Haven Street and Arrow Highway ("Point of Beginning") in Cucamonga California, go N5º 33´W; 1804 feet to the second fence corner referred to as the "True Point of Beginning (Starting Point)." Starting at the NW fence corner, go S89º 19´E, 2664 feet; at the NE fence corner, go S0º 32´E for 1302 feet along the stone wall to the iron pin; at the SE corner, go N89º 11´W for 2550; at the SW corner, go N5º 33´W 1804 feet back to the starting point.

B. COURSES AND DISTANCES

Once the true point of beginning is established, the metes and bounds description proceeds to describe each boundary of the property. *METES describe the direction one moves from one reference point to another and the distances between points.* One moves from one point to another by knowing the courses of each point. *COURSES are degrees, minutes, and seconds of angle from north or south.* The boundaries are described in sequential order, ending up back at the true point of beginning.

There are 360 degrees in a circle, so 1 degree (1º) is an angle 1/360th of a circle. One minute is 1/60th of 1 degree (1') and one second is 1/60th of 1 minute (1").

1. Metes and Bounds Descriptions in Appraisals

Metes and bounds descriptions can be very long and complex, which creates opportunities for errors whenever the description must be copied. For this reason, the description is often photocopied from a deed or other document, and the photocopy is attached as an addendum to the appraisal. This does not guarantee the accuracy of the description, but it at least prevents errors in its transcription. Appraisers can calculate a parcel area imputing the metes and bounds description into a computer program. The computer program can also simulate a survey around the boundary of the property to see if the description ends at exactly the point of beginning.

The laser transit used by surveyors has made for more accurate determinations of points, directions and distances. Uncertainty with regards to points of beginning has largely been eliminated through the use of established *BENCH MARKS, which are survey markers set in heavy concrete monuments.* Satellite technology has also been utilized by surveyors to locate points.

The metes and bounds system is often used instead of the rectangular survey system, and is especially good when describing unusual or odd-shaped parcels of land.

III. Rectangular (U.S. Government) Survey System

The second major system of property description is the rectangular survey system, also known as the United States government survey system. In this system, property is described in relation to a rectangular grid that has been established by federal government survey.

The rectangular survey system was established by law in 1785.

It covers most areas of the country that were not already settled as of the date the system was established. Separate rectangular grid systems have been surveyed for most areas of the country, the main exception being the eastern states.

A. BASE LINE AND MERIDIAN

Each main grid in the rectangular survey system has an initial reference point, which serves as the basis for locating all properties in the grid. The initial reference point is the intersection between the *PRINCIPAL MERIDIAN, running north and south,* and the *BASE LINE, which runs east and west.*

These baselines and meridians are simply surveyor reference lines. Land is measured from the intersection of these baselines and meridians.

Each grid system has its own unique name, corresponding to the name of its principal meridian. Property descriptions that use the rectangular survey system must refer to the name of the particular grid that is the reference for the description.

Case/Example: The rectangular survey in Southern California is based on the San Bernardino Principal Meridian and Base Line. A rectangular survey description in this area would refer to the "San Bernardino Base and Meridian," or "S.B.B. & M" (see **Figure 4-2**).

B. TOWNSHIPS

Each rectangular survey grid consists of a series of lines that run parallel to the principal meridian and the base line, at intervals of six miles. *The east-west lines (running parallel to the base line) are called TIER LINES. The north-south lines (parallel to the principal meridian) are referred to as RANGE LINES.* **Figure 4-3** shows principal meridian, base line, tiers and ranges.

Township lines divide the land into a series of east-west strips, called TIERS. Range lines divide the land into north-south strips called RANGES. Where a tier intersects with a range, the result is a six miles by six miles square of land known as a TOWNSHIP. Thus, each township contains 36 square miles. Townships are the main divisions of land in the rectangular survey system. Each township is identified according to its distance from the principal meridian and base line.

Case/Example: The township that is located at the intersection of the first township tier north of the base line, and the third range east of the principal meridian, is called:

"Township 1 North, Range 3 East", or "T1N, R3E"

Figure 4-2

San Bernardino Base and Meridian - S.B.B. & M.

Figure 4-3

Tiers, Ranges, and Townships

116

C. SECTIONS

Each six-mile-square township is divided into an even smaller rectangular grid, with grid lines (called section lines) spaced one mile apart. The section lines run both north-south and east-west within the township. The result is that each township contains 36 sections, each *SECTION measuring one mile on a side and containing 640 acres.* The sections are numbered from 1 to 36, starting with Section 1 in the northeast corner of the township and continuing across and down in snake-like fashion to Section 36 in the southeast corner (see **Figure 4-4**).

Figure 4-4

6	5	4	3	2	1
7	8	9	10	11	12
18	17	16	15	14	13
19	20	21	22	23	24
30	29	28	27	26	25
31	32	33	34	35	36

D. PARTIAL SECTIONS

Sections may be broken down into even smaller rectangular blocks. This is done by first dividing the section into quarters, and then progressively dividing the quarter sections into quarters or halves, as shown in **Figure 4-5 (Section 29)**. Partial sections are described by simply listing the sequence of the divisions, starting with the smallest one and ending with the largest.

Case/Example: The partial section that is highlighted in Figure 4-5 would be described as "Southwest quarter of the Northeast quarter (SW 1/4 of NE 1/4)."

Figure 4-5   **Section 29**

NORTHWEST QUARTER (NW ¼) 160 ACRES	(NW ¼ NE ¼)	(NE ¼ NE ¼)
	(SW ¼ NE ¼)	(SE ¼ NE ¼)

N ↑

| WEST HALF OF SOUTHWEST QUARTER (W ½ SW ¼) 80 Acres | EAST HALF OF SOUTHWEST QUARTER (E ½ SW ¼) 80 Acres | 40 Acres | 10 Acres / 10 Acres 10 Acres (2 1/2 Acres, 2 1/2 Acres, 2 1/2 Acres, 2 1/2 Acres) |
| | | 40 Acres | 40 Acres |

E. ADJUSTMENTS AND GOVERNMENT LOTS

The range lines in the rectangular survey are supposed to run true north and south. They are also supposed to be parallel, spaced six miles apart. Due to the fact that the earth is not flat, however, lines running north and south are not parallel to each other, they tend to converge (get closer together) as they approach the poles. To account for this convergence, the range lines in the rectangular survey must be adjusted.

To maintain an approximate distance of six miles between range lines, they are adjusted at intervals of every 24 miles (every fourth township line) north and south of the base line. *The township lines where the adjustments are made are referred to as CORRECTION LINES or STANDARD PARALLELS. Similarly, every fourth range line east and west of the principle meridian is referred to as a GUIDE MERIDIAN.*

Irregularities due to convergence or other factors are usually accounted for along the north and west boundaries of a township. For this reason, the quarter sections that lie along these boundaries are often somewhat irregular in size and shape. Irregular parcels in a township can also result when land abuts a body of water such as a river, lake or ocean. *An irregular parcel that does not constitute a full section or quarter section is known as a GOVERNMENT LOT*, and is identified by a special government lot number.

F. RECTANGULAR SURVEY SYSTEM DESCRIPTIONS

Land descriptions using the rectangular survey system are relatively simple. The standard procedure is to begin with the smallest division that identifies the parcel, and then list each larger division in sequence. At the end, the description must refer to the base and meridian that is the reference for the grid.

Case/Example: A typical rectangular survey description might read "The Northwest quarter of the Southwest quarter of Section 33, Township 6 South, Range 13 West, San Bernardino Base and Meridian," or "The NW 1/4 of the SW 1/4 of Sec. 33, T6S, R13W, S.B.B. & M."

(Note: descriptions usually include county and state as well to avoid confusion.)

G. GEODETIC SURVEY SYSTEM

As part of the government survey system, the U. S. Department of the Interior Geological Survey maintains a geodetic survey system and publishes detailed topographic maps. These maps, called *QUADRANGLES, ordinarily contain the base lines and principal meridians, section lines, and most major topographic features, including towns, roads, bodies of water, and contour lines and elevations of land.*

IV. Lot, Block, and Tract System

The rectangular survey is a simple and convenient way to describe large parcels of land. The lot and block system, on the other hand, is better suited for describing smaller parcels, such as building lots. This *LOT, BLOCK, AND TRACT SYSTEM allows land to be described by reference to an official map showing the boundaries of the parcel.* This description is also known as a **subdivision map**.

Reference Table

One **ACRE** is 43,560 square feet; 4,840 square yards.
One **SQUARE ACRE** is 208.71 feet on each side, but this number is generally rounded off to 209 feet.
One **MILE** is 5,280 feet long.
One **SQUARE MILE** contains 640 acres.
One **SECTION** is one square mile, containing 640 acres.
One **TOWNSHIP** (standard) is six miles square (36 square miles).
One **COMMERCIAL ACRE** is an acre minus any required public dedications.
One **ROD** is 16.5 feet long (5.5 yards). There are four rods, or 66 feet, to one chain, and 320 rods to a mile.

For subdivided property, the lot, block, and tract system is the most widely used legal description system.

When a section or partial section is subdivided, the land is surveyed and a map is drawn to show the exact boundaries of each lot in the subdivision. The map is similar to a metes and bounds description; it shows a fixed reference point (such as a section corner) that locates the survey in relation to surrounding properties, and identifies the boundaries of each lot by course and distance. Maps usually indicate the public streets, easements and lot lines.

Each lot on the subdivision map is identified by a number or letter. Once the map has been filed in the local county records office, a lot can be described by simply referring to its lot number, and identifying the map that contains its description (See **Figure 4-6**).

Case/Example: The description of a lot in a subdivision known as Short Line Beach Subdivision No. 2 might read "LOT 22 in BLOCK 21 of Short Line Beach Subdivision No. 2 as per map recorded in Book 4, Page 42 of Maps in the Office of the County Recorder of Los Angeles.

V. Appraisal Math

Appraisers use math in a wide variety of situations, from calculating the living area of a house to capitalizing the value of an income property. In the next part of this chapter, we will examine some of the more common applications of math in appraisal practice, including area and volume calculations, percentage and interest calculations, income capitalization, and financial calculations involving compound interest. The more advanced mathematical techniques that are used by appraisers, such as statistical analysis and regression techniques, are beyond the scope of this textbook.

A. DISTANCE, AREA, AND VOLUME

Appraisers are often called upon to determine the size of something, such as a lot or a building. The size may be a distance, an area or even a volume.

DISTANCE is a measurement of one dimension only, such as the width of a lot or the height of a building. Distance is normally determined by direct measurement, as when an appraiser measures the perimeter walls of a house.

AREA is the size of something in two dimensions. It doesn't matter what the dimensions are called: length and width, width and height, width and depth, length and height, and so on. What matters is that there are only two dimensions. Unlike distance, area cannot be measured directly; each of the two dimensions can be measured, but the area must be calculated mathematically.

For a home, area would be calculated by using the exterior dimensions (excluding the garage) and would customarily be expressed in square feet.

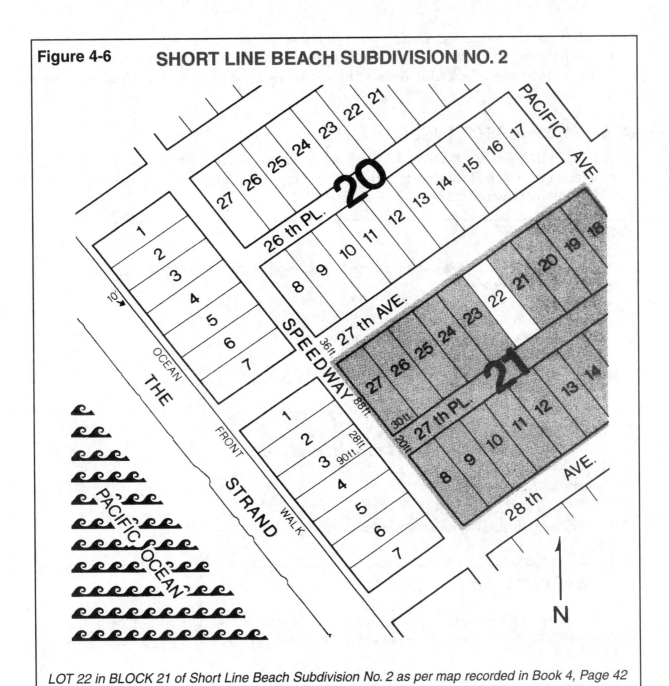

Figure 4-6   SHORT LINE BEACH SUBDIVISION NO. 2

LOT 22 in BLOCK 21 of Short Line Beach Subdivision No. 2 as per map recorded in Book 4, Page 42 of Maps, in the office of the County Recorder of Los Angeles.

The area of an object can be calculated from its dimensions. The formula used to calculate area depends on the shape of the object; different formulas are used to calculate the areas of rectangles, triangles, circles and other shapes.

Like area, **VOLUME** *is the size of something in more than one dimension. In the case of volume, the thing to be measured has three dimensions.* Here again, it doesn't matter what the dimensions are called, it only matters that there are three of them. And as is the case with area, each of the dimensions may be measured directly, but the volume itself must be calculated. The following sections explain the procedures for calculating areas and volumes.

B. AREA OF A RECTANGLE

A *RECTANGLE is any four-sided figure whose sides all meet at right angles (90°).* The area of a rectangle can be found by simply multiplying the dimensions of any two adjacent sides (the length and the width). See **Figure 4-7**.

Figure 4-7

EXAMPLE: How many square feet would there be in a rectangular parcel 100 feet long and 50 feet wide?

100'

?
AREA

50'

A = L x W

AREA = LENGTH x WIDTH

AREA = 100 FEET x 50 FEET

A = 100 x 50

A = 5,000 SQUARE FEET

ANSWER: The area of this lot is calculated to be **5,000 square feet**.

Area of Rectangle = Length x Width

Case/Example: A rectangular garage measures 24 feet by 30 feet. The area of the garage can be calculated by multiplying the length by the width (24 x 30 = 720), so the garage has an area of 720 square feet.

C. UNITS OF AREA

As seen in the previous example, the result of an area calculation is expressed as square units. The units can be square inches, square feet, square yards, etc., depending on the units of distance (length) that are used to express the dimensions (length and width) of the object.

The most common units of area are square inches, square feet, square yards, square miles and acres. A square inch is equivalent to the area of a square that measures one inch on each side. Similarly, a square foot is equal to the area of a one-foot square, a square yard is equal to the area of a one-yard square, and a square mile is equal to the area of a square measuring one mile by one mile. An acre is an area that is equivalent to 43,560 square feet.

D. CONVERTING UNITS

When calculating areas, it is essential that the same units of distance be used to express each of the two dimensions.

If one dimension is expressed in feet and the other is expressed in yards, for example, one of the dimensions will have to be converted to match the unit of the other before area can be calculated (see **Figure 4-8**).

Figure 4-8

CONVERSION: SQUARE FEET TO SQUARE YARDS

Many questions on area will ask that you present the answer in square yards, then square feet. Conversion of square feet to square yards is a simple matter of dividing the answer by nine, because there are nine square feet in a square yard.

(3 FEET X 3 FEET = 9 SQUARE FEET OR 1 SQUARE YARD)

Square yards, likewise, may be converted into square feet through multiplication by nine.

SQUARE YARDS = SQUARE FEET / 9

SQUARE FEET = SQUARE YARDS x 9

Case/Example: A rectangular building is 45 feet long and 7 yards wide. To calculate the floor area of the building, one of the dimensions must first be converted. One yard is equal to 3 feet, so 7 yards can be converted to feet by multiplying by 3.

7 yards x 3 (feet per yard) = 21 feet

Now both dimensions are expressed in feet, so the area can be calculated.

21 feet x 45 feet = 945 square feet.

Instead of converting the width to feet, we could have converted length to yards. In this case the length of 45 feet is divided by 3 to get the equivalent number of yards.

45 ÷ 3 (feet per yard) = 15 yards

The area can then be calculated as follows.

15 yards x 7 yards = 105 square yards

In the preceding example, we obtained two different answers for the area of the building, depending on the units we used for the dimensions. When the dimensions were expressed as feet, the answer was an area in square feet; when the dimensions were expressed as yards, the answer was square yards. Units of area can be converted, just like units of distance. In this case, one square yard is equal to 9 square feet, so the calculated area of 105 square yards is equivalent to the calculated area of 945 square feet.

105 sq. yd. x 9 (sq. ft. per sq. yd.) = 945 sq. ft.

Sometimes, dimensions are expressed in a combination of units, such as 12 feet 4 inches (12'4"). Dimensions that use a combination of units cannot be used to calculate area; they must be converted to a single unit. Only one part of the dimension is converted, and then added to the other part to get the dimension in a single unit.

Case/Example: To convert 12' 4" to feet, only the 4" is converted. 4 inches ÷ 12 (inches per foot) = 0.33 feet. The result of the conversion is then added to the other part of the dimension (the 12 feet).

0.33 feet + 12 feet = 12.33 feet

If we wanted to convert 12' 4" to inches, we would convert the 12 feet to inches and then add the result to 4 inches.

12 feet x (12 inches per foot) = 144 inches
144 inches + 4 inches = 148 inches

To change square inches to square feet, divide the square inches by 144 (12" x 12" = 144 square inches.)

E. AREA OF A TRIANGLE

A *TRIANGLE is any three-sided figure whose sides are straight lines.* To calculate the area of a triangle, two dimensions must be known: the base and the height. The *BASE is simply the length of one of the sides of the triangle.* The *HEIGHT is the perpendicular distance (the distance measured at a right angle—90 degrees to the base) from the base to the opposite point (angle) of the triangle.*

To calculate the area of a triangle, multiply the base by the height, then multiply the result by ½ (or divide by 2).

Area of a Triangle = 1/2 x Base x Height

Case/Example: A triangular area has a base of 14 feet and a height of 10 feet. To find the area, multiply ½ times the base by the height.

1/2 x 14 feet x 10 feet = 70 square feet

Case/Example: How many square feet would there be in a triangular lot with a 150 foot base and a height of 100 feet? (See **Figure 4-9**.)

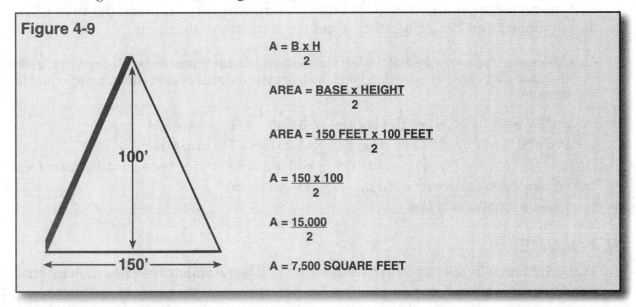

Figure 4-9

$$A = \frac{B \times H}{2}$$

$$AREA = \frac{BASE \times HEIGHT}{2}$$

$$AREA = \frac{150\ FEET \times 100\ FEET}{2}$$

$$A = \frac{150 \times 100}{2}$$

$$A = \frac{15,000}{2}$$

$$A = 7,500\ SQUARE\ FEET$$

As is the case with any area calculation, it is essential that both dimensions (the height and the base) be expressed in the same unit of measurement. If necessary, the dimensions may have to be converted to a common unit before calculating the area.

When calculating the area of a triangle, it does not matter which side of the triangle is used as the base. What is important is that the height measurement must correspond to the base measurement. In other words, the height must be the perpendicular distance from the base to the opposite point of the triangle.

F. RIGHT TRIANGLES

A *RIGHT TRIANGLE is a triangle where two of the sides meet at a right angle (90°).* When calculating the area of a right triangle, the dimensions of the two sides that meet at a right angle can be used as the base and the height. The formula for calculating the area is the same as for any other triangle:

Area = 1/2 x Base x Height

Case/Example: Because the triangle illustrated below contains a right angle, the dimensions of the two sides that meet at the right angle can be used as the base and the height to calculate the area of the triangle.

1/2 x 12 feet x 20 feet = 120 square feet

G. AREAS OF COMPLEX FIGURES

To calculate the area of a complex figure (such as the lot outlined in **Figure 4-10**), the figure is first divided up into simple shapes. Virtually any figure with straight sides can be divided into a series of rectangles and/or triangles. The area of each component rectangle and triangle is calculated individually, and then the areas of all the components are added together to get the total area of the figure.

Case/Example: To find the area of the lot, we must first divide it into rectangles and triangles. Figure 4-10 shows one way to do this. Next, we calculate the area of each component rectangle and triangle.

Square "S" is 40' by 40', so its area is 40 feet x 40 feet = 1,600 square feet.

Rectangle "R" is 30' by 25', so its area is 30 feet x 25 feet = 750 square feet.

Triangle "T" is 30' by 30', so its area is 30 feet x 30 feet = 900 square feet ÷ 2 = 450 square feet.

Total Area = 1,600 square feet + 750 square feet + 450 square feet.

Total Area = 2,800 square feet.

H. VOLUME

VOLUME is the size of an object in three dimensions. It is the amount of three dimensional space that is enclosed or occupied by the object. Just as area can be calculated by multiplying two dimensions to find square units, volume is calculated by multiplying three dimensions to find cubic units. Cubic units are similar to square units, except that they have three dimensions instead of two. For example, a cubic inch is equal to the volume of a cube measuring one inch on each side and a cubic foot is the volume of a cube with sides measuring 1 foot.

The rule that all dimensions must be expressed in the same unit of measurement applies to volume calculations, just as it does to area calculations.

If all three of the dimensions are not expressed in identical units (all in feet, all in inches, etc.), then they must be converted to a consistent unit before the volume is calculated.

Case/Example: How many cubic feet would there be in a room that is 15 feet long, 10 feet wide and 10 feet high? See **Figure 4-11.**

Cubic measurements are important in the appraisal of warehouses where a price per cubic unit becomes important because cubic measurements determine storage capability.

Figure 4-10

An Irregular Lot Problem

EXAMPLE: What would be the total area of the irregular lot shown below? Use the dimensions given to calculate your answer.

ANSWER: The irregular lot is broken up into a square, a rectangle and a triangle. The area of the parcel is the total of the areas of each of these.

TOTAL AREA = AREA (S) + AREA (R) + AREA (T)
TOTAL AREA = AREA SQUARE + AREA RECTANGLE + AREA TRIANGLE

AREA (S) = L x W
AREA (S) = LENGTH X WIDTH
AREA (S) = 40 FEET X 40 FEET
AREA (S) = 40 X 40
AREA (S) = 1,600 SQUARE FEET

The area of the square is **1,600 square feet**.

750
Square Feet
(R)

30'

25'

AREA (R) = L x W

AREA (R) = LENGTH x WIDTH

AREA (R) = 30 FEET x 25 FEET

AREA (R) = 30 X 25

AREA (R) = 750 SQUARE FEET

The area of the rectangular section is 750 square feet.

450
Square
Feet
(T)

30'

30'

$$AREA (T) = \frac{B \times H}{2}$$

$$AREA (T) = \frac{BASE \times HEIGHT}{2}$$

$$AREA (T) = \frac{30 \text{ FEET} \times 30 \text{ FEET}}{2}$$

$$AREA (T) = \frac{30 \times 30}{2}$$

$$AREA (T) = \frac{900}{2}$$

AREA (T) = 450 SQUARE FEET

The area of the triangle is 450 square feet.

IRREGULAR LOT PROBLEM SOLUTION

AREA (S) = 1,600 SQUARE FEET

AREA (R) = 750 SQUARE FEET

AREA (T) = 450 SQUARE FEET

TOTAL AREA = AREA (S) + AREA (R) + AREA (T)

TOTAL AREA = 1,600 + 750 + 450

TOTAL AREA = 2,800 SQUARE FEET

The total area of this irregular lot is 2,800 square feet.

Figure 4-11

VOLUME PROBLEM

V = L x W x H

VOLUME = LENGTH x WIDTH x HEIGHT

VOLUME = 15 FEET x 10 FEET x 10 FEET

VOLUME = 15 x 10 x 10

VOLUME = 150 x 10

VOLUME = 1,500 CUBIC FEET

ANSWER: The cubic volume of this room would be **1,500 cubic feet**.

I. RECIPROCALS

The *RECIPROCAL OF A NUMBER is equal to 1 divided by the number*. For example, the reciprocal of 2 is equal to $1 \div 2$, or ½ (0.5). Reciprocals always come in pairs. If "A" is the reciprocal of "B," then "B" is also the reciprocal of "A."

Case/Example: 0.5 is the reciprocal of 2. So 2 is the reciprocal of 0.5.

1 ÷ 2 = 0.5
1 ÷ 0.5 = 2

Reciprocals can be useful in performing multiplication and division calculations. The reason is that multiplication by a number is the same as division by its reciprocal; and division by a number is the same as multiplication by its reciprocal.

Case/Example: Multiplication by 0.5 is the same as division by 2 (the reciprocal of 0.5); and division by 0.5 is the same as multiplication by 2.

10 x 0.5 = 5 or 10 ÷ 2 = 5
10 ÷ 0.5 = 20 or 10 x 2 = 20

J. PERCENTAGES

The use of percentages is common in appraisals. Allocation, direct capitalization, sales comparison, and many other appraisal techniques use percentages. In ordinary language, we often say that one number is a certain percentage of another number. In mathematics, "percent of" means "percent times," so the general formula for percent calculations is:

Part = Percentage x (of) Whole

Case/Example: $10.00 is 10% of $100.00.
Part = Percentage x Whole
$10.00 = 10% x $100.00

The symbol "%" is used to designate a percentage. "Percent," or "%," means "divided by 100," so a ***PERCENTAGE*** *is simply a number divided by 100*. For example, 10% means 10 divided by 100.

In mathematical calculations using percentages, the percentage is always converted to a decimal number (by dividing by 100) before performing the calculation.

Because a percentage is nothing more than a number divided by 100, it is easy to convert percentages to decimals, and decimals to percentages. To convert a percentage to a decimal, move the decimal point two places to the left (adding zeros if necessary) and drop the percent sign. Reverse the process to convert a decimal to a percentage: move the decimal point two places to the right (again adding zeros if necessary), and add a percent sign.

Case/Example: To convert 8.5% to a decimal, move the decimal point two places to the left and drop the percent sign.

> **PERCENT TO DECIMAL**
>
> 8.5% = .085

Case/Example: To convert .095 to a percentage, move the decimal point two places to the right and add the percent sign.

> **DECIMAL TO PERCENT**
>
> .095 = 9.5%

Any mathematical formula that can be written in the form A = B x C, such as the basic percentage formula (Part [A] = Percentage [B] x Whole [C]), can be solved in three different ways, depending on whether A, B or C is the unknown quantity. To find the value of one of the variables, simply perform the operation indicated by **Figure 4-12** on the other two: to find A, multiply B by C (A = B x C); to find B, divide A by C (B = A ÷ C); and to find C, divide A by B (C = A ÷ B).

Case/Example: A 1,500 square foot house is located on a 7,500 square foot lot. What percentage of the lot is occupied by the house?

Figure 4-12

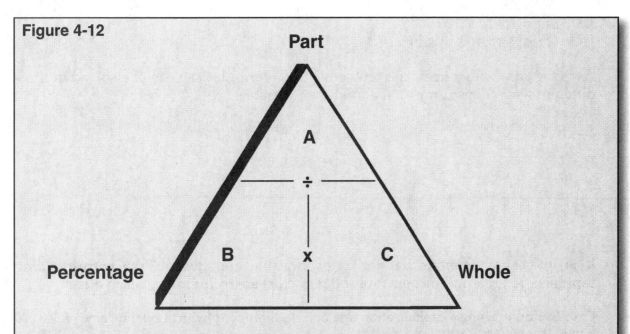

The pyramid consists of three sections, or chambers (which can be modified to four chambers for certain problems). The top chamber is the **PART (A)** chamber. It is separated from the other two chambers by a division sign. The bottom left chamber is the **PERCENTAGE (B)** chamber. The bottom right chamber is the **WHOLE (C)** chamber. It is separated from the **PERCENTAGE** chamber by a multiplication sign.

1. To find A, cover A and multiply B x C
2. To find B, cover B and divide A by C
3. To find C, cover C and divide A by B

We are looking for the percentage of the lot, so the lot represents the whole, and the house is the part.

Part (A) = Percentage (B) x Whole (C), so
Percentage (B) = Part (A) ÷ Whole (C)
Percentage = 1,500 sq. ft. ÷ 7,500 sq. ft = 0. 2.

If we convert the decimal to a percentage, we can see that the house covers 20% of the lot area.

K. DIRECT CAPITALIZATION

Direct capitalization problems are very similar to percentage problems; they both use formulas that can be written as A = B x C. In direct capitalization, there are these formulas, depending on whether the calculation involves a capitalization rate or an income multiplier (factor).

Income = Rate x Value
IRV (The Appraiser's Friend)

As is the case with percentage problems, these formulas can each be solved in three different ways, depending on the unknown variable.

I = R x V

$$R = \frac{I}{V}$$

$$V = \frac{I}{R}$$

It is interesting to note that for a given value and income, the corresponding capitalization rate and income multiplier (factor) are reciprocals of each other.

Case/Example: Using a capitalization rate of 25%, a property with annual income of $40,000 would be assigned a value of $160,000.

Value = Income ÷ by Rate

Value = $40,000 ÷ 25% (0.25) = $160,000

The corresponding income multiplier is 4, which is the reciprocal of 0.25 (1 ÷ 0.25 = 4).

Rate (Factor) = Income ÷ Value

Rate (Factor) = $40,000 ÷ $160,000 = .25

L. INTEREST

Simple interest problems are also similar to percentage and capitalization problems, but they involve an additional factor: time. The formula for calculating interest is:

Interest = Principal x Rate x Time

Instead of our usual A = B x C, we now have A = B x C x D. Fortunately, we can still use the same approach to solving for each of the four variables. D represents Time for one year (one year is 1, two years is 2, and six months is 1/2). The basic interest formula can be stated in four ways:

Interest (A) = Principal (B) x Rate (C) x Time (D)

Principal (B) = Interest (A) ÷ (Rate [C] x Time [D])

Rate (C) = Interest (A) ÷ (Principal [B] x Time [D])

Time (D) = Interest (A) ÷ (Principal [B] x Rate [C])

An important point to keep in mind when solving interest problems is that an interest rate is always a rate per one year time period, such as 10% per year, or 2% per month, which should be converted to 24% a year. It is essential that the time variable in the interest equation be expressed in the same units as the time period of the interest rate. If necessary, either the rate or the time should be converted before performing the calculation.

Case/Example: An investment earns 12% interest per year. How much interest will be earned in six months on an investment of $1,000? Here, the interest rate is an annual rate, but the time is given in months. Either the interest rate must be converted to a monthly rate, or the time must be converted to years.

Interest = Principal x Rate x Time

Interest = $1,000 x .12 (12 percent per year) x 6/12 (year) = $60, or

Interest = $1,000 x 0.12 (12% per year) x 0.5 (years) = $60

VI. Financial Calculations

According to folk wisdom, "time is money." The value of a dollar depends on when it is received. One dollar that is received today is worth more now than one dollar that will be paid a year from now. The so-called "time value" of money is a critical factor in analyzing property values with the income approach.

In the past, financial calculations were performed using complex formulas and huge tables of factors. Now, these manual techniques have been largely replaced by computer programs and inexpensive financial calculators. Financial calculations can now be performed accurately and quickly with the push of a few buttons.

Computer programs and financial calculators may simplify much of the work of financial calculations, but the appraiser still needs to understand the fundamental concepts that these computers are designed to apply. The following section will discuss the basic concepts that underlie all financial calculations.

A. PRESENT AND FUTURE VALUE

If you put $100 into a savings account that pays 10% interest per year, after one year your account will hold $110: the original $100 plus one year's interest of 10%, or $10. In this case, the present value of $100 is equal to a future value of $110. ***PRESENT VALUE*** *is the value of money today;* ***FUTURE VALUE*** *is the value of money at some date in the future. The process of calculating the present value of a future payment amount is known as* ***DISCOUNTING***.

The relationship between present value and future value depends on the amount of interest that can be earned between the present date and the future date. Earlier in this chapter, we saw that interest can be calculated with the formula: Interest = Principal x Rate x Time. This formula is used to calculate simple interest, which is interest that is earned by the principal only. However, most financial calculations involve compound interest.

B. INTEREST COMPOUNDING

COMPOUND INTEREST is interest that is earned on both principal and accrued (paid) interest. In our savings account example, the initial $100 account balance grew to $110 after one year. If the account pays compound interest, the interest for the second year will be calculated on the new balance of $110 ($100 principal and $10 accrued interest). So in the second year, the account will earn interest of $11 (10% x $110), rather than just $10 as in the first year.

A critical factor in calculating compound interest is the *COMPOUNDING PERIOD. This is the interval at which interest is actually paid on the investment.* If interest is compounded annually, for example, the interest payments are made once per year. With monthly compounding, interest is paid each month, so the balance of principal plus accrued interest grows each month.

Case/Example: If the 10% interest on our savings account were compounded quarterly, an interest payment would be added to the account after each three months, 10% annual interest corresponds to 2.5% quarterly interest (10% ÷ 4 = 2.5%, or 0.025), so the interest on the account for one year would be calculated as follows:

$100.00 x 0.025 = $2.50 interest for 1st quarter
$100.00 + $2.50 = $102.50 account balance after 1st quarter
$102.50 x 0.025 = $2.56 interest for 2nd quarter
$102.50 + $2.56 = $105.06 account balance after 2nd quarter
$105.06 x 0.025 = $2.63 interest for 3rd quarter
$105.06 + $2.63 = $107.69 account balance after 3rd quarter
$107.69 x 0.025 = $2.69 interest for 4th quarter
$107.69 + $2.69 = $110.38 account balance after 4th quarter (1 year)

With quarterly compounding at a 10% annual rate of interest, the present value of $100 equals a future value (after one year) of $110.38. We have seen that the relationship between present value and future value depends on the amount of interest that is earned between the present date and the future date. The amount of interest earned by an investment depends on two factors:

1. the interest rate per compounding period; and
2. the number of compounding periods during the life of the investment.

In the example above, we calculated the future value of $100, based on an interest rate of 2.5% per compounding period (10% annual interest with quarterly compounding), and a total of four compounding periods (1 year = 4 quarters). The basic process is fairly simple: for each compounding period during the life of the investment, the interest for the period is calculated and added to the investment balance. To calculate the present value of a future amount the process is simply reversed.

Although the formulas for calculating present value and future value are fairly simple, they can be lengthy without a financial calculator.

C. "HOSKOLD" OR SINKING FUND METHOD

The **HOSKOLD METHOD** *gives the present value of annual recapture amounts on an investment, if put into a sinking fund account earning interest at a safe rate* (the equivalent to U.S. government bond rate). An income stream from wasting assets like mineral deposits might be recaptured using this method. While the premise may be sound, it is rarely used anymore, because modern day investors prefer to earn a higher rate of return on an investment.

D. "INWOOD" METHOD

The **INWOOD METHOD** *holds that the present value of recapturing an investment from an income stream is based on a single discount rate.* An annual recapture amount, assuming a level annual income, is capable of earning compound interest, and is amortized or "paid off" just like a loan. Complicated methods like these are described in greater detail in advanced appraisal textbooks.

VII. Measures of Central Tendency

Appraisers often calculate averages to determine predominant values in a neighborhood, average rent prices, and gross rent multipliers. Additionally, information from the U.S. Bureau of the Census and other statistical data is often presented as an average. Calling something average has a number of different meanings and the appraiser has to be conversant with them all. The common ways to measure central tendency (average) are the **mean**, **median**, and **mode**.

In the sample of values listed below:

1
2
3
4
4

2.8 is the mean
3 is the median

4 is the mode
1-4 is the range

MEAN is the arithmetic average, which is calculated by adding all the values in the sample to arrive at a sum and then dividing by the number of items in the sample. This method is generally used by real estate agents when referring to "average" square footage or "average" price.

MEDIAN is the middle value in a sample of values. In the sample above 3 is the median because there are an equal number of value above and below it (two higher and two lower). Real estate publications often refer to the median price of housing in a particular state, city, or county.

MODE is the most frequently occurring value in a sample. In the sample above 4 is the mode. Modal prices of similar housing would be of interest to an appraiser in developing comparables.

RANGE is the spread between the lowest and highest numbers in the sample. Appraisers, for instance, would be interested in the lowest and highest prices paid for housing in a neighborhood.

STANDARD DEVIATION is a mathematical formula that measures how far the prices vary from the mean (arithmetic average). For example, a small standard deviation would mean that most of the prices are approximately the same. The greater the standard deviation the more the prices would vary.

VIII. CHAPTER SUMMARY

I. In appraisals, real estate is identified by its legal description.

    A. A metes and bounds description describes the boundaries of a parcel of land by listing the course and distance for each boundary.

        1. Reference points or monuments are natural or man-made landmarks that are used to locate property boundaries.

        2. The point where the actual description of the property boundaries begins and ends is the true point of beginning.

        3. Courses in a metes and bounds description are described according to their deviation from true north or south.

    B. The rectangular (government) survey divides land into rectangular grids for purposes of identification.

        1. Each grid system is identified by the name of its principal meridian (north-south) and base line (east-west line).

        2. Township lines (east-west) and range lines (north-south) divide the land into townships measuring six miles on each side. The townships are numbered according to their distance from the principal meridian and base line, e.g., Township 3 North, Range 2 West.

        3. Townships are divided into 36 numbered sections, each measuring 1 mile on a side and containing 640 acres.

        4. Sections may be further divided into quarter sections, quarter-quarter sections, etc.

        5. Adjustments to account for convergence are made at intervals of 24 miles north and south of the base line, at correction lines (standard parallels). The range lines at intervals of 24 miles east and west of the principal meridian are called guide meridians.

        6. Partial sections (resulting from convergence, bodies of water, or other causes) may be identified as government lots, with a special identifying number.

    C. The lot, block, and tract system identifies land by referring to a numbered parcel on an official map that is kept in the local county recorder's office.

II. Area is the size of something in two dimensions, measured in square units (square feet, square yards, etc.).

    A. Area of a Rectangle = Length x Width.

    B. Area of a Triangle = 1/2 Base x Height.

1. The base can be any side of the triangle. The corresponding height is the perpendicular distance from the base to the opposite point of the triangle.

C. Irregular figures can be divided into component rectangles and triangles, and the areas of the components added together to find the area of the whole.

D. In area calculations, both dimensions must be expressed in the same unit of measurement.

III. Volume is the size of something in three dimensions, measured in cubic units (cubic feet, cubic yards, etc.).

A. Volume of a rectangular room = area of floor (length x width) x height of room.

B. In volume calculations, all three dimensions must be expressed in the same unit of measurement.

IV. The reciprocal of a number is equal to 1 divided by the number. Reciprocals always come in pairs, with each one of the pair being the reciprocal of the other.

V. Formulas in the form of A = B x C can also be expressed as B = A ÷ C or C = A divided by B, depending on which variable is unknown.

A. The formula for percentage problems is Part = Percentage x Whole.

1. Percent (%) means "divided by 100."

B. The formula for capitalization is Income = Rate x Value.

C. The formula for simple interest is Interest = Principal x Rate x Time. Rate and time must be expressed in corresponding units, e.g. 10% per year for five years.

VI. Financial problems involving compound interest are usually too complex to solve by hand. Most appraisers use computers, calculators or tables of financial factors to solve these problems.

A. Most financial calculations involve the following variables: present value, future value, interest rate per compounding period, total number of compounding periods, and annuity payment amount. Given any four of these five variables, a financial computer program or calculator can calculate the missing 5th variable.

B. Factors from financial tables can also be used to solve financial calculations. Financial tables contain listings of factors that correspond to different combinations of interest rate, compounding period and investment term.

VII. The mean, the median, and the mode are measures of central tendency. Range is the spread between the lowest and highest numbers in a sample. Standard deviation measures how far prices vary from the mean.

IX. CHAPTER QUIZ

1. The Southeast quarter of the Southwest quarter of Section 25 contains:
    a. 40 acres.
    b. 80 acres.
    c. 160 acres.
    d. 640 acres.

2. Courses in metes and bounds descriptions are given according to:
    a. the angle of deviation from north or south.
    b. the angle of deviation from east or west.
    c. either of the above.
    d. neither of the above.

3. The primary north-south line in a rectangular survey grid is called the:
    a. base line.
    b. guide meridian.
    c. principal meridian.
    d. correction line.

4. The system used to describe land by referring to a recorded map showing its boundaries is known as the:
    a. record title system.
    b. registration system.
    c. subdivision system.
    d. lot and block system.

5. A natural or man-made landmark that is used in a metes and bounds description is called a:
    a. marker.
    b. monument.
    c. base line.
    d. point of beginning.

6. If compound interest of 12% per year is paid on an account, how much interest will be earned after two years by an investment of $100?
    a. $12.00
    b. $24.00
    c. $25.44
    d. $124.00

7. A 4 inch thick concrete slab is 20 feet wide and 30 feet long. How many cubic yards of concrete are contained in the slab?

    a. 7.4
    b. 22.2
    c. 200.00
    d. 240.00

8. How many acres are contained in a square parcel of land that measures 330′ on each side?

    a. 2.5
    b. 5.0
    c. 7.5
    d. 10.0

9. A property was valued at $124,000, based on an annual direct capitalization rate of 13%. What is the property's annual income?

    a. $13,000
    b. $16,120
    c. $21,400
    d. None of the above

10. An iron stake at a corner of a property would be a(n):

    a. benchmark.
    b. natural monument.
    c. artificial monument.
    d. standard parallel.

Chapter 5
Data Collection and Analysis

KEY WORDS AND TERMS

Comparable Property Data
Economic Base
Energy Efficiency Ratio (EER)
General Data
Infrastructure
Internet Data Searches
Neighborhood
Neighborhood Data

Primary Data
Regional and Community Data
Secondary Data
Site Data
Specific Data
Subject Property Data
Supply and Demand Data
Trend Data

LEARNING OBJECTIVES

After completing this chapter, you should be able to:

1. identify the types of forces that influence value on regional, community and neighborhood levels;

2. identify common sources of general appraisal data;

3. describe the way appraisers define neighborhoods;

4. list neighborhood characteristics that are important to appraisers;

5. describe the data necessary for a site description;

6. describe the data necessary for a building description;

7. describe the data that is collected for comparable properties; and

8. know how to complete Page 1 (Property Description) of the Uniform Residential Appraisal Report (URAR).

CHAPTER OUTLINE

I. Understanding Data

Data collection and analysis is the third step in the orderly process of appraisal.

Data selection and gathering, as well as analysis, is an integral and ongoing part of virtually the entire appraisal process.

As an appraiser estimates the value of property, he or she is constantly analyzing data, discarding data that is not reliable, selecting data that is most relevant to the appraisal problem, and gathering additional necessary data.

Appraisal data may be classified in several different ways. Data may be classified as either **GENERAL DATA** *(pertaining to real estate values in general, on a national, regional and local level)* or **SPECIFIC DATA** *(pertaining to a particular property).*

General data may be further classified as *broad market* **TREND DATA** *or more localized competitive* **SUPPLY AND DEMAND DATA**. Data is also categorized as **PRIMARY** or **SECONDARY**, *depending on whether it is generated directly by the appraiser or obtained from published sources.*

Another way to categorize data is according to its application in the appraisal process. Appraisal data is gathered for four basic reasons, including:

1. to identify relevant market trends that may affect real estate values;
2. to identify the probable future supply and demand of competitive properties in the market;
3. to identify the characteristics of the subject property that may affect its value; and
4. to identify the characteristics of comparable properties that may affect their values.

A. MARKET TREND DATA

The terms *MARKET TREND DATA* and *GENERAL DATA both refer to the same thing: information about the ways that social, economic, governmental and environmental (physical) forces interact to affect value.*

Other Forms of Data	
Primary Data:	Data generated by the appraiser
Secondary Data:	Data generated by other sources
Market Trend Data:	Data regarding the interactions of the four forces that affect value
Competitive Supply and Demand Data:	Data regarding the prospective (future) supply and demand for competitive properties in the market
Subject Property Data:	Characteristics of the subject property
Comparable Property Data:	Characteristics of comparable properties

All data may not be relevant. The appraiser should analyze data for relevancy.

Case/Example: Government statistics indicate a trend for smaller households (number of persons within a household). This would seem to indicate that demand should be increasing for smaller homes. However, government statistics also indicate an increasing trend for multiple income households. This data is apparently more relevant than household size in that the demand for larger homes has been related more to household income and interest rates than to the size of the household.

Appraisers should keep abreast of international and national market trends by subscribing to financial publications like the *Wall Street Journal* and the *Economist*. Not only can you view this material online, but with portable Internet devices like smartphones, you can also keep up to date through social networking apps like Facebook® and Twitter®.

B. COMPETITIVE SUPPLY AND DEMAND DATA

"Competitive supply and demand data" is a form of market trend data, one that is more closely tied to a particular (local) market.

The appraiser must identify, collect and analyze data for both competitive supply and competitive demand. *SUPPLY DATA includes the numbers of existing and proposed properties that may be offered on the market, and also data about the rates at which new properties are absorbed into the market. DEMAND DATA includes items such as wage and employment levels and population shifts, which drive demand in the local market.*

Case/Example: In analyzing the competitive supply of single-family residences in a market, an appraiser would consider the existing supply of houses, the supply of vacant land available for residential development, and also the supply of properties that might reasonably be converted to residential use in the future. All of these might prove competitive to the subject property in its future market.

C. SUBJECT PROPERTY DATA

SUBJECT PROPERTY DATA is any data that pertains specifically to the subject property. This includes physical characteristics such as size and number of rooms, floor plan, architectural features, landscaping, special amenities and also includes other specific data that affects the value of the property, such as terms of sale or special financing arrangements.

Knowledge of the market will guide the appraiser in identifying the relevant data concerning the subject property. Certain property data, such as size, location and condition of improvements, is virtually always relevant to an estimate of value. But the relevance of other property data may depend on the market. For example, a pool may be considered desirable in one market, undesirable in another and of no relevance at all in a third.

D. COMPARABLE PROPERTY DATA

Much of the data required for an appraisal is about comparable properties. A *COMPARABLE PROPERTY is a property that is similar to the subject property in certain key characteristics.* For a property to be truly comparable, it must:

1. have similar physical characteristics to the subject property;
2. be competitive with the subject property, that is, appeal to the same kinds of buyers in the market;
3. be located in the same market area as the subject property; and
4. have sold within a limited time from the valuation date (normally within six months).

Case/Example: If the subject property is a 3-bedroom, 2-bath ranch-style house located in a neighborhood of similar houses, the best comparables will be other 3-bedroom, 2-bath ranch-style homes in the same neighborhood, that have sold within the last six months. A similar (or even identical) home in a different neighborhood may not be a true comparable, since those neighborhood characteristics may appeal to a different group of buyers.

The appraiser will use comparable property data in each of the three approaches to value.

In the sales comparison approach, the appraiser analyzes the sales of improved properties that are comparable to the subject property. In the cost approach, the appraiser analyzes sales of vacant lots that are comparable to the subject property's lot. Sales prices and rents for comparable properties are the basis of the income approach.

An appraiser can begin to identify potential comparables as soon as a general description of the subject property is known.

Often the appraiser will be familiar with the subject property's market, and will have some idea of the relative scarcity or abundance of suitable comparables. This knowledge is useful for assessing the amount of time and effort that will be necessary to complete the appraisal assignment.

Early in the appraisal process, the appraiser will normally inspect the subject property.

The information obtained from this inspection, together with additional information gathered in regard to the rights and restrictions applicable to the property, allows the appraiser to refine the list of potential comparables, discarding those that are not truly comparable, and perhaps adding new ones that more clearly match the subject property's characteristics.

For the purposes of this chapter, we will be considering different types of data according to the third method of classification—data collection and analysis—used in the appraisal process.

These types of appraisal data are broken down into the following categories:

1. Regional and Community Data
2. Neighborhood Data
3. Site Data
4. Building (Improvement) Data
5. Specific Market Data

II. Regional and Community Data

REGIONAL AND COMMUNITY DATA reflect the effects of local social, economic, governmental and physical forces on value. The interaction of these forces influence real estate values, either for better or for worse.

Case/Example: Property values in an exclusive neighborhood of expensive homes may be enhanced by the scarcity of similar neighborhoods in a community. On the other hand, if the regional economy is in a slump, the demand for high-priced homes may lessen, causing neighborhood values to decline. In either case, the value of homes in the neighborhood cannot be analyzed without appreciating outside influences and trends on the regional and community level.

A. USE OF REGIONAL AND COMMUNITY DATA

The collection and analysis of regional and community data is essential to the appraisal process for several reasons. First, it helps the appraiser identify the particular characteristics of properties that increase or decrease value.

Case/Example: A region's climate has a significant effect on the desirability of various architectural styles and methods of construction. Buyer's in areas with extreme winter or summer temperatures may place a high value on extra insulation and other energy-efficient construction details, while buyers in areas with more moderate climates may consider such features to be excessive and not worth their extra cost.

When included in an appraisal report, regional and community data also helps the appraisal client, or other reader, to understand why buyers in the market value specific property characteristics.

A second reason for including regional and community data in an appraisal is to identify large scale patterns of value fluctuations. Economic cycles are particularly important to an appraiser.

The study of regional and community data helps the appraiser to anticipate shifts in the economy, either from a period of growth to one of stagnation or decline, or vice versa.

Case/Example: Defense contracting is one of the mainstays of the economy of Southern California. The vast sums invested by the government in defense spending during the 1980s created an economic stimulus in the area, which contributed to an increase in property values. In contrast, the trend during the early to mid '90s toward reduced spending on defense had a dampening effect on the Southern California economy, with a resulting decline in property values.

Economic cycles are not the only large-scale patterns that affect value. Social and political trends are also significant. The general aging of the population, for example, has been a factor in the population growth of the South and Southwest regions of the country, as growing numbers of retirees seek out warmer places to live. Changing political winds, especially on the state and local levels, have a big effect on value indicators such as property tax rates and regional economic climates.

A third reason to consider regional and community data is to provide a context for the analysis of local influences on value. Neighborhoods do not exist in isolation, but are part of larger communities and regions.

To understand the desirability of a particular neighborhood, it must be viewed in the context of the surrounding area.

Case/Example: A boom of new housing construction in a city may adversely affect property values in a neighborhood of older homes located in the same city. In addition to increasing the overall supply of housing, the new homes may have more modern designs and features that make the older homes seem less desirable by comparison.

B. REGIONAL AND COMMUNITY VALUE INDICATIONS

All data used in an appraisal is collected for one purpose: to help form a value estimate for a particular subject property. But this does not mean that the appraiser must collect new regional and community data for each appraisal assignment.

Regional and community data is often collected in advance, without reference to any particular subject property. Appraisers maintain files of regional and community data pertaining to the geographic areas in which they practice.

These files are updated on an on-going basis, to reflect changes and developments in the market. When the appraiser receives a particular appraisal assignment, he or she simply determines which regional and community data is relevant to the appraisal problem.

Appraisers maintain regional and community data on a wide range of subjects. Some of the more common regional and community value indicators include:

1. Natural Environmental Factors
2. Economic Characteristics
3. Infrastructure

1. Natural Environmental Factors (Physical Features)

Natural environmental factors (physical features) that can influence value include climate, topography (the shape of the land and the location of physical features such as lakes and streams), potential hazards (such as earthquakes, floods, or tornadoes), and the presence of natural resources. A major environmental consideration is the attitude of regional and city governments towards the development and/or preservation of area resources.

Case/Example: Environmental regulations and restrictions on new development may enhance the value of property that is already developed. The regulations and restrictions reduce the supply of developable land, and may also be seen as enhancing the quality of life in a region. On the other hand, the same regulations and restrictions will often have a negative effect on the value of vacant land, since they limit the potential uses of such land.

2. Economic Characteristics

The appraiser must be aware of the economic forces at work in the area. A major factor here is the area's economic base. The *ECONOMIC BASE is the economic activities that support the people living in the area.*

Areas with strong economic bases draw income from other areas, increasing local wealth and property values. In contrast, a weak economic base negatively affects values.

Case/Example: The computer industry is a major part of the economic base of the San Francisco Bay area. Computer hardware and software products developed in the area are sold all over the country and the world, drawing income from outside areas into the Bay Area. The strength of this economic base has a major influence on real estate values in the area.

To understand an area's economic base, and its potential effect on values, the appraiser collects a variety of data. What are the major industries in the area? Are these industries growing, stable, or in decline? How many people do they employ, and at what wage and skill levels? Is the economy diversified, or is the region dependent on only one or a handful of industries? What forces may affect the economic base for better or for worse in the future?

In addition to the economic base, other economic factors that affect values in a region or community include: employment and unemployment levels, price levels, interest rates, construction activity and government regulation and taxation of business and development.

3. Infrastructure

INFRASTRUCTURE refers to public improvements that support basic needs, such as transportation and utilities. Infrastructure contributes to the quality of life in an area, and can also have a major affect on business activity and regional growth. Appraisers collect infrastructure data that includes:

1. public transportation facilities (airlines, railroads, busses);
2. highways;
3. power and water supplies; and
4. sanitation facilities (sewage treatment and solid waste disposal).

The appraiser should be aware of the availability of these services in the area, their quality, their costs and benefits, and their capacity to support new growth.

Case/Example: In many areas of the West, agricultural communities are dependent on irrigation water that is supplied from a system of dams and canals. This infrastructure of dams and canals has converted thousands of square miles of "worthless desert" into valuable and productive farm land. The value of that land is threatened, however, by the possibility that irrigation rights may be curtailed in order to provide more water to support fisheries resources, or to supply domestic water needs in urban areas.

C. HOUSING SUPPLY AND DEMAND

It is a fundamental rule of appraisal that supply and demand affects value.

Data about the supply of housing in an area includes the existing supply of housing of various types and ages, the supply of vacant land for residential development, the current level of housing construction activity, the number of building permits being issued or processed, construction costs (for capital, materials and labor), vacancy rates and time to sell properties.

These types of data are also relevant to the demand for housing, since they indicate the level of purchasing power of potential buyers. Demand data also includes population characteristics of the region. Is the population increasing or decreasing? What is the age profile of the region, and how is the age profile changing, if at all? How does the population break down according to income level, education level, and size/composition of the household? What population characteristics are likely to change in the future? The answers to these questions give an indication as to the level of demand in the market.

Case/Example: An increase in household income within a marketplace would likely increase the demand for more expensive housing.

Housing demand within a marketplace is not homogeneous.

It is stratified; the demand for low-priced homes could be different than for luxury homes. As an example, the average time to sell lower-priced homes could be 38 days, but the average time to sell luxury homes could be 9 1/2 months. Similarly, the demand could be different for condominiums than for single-family homes. Many areas have a glut of condominiums with stagnant or falling values, while they have a strong market for single-family homes with increasing values.

1. Social Attitudes

Population data such as age, income level or household size are important indicators of SOCIAL ATTITUDES. Young families with small children tend to want different types of housing than retired persons, for example. Another important indicator of social attitudes is the level and type of government regulation. For example, high development fees or other taxes may indicate an anti-growth attitude, while tax incentives to businesses or other groups may indicate a strong desire for growth in the region. Appraisers must be aware of regional and city government regulations pertaining to zoning, environmental protection, building standards and the taxation of income, business activities and property ownership.

2. Data Sources

Some regional and city data, such as climate and topography, can be gathered through direct observation by the appraiser. Other data can be obtained from interviews with property owners, real estate brokers, lenders, property managers, building professionals (contractors, architects, etc.) and other real estate appraisers.

But for the most part, regional and community data come from published sources. Some of the more common sources of published regional and community data are listed below.

a. City, County, and State Public Agencies

In particular, agencies dealing with public records, planning, zoning, taxation, employment, housing and transportation—for information on environmental, zoning and building regulations, tax laws, tax assessments, ownership transfers, public improvements, building permits, current and proposed infrastructure, local industries and employment and population and household statistics.

b. Federal Government Agencies

In particular, the Departments of Commerce (Bureau of the Census and Bureau of Economic Analysis), Housing and Urban Development, and Labor (Bureau of Labor Statistics), the Council of Economic Advisors and the Federal Reserve Board—for national, regional, and local statistics on business activity, income, employment, housing and housing construction, financial markets, population demographics and price levels.

c. Trade Associations

Included are Chambers of Commerce, Boards of Realtors®, multiple listing services and home builders associations—for information on housing sales, housing costs and construction, financing, business activity and demographics.

Note: Many Chambers of Commerce Boards of REALTORS® and MLS sites can be "followed" on social networking sites like Twitter®, Facebook®, LinkedIn®, ActiveRain®, etc.

d. The Internet

The Internet is your window to literally thousands of sites offering data that can be relevant to appraisal. It would not be feasible to search every site but, with experience, you should be able to locate sites which provide information relevant to your appraisal needs. Some of the following sites might be useful:

Appraisal-Related Internet Sites

Fedworld information network (a hyperlink to most federal sites):
fedworld.gov

Webcrawler (a search engine for government sites):
http://msxml.webcrawler.com/info.wbcrwl/search/web/Appraisal

▼

State and Local Government on the Net:
statelocalgov.net/

U.S. Census Bureau:
census.gov

Environmental Protection Agency:
epa.gov

Department of Housing and Urban Development (HUD):
hud.gov

U.S. Department of Labor:
dol.gov

Bureau of Labor Statistics:
stats.bls.gov

U.S. Department of Transportation:
dot.gov

Bureau of Transportation Statistics:
bts.gov

Federal Reserve Board:
federalreserve.gov/

Federal Emergency Management Agency (FEMA):
fema.gov

Department of Commerce, Bureau of Economic Analysis:
bea.gov

U.S. Congress Economic Indicators of the Joint Economic Committee:
gpoaccess.gov/indicators/index.html

III. Neighborhood Data

For appraisal purposes, a **NEIGHBORHOOD** *can be defined as a geographical area in which land uses are complementary and in which all properties are influenced in a similar way by the forces affecting value.* A neighborhood may have more than one type of use. For example, a neighborhood may include residences, schools and retail shops, all of which complement each other. *When a neighborhood includes only one type of land use, it is sometimes referred to as a **DISTRICT**.*

A. DEFINING NEIGHBORHOOD BOUNDARIES

Neighborhoods have some degree or type of conformity that sets them apart from surrounding areas. The conformity may relate to the age or architectural style of buildings in the neighborhood, to its zoning classification, to the economic status of its residents or to some other factor or combination of factors.

Neighborhood boundaries are often (but not always) some type of physical feature.

Common examples include highways or arteries, railroads, waterways and other geographic boundaries. The boundaries can also be established by zoning differences, with one neighborhood ending and another beginning at the point where different land uses are permitted. School district boundaries can also be neighborhood boundaries where a particular district is highly desirable. In some case, political subdivisions create the boundaries with the change in address creating a significant difference.

In many states, the subdivisions themselves are the neighborhoods. This is especially true in walled and/or gated subdivisions.

When defining a neighborhood boundary, an appraiser must keep in mind that just because a group of properties appears to be similar does not mean that they are all subject to the same value influences. Nor does a physical barrier necessarily indicate the boundary of a neighborhood.

[The appraiser should provide an outline of the neighborhood boundaries, which should be clearly delineated using 'North', 'South', 'East', and 'West'. These boundaries may include, but are not limited to, streets, legally recognized neighborhood boundaries, waterways, or other natural boundaries that define the separation of one neighborhood from another. Appraisers should not reference a map or other addendum as the only example of the neighborhood boundaries.]

Case/Example: A residential subdivision may contain homes of similar size, construction style, and lot size. At first glance, the subdivision may appear to be a distinct neighborhood. But if one side of the subdivision borders on a park or waterfront, while the other side borders on a busy freeway, the appraiser may decide that the subdivision is actually comprised of two or more distinct neighborhoods (or sub-neighborhoods), despite the superficial similarities between the homes.

It is important for the appraiser to establish and justify neighborhood boundaries for each subject property that is appraised.

The boundaries established for the subject property's neighborhood will define the area for which neighborhood data will be gathered, and from which the most reliable comparable properties can be chosen.

B. NEIGHBORHOOD VALUE INDICATORS

Neighborhood data helps define the potential market for the subject property.

Neighborhood data also helps indicate the desirability of the subject property in relation to homes in competing neighborhoods. And, if it becomes necessary to use comparable properties from other neighborhoods, neighborhood data helps the appraiser identify similar neighborhoods, and adjust the values of the comparables for differences in neighborhood characteristics.

Case/Example: An appraiser determines that the subject property neighborhood consists of an area of single-family, 2- and 3-bedroom homes, located 2 miles from the city center. Due to a shortage of recent comparable sales in the subject neighborhood, the appraiser must use comparables from another, similar neighborhood. The second neighborhood has homes of similar size, age, and appeal as the subject neighborhood, but is located 5 miles from the city center. In this case, the appraiser must investigate whether the added distance from the area business core has an affect on neighborhood values, and possibly adjust the sales prices of the comparables from the second neighborhood to account for any observed value difference.

The section entitled "**Neighborhood**," from the Uniform Residential Appraisal Report (URAR), is shown as **Figure 5-1** and includes the following categories:

Figure 5-1

Neighborhood Section - URAR

Note: Race and the racial composition of the neighborhood are not appraisal factors.									
Neighborhood Characteristics			**One-Unit Housing Trends**			**One-Unit Housing**		**Present Land Use %**	
Location 52 Urban 53 Suburban 54 Rural			Property Values 61 Increasing 62 Stable 63 Declining			PRICE AGE		One-Unit 76 %	
Built-Up 55 Over 75% 56 25–75% 57 Under 25%			Demand/Supply 64 Shortage 65 In Balance 66 Over Supply			$ (000) (yrs)		2-4 Unit 77 %	
Growth 58 Rapid 59 Stable 60 Slow			Marketing Time 67 Under 3 mths 68 3–6 mths 69 Over 6 mths			70 Low 73		Multi-Family 78 %	
Neighborhood Boundaries 82						71 High 74		Commercial 79 %	
						72 Pred. 75		Other 81 %	
Neighborhood Description 83									
Market Conditions (including support for the above conclusions) 84									

Location: Can be checked as *URBAN (city), SUBURBAN (a community beyond the central city but linked physically and/or economically to the central city)* or *RURAL (primarily agricultural or undeveloped).*

Built-Up: Rrefers to the percentage of property that has been developed in an area. It allows the lender to gain an understanding of the state of development. Over 75 percent would indicate a mostly developed area, 25 percent to 75 percent would indicate an area with room for further development, and under 25 percent would indicate a mostly undeveloped area.

Growth: Would be shown as rapid, stable or slow. Building permit data could be the basis of the appraiser's opinion.

Property Values: Would be shown as increasing, stable or declining, based upon data which the appraiser has gathered as to the neighborhood.

Demand/Supply: Evaluation of the neighborhood could be checked as a shortage (normally evidenced by a relatively short time to sell and increasing values), in balance (normally evidenced by a reasonable time to sell and relatively stable values) or declining (evidenced by an unusually lengthy period to sell and a trend toward lower prices).

Marketing Time: If under three months for the average sale, would indicate a seller's market. From three to five months would indicate a reasonable marketplace, while over six months would be indicative of a buyer's market.

There is an interrelationship between the last three sectikon categories.

The form has eliminated questions regarding the **Predominant Occupancy** of the neighborhood and vacancy factors. It is an axiom that owner-occupied neighborhoods enjoy more stable values than tenant-occupied single-family housing. Vacancy factors over 5% for single-family housing can indicate market problems.

Practical Tip: While there is no longer an individual's space to report this analysis on the form, the appraiser might include this information under "Market Conditions."

One-Unit Housing: This block allows the appraiser to show the range of prices and age of properties within a neighborhood, as well as the predominant or average price and age of neighborhood housing. A value at the top or bottom of the price range could be considered relevant by a lender when considering the principles of progression and regression.

Present Land Use %: This would provide information as to the composition of the neighborhood as to use. Many residential appraisals will show neighborhoods of 100 percent single-family homes.

The concept of change is one of the pillars supporting valuation and appraisal theory. Regardless of the removal of **Land Use Change** from the form, it is an issue that must be confronted in every appraisal analysis.

Practical Tip: If there is evidence of change, this should be discussed in the "Neighborhood Description" area and its effect on value should be discussed in the "Market Conditions" area.

Race and racial composition are NOT to be used as appraisal characteristics.

Minimal space is provided for the appraiser to discuss and analyze the **Neighborhood Boundaries, Neighborhood Description, and Market Conditions.** Because the space is seldom adequate, the appraiser may have to attach an addendum to the report and reference the addendum in the spaces provided on the report.

For complicated boundaries, the appraiser might want to use a map, marked to indicate boundaries.

Characteristics of the neighborhood could include reference to factors checked in the blocks above.

The factors that affect the marketability of properties in the neighborhood might include negative factors as well as positive factors. Negative factors could include the presence of noise, dust, odors, traffic problems, etc. Positive factors could include well lighted, quiet streets, convenient access to major transportation routes, employment and/or shopping, quality of schools, cultural activities, etc.

Market conditions in the neighborhood could include average time to sell, including any trend as to changes in time to sell, number of properties on the market, concessions given to buyers and/or renters, relationship of sale prices to list prices and any recent change in the relationship.

Assume an MLS service reports that the average sale during the last six months was at 89 percent of list price but for the neighborhood being evaluated, the average sale was at 93 percent of list price. This would be indicative of a stronger market than for other areas.

C. SOURCES OF NEIGHBORHOOD DATA

Many of the sources of neighborhood data are the same as the sources of regional and community data.

In particular, local government agencies and trade associations can often provide useful data concerning *NEIGHBORHOOD DATA, which includes growth rates, zoning regulations, population characteristics, taxes and public services.* Interviews with local real estate professionals (brokers, appraisers, lenders and property managers) and property owners are another valuable source of neighborhood data. But to a far greater extent than is the case with regional and community data, the major source of neighborhood data is personal inspection by the appraiser.

D. NEIGHBORHOOD INSPECTION

The appraiser's first task in inspecting a neighborhood is to determine its boundaries.

The appraiser may already have some idea of the boundaries of the subject property's neighborhood, either from past experience or from secondary data sources. But it is important to inspect the area surrounding the subject property to note any unusual influences that may apply.

Properties located near the edge of a neighborhood, for example, may be subject to greater value influences from adjoining uses than are properties located in the center of the neighborhood.

It is usually helpful to outline the neighborhood boundaries on an area map. (A neighborhood map, showing the locations of the subject property and any comparables used in the appraisal, is usually attached as an exhibit to the appraisal.) In mapping the neighborhood boundaries, the appraiser should note the characteristics (physical barriers, land use changes, changes in school district, etc.) that define each boundary (see **Figure 5-2**).

Figure 5-2 — Neighborhood Boundary Map

The boundaries of a neighborhood could be as simple as a particular subdivision (**Figure 5-3**), however, a neighborhood could encompass a greater or lesser area than a subdivision.

Figure 5-3

Subdivision

In addition to determining the boundaries of the neighborhood, the appraiser will observe and note its essential characteristics. Important data to be gathered or verified by inspection include:

1. the type of neighborhood;
2. physical characteristics and layout;
3. percent of development;
4. evidence of change (new construction, remodeling, degree of maintenance);
5. quantity, age, and condition of various types of properties;
6. traffic patterns;
7. presence of negative value influences; and
8. overall neighborhood quality and appeal.

Important features may be noted on the neighborhood map, either for later reference by the appraiser, or for inclusion in the appraisal report.

IV. Site Data

SITE DATA is specific data regarding the subject property site. A site is defined as land that has been prepared for use, for example by clearing, grading and development of access and utilities. In an appraisal, the site is distinguished from its improvements (buildings, etc.) for several reasons, including:

1. for highest and best use analysis;
2. to provide data for certain valuation techniques (such as the cost approach to value); and
3. sometimes as a requirement of the appraisal assignment (as in appraisals for tax assessment purposes).

A. SITE DESCRIPTION

When preparing a site description, the appraiser should note whether the property boundaries appear to match the legal description of the property, and whether there are any apparent encroachments, either by the subject upon adjoining properties or vice versa. The appraiser should also note the location of any easements that benefit or burden the property. For example, the property may benefit from an access easement across adjoining land, or may be burdened by an easement for the installation and maintenance of underground utilities. The location of easements and encroachments should be noted on the site map.

The appraiser should verify the property boundaries as shown on the site map, and note the locations of any easements and apparent encroachments. The appraiser will note the width and depth of the lot and also identify the location and dimension of any frontage. *WIDTH is the dimension of the site measured parallel to the street on which the site address is located. DEPTH is the opposite dimension, perpendicular to the street.*

For irregularly shaped lots, width or depth are sometimes stated as averages (average width, average depth).

FRONTAGE (or front footage) is the length of a property's boundary where it adjoins a street or body of water. It is sometimes used as a measure of value, but only when market data clearly indicates a relationship between frontage and value.

Street frontage is normally more important for commercial properties than for residential properties.

Case/Example: In a residential neighborhood where street frontages vary from 80 feet to 100 feet, the difference in frontage will probably not affect value to any significant extent. On the other hand, residential properties bordering on a lake or stream may show significant value differences based on the amount of water frontage for each lot.

Chapter 5

Other land characteristics that are relevant to site description include the contour (slope) of the land, soil characteristics and climate. The appraiser should note any characteristics that might pose problems such as steep slopes, poor drainage or exposure to high winds, as well as favorable characteristics such as a sunny exposure, gently rolling topography or pleasant views. (Refer to the UAD Field Specific Standardization Requirements at **efanniemae.com** or **Appendix 5** of this textbook for the appropriate responses to this section.)

B. PHYSICAL DATA

The majority of the data needed for the site description is generated by a personal inspection of the subject site. Physical site data includes information about the land itself, its location and any site improvements.

The section entitled "**Site**" from the Uniform Residential Appraisal Report is shown as **Figure 5-4**.

Figure 5-4

Site Selection - URAR

Dimensions 85		Area 86		Shape 87		View e-5; e-6; e-7		
Specific Zoning Classification 89		Zoning Description 90						
Zoning Compliance [91] Legal [92] Legal Nonconforming (Grandfathered Use) [93] No Zoning [94] Illegal (describe) 95								
Is the highest and best use of the subject property as improved (or as proposed per plans and specifications) the present use? [96] Yes [97] No If No, describe 98								

Utilities	Public	Other (describe)		Public	Other (describe)	Off-site Improvements—Type	Public	Private
Electricity	[99]	[100] 101	Water	[105]	[106] 107	Street 111	[112]	[113]
Gas	[102]	[103] 104	Sanitary Sewer	[108]	[109] 110	Alley 114	[115]	[116]
FEMA Special Flood Hazard Area [117] Yes [118] No FEMA Flood Zone 119 FEMA Map # 120						FEMA Map Date 121		
Are the utilities and off-site improvements typical for the market area? [122] Yes [123] No If No, describe 124								
Are there any adverse site conditions or external factors (easements, encroachments, environmental conditions, land uses, etc.)? [125] Yes [126] No If Yes, describe								
127								

The section provides for:

Dimensions: These would be shown by feet if subject site is a regularly shaped rectangular lot. If not, a plot plan or a section of a plot map can be included as an attachment to the report. However, the dimensions should be clearly shown.

[For sites/parcels that have an area of less than one acre, the size must be reported in square feet. For sites/parcels that have an area of one acre or greater, the size must be reported in acreage to two decimal places. The unit of measure must be indicated as either 'sf' for square feet or 'ac' for acres. A numeric value must be entered followed by the appropriate unit of measure. The total size of the entire site/parcel must be entered. No other data is permitted.]

Site Area: The area in square feet or acreage should be shown. If the total area cannot be exactly calculated, such as a lot along a meandering river, the area can be expressed as _____ sq. ft. MOL for "More or Less." (Surveyor maps would normally indicate acreage or square feet for irregular shaped parcels.)

Shape: The appraiser should describe the shape of the lot. Rectangular, triangular, and irregular are several descriptions that come to mind.

View: The Field Specific Standardization Requirements section of the UAD has defined the appropriate responses to the "View" section of the URAR as shown in the chat below.

Specific Zoning Classification: Provide the specific zoning classification.

Zoning Description: For anything other than single-family residential zoning, an attachment from the zoning authorities may be required describing the uses that the zoning category allows.

Zoning Compliance: By checking the appropriate block, the appraiser can indicate if the present use is legal, legal but a nonconforming use allowed by use before zoning (Grandfathered Use), no zoning at all, or illegal use. Any illegal use must be explained either in the space provided or more likely in an addendum referenced here.

Highest and Best Use: If the site is or is not being used at its highest and best use, the appropriate block should be marked. As an example, if a site is currently being utilized as a single-family residence where the zoning would allow 20 units, the site would not be at its highest and best use. The appraiser must analyze and describe the effect on value of a different highest and best use other than the present one for the site.

Utilities: By checking the appropriate block, the appraiser can show if the utilities (electricity, gas, water, and sanitary sewers) are public or private. If private is not available, the appraiser should state what they are (propane, well, septic system, etc.) under "Other."

Off-site Improvements: The current check boxes only cover the street or an alleyway. Curbs, gutters, and lighting are also important, and the presence, or lack of them, should be covered in an addendum. *[Indicate if street or alleyway is public or private.]*

FEMA Special Flood Hazard Area: The appraiser should indicate if the property is in a flood hazard area as indicated by a FEMA map. Check the "Yes" box if the zone has an "A" or "V" designation. Check "No" for "B," "C," "D," etc. Enter zone, map date, and map number in the spaces provided.

Are the utilities and off-site improvements typical for the market area?: Check "Yes" or "No."

Sales Comparison Approach Section	Forms	Requirement or Instruction
Site For sites/parcels that have an area of less than one acre, the size must be reported in square feet. For sites/parcels that have an area of one acre or greater, the size must be reported in acreage to two decimal places. The unit of measure must be indicated as either 'sf' for square feet or 'ac' for acres. A numeric value must be entered followed by the appropriate unit of measure. The total size of the entire site/parcel must be entered. No other data is permitted in this field. **Reporting Format:** Area less than one acre -- whole numbers only Area equal to one acre or more -- numeric to 2 decimals Indicate the unit of measure as either 'sf' for square feet or 'ac' for acres as appropriate. **Examples:** 6400 sf 3.40 ac	1004/70 2055/2055	REQUIREMENT
View The appraiser must provide one of the ratings from the list below to describe the overall effect on value and marketability of the view factor(s) associated with the subject property and each comparable property.	1004/70 2055/2055 1073/465 1075/466	REQUIREMENT

ABBREVIATED ENTRY	OVERALL VIEW RATING
N	Neutral
B	Beneficial
A	Adverse

The appraiser must also provide at least one, but not more than two, view factor(s) from the list below to provide details about the overall view rating selected above.

ABBREVIATED ENTRY	VIEW FACTOR
Wtr	Water View
Pstrl	Pastoral View
Woods	Woods View
Prk	Park View
Glfvw	Golf Course View
CtySky	City View Skyline View
Mtn	Mountain View
Res	Residential View
CtyStr	City Street View
Ind	Industrial View
PwrLn	Power Lines
LtdSght	Limited Sight
See Instruction Below	Other -- Appraiser to enter a description of the view*

*Other: If a view factor not on this list materially affects the value of the property, the appraiser must enter a description of the view associated with the property (see second example below). Descriptions should be entered carefully because the text will be represented in both the Site Section and the Sales Comparison Approach section for the subject property. The description entered must allow a reader of the appraisal report to understand what the view is that is associated with the property. Descriptors such as 'None', 'N/A', 'Typical', 'Average', etc., are unacceptable. The text must fit in the allowable space.

The above box in burgundy is from the Sales Comparison Approach Section of the UAD. It can be seen in it's entirety on page 553 of Appendix 5 at the end of this book. It specifically refers to new abbreviations or overall view ratings and view factors, the purpose of which is to make sure all lenders and appraisers understand the same terminology and descriptions that were used to value the property.

For loan Purposes of Fannie Mae and Freddie Mac, the appraiser must rate the effect of the view on the value and marketability of the property by rating the view as either normal, beneficial, or adverse, and also by describing the nature of the view as, among other things, water, pastoral, woods, etc. For appraisals other than for Fannie Mae and Freddie Mac loan purposes, the appraiser may described the property in any manner the appraiser deems fit.

Are there any adverse site conditions or external factors (easements, encroachments, environmental conditions, land uses, etc.)?: Check "Yes" or "No." If yes, describe.

Appraisers are not required to check the title for recorded easements for the Uniform Residential Appraisal Report, but should note any adverse use as it might be a prescriptive easement that could reduce value.

The form has omitted any discussion of **Topography, Drainage,** or **Landscaping**. Topography is important in that it can limit not only the placement of a structure and other improvements upon a property, but the size and type of the structure. This does, of course, have a major impact on value. The appraiser needs to note in an addendum whether the lot is flat or sloped and the degree of slope. Tied into this is the adequacy of the apparent drainage of the property. If there is evidence of water damage, the appraiser should make inquires and note the damage and the result of his or her inquires. **Note:** The drainage from a property has nothing to do with a property's location inside or outside of a flood zone. That is a separate issue. The appraiser should also note the type and quality of landscaping in an addendum. All of these non-listed items contribute to value.

Practical Tip: In some areas, cable T.V. and presence of online local services for the Internet are a consideration and should be included in comments. Also, in areas where there is no public garbage pickup, the need for a private service should be noted.

Any adverse aspects of the site should be reported. Adverse examples would include a structure that appears to encroach from another site or appears to be over an established lot setback. Severe hillside erosion may be indicative of serious soil problems. In such an eventuality, it may be necessary for the appraiser to suggest that the client obtain expert advice from a surveyor or soil expert for their own protection.

V. Building Data

Building data for the subject property is collected for two main reasons. First, it is used to help identify and analyze comparable properties. A good comparable should not only be similar to the subject property in neighborhood and site characteristics, but in building characteristics as well (see **Figure 5-5**).

Figure 5-5

Comparable Property Information

✔ House – Ranch style
✔ 1,800 square feet
✔ Built in 1975
✔ 3-Bedroom – #1 14x16 master bedroom, walk-in closet; #2 10x12; #3 12x12
✔ 2-Full Baths – #1 off master bedroom, tiled, sunken cast iron tub; #2 off hallway
✔ Remodeled kitchen – built-in gas range, oven, dishwasher (medium quality),
   white maple cabinets, Corian countertops, linoleum flooring
✔ Fireplace – masonry, 8 feet wide, gas and wood burning
✔ Detached two-car garage – 800 square feet
✔ Lathe and plaster interior with hardwood doors; above average condition
✔ Stucco exterior – slight cracks near rear door
✔ Slab on grade foundation; good condition
✔ Medium grade shingle roof with gutters; good condition
✔ Septic tank system/80 gallon water heater
✔ Copper plumbing throughout
✔ Forced air/heating and cooling – gas
✔ Fiberglass insulation attic
✔ Outdoor jacuzzi

Knowledge of the detailed building data will also help the appraiser make any necessary adjustments for differences between the subject improvements and those of the comparables.

Case/Example: If the subject property is a 3-bedroom, 1-bath, ranch-style house, the appraiser will look for other 3-bedroom, 1-bath ranch-style houses to serve as comparables for the sales comparison approach to value. The appraiser will then adjust the values of the comparables to account for differences in building characteristics, such as differences in total square footage, building age, or quality of construction.

The second main reason for collecting building data is for use in the cost approach to value.

This data is useful in estimating the reproduction or replacement cost of the improvements, and also in the analysis of depreciation due to deterioration or other causes.

Virtually all building data for the subject property is collected or verified by personal inspection, normally when the appraiser inspects the neighborhood and site. A solid knowledge of construction fundamentals is essential for this step in the appraisal process, since the appraiser must not only describe the improvements in terms of their size, style and materials, but must rate their quality and condition as well. (Aspects of residential construction are discussed in detail in Chapter 7.)

A. CATEGORIES OF BUILDING DATA

There are any number of ways to categorize building data, and no one way is "the best." For our purposes here, we will categorize building data according to the following eight areas:

1. General Data
2. Building Dimensions
3. Sub-Structure Data
4. Exterior Data
5. Interior Data
6. Equipment/Appliance Data
7. Energy Efficiency Data
8. Special Feature Data

1. General Building Data

The first item of general data is a general description of the building: its overall size, number of living units, number of stories, architectural style and placement on the site.

General data also includes a general description of each room in the structure, including its function (bedroom, living room, kitchen, etc.), and location (basement, first floor, second floor, etc.). In addition to counting rooms, the appraiser will also photograph the building. The front and rear view photos are taken at an angle to show the sides of the house and a view of the street. The appraiser indicates the building's location on the site map, and makes a sketch of the floor plan.

2. Building Dimensions

The overall size of a building is measured by its outside dimensions.

The appraiser measures each exterior wall of the structure, then calculates the gross living area. For purposes of this calculation, only above-grade living space is included; garage space, finished or unfinished basement space, or attic space is not considered part of the gross living area but may be indicated separately.

3. Sub-Structure Data

SUB-STRUCTURE DATA (also known as foundation data) is information about the parts of the building that are below (or mostly below) grade level: the foundation and, if applicable, the basement or crawl space. The foundation must be described in terms of its type and condition. Common foundation types include slab-on-grade, full basement, and crawl space foundations. Most modern foundations are constructed of reinforced concrete, with footings and/or piers that distribute the weight of the structure to the subsoil, and foundation walls, columns or posts that rest on the footings and support the super-structure of the building.

When inspecting the sub-structure, the appraiser should pay careful attention to evidence of settling (cracked, broken, or uneven foundation components), moisture penetration (damp foundation slabs or walls, accumulated water in crawl spaces or basements, presence of mold or fungus, moisture damage to wooden foundation members or floor framing), or infestation by termites, rodents or other pests. The existence and condition of any floor insulation and vapor barrier are also noted.

In the case of basements, the appraiser will note the size of the basement area, and describe the ceiling, wall, and floor finishes of any finished areas of the basement. The appraiser should also describe any features (such as sump pumps or drains) designed to remove water from the basement. If the basement includes an outside access door, this fact is also noted.

4. Exterior Data

Important *EXTERIOR BUILDING DATA includes the type and condition of roofing materials, gutters and downspouts, exterior siding and trim, windows and window accessories, and exterior doors.* Some types of roofing materials may last the lifetime of the building, but most tend to require replacement at some point, at a substantial cost. Thus, the type and condition of the roofing material can have a significant affect on value. The appraiser should also note any damaged or missing shingles, as well as any evidence of rot or moss accumulation.

Gutters and downspouts are designed to carry runoff water from the roof. They should be in sound condition, with no leaks or broken connections, and water should drain through the downspouts in the opposite direction from the building, in a way that does not cause soil erosion.

Exterior wall materials come in a wide variety, including masonry (brick, block, stucco, concrete), wood (plywood, board siding, shingles), metal (steel, aluminum), and vinyl plastic. In addition to identifying the type (or types) of exterior wall covering, the appraiser looks for signs of damage or poor workmanship, such as cracks in masonry walls, moisture damage, warped, broken, rotten or missing boards, etc. The condition of any painted surfaces is also noted.

With regard to **windows**, the appraiser should identify the type of windows (casement, sliding, double-hung, etc.), the type of sash (wood, metal, vinyl-clad), and the type of glazing (single-panel, double-panel, etc.). If known, the window manufacturer's name may be noted. All non-fixed (opening) windows should operate smoothly and be equipped with screens. Wood frame windows should be checked for rot or decay, and all windows should be well caulked around their edges to prevent air leakage. Similar considerations apply to storm windows, if applicable.

The final component of exterior building data is the **exterior doors**. Most exterior doors for residential construction are wood or glass. Exterior wood doors should be solid (not hollow), and glass doors, whether swinging or sliding, should be made of tempered safety glass. All exterior doors should have adequate weather stripping. Door widths should be a minimum of 2'8", with a minimum width of 3'0" for entry doors.

Exterior doors can run from less than $100 for a prehung door to over $10,000 for a quality double door.

5. Interior Data

INTERIOR DATA is concerned with the type and quality of interior finishes. This data not only reveals any repairs that may be necessary, but gives a good indication of the overall quality of the building's construction. The quality of interior finishes has a big impact on the construction cost of a home, and has the potential for a similar impact on value.

In general, the appraiser will note the materials used to cover the walls, ceilings and floors in each room of the house. Wall and ceiling coverings are typically drywall, plaster or wood. Floor coverings include carpet, wood, stone and ceramic or vinyl tile, all of which can vary considerably in quality. Particular attention is paid to bathroom and kitchen finishes, as these tend to be more expensive (tiled walls, for example) and also more subject to water damage, requiring costly repairs.

The quality and condition of cabinetry, interior doors and trim is also noted.

Some wood-appearing cabinets are actually chipboard with a vinyl finish and wood grain photographic finish. Such cabinetry may be a fraction of the value of solid oak, birch or other hardwood cabinetry. The hardware used and door construction and suspension are good indications of cabinet quality.

Countertops can be Formica, (relatively inexpensive) or one-piece Corian or granite. Corian and granite countertops run over $100 per foot and $5,000 to $8,000 countertops costs are not unusual. Tile also varies in cost. New homes typically have what is known as *PROJECT CARPETS (minimum FHA requirements for carpet and pad)* and vinyl flooring. A builder's allowance for an entire house might be $1,500 to $5,000 but typically buyers will spend from $5,000 to $25,000 for carpet and floor tile.

Solid hardwood trim, such as oak, is a costly feature and expected in many areas of the country. However, in some areas of Arizona and California, luxury homes have no window trim and painted door trim.

Cheap locks and other hardware are a sign of minimum construction standards.

Hollow core masonite or mahogany doors are generally low cost, but solid core interior doors are a sign of quality.

Area standards vary. In some areas, Formica counters would be acceptable in more expensive homes, while in other areas, they would only be used in rental housing.

You will often find a luxury feature in otherwise lower quality construction or a low quality feature in an otherwise quality built home. You have to evaluate many of the features to determine an overall quality.

The quality of these items, like that of all interior finishes, should be comparable to other homes in the market.

Substandard quality may detract from value, and an above-normal quality may not add significantly to the home's value.

6. Equipment/Appliance Data
The appraiser must note the specifications of the major equipment systems of the subject property, and identify any appliances that are included in the value estimate.

Major equipment systems for most residences include electrical, plumbing and heating systems; cooling systems are also standard features in many parts of the country.

With regard to the electrical system, the appraiser should verify that the electrical service is adequate to supply the needs of the residence. 110-volt, 100-amp service is considered basic for residences in most areas; higher amperage service may be necessary in homes with electric-powered heating and/or cooling systems.

Important plumbing system data includes the type of piping used for water supply and drain pipes, evidence of leakage or water backup, and the quality and condition of plumbing fixtures in kitchens and baths. The type, condition, and capacity of the water heater is also noted.

Bath fixtures might include expensive, one-piece, low-noise commodes or very cheap reverse-flow toilets with separate tanks. Tubs may be cast iron (the best), steel, or low-price fiberglass. Shower stalls might be quality all ceramic enclosures or bottom-of-the-line one piece fiberglass tub and shower combinations.

Heating and air conditioning systems vary greatly in quality. A heat pump is a superior installation and hot water heat is normally more desirable than a hot air system.

The appraiser should identify the type of system(s) used for heating and cooling in the house, and the type(s) of fuel (gas, oil, electricity, etc.) used to operate the system(s). The capacity of the systems should be adequate for the local climate and the size of the building. The condition of these systems should be noted as well, including any need for immediate repairs. For houses that are heated (or once were) with oil, the appraiser must note the location and condition of the oil storage tank, since this is a potential source of environmental pollution.

Finally, the appraiser will record the make, model, and condition of any appliances included in the appraisal. Such appliances commonly include refrigerators, ovens, ranges, microwave ovens, dishwashers, disposals, kitchen exhaust fans/hoods and washers and dryers.

The importance of evaluating quality CANNOT be minimized. Comparing apples with oranges creates flawed results.

7. Energy Efficiency Data

As energy costs rise, buyers place greater and greater value on the energy efficiency of a house, especially in areas of extreme winter cold and/or summer heat. Energy efficient design, construction and equipment can improve the value of a home by reducing the annual cost of heating and cooling.

EER (Energy Efficiency Ratio) is a measure of energy efficiency; the higher the EER the higher the efficiency.

Energy efficiency items that can influence value include above (or below) average building insulation (in ceilings, walls and floors), insulated doors and windows, weather-stripping and caulking and insulation of hot water systems (water heater and hot water pipes) and central heating ducts. Energy efficient heating and cooling equipment, as well as solar design features, may also provide desirable energy cost savings.

A "tankless" water heater is a "green improvement" that saves both energy and heating costs.

8. Special Feature Data

SPECIAL FEATURE DATA includes any items that may affect value. Some common special feature data include:

1. size and type of car storage (attached or detached garage or carport);
2. type of attic access, and attic improvements (flooring, heating, finished areas);
3. porches, patios and decks;
4. outbuildings (sheds, gazebos, storage buildings);
5. fences and walls;
6. fireplaces; and
7. pools, spas, and saunas.

VI. Specific Market Data

The category of data collected by appraisers is specific market data. This is data that relates to "comparable properties" in the marketplace.

To identify the comparable properties in the first place, the appraiser must identify their neighborhood, site and building characteristics. Once the comparables have been identified, data can be collected in regard to price and terms of sale (for the sales comparison and income approaches to value), construction costs (for the cost approach) and income and expenses (for the income approach).

The site and building data needed for comparable properties is similar to that required for the subject property.

Indeed, some of the most reliable comparable property data is obtained from the appraiser's own files on previous appraisals. Comparable property data is also commonly gathered from secondary sources (such as multiple listing services or computer data banks).

Verification (by personal inspection) of site and building data for comparable properties is not as critical as it is for the subject property.

Significant errors in comparable property site or building data are likely to show up in sales prices or rental incomes. When this happens, the nonconforming comparable is generally considered unreliable as a value indicator, and is either discarded from consideration or subjected to further investigation to determine the cause of the discrepancy.

A. PRICES AND TERMS OF SALE

One of the key pieces of data for the sales comparison approach to value (and also for the income approach) is the sales prices of comparable properties.

But price alone is not a sufficient indicator of value, even for a comparable that is identical to the subject property. The appraiser must also gather data on the conditions of the sale. Of particular importance are the date of the comparable's sale, its financing terms, and any special circumstances associated with the sale.

B. DATE OF SALE

The date of the comparable sale is important because market values are subject to change.

Just as the subject property is valued as of a specific date, the value of a comparable, as indicated by its sales price, is tied to the date of its sale. The sales dates of comparable properties should be within six months of the effective date of the appraisal. And in a rapidly changing market, the appraiser may still have to adjust the comparable sales prices for market trends.

C. FINANCING

Financing terms have a large impact on sales prices of property. When favorable financing is available, buyers are more willing, and more able, to pay higher prices for housing. Normally, financing is available on equal terms to all buyers in a market. But when a sale includes financing that is not typical of the market, the appraiser must take into account the effect of the financing terms on the price paid for the property.

D. SALE CONDITIONS

Conditions of sale that affect value also include special concessions by the seller, such as agreeing to pay some or all of the buyer's loan costs.

Any such concessions that are not typical of the local market must be accounted for by the appraiser. The appraiser must also identify any unusual circumstances that may have applied to the comparable sale: whether either party was under unusual pressure to sell or to buy, for example, or whether there was a family or business relationship between the parties. Comparable sales that are not "arm's length transactions" are generally unreliable as value indicators, due to the difficulty of adjusting the sales prices to account for the circumstances of the sale.

Common sources for obtaining and/or verifying comparable price and terms data include: real estate brokers, lenders, public records and interviews with the buyers and sellers themselves.

E. COST DATA

The second type of specific market data, *COST DATA, is used in the cost approach to value. It is used to determine the replacement or reproduction cost of the subject property.* Building cost estimates can be highly complex and require considerable skill and experience to prepare. For residential appraisals, cost estimates usually use a simple cost per square foot measure. The average cost per square foot to construct a building similar to the subject property is multiplied by the gross living area of the subject to give an indication of cost.

Case/Example: Data collected from costing manuals and services and local building contractors indicates that typical residential building costs run $60 per square foot for homes that are comparable in features to the subject property. If the subject property is a 2,500 square foot residence, its cost would be estimated as:

2,500 sq.ft. x $60 sq.ft = $150,000.

(The cost approach to value is discussed in detail in Chapter 8.)

F. INCOME AND EXPENSE DATA

If the property subject to an appraisal is (or will be) used for income production, data must be collected for the income approach to value. Income and expense data can be obtained from owners, brokers, and property managers. This data is collected for both the subject property and for comparable income properties. For the comparable properties, information on sales prices and terms is also necessary to determine the appropriate multiplier(s) to use in the income approach.

Important income and expense data include:

1. monthly or annual rental rates;
2. the terms of rental agreements;
3. vacancy and bad debt rates;
4. operating costs for salaries, utilities, repairs, maintenance and management and professional fees;
5. real estate taxes and insurance costs;
6. annual replacement reserve costs for items such as roofing and mechanical systems;
7. depreciation rates;
8. the mortgage interest rate; and
9. equity investment rates of return.

The income approach to value is discussed in detail in Chapter 10.

Exhibit 3: Requirements – Abbreviations Used in Data Standardization Text

Abbreviation	Full Name	Appropriate Fields
ac	Acres	Area, Site
AdjPrk	Adjacent to Park	Location
AdjPwr	Adjacent to Power Lines	Location
A	Adverse	Location & View
ArmLth	Arms Length Sale	Sale or Financing Concessions
ba	Bathroom(s)	Basement & Finished Rooms Below Grade
br	Bedroom	Basement & Finished Rooms Below Grade
B	Beneficial	Location & View
Cash	Cash	Sale or Financing Concessions
CtySky	City View Skyline View	View
CtyStr	City Street View	View
Comm	Commercial Influence	Location
c	Contracted Date	Date of Sale/Time
Conv	Conventional	Sale or Financing Concessions
CrtOrd	Court Ordered Sale	Sale or Financing Concessions
DOM	Days On Market	Data Sources
e	Expiration Date	Date of Sale/Time
Estate	Estate Sale	Sale or Financing Concessions
FHA	Federal Housing Authority	Sale or Financing Concessions
GlfCse	Golf Course	Location
Glfvw	Golf Course View	View
Ind	Industrial	Location & View
in	Interior Only Stairs	Basement & Finished Rooms Below Grade
Lndfl	Landfill	Location
LtdSght	Limited Sight	View
Listing	Listing	Sale or Financing Concessions
Mtn	Mountain View	View
N	Neutral	Location & View
NonArm	Non-Arms Length Sale	Sale or Financing Concessions
BsyRd	Busy Road	Location
o	Other	Basement & Finished Rooms Below Grade
Prk	Park View	View
Pstrl	Pastoral View	View
PwrLn	Power Lines	View
PubTrn	Public Transportation	Location
rr	Recreational (Rec) Room	Basement & Finished Rooms Below Grade
Relo	Relocation Sale	Sale or Financing Concessions
REO	REO Sale	Sale or Financing Concessions
Res	Residential	Location & View
RH	USDA –Rural Housing	Sale or Financing Concessions
s	Settlement Date	Date of Sale/Time
Short	Short Sale	Sale or Financing Concessions
sf	Square Feet	Area, Site, Basement
Unk	Unknown	Date of Sale/Time
VA	Veterans Administration	Sale or Financing Concessions
w	Withdrawn Date	Date of Sale/Time
wo	Walk Out Basement	Basement & Finished Rooms Below Grade
wu	Walk Up Basement	Basement & Finished Rooms Below Grade
WtrFr	Water Frontage	Location
Wtr	Water View	View
Woods	Woods View	View

Exhibit 3: Requirements, is an example of the standardized abbreviations that are required by Fannie Mae and Freddie MAC to allow more information to fit on the printed appraisal forms when electronically submitting appraisal loan reports.

VII. CHAPTER SUMMARY

I. Regional and Community Data.

    A. Describes broad-scale market forces that affect value.

    B. Useful as background information, and for identifying property characteristics and economic and social trends that enhance or detract from value.

    C. Includes data on the regional and community natural environment, economic characteristics, infrastructure, housing supply and demand, and social attitudes.

    D. Important sources include publications by federal, state and local government agencies and business trade associations.

II. Neighborhood Data.

    A. A neighborhood is a geographical area of complementary land uses.

        1. Neighborhood boundaries are defined by changing market influences. They may or may not coincide with physical boundaries or changes in land use.

    B. Neighborhood value indicators include:

        1. physical characteristics, type of neighborhood, property uses, changes in use;

        2. percent of development, rate of growth, relative supply and demand of housing;

        3. turnover rate, marketing time, sale terms;

        4. age, size, price, condition and occupancy of properties;

        5. population characteristics;

        6. distance to services, quality of services and utilities;

        7. taxes and special assessments; and

        8. negative value influences.

    C. Major neighborhood data sources include government agencies, trade groups and personal inspection.

III. Site Data.

    A. Site description includes the legal description of the subject property, and information relating to zoning and property taxes and assessments.

B. Data describing the physical characteristics of the size include:

   1. dimensions, size, topography, soil characteristics, climate and views;

   2. orientation, access, distance to amenities, hazards and nuisances; and

   3. on-site and off-site improvements

IV. Building Data.

A. Building data is used to select and analyze comparables, and to estimate improvement costs in the cost approach to value.

B. Appraisers collect building data to describe the improvements in terms of size, style, materials, and quality.

C. Building value indicators include:

   1. building size, number of living units, number of stories, architectural style, lot placement, number/size/type of rooms;

   2. type and condition of foundation, basement size and features;

   3. type and condition of roofing, gutters, exterior walls, windows and exterior doors

   4. type and condition of interior wall/ceiling/floor finishes, bathroom and kitchen finishes, cabinetry and doors;

   5. type and condition of electrical and plumbing systems, type, age and capacity of heating and cooling systems, age, and type of appliances included in appraisal;

   6. insulation, efficiency of heating/cooling, solar design; and

   7. attics, car storage, patios, decks, fireplaces, outbuildings, pools, etc.

V. Specific Market Data.

A. Site and building data for comparable properties is necessary in order to make comparisons with the subject property.

B. Date of sale, financing terms, and sale conditions can all affect the price paid for a comparable property.

C. Building cost estimates for residential appraisals are usually made on a "per square foot" basis.

D. Comparable income and expense data must be collected when the subject property is, or will be, used for rental purposes.

VIII. CHAPTER QUIZ

1. Which of the following types of data is most likely to be derived from secondary data sources?

    a. Building data
    b. Site data
    c. Neighborhood data
    d. Regional data

2. Which of the following is NOT a regional value indicator?

    a. Economic base
    b. Transportation systems
    c. Neighborhood boundaries
    d. Average household size

3. Neighborhood boundaries:

    a. are determined by market influences.
    b. always correspond to physical barriers such as roads or streams.
    c. never correspond to physical barriers such as roads or streams.
    d. are the same as subdivision boundaries.

4. Neighborhood data in an appraisal is used to:

    a. identify comparable properties for analysis (sales comparison approach).
    b. identify value influences that affect the subject property.
    c. support the appraiser's estimate of value.
    d. all of the above.

5. Off-site improvements that are relevant to a site description include:

    a. streets.
    b. neighborhood utilities.
    c. storm sewers.
    d. all of the above.

6. In an appraisal of residential property, building data would NOT be used to:

    a. determine highest and best use of the land as if vacant.
    b. adjust the sales prices of comparable properties (sales comparison approach).
    c. estimate reproduction cost or replacement cost in the cost approach to value.
    d. identify comparable properties for analysis.

7. The most reliable building data for the subject property is acquired by:
    a. reviewing the plans and specifications.
    b. interviewing the property owner.
    c. personal inspection.
    d. reviewing previous appraisal report on the property.

8. The sales price of a comparable property may need to be adjusted to account for:
    a. financing terms.
    b. date of sale.
    c. building size.
    d. all of the above.

9. If market interest rates are 8%, and a comparable property is sold with seller financing at 6%, the price paid for the comparable property is likely to be:
    a. higher than market value.
    b. lower than market value.
    c. the same as market value.
    d. none of the above.

10. In a comparable sale, the seller paid closing costs for real estate transfer taxes. This fact would be relevant to the appraisal:
    a. if not customary in the market for the seller to pay the transfer taxes.
    b. only if the transfer taxes exceeded $500.
    c. only if the sale was an arm's length transaction.
    d. in all cases.

ANSWERS: 1. d; 2. c; 3. a; 4. d; 5. d; 6. a; 7. c; 8. d; 9. a; 10. a

Chapter 6
Site Valuation

KEY WORDS AND TERMS

Allocation Method
Consistent Use
Development Method
Depth Tables
Elements of Comparison
Excess Land
Extraction Method
Ground Rent Capitalization
Highest and Best Use

Interim Use
Land Residual Method
Legal Nonconforming Use
Legally Permitted Use
Maximally Productive Use
Physically Possible Use
Plottage
Principle of Anticipation
Sales Comparison Method

LEARNING OBJECTIVES

After completing this chapter, you should be able to:

1. define highest and best use, and understand its importance in the appraisal of real estate;

2. list the four characteristics of highest and best use;

3. understand the distinction between the highest and best use of land as if vacant, and the highest and best use of property as improved, and the significance of each;

4. understand the concepts of interim use and legal nonconforming use;

5. understand the concepts of excess land and plottage;

6. identify the six common methods for appraising land, and describe their basic procedures; and

7. identify the critical data needed for each of the six land valuation methods.

CHAPTER OUTLINE

I. Highest and Best Use

The orderly process of appraisal is totally dependant on an accurate analysis of highest and best use.

There are a variety of reasons for estimating the value of land or a site. It may simply be that the subject property is in fact vacant land. Or in the case of improved property, a separate valuation of the site may be required in order to apply a valuation technique (such as the cost approach to value), or as part of the scope of the appraisal. In this chapter, we will examine the concept of site valuation. We will begin by exploring the doctrine of highest and best use, which underlies every estimate of the market value of land. We will then review some of the more commonly used techniques for estimating land value.

We have seen that real estate is not simply the land and its improvements, but the rights that go with the land, such as the right to use, subdivide, or transfer the land. The concept of highest and best use recognizes this fact—and the fact that the value of real estate depends on how it is used. For example, a particular property may be worth more for commercial development than it is for agricultural purposes. In real estate appraisal, the market value of property always depends on its highest and best use.

A. HIGHEST AND BEST USE DEFINED

The *HIGHEST AND BEST USE of property is the use that is reasonable and probable and that results in the highest present value, as of the date of the appraisal.* Highest and best use assumes that the market will view the value of the property in light of all its possible uses (see **Figure 6-1**).

If there is more than one possible use for the property, its value will be determined by the most productive (profitable) use.

Highest and best use is also defined as the use that gives the greatest value attributable to the land.

Case/Example: Assume a site could be utilized as a mini-warehouse or a parking garage. Assume that the construction costs to build the warehouse would be $1,000,000, but when completed, the site land and improvements would have a value of $1,500,000. For use as a mini-warehouse the site would therefore have a value of $ 500,000:

Value of mini-warehouse	$1,500,000.00
Cost to construct	-1,000,000.00
Value attributable to land	$ 500,000.00

Assume a parking structure on the same site would cost $2,000,000 to construct but the value of the structure and land would be $3,000,000. In this case, the parking structure would be a higher and better use than the mini-warehouse since the land value for this use would be $1,000,000:

Chapter 6

Figure 6-1

Analyzing a Property for Highest and Best Use

It is of extreme importance to the accuracy of the appraisal.

Suppose, for example, that an appraiser concludes the highest and best use of a parcel to be for single-family detached homes when, in actuality, it has a potential for apartments. Consequently, as a result of this initial mistake, the appraiser would obtain zoning, construction, rental income and expense, and sales information for single-family homes rather than for the more intensive and valuable use as apartments. Great care must be taken to truly analyze a property at its highest and best use, rather than just including a brief and incomplete statement concerning its optimum use.

If the appraiser mistakenly judges a property's highest and best use, all subsequent work and analysis in arriving at the property's value is wasted.

Value of parking structure	$3,000,000.00
Cost to construct	-2,000,000.00
Value attributable to land	$1,000,000.00

B. PURPOSE OF HIGHEST AND BEST USE ANALYSIS

Appraisers must identify the highest and best use of a property for three reasons:

1. Highest and best use influences the value of the property, since the market value depends on the most profitable use.

2. Highest and best use guides the appraiser in the separate valuation of land and improvements. The principle of consistent use requires both land and improvements to be appraised for the same use, which should be the highest and best use of the property.

3. Highest and best use helps identify comparable properties for the sales comparison approach to value. Both comparable vacant lots and comparable improved properties should have the same highest and best use as the subject property.

C. CHARACTERISTICS OF HIGHEST AND BEST USE

To qualify as the highest and best use, the use must result in the highest value.

But the use must also be reasonable and profitable.

Uses that are NOT "reasonable" and "profitable" due to legal, economic, or physical limitations cannot qualify as the highest and best use.

184

Case/Example: The most profitable use of a site may be to construct a 20-story office tower on it. But if current building regulations restrict maximum building height to 10 stories, then a 20-story building is not likely to be erected on the site. Although a 20-story office building would be the most profitable use of the land, it is not the highest and best use because it is not reasonably likely to occur.

Highest and best use analysis can be seen as a process of elimination.

To begin with, the appraiser eliminates any uses that would be illegal under existing or proposed laws, regulations, deed restrictions or contractual agreements. Next, uses that are not possible due to the physical characteristics of the land itself are eliminated from consideration.

The remaining potential uses are then analyzed to see whether they would generate any financial return. Uses that do not generate an adequate positive return are discarded as economically unfeasible, and the others are evaluated to determine which one would generate the highest return. The result is the highest and best use.

"Highest and best use" is often defined as the use that is legally permitted, physically possible, economically feasible, and maximally productive.

This definition reflects the process used to determine highest and best use as described above. Keep in mind, that the legal, physical, and economic probabilities of a particular use are often interrelated (see **Figure 6-2**).

1. Legally Permitted Use

A review of the legal restrictions that apply to the subject property is usually completed first. These restrictions include a wide variety of government regulations such as zoning, environmental and tax regulations, and also private legal restrictions, such as easements, deed restrictions or lease conditions.

Case/Example: A particular site may be more valuable for commercial purposes than for residential use. But if the site's zoning only allows residential use, a commercial use would be illegal and therefore could not be the highest and best use of the land.

Legal restrictions affect the use of land in a variety of ways. For instance, zoning laws may limit use by such means as setback requirements, and maximum or minimum limits on lot and building size.

Legal restrictions may also influence land use by influencing the cost of various types of development. Examples of this include special property tax breaks that encourage agricultural use of property, or development fees and regulatory procedures that drive up the cost of building a new housing.

Figure 6-2

Four Characteristics of Highest and Best Use

1. Legally Permitted Use

A review of the legal restrictions that apply to the subject property is first. These restrictions include: government regulations such as zoning, environmental and tax regulations, and private legal restrictions, such as easements, deed restrictions, or lease conditions. Zoning laws may limit use by setback requirements, and maximum or minimum limits on lot and building size.

2. Physically Possible Use

The size, shape, soil, topography, and other physical characteristics of a site are important considerations in determining its highest and best use. For determining potential use the soil must be capable of supporting the necessary improvements.

3. Economically Feasible Use

The appraiser must also consider whether a given use is probable from an economic standpoint. For a use to be economically feasible, it must result in a positive economic return.

4. Maximally Productive Use

Maximally productive use is just another way of saying "the use that results in the highest value." If highest and best use is the use that results in the highest value, then it's maximally productive.

2. Physically Possible Use

The size, shape, soil, topography, and other physical characteristics of a site are important considerations in determining its highest and best use. For example, the site must be large enough to accommodate the potential use, and the soil must be capable of supporting the necessary improvements. Water and other utilities must be available and adequate, and the climate must be suitable.

3. Economically Feasible Use

The appraiser must also consider whether a given use is probable from an economic standpoint. For a use to be economically feasible, it must result in a positive economic return. If a use would result in economic loss, it is removed from consideration.

The supply of and demand for properties with a particular use is a major factor in analyzing economic feasibility.

If there is already an oversupply of one type of property (such as office space or warehouses), it may not be economically feasible to develop additional property for that use, even if existing properties are profitable.

Case/Example: An appraiser is analyzing the highest and best use of a commercial site in a small town. One of the potential uses of the site is as a gas station. The appraiser notes that the two existing gas stations in town are both profitable, but determines that there is not sufficient demand in town to support three stations. Although supply and demand are currently in balance, development of a third station would create an oversupply. In this case, the appraiser would conclude that use as a gas station could not be the highest and best use of the site, because it was not economically feasible.

4. Maximally Productive Use

MAXIMALLY PRODUCTIVE USE is just another way of saying "the use that results in the highest value." Value can be measured in terms of productivity, the ability of an asset to create wealth. The greater the productivity, the greater the value, and vice versa. If highest and best use is the use that results in the highest value, then it can also be defined as the use that is maximally productive.

D. IMPORTANCE OF THE PRINCIPLE OF ANTICIPATION

The *PRINCIPLE OF ANTICIPATION states that the value of property is affected by the potential future benefits of its ownership.* So when analyzing highest and best use, the appraiser must always consider the possible future uses of the property.

A site's legal restrictions, economic circumstances, and even physical characteristics are all subject to change. Zoning and other laws can become more restrictive, or less so. Supply and demand for particular types of properties can go up or down. Physical characteristics, such as the availability of water, can also change. Highest and best use analysis requires the appraiser to evaluate the likelihood of any changes that may affect the potential use of the property.

Case/Example: A site is zoned for office buildings of up to three stories. The area is economically suitable for office development, and so it may appear that a three-story office building would be the highest and best use of the site. However, if the site is likely to be rezoned in the near future to allow for ten-story office buildings, it may be more profitable to wait and develop the site more intensively after the new zoning takes effect, rather than to immediately develop a three-story office building that will shortly become an underimprovement. In this case, the current highest and best use of the land may be to do nothing with it, to simply hold it for speculation.

When conditions are such that a change in legal, economic, or physical restrictions on property use seems likely to occur, an appraiser may (and should) take this fact into consideration when determining highest and best use.

E. INTERIM USES

When the current highest and best use of land is expected to change in the near future, the use to which the land is put while awaiting the change is called an interim use. An *INTERIM USE is a current highest and best use that is viewed as only temporary.*

A common example of an "interim use" is agricultural land that is currently being farmed but will soon be converted for residential or commercial development.

In urban areas, parking lots are a frequent interim use of land that is not yet ready for development (due to lack of demand or some other reason). Another example of an interim use is an older building that is a candidate for replacement or extensive renovation to allow for a more productive use of the land.

Because they are expected to change in a relatively short period of time, interim uses do not usually involve expensive improvements. In the first place, it does not make economic sense to put a lot of money into improvements that will have to be torn down in a few years.

II. Vacant and Improved Land

Highest and best use may vary, depending on whether land is vacant (or assumed to be vacant) or improved.

Appraisers make a distinction between the highest and best use of land as if vacant, and the highest and best use of property as improved.

To determine the highest and best use of land as if vacant, the appraiser assumes that any existing improvements on the land do not exist. The highest and best use becomes the use that would result in the highest value if the land were vacant and ready for any kind of development. In the case of property that is actually vacant land, this assumption simply reflects the true state of affairs.

But improved property may also be analyzed in this manner.

Case/Example: A property is improved with a single-family residence. If vacant, the value of the site for residential use would be $40,000. However, the zoning allows for commercial development, and the site would be worth $80,000 if vacant and available for commercial development. In this case, the highest and best use of the land as if vacant would be commercial use. The fact that the land is already improved for residential use has no effect on this determination.

The highest and best use of the property as improved takes into account the contribution of existing improvements, and also the cost of their removal (if necessary) to allow for some different use.

Site Valuation

Case/Example: Using the facts of the example above, assume the value of the property (land and buildings), as currently improved for residential use, is $120,000 ($40,000 land value, plus $80,000 value contribution from the improvements). Also assume that it would cost $10,000 to remove the existing structure to allow for commercial use development.

In this case, the value of the property as improved for commercial use can be calculated as follows:

$80,000.00 = value of land if vacant
- 10,000.00 = cost to remove existing improvements
$70,000.00 = value of property as improved for commercial use

These figures indicate that the highest and best use of the property as improved is the current residential use, since the value of the property as improved ($120,000) is higher for residential than for commercial use.

In considering the highest and best use of property as improved, keep in mind that existing improvements do not necessarily add to the value of the property, and may actually detract from it. Even when an improvement is physically sound, it may be functionally obsolete, and the necessary cost of removing it to make way for a newer structure could have a negative impact on overall property value.

Case/Example: In some areas of the country, where there is a strong demand for luxury housing, but little or no supply of vacant land for new development, existing homes in good condition may be purchased and then razed to make way for more luxurious residences. Even though the existing residences are perfectly livable, they represent a negative contribution to value, since the building-lots would be worth more if they were vacant.

A. LEGAL NONCONFORMING USES

When zoning laws are changed to become more restrictive, existing uses may become nonconforming.

For example, an area that once allowed both commercial and residential uses may be rezoned to permit residential use only. In that case, an existing commercial building would no longer conform to the zoning laws.

When zoning laws allow the continuation of existing uses that have become nonconforming due to changes in zoning regulation, they are referred to as LEGALLY NONCONFORMING USES. Such uses are allowed to continue, but usually may not be rebuilt or expanded. A legal nonconforming use may be the highest and best use of property as improved, but generally cannot be the highest and best use of the land as if vacant, because if the land were vacant, the nonconforming use would no longer be legal.

B. TRUE HIGHEST AND BEST USE

For appraisal purposes, there can be only one highest and best use.

When a property's highest and best use as if vacant is different from its highest and best use as improved, the appraiser must determine which one should serve as the basis of the appraisal. This is actually an easy procedure, since highest and best use is simply the use that results in the highest value.

If the highest and best use of the land as if vacant results in a higher value than the highest and best use of the property as improved, then it is the true highest and best use of the property, and the opposite is also true. Remember though, that the value indicated by the highest and best use of the land as if vacant may need to be adjusted to reflect the costs of removing existing improvements.

Case/Example: In preceding examples, we looked at a property whose value for its highest and best use as improved ($120,000 for residential use) was greater than the adjusted value for its highest and best use as if vacant ($70,000 for commercial use). An appraiser in this case would conclude that the highest and best use of the subject property was residential use, since it resulted in the highest value.

Comparing the highest and best use of land as if vacant to the highest and best use of property as improved helps determine whether an existing use should continue or not.

If the existing use is not the true highest and best use (because the adjusted value of the land as if vacant is greater than the value of the property as improved), then a change in the use of the property is indicated (see **Figure 6-3**).

Figure 6-3

True Highest and Best Use

I. Current Use Should Change When:

Vacant Land Value > Improved Property Value + Demolition Cost

(True HBU is HBU as if vacant)

II. Current Use Should Continue When:

Vacant Land Value < Improved Property Value + Demolition Cost

(True HBU is HBU as improved)

Case/Example: A particular site, if vacant, would have a market value of $100,000 for commercial purposes. The value of the site if vacant for residential use is only $75,000. However, if the value of the site as currently improved for residential purposes is $120,000, the current residential use is the true highest and best use and should be continued. The property as improved can sell for $120,000, which is more than its value if vacant for commercial use, so a change to commercial use is not indicated.

C. PRINCIPLE OF CONSISTENT USE

Several appraisal methods (including residual techniques and the cost approach to value) rely on the separate valuation of land and improvements.

When using these techniques, the appraiser must bear in mind the principle of consistent use: both land and improvements must be appraised for the same use.

Once the appraiser determines the true highest and best use for the property, he or she may then consider the individual values of site and improvements that are indicated by that use.

Case/Example: Returning to the facts of our ongoing example, an appraiser would decide that the value of the subject site was $40,000, which is its value for residential purposes. Since residential use was determined to be the highest and best use of the property, both the land and the improvements must be valued on the basis of residential use. This would be the case even though the land was found to be worth more for commercial use.

D. EXCESS or SURPLUS LAND

For any given use, there is usually an optimum amount of land associated with the use. When a parcel of land includes more land than is necessary to support its highest and best use, it is said to contain excess or surplus land. *EXCESS or SURPLUS LAND is land that is not needed for the highest and best use of the site.*

Excess land may be held for future expansion. It may also be subdivided for some other use. In such a case, it may have a similar or different highest and best use.

Case/Example: The highest and best use of a two acre site is for a grocery store. However, the amount of land needed to support the grocery store use is only one acre. If the site can be subdivided, the excess one acre of land may have value for some other use, such as a fast food franchise.

Surplus land not necessary to the highest and best use of the site may not be subdivided. Thus, it can lead to a condition known as "under improvement".

Case/Example: Water restrictions require that lots for residences, in a particular district, must be twenty acres minimum and may not be subdivided. Surrounding districts allow one acre parcels. Additional taxes as well as maintenance of the large parcel may make it undesirable to develop. On the other hand, it might be desirable to someone who wishes to build a very large estate property.

E. PLOTTAGE

A concept related to excess land is the concept of plottage. *PLOTTAGE refers to the increase in value that results from combining two or more lots to allow for a more profitable highest and best use. If two lots were worth more when combined than they were separately, the added value is called the PLOTTAGE VALUE or PLOTTAGE INCREMENT.*

Case/Example: Two adjoining lots are each valued at $50,000. They are each too small to support a building of the size typical in the neighborhood. But if the two lots are combined, the resulting parcel is comparable in size to other neighborhood sites, and the value of the combined property is $150,000. The extra $50,000 in value is the plottage value.

F. HIGHEST AND BEST USE IN RESIDENTIAL APPRAISALS

Strictly speaking, an analysis of highest and best use should determine the optimum use for the subject property in very specific terms. For example, a determination that residential use is the highest and best use of the subject property should also specify the characteristics of the residential improvements (optimum size, number of bedrooms, etc.). As a practical matter, most residential appraisals do not require such a detailed analysis. Unless otherwise required, an appraiser may assume that the current use of improved residential property is its highest and best use if:

1. the value of the property as improved is higher than the value of the site as if vacant, and
2. there is adequate comparable sales data to show that the existing improvements are typical of properties for which there is demand in the local market.

III. Methods of Site Valuation

There are six commonly recognized methods for appraising the value of land (see **Figure 6-4**).

> *Since the sales comparison method is by far the most reliable, it is the most often used method of valuing land.*

The other methods are used only when the sales comparison method is impossible or impractical. This may be due to a lack of adequate comparable sales data or because of cost considerations (as in property tax assessments, which commonly use allocation to determine land value). It may also be used to support the value estimate determined by the sales comparison method (as in an investment analysis which calculates the potential profit and loss from a development).

Residential appraisers rely primarily on the sales comparison method for site valuation, if adequate comparable sales data are available. Allocation and extraction are also used

---

Figure 6-4   **Six Methods of Land Valuation**

The six commonly recognized methods for appraising the value of land are:

1. Sales Comparison Method

It is considered the most reliable, relies on sales of similar vacant parcels to determine the value of the subject land or site.

2. Allocation Method

3. Extraction Method

Allocation and extraction are used to value the land component of total improved property, either by applying a ratio of land value to total property value (allocation) or deducting depreciated improvement value from total value (extraction).

4. Development Method

In the development method, the appraiser analyzes the costs of developing, then deducts these costs from the anticipated sales price of the developed property to arrive at the value of the raw land.

5. Land Residual Method

6. Ground Rent Capitalization Method

The land residual and ground rent capitalization methods analyze the income attributable to the land, and calculate the value of the land by capitalizing its income.

---

in residential appraisals, with extraction generally preferred over allocation. Commercial (general) appraisals may use any of the six methods for valuing land or sites.

A. SALES COMPARISON METHOD (First and Most Important Method)

The "sales comparison method" is considered the most important and reliable approach to land valuation, because it relies on an analysis of actual sales in the marketplace to arrive at the value of the subject property.

According to the sales comparison method, the value of the subject land or site is indicated by the prices paid for similar parcels (see **Figure 6-5**).

Identifying comparable properties and adjusting their sales prices are really two sides of the same coin. The sales that are the most reliable indicators of the subject property's value—those that are the most "comparable"—are the ones that require the

Figure 6-5

Sales Comparison Method						
Sale No.	Time of Sale	Sale Price	Utility (Size, Shape, etc.)	Location	Time	Indicated Value of Subjects
1.	1 year ago	$56,000	5,000	Equal	2,000	$63,000
2.	1 month ago	$53,700	3,700	5,000	Equal	$62,400
3.	2 years ago	$43,000	4,000	10,000	5,000	$62,000
4.	Presently listed for sale (asking price)	$75,000	-4,500	-10,000	Equal	$60,500

fewest and smallest adjustments to account for differences from the subject property. On the other hand, sales that require significant adjustments may not be considered comparable at all.

1. Sources of Data

Sales data for comparable vacant land can be found through interviews with owners, buyers, sellers, real estate brokers and land developers. The appraiser can get information if he or she is a member of a multiple listing service or computerized online information service, such as FNC, Inc.

fncinc.com
FNC, Inc.

Some information is on CD from subscription services such as FNC, sales periodicals, title insurance companies, other appraisers, banks, mortgage loan officers and county recorders' offices.

Commercial computerized online and CD data services are now considered efficient resources for gathering information compiled from the county tax assessor and title company records. These types of services offer sales histories, prices and dates of sale, document numbers, statistics about property and improvements. They also may include plat maps, as well as access to flood zone and demographic information. These computer systems offer computer search capabilities that seek comparable properties within a given geographic area, based on similar characteristics of the subject property.

2. Sales of Improved Property

In some cases, sales of improved property can be used as comparables for the purpose of site valuation. If a property is purchased for the purpose of demolishing the existing improvements, and rebuilding new ones, the sale can serve as an indicator of site value. The appraiser would deduct the cost of demolishing the existing improvements from the sales price of the property to arrive at an indicator for the value of the site as if vacant. This application of the sales comparison method can be quite useful in built-up areas where sales of actual vacant sites are few or non-existent.

3. Elements of Comparison

An *ELEMENT OF COMPARISON is a factor that may indicate a difference in value between the subject property and a comparable.* With respect to land, the most important elements of comparison include location, time of sale, financing and other terms of sale, highest and best use, property rights and restrictions, physical characteristics and degree of development (see **Figure 6-6**).

Figure 6-6	**Elements of Comparison for Land**
● **Real Property Rights Conveyed**	● **Market Conditions Adjustment**
● **Financing Terms**	● **Location Adjustments**
● **Conditions of Sale**	● **Physical Characteristics**
● **Expenditures Immediately After Sale**	● **Economic Characteristics**

a. Real Property Rights Conyeyed

A precise identifi cation of the real property rights conveyed in each comparable transaction, selected for analysis, is essential because the transaction price is always predicated on the property interest conveyed. Comparable sales must be adjusted for any differences in the property rights conveyed in the sale, and also for any differences in property restrictions such as zoning, easements, property tax rates, and private deed restrictions.

b. Financing Terms

The definition of market value requires that the subject property be appraised on the basis of a cash (or cash equivalent) transaction. Otherwise, the specific financing terms must be spelled out in the appraisal. Market value also assumes that there are no undue influences or pressures on either the buyer or the seller. In other words, the sale is an arm's length transaction. If a comparable sale includes financing concessions or other terms that are not typical of the market, their effect must be accounted for by adjusting the comparable's sale price.

Case/Example: A comparable property sold recently on terms which required the seller to buy down the buyer's mortgage interest rate by 1 %. In this case, the appraiser must adjust the sales price of the comparable to account for any increase in price that may be attributed to the interest rate buydown.

c. Condtions of Sale

The special motivations of the parties to the transaction in many situations can affect the prices paid and even render some transactions as non-market. Examples of special conditions of sale include a higher price paid by a buyer because the parcel had synergistic, or marriage, value; a lower price paid because a seller was in a hurry to conclude the sale; a financial, business, or family relationship between the parties involved in the transaction; unusual tax considerations; lack of exposure of the property in the (open) market; or the prospect of lengthy `litigation proceedings.

d. Expenditures Immediately After Sale

These are expenditures that would have to be made upon purchase of the property and that a knowledgeable buyer may negotiate into the purchase price. Examples include the cost to repair or replace structures or parts of structures, the cost to remediate environmental contamination, or the costs associated with zoning changes to permit development. These expenditures should be included in the sales contract. **The appraiser is not responsible for hidden defects or conditions that are not disclosed by other parties.**

e. Market Condtions Adjustment

The date of a comparable sale is significant because market forces (and therefore values) change over time. In general, the greater the difference between the date of the comparable sale and the effective date of the subject property appraisal, the less reliable the comparable is as a value indicator. However, the rate at which market conditions are changing is a significant factor as well. A comparable sale that took place six months prior to the appraisal of the subject property is ordinarily considered fairly reliable, but might require significant adjustment in a rapidly changing market.

Case/Example: A comparable property was sold three months prior to the date of the subject appraisal. Since that time, however, market values have declined by an average of 10% due to an announcement of major layoffs by the town's principal employer. Even though the comparable sale is fairly recent, its price will need to be adjusted to reflect the change in market conditions.

f. Location Adjustments

Ideally, comparable sales should be located in the same neighborhood as the subject property. As defined in Chapter 5, a neighborhood is an area where market forces operate in a similar way on all properties in the area. If comparable sales from the subject property neighborhood are not available, the appraiser may consider sales from nearby neighborhoods that are subject to similar market influences. However, the appraiser will have to make adjustments for any differences in neighborhood characteristics.

Case/Example: Two neighborhoods in a city are similar in most respects, the major differences being that Neighborhood "A" is located in an area of rolling hills, while Neighborhood "B" is mostly flat in topography. An appraisal of a property in Neighborhood "A" may use a comparable sale from Neighborhood "B", but the sales price of the comparable will have to be adjusted to account for any difference in desirability related to topography.

g. Physical Characteristics

Differences in physical characteristics may include such items as size, shape, topography and soil characteristics. When evaluating the effects of size differences between the subject and comparable properties, the appraiser must bear in mind that most land uses are associated with an optimum size. Therefore, size differences between sites with the same highest and best use do not usually result in a proportionate difference in value.

Case/Example: Two lots are each found to have a highest and best use as single-family residential properties with comparable size homes. One lot is 20,000 square feet, while the other is 22,000 square feet. All other factors being equal, the 10% greater size of the second lot is not likely to result in a 10% difference in value, because both lots are capable of supporting the same highest and best use. However, the greater size will still contribute to value.

The geological characteristics of soil have become very important in determining value in recent years. Soil conditions may make building improvements difficult, expensive, or virtually impossible for a number of reasons. These reasons may include natural environmental contamination, such as radon or the leaching of chemicals from nearby sites. The site may be full of boulders or rocks that require removal or, in extreme cases, blasting before construction is possible. *SOIL LIQUEFACTION may also be present. This is a soil condition in which the soil becomes virtually a liquid during an earthquake.* High groundwater levels can create the need for sump pumps. Finally, certain clay deposits may create slide conditions on hillsides. If an appraiser suspects any of these conditions, he/she should notify the client, and the appraisal may need to be carried out utilizing an **Extraordinary Assumption**, a **Hypothetical Condition**, or both.

h. Economic Characteristics

Qualities such as income, operating expenses, lease provisions, management, and tenant mix are used to analyse income-producing properties.

4. Comparable Sale Price Adjustments

Adjustments must be made, or at least considered, for each element of comparison (location, date of sale, etc.) that may affect the value of the subject property. (The techniques for determining the amounts of comparable price adjustments are discussed in Chapter 9.)

The adjustment is always applied to the price of the comparable, rather than to the subject property.

If the comparable is superior in some respect, its price is adjusted downward; if it is inferior to the subject property, its price is adjusted upward.

Case/Example: A comparable lot sold recently for $45,000. The comparable has a superior location, which makes it $5,000 more valuable that the subject lot. Because the comparable is superior in location, its price is adjusted downward.

$45,000 - $5,000 = $40,000

The indicated value of the subject lot is $40,000.

Depending on the data, adjustments may be in the form of a dollar amount or a percentage of the comparable sales price.

When the adjustment is a percentage, the dollar amount of the percentage is calculated and then added to or subtracted from the comparable sale price.

Case/Example: The sales price of a comparable lot is $45,000. Market data suggest that the subject lot is worth 10% less than the comparable lot, due to changes in the market since the date of the comparable sale. The amount of the adjustment is 10% of $45,000 (.10 x 45,000), or $4,500. Since the comparable is more valuable, the adjustment is made by subtracting the difference in value from the comparable sales price.

$45,000 - $4,500 = $40,500

The indicated value of the subject lot is $40,500.

When calculating percentage adjustments, the order in which the adjustments are calculated can affect the results of the calculation. For this reason, adjustments are normally calculated in a particular order or sequence. The sequence used to calculate the adjustments will depend on the appraiser's analysis of the market, but in general, adjustments for property rights, financing and sale terms, and market conditions are made first, before adjustments for location and physical characteristics.

Case/Example: An appraiser determines that a comparable sales price must be adjusted downward by 10% to account for the value of financing concessions in the comparable sale. In addition, the subject property is worth $5,000 more than the comparable due to superior utility service. The sales price of the comparable is $100,000. In this case, the amount of the adjustment for financing terms will depend on whether it is made before or after the adjustment for utilities. If the adjustment for financing terms is made first, the result is as follows.

$100,000 x 10% (.10) = $10,000 financing adjustment

$100,000 - $10,000 = $90,000 value adjusted for financing

$90,000 + $5,000 = $95,000 value adjusted for financing and utilities

If the adjustment for utilities is made first, the result is a different indicated value for the subject lot.

$100,000 + $5,000 = $105,000 value adjusted for utilities

$105,000 x 10% (.10) = $10,500 financing adjustment

$105,000 - $10,500 = $94,500 value adjusted for financing and utilities

B. ALLOCATION METHOD (Second Method)

ALLOCATION is a method of estimating the land value for an improved property. This method assumes that a certain percentage of a property's value is attributable to its improvements and the remaining percentage is attributable to the land. In other words, it assumes that similar properties will have similar ratios of land value to building value. For example, if a typical building value to land value ratio is 3 to 1 (i.e., buildings are typically worth three times as much as their lots), then 25% (¼) of the property's total value is allocated to the land, and 75% (¾) to the improvements. If the value of the property as a whole can be established, then determining the value of the land is simply a matter of multiplying by the appropriate percentage.

Case/Example: An appraiser has estimated that a property is worth a total of $200,000, and that the ratio of building value to land value for similar properties is 3:2 (3 to 2). In this case, 60% (3/5) of the property's value is allocated to the improvements, and 40% (2/5) is allocated to the land.

$200,000 x 40% (A) = $80,000 allocated land value

A variation of the allocation approach is to use the property tax assessor's estimate of the land value as a percentage of the total property.

This land amount is usually stated separately from the improvements and can be used if the land has been recently reassessed.

Allocation suffers from two serious drawbacks. First, in order to determine the correct ratio or percentage to apply, it is necessary to have market data: how much have builders and developers paid for land in relation to the value of the improvements that they constructed? But if reliable market data is available, there is no reason to resort to allocation; the sales comparison method is always preferable when adequate comparable sales data exists.

The second problem with allocation is that it is inherently inaccurate. At best, an allocation percentage will represent an average for a particular type of property. Lots of the same size and type (such as residential), with equal value, can be improved with buildings of different sizes, styles, and functionality. The allocation method does not take this variation in the value of improvements into consideration.

Allocation alone is NOT a very reliable indicator of land or site value.

Accordingly, it is only used when more reliable methods are impossible (due to lack of market data) or impractical (as in the case of property tax assessment, where the values of thousands of properties must be allocated between land and improvements). Allocation is also used sometimes as a check on the values indicated by other methods of land valuation.

C. EXTRACTION METHOD (Third Method)

Extraction is another method that is sometimes used to value land (either vacant land, or the land component of improved property) when data for comparable sales of vacant land is not available. In a sense, extraction is the cost approach to value in reverse. In the cost approach, appraisers add the value of the land to the depreciated cost of the improvements to arrive at the total value of the property.

With the **EXTRACTION METHOD**, *the depreciated cost of improvements is subtracted from the total value of the property to arrive at the value of the land.*

The extraction method is applied to comparable sales of improved property when comparable sales of vacant land are not available. By extraction, the appraiser estimates the value of the land component of the comparable sale, and then uses this data to estimate the land value of the subject property. Extraction cannot be considered reliable unless one or both of the following conditions is true:

1. the value of the comparable improvements can be reliably estimated, or
2. the value of the comparable improvements is very small in relation to the total value of the comparable property.

The most common use of extraction is probably for rural properties, where the value of land tends to represent a higher percentage of the total property value.

Case/Example: A comparable rural property sold recently for $650,000. The appraiser estimates that the depreciated value of the comparable's improvements is between $80,000 to $100,000.

By extraction, the value of the comparable's land is in the range of $550,000 to $570,000. Because the improvements represent a fairly small portion of the total value, extraction yields a range of land values that varies by less than 5%, even though the appraiser was only able to estimate improvement value to within a range of 25%.

D. DEVELOPMENT METHOD (Fourth Method)

The land development method is often applied to large "raw" or undeveloped vacant parcels of land for the purposes of subdivision.

This method utilizes ***DISCOUNTED CASH FLOW TECHNIQUES***. *Subdivision is often carried out over a period of several years. This method requires that future net cash flows projected from sales after deduction of expenses be discounted to arrive at the present value of the land.* Discounting is a means of calculating the present value of a future amount.

To properly carry out the analysis, the appraiser must first determine the highest and best use of the land. In addition, the appraiser must create a sound development plan, calculate a realistic pricing schedule, calculate an absorption rate for the sale of the individual parcels, calculate the expenses of the land development, estimate marketing costs, estimate annual taxes over the period of development and sales, and allow for reasonable overhead and profit allowances for the project.

Then the appraiser researches the market to determine an appropriate discount rate that is proper for this type of investment and that takes into account the timing of the sales within the subdivision. Typically, subdivisions are sold over a period of several years and each year's income and expenses over the development period must be properly allocated and discounted. The appraiser may use a financial calculator or a table of reversion factors to apply the proper reversion factor to the problem. **Figure 6-7** shows a table of reversion factors.

This method may produce unrealistically high value conclusions if the highest and best use analysis is incorrect, income is either overstated or not properly graduated, all expenses are not accounted for properly, or the rate selected is either incorrect or improperly applied. The proper application of the development method utilizes advanced appraisal methodology and is described in more depth and detail in advanced income appraisal texts.

E. LAND RESIDUAL METHOD (Fifth Method)

The *LAND RESIDUAL METHOD is a form of the income capitalization approach to value.* (Income capitalization is discussed in detail in Chapter 10.) Income capitalization measures value as a function of income.

The basic formula for income capitalization is:

Income (I) = Value (V) x Capitalization Rate (R)

Figure 6-7

Table of Reversion Factors					
Years	8%	9%	10%	11%	12%
1	.9259	.9174	.9091	.9009	.8929
2	.8573	.8417	.8264	.8116	.7972
3	.7938	.7722	.7513	.7312	.7118
4	.7350	.7084	.6830	.6587	.6355
5	.6806	.6499	.6209	.5935	.5674
6	.6302	.5963	.5645	.5346	.5066
7	.5835	.5470	.5132	.4816	.4523
8	.5403	.5019	.4665	.4339	.4039
9	.5002	.4604	.4241	.3909	.3606
10	.4632	.4224	.3855	.3522	.3220
11	.4289	.3875	.3505	.3173	.2875
12	.3971	.3555	.3186	.2858	.2567
13	.3677	.3262	.2897	.2575	.2292
14	.3405	.2992	.2633	.2320	.2046
15	.3152	.2745	.2394	.2090	.1827
16	.2919	.2519	.2176	.1183	.1631
17	.2703	.2311	.1978	.1696	.1456
18	.2502	.2120	.1799	.1528	.1300
19	.2317	.1945	.1635	.1377	.1161
20	.2145	.1784	.1486	.1240	.1037
21	.1987	.1637	.1351	.1117	.0925
22	.1839	.1502	.1228	.1007	.0826
23	.1703	.1378	.1117	.0907	.0738
24	.1577	.1264	.1015	.0817	.0659
25	.1460	.1160	.0923	.0736	.0588
26	.1352	.1064	.0839	.0663	.0525
27	.1252	.0976	.0763	.0597	.0469
28	.1159	.0895	.0693	.0538	.0419
29	.1073	.0822	.0630	.0485	.0374
30	.0994	.0754	.0573	.0437	.0334

Chapter 6

This formula can also be expressed as:

Value (V) = Income (I) ÷ Capitalization Rate (R)

Case/Example: A property's net annual income is $12,000. If market data indicates a capitalization rate of 10%, then the value of the property can be estimated by income capitalization as follows:

V = I ÷ R
V = $12,000 ÷ .10 (10%)
V = $120,000 indicated value of property

To apply the land residual technique, the appraiser must be able to reliably determine four critical pieces of data:

1. the value (depreciated cost) of the improvement;
2. the market capitalization rates for land;
3. the market capitalization rates for buildings; and
4. the property's total net operating income.

By multiplying the building capitalization rate times the value of the improvements, the appraiser can determine the amount of the property's income that is attributable to the improvements (I = V x R). This amount is then subtracted from the total net income of the property to find the amount of income that is attributable to the land. Finally, the land income is converted to a value figure by means of the land capitalization rate.

Case/Example: The highest and best use of a parcel of land is determined to be a retail shopping center. The cost to construct the improvements is estimated at $1.2 million dollars, and the property is projected to generate net annual income of $208,000. Market data indicate capitalization rates for this type of property to be 8% for land and 12% for improvements. The first step is to calculate the income attributable to the improvements, by multiplying the improvement capitalization rate by the value of the improvements.

I = V x R
I = $1,200,000 x .12 (12%)
I = $144,000 income attributable to improvements

Next, the improvement income is subtracted from the total net income to find the income attributable to the land.

$208,000 - $144,000 = $64,000 income attributable to land

Finally, the land income is capitalized by dividing it by the land capitalization rate.

V = I ÷ R
V = $64,000 ÷ .08 (8%)
V = $800,000 indicated land value

F. GROUND RENT CAPITALIZATION METHOD (Sixth Method)

Ground rent capitalization is another means of applying the income capitalization approach to estimating the value of land.

In a **GROUND LEASE** *the tenant leases the land from the landlord, and constructs a building on the site.* Ground leases are usually long-term leases of 50 or more years, to allow the tenant to have the use of building for the course of its useful life. *The rent paid by the tenant of a ground lease is called* **GROUND RENT**.

When property is subject to a ground lease, its value can be estimated by capitalizing the amount of ground rent, using the formula V = I ÷ R. This is often more complicated than it sounds, however, since other factors (such as the amount of time remaining on the lease, any provisions for escalation of rent, etc.) must be taken into account. (Refer to Chapter 10 for a more detailed discussion of capitalization techniques.)

Case/Example: A property's ground rent is $50,000 a year for 50 years. If market data indicates a capitalization rate of 10%, then the value of the property can be estimated by income capitalization as follows:

V = I ÷ R
V = $50,000 ÷ .10 (10%)
V = $500,000 indicated land value

The land residual and ground rent capitalization methods analyze the income attributable to the land, and calculate the value of the land by capitalizing its income.

G. DEPTH TABLES ("4-3-2-1 Method")

There are appraisal tables which show the additional value for additional depth. A depth table is a percentage table that illustrates how the highest value is located in the front part of a lot. **Figure 6-8** is an example of the "4-3-2-1" depth table.

Case/Example: If a property lost the rear 25 percent of its depth, the value would decline, but the loss in value would be less than 25 percent. While there are complex mathematical tables, a simple evaluation method is the "4-3-2-1 Method."

The appraiser assumes that the value of the parcel is as follows:

1st ¼ = 40% of Value
2nd ¼ = 30% of Value
3rd ¼ = 20% of Value
4th ¼ = 10% of Value

Based on this rough formula, you will see that the loss of the rear 25 percent (¼th) would only reduce the value by 10 percent.

Figure 6-8

The "4-3-2-1" Depth Table

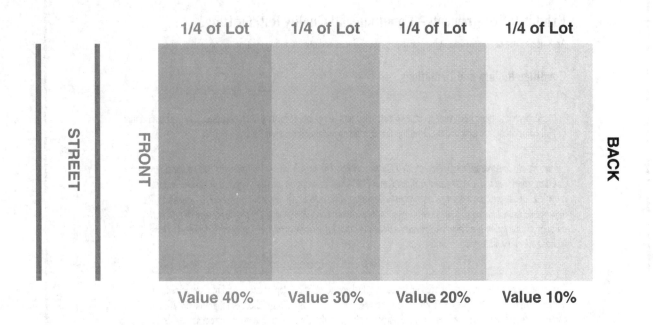

Depth tables give a ballpark idea of value in relationship to depth. They are NOT accurate because they do NOT consider the need for depth of particular users.

All land (the site) is unique: no property is the same as any other property. When an appraiser of a loan takes into consideration the highest and best use of the land, the appraiser considers the quality and condition of the residential property as a whole, which is the focus of the following Exhibit 1.

EXHIBITS

Exhibit 1: Requirements – Condition and Quality Ratings Usage

Appraisers must utilize the following standardized condition and quality ratings within the appraisal report.

Condition Ratings and Definitions

C1

The improvements have been very recently constructed and have not previously been occupied. The entire structure and all components are new and the dwelling features no physical depreciation.*

Note: Newly constructed improvements that feature recycled materials and/or components can be considered new dwellings provided that the dwelling is placed on a 100% new foundation and the recycled materials and the recycled components have been rehabilitated/re-manufactured into like-new condition. Recently constructed improvements that have not been previously occupied are not considered "new" if they have any significant physical depreciation (i.e., newly constructed dwellings that have been vacant for an extended period of time without adequate maintenance or upkeep).

C2

The improvements feature no deferred maintenance, little or no physical depreciation, and require no repairs. Virtually all building components are new or have been recently repaired, refinished, or rehabilitated. All outdated components and finishes have been updated and/or replaced with components that meet current standards. Dwellings in this category either are almost new or have been recently completely renovated and are similar in condition to new construction.

C3

The improvements are well maintained and feature limited physical depreciation due to normal wear and tear. Some components, but not every major building component, may be updated or recently rehabilitated. The structure has been well maintained.

C4

The improvements feature some minor deferred maintenance and physical deterioration due to normal wear and tear. The dwelling has been adequately maintained and requires only minimal repairs to building components/mechanical systems and cosmetic repairs. All major building components have been adequately maintained and are functionally adequate.

C5

The improvements feature obvious deferred maintenance and are in need of some significant repairs. Some building components need repairs, rehabilitation, or updating. The functional utility and overall livability is somewhat diminished due to condition, but the dwelling remains useable and functional as a residence.

C6

The improvements have substantial damage or deferred maintenance with deficiencies or defects that are severe enough to affect the safety, soundness, or structural integrity of the improvements. The improvements are in need of substantial repairs and rehabilitation, including many or most major components.

EXHIBITS

Quality Ratings and Definitions

Q1

Dwellings with this quality rating are usually unique structures that are individually designed by an architect for a specified user. Such residences typically are constructed from detailed architectural plans and specifications and feature an exceptionally high level of workmanship and exceptionally high-grade materials throughout the interior and exterior of the structure. The design features exceptionally high-quality exterior refinements and ornamentation, and exceptionally high-quality interior refinements. The workmanship, materials, and finishes throughout the dwelling are of exceptionally high quality.

Q2

Dwellings with this quality rating are often custom designed for construction on an individual property owner's site. However, dwellings in this quality grade are also found in high-quality tract developments featuring residences constructed from individual plans or from highly modified or upgraded plans. The design features detailed, high-quality exterior ornamentation, high-quality interior refinements, and detail. The workmanship, materials, and finishes throughout the dwelling are generally of high or very high quality.

Q3

Dwellings with this quality rating are residences of higher quality built from individual or readily available designer plans in above-standard residential tract developments or on an individual property owner's site. The design includes significant exterior ornamentation and interiors that are well finished. The workmanship exceeds acceptable standards and many materials and finishes throughout the dwelling have been upgraded from "stock" standards.

Q4

Dwellings with this quality rating meet or exceed the requirements of applicable building codes. Standard or modified standard building plans are utilized and the design includes adequate fenestration and some exterior ornamentation and interior refinements. Materials, workmanship, finish, and equipment are of stock or builder grade and may feature some upgrades.

Q5

Dwellings with this quality rating feature economy of construction and basic functionality as main considerations. Such dwellings feature a plain design using readily available or basic floor plans featuring minimal fenestration and basic finishes with minimal exterior ornamentation and limited interior detail. These dwellings meet minimum building codes and are constructed with inexpensive, stock materials with limited refinements and upgrades.

Q6

Dwellings with this quality rating are of basic quality and lower cost; some may not be suitable for year-round occupancy. Such dwellings are often built with simple plans or without plans, often utilizing the lowest quality building materials. Such dwellings are often built or expanded by persons who are professionally unskilled or possess only minimal construction skills. Electrical, plumbing, and other mechanical systems and equipment may be minimal or non-existent. Older dwellings may feature one or more substandard or non-conforming additions to the original structure.

IV. CHAPTER SUMMARY

I. Market value of a property is always determined by its highest and best use, the use that is reasonably probable and results in the highest value.

A. The highest and best use must be legally permitted, physically possible, economically feasible and maximally productive.

B. The appraiser eliminates uses that are not likely to occur, then analyzes the remaining possible uses to determine which is the most profitable.

C. Appraisers must consider whether probable uses of the property are likely to change in the future.

    1. An interim use is a temporary highest and best use that is likely to be replaced by a more profitable use in the near future.

D. In the case of improved property, the appraiser must consider both the highest and best use of the land as if vacant, and the highest and best use of the property as improved.

    1. Highest and best use of land as if vacant assumes that the property is vacant and ready for development.

    2. Highest and best use of property as improved takes into account the value contribution of any improvements, and also the cost that would be necessary to remove existing improvements to allow for a change in use.

    3. A legal nonconforming use may be the highest and best use of property as improved, but cannot be considered as the highest and best use of the land as if vacant.

    4. When the highest and best use of the land as if vacant is different than the highest and best use of the property as improved, the use that results in the highest value is the true highest and best use.

        a. The cost of removing existing improvements must be taken into account when comparing the values of existing and potential uses.

E. Both land and improvements must be valued for the same use, which is the highest and best use of the property.

F. Excess land is land that is not needed for the primary highest and best use of a site, and that is adaptable to some other use.

G. Plottage is the combination of two or more parcels of land to create a larger parcel with a more profitable highest and best use. The overall value increase due to combining the parcels is called the plottage value.

II. Land or a site may be valued by several different techniques.

  A. The sales comparison method is always the preferred approach to estimating market value, and should always be used when adequate comparable sales data exists.

    1. Sales prices of vacant lots that are similar to the subject property indicate the value of the subject property.

    2. Adjustments to the sales prices of the comparables must be made to account for differences in real property rights conveyed, financing terms, condtions of sale, expenditures immediately after sale, market condtions adjustment, location adjustments, physical characteristics, and economic characteristics.

      a. Comparable sales prices are adjusted upward when the subject property is superior to the comparable, and downward when the comparable has more valuable characteristics.

      b. The appraiser must consider the sequence of adjustments when using percentage type adjustments.

  B. Allocation assumes that there is a typical or standard ratio between the value of land and the value of improvements on the land. The land value is estimated by multiplying the total property value by the percentage allocated to land.

  C. Extraction is used when the value of improvements can be reliably estimated, or when the value of the improvements is relatively insignificant in relation to the total property value. The depreciated value of the improvements is subtracted from the total value, to find the value of the land.

  D. The subdivision development method can be used to estimate the value of land whose highest and best use is for subdivision and development. The costs of development are subtracted from the projected sales of the finished lots, to arrive at the current value of the raw land.

    1. Subdivision development analysis often requires discounting of sales and cost figures to take into account the time value of money. A future payment or expense can be discounted to its present value by multiplying it times a reversion factor. The reversion factor depends on the selected discount rate, and the length of time until the payment will be made or received.

  E. In the land residual method, the appraiser calculates the amount of income that is attributable to a property's improvements, and then subtracts it from the total net income of the property. The result is the income that is attributable to the land, which can then be capitalized to determine land value.

  F. Ground rent capitalization is another form of capitalizing land income to determine land value. The land income in this case is the rent paid by a long-term tenant under a ground lease.

  G. Depth tables show value in relationship to depth.

7. The formula used to express the relationship between income and value is:

    a. income = value x capitalization rate.
    b. income = value divided by capitalization rate.
    c. value = income x capitalization rate.
    d. value = capitalization rate divided by income.

8. With regard to sales of vacant land, all of the following are appropriate elements of comparison, except:

    a. location.
    b. financing terms.
    c. zoning.
    d. no exceptions.

9. Which of the following is an example of the income approach to value?

    a. Land residual method
    b. Ground rent capitalization
    c. Both of the above
    d. Neither of the above

10. The primary reason for using a technique other than the sales comparison method in order to estimate land value is:

    a. lack of comparable sales data for sales of vacant land.
    b. lack of comparable sales data for sales of improved properties.
    c. lack of income data for the subject property.
    d. to save time and money.

ANSWERS: 1. c; 2. c; 3. b; 4. a; 5. b; 6. d; 7. a; 8. d; 9. c; 10. a

Chapter 7
Residential Construction

KEY WORDS AND TERMS

Balloon Framing
Bamboo Flooring
Basement
Detached House
Dormer
Fenestration
Floor Plan
Footing
Foundation Wall
Framing
Functional Utility
Gable Roof
Green Technology
Jamb
Joists

Monolithic Slab (Floating Foundation)
Multiple Pane
Pier and Beam
Platform Framing
Post and Beam Framing
Rafter
Renewable Resource
Sheathing
Siding
Sill
Studs
Tankless Water Heaters
Taping
Truss Roof Systems

LEARNING OBJECTIVES

The orderly process of appraisal requires that appraisers have a basic understanding of residential construction for a number of reasons. To properly describe the building in the appraisal report, appraisers must understand the terminology that is used to describe the various features of a house. Appraisers need to be familiar with the "pros" and "cons" of different building materials, techniques, and styles in order to judge the overall quality of improvements. And they must be able to identify defects or shortcomings in design, workmanship, and materials, and to determine whether such defects can be cured, and if so, at what cost.

In this chapter, we will examine the various types and styles of homes and the features that characterize good home design. We will also discuss the basic materials and techniques that are common in residential construction. After completing this chapter, you should be able to:

CHAPTER OUTLINE

1. list the five basic types of houses and describe their characteristics;
2. understand the impact of architectural style on value;
3. describe the factors that influence proper siting of a house on its lot;
4. list the three basic activity zones of a house and describe their relationships to each other;
5. describe the characteristics that affect functional utility in the various rooms of a house;
6. identify the characteristics of various building components that can affect value; and
7. understand the technical terminology used to describe residential construction.

I. Classification of Houses

Houses are generally classified on the basis of four characteristics: the number of units, whether the building is attached or detached, the number of stories and the architectural style.

The **NUMBER OF UNITS** *refers to the number of separate households that the building is designed to accommodate. Although usage may vary in different areas, the term "house" is most often used to refer to a* **SINGLE-FAMILY RESIDENCE**. *If a building has multiple units that share a common access and other common areas, it is usually referred to as an* **APARTMENT BUILDING**.

A **DETACHED HOUSE** *is one that is not connected to any other property.* **ATTACHED HOUSES** *share one or more walls, called "party walls," that are jointly owned by the two adjoining properties.* **ROW HOUSES**, *common in many urban areas, are an example of attached dwellings. Ownership of an attached dwelling often involves a* **PARTY WALL AGREEMENT**, *which assigns responsibility for maintenance and repair of the party wall(s) (see* **Figure 7-1**).

A. TYPES OF HOUSES

The "type of house" refers to the number of stories or levels in the house, and their relationship to each other.

Figure 7-1   Attached Houses

Multiples (Apartments)

Town House

Duplexes

Row House

Illustrations courtesy of Marshall & Swift

Figure 7-2   Types of Houses

One Story

Bi-Level

One and One-Half Story

Two Story

Split Level

Illustrations courtesy of Marshall & Swift

Although modern construction methods allow for all sorts of variations, the vast majority of houses fall into five basic "type" categories (see **Figure 7-2**):

1. one-story;
2. one and one-half story;
3. two-story;
4. split-level; and
5. bi-level (also known as split-entry or raised ranch).

1. One-Story House

A *ONE-STORY HOUSE, often called a "ranch" or "rambler," has its entire living area on the ground floor. It may or may not have a BASEMENT, which is a room of full story height located below the first floor, at least partially below ground level, and primarily not used for living accommodations.*

The advantages of one-story houses include: ease of exterior maintenance, flexibility of floor plan design and the fact that there are no stairs to climb.

On the down side, this type of house is relatively expensive to build; by comparison, a two-story house with the same exterior dimensions has twice the living area, with essentially no extra cost for roof or foundation. (Roof costs for a one-story house are often minimized by using a low pitched roofline.)

One-story houses also require a greater amount of lot space in relation to the amount of living area, so they may be inappropriate or impractical on small or narrow lots.

2. One and One-Half Story House

Also known as a Cape Cod, the *ONE AND ONE-HALF STORY HOUSE has a steeply pitched roof that permits part of the attic area to be used for living space.* Roof dormers, which add to the amount of usable upstairs space, are a common feature of this type of house. As in the case of one-story houses, the foundation may or may not include a basement. Construction costs per square foot tend to be lower for one and one-half story houses than for one-story houses.

One and one-half story houses are often built with expandability in mind. Because the ground floor normally has at least one bedroom (and sometimes two), the upstairs level can be left unfinished until the extra space is needed. However, ease of expandability will depend on the quality of the original design and construction, which should allow for adequate access (stairs), ventilation (windows) and plumbing (bathrooms) on the attic level.

3. Two-Story House

Compared to a one-story or one and one-half story house, the two-story house is more economical in terms of construction cost per square foot of living space.

The reason for the economy is that square footage can be doubled without doubling foundation and roof system costs. This design also allows for the most living space on a given size of lot. Bedrooms are normally located on the upper floor, providing a natural separation between the public and private areas of the house.

A concern with all multi-level houses is the design and efficiency of heating and cooling systems. Because heat rises, a poorly designed system will make it difficult to keep the lower level warm in winter, and the upstairs cool in the summer.

With a well designed system, however, heating and cooling efficiency may actually be greater than for single-story houses, since the building has less exterior surface area relative to the amount of heated or cooled interior space.

4. Split-Level House

A *SPLIT-LEVEL HOUSE has three or four different levels, which are staggered so that each level is separated from the next by half of a flight of stairs.* Bedrooms and baths are located on the top level. Half a flight down are the main entry, living room, dining room and kitchen. Down another half-story, beneath the bedroom level, is space for a family room, den or spare bedroom; the garage is often located on this level as well. A fourth level, equivalent to a basement, may be located below the living/dining/kitchen space.

The design of a split-level home lends itself to a sloped lot, where the garage and main entry can both open out at grade level. On a flat site, the main entry will be raised one-half story above the finished grade.

A split-level house has some of the same benefits as a two-story house in terms of construction, cost efficiency and natural separation of the various functional areas of the home.

5. Bi-Level House

A *BI-LEVEL or SPLIT-ENTRY HOUSE has two main levels, one atop the other, with an entry or foyer located on a level halfway between.* The lower level is sunk about halfway below ground, so the entry is even with the grade level. This design is sometimes called a "raised ranch," since it is essentially a one-story home with a finished basement that has been raised partially out of the ground. The main rooms of the house are all on the upper level, with the lower story used for a family room or rec room, and perhaps a spare bedroom.

Since the lower level of a split-entry house is partly below ground, special care must be taken to provide adequate insulation and moisture proofing. Another drawback to this design is the lack of a basement or crawlspace in which to run pipes and ductwork.

Nevertheless, split-entry homes are cost-effective to build, and the finished lower level space is considered part of the "gross living area" for appraisal purposes in many parts of the country.

II. Architectural Styles

ARCHITECTURAL STYLE is the character of a building's form and ornamentation.

If homebuyers in a particular area do not find a particular architectural style desirable, homes of that style are likely to sell for less than similar size homes having architectural styles which are more desirable within that community.

Architectural styles have traditionally been influenced by local factors such as climate and the availability of different building materials.

There are many examples of traditional architectural styles that are adapted to a particular location: Spanish style houses with thick adobe walls and tile roofs in the southwest desert, Southern Colonial houses with deep shaded porches in the hot, humid South, or Cape Cod style homes designed for protection from cold northern winds in New England (see **Figure 7-3**).

Local traditional styles can still be found in many areas, but location is much less of an influence on architectural style than it used to be.

Builders are no longer limited to using local materials, since modern transportation systems make different building materials widely available at reasonable costs. The invention of central heating and cooling, as well as improved insulating materials, has broadened the range of architectural styles that can be adapted to local climates.

A. COMPATIBILITY

COMPATIBILITY means that a building is in harmony with its use or uses and its environment. In terms of value, one type or style of house is not inherently better or worse than any other. What is most important to value is the compatibility of the design. Compatibility has several different aspects. To maximize value, the design of a house should be compatible with the designs of other homes in the area, with the physical and environmental characteristics of the building site, with the materials used in the construction, and with the preferences of the local market.

Figure 7-3

Examples of Different Architectural Styles

Colonial

Cape Cod (1)

Cape Cod (2)

Cottage

Victorian

Mediterranean

Southern

Saltbox

Ranch

Chalet

"A" Frame

Contemporary

Illustrations courtesy of Marshall & Swift

First of all, the design of a house should be compatible with the styles of other houses in the local neighborhood.

The market may welcome a limited degree of uniqueness in design, but value will generally suffer if the design contrasts too radically with surrounding houses.

Subdivision developers often impose design restrictions on their developments, because they know that compatibility of design will have a positive impact on property values in the subdivision.

Case/Example: A contemporary style house located in a neighborhood of other contemporary style houses is likely to be viewed positively by the market. But the same house located in a neighborhood of traditional style homes might seem "out-of-place," and its value could suffer as a result.

Compatibility of design also refers to the suitability of the design for the particular building lot and location. Value is enhanced by a design that takes advantage of physical site characteristics, such as views. The design should also be appropriate for the topography of the site. For example, split-level designs often work well on hilly sites, while colonial style houses do not. Finally, the design should be appropriate for the local climate. A design that is specifically adapted to a hot desert climate, for example, would be inappropriate in an area with cool, rainy weather.

A building's architectural style is often defined at least in part by the materials used in its construction. Spanish style homes have clay tile roofs, Tudor's utilize timber framing, contemporary designs incorporate large areas of glass. A compatible design is one where the materials are appropriate to the style.

Case/Example: A clay tile roof on a Cape Cod house would look ridiculous to most potential homebuyers.

The final aspect of design compatibility is perhaps the most important: the design must be compatible with the demands of the market.

The popularity of any given design is influenced by the economic and social forces that affect value. As lifestyles and demographics change, so does the demand for different design features in housing.

Ultimately, it is the local market that determines what is a "good" design, and what is a "bad" one.

Case/Example: A development of new contemporary style houses is built in an older community with mostly traditional style housing. If the market places an emphasis on the historic character of the community, the contemporary homes will be viewed as incompatible, and their value will suffer. On the other hand, if market forces are creating a demand for more modern housing in the community, the contemporary homes may not be incompatible at all, but may simply represent a new trend in community standards.

III. Elements of House Design

An appraiser must be able to identify the various elements of house design and evaluate any defects in those elements. The elements of house design include siting, interior functional zones, and room characteristics.

A. SITING

SITING refers to the placement of the house on the building lot. Placement is normally limited to some extent by building code set-back requirements, which call for minimum distances between the house and the property's boundaries. Topographic considerations such as slopes or poor soil conditions may also limit where the house may be placed on the lot. Within these limits, however, careful placement of the house on the lot can have a significant impact on value.

There are four basic considerations in designing the placement of a house on its lot: orientation to the sun, orientation to prevailing storm winds, orientation to views, and the division of the lot into functional zones (see **Figure 7-4**).

Figure 7-4

Exterior Functional Zone Example - Windbreak Layout

Orientation to the sun affects the amount of light and heat that can enter the house. In most areas, a design where the living areas of the house face south is considered optimum. This orientation takes best advantage of natural lighting in the most used areas of the home, and helps maximize solar heat gain in the winter. Excessive summer heat gain can be avoided by using wide roof overhangs, which shade the house in summer when the sun is high in the sky, but allow light and heat to penetrate in the winter when the sun's path is lower.

Screening with deciduous trees is another effective way to block the summer sun but still allow it to shine through in the winter when the trees are bare.

In some areas, **orientation to prevailing storm winds** is an important siting consideration. In areas that are subject to frequent or heavy storms from a particular direction, it is best to minimize the amount of window area that is directly exposed to the winds, in order to cut down on heat loss. Entries should also be sheltered from the direct path of the storms.

An attractive **view** can add significantly to the value of a house. Views should be visible from the most used areas of the house. Even if the site does not have an attractive territorial view, careful landscaping can provide a pleasant view of the lot from the living area.

The last aspect of house siting is the division of the lot into **functional areas** or **zones**, the so-called public, private, and service zones. The area that can be viewed from the street frontage is the public zone. Areas shielded from the street by the house, or by fencing or other landscaping, constitute the private area. The service area includes access ways (driveway, walkways, etc.) and outdoor storage areas. Good design maximizes the amount of private area available for household activities.

B. INTERIOR FUNCTIONAL ZONE

An appraiser cannot underestimate the importance of *FUNCTIONAL UTILITY*, *which concerns a building's ability to perform the function for which it is intended according to current market tastes and standards; as well as the efficiency of use in terms of architectural style, design and layout, traffic patterns, and the size and type of rooms.*

A well-designed house should provide space for three basic activities: living, working, and sleeping.

Ideally, the spaces provided for each of these activities should be separated, so that one activity does not interfere with another. For example, bedrooms should be located where they will not be disturbed by activities in the living and working areas of the house.

Figure 7-5 shows how the spaces for the three different activities can be separated into zones. The *LIVING ZONE includes the public areas of the house: the living room, dining room, family room and guest bath.* The *WORKING ZONE is comprised of the kitchen and laundry/utility room. Bedrooms and private baths are located in the SLEEPING ZONE.*

The separate activity areas of the home are connected by hallways, stairs and entry ways, which are sometimes referred to as a fourth zone of the house, the CIRCULATION ZONE. While the three activity zones should be designed to provide separation of the activities, they should also allow for easy circulation between and within zones.

Design features that affect desirability affect value because value is determined by supply and demand features of the marketplace.

A house's value is affected by the building's *FLOOR PLAN, which is an architectural drawing indicating the exact layout of rooms and illustrating the functional or nonfunctional relationship between them.* Structures with wasted space might lack space where it is otherwise desired so that the property will be less desirable to buyers than similar size homes.

How the designer allocates space affects desirability for many buyers. An example is while a custom 3,000 square foot home might have only two bedrooms because that is what the original owner wanted, to most potential buyers, the design would be a negative feature.

Case/Example: In a retirement oriented community, a two-story home without a bedroom on the first level is likely to be far less desirable than one with this feature.

C. ROOM CHARACTERISTICS

1. Kitchens

The kitchen is commonly the most used room of the house, so its design and location have a large impact on the functionality of the overall floor plan.

Kitchens should be conveniently accessible from both the main entrance and service entrance of the house, and should be located adjacent to the dining room and family room, if these rooms are included in the design. Also, the kitchen should be designed so that it is not necessary to walk through the working area in order to reach other rooms of the house.

A critical aspect of kitchen design is the work triangle, which is formed by the sink, refrigerator, and range. The distances between the three points of the work triangle can make the difference between an efficient kitchen design and a poor one. If the distances are too small, the kitchen will be cramped; if they are too great, preparing a meal will seem like a five-mile hike. A distance of four to seven feet between each point of the work triangle is considered optimal (see **Figure 7-6**).

Figure 7-6

Kitchen Work Triangle

SINK

REFRIGERATOR

STOVE

Kitchen sizes vary considerably. Eighty square feet of space (8' x 10') is considered a minimum, but kitchens twice that size are not uncommon. Larger kitchens often include an eating area or family activity area. The design should include adequate counter and cabinet space, and plenty of electrical outlets for kitchen appliances.

Lighting and ventilation are important considerations in kitchen design. Overhead lights should illuminate all areas of the kitchen, and a vent or fan should be located over the cooking area to allow cooking fumes to escape. Natural lighting is desirable, but the placement of windows can be a problem. The best location for a kitchen window is over the sink. Additional windows are desirable so long as they do not take up space needed for wall cabinets.

Windows should never be placed over the cooking area.

2. Laundry/Utility Rooms

Laundry areas are best located where they are convenient to the sleeping area of the house, off the bedroom hallway for example. However, location of the laundry area is not as critical as most other rooms of the house, and laundries are often located in the garage or basement.

The laundry area should be well-ventilated, and located where noise from the appliances will not disturb others.

3. Living Rooms

The living room is the main public room of the house.

It should be located near the main (guest) entry, be separated from the sleeping area, and preferably be on the south side of the house. If the house has a dining room, it should be next to the living room. It should not be necessary to cross through the living room in order to reach the kitchen or bedrooms.

The size and shape of the living room should allow for easy arrangement of furniture. About 200 square feet is the minimum size, and rectangular shaped rooms tend to work best for furniture placement. The modern trend is for smaller living rooms, particularly in homes with a separate family/recreation room.

4. Family Rooms

In many areas, the *FAMILY ROOM (also called a recreation room) has taken over the role of the living room as the main center of entertainment and socializing in the house.* As part of the living zone, the family room should be separated from the sleeping zone; however, it is usually considered an advantage if the family room is next to (or near) the kitchen.

Since the family room is a center of activity for household members, direct access to the outside is also an asset.

5. Dining Rooms

Dining rooms may be formal or informal. A formal dining room or area is a separate room that is designed for that purpose. Informal dining areas are usually attached to or part of the kitchen itself, and may take the form of a nook or alcove.

The main considerations for the dining area are that it should be large enough to accommodate a dining table and chairs (including room to get in and out of the table), and it should have easy access to the kitchen so that food does not have to be carried through other areas of the house.

6. Bedrooms

The number of bedrooms has a major effect on house value.

Normally, homes with different numbers of bedrooms appeal to different segments of the market, that is, to families of different sizes or lifestyles. The average household size in the market will have a large impact on the desirability of three- or four-bedroom homes, as opposed to two-bedroom homes.

Ideally, bedrooms should all be located in a separate sleeping zone, to provide both privacy and noise insulation. The most common arrangement is to locate the bedrooms on a separate story or wing. Each bedroom should have convenient access to a bathroom, either directly or via a private hallway. Also, it should not be necessary to go through a bedroom to reach another room (other than a private bath).

Depending on the room layout, a size of 9' x 10' is the minimum needed to allow for a single bed, 10' x 12' for a double bed. Whether larger room sizes will add to value depends on local market preferences. *Most homes have at least one bedroom that is larger than the others, the MASTER BEDROOM*. Modern master bedrooms will often have walk-in closets and other amenities.

Each bedroom should have its own closet, with a minimum of four linear feet of closet space per occupant.

More generous amounts of closet space are usually desirable, especially if the house lacks other storage areas, such as a basement or attic.

Locating closets along common walls (either between bedrooms, or between a bedroom and the public area of the house) can help to provide insulation from noise.

7. Bathrooms

Bathrooms are classified according to the types of fixtures they include.

Chapter 7

The following charts indicate the appropriate way to fill out the Uniform Residential Appraisal Report (URAR) as mandated by Fannie Mae and Freddie Mac. It asks for specific language and numerical information that is or will come to be used in almost all residential appraisal forms, including those used for VA and FHA loans.

Improvements Section	Forms	Requirement or Instruction
# of Stories The appraiser must indicate the number of stories for the subject property. Do not use any designators or descriptors, such as '1 story' or 'one story and a half.' For condominiums, the appraiser must enter the number of stories for the building in which the subject unit is located. **Reporting Format**: # of Stories – Numeric to 2 decimal places	1004/70 2055/2055 1073*/465* 1075*/466* *FIELD IS LOCATED IN PROJECT INFORMATION SECTION	REQUIREMENT
# of Levels The appraiser must indicate the number of levels for the subject unit. Do not use any designators or descriptors, such as '1 level'. **Reporting Format**: # of Levels – Numeric, whole numbers only	1073*/465* 1075*/466* *FIELD IS LOCATED IN UNIT DESCRIPTION SECTION	REQUIREMENT
Design (Style) The appraiser should enter an appropriate architectural design (style) type descriptor that best describes the subject property. Valid descriptions include, but are not limited to, 'Colonial,' 'Rambler,' 'Georgian,' 'Farmhouse'. Do not use descriptors such as 'brick,' '2 stories,' 'average,' 'conventional,' or 'typical' as these are not architectural styles. Design style names may vary by locality. The appraiser should report the name of the design style that is applicable within the local market area. **Reporting Format**: Design (Style) – Text	1004/70 2055/2055	INSTRUCTION
Year Built The appraiser must indicate the year the subject property was built. If it is unknown or unavailable to the appraiser within the normal course of business, the appraiser must estimate the year the subject property was built. **Reporting Format:** Year Built – 4-digit number, yyyy Estimation of Year Built – A tilde (~) must precede the year built **Examples:** 1978 ~1950 (The PDF creator will insert the tilde)	1004/70 2055/2055 1073*/465* 1075*/466* *FIELD IS LOCATED IN PROJECT INFORMATION SECTION	REQUIREMENT

Form Friendly Dataset (watermark)

Improvements Section	Forms	Requirement or Instruction
Basement Area, Basement Finish If a basement exists, the appraiser must indicate the basement size in square feet and the percentage of the basement that is finished. If there is no basement, enter the numeral zero (0) in both fields. **Reporting Format:** Basement Area – Numeric to 5 digits, whole numbers only Basement Finish – Numeric to 3 digits, whole numbers only	1004/70 2055/2055	REQUIREMENT
Heating, Cooling The appraiser should select the heating and/or cooling types. If there is no heating or cooling source, the appraiser should indicate 'Other' and enter 'None'. **Reporting Format:** Heating Types (for 1004 and 2055) – Checkbox(es) designated with an 'x' Cooling Types – Checkbox(es) designated with an 'x' Description of 'Other' (if applicable) – Text	1004/70 2055/2055	INSTRUCTION
Heating, Cooling -- *(for Condominiums)* The appraiser should indicate the heating and cooling types. If there is no heating source, the appraiser should indicate 'None'. If there is no cooling source, the appraiser should indicate 'Other' and enter 'None'. **Reporting Format:** Heating Types (for 1073 and 1075) – Text Cooling Types – Checkbox(es) designated with an 'x' Description of 'Other' (if applicable) – Text	1073*/465* 1075**/466** *FIELD IS LOCATED IN THE UNIT DESCRIPTION SECTION **FIELD IS LOCATED IN THE UNIT IMPROVEMENTS SECTION	INSTRUCTION
Amenities The appraiser should select the appropriate checkbox(es) to indicate the amenities available. The appraiser should enter the numeral zero (0) in the appropriate space if there are no fireplaces or woodstoves. The appraiser should enter 'None' in the appropriate space if there is no patio/deck, pool, fence, porch, or other amenity. **Reporting Format:** Amenity Types – Checkbox(es) designated with an 'x' Description of Amenity – Text	1004/70 2055/2055 1073*/465* 1075**/466** *FIELD IS LOCATED IN THE UNIT DESCRIPTION SECTION **FIELD IS LOCATED IN THE UNIT IMPROVEMENTS SECTION	INSTRUCTION

Improvements Section	Forms	Requirement or Instruction
Car Storage, Driveway, Garage, Carport The appraiser must indicate whether the subject property has a driveway, garage, and/or carport, or has no car storage. If the subject property has a driveway, garage, and/or carport, the appraiser must enter the number of spaces for each type of car storage; if none, enter the numeral zero (0). Reporting Format: Car Storage Types – Checkbox(es) designated with an 'x' # of Cars - Numeric to 2 digits, whole numbers only	1004/70 2055/2055 1073*/465* 1075*/466* *CAR STORAGE AND # CARS FIELDS ARE LOCATED IN UNIT DESCRIPTION SECTION	REQUIREMENT
Finished Area Above Grade Contains _____Rooms The appraiser must enter the total number of finished rooms above grade. Reporting Format: # of Rooms – Numeric to 2 digits, whole numbers only	1004/70 2055/2055 1073*/465* 1075*/466* *FIELD IS LOCATED IN UNIT DESCRIPTION SECTION	REQUIREMENT
Finished Area Above Grade Contains _____Bedrooms This appraiser must enter the total number of bedrooms above grade. Reporting Format: # of Bedrooms – Numeric to 2 digits, whole numbers only	1004/70 2055/2055 1073*/465* 1075*/466* *FIELD IS LOCATED IN UNIT DESCRIPTION SECTION	REQUIREMENT
Finished Area Above Grade Contains _____Bath(s) The appraiser must enter the total number of full baths and partial baths above grade. A three-quarter bath is to be counted as a full bath in all cases. Quarter baths (baths that feature only a toilet) are not to be included in the bathroom count. The number of full and half baths must be entered, separated by a period. The full bath count is represented to the left of the period. The half bath count is represented to the right of the period. Reporting Format: # of Bath(s) – Numeric to 2 decimal places Separate full bath count from half bath count with a period (.), nn.nn Example: 3.2 indicates three full baths and two half baths above grade.	1004/70 2055/2055 1073*/465* 1075*/466* *FIELD IS LOCATED IN UNIT DESCRIPTION SECTION	REQUIREMENT
Square Feet of Gross Living Area Above Grade The appraiser must enter the total square footage of the above grade living area. Reporting Format: Square Feet of GLA – Numeric to 5 digits, whole numbers only	1004/70 2055/2055 1073*/465* 1075*/466* *FIELD IS LOCATED IN UNIT DESCRIPTION SECTION	REQUIREMENT

Improvements Section	Forms	Requirement or Instruction

Describe the condition of the property (including needed repairs, deterioration, renovations, remodeling, etc.)
 	
Interior/Exterior Complete Inspection Reports:
The appraiser must provide the following information:
 	
Overall Condition Rating – The appraiser must select one of the following ratings that best describes the overall condition of the subject property or unit. For condominium properties, the rating must reflect the overall condition for the individual unit being appraised. Only one selection is permitted. The rating for the subject property must match the overall condition rating that is reported in the Sales Comparison Approach section.
 	
    ▪ C1
    ▪ C2
    ▪ C3
    ▪ C4
    ▪ C5
    ▪ C6
 	
The definitions for the ratings listed above are provided in Exhibit 1: Requirements – Condition and Quality Ratings Usage.
 	
The appraiser must indicate 'Yes' or 'No' if there has been any material work done to the kitchen(s) or bathroom(s) in the prior 15 years. If 'No', the text 'No updates in the prior 15 years' must be provided. If 'Yes', additional information for kitchens and bathrooms must be provided.
 	
Kitchen(s) and Bathroom(s) – Level of Work Completed and Timeframes – The appraiser must identify any work completed in the kitchen(s) and bathroom(s) along with the timeframes in which the work was completed. The appraiser must select one of the values from the lists below for both the kitchen(s) and the bathroom(s).
 	
Level of Work Completed:
    ▪ not updated
    ▪ updated
    ▪ remodeled
 	
Definitions for the Level of Work Completed are provided in Exhibit 2: Requirements – Definitions of Not Updated, Updated, and Remodeled.
 	
Timeframes:
    ▪ less than one year ago
    ▪ one to five years ago
    ▪ six to ten years ago
    ▪ eleven to fifteen years ago
    ▪ timeframe unknown
 	
Timeframes represent the time period in which the majority of the improvements were completed.
 	
Descriptions or Comments – The appraiser must provide a description of the condition of the improvements to the subject property.
	1004/70
	1073*/465*
	
	*FIELD IS LOCATED IN UNIT DESCRIPTION SECTION
		REQUIREMENT

Improvements Section	Forms	Requirement or Instruction
Reporting Format: Condition Rating – Appraiser must select one value from the specified list Indicator of Work Completed in Prior 15 Years – 'Yes' or 'No' response Level of Work Completed for Kitchen(s) and Bathroom(s) – Appraiser must select one value from the specified list Timeframes for Work Completed for the Kitchen(s) and Bathroom(s) – Appraiser must select one value from the specified list Description of Condition of Improvements – Text The PDF creator will populate the selected text from the specified lists for 'Overall Condition Rating' (Improvement Area), 'Level of Work Completed,' and 'Timeframe for Work Completed.' A semicolon will be used to separate the overall condition rating from the kitchen and bathroom improvements. **Examples:** C4;No updates in the prior 15 years;[enter description of property condition] C3;Kitchen-updated-less than one year ago;Bathrooms-remodeled-one to five years ago;[enter description of property condition] C2;Kitchen-not updated;Bathrooms-remodeled-less than one year ago;[enter description of property condition]		
Exterior-Only Inspection Residential Appraisal Report Forms: The appraiser must report the overall condition of the property or unit using one of the overall condition ratings. **Reporting Format:** Condition Rating – Appraiser must select one value from the specified list Description of Condition of Improvements – Text	2055/2055 1075*/ 466* *FIELD IS LOCATED IN UNIT DESCRIPTION SECTION	REQUIREMENT

A *FULL BATH* includes *a tub, sink and toilet.* In a *THREE-QUARTER BATH*, *the tub is replaced by a stand up shower.* A *HALF BATH* has *neither shower nor tub, only a sink and toilet.* Half baths may also be known as powder rooms, lavatories or two-third baths.

As is the case with bedrooms, the number of baths in a house has a significant impact on value.

Although market preferences are the deciding factor, one-and-a-half to two baths is considered a minimum in most areas. There should be at least one full bath in the private area of the house, and a half bath in the public area. In a multi-story house, each story should have its own bath.

Bathrooms tend to be built as small as possible; 5' x 7' is the minimum needed for a full bath, and most are no larger than 6' x 8'. The exception is the private master bath, which has grown in size and amenities along with the master bedroom.

IV. Construction Methods and Materials

Understanding construction methods and materials is important for various reasons: an appraiser must understand construction terminology to properly describe the building in the appraisal report, the appraiser must be familiar with the advantages and disadvantages of different construction methods and materials to judge the quality of the building, and the appraiser must be able to spot construction defects and wear and tear, and know whether they can be repaired and what the cost of the repair would be.

For simplicity's sake, we will divide the various construction methods and materials used to build a home into several categories:

1. Foundations
2. Framing and Sheathing
3. Exterior Finishes
4. Doors and Windows
5. Insulation
6. Interior Finishes
7. Plumbing
8. Heating and Air Conditioning
9. Electrical Systems

A. FOUNDATIONS

Foundations perform two essential functions: they distribute the weight of the house to the subsoil, and they provide a platform to support the superstructure (the part of the house that is above ground level). In some cases, the foundation also provides usable space in the form of a basement (see **Figure 7-7**).

Figure 7-7

Foundation and Substructure
BASEMENT

31. Basement stair riser
32. Stair stringer
33. Girder post
34. Chair rail
35. Cleanout door
36. Furring strips
37. Corner stud
38. Girder
39. Cinder or gravel fill
40. Concrete basement floor
41. Footing for foundation wall
42. Tar paper strip
43. Foundation drain tile
44. Diagonal subflooring
45. Foundation wall
46. Mudsill
47. Backfill
48. Termite shield
49. Areaway wall
50. Grade line
51. Basement sash
52. Areaway

Illustrations courtesy of Marshall & Swift

1. Types of Foundations

There are three common types of foundations: foundation wall, pier and beam, and monolithic slab.

In a **FOUNDATION WALL** *type of foundation, the perimeter of the house is supported by a solid concrete wall which rests on a continuous footing.* Foundation wall foundations may also utilize piers, posts, and beams to support the central portion of the superstructure. The foundation wall should extend far enough above grade (6" or more) to prevent any problems with moisture damaging the superstructure.

An important benefit of foundation wall construction is that it allows for usable space below the superstructure, in the form of a basement or crawlspace, depending on the depth of the excavation.

In a **PIER AND BEAM FOUNDATION**, *each footing is a separate concrete pad that supports a raised block of concrete, or pier.* The piers in turn support a network of posts and beams that form a platform for the superstructure. This type of foundation is distinguished from the foundation wall type, primarily by the absence of a continuous perimeter foundation wall.

The **MONOLITHIC SLAB FOUNDATION (FLOATING FOUNDATION)** *consists of a single poured concrete slab that rests directly on the soil.* Certain parts of the slab, such as the perimeter, are thicker in order to provide more strength at weight bearing locations. This type of foundation is relatively inexpensive, but has two significant drawbacks. First, there is no space under the house, so plumbing must be in the slab, which makes repairs costly. Secondly, the superstructure is raised only slightly above grade level, so the danger of moisture damage is high unless proper drainage is carefully provided for.

Slab foundations and basement slab floors should generally have a "vapor barrier," such as plastic sheeting, under the slab. In many areas of the country, the ground is also treated for termites prior to pouring the slab.

Foundation wall and pier and beam foundations are similar in many respects. Each uses **FOOTINGS**, *which are concrete pads or beams that transmit the weight of the structure to the soil.* In order to distribute the weight over a larger soil surface area, footings are built wider than the foundation walls or piers that rest on them.

The bottom of the footings should always extend below the ground freezing level for the area.

2. Foundation Materials

Reinforced concrete is by far the most common material used for modern foundations. The various components of the foundation are created by digging holes or trenches in the soil (for footings), or by constructing forms (for foundation walls and columns), and then filling them with wet concrete. After the concrete has hardened, the forms (if any) are removed.

Steel rods called **REINFORCING BARS**, *or "rebar," are embedded in the concrete to increase its load-bearing capacity and help resist cracking.* (The reinforcement is put in place first, then the concrete is poured around it.) In the case of concrete slabs, heavy wire mesh is often used instead of rebar for reinforcement.

Fiberglass filaments can also be added to the concrete mix to provide added strength.

B. FRAMING AND SHEATHING

Most modern houses utilize frame construction, in which the walls, floors, ceilings and roof are constructed as a framework which is then covered by sheathing. The *FRAMING is typically built from wooden boards,* although metal framing is gaining in popularity as the price of lumber continues to rise.

Figure 7-8 shows framing elements, including construction nomenclature, while **Figure 7-9** shows framing for masonry construction.

1. Framing Lumber

FRAMING LUMBER is identified by its size in cross section, by its moisture content and by the species of wood from which it is made. In addition, there are various grading systems which rate the structural strength of individual boards. The most common sizes are all multiples of two inches: 2x4, 2x6, 2x8, 4x4, 4x6, etc. The actual size of a finished board is usually about ½" smaller than its nominal dimension, so a 2x4 (rough) is really 1½" x 3½" (finished).

The moisture content of lumber is denoted by the terms dry or green. *DRY LUMBER has a moisture content of 19% or less.* Dry lumber is preferred because it is more stable. *GREEN LUMBER tends to shrink, and perhaps warp, as it loses its moisture content.*

Shrinkage occurs mainly in cross-section, NOT lengthwise; boards get thinner, not shorter.

Structural strength is most important for horizontal load bearing elements such as beams, headers and joists. (These terms are defined in the next section.) Building codes commonly specify the acceptable species and grades for these elements, since both wood species and grade affect structural strength.

2. Framing Terminology

The different elements of a house frame all have special names, depending on their position and use in the frame. *In a wall frame, the vertical pieces are called STUDS, and the horizontal pieces to which the studs are attached at top and bottom are called PLATES (top*

Figure 7-8

Residential Construction Nomenclature

1	Gable stud	20	Downspout, leader or conductor	39	Cinder or gravel fill
2	Collar beam			40	Concrete basement floor
3	Ceiling joist	21	Double plate		
4	Ridgeboard	22	Entrance canopy	41	Footing for foundation wall
5	Insulation	23	Garage cornice		
6	Chimney cap	24	Frieze	42	Tarpaper strip
7	Chimney pot	25	Doorjamb	43	Foundation drain tile
8	Chimney	26	Garage door	44	Diagonal subflooring
9	Chimney flashing	27	Downspout or leader shoe	45	Foundation wall
10	Rafters			46	Mudsill
11	Ridge	28	Sidewalk	47	Backfill
12	Roof boards	29	Entrance post	48	Termite shield
13	Stud	30	Entrance platform	49	Areaway wall
14	Eave trough or gutter	31	Basement stair riser	50	Grade line
15	Roofing	32	Stair stringer	51	Basement sash
16	Blind or shutter	33	Girder post	52	Areaway
17	Bevel siding	34	Chair rail	53	Corner brace
18	Downspout or leader gooseneck	35	Cleanout door	54	Corner studs
		36	Furring strips	55	Window frame
19	Downspout or leader strap	37	Corner stud	56	Window light
		38	Girder	57	Wall studs

58	Header	79	Fire brick
59	Window cripple	80	Sole plate
60	Wall sheathing	81	Stair tread
61	Building paper	82	Finish stringer
62	Frieze or barge board	83	Stair rail
63	Rough header	84	Balusters
64	Cripple stud	85	Plaster arch
65	Cornice moulding	86	Mantel
66	Fascia board	87	Floor joist
67	Window casing	88	Bridging
68	Lath	89	Lookout
69	Insulation	90	Attic space
70	Wainscoting	91	Metal lath
71	Baseboard	92	Window sash
72	Building paper	93	Chimney breast
73	Finish floor	94	Newel post
74	Ash dump		
75	Door trim		
76	Fireplace hearth		
77	Floor joists		
78	Stair riser		

Illustrations courtesy of Marshall & Swift

Figure 7-9

Framing Methods for Masonry Construction

1. Common brick
2. Windows
3. Doors
4. Waterproofing
5. Block backup (reinforced)
6. Rebar (reinforcing steel)

Illustrations courtesy of Marshall & Swift

*plate on the top, sole plate on the bottom). A horizontal piece across the top of a door or window opening is called a **HEADER**. A horizontal piece at the bottom of a window is a **SILL**.*

Historically, 2" x 4" studs were used for framing. In climactic areas where heating or cooling costs are significant, exterior walls may have 2" x 6" studs. The wider studs allow for more sidewall insulation and thus lower heating and/or cooling costs.

JOISTS are structural parts supporting floor or ceiling loads. Both floor and wall frames may also have **BLOCKING**, *which are short pieces between the studs or joists to add strength to the frame and to block the passage of fire through the frame. A larger horizontal piece used to support a floor or ceiling frame is called a **BEAM**. The vertical pieces that support a beam are called **POSTS**.* Beams and posts are normally four inches thick (4x) or larger.

Some other common framing terms are rafter and sill plate. A *RAFTER is a sloped piece of the roof frame. A **SOLE PLATE** is a horizontal board that is attached to the* *foundation wall (or slab) by means of anchor bolts, the first floor or wall frame is then attached to the sill plate.*

Because the sole plate is in contact with the foundation, it must be made of decay-resistant material (redwood) or pressure-treated lumber.

3. Framing Methods

There are several different styles or methods of framing. The most common are platform framing, balloon framing and post and beam framing.

In *PLATFORM FRAMING, the floor frame is built first, forming a platform.* Then the first floor walls are framed and erected on the platform. If the building is multi-story, the process is repeated, with the second floor frame constructed on top of the first floor walls, and the second floor walls built on the platform of the second floor frame.

In *BALLOON FRAMING, the walls are built first, and they are constructed as a single frame that is the full height of the house.* For a two-story house, for example, the wall frame is a single unit, two stories high. The floor frames are then attached to wall frames. This method has the advantage of leaving no breaks or irregularities on the exterior of the frame, and eliminating the effects of shrinkage of the floor frame(s). It is used most often when the exterior wall finish will be a rigid material such as stucco or brick.

POST AND BEAM FRAMING uses larger size lumber than the other framing methods, so the framing members can be spaced farther apart. Framing timbers are often left exposed on the interior for a dramatic effect.

a. Roof Framing

A roof is designed and constructed to support its own weight and weight of pressures from snow, ice and wind.

The style of roof framing can add considerably to the character (and cost) of a house. There are several basic roof framing styles, and endless variations. The most basic roof styles are the shed, gable and hip roofs. A *SHED ROOF consists of a single inclined surface, sloping from one side of the house to the other. GABLE ROOFS have two inclined surfaces, which rise from opposite sides of the house and meet at a ridge.* ("Gable" is the name for the triangular wall area formed by this type of roof.) With a *HIP ROOF, inclined roof surfaces rise from every wall of the house* (see **Figure 7-10**).

A structure that protrudes through a roof surface is called a DORMER. Dormers are also classified according to their roof styles: shed dormers and gable dormers (sometimes called single dormers) are the most common.

239

Figure 7-10

Roof Styles

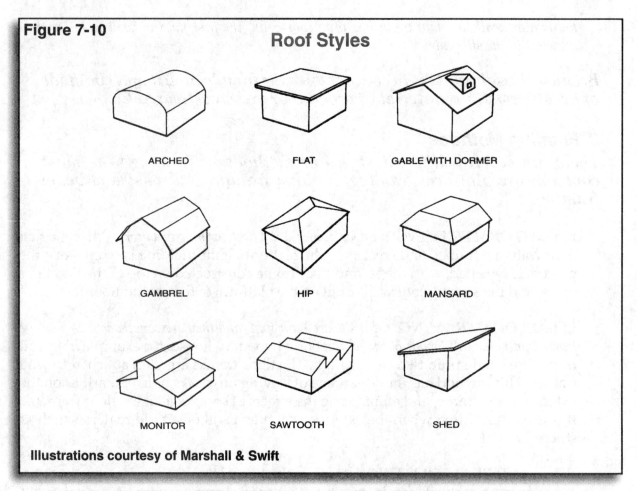

ARCHED   FLAT   GABLE WITH DORMER

GAMBREL   HIP   MANSARD

MONITOR   SAWTOOTH   SHED

Illustrations courtesy of Marshall & Swift

Roofs may be framed with a joist and rafter system, or by means of trusses (see **Figure 7-11**). A *TRUSS ROOF SYSTEM has the advantage of being able to span wider distances, eliminating the need for interior bearing walls. They are also easier to install than joist and rafter roof framing. Trusses are most effective for simple roof designs.* **Figure 7-12** will help you understand roof terminology.

b. Chimneys, Stacks, and Vents

Chimneys, stacks, and vents should be constructed and installed to be structurally safe, durable and smoketight, and be capable of withstanding the action of flue gasses. The construction of chimneys, stacks, and vents range from simple metal vents and flues to complex masonry fireplaces and ventilation systems. These items and their apparent condition are described in an appraisal report.

c. Sheathing

SHEATHING is the "skin" that is attached to the frame of the house. It may be a structural component of the house, meaning that one of its functions is to add strength to the structure, and/or to carry a weight load. Boards may be used for sheathing in some applications, but it is more common (and often required

240

Figure 7-11

Joist and Rafter – Truss Roof Systems

SPACED SHEATHING

BRACE

PURLINS

WOOD SHAKE

RAFTER

CEILING JOIST

BOWSTRING TRUSS

FLAT HOWE

BELGIAN TRIANGULAR

Illustrations courtesy of Marshall & Swift

Figure 7-12

Roof Terminology

1. Rake
2. Ridge Vent
3. Ridge
4. Valley
5. Hip
6. Gable End
7. Eaves

Illustrations courtesy of Marshall & Swift

by building codes) to use panels such as plywood, waferboard, gypsum board, etc. *The sheathing applied to a floor frame is often referred to as SUBFLOORING, and for a roof it would be ROOF SHEATHING.*

Floor and roof sheathing would generally be plywood, with the thickness determined by the distance between joists for rafters.

Insulation material, such as styrofoam panels, may also be used as wall sheathing. Insulation material might be used in connection with another type of sheathing such as plywood.

C. EXTERIOR FINISHES

EXTERIOR FINISHES are the materials applied to the outside of the frame. Their function is to protect the structure from the elements, and to provide visual appeal. The exterior finish is attached to the sheathing, usually with a layer of waterproof paper or felt sandwiched in between. *The exterior finish for the walls is called SIDING. The exterior finish for the roof is called ROOFING.*

The pitch of the roof is measured by the vertical drop per horizontal foot. A 4/12 pitch would drop 4 inches per horizontal foot. The pitch will determine what roofing materials may be used.

For pitched roofs, roofing material can be tile, slate, asphalt composition shingles, wood sawed shingles or split cedar shakes or roll roofing. There are various qualities of roofing for the types listed. As an example, tile roofs can cover a wide cost spectrum from double clay tile roofs to simple cement tile. Flat roofs generally have a built up roof composed of layers of roofing felt and tar, although a quality rubber roof or even a foam roof could be used.

Exterior finishes also include the detailing of roof overhangs, and the trim applied around doors and windows and on the corners of the house. *Roof edges are normally finished off with a FASCIA BOARD that is attached to the ends of the rafters. The eaves of the roof may be left open (exposed), or may be enclosed by covering them with a SOFFIT. Soffits are often trimmed out with a frieze board where they meet the wall.*

D. DOORS AND WINDOWS

The arrangement of the windows and other openings on the wall of the house is called FENESTRATION. Doors and windows can have a significant effect on construction cost. Whether the cost of the doors and windows translates into value depends mainly on whether their quality is in line with the quality of the other components of the building. Value is maximized when all aspects of the construction are compatible in quality.

Windows and doors are attached to frames called JAMBS. The bottom of a door frame is called a THRESHOLD; the bottom of a window frame is a SILL.

1. Doors

Doors are classified as either swinging or sliding, and are further classified by their materials and style of construction. *EXTERIOR DOORS are (water resistant) usually made of either wood, steel or glass, while INTERIOR DOORS are almost always wood or plastic.* Exterior doors should also be solid (not hollow), and are usually thicker (1- 3/4") than interior doors (1-3/8").

Wood doors come in two basic styles: flush and panel.

A *FLUSH DOOR has a hollow or solid core sandwiched between two thin sheets of veneer; the entire surface is even (flush), with no visible joints. A PANEL DOOR has solid wood stiles (vertical pieces) and rails (horizontal pieces), that frame one or more thinner panels (made of wood, plywood or glass).* Although panel doors tend to be more expensive, and also more difficult to maintain than flush doors, their traditional style appeals to many people.

SLIDING GLASS DOORS (patio doors) are popular in many areas of the country. These doors have one fixed panel, and one or two sliding panels, each consisting of a large sheet of glass in a metal or wooden frame. Tempered safety glass should be used in all glass doors, and insulated (double- or triple-pane) glass is important in areas with high heating and/or cooling costs.

2. Windows

Windows are classified by three criteria: type of glass, type of frame and method of opening (if any). The type of glass may be regular or safety tempered; building codes require tempered glass for windows that are a certain distance from the floor. Glass may also be single or multiple pane. Multiple pane glass is more efficient in terms of insulating value (see **Figure 7-13** for window terminology).

Window frames can be made of wood or metal (usually aluminum). Wood frames have better insulating value than metal, but are typically more expensive and require more maintenance. Wood frames are sometimes coated with vinyl (vinyl-clad windows) to minimize maintenance requirements.

Some of the more common styles of windows are shown in **Figure 7-14**. Horizontal sliders open by sliding back and forth. Single or double hung windows slide up and down. Casements, awnings, and hoppers pivot on one edge: casements at the side, awnings at the top and hoppers at the bottom. A *JALOUSIE has a series of glass slats like a venetian blind, that may be opened or closed with a crank or handle.*

E. INSULATION

As energy costs increase, insulation becomes a more and more important feature of house construction. The amount of insulation required by building codes for new

Figure 7-13

Window Terminology

1. Inside Casing
2. Upper Sash
3. Lower Sash
4. Jamb
5. Stop
6. Stool
7. Apron
8. Stop

9. Outside Casing
10. Parting Stop
11. Rail
12. Glazing
13. Check Rail or Meeting Rail
14. Rail
15. Sill

Illustrations courtesy of Marshall & Swift

Figure 7-14

Types of Windows

Double-Hung

Casement

Fixed

Sliding

Awning

Bay

Bow

construction has increased steadily over the past few decades. Older homes are often retro-fitted with additional insulation, as well as insulated glass and other energy-saving measures, to make them more attractive to modern energy-conscious home buyers.

INSULATION is a material that resists the transfer of heat. Its effectiveness is measured in terms of R-VALUE (RESISTANCE TO HEAT TRANSFER). The higher the R-value, the better the insulation. Since most heat transfer tends to occur in the roof of a house, insulation R-value requirements for roofs are usually higher than those for walls and floors.

Common insulating materials include fiberglass, rock, wool, and rigid foam. Fiberglass insulation comes in rolls or batts that are attached between studs, joists or rafters. The fiberglass may be lined with building paper or foil to serve as a vapor barrier and to reflect heat.

Rock wool is available either as loose material or in batts. Loose rock wool is sometimes called "blown-in" insulation, because it is installed by blowing it through a large hose. Blown-in insulation can be used to fill the space between studs in existing walls, but it will tend to settle over time, leaving the upper portion of the wall uninsulated.

Rigid foam insulation comes in large sheets similar to plywood. This type of insulation is useful when the thickness of the framing is not sufficient to accommodate insulation of the desired R-value, since it can be applied on top of (instead of between) the framing.

Insulation can help save energy costs in other areas besides walls, floors, and ceilings. Water heaters normally have built-in insulation, which can be enhanced by wrapping the heater in an insulating "blanket" designed for that purpose. In addition, any hot water pipes or heating or cooling ducts that are not located within an insulated area of the house can be wrapped with insulation to reduce energy consumption and cost.

F. VENTILATION

Ventilation is required to reduce heat in closed-off areas such as attics, basement-less spaces, and spaces behind walls. It also prevents the condensation of water that collects in unventilated spaces, which causes building materials to rot and decay. When water condensation seeps into insulation, it reduces the R rating.

The higher the R rating, the better the insulation.

G. INTERIOR FINISHES

Interior finishes include floor and wall coverings, cabinets and countertops, and interior trim. Interior finishes should be comparable in quality to the other components of the house.

1. Wall Finishes

LATH AND PLASTER, once the most common type of wall and ceiling finish, has been largely replaced in modern construction by DRYWALL (also known as wallboard or plasterboard). Drywall comes in sheets (usually 4' x 8') of varying thickness: 1/2" is standard for most interior walls, but fire codes often require 5/8" in areas such as attached garages. A special type of water-resistant drywall is used for bathrooms and other areas of heavy moisture.

Drywall is nailed or screwed to the studs, and the joints and corners are then sealed with a paper or plastic tape imbedded in plaster-like joint compound. Outside corners are protected by applying a strip of angled metal, which is also covered with joint compound. *The process of sealing the joints in drywall is called TAPING.*

Joint compound is also used to cover the nails and screws used to attach the drywall, and to smooth any irregularities in the wall or ceiling surface. This is known as FLOATING, and produces a smooth-wall finish. Texturing may be applied over the floated finish, either by spraying or rolling. Textured walls are normally finished with paint, while smooth walls may be painted, wall-papered, tiled, or covered with wood or synthetic paneling.

2. Floor Finishes

Floor finishes are applied over the subflooring of wood, plywood or concrete. Hardwood or carpet are appropriate floor finishes for most rooms in the house. Areas subject to drips and spills, such as kitchens, baths, and utility rooms, are often floored with ceramic or vinyl tile or rolled linoleum. Tile or stone is often used for flooring in entry ways.

Bamboo flooring is now often used in place of hardwood as it is a fast-growing "green technology" renewable resource alternative.

3. Cabinets and Countertops

Most modern cabinet work is prefabricated in a shop or mill and then installed on the building site. Cabinets may be solid wood or metal, or made of composite material covered with a wood or plastic veneer. Cabinets must be set true and level, and securely fastened in place in order to operate properly.

Plastic laminate (also called **Formica®**) and ceramic tile are the most commonly used materials for countertops in kitchens and baths. Luxury homes generally use **granite, granite tile**, or **Corian®** for countertops.

Counters should have a backsplash at least four inches high, and all joints should be well sealed to prevent moisture damage.

4. Interior Trim

Interior trim consists of the moldings used around doors and windows, at the top and base of the walls, and in various other areas. Moldings are usually made of wood, and may be painted or stained. They come in hundreds of shapes and sizes, and are often used for decorative effect. The most commonly found moldings are casings (used around openings) and baseboard (used at the base of walls).

H. PLUMBING

The *PLUMBING SYSTEM in a house consists of hot and cold water supply lines, drain lines, plumbing fixtures and appliances such as water heaters and water softeners.*

Supply lines carry water under pressure from a well or water system. There are two sets of supply lines, one for cold water and one for hot. Galvanized steel pipe was once the standard for water supply lines, but the majority of modern construction uses copper or plastic water pipes.

Drain lines are not pressurized; water and waste flows through the drain lines under the force of gravity. For this reason, drain lines must be sloped to allow the water to drain properly. Where the drain lines connect to a fixture, a U-shaped bend is used to prevent gasses from escaping into the house. The drain lines for each fixture are also connected to a system of vent pipes. Most drain lines are made from either cast iron or plastic.

The hot water supply for a house is provided by a water heater, which is basically a tank of water that is kept heated to a pre-set temperature by electricity or gas. The capacity of the water heater should be adequate to meet the needs of the occupants of the house; 40-50 gallon water heaters are typical for an average residence. Water heaters eventually corrode and leak, and must be replaced periodically.

Water in many areas contains minerals that react unfavorably with soap and form a curd-like substance that is difficult to rinse from clothing, hair, and skin. This condition is known as "hard water."

It can cause damage to plumbing systems by causing a mineral build up that constricts water flow in the supply lines. A water softener is a device designed to neutralize the mineral salts in water. By filtering the water supply through a water softener, these problems can be eliminated.

Water pipes may have to be replaced if they are rusted (or corroded). It is often hard for the appraiser to ascertain pipe degeneration unless there is outside evidence of leaks.

1. Green Machines (Tankless Water Heaters)

Recently, new construction and older residences are replacing traditional water heaters with "tankless water heaters." Those units provide unlimited quantities of hot water instantly and do not operate continuously like traditional systems. Thus, they save energy.

I. HEATING AND AIR CONDITIONING

Most heating and air conditioning systems utilize a central, forced-air system. This type of system has a central heating or cooling unit connected to a series of ducts. Hot or cold air is blown through the ducts and out through registers in the different rooms of the house. Return air registers and ducts then draw the air back to the central unit, where it is re-heated or re-cooled.

Heating and cooling systems are designed by mechanical engineers, who calculate the capacity of the heating or cooling equipment necessary to serve the house, and also design the layout and sizes of the duct work. An improperly designed system can result in some areas of the house being too hot or too cold, or in a system that is not powerful enough to provide adequate heating or cooling throughout the house.

Furnaces and air conditioners are rated according to their capacity in British Thermal Units (BTUs). A *BTU is the quantity of heat required to raise one pound of water one degree Fahrenheit.* Air conditioners are also sometimes rated in tons (1 ton = 12,000 BTUs).

The *EER (ENERGY EFFICIENCY RATIO) is a measure of energy efficiency, the higher the EER the higher the efficiency.* As discussed earlier R-Value is a measure used to calculate the heat resistance of insulation (the higher the better.)

J. ELECTRICAL

The *ELECTRICAL SYSTEM in a house consists of a main panel (breaker box or fuse box), wiring, switches, lights, and outlets.* The power supply is connected to the house at the main panel. Standard residential power is either 110/120 volts or 220/240 volts. 110V power is adequate for lighting and small appliances, but 220V is required for electric heating or larger electric appliances such as ranges or clothes dryers.

The breaker box or fuse box is rated as to how much current (amperage) it can distribute. 100 amp service is generally the minimum for a residence. A large capacity panel is required to handle electric heating or power-hungry appliances. Most new homes today have 200 amp service.

At the main panel, the current is divided into circuits, each controlled by its own circuit breaker or fuse. Each major electrical appliance will normally have its own separate circuit, while several lights or outlets can be grouped together on a single circuit.

The wiring of each circuit must be rated for the amount of current that the circuit breaker or fuse can carry. Too much current can cause the wiring to overheat, posing a severe fire danger. For this reason, most electrical wire is copper wire.

K. QUALITY

While appraisers are not expected to have the level of construction knowledge that a home inspection specialist should possess, appraisers should be able to judge construction quality.

The quality of cabinetry, countertops, floor coverings, windows, doors, hardware, appliances, heating and cooling systems, bath fixtures and even ceiling height will affect value (see **Figure 7-15**).

A visit to a large building supply store will quickly show the tremendous price difference that quality can make. As an example, exterior doors may range from one hundred dollars to many thousands of dollars.

The quality of construction material should be viewed in total context. The presence or absence of one or more features would not by themselves mean that construction quality was superior or just met minimum standards. The appraiser should consider overall quality in balancing out comparables. As an example, a jacuzzi tub and tile floors are glitz features but should be balanced out with the quality of air conditioners and cooling systems, windows, etc.

Figure 7-15

Quality Classification

QUALITY	ROOFS		QUALITY	DOORS	
	Shape	**Material**		**Exterior, Front**	**Material**
Excellent	A-fr. Chalet	Copper	**Excellent**	Hand-carved solid double doors with etched side-panel window(s)	Solid, patterned
	Mansard	Slate			
Good		Tile			
	Gambrel	Hardy Shake	**Good**	Hand-carved solid oak single door with etched side-panel window(s)	Solid plain
Average	Hip	Heavy Shake			
		Light Shake			
	Gable	Wood Shingle			
Fair	Shed	Composition	**Average**	Steel door with wood veneer	Hollow plywood with precast pattern/pane
		Tar & Gravel			
Poor		Tar Paper	**Fair**	Hollow-core wood door with pre-cast panels	Plain, hollow-core doors
	Flat				
			Poor	Plain hollow-core wood	Plywood

Because quality is a subjective term and variables, such as workmanship, contribute to value, this chart is merely an approximation.

Chart courtesy of Marty Carrick, Shasta College

V. CHAPTER SUMMARY

I. Classification of Houses.

   A. A house is a single-family residence.

   B. Houses may be attached or detached.

      1. Attached houses share party walls.

   C. Types of houses.

      1. One-story, ranch or rambler: flexible design, easy maintenance, no stairs, relatively expensive.

      2. One and one-half-story: expandable living area, lower construction costs.

      3. Two-story: most cost effective, natural separation of living zones, potential heating/cooling problems.

      4. Split-level: three or four levels offset by a half-story, benefits similar to two-story houses, adaptable to sloped sites.

      5. Split-entry or raised ranch: similar to a one-story house with a raised basement.

   D. Architectural Styles.

      1. Regional style was traditionally influenced by climate and local building materials.

      2. Contemporary styles are more uniform, due to central heating, modern transportation, new construction techniques, and uniform building codes.

      3. The effect of style on value depends on its compatibility. The most important aspect of compatibility is the demand of the market.

II. Elements of House Design.

   A. Siting is the location of the house on its lot.

      1. Living areas should face south if possible.

      2. Windows and doors should be protected from prevailing storm winds.

      3. Living areas should face the view.

      4. Siting should maximize the private area of the lot, and minimize public and service areas.

   B. Houses have three functional zones, which should be properly located in relation to one another.

      1. The public living zone includes the living room, dining room, family or rec room, and guest bath.

      2. The working zone includes the kitchen and laundry area.

      3. The private sleeping zone includes bedrooms and non-guest baths.

C. Room characteristics.

1. Kitchens should have convenient access to the main and service entrances, and be located next to any dining or family rooms. The sink, range and refrigerator form the work triangle; they should each be four to seven feet apart. Lighting and ventilation are critical.

2. Laundries require adequate ventilation, and should be located where their noise will not be a disturbance.

3. Living rooms should be near the main entry, next to any dining room, and separated from the sleeping area. Rectangular layouts are best for furniture arranging.

4. The family room should be near the kitchen and away from the sleeping zone. Direct outside access is preferable.

5. The dining area should have direct access to the kitchen. A dining area may be a separate room for formal dining, and/or an area in the kitchen (informal).

6. Bedrooms should be located away from the living and working areas of the house. Ample closet space is important, as is access to baths. The number of bedrooms has a greater impact on value than their size. There is a trend toward larger master bedrooms.

7. Baths can be half (sink and toilet), three-quarter (sink, toilet, and shower) or full (sink, toilet, and tub). The number of baths is an important value indicator. The sleeping area should have at least one full bath, and the public area a half bath. Two-story houses should have a bath on each story.

III. Construction Methods and Materials.

A. Foundations provide support for the superstructure.

1. A monolithic slab is a single poured concrete slab. It has no crawl space or basement.

2. Pier and beam foundations support the house on a framework of beams, which rests on raised piers set in concrete footings.

3. A foundation wall foundation is similar to a pier and beam foundation, but has a continuous concrete wall around the perimeter, resting on a continuous perimeter footing. The space enclosed by the foundation walls can be a crawl space or basement.

4. Most foundations are made from reinforced concrete.

B. Framing and sheathing provide the structural strength of the superstructure.

1. Framing lumber is identified by its cross-section dimensions, moisture content, wood species and grade.

2. Pieces of the frame are identified by their position and use, such as studs, plates (top plate, sole plate, sill plate), headers, sills, joists, blocking, posts, beams, and rafters.

3. The three common framing systems are platform framing, balloon framing, and post and beam framing.

4. Roof frames have many different styles, most of them variations or combinations of the shed, gable, and hip roof styles. The roof frame may be constructed of joists and rafters, or roof trusses. Projecting dormers add usable space to the upper floor of the house.

5. The exterior of the wall and roof frames, and the top of the floor frames is covered with sheathing, which gives more structural strength and supports the finish materials.

C. Exterior finishes provide weather protection and visual appeal. Siding and roofing are available in a wide range of materials. Exterior finishes may include flashing, soffits, fascias, and frieze boards.

D. Doors and windows are set in frames called jambs, with a threshold or sill at the bottom.

1. Doors are identified by thickness (1-3/8", 1-3/4"), material (wood, plastic, steel, glass), type of construction (hollow/solid, flush/panel), and method of opening (swinging, sliding).

2. Windows are classified by type of glass (regular, tempered, single/multiple pane), frame material (wood, aluminum, vinyl clad, plastic), and method of opening (fixed, slider, casement, single/double hung, awning, hopper, jalousie).

E. Insulation is rated for R-value: its resistance to heat transfer. It is commonly available in fiberglass (rolls or bats), rock wool (bats or blown-in) and rigid foam (panels).

F. Interior finishes.

1. Most walls are constructed of drywall, which is taped and floated with joint compound, and may be textured, painted, papered or paneled.

2. Floor finishes include wood, carpet, ceramic or vinyl tile, linoleum, and other materials. Bamboo flooring is the latest in "green" building materials.

3. Cabinets, countertops and trim complete the interior finish.

G. Plumbing systems include pressurized hot and cold water supply pipes, sloping drain pipes with vents, the hot water heater, and sometimes a water softener to remove mineral salts from the water supply.

H. Modern heating and cooling systems usually have a central furnace or air conditioner that supplies hot or cold air through a system of ducts and registers. The systems are rated for capacity in BTUs or tons (12,000 BTU).

1. Electric service of 110 or 220 volts is connected to a main panel (fuse box or breaker box) that routes the power into circuits to serve appliances, lights and outlets. The amount of current (amperage) available to a circuit is limited by the fuse or circuit breaker to prevent fire danger.

VI. CHAPTER QUIZ

1. A split-entry house is also known as a:

    a. split-level.
    b. rambler.
    c. raised ranch.
    d. cape cod.

2. A house with a party wall would be considered:

    a. attached.
    b. detached.
    c. multi-family.
    d. manufactured.

3. It is generally preferable for a house to be sited so that the living area faces:

    a. north.
    b. south.
    c. east.
    d. west.

4. In which room would direct outside access be considered most desirable?

    a. Living room
    b. Dining room
    c. Family room
    d. Bedroom

5. Kitchens should be located with convenient access to:

    a. the service entrance.
    b. the main entrance.
    c. the dining room.
    d. all of the above.

6. The vertical pieces in a wall frame are called:

    a. studs.
    b. plates.
    c. headers.
    d. joists.

7. Which of the following would not be found in a wall frame?

    a. Stud
    b. Plate
    c. Header
    d. Joist

8. R-value is a measure of:

    a. electric current.
    b. heating capacity.
    c. insulation efficiency.
    d. wall thickness.

9. The terms "stile" and "rail" refer to parts of a:

    a. door.
    b. window.
    c. staircase.
    d. soffit.

10. The heating capacity of a furnace is measured in:

    a. volts.
    b. amps.
    c. BTUs.
    d. kilos.

ANSWERS: 1. c; 2. a; 3. b; 4. c; 5. d; 6. a; 7. d; 8. c; 9. a; 10. c

Chapter 8
Cost Approach to Value

KEY WORDS AND TERMS

Accrued Depreciation
Comparative Unit Method
Cost to Cure Method
Curable Depreciation
Economic Life
Economic Age-Life Method
Economic Obsolescence
Effective Age
Entrepreneurial Profit
External Obsolescence
Functional Obsolescence

Incurable Depreciation
Long-Lived Items
Physical Life
Quantity Survey Method
Replacement Cost
Reproduction Cost
Short-lived Items
Straight-Line Depreciation
Superadequacies
Unit-in-Place Method

LEARNING OBJECTIVES

After completing this chapter, you should be able to:

1. describe the relationship between cost, value, and depreciation;

2. list the steps in the cost approach to estimating value;

3. distinguish between replacement cost and reproduction cost, and understand the significance of this distinction for appraisal purposes;

4. describe the types of costs that are included in an improvement cost estimate;

5. describe the comparative unit, unit-in-place, quantity survey, and cost index methods for estimating improvement costs, and list the advantages and disadvantages of each method;

Chapter 8

CHAPTER OUTLINE

6. identify the sources of data for construction unit costs;

7. define the term depreciation as it is used in appraisal practice;

8. describe the difference between an improvement's physical life and economic life and its actual age and effective age;

9. list the five major categories of depreciation and define the kinds of items included in each category; and

10. calculate depreciation using the economic age-life method, sales comparison method, capitalization method and cost to cure method, and describe how each of these techniques can be used in the observed condition method.

I. Basics of the Cost Approach

The **COST APPROACH METHOD** *is an orderly process which assumes that the value of improved property is indicated by the value of the site, plus the cost (new) to construct the improvements, less any depreciation from any cause that the improvements have suffered.* **DEPRECIATION** *is the difference in value between the cost (new) of the improvements and their current value, regardless of the reasons for the difference.* In the cost approach, cost is related to value by the formula:

Value = Cost - Depreciation

In this formula, cost refers to the cost to reproduce or replace the property's improvements. Depreciation is the difference between cost and value, from whatever cause. This basic formula applies only to the value of the improvements. The value of the land or site is determined separately (for example, by using the sales comparison method), and then added to the estimated value of the improvements to reach the total value of the property. So the process of the cost approach to value can be summarized by the formula:

Property Value (by Cost Approach)
   = Reproduction or Replacement Cost of Improvements
   - Depreciation of Improvements
   + Land Value (determined separately)

This formula requires three separate steps, which include:

1. estimating the reproduction or replacement cost of the improvements;

2. estimating depreciation; and

3. estimating the value of the land.

The first part of this chapter will examine the techniques for estimating cost, and the second section will discuss depreciation. (Estimation of land value was covered in Chapter 6.)

II. Application of the Cost Approach

The cost approach to value is the best approach for service type buildings where there are few comparables and the income is not appropriate.

As an example, an appraiser would use the cost approach to appraise an athletic stadium.

The cost approach is also appropriate for newer structures. The older the structure the less reliable is the approach, since the determination of accrued depreciation is somewhat subjective. As an example, the cost approach could be used for a new home but would likely provide an unrealistic value in appraising a 40-year-old single-family residence.

III. Estimating Cost

A. REPRODUCTION AND REPLACEMENT COST

Before discussing the methods of estimating cost, it is important to again distinguish reproduction cost from replacement cost. The **REPLACEMENT COST** *that is estimated is the cost to build a new substitute improvement at current prices with modern materials, and according to current standards, design and layout, as of the effective date of the appraisal.* **REPRODUCTION COST** *is obtained by estimating the cost to create an exact replica of the improvements, at current prices, using the same materials, design, layout and level of craftsmanship, and embodying all the deficiencies, superadequacies and obsolescence of the subject building.*

Replacement cost estimates are usually lower than reproduction cost estimates, because it usually costs less to build a structure using modern materials and techniques.

In addition, reproduction cost must account for the cost to reproduce any features that are excessive in quality or design, known as **SUPERADEQUACIES**. Replacement cost only takes into account the cost needed to create equal utility, so superadequacies are ignored.

Case/Example: An older home has 3/4" thick oak plank flooring. Modern homes are using less expensive 1/2" planks, which the market views as comparable in terms of utility. A reproduction cost estimate would account for the cost of the more expensive 3/4" flooring, while replacement cost would only consider the cost of the cheaper, but functionally equivalent, 1/2" flooring.

The choice of either reproduction cost or replacement cost can affect the calculation of depreciation. When reproduction cost is the basis of the cost estimate, the appraiser must estimate depreciation from all causes. When replacement cost is used, some forms of depreciation (such as functional obsolescence due to superadequacies) are accounted for in the cost estimation step, and so they are not included in the depreciation estimate. This distinction will be discussed in more detail in the second section of this chapter.

B. TYPES OF COST

Whether the appraiser is estimating reproduction cost or replacement cost, he or she must account for all of the types of costs necessary to construct the improvements. These include so-called hard costs (also called direct costs), such as the costs for labor, materials and equipment used in the construction, as well as soft costs, which are indirect costs, such as architects' fees, construction loan interest, property taxes during the development period and real estate sales commissions.

The appraiser must also account for the cost of *ENTREPRENEURIAL PROFIT, which is the amount that the owner/developer would expect to make from improving the property.* Entrepreneurial profit is not the same thing as the actual profit or loss on a project. It is an amount (usually a percentage) that an investor would expect to earn when deciding to undertake a similar type of project.

Case/Example: An appraiser estimates that total hard and soft costs for an office building at current prices would be $176,000. Developers of office property in the current market desire a 12% return on their developments. So 12% of the total cost will be allocated to entrepreneurial profit, and the remaining 88% is the hard and soft costs. The total cost can be calculated as:

$176,000 ÷ .88 (88%) = $200,000 total costs
$200,000 total cost - $176,000 hard and soft costs =
$24,000 entrepreneurial profit.

(**NOTE:** All cost figures in this and other examples are for illustration purposes only, and are strictly hypothetical.)

IV. Cost Estimating Techniques

Cost estimating can be quite complex in practice, but in theory it is a very simple concept.

The appraiser measures some feature of the improvement (such as square footage of building area, or number of doors) and multiplies it by the estimated unit cost for the feature. This procedure can be summarized as a formula:

Cost = Number of Units x Cost per unit (unit cost).

The most common cost estimating techniques all apply this same procedure. The primary difference between the techniques is in the level of detail.

The simpler cost estimating techniques apply unit costs to broad-scale features such as building square footage, while the more detailed techniques apply unit costs to individual features of the construction and then add them up to find the total cost.

The choice of technique is determined by the scope of the appraisal; the more detailed methods generally provide a more reliable cost estimate.

The most common cost estimating techniques are the:

A. Comparative Unit Method
B. Unit-in-Place Method
C. Quantity Survey Method
D. Cost Index Trending

A. COMPARATIVE UNIT METHOD

In the *COMPARATIVE UNIT METHOD cost is estimated on the basis of the square footage of building area, or the cubic footage of building volume.* Residential cost estimates using this technique almost always use square footage, so it is often referred to as the square foot method.

Square footage is calculated by measuring and multiplying the outside dimensions (length x width) of the building.

SQUARE FOOTAGE is determined by multiplying length times width (first measuring the outside dimensions of the building to break it down into rectangles and triangles). COST PER SQUARE FOOTAGE is obtained by multiplying the square footage by the estimated cost per square foot. Different costs per square foot are applied to different areas of the structure. For example, one figure is applied to the living area and another is applied to the garage. The cost of site improvements such as landscaping is also estimated separately.

Case/Example: Figure 8-1 shows the outline (perimeter) of a new 1-story house that does not suffer from any depreciation. The living area is 1280 square feet (32 ft. x 40 ft. = 1280 sq. ft.) and there is a 576 sq. ft. attached garage (24 ft. x 24 ft. = 576 sq. ft.). The appraiser has determined that current construction costs for similar buildings are $60 per square foot for living area, and $25 per square foot for garage space. The site has been valued at $35,000, and the appraiser estimates the value of site improvements (driveway, landscaping, etc.) to be $8,500. In this case, the value of the property can be estimated by the cost approach using the square foot method as follows (also see Figure 8-1):

Cost of living area = 1280 sq. ft. x $60 a sq. ft. = $76,800
Cost of garage = 576 sq. ft. x $25 a sq. ft. = $14,400
Total cost of building = $76,800 (living area) + $14,400 (garage) = $91,200
Total cost of improvements = $91,200 (building) + $8,500 (other improvements)
= $99,700 (indicated improvement value) = $99,700 (improvement cost) + $35,000 (site value)
= **$134,700**

Figure 8-1

Houses and Garage Dimensions for Previous Example

32 ft. x 40 ft. = 1,280 sq. ft.

24 ft. x 24 ft. = 576 sq. ft.

Calculating the building areas for the square foot method is a fairly simple process. The hard part is determining the appropriate unit cost per square foot. Unit costs may be derived in two ways:

1. by market analysis, or
2. by use of cost estimating manuals or services.

1. Market Analysis

To establish *UNIT COST BY MARKET ANALYSIS, the appraiser gathers data on the sales of comparable new homes.* The comparables must be similar to the subject property in both size and quality of construction, and the appraiser must be able to determine the site values for the comparables. The appraiser subtracts the site value from the sales price, and then divides the result by the square footage of the comparable. The result is a unit cost.

Case/Example: A new 1,500 square foot rambler sold recently for $120,000. Market data support the appraiser's estimate of the site value for this property of $30,000, so the building value is $90,000 ($120,000 sales price, $30,000 site value). Assuming the home does not suffer from any depreciation, its value should be equivalent to its cost. So the appraiser takes $90,000 (the building value or cost) and divides that by 1,500 (the size in square feet). The result, $60 per square foot, becomes the unit cost.

Choosing comparables of similar size to the subject property is important.

Many types of construction costs do not vary in direct proportion to the size of the building. So, as a general rule, the unit costs per square foot will be higher for a smaller building than they will be for a larger building with the same quality and style.

Case/Example: A 1,000 square foot house and a 1,400 square foot house each have only one kitchen. The plumbing, electrical work, cabinetry, countertops, and built-in appliances required for a kitchen are relatively expensive in relation to the rest of the house, and these costs will be about the same for both houses. Therefore, the unit cost of the 1,000 square foot house will be higher than the unit cost of the 1,400 square foot house, because the kitchen costs are divided between fewer square feet in the smaller house.

Cost per square foot is also influenced by the complexity of the building design, as illustrated in **Figure 8-2**. A square building with a perimeter of 20' x 20' has 80 linear feet of perimeter wall for 400 square feet of area. The L-shaped building with the same area has a larger amount of perimeter wall, so the unit cost per square foot is higher.

Figure 8-2

Illustration of square building with perimeter of 20x20 linear feet of perimeter wall for 400 square feet of area. L-shaped building with same area, larger amount of perimeter wall.

400 sq. ft.
80 linear ft.

A = 100 sq. ft.
B = 300 sq. ft.
A + B = 400 sq. ft.
A + B = 100 linear ft.

2. Cost Estimating Manuals or Services

Instead of estimating the unit cost, an appraiser may use local builders and developers, as well as published cost manuals and professional costing services, to find the unit cost. Some widely used cost manuals are published by Boeckh Publications, F. W. Dodge Corporation (owned by Marshall and Swift Publication Company), Marshall and Swift Publication Company, and R. S. Means Company. Cost manuals are published periodically (usually quarterly) and list the average unit costs for different sizes and styles of construction.

Unit cost figures must be adjusted to account for differences in construction features, size and shape, time, and location.

Also, the appraiser must have a clear understanding of what the unit cost figures include, and make additional adjustments for any cost items that are not included in the published cost figures.

Case/Example: The calculation shown below is based on the following hypothetical fact situation. According to a cost manual, the average cost per square foot for an average quality one-story house of 1,500 square feet with a 160 lineal foot perimeter is $55.50. The manual also indicates that construction costs in the area where the subject property is located are 11% higher than average. The subject property has above-average exterior finishes, which add $3.50 per square foot to its cost. It also has 2,000 square feet of living area, which the appraiser estimates should reduce the unit cost by 8%. Since the date of publication of the manual, construction costs have declined by 5% due to a slowdown in the economy. A review of the cost manual indicates that its figures do not include entrepreneurial profit, which the appraiser has determined should be 10% for this type of property (see **Figure 8-3**).

Published cost per square foot	$55.50
Adjustment for exterior finishes	+ 3.50
Subtotal	**$59.00**
Adjustment for larger size (100% - 8% = 92%)	x 0.92
Subtotal	**$54.28**
Adjustment for time (current cost) (100% - 5% = 95%)	x 0.95
Subtotal	**$51.57**
Adjustment for location (local cost) (100% + 11 % = 111 %)	x 1.11
Subtotal	**$57.24**
Adjustment for entrepreneurial profit (x10%)	x .10
Subtotal	**+5.72**
Total cost per square foot	**$62.96**

$62.96 x 2,000 sq. ft. = $125,920 estimated cost of improvement (building)

Figure 8-3

50 ft. x. 30 ft. =1,500 sq. ft.

COMPARABLE PROPERTY

Cost Manual = $55.50 per sq. ft.

50 ft. x. 40 ft. = 2,000 sq. ft.

SUBJECT PROPERTY

Larger Structure
Above Average $3.50 Exterior
Location is 11% Better
5% Slowdown in Economy
10% Entrepreneurial Profit

B. UNIT-IN-PLACE METHOD

The *UNIT-IN-PLACE METHOD* *requires the appraiser to measure the quantities of various building components, such as foundation, floor, walls, roof, doors, windows, etc.* The quantity of each item is then multiplied by its appropriate unit cost, and the subtotals for the building components are added together to get the total cost (see **Figure 8-4**).

Figure 8-4

Page From Cost Manual Showing Unit-in-Place Costs

Floors	5,000 sq. ft. @ $7 =	$35,000
Walls	300 linear ft. @ $200 =	60,000
Roof structure	5,000 sq. ft. @ $15 =	75,000
Interior partitions	100 linear ft. @ $40 =	4,000
Ceilings	5,000 sq. ft. @ $4 =	20,000
Doors and windows		5,000
Roof cover		10,000
Plumbing lines and fixtures		5,500
Electrical system		5,000
Heating and cooling		20,000
Hardware and all other costs		10,000
Total direct and indirect costs		$249,500

Unit-in-Place Cost Estimate for a Small Commercial Building

Unit costs for the unit-in-place method may be obtained from local builders and developers, and by referring to cost manuals or costing services.

The appraiser must be sure that the measurements used for the different building components are the same as the measurements for which the costs are stated.

Case/Example: Wall framing costs may be stated as so much per lineal foot of wall, while the cost for painting the walls may be quoted as a cost per square foot of wall surface. Other costs, such as unit costs for plumbing or electrical systems, may be given as costs per square foot of building area. The appraiser must be sure to measure framing in terms of lineal foot of wall, painting in terms of square foot of wall surface, and plumbing and electrical systems in terms of square foot of building area. If the appraiser measures painting in terms of square yards of wall surface instead of square feet, he or she will not be able to apply the unit cost without making the appropriate adjustments.

As is the case with the square foot method, the cost calculated by the unit-in-place method must be adjusted to account for differences in time (current cost) and location (local cost), and also for any cost items that are not included in the unit cost figures (such as indirect costs and entrepreneurial profit). Adjustments for differences in construction features, size and complexity are generally not required in the unit-in-place method, since the procedure takes these differences into account.

Case/Example: Figure 8-5 shows how the amount of exterior wall framing can vary depending on the shape of the building, even in buildings with the same square footage. The square foot method must make an adjustment to account for this variation. In the unit-in-place method, however, the actual amount of exterior wall framing is calculated (by measuring and then multiplied by its unit cost), so no adjustment is necessary.

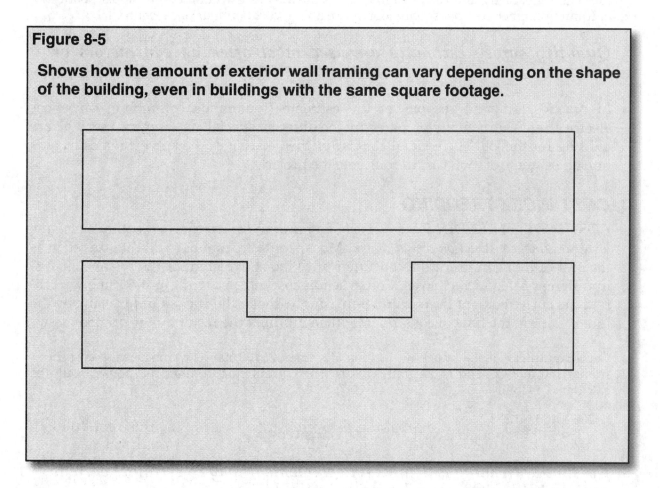

Figure 8-5

Shows how the amount of exterior wall framing can vary depending on the shape of the building, even in buildings with the same square footage.

The unit-in-place method gets its name from the fact that the unit costs for each construction item represent the total cost to install or build the item, including the cost of materials, labor, equipment and overhead.

C. QUANTITY SURVEY METHOD

The *QUANTITY SURVEY METHOD is the most detailed and most reliable method for estimating construction costs.* It is similar to the unit-in-place method, in that the cost of each construction component is estimated separately, and the component costs are then added together to find the total cost. However, in the quantity survey, the costs for labor, materials, equipment and overhead are each calculated separately. Also, the level of detail in a quantity survey estimate is greater than in a unit-in-place estimate.

Case/Example: In the unit-in-place method, a single unit cost is used to calculate the cost of exterior wall framing, including the cost for the framing lumber, sheathing, carpentry labor, scaffolding, etc. In the quantity survey method, the quantities of each of these items would be estimated separately, and each would be multiplied by its own unit cost (cost per board foot of framing lumber, cost per square foot of sheathing, cost per hour of carpentry labor, etc.).

Quantity survey estimates are used most often by contractors or builders.

In practice, different sections of the estimate (foundation, plumbing, carpentry, electrical, etc.) are actually prepared by the different specialty subcontractors who are bidding for the job. The general contractor then combines the sub-estimates or bids into an estimate of total cost to complete the project.

D. COST INDEX TRENDING

COST INDEX TRENDING is a method of estimating the reproduction cost of a building whose original construction cost is known. Most people are familiar with indexes such as the cost-of-living index or the consumer price index, which track the relative change in different categories of costs. Construction cost indexes work in the same way. To find the current cost of the construction, simply divide the current index value by the index value at the time of construction, then multiply the result by the original cost.

Case/Example: A house was built in 1980 at a cost of $100,000. The construction cost index was at 150 in 1980, and is currently at 200. The current cost to build the house would be calculated as follows:

200 ÷ 150 = 1.33
1.33 x $100,000 (original cost) = $133,000 current cost

Cost index trending is a quick and convenient way to estimate current cost, but it is NOT considered very reliable.

Even when the original construction cost of an improvement is known, there is no guarantee that the actual cost was typical for similar improvements that were built at the same time. This method is most appropriate for double-checking the results of some other, more reliable, cost estimating procedure.

V. Estimating Depreciation

Estimating the reproduction or replacement cost of an improvement is only the first step in the cost approach to value. In the second step, the appraiser must estimate the amount of depreciation that the subject improvement has suffered. By deducting the total depreciation from the estimated cost, the appraiser can estimate the value of the improvement.

A. DEPRECIATION TERMINOLOGY

For purposes of appraisal, the term **DEPRECIATION** *refers to a loss in the value of an improvement (as compared to its cost) due to any reason whatsoever.* Depreciation is the difference between the market value of the improvement and its cost.

*The amount of depreciation that has occurred between the time the improvement was built and the effective date of the appraisal is called the **ACCRUED DEPRECIATION**.*

The term depreciation is also widely used to refer to the amount of an asset's capital value that has been "written off" for accounting or tax purposes. This kind of depreciation is sometimes called book depreciation, and has no significance from an appraisal standpoint.

B. AGE AND ECONOMIC LIFE

Depreciation is related to the age of an improvement. Improvements have an actual age and an effective age. **ACTUAL AGE** *(also called chronological or historical age) is the actual amount of time that the improvement has been in existence.*

EFFECTIVE AGE *is the apparent or functional age of the improvement, based on its current conditions and the current conditions in the market.* Effective age may be the same as actual age, or it may be greater or less than actual age. Effective age is related to remaining economic life.

Improvements are said to have an **ECONOMIC LIFE** *(also called useful life), which is the length of time during which the improvement will contribute to the value of the property.* Economic life is distinguished from **PHYSICAL LIFE**, *which is the length of time that an improvement would be expected to last with normal maintenance.*

Case/Example: An exceptionally well maintained building might have a chronological age of 20 years but an appraiser might use an effective age of 14 years to determine the depreciation. On the other extreme, the appraiser might determine that a poorly maintained 20-year-old property should have an effective age of 26 years.

The economic life of an improvement comes to an end when it no longer represents the highest and best use of the property as improved.

Exhibit 2: Definitions of Not Updated, Updated, and Remodeled Residential Properties

A "Not Updated" residential property shows little or no updaating or modernization. Properties over 15 years of age are considered not updated if no major components have been replaced or updated.

An "Updated" residential property would include refurbishing and/or replacing components to meet existing market exppectations. This does not include significant alterations to the existing structure.

A "Remodeled" area would shown fundamental changes that include multiple alterations. This would include a complete gutting and rebuild.

VI. Types of Depreciation

Depreciation is categorized according to the cause of the decrease in value, and also according to whether the decrease can be remedied. The three causes of depreciation are:

1. physical deterioration;
2. functional obsolescence; and
3. external (economic) obsolescence.

Depreciation can be curable or incurable. If depreciation can be remedied, it is said to be "curable." If a remedy is NOT possible or practical, the depreciation is "incurable."

A. PHYSICAL DETERIORATION

PHYSICAL DETERIORATION is depreciation that is caused by wear and tear of, or damage to, the physical components of the improvement. Broken windows, leaky roofs, peeling paint, termite damage or worn carpeting are all examples of physical deterioration.

Physical deterioration can be curable or incurable.

If the cost to correct the deterioration is less than the added value that would result from the correction, then it is CURABLE. Otherwise, it is INCURABLE.

Case/Example: The need for repainting is usually curable, since a fresh coat of paint often adds more to the value of a house than the cost of the painting. On the other hand, the cost to repair a cracked foundation may far exceed any increase in value that would result from the repairs. In this case, the cracked foundation would be considered incurable physical deterioration.

When analyzing the physical deterioration of an improvement, a distinction is sometimes made between long-lived items and short-lived items.

A *LONG-LIVED ITEM is a component of the improvement that is expected to last as long as the building itself does. SHORT-LIVED components can be expected to need replacement during the improvement's economic life.*

An example of a long-lived item is the foundation, which normally lasts for the life of the building. Paint and carpeting are short-lived items, which require periodic replacement.

The economic life of a short-lived improvement is normally the same as its physical life. The physical life of a long-lived improvement, on the other hand, is usually longer than its economic life: buildings are usually torn down before they fall down.

B. FUNCTIONAL OBSOLESCENCE

Functional obsolescence is "built-in" obsolescence.

In addition to physical wear and tear, an improvement can suffer from depreciation that is caused by design defects. This form of depreciation is called FUNCTIONAL OBSOLESCENCE. Whether the design is defective from the start or simply becomes outdated with the passage of time, the resulting loss in value is treated as functional obsolescence.

Case/Example: At one time homes were frequently built without bedroom closets. Clothing was stored in chests or wardrobe cabinets. At the time, people owned limited clothing. This design would not be adequate for modern needs.

Design defects that cause functional obsolescence can be either deficiencies (such as inadequate insulation) or superadequacies. *SUPERADEQUACIES are forms of overimprovement; design features whose costs are greater than their contribution to value.*

Case/Example: Most modern housing uses 2' x 4' or 2' x 6' framing for wall construction. A house that was built with 2' x 12' wall framing would probably suffer from functional obsolescence due to a superadequacy. The cost of the superadequate wall framing would more than likely exceed any resulting value increase.

Like physical deterioration, functional obsolescence is either curable or incurable.

The same test applies: if the defect can be remedied at a cost that is less than the resulting increase in value, then it is curable. Otherwise, it is incurable.

Case/Example: Inadequate insulation in the ceiling of a house is usually a curable form of functional obsolescence, because additional insulation can be installed at a reasonable cost. A house with substandard ceiling heights, on the other hand, probably suffers from incurable functional obsolescence, since it would be prohibitively expensive to increase the height of the walls.

C. EXTERNAL (ECONOMIC) OBSOLESCENCE

The third form of depreciation is *EXTERNAL (ECONOMIC) OBSOLESCENCE, which is a loss in value resulting from causes arising outside of the property itself.* The most common causes of external obsolescence are negative influences from surrounding properties, and poor local economic conditions.

Case/Example: A residence located in an industrial area will suffer a loss in value due to its poor location. External obsolescence will also occur if a community's sole employer (such as the mill owner in a logging community) goes out of business or closes its operations in the community.

External or economic obsolescence is generally regarded as "incurable obsolescence" since the property owner has no control over the forces outside his or her property.

VII. Methods of Estimating Depreciation

Properly estimating depreciation is the most difficult part of the cost approach.

This is particularly true of older properties, which may suffer from several types and causes of depreciation. The simpler methods of calculating depreciation rely on assumptions that do not necessarily apply in every case, while the more complex methods require market data which often is not available. This is one reason why the cost approach to value tends to be less reliable than the sales comparison or income approaches.

The methods of estimating depreciation are:

A. Economic Age-Life Method
B. Sales Comparison Method
C. Capitalization Method
D. Cost to Cure Method
E. Observed Condition Method

A. ECONOMIC AGE-LIFE METHOD

The *ECONOMIC AGE-LIFE METHOD of estimating depreciation is based on the assumption that an improvement loses value at a steady rate over the course of its economic life. According to this assumption, a graph of the depreciated value of an improvement versus its age would appear as a STRAIGHT-LINE,* as shown in **Figure 8-6**.

The economic age-life method is sometimes called the "straight-line method."

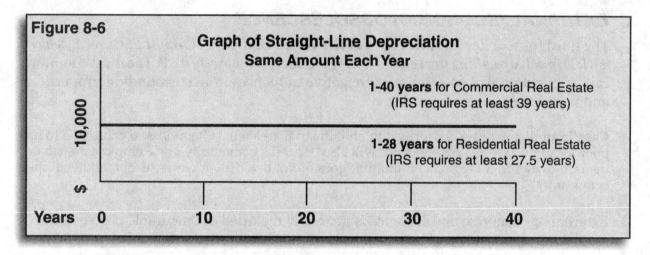

Figure 8-6

Graph of Straight-Line Depreciation
Same Amount Each Year

1-40 years for Commercial Real Estate
(IRS requires at least 39 years)

1-28 years for Residential Real Estate
(IRS requires at least 27.5 years)

10,000

$

Years   0   10   20   30   40

To use the economic age-life method, the appraiser must first estimate the effective age and the economic life of the improvement. The ratio of effective age to economic life (called the accrued depreciation rate) is then multiplied by the estimated cost to determine the amount of depreciation.

Depreciation = (Effective Age ÷ Economic Life) x Cost

Appraisers would use a realistic life for a building in determining depreciation. Accountants, on the other hand, use the shortest life allowed by the IRS.

Appraisers use age-life tables based on the type of building and its construction. As an example, while a frame building may have a 40-year life for depreciation purposes, a solid masonry building may have a 50-year life.

Case/Example: An appraiser estimates the reproduction cost of a home at $220,000. The home has an economic life of 60 years, and an effective age of 15 years. Under the economic age-life method, depreciation would be calculated as follows:

15 ÷ 60 = 0.25 (25%) accrued depreciation rate 0.25 x $220,000
= $55,000 accrued depreciation
$220,000 - $55,000 = $165,000 depreciated value of improvement

In an alternative version of the economic age-life method, depreciation that is caused by curable physical deterioration and curable functional obsolescence is assumed to be equal to the cost of curing the defects. This cost to cure is deducted from the total estimated reproduction or replacement cost, and the ratio of effective age to economic life is then applied to the remaining cost of the improvement.

When estimating effective age, the appraiser takes into account any change in effective age that would result from curing the curable physical and functional defects.

Case/Example: Using the same figures as the example above, assume that it would cost $5,000 to remedy the curable physical and functional defects in the house, and that curing these defects would result in the house having an effective age of only 12 years. The calculation of depreciation in this case is as follows:

$220,000 - $5,000 = $215,000 cost (adjusted for curable items)
12 ÷ 60 = 0.20 (20%) accrued depreciation rate
0.20 x $215,000 = $43,000 incurable depreciation
$43,000 + $5,000 = $48,000 total depreciation
$220,000 - $48,000 = $172,000 depreciated value of improvement

The economic age-life method is most appropriate for measuring depreciation due to physical deterioration.

This method is not reliable in calculating for depreciation that is due to functional or external causes.

B. SALES COMPARISON METHOD

When adequate data are available, sales comparison is a useful tool for measuring depreciation. To use the *SALES COMPARISON METHOD, the appraiser must be able to identify comparable properties that have the same defect as the subject property, and other comparable properties that do not have the defect.* The difference in selling prices between the two sets of comparable sales represents the amount of depreciation. This is an example of "paired data set analysis," which is discussed in detail in Chapter 9.

Case/Example: A subject property suffers from functional obsolescence due to a poor floor plan. Market analysis reveals that comparable houses with similar floor plans sell for $110,000, while comparable houses with more functional floor plans sell for $120,000. This indicates that the functional obsolescence due to the poor floor plan causes depreciation of $10,000 ($120,000 - $110,000 = $10,000).

Sales comparison data are more likely to be available for depreciation due to functional or external causes, but this method can be used to calculate any type of depreciation when there is adequate data.

C. CAPITALIZATION METHOD

The *CAPITALIZATION METHOD of estimating depreciation is similar to the sales comparison method.* As in the sales comparison method, the appraiser must be able to identify comparable rental properties that contain the particular defect, and those that do not. The difference in income between the two sets of properties is then capitalized to arrive at a figure for the amount of depreciation caused by the defect. (Income capitalization techniques are discussed in detail in Chapter 10.)

Case/Example: A subject property suffers from external obsolescence due to its location near a busy airport. Comparable properties in similar locations rent for $800 per month, while comparables in more favorable locations command monthly rents of $900. The $100 difference in monthly rent is multiplied by 12 (months) to give an annual difference. This difference is then divided by a capitalization rate. If the rate were eight percent, then $1,200 divided by .08 would mean the locational difference would be $15,000.

A variant of the capitalization method is the multiplier. If property of this type customarily sells for 150 times the monthly gross, then the loss in rent ($100) times the 150 multiplier would show a loss (depreciation) of $15, 000 because of locational influences.

D. COST TO CURE METHOD

The *COST TO CURE METHOD takes into account the amount of depreciation due to curable items (curable physical deterioration or curable functional obsolescence) which is considered to be equal to the cost of curing the defects.* For example, the amount of depreciation due to worn out carpeting in a house would be equal to the cost of replacing the carpets.

Before using the cost to cure method, the appraiser must verify that the particular item of depreciation is in fact curable. For a defect to be curable the repairs must be physically and legally possible, and their cost must not exceed the resulting increase in value.

E. OBSERVED CONDITION METHOD

In the *OBSERVED CONDITION METHOD (also known as the breakdown method), the appraiser estimates the amounts of each of the types of depreciation separately.* When estimating the various types of depreciation, the appraiser may utilize straight-line, sales comparison, and capitalization techniques, as well as cost to cure estimates.

The observed condition method (seldom used in residential real estate appraisals), provides a good illustration of the theory of depreciation as it applies to appraisal.

VIII. Uniform Residential Appraisal Report (URAR)

The Uniform Residential Appraisal Report (URAR) has a section for the cost approach (see **Figure 8-7**).

You will see that the following information is required:

1. Estimated Site Value
2. Estimated, Reproduction, or Replacement Cost New, which is determined by square footage of house and garage
3. Depreciated Cost of Improvements
4. "As-is" Value of Site Improvements

The URAR leaves room for comments as to the source of cost estimate, site valuation, square foot calculation, and estimated remaining economic life. Because the space provided may not be adequate, an addendum may be necessary.

Figure 8-7

Cost Approach Section - URAR

COST APPROACH TO VALUE (not required by Fannie Mae)						
Provide adequate information for the lender/client to replicate the below cost figures and calculations.						
Support for the opinion of site value (summary of comparable land sales or other methods for estimating site value) 6						
ESTIMATED ☐7 REPRODUCTION OR ☐8 REPLACEMENT COST NEW		OPINION OF SITE VALUE			= $	14
Source of cost data 9		Dwelling 15	Sq. Ft. @ $ 16		=$	17
Quality rating from cost service 10 Effective date of cost data 11		18 19	Sq. Ft. @ $ 20		=$	21
Comments on Cost Approach (gross living area calculations, depreciation, etc.)		22				23
12		Garage/Carport 24	Sq. Ft. @ $ 25		=$	26
		Total Estimate of Cost-New			= $	27
		Less Physical	Functional	External		
		Depreciation 29	31	33	=$(	34)
		Depreciated Cost of Improvements			=$	35
		"As-is" Value of Site Improvements			=$	36
Estimated Remaining Economic Life (HUD and VA only) 13 Years		Indicated Value By Cost Approach			=$	37

IX. CHAPTER SUMMARY

I. In the cost approach, value is determined by adding the estimated value of the site to the depreciated cost of the improvements.

   A. The value of an improvement is indicated by the difference between its cost and depreciation.

II. Cost is estimated as the cost to build a new substitute improvement, at current prices as of the effective date of the appraisal.

   A. Reproduction cost is the cost to create an exact replica.

   B. Replacement cost is the cost to create an improvement of equal utility, using modern methods and materials.

   C. The cost estimate must include hard (direct) costs and soft (indirect) costs, as well as entrepreneurial profit.

   D. In the comparative unit (square foot) method, cost is estimated by multiplying the amount of building area by a cost per square foot.

   1. Separate unit costs are used for areas of different construction, living area, garage, etc.

2. The value of site improvements must be estimated separately.

3. Unit costs may be derived from market data, or obtained from costing manuals, local builders, and other sources.

4. Costs must be adjusted for differences in construction features, size and complexity, as well as for differences in time (current cost) and location (local cost). An adjustment must also be made for any costs that are not included in the unit cost figure, such as indirect costs.

E. In the unit-in-place method, the appraiser applies unit costs to each of the items in a breakdown of the building's components.

1. The unit costs represent the total costs for each item, including labor, materials, equipment, etc.

2. Costs must be adjusted for current cost and local cost, and for any indirect costs that are not included.

F. A quantity survey involves a detailed estimate of the cost for each building component, including separate cost estimates for materials, labor, equipment, overhead items and other costs of construction.

G. Cost may be estimated by means of construction cost indexes when the original construction cost is known, but this method tends to be unreliable.

III. Depreciation is the difference between value and cost. It represents the loss in value of an improvement from all causes.

A. Depreciation is caused by physical deterioration, functional obsolescence, and external obsolescence. The depreciation is curable if it is possible and economically practical to fix it; otherwise it is incurable.

1. Physical deterioration (deferred maintenance) is depreciation caused by physical damage or wear and tear. It may be curable or incurable.

2. Functional obsolescence is depreciation caused by design defects. The defect may be a deficiency (something lacking) or a superadequacy, (overimprovement). It may be curable or incurable.

3. External obsolescence is depreciation caused by something outside the property itself, such as surrounding property influences or market conditions. It is incurable.

B. The economic age-life (straight-line) method measures depreciation by applying an accrued depreciation rate to the cost of the improvements.

1. The accrued depreciation rate is equal to the effective age of the improvement divided by its economic life.

> 2. This method is used to measure physical deterioration, but is unreliable for measuring functional or external obsolescence.
>
> C. The difference in selling prices (or incomes) between comparable properties that include a defect and those that don't, can be used to measure the amount of depreciation caused by the defect.
>
>   1. In the case of a difference in income, the income difference must be capitalized to determine the difference in value.
>
> D. The amount of depreciation caused by a curable defect is equivalent to the cost of curing the defect.
>
> E. The observed condition method uses a variety of techniques to separately calculate each item of depreciation in an improvement.

X. CHAPTER QUIZ

1. Which of the following cost estimating techniques would include an estimate of the labor rates and man hours necessary to install the plumbing system in a house?

    a. Unit-in-place method
    b. Cost index trending method
    c. Quantity survey method
    d. Comparative unit method

2. Which of the following is the most commonly used method by appraisers to estimate cost of residential properties?

    a. Cost index trending
    b. Quantity survey method
    c. Comparative unit method
    d. None of the above

3. The unit costs used with the unit-in-place method include the costs of:

    a. labor.
    b. materials.
    c. equipment.
    d. all of the above.

4. If construction costs are 10% higher in the local market than the average costs listed in a costing manual, the appraiser should adjust the unit costs used in the cost estimate by:

    a. multiplying them by 10%.
    b. multiplying them by 110%.
    c. multiplying them by 90%.
    d. dividing them by 90%.

5. A poor floor plan design is an example of:

    a. deferred maintenance.
    b. a superadequacy.
    c. functional obsolescence.
    d. economic obsolescence.

6. Which of the following types of depreciation is always incurable?

    a. Physical deterioration
    b. Functional obsolescence
    c. External obsolescence
    d. None of the above

7. Worn out carpeting in a house **would most likely fall** into the category of:

    a. curable physical deterioration.
    b. incurable physical deterioration.
    c. curable functional obsolescence.
    d. incurable functional obsolescence.

8. Estimates of depreciation are **generally more reliable** in the case of:

    a. older homes.
    b. newer homes.
    c. larger homes.
    d. smaller homes.

9. The effective age of an improvement:

    a. depends on the actual age of the improvement.
    b. is the difference between actual age and economic life.
    c. is the difference between actual age and remaining economic life.
    d. is the difference between economic life and remaining economic life.

10. Depreciation may be measured by:

    a. market comparison.
    b. income capitalization.
    c. cost to cure.
    d. any of the above.

ANSWERS: 1. c; 2. c; 3. d; 4. b; 5. c; 6. c; 7. a; 8. b; 9. d; 10. d

Chapter 9
Sales Comparison Approach to Value

KEY WORDS AND TERMS

Adjustment Process
Comparable Sales
Data Collection
Elements of Comparison
Financing Terms
Gross Adjustment
Leased Fee
Market Theory of Value

Net Adjustment
Paired Data Analysis
Percentage Adjustments
Relative Comparison Analysis
Reconciliation of Comparables
Sequence of Adjustment
Units of Comparison
Verification of Data

LEARNING OBJECTIVES

After completing this chapter, you should be able to:

1. describe the characteristics of a real estate market, and explain the significance of real estate markets to the sales comparison approach to value;

2. list the basic steps in the sales comparison approach to value;

3. explain what makes a sale "comparable" for appraisal purposes;

4. list the elements of comparison that are commonly used to analyze comparable sales in residential appraisals;

5. understand the difference between units of comparison and elements of comparison, and describe their roles in the sales comparison approach;

Chapter 9

CHAPTER OUTLINE

6. describe how adjustments are made to the prices of comparable sales;

7. understand the effect of financing terms on sales prices, and explain what is meant by cash equivalent financing terms;

8. apply the techniques of paired data analysis and relative comparison analysis to obtain adjustment values for any differences in the elements of comparison;

9. describe the significance of the sequence in which adjustments are made to comparable sales prices; and

10. describe the process by which the value indicators from the sales comparison approach are reconciled into a single indicator of the subject property's value.

I. Market Theory of Value

In the sales comparison approach, an appraiser utilizes an orderly process to analyze the sales of similar properties in order to estimate the value of the subject property. The sales comparison method is the best method to appraise single-family dwellings.

More emphasis is placed on the sales comparison approach to value than on either the cost or income approaches. The sales comparison approach is preferred because it is easy for non-professionals to understand and it is usually considered quite reliable. In this chapter, we will discuss the various steps to the sales comparison approach.

In the *SALES COMPARISON APPROACH* (*also known as the market comparison or market data approach*), *the appraiser uses data from actual market transactions to arrive at an indicator of value for the subject property*. The sales comparison approach to value is based on the market theory of value.

> *The market theory states that value is determined by the actions of buyers and sellers in the marketplace in response to the influences of supply and demand.*

(The market theory of value is covered in detail in Chapter 2.)

The principle of substitution underlies both the sales comparison approach and the market theory of value. According to the *PRINCIPLE OF SUBSTITUTION*, *a buyer will not pay more for a property than it would cost to acquire a substitute property of equal utility, assuming the substitute property could be acquired within a reasonable length of time*. Thus, in an active market where many equivalent properties are available, the value of any one property should be equivalent to the prices paid for similar properties.

> *It is a truism of real estate that no two pieces of property are exactly alike; in fact each is unique.*

So appraisers must identify the differences that exist between the subject property and the comparable sales, and make price adjustments to account for those differences. The basic formula for the sales comparison approach can be stated as follows:

Value of Subject Property = Sales Prices of Comparable Properties +/- Adjustments for Differences Between the Subject and Comparable Sales.

II. Real Estate Markets

The concept of a real estate market is central to the sales comparison approach. A *REAL ESTATE MARKET is a distinct group of buyers and sellers whose actions are influenced in similar ways by similar forces of supply and demand.* Prices paid for properties within a given market should indicate the value of other similar properties in that market, but usually do not indicate the value of properties in a different market.

Case/Example: Prices paid for homes in a community with a strong economic base and high wage levels are likely to be much higher than prices paid for similar homes in a depressed community.

In applying the sales comparison approach, the appraiser must be keenly aware of the market in which the subject property is located. The geographic boundaries of a market may be large or small, depending on the type of property.

Markets for residential property tend to be smaller, encompassing neighborhoods or districts, while markets for large commercial properties may be national or even international.

Markets are sometimes defined by physical boundaries, but the critical factor in defining a market for appraisal purposes is similarity in the forces (economic, social, governmental and physical/environmental) that influence value. And if these forces are rapidly changing, it becomes much more difficult to identify comparable sales, and the sales comparison approach becomes much less reliable.

Case/Example: In a period of rapid inflation, the pool of buyers who can afford to purchase a particular size of house may change almost daily, and sales of similar properties that closed a month ago may no longer be representative of the present market.

For the comparison approach to value, it is necessary to know about the subject property for which comparables are to be used in order to estimate value of the subject property.

The appraiser's physical inspection of the property will provide much of the information needed as to the subject property.

A. DESCRIPTION OF IMPROVEMENTS (URAR)

The Uniform Residential Appraisal Report (URAR) includes a section with a series of blocks which, when completed, along with any additional comments needed, will set forth an understandable description of a residential property (see **Figure 9-1**).

The **General Description** block asks the following questions:

Units: Either one unit or one unit with a guest house (accessory unit).

Number of Stories: One, Two, Three, etc.

Type: Detached, Attached, End Unit.

Is the house **Existing, Proposed,** or **Under Construction**? Check the applicable box.

Design: The architectural style of the subject such as Cape Cod, Tudor, etc.

Year Built: The calendar year in which the subject was built.

Figure 9-1

Improvements Section – URAR

General Description	Foundation	Exterior Description materials/condition	Interior materials/condition
Units 128 One 129 One with Accessory Unit	140 Concrete Slab 141 Crawl Space	Foundation Walls 152	Floors 159
# of Stories 130	142 Full Basement 143 Partial Basement	Exterior Walls 153	Walls 160
Type 131 Det. 132 Att. 133 S-Det./End Unit	Basement Area 144 sq. ft.	Roof Surface 154	Trim/Finish 161
134 Existing 135 Proposed 136 Under Const.	Basement Finish 145 %	Gutters & Downspouts 155	Bath Floor 162
Design (Style) 137	146 Outside Entry/Exit 147 Sump Pump	Window Type 156	Bath Wainscot 163
Year Built e-8; 138	Evidence of 148 Infestation	Storm Sash/Insulated 157	Car Storage 195 None
Effective Age (Yrs) 139	150 Dampness 151 Settlement	Screens 158	196 Driveway # of Cars 197
Attic 164 None	Heating 171 FWA 172 HWBB 173 Radiant	Amenities 187 Woodstove(s) # 188	Driveway Surface 198
165 Drop Stair 166 Stairs	174 Other 175 Fuel 176	181 Fireplace(s)# 182 189 Fence 190	199 Garage # of Cars 200
167 Floor 168 Scuttle	Cooling 177 Central Air Conditioning	183 Patio/Deck 184 191 Porch 192	201 Carport # of Cars 202
169 Finished 170 Heated	178 Individual 179 Other 180	185 Pool 186 193 Other 194	203 Att. 204 Det. 205 Built-in

Appliances 206 Refrigerator 207 Range/Oven 208 Dishwasher 209 Disposal 210 Microwave 211 Washer/Dryer 212 Other (describe) 213

Finished area **above grade** contains: 214 Rooms 215 Bedrooms 216 Bath(s) 217 Square Feet of Gross Living Area Above Grade

Additional features (special energy efficient items, etc.) 218

Describe the condition of the property (including needed repairs, deterioration, renovations, remodeling, etc.). e-9; e-10; e-11; e-12; e-13; 219

Are there any physical deficiencies or adverse conditions that affect the livability, soundness, or structural integrity of the property? 220 Yes 221 No If Yes, describe 222

Does the property generally conform to the neighborhood (functional utility, style, condition, use, construction, etc.)? 223 Yes 224 No If No, describe 225

Effective Age: The effective age in years.

Directly under the question on effective age are a series of questions regarding the area above the ceiling. Many homes throughout the country have fully finished attics, in which it is possible for an individual to stand up, that may be used for storage or recreational activities. There are perhaps as many others that have only a torturous crawlspace between the roof and the ceiling. The following questions are designed to elicit this information. A fully finished attic adds additional value to a residence. Depending on the quality and degree of finish, additional information describing the attic may have to be provided in an addendum.

Attic: If there is no attic mark the **"None"** box. Otherwise, answer whether or not the attic has a **Drop Stair**, regular **Stairs**, a **Floor**, and is **Finished** and **Heated**. If there are no stairs, is the area accessed by a scuttle? Place an **"X"** only in the pertinent boxes.

The **Foundation** block has a series of check boxes that are intended to elicit information regarding the foundation and basement areas. These boxes will work for the vast majority of housing in the nation. However, additional information regarding certain types of raised foundations, sump pump systems, and basements might need to be described in an addendum. It should also be noted that a fully finished basement also can add significant value to a home, and may need to be described in an addendum, as well.

Is the house built with a **Concrete Slab** (no basement!) or with a raised foundation with a **Crawl Space**? Does it have a **Full Basement** or a **Partial Basement**? If there is a basement, what is the **Area** of the basement in square feet (a number is required here)? By what percentage is the basement **Finished** (fully finished = 100%)? Does the basement have an **Outside Entry**? Is there a **Sump Pump**? A sump pump is used in high ground water areas to prevent flooding either under a foundation or in a basement. Obviously, if this pump is not functioning properly there may be a possibility of damage to the foundation or the buildup of mold as a result of water damage. The question that follows asks whether there is evidence of **Dampness, Infestation,** or **Settlement**. Once again, place an **"X"** in the pertinent boxes. Evidence of infestation, mold, or dampness must be described.

Directly under the foundation block, there are a series of questions regarding the heating and cooling systems of the subject residence. These are to be answered, for the most part, with an "X" in the pertinent box if they apply. The following translation of the form's abbreviations apply:

FWA – Forced Warm Air. This is also known in the west as either FAU (Forced Air Unit) or FAH (Forced Air Heating). It is perhaps the most common system.

HWBB – Hot Water Baseboard.

Radiant – Uses radiators that are supplied by hot water or steam from a furnace. Typically, heating is provided to each individual room and there is no provision for exhausting stale air.

Both the hot water baseboard and radiant systems are more common in the east and mid-west. Gas heated forced air systems tend to be popular in the west.

Other: Floor and wall heaters.

Cooling: Central Air Conditioning Systems.

Individual: Window or wall units. Window units are considered personal property.

Other: Evaporative Cooling Units (popular in the dry climates of the western states).

The **Exterior Description** block is intended to allow the appraiser to describe both the materials utilized to build the major components of the residence as well as their condition at the time of inspection. Typical **Condition** comments would be Poor, Fair, Average, Good, Very Good, and Excellent. Typical **Materials** utilized in residential construction are listed below. They are not all inclusive.

Foundation Walls – Enter the type, such as poured concrete, concrete block, or treated wood.

Exterior Walls – Exterior walls could be stucco, brick, solid masonry, or wood siding.

Roof Surface – Enter the roofing type, such as asphalt shingle, wood shingle, clay tile, or concrete tile.

Gutters and Downspouts – Enter whether made of steel, aluminum, or vinyl.

Window Type – This may be vinyl or aluminum sliders, casement, or wooden double hung windows.

Storm Sash/Insulated – A storm sash is a separate outer window that is fitted over a single pane window during the winter. These are found in the east and mid-west on older homes. They are gradually being phased out by modern energy efficient dual pane windows.

Screens – Are fitted to windows in all areas of the country to keep out disease bearing insects such as flies and mosquitos. If any are missing they must be replaced.

The area directly below the exterior description contains a series of check boxes for the subject's Amenities. This is another area of the form that will require the use of addendums.

Woodstove(s) – If present, check the box, enter the number of these items.

Fireplace(s) – If present, check the box and enter the number of fireplaces. This is an example of the need for an addendum. The quality of the materials used in the construction of the fireplace(s) and mantle(s) can have a major value impact.

Fence – Check the box if there is one. Note in the addendum what material it is built from (wire, split rail, cedar, redwood, blockwall, etc). The quantity and quality of the materials used to build the fence can have a major impact on overall property value.

Patio/Deck – If present check the box. Again, this is an addendum item. The appraiser must note in an addendum just which of the "Patio Triplets" is present— a deck, a covered patio, or an enclosed patio. A glass enclosed sunroom patio can add a great deal of market value to a residence. Also, note if there is more than one patio attached to the residence.

Porch – This may be merely a five-foot by five-foot roofed over area at a front or rear entrance or a wide screened-in traditional wooden porch complete with rocking chairs! Once again, the appraiser will have to utilize an addendum to indicate quality and value.

Pool – If there is a pool present, check the box. Describe it in an addendum.

Other – Balconies, in-ground spas, gazebos, tennis courts, guest quarters, equestrian facilities, etc. are just a few of the items that fit this checkbox. They can add enormous value, so they need to be covered in depth in an addendum.

The next block covers the **Interior** description. Once again, the appraiser is asked to describe both the materials utilized and a judgment regarding their condition (Poor to Excellent).

Floors – Wood, vinyl, carpet, ceramic tile, etc. Note the material that is predominant.

Walls – Plaster, drywall, wood panel.

Trim/Finish – Paint grade wood, stain grade wood, vinyl.

Bath Floor – Vinyl, ceramic tile, marble, etc.

Bath Wainscot – Fiberglass, ceramic tile, plaster, marble, etc.

Below the Interior block is a section that covers car storage. There is a check box that says none. Do not check this unless there really is no provision for car storage on the subject property.

Driveway – Check the box if there is one. Also, note the number of cars that may be parked in this space.

Driveway Surface – Concrete, asphalt, gravel, etc.

Garage – Check the box if the answer is yes. Note the number of cars it holds.

Carport – A carport is a structure that is covered and it may also have up to three walls enclosing it (sort of like a garage without a door). If a carport is present, check the box. Note the number of vehicles the carport can hold.

Finally, note whether the garage or carport is **Attached**, **Detached**, or **Built-in** to the residence.

The final check blocks for this section ask the appraiser to give a room count and square footage figure for the subject property. This consists of **Total Rooms (not including bathrooms)**, **Total Bedrooms**, **Total Bathrooms**, and **Total Square Footage** for the house.

A series of questions that require descriptive answers follows:

Are there any **Additional Features?** In particular, the form asks for energy efficient fixtures. However the appraiser may be able to fit other additional features in here as well.

Describe the **Condition of the Property**. Discuss repairs, refurbishment, and remodeling. An additional addendum may be necessary.

Are there any **Physical Deficiencies**, or any other **Adverse Conditions**? If yes describe. These may include repairs needed, health and safety violations, possible environmental contamination problems, etc. Keep in mind that even if you check the box NO that most underwriters will require you to state that you saw none of the above.

Is the property **Conforming**? Check the YES or NO box. Describe any problems of **Functional Utility**, **Style**, **Condition**, **Use**, **Construction Quality**, etc. If there were no problems seen, provide a statement to that effect.

Authors' Comment – It appears that the new URAR has been formatted with the Automated Valuation Model (AVM) computer programs in mind. The check box format seems to continue recent trends in the marketplace to provide "one size fits all" answers for appraisal documents. This trend ignores the fact that real estate is not a homogenous (similar) product. Homogeneity allows us to assume, for instance, that a share of Apple, Inc. stock looks like any other share of Apple, Inc. stock and is worth the same price as any other share. ▼

> *A computer AVM of 1500 square foot houses can lead to the same sort of conclusion, not because of what it says, but because of what it does not say. In general, owner upgrades and refurbishment, as well as differences in quality and type of certain additional features, are often ignored and given no value in a check box format.*
>
> *The computer programs used to create comparable AVM information are often unable to properly scan in information that is written in the commentary fields unless the wording is exactly the same each and every time. Otherwise, the machine does not know where to transfer the information from the appraisal into the AVM program. It is this weakness that the check box formula is attempting to address.*

III. Comparable Sales

For a sale to be considered comparable, it must compete with the subject property. In other words, a *COMPARABLE SALE must be in the same market as the subject property and appeal to the same sorts of buyers.*

> *The sales comparison approach to value is the preferred approach for many appraisal purposes, including residential and vacant land appraisals.*

The values indicated by this approach are viewed as highly reliable in most cases. The strength of this approach, its reliance on market data, is also its weakness, however.

> *If data for comparable sales is inadequate, or totally lacking, the sales comparison approach CANNOT be properly applied.*

This is often the case for special use properties such as public buildings, so the sales comparison approach is rarely used in appraising special use properties.

IV. Steps in the Sales Comparison Approach

There are five basic steps to the sales comparison approach:

1. Data collection
2. Verification of data
3. Selecting units of comparison
4. Analysis and adjustments of comparable prices
5. Reconciliation of comparable value indicators

A. DATA COLLECTION

Each appraiser develops sources for sales data.

Appraisers must go through a lengthy training program to be licensed or certified in a particular state. The list of **State Real Estate Appraiser Regulatory Boards**, responsible for licensing appraisers in each state, can be found in Chapter 14 of this book. By the time an appraiser reaches this stage in his or her career, they will have used many data sources such as those set forth in **Figure 9-2**.

Figure 9-2

Sources of Data

1. **County Recorder's office.** Maintains a file of all documents recorded in the county offices, including all deeds transferring ownership of real estate. The assessor's office has detailed maps of most lots and tracts.

2. **Title Insurance companies.** Maintain files of all recorded county documents.

3. **Real Estate Board MLS.** As technology increases, the number of "local boards" Multiple Listing Services (MLS) keeps consolidating. In effect, the geographical area covered by a membership keeps increasing.

4. **Published services. FNC, REDI.** There are several publishing services that collect data about sales prices and the associated loans.

5. **Computerized services.** On-line, such as DataQuick, and CD-ROM services.

To begin with, the appraiser must gather data on comparable properties in the market. Relevant data include sales prices, listing prices, contract prices for pending sales, option prices, and offering prices of pending offers. The appraiser must also gather data concerning the characteristics (physical, legal, and economic) of the comparable properties, and the terms and conditions of the property transactions (see **Figure 9-3**).

B. VERIFICATION OF DATA

In step two, the appraiser must verify the data that will be used. Not only does verification establish the reliability of the data, it also allows the appraiser to determine the circumstances surrounding the transaction. For example, if the buyer or seller was not typically motivated, the transaction may not have been at arm's length and will not be a reliable value indicator.

Sales Comparison Approach Section	Forms	Requirement or Instruction
Date of Sale/Time For each comparable property, the appraiser must first identify the status type from the list of options below.	1004/70 2055/2055 1073/465 1075/466	REQUIREMENT

Status Type
Active
Contract
Expired
Withdrawn
Settled sale

- If the comparable property is an active listing, the appraiser must specify 'Active'.
- If the comparable property is under contract, or an expired or withdrawn listing, the appraiser must first indicate the date status type using the abbreviations below followed by the corresponding contract, expiration, or withdrawal date in mm/yy format. Use 'c' for contract, 'w' for withdrawn listings, and 'e' for expired listings.

Abbreviated Entry	Date Status Type
c	Contract Date
s	Settlement Date
w	Withdrawn Date
e	Expiration Date

- If the comparable property is a settled sale and the contract date is known, the appraiser must first indicate the date status type 's' followed by the settlement date (mm/yy), and then the date status type 'c' followed by the contract date (mm/yy). For settled sales for which the contract date is unavailable to the appraiser in the normal course of business, the appraiser must enter the abbreviation 'Unk', for unknown, in place of the contract date.

Reporting Format:
Status Type – Appraiser must select one value from the specified list
Date – mm/yy
Contract Date Unknown Indicator (for Settled Sales only) – Select 'Yes' or 'No'
The PDF creator will automatically insert the abbreviated Date Status type and a semicolon to separate the data values (for settled sales only). If the appraiser indicates the contract date is unknown, the PDF creator will populate 'Unk' after the semicolon.

Examples:
Active listing: Active
Contract: c04/10
Expired listing: e04/10
Withdrawn listing: w04/10
Settled sale (contract date known): s04/10;c02/10
Settled sale (contract date unknown): s04/10;Unk

The previous burgundy-framed box can be found in Appendix 5 at the end of this textbook. The abbreviations will be recognizable to real estate salespeople and brokers as those commonly used in MLS listings. Now, with the Fannie Mae and Freddie Mac mandatory usage of these abbreviations, real estate, lending, and appraisal professionals will all be progressing towards using a common language. This should also help the general public to understand the terminology used for comparables. If any part of the UAD contradicts or does not fulfill the requirements of USPAP (the body that governs appraisers), then an addendum must be included that does fulfill these requirements.

Figure 9-3

Sale Data Form

The sale data form includes the following information:

1. **Terms of sale**

2. **Any extenuating circumstances in the sale (imminent foreclosure)**

3. **Description of improvements (number of rooms, baths, etc.)**

4. **Occupancy status**

5. **Rental, if not owner-occupied**

6. **Condition of property at the date of sale**

7. **Personal property included in the sale**

8. **Assessments or encumbrances against the property at the date of sale**

Interviewing a party to the transaction is considered the most reliable way to verify transaction data. Physical inspection is the most reliable way to verify physical data. (Refer to Chapter 5 for more information on data collection and verification.)

C. SELECTING UNITS OF COMPARISON

The third step is selecting units of comparison. That unit may be an acre, a front foot or a square foot. For example, the price of vacant land is often stated as a price per acre, per square foot or per front foot.

In residential appraisals, the price per square foot of living area, or the price for the entire property are commonly used units of comparison.

When comparing different properties, it is important for the price of each property to be stated in the same unit of comparison. It would make no sense, for example, to compare one property's price per square foot of living area to another property's price per front foot of water frontage.

In the sales comparison method, the appraiser must choose the unit or units of comparison that are most appropriate for the particular property being appraised. More than one unit may be appropriate, and the appraiser will make a comparison for each of the applicable units. If comparing several different units of comparison leads to a consistent indicator of value, that indicator of value will be more reliable. If a wide range of values results from using different units of comparison, the appraiser will want to investigate the cause for the discrepancy.

D. ANALYSIS AND ADJUSTMENT OF COMPARABLE PRICES

The unit prices of the comparables must be analyzed and adjusted to account for differences between the comparables and the subject property.

The appraiser first identifies the elements of comparison that may affect the value of the subject property. For each element of comparison, the characteristics of the subject property are compared to those of the comparable; any differences are measured and an appropriate price adjustment is made. The net total of all the adjustments for each comparable is then added to (or subtracted from) the price of the comparable to arrive at an indication of value for the subject property. (The process of calculating and applying adjustments is discussed in greater detail later in this chapter.)

1. General Rules as to Comparables

a. Avoid forced sales (foreclosure and tax sales).

b. Avoid comparables more than 20 percent different in size. (The greater the size difference, the greater the likelihood of an unrealistic appraisal.)

c. Avoid comparables that are not in the same general age range as the property being appraised.

d. Use the same neighborhood for comparables or one as geographically close as possible.

e. If the gross adjustments are greater than 25 percent of the sale price of the comparable, it is likely not a comparable (or if net adjustments exceed 15%).

f. Consider marketability. A comparable with serious marketability problems should not be used as a comparable unless the subject property has similar problems. As an example, a 2,500 square foot home with only one bath used as a comparable would likely result in an unrealistically low value for the property being appraised, even after the comparable's sale price was adjusted for a second bath.

g. Add-on space is not comparable space if the addition is obvious.

h. You must use comparables where you have seen the exterior. (If you have seen the interior, it would be a better comparable.)

i. Comparables which vary greatly from other comparables should be discarded.

E. RECONCILIATION OF COMPARABLE VALUE INDICATORS

The final step in the sales comparison approach is reconciliation. For the sales comparison approach, the appraiser will always analyze at least three different comparable properties, and each analysis of a comparable leads to a value indicator for the subject property. Typically, the subject property's value will fall somewhere between the highest and lowest value indicator. In *RECONCILING THE VALUE INDICATORS*, *the appraiser estimates where within the range of values the subject property's value lies.*

Reconciliation is NOT a simple averaging of the value indicators.

The appraiser must evaluate the characteristics of each comparable and determine which is most reliable. As a general rule, the comparables that are most similar to the subject property are considered the most reliable indicator's of the subjects value.

Case/Example: The adjusted sales prices of four comparable properties indicate the following range of values for the subject property:

Comparable	Indicated Subject Value
#1.	$102,300.00
#2.	$97,700.00
#3.	$105,100.00
#4.	$103,700.00

Comparable #1 is the most similar to the subject property and requires the fewest adjustments. Therefore, the appraiser concludes that the indicated value of the subject property is $102,000.

V. The Adjustment Process

We turn our attention now to a more detailed look at the fourth step in the sales comparison approach, the adjustment process. Appraisers use a number of techniques to determine what adjustments to make to comparable sale prices. Some of these techniques involve sophisticated statistical analysis that is beyond the scope of this book. However, for most residential appraisals, it is usually enough to make adjustments on the basis of comparative analysis.

Comparative analysis includes four steps:

Step 1: Identify the elements of comparison.

Step 2: For each element of comparison, measure the differences between the subject and each comparable, and determine an appropriate adjustment to account for each difference.

Step 3: Calculate the net total of adjustments for each comparable, and add or subtract the net total to or from the comparable's sales price.

Step 4: Based on the analysis of the comparables, determine a single indicated value for the subject. (This is the same as the reconciliation step in the overall sales comparison approach.)

A. ELEMENTS OF COMPARISON

The first step in the comparative analysis is to identify the elements of comparison. An *ELEMENT OF COMPARISON is any aspect of a real estate transaction that may affect the sales price, including the terms and conditions of the sale and the characteristics of the property itself.* The appraiser then compares each element of comparison in the subject property to the same element in each comparable sale, and adjusts the comparable sales' prices for any differences.

Case/Example: An appraiser knows that the number of baths in a house has an affect on its sale price, so the number of baths is identified as an element of comparison. If the subject property has two baths, but the comparable property has only one, the appraiser will adjust the sales price of the comparable property to account for the difference in this element of comparison.

If an adjustment is NOT possible or practical (for example, because there is no data for estimating the amount of the adjustment), the appraiser must reject the comparable.

Commonly used elements of comparison for residential appraisals include:

1. Real property rights conveyed (fee simple or other interest);
2. Financing terms;
3. Conditions of sale (the motivation of the buyer and the seller);
4. Expenditures immediately after sale;
5. Market conditions adjustment (date of sale);
6. Location adjustments;
7. Physical characteristics (size, quality, etc.);
8. Economic characteristics;
9. Use; and
10. Non-Realty Components of Sale

1. Real Property Rights Conveyed

In most residential transactions, the real property rights conveyed include the full fee simple interest in the property.

If the real property interest that is being appraised differs from the interest conveyed in a comparable (leasehold vs. leased fee), an adjustment will be necessary.

Two common examples of non-fee interests are the leasehold and the leased fee. A **LEASEHOLD INTEREST** *includes the rights to use property under the terms of a lease. The interest of the owner of the leased property is called the* **LEASED FEE**. Residential appraisals of leasehold estates usually involve long-term ground leases, where the tenant has constructed a building on the leased land.

Easements can also affect the value of property.

An easement that is typical for most properties, such as an easement for maintenance of electric service lines, does not ordinarily affect value. Easements that are not typical, such as a right of public access across a property, may have a significant effect on value.

The UAD burgundy-framed box on the following page contains abbreviations for overall location rating and Abbreviated entries for locations factors. While the location factors abbreviations are helpful to clarify what letters an appraiser uses to abbreviate certain common elements, the overall location rating of Neutral, Beneficial and Adverse are controversial to many appraisers as it may be misleading in terms of an appropriate appraisal. It is highly recommended that the appraiser expand upon these very limited terms in an attached addendum to fulfill USPAP requirements.

The appraiser must also consider whether the property includes any special rights, such as water rights, or whether any rights, such as mineral rights, have been reserved by a previous owner.

2. Financing Terms

If the financing terms do not affect the price paid for the property, the financing is referred to as **CASH EQUIVALENT**. Sales that are cash equivalent do not require any price adjustment for financing terms. However, when financing terms are not typical of those available in the market, they will usually affect the sales price of the comparable.

Non-standard financing can take a wide variety of forms, from seller financing to interest rate buy-downs to loan assumptions. In some cases, the monetary effect may be fairly obvious. For example, if the seller pays some or all of the points on the buyer's loan, the effect on the sales price is likely to equal the amount paid by the seller. Other cases are not so clear-cut. In a sale that involves seller financing, for instance, the buyer may benefit in any of several ways. A below-market interest rate, small down payment, reduced (or zero) loan fees, and easier loan qualification are some of the possible benefits of seller financing.

Sales Comparison Approach Section	Forms	Requirement or Instruction
Location The appraiser must select one of the following ratings to describe the overall effect on value and marketability of the location factor(s) associated with the subject property and each comparable property. The abbreviation for the rating must be entered.	1004/70 2055/2055 1073/465 1075/466	REQUIREMENT

ABBREVIATED ENTRY	OVERALL LOCATION RATING
N	Neutral
B	Beneficial
A	Adverse

The appraiser must also select at least one, but not more than two, location factor(s) from the list below. If two factors are entered, separate them with a semicolon. The abbreviation for the factor must be entered, with the exception of 'Other'.

ABBREVIATED ENTRY	LOCATION FACTOR
Res	Residential
Ind	Industrial
Comm	Commercial
BsyRd	Busy Road
WtrFr	Water Front
GlfCse	Golf Course
AdjPrk	Adjacent to Park
AdjPwr	Adjacent to Power Lines
Lndfl	Landfill
PubTrn	Public Transportation
See Instruction Below	Other – Appraiser to enter a description of the location*

*Other: If a location factor not on this list materially affects the value of the property, the appraiser must enter a description of the location associated with the property. The description entered must allow a reader of the appraisal report to understand the location factor(s) that is associated with the property. Descriptors such as 'None', 'N/A', 'Typical', 'Average', etc., are unacceptable. The text must fit in the allowable space.

A list of acceptable abbreviations and definitions is also provided at the end of this document in Exhibit 3: Requirements – Abbreviations.

Reporting Format:
Location Rating – Appraiser must select one value from the specified list
Location Factors – Appraiser must select one or two factors from the specified list
Description of 'Other' (if applicable) – Text
The PDF creator will automatically insert a semicolon to separate the data values.

Example:
B;AdjPrk;WtrFr

Sales Comparison Approach Section	Forms	Requirement or Instruction
Sale or Financing Concessions *Note: This field, comprised of two lines, is used to capture sale type, financing type, and any concessions. The information must be entered on line 1 and line 2 as indicated.* **Line 1** The appraiser must indicate the sale type for each comparable property. If more than one sale type applies to the comparable property, the appraiser must start at the top of the list and identify the first sale type that applies. The valid values are:	1004/70 2055/2055 1073/465 1075/466	REQUIREMENT

ABBREVIATED ENTRY	SALE TYPE
REO	REO sale
Short	Short sale
CrtOrd	Court ordered sale
Estate	Estate sale
Relo	Relocation sale
NonArm	Non-arms length sale
ArmLth	Arms length sale
Listing	Listing

Line 2
The appraiser must enter the financing type from the list below and the total amount of concessions, if any, for each settled sale. If there are no sales or financing concessions, enter the numeral zero (0).

ABBREVIATED ENTRY	FINANCING TYPE
FHA	FHA
VA	VA
Conv	Conventional
Seller	Seller
Cash	Cash
RH	USDA – Rural housing
See Instruction Below	Other – Appraiser to enter a description of the financing type*

*Other: If the financing type is not on this list, the appraiser must enter a description of the financing type. The text must fit in the allowable space.

Note: Below-market financing can have an impact on market values and therefore is of particular importance. A variety of government programs, such as state and local bond programs, provide below-market financing. The appraiser must indicate if sales transactions with below-market financing are used for comparable sales.

Reporting Format:
Line 1: Sale Type – Appraiser must select one value from the specified list

Line 2: Financing Type – Appraiser must select one value from the specified list
Description of 'Other Financing Type' (if applicable) – Text
Concession Amount – Numeric, whole numbers only
The PDF creator will automatically insert a semicolon to separate the data values.

Example:
Line 1: ArmLth
Line 2: FHA;5000

In addition to checking the blocks for location factors, the appraiser is given the opportunity to fill in the "text" box to further describe the location in his or her own words. Note: If the boxes or spaces for text do not adequately allow for USPAP compliance, the appraiser is required to

Chapter 9

provide an attached addendum. If it is for a federally related transaction, the appraiser is required to provide an addendum that provides sufficient information that will not be misleading or cause confusion in the marketplace and to make the appraisal USPAP compliant.

> *To estimate the effect of non-standard financing on price, the appraiser should compare the sales of properties with similar non-standard financing to sales with standard market financing.*

The difference in the prices paid for the two classes of properties will indicate the effect the non-standard financing has on market price.

The appraiser can also try to compare the amount the buyer must pay under the non-standard financing terms to the amount that would be required with standard financing.

Case/Example: In a sale for $120,000, the buyer paid $20,000 down and financed the balance with a $100,000 seller financed loan at 8% interest. If market interest rates are 10%, the appraiser could compare the amount of the buyer's monthly payment at 8% to the amount the buyer would have to pay at 10% interest. The monthly payment on a $100,000 loan with a term of 30 years is $733.76 at 8%, and $877.57 at 10%. The actual payment (at 8%) is 83.6% (733.76 ÷ 877.57 = 0.836) of what it would be at market rates (10%), so the loan amount is multiplied by 83.6% divided by $100,000 x 83.6% = $83,600. Adding the down payment of $20,000 indicates a cash equivalent price of $103,600.

A more detailed approach is to estimate the present value of the payments to be made by the buyer. Present value is determined by discounting the buyer's payments at the current market interest rate. This approach allows the appraiser to take into account such factors as balloon payments and early payoff of the loan. (Most mortgage loans are paid off before the ends of their terms, either because of refinancing or resale of the mortgaged property.)

Case/Example: Using the same facts as the previous example, the appraiser notes that the average life of a mortgage loan in the market is seven years. The appraiser calculates the present value of seven years worth of monthly payments of $733.76, discounted at the market interest rate of 10%, which comes to $44,200 (rounded). Next, the appraiser determines the amount of the remaining loan balance after seven years: $92,500 (rounded), and discounts this amount to its present value at 10%: $46,000 (rounded, assuming monthly compounding of interest). The sum of these two amounts indicates the cash equivalent of the seller financed loan: $44,200 + $46,000 = $90,200. Adding the amount of the down payment gives a cash equivalent sales price of $110,200. (**Note:** The procedure for discounting payments to present value is discussed in detail in Chapter 10.)

The preceding examples illustrate that calculating the monetary effect of non-standard financing is not a simple task. The amount of the calculated adjustment will vary depending on the assumptions used in the calculation process. For this reason, the appraiser must always look to market data as the primary indicator of the effect of non-standard financing.

If adequate market data is NOT available to make this determination, the property with non-standard financing should be rejected as a comparable.

3. Conditions of Sale

CONDITIONS OF SALE *refers to the motivations of the buyer and seller in a particular transaction.* These conditions of sale as well as financing terms are typically contained within the **Real Estate Purchase Agreement** (see **Figure 9-4** for page one of a California example and **Figure 9-5** for page one of a Texas example). The appraiser must be provided with a copy of the subject's sales contract to determine whether the conditions of sale and the financing terms are typical of the market.

If the buyer and seller are NOT typically motivated, the price paid for the property may not reflect market value.

For example, a seller who has been transferred to another city may accept a low offer to make a quick sale, or a developer may pay a higher than market price for a property that is necessary to complete a certain project. If there is a family or business relationship between the buyer and seller, the appraiser must assume that the motivation of the parties is not typical.

When the buyer and/or seller are not typically motivated, the sale is most likely not an arm's length transaction. Such sales are rarely used as comparables; the price paid is not a reliable indicator of market value, because the buyer and seller are acting under the influence of forces that do not affect the market in general.

The adjustment for conditions of sale is sometimes combined with the adjustment for financing terms (discussed below), since financing concessions may reflect unusual motivation on the part of the buyer or seller. For example, a seller who needs a quick sale may offer seller financing with below market interest or a very low down payment.

4. Expenditures Immediately After Sale

These are expenditures that would have to be made upon purchase of the property and that a knowledgeable buyer may negotiate into the purchase price. Examples include the cost to repair or replace structures or parts of structures, the cost to remediate environmental contamination, or the costs associated with zoning changes to permit development.

5. Market Conditions

The price paid for a comparable property reflects the state of the market as of the date the property was sold, but the forces that affect value are subject to constant change.

Every state uses a different purchase agreement/deposit receipt/agreement of sale. The form used in Figure 9-4 is the most commonly used by REALTORS® in California. In Texas real estate contract forms are promulgated by the Texas Real Estate Commission (TREC) (see Figure 9-5). Only the first pages of each form are shown here. As an appraiser, you should become familiar with the most commonly used local form in your state. It's especially important to take note of the purchase price, down payment, and financing sections.

Figure 9-4

CALIFORNIA
ASSOCIATION
OF REALTORS®

CALIFORNIA
RESIDENTIAL PURCHASE AGREEMENT
AND JOINT ESCROW INSTRUCTIONS
For Use With Single Family Residential Property — Attached or Detached
(C.A.R. Form RPA-CA, Revised 4/10)

Date _June 14, 20xx_

1. OFFER:
   A. THIS IS AN OFFER FROM _____ _Walter Buyer, Debbie Buyer_ _____ ("Buyer").
   B. THE REAL PROPERTY TO BE ACQUIRED is described as _264 Beach Lane, Costa Mesa CA 92627_ _____, Assessor's Parcel No. _____, situated in _Costa Mesa_, County of _Orange_, California, ("Property").
   C. THE PURCHASE PRICE offered is _Eight Hundred Thousand_ _____ (Dollars $ _800,000.00_).
   D. CLOSE OF ESCROW shall occur on _____ (date) (or ☒ _90_ Days After Acceptance).
2. AGENCY:
   A. DISCLOSURE: Buyer and Seller each acknowledge prior receipt of a "Disclosure Regarding Real Estate Agency Relationships" (C.A.R. Form AD).
   B. POTENTIALLY COMPETING BUYERS AND SELLERS: Buyer and Seller each acknowledge receipt of a disclosure of the possibility of multiple representation by the Broker representing that principal. This disclosure may be part of a listing agreement, buyer representation agreement or separate document (C.A.R. Form DA). Buyer understands that Broker representing Buyer may also represent other potential buyers, who may consider, make offers on or ultimately acquire the Property. Seller understands that Broker representing Seller may also represent other sellers with competing properties of interest to this Buyer.
   C. CONFIRMATION: The following agency relationships are hereby confirmed for this transaction:
      Listing Agent _____ _Sail Realty_ _____ (Print Firm Name) is the agent of (check one): ☒ the Seller exclusively; or ☐ both the Buyer and Seller.
      Selling Agent _____ _Ramos Realty_ _____ (Print Firm Name) (if not the same as the Listing Agent) is the agent of (check one): ☒ the Buyer exclusively; or ☐ the Seller exclusively; or ☐ both the Buyer and Seller. Real Estate Brokers are not parties to the Agreement between Buyer and Seller.
3. FINANCE TERMS: Buyer represents that funds will be good when deposited with Escrow Holder.
   A. INITIAL DEPOSIT: Deposit shall be in the amount of . . . . $ _10,000.00_
      (1) Buyer shall deliver deposit directly to Escrow Holder by personal check, ☐ electronic funds transfer, ☐ Other _____ within **3** business days after acceptance (or ☐ Other _____);
      OR (2) (If checked) ☒ Buyer has given the deposit by personal check (or ☐ _____) to the agent submitting the offer (or to ☒ _____), made payable to _____ _ABC Escrow_ _____. The deposit shall be held uncashed until Acceptance and then deposited with Escrow Holder (or ☐ into Broker's trust account) within **3** business days after Acceptance (or ☐ Other _____).
   B. INCREASED DEPOSIT: Buyer shall deposit with Escrow Holder an increased deposit in the amount of . . . . $ _____
      within _____ Days After Acceptance, or ☐ _____
      If a liquidated damages clause is incorporated into this Agreement, Buyer and Seller shall sign a separate liquidated damages clause (C.A.R. Form RID) for any increased deposit at the time it is deposited.
   C. LOAN(S):
      (1) FIRST LOAN: in the amount of . . . . $ _640,000.00_
          This loan will be conventional financing or, if checked, ☐ FHA, ☐ VA, ☐ Seller (C.A.R. Form SFA), ☐ assumed financing (C.A.R. Form PAA), ☐ Other _____ . This loan shall be at a fixed rate not to exceed _8.000_ % or, ☐ an adjustable rate loan with initial rate not to exceed _____ %. Regardless of the type of loan, Buyer shall pay points not to exceed _2.00_ % of the loan amount.
      (2) ☐ SECOND LOAN: in the amount of . . . . $ _____
          This loan will be conventional financing or, if checked, ☐ Seller (C.A.R. Form SFA), ☐ assumed financing (C.A.R. Form PAA), ☐ Other _____ . This loan shall be at a fixed rate not to exceed _____ % or, ☐ an adjustable rate loan with initial rate not to exceed _____ %. Regardless of the type of loan, Buyer shall pay points not to exceed _____ % of the loan amount.
      (3) FHA/VA: For any FHA or VA loan specified above, Buyer has 17 (or ☐ _____) Days After Acceptance to Deliver to Seller written notice (C.A.R. Form FVA) of any lender-required repairs or costs that Buyer requests Seller to pay for or repair. Seller has no obligation to pay for repairs or satisfy lender requirements unless otherwise agreed in writing.
   D. ADDITIONAL FINANCING TERMS: _____

   E. BALANCE OF PURCHASE PRICE OR DOWN PAYMENT: in the amount of . . . . $ _150,000.00_
      to be deposited with Escrow Holder within sufficient time to close escrow.
   F. PURCHASE PRICE (TOTAL): . . . . $ _800,000.00_

Buyer's Initials (_____) (_____)   Seller's Initials (_____) (_____)

EQUAL HOUSING OPPORTUNITY

RPA-CA REVISED 4/10 (PAGE 1 OF 8)

CALIFORNIA RESIDENTIAL PURCHASE AGREEMENT (RPA-CA PAGE 1 OF 8)

Agent: WALT HUBER	Phone:	Fax:	Prepared using zipForm® software
Broker: WALT HUBER REALTOR			

Figure 9-5

EQUAL HOUSING
OPPORTUNITY

02-14-2011

PROMULGATED BY THE TEXAS REAL ESTATE COMMISSION (TREC)
ONE TO FOUR FAMILY RESIDENTIAL CONTRACT (RESALE)

NOTICE: Not For Use For Condominium Transactions

1. PARTIES: The parties to this contract are _____(Seller) and _____(Buyer). Seller agrees to sell and convey to Buyer and Buyer agrees to buy from Seller the Property defined below.

2. PROPERTY:
  A. LAND: Lot _____ Block_____, _____
     Addition, City of _____ , County of _____,
     Texas, known as _____
     (address/zip code), or as described on attached exhibit.
  B. IMPROVEMENTS: The house, garage and all other fixtures and improvements attached to the above-described real property, including without limitation, the following **permanently installed and built-in items,** if any: all equipment and appliances, valances, screens, shutters, awnings, wall-to-wall carpeting, mirrors, ceiling fans, attic fans, mail boxes, television antennas and satellite dish system and equipment, mounts and brackets for televisions and speakers, heating and air-conditioning units, security and fire detection equipment, wiring, plumbing and lighting fixtures, chandeliers, water softener system, kitchen equipment, garage door openers, cleaning equipment, shrubbery, landscaping, outdoor cooking equipment, and all other property owned by Seller and attached to the above described real property.
  C. ACCESSORIES: The following described related accessories, if any: window air conditioning units, stove, fireplace screens, curtains and rods, blinds, window shades, draperies and rods, door keys, mailbox keys, above ground pool, swimming pool equipment and maintenance accessories, artificial fireplace logs, and controls for: (i) satellite dish systems, (ii) garage doors, (iii) entry gates, and (iv) other improvements and accessories.
  D. EXCLUSIONS: The following improvements and accessories will be retained by Seller and must be removed prior to delivery of possession:_____
     _____.

The land, improvements and accessories are collectively referred to as the "Property".

3. SALES PRICE:
  A. Cash portion of Sales Price payable by Buyer at closing ....$_____
  B. Sum of all financing described below (excluding any loan funding
     fee or mortgage insurance premium) ....$_____
  C. Sales Price (Sum of A and B) ....$_____

4. FINANCING: The portion of Sales Price not payable in cash will be paid as follows: (Check applicable boxes below)
  ❑ A. THIRD PARTY FINANCING: One or more third party mortgage loans in the total amount of
     $_____ (excluding any loan funding fee or mortgage insurance premium).
     (1) Property Approval: If the Property does not satisfy the lenders' underwriting requirements for the loan(s) (including, but not limited to appraisal, insurability and lender required repairs), Buyer may terminate this contract by giving notice to Seller prior to closing and the earnest money will be refunded to Buyer.
     (2) Credit Approval: (Check one box only)
       ❑ (a) This contract is subject to Buyer being approved for the financing described in the attached Third Party Financing Addendum for Credit Approval.
       ❑ (b) This contract is not subject to Buyer being approved for financing and does not involve FHA or VA financing.
  ❑ B. ASSUMPTION: The assumption of the unpaid principal balance of one or more promissory notes described in the attached TREC Loan Assumption Addendum.
  ❑ C. SELLER FINANCING: A promissory note from Buyer to Seller of $_____, secured by vendor's and deed of trust liens, and containing the terms and conditions described in the attached TREC Seller Financing Addendum. If an owner policy of title insurance is furnished, Buyer shall furnish Seller with a mortgagee policy of title insurance.

Initialed for identification by Buyer_____ _____ and Seller _____ _____   TREC NO. 20-10

If market conditions have changed between the date of the comparable sale and the effective date of the appraisal, an adjustment must be made to account for this fact.

The closer a comparable sale is to the effective date of the appraisal, the more reliable it will be as a value indicator.

Comparables that sold within 6 months of the appraisal date do not usually require an adjustment for market conditions, unless there has been a significant change in the market since the date of the comparable sale. On the other hand, comparables older than 1 year are not considered, regardless of any obvious change in market conditions.

Case/Example: If the effective date of an appraisal is January 1, 2005, sales that took place prior to 2004 would not be considered as possible comparables. A sale that occurred on July 15, 2004, could be considered a comparable, but it may require an adjustment for market conditions if there was a significant change in the market during the intervening period.

One of the forces that can affect values is the construction of new housing projects in a market area. Newer housing may create some rate of progression for the sales prices of older housing within the area over time. However, this might not occur immediately, especially if the new housing is priced similarly to the old. Indeed, the market for all housing, both old and new, could drop due to over supply. In areas where new housing is coming online it may be necessary to carry out an **Absorption Analysis** to determine how long it will take the market to absorb the expected available supply of housing. This analysis would take into account the future demand based on increase of population in the area, expected employment and business and infrastructure growth patterns.

6. Location Adjustments

Another important element of comparison is the location of the comparable in comparison to the location of the subject property.

Ideally, the comparable should be in the same neighborhood as the subject.

If sufficient recent comparables are not available from the subject neighborhood, the appraiser will consider sales from nearby similar neighborhoods. Even if the comparable is located in the same neighborhood as the subject, however, the appraiser must consider any differences in value that result from location.

Case/Example: Two identical properties located one block apart in the same neighborhood may have different values if one of the properties has a pleasant view, while the other does not. The values of the properties could also differ if one was located on a busy main avenue, while the other was on a quiet side street.

Adjustments for locational differences normally represent differences in site value, but they may also represent differences in external obsolescence of the improvements. In the latter case, the appraiser must be careful not to make duplicate adjustments (under location and under physical characteristics) for the same item.

7. Physical Characteristics

Most adjustments in residential appraisals are made for differences in the physical characteristics of the site or the improvements.

Comparables with differences in market conditions, conditions of sale, financing terms, property rights or location are more likely to simply be rejected from consideration.

There is a wide range of physical characteristics that can affect the price paid for a property. The appraiser must consider all of these potential differences, and make the appropriate adjustment for each characteristic where the subject differs from the comparable. Physical characteristics that are elements of comparison in residential appraisals include:

1. size and shape of lot,
2. age and condition of improvements,
3. architectural style and compatibility,
4. type and quality of building materials,
5. square footage of living area/basement/garage,
6. number of rooms,
7. functional utility,
8. equipment and amenities, and
9. site improvements.

If the residence is a sale, the appraiser should obtain a copy of the **Real Estate Transfer Disclosure Statement** (see **Figure 9-6** for California example). This statement should contain a disclosure of any physical problems with the property.

8. Economic Characteristics

Qualities such as income, operating expenses, lease provisions, management, and tenant mix are used to analyse income-producing properties.

9. Use

Zoning and other restrictions or limitations affect the use of a property. If there is a difference in the current use or highest and best use of a comparable property and that of the subject property, its impact on value shall be carefully considered.

This three-page form is an example of disclosures made by buyers in California. Your state's form may vary, but all detail important disclosures concerning the improvements (including the conditions and quality of the fixtures, appliances, etc.). Look carefully at items of importance, such as zoning, assessments, and CC&Rs.

Figure 9-6

CALIFORNIA ASSOCIATION OF REALTORS®

REAL ESTATE TRANSFER DISCLOSURE STATEMENT
(CALIFORNIA CIVIL CODE §1102, ET SEQ.)
(C.A.R. Form TDS, Revised 11/10)

THIS DISCLOSURE STATEMENT CONCERNS THE REAL PROPERTY SITUATED IN THE CITY OF _____Marina del Rey_____, COUNTY OF _____, STATE OF CALIFORNIA, DESCRIBED AS _____123 Sail Avenue, Marina del Rey CA 90292_____
THIS STATEMENT IS A DISCLOSURE OF THE CONDITION OF THE ABOVE DESCRIBED PROPERTY IN COMPLIANCE WITH SECTION 1102 OF THE CIVIL CODE AS OF (date) _____. IT IS NOT A WARRANTY OF ANY KIND BY THE SELLER(S) OR ANY AGENT(S) REPRESENTING ANY PRINCIPAL(S) IN THIS TRANSACTION, AND IS NOT A SUBSTITUTE FOR ANY INSPECTIONS OR WARRANTIES THE PRINCIPAL(S) MAY WISH TO OBTAIN.

I. COORDINATION WITH OTHER DISCLOSURE FORMS

This Real Estate Transfer Disclosure Statement is made pursuant to Section 1102 of the Civil Code. Other statutes require disclosures, depending upon the details of the particular real estate transaction (for example: special study zone and purchase-money liens on residential property).

Substituted Disclosures: The following disclosures and other disclosures required by law, including the Natural Hazard Disclosure Report/Statement that may include airport annoyances, earthquake, fire, flood, or special assessment information, have or will be made in connection with this real estate transfer, and are intended to satisfy the disclosure obligations on this form, where the subject matter is the same:

☐ Inspection reports completed pursuant to the contract of sale or receipt for deposit.
☐ Additional inspection reports or disclosures: _____

II. SELLER'S INFORMATION

The Seller discloses the following information with the knowledge that even though this is not a warranty, prospective Buyers may rely on this information in deciding whether and on what terms to purchase the subject property. Seller hereby authorizes any agent(s) representing any principal(s) in this transaction to provide a copy of this statement to any person or entity in connection with any actual or anticipated sale of the property.

THE FOLLOWING ARE REPRESENTATIONS MADE BY THE SELLER(S) AND ARE NOT THE REPRESENTATIONS OF THE AGENT(S), IF ANY. THIS INFORMATION IS A DISCLOSURE AND IS NOT INTENDED TO BE PART OF ANY CONTRACT BETWEEN THE BUYER AND SELLER.

Seller ☐ is ☐ is not occupying the property.

A. The subject property has the items checked below:

☐ Range	☐ Wall/Window Air Conditioning	☐ Pool:
☐ Oven	☐ Sprinklers	☐ Child Resistant Barrier*
☐ Microwave	☐ Public Sewer System	☐ Pool/Spa Heater:
☐ Dishwasher	☐ Septic Tank	☐ Gas ☐ Solar ☐ Electric
☐ Trash Compactor	☐ Sump Pump	☐ Water Heater:
☐ Garbage Disposal	☐ Water Softener	☐ Gas ☐ Solar ☐ Electric
☐ Washer/Dryer Hookups	☐ Patio/Decking	☐ Water Supply:
☐ Rain Gutters	☐ Built-in Barbecue	☐ City ☐ Well
☐ Burglar Alarms	☐ Gazebo	☐ Private Utility or
☐ Carbon Monoxide Device(s)	☐ Security Gate(s)	Other _____
☐ Smoke Detector(s)	☐ Garage:	☐ Gas Supply:
☐ Fire Alarm	☐ Attached ☐ Not Attached	☐ Utility ☐ Bottled (Tank)
☐ TV Antenna	☐ Carport	☐ Window Screens
☐ Satellite Dish	☐ Automatic Garage Door Opener(s)*	☐ Window Security Bars
☐ Intercom	☐ Number Remote Controls _____	☐ Quick Release Mechanism on
☐ Central Heating	☐ Sauna	Bedroom Windows*
☐ Central Air Conditioning	☐ Hot/Tub Spa:	
☐ Evaporator Cooler(s)	☐ Locking Safety Cover*	

Exhaust Fan(s) in _____ 220 Volt Wiring in _____ Fireplace(s) in _____
☐ Gas Starter _____ ☐ Roof(s): Type: _____ Age: _____ (approx.)
☐ Other: _____

Are there, to the best of your (Seller's) knowledge, any of the above that are not in operating condition? ☐ Yes ☐ No. If yes, then describe. (Attach additional sheets if necessary): _____

(*see footnote on page 2)

Buyer's Initials (_____) (_____)   Seller's Initials (_____) (_____)

EQUAL HOUSING OPPORTUNITY

TDS REVISED 11/10 (PAGE 1 OF 3)   Reviewed by _____ Date _____
REAL ESTATE TRANSFER DISCLOSURE STATEMENT (TDS PAGE 1 OF 3)

Agent: WALT HUBER   Phone: Fax: Prepared using zipForm® software
Broker: WALT HUBER REALTOR

Property Address: *123 Sail Avenue, Marina del Rey, CA 90292* _____ Date: _____

B. Are you (Seller) aware of any significant defects/malfunctions in any of the following? ☐ Yes ☐ No. If yes, check appropriate space(s) below.

☐ Interior Walls ☐ Ceilings ☐ Floors ☐ Exterior Walls ☐ Insulation ☐ Roof(s) ☐ Windows ☐ Doors ☐ Foundation ☐ Slab(s) ☐ Driveways ☐ Sidewalks ☐ Walls/Fences ☐ Electrical Systems ☐ Plumbing/Sewers/Septics ☐ Other Structural Components

(Describe: _____

_____

_____)

If any of the above is checked, explain. (Attach additional sheets if necessary.): _____

_____

_____

*Installation of a listed appliance, device, or amenity is not a precondition of sale or transfer of the dwelling. The carbon monoxide device, garage door opener, or child-resistant pool barrier may not be in compliance with the safety standards relating to, respectively, carbon monoxide device standards of Chapter 8 (commencing with Section 13260) of Part 2 of Division 12 of, automatic reversing device standards of Chapter 12.5 (commencing with Section 19890) of Part 3 of Division 13 of, or the pool safety standards of Article 2.5 (commencing with Section 115920) of Chapter 5 of Part 10 of Division 104 of, the Health and Safety Code. Window security bars may not have quick-release mechanisms in compliance with the 1995 edition of the California Building Standards Code.

C. Are you (Seller) aware of any the following:

1. Substances, materials, or products which may be an environmental hazard such as, but not limited to, asbestos, formaldehyde, radon gas, lead-based paint, mold, fuel or chemical storage tanks, and contaminated soil or water on the subject property . . . . ☐ Yes ☐ No
2. Features of the property shared in common with adjoining landowners, such as walls, fences, and driveways, whose use or responsibility for maintenance may have an effect on the subject property . . . . . . ☐ Yes ☐ No
3. Any encroachments, easements or similar matters that may affect your interest in the subject property . . . . . . ☐ Yes ☐ No
4. Room additions, structural modifications, or other alterations or repairs made without necessary permits. . . . . . ☐ Yes ☐ No
5. Room additions, structural modifications, or other alterations or repairs not in compliance with building codes. . . . ☐ Yes ☐ No
6. Fill (compacted or otherwise) on the property or any portion thereof . . . . . . ☐ Yes ☐ No
7. Any settling from any cause, or slippage, sliding, or other soil problems . . . . . . ☐ Yes ☐ No
8. Flooding, drainage or grading problems . . . . . . ☐ Yes ☐ No
9. Major damage to the property or any of the structures from fire, earthquake, floods, or landslides . . . . . . ☐ Yes ☐ No
10. Any zoning violations, nonconforming uses, violations of "setback" requirements . . . . . . ☐ Yes ☐ No
11. Neighborhood noise problems or other nuisances . . . . . . ☐ Yes ☐ No
12. CC&R's or other deed restrictions or obligations . . . . . . ☐ Yes ☐ No
13. Homeowners' Association which has any authority over the subject property . . . . . . ☐ Yes ☐ No
14. Any "common area" (facilities such as pools, tennis courts, walkways, or other areas co-owned in undivided interest with others) . . . . . . ☐ Yes ☐ No
15. Any notices of abatement or citations against the property . . . . . . ☐ Yes ☐ No
16. Any lawsuits by or against the Seller threatening to or affecting this real property, including any lawsuits alleging a defect or deficiency in this real property or "common areas" (facilities such as pools, tennis courts, walkways, or other areas, co-owned in undivided interest with others) . . . . . . ☐ Yes ☐ No

If the answer to any of these is yes, explain. (Attach additional sheets if necessary.) _____

_____

_____

D. 1. The Seller certifies that the property, as of the close of escrow, will be in compliance with Section 13113.8 of the Health and Safety Code by having operable smoke detector(s) which are approved, listed, and installed in accordance with the State Fire Marshal's regulations and applicable local standards.

2. The Seller certifies that the property, as of the close of escrow, will be in compliance with Section 19211 of the Health and Safety Code by having the water heater tank(s) braced, anchored, or strapped in place in accordance with applicable law.

Seller certifies that the information herein is true and correct to the best of the Seller's knowledge as of the date signed by the Seller.

Seller _____ Date _____

Seller _____ Date _____

Buyer's Initials (_____) (_____)

Reviewed by _____ Date _____

TDS REVISED 11/10 (PAGE 2 OF 3)

REAL ESTATE TRANSFER DISCLOSURE STATEMENT (TDS PAGE 2 OF 3)   TDS

Property Address: 123 Sail Avenue
Marina del Rey, CA 90292 _____ Date: _____

III. AGENT'S INSPECTION DISCLOSURE
(To be completed only if the Seller is represented by an agent in this transaction.)

THE UNDERSIGNED, BASED ON THE ABOVE INQUIRY OF THE SELLER(S) AS TO THE CONDITION OF THE PROPERTY AND BASED ON A REASONABLY COMPETENT AND DILIGENT VISUAL INSPECTION OF THE ACCESSIBLE AREAS OF THE PROPERTY IN CONJUNCTION WITH THAT INQUIRY, STATES THE FOLLOWING:

☐ See attached Agent Visual Inspection Disclosure (AVID Form)
☐ Agent notes no items for disclosure.
☐ Agent notes the following items: _____

Agent (Broker Representing Seller) _____ By _____ Date _____
(Please Print) (Associate Licensee or Broker Signature)

IV. AGENT'S INSPECTION DISCLOSURE
(To be completed only if the agent who has obtained the offer is other than the agent above.)

THE UNDERSIGNED, BASED ON A REASONABLY COMPETENT AND DILIGENT VISUAL INSPECTION OF THE ACCESSIBLE AREAS OF THE PROPERTY, STATES THE FOLLOWING:

☐ See attached Agent Visual Inspection Disclosure (AVID Form)
☐ Agent notes no items for disclosure.
☐ Agent notes the following items: _____

Agent (Broker Obtaining the Offer) _____ By _____ Date _____
(Please Print) (Associate Licensee or Broker Signature)

V. BUYER(S) AND SELLER(S) MAY WISH TO OBTAIN PROFESSIONAL ADVICE AND/OR INSPECTIONS OF THE PROPERTY AND TO PROVIDE FOR APPROPRIATE PROVISIONS IN A CONTRACT BETWEEN BUYER AND SELLER(S) WITH RESPECT TO ANY ADVICE/INSPECTIONS/DEFECTS.

I/WE ACKNOWLEDGE RECEIPT OF A COPY OF THIS STATEMENT.

Seller _____ Date _____ Buyer _____ Date _____

Seller _____ Date _____ Buyer _____ Date _____

Agent (Broker Representing Seller) _____ By _____ Date _____
(Please Print) (Associate Licensee or Broker Signature)

Agent (Broker Obtaining the Offer) _____ By _____ Date _____
(Please Print) (Associate Licensee or Broker Signature)

SECTION 1102.3 OF THE CIVIL CODE PROVIDES A BUYER WITH THE RIGHT TO RESCIND A PURCHASE CONTRACT FOR AT LEAST THREE DAYS AFTER THE DELIVERY OF THIS DISCLOSURE IF DELIVERY OCCURS AFTER THE SIGNING OF AN OFFER TO PURCHASE. IF YOU WISH TO RESCIND THE CONTRACT, YOU MUST ACT WITHIN THE PRESCRIBED PERIOD.

A REAL ESTATE BROKER IS QUALIFIED TO ADVISE ON REAL ESTATE. IF YOU DESIRE LEGAL ADVICE, CONSULT YOUR ATTORNEY.

THIS FORM HAS BEEN APPROVED BY THE CALIFORNIA ASSOCIATION OF REALTORS® (C.A.R.). NO REPRESENTATION IS MADE AS TO THE LEGAL VALIDITY OR ADEQUACY OF ANY PROVISION IN ANY SPECIFIC TRANSACTION. A REAL ESTATE BROKER IS THE PERSON QUALIFIED TO ADVISE ON REAL ESTATE TRANSACTIONS. IF YOU DESIRE LEGAL OR TAX ADVICE, CONSULT AN APPROPRIATE PROFESSIONAL.
This form is available for use by the entire real estate industry. It is not intended to identify the user as a REALTOR®. REALTOR® is a registered collective membership mark which may be used only by members of the NATIONAL ASSOCIATION OF REALTORS® who subscribe to its Code of Ethics.

Published and Distributed by:
REAL ESTATE BUSINESS SERVICES, INC.
a subsidiary of the California Association of REALTORS®
525 South Virgil Avenue, Los Angeles, California 90020
TDS REVISED 11/10 (PAGE 3 OF 3)

Reviewed by _____ Date _____

REAL ESTATE TRANSFER DISCLOSURE STATEMENT (TDS PAGE 3 OF 3)

TDS

Generally, only properties with the same or similar highest and best uses are used in comparable analysis.

10. Non-Realty Components of Sale

Personal property, business interests, or other items that do not constitute real property may be included in either the transaction price or the ownership interest in the property being valued. These components shall be analyzed separately from the real property. Typical examples of personal property are furniture, fixtures, and equipment (FF&E) in a hotel or restaurant.

VI. Adjustment Techniques

After identifying the appropriate elements of comparison, the appraiser measures the difference in each element of comparison between the subject property and each comparable.

The measurements may be in "quantitative terms" (a dollar amount or percentage) or in "qualitative terms" (superior, inferior, or same).

The technique used for quantitative adjustments is called **paired data analysis**; qualitative adjustments are the result of **relative comparison analysis**.

For each measured difference in an element of comparison, the appraiser must make an adjustment to account for the resulting difference in value. Adjustments are made to the prices of the comparables. If a comparable is superior to the subject in some respect, its price is adjusted downward (minus adjustment). If the comparable is inferior to the subject, its price is adjusted upward (plus adjustment).

Case/Example: A comparable that sold for $220,000 has a good view, while the subject does not. The difference in value attributable to the view is $10,000. Since the comparable is superior to the subject, the $10,000 is subtracted from the comparable sales price, to give an indicated value for the subject of $210,000. If the subject had the good view and the comparable did not, the price of the comparable would be adjusted upward (comparable inferior to subject), to give an indicated value of $230,000 for the subject.

Figure 9-7 will help you in understanding the adjustment process.

A. PAIRED DATA ANALYSIS

PAIRED DATA ANALYSIS (also known as "matched pairs analysis," or "paired data set analysis") is a technique for measuring the effect on value that is caused by differences in a single element of comparison. The process involves identifying properties that are identical (or very similar) in all aspects except one. Any difference in the sales prices of the properties is then attributed to the difference in the characteristic that varies.

Figure 9-7

Memory Tool

Positive = Negative Adjustment

Negative = Positive Adjustment

If the comparable has a positive feature or is in any way better than the property being appraised—reduce the sale price of the comparable.

If the comparable has a negative feature or is in any way less desirable than the property being appraised—increase the sale price of the comparable.

The values determined in this fashion can then be used to make adjustments to the sales prices of comparables used in actual appraisals.

Paired data analysis is best illustrated by means of an example. **Figure 9-8** shows a market data grid listing several elements of comparison for five different properties.

Figure 9-8

Comparables for a Two-Bedroom, One and One-Half Bath

1. Two-Bedroom, One and One-Half Bath
2. One or Two-Car Garage
3. Number of Square Feet in Structure
4. Number of Square Feet in Lot
5. Fireplace

The first step is to identify pairs of properties that vary in only one characteristic (**Figure 9-9**). In this example, properties #1 and #2 are identical in all respects except that property #1 has a two-car garage, while property #2 has a one-car garage. Since the price paid for property #1 is $10,000 higher than the price of property #2, an appraiser would conclude that the market value of the extra garage space was $10,000.

Continuing with this example, we can see that properties #1 and #3 (**Figure 9-10**) are identical except for the size of the living area. Property #3 has an additional 100 square

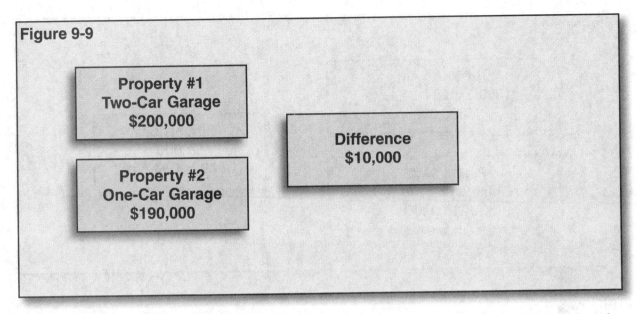

Figure 9-9

Property #1
Two-Car Garage
$200,000

Property #2
One-Car Garage
$190,000

Difference
$10,000

feet of living area, and sold for $6,000 more than property #1. This indicates that the market places a value of $60 per square foot on the additional living space.

Properties #3 and #5 vary only in the size of their lots (**Figure 9-11**). The difference in sales prices indicates a value of $4,000 for an additional 1,000 square feet of lot area.

Finally, properties #4 and #5 (**Figure 9-12**) have all the same characteristics, except that property #4 is lacking a fireplace. Based on the difference in sales prices, the indicated value of a fireplace is $5,000.

The appraiser in this example has now identified adjustment values for four elements

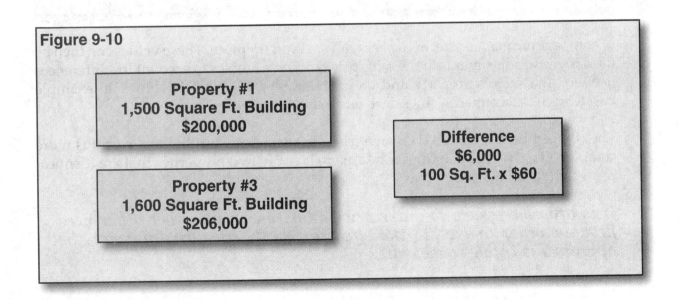

Figure 9-10

Property #1
1,500 Square Ft. Building
$200,000

Property #3
1,600 Square Ft. Building
$206,000

Difference
$6,000
100 Sq. Ft. x $60

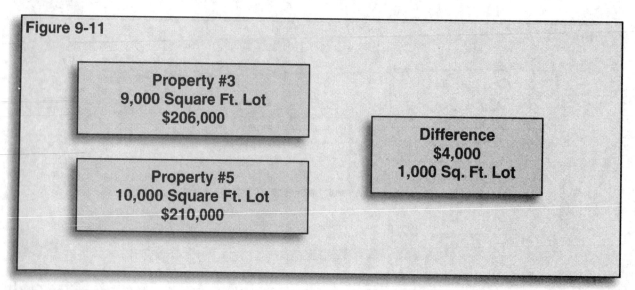

Figure 9-11

> **Property #3**
> **9,000 Square Ft. Lot**
> **$206,000**

> **Property #5**
> **10,000 Square Ft. Lot**
> **$210,000**

> **Difference**
> **$4,000**
> **1,000 Sq. Ft. Lot**

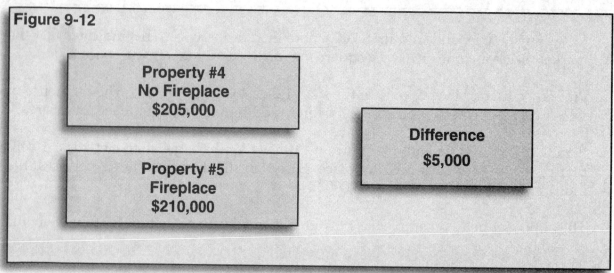

Figure 9-12

> **Property #4**
> **No Fireplace**
> **$205,000**

> **Property #5**
> **Fireplace**
> **$210,000**

> **Difference**
> **$5,000**

of comparison: garage size, living area, lot size and fireplace. These values can then be used to make adjustments to the sales prices of comparables to account for differences between the subject property and the comparables. **Figure 9-13** shows an example based on the adjustment values derived from the preceding examples.

The concept behind paired data analysis is fairly simple. But the real world is more complex. Rarely will an appraiser be able to identify two properties that are identical in all characteristics except one.

It is often necessary to make price adjustments for other differences first, in order to isolate the effect of the particular difference the appraiser is trying to measure.

Figure 9-13

#1	#2	#3	#4	#5
Property 2 Bed., 1 Bath Two C. Garage 1,500 Sq. Ft. Build. 9,000 Sq. Ft. Lot Fireplace	Property 2 Bed., 1 Bath One C. Garage 1,500 Sq. Ft. Build. 9,000 Sq. Ft. Lot Fireplace	Property 2 Bed., 1 Bath Two C. Garage 1,600 Sq. Ft. Build. 9,000 Sq. Ft. Lot Fireplace	Property 2 Bed., 1 Bath Two C. Garage 1,600 Sq. Ft. Build. 10,000 Sq. Ft. Lot No Fireplace	Property 2 Bed., 1 Bath Two C. Garage 1,600 Sq. Ft. Build. 10,000 Sq. Ft. Lot No Fireplace
$200,000	$190,000	$206,000	$205,000	$210,000

Case/Example: An appraiser is analyzing property data to determine the effect of a property's age on value. Property A is ten years old and has 1,300 square feet of living area. It sold recently for $77,000. Property B is similar, except that it is 18 years old and contains 1,400 square feet. Its sales price was $74,000. In this case, the appraiser must first make an adjustment for the size difference between the two properties, in order to isolate the effect on value of the difference in age. If the appraiser estimates that the extra 100 square feet in Property B adds $4,000 to its value, this amount would be subtracted from Property B's sales price. The difference between the adjusted price of Property B ($70,000) and the price of Property A ($77,000) could then be used to indicate the effect on value of the difference in the age of the improvements.

The example above raises another issue that comes into play when using paired data analysis. That is, the effect of one characteristic on value can often depend on another characteristic. In the example above, the amount of the adjustment to account for the difference in the size of the improvements may well depend on the age of the improvements. 100 square feet of living space may add more value (in terms of dollar amount) to a ten-year-old home than it does to an 18-year-old home.

In practice, appraisers must analyze and compare hundreds or thousands of sales transactions in order to gain an understanding of the effects on value caused by different elements of comparison.

Paired data analysis is a useful tool in this process, but more sophisticated statistical analysis is often necessary as well.

B. RELATIVE COMPARISON ANALYSIS

Relative comparison analysis uses essentially the same procedure as paired data analysis. Market data is analyzed to isolate the effect on value of different elements of comparison, and the resulting value indications are used to adjust the sales prices of the comparables in the actual appraisal. In *RELATIVE COMPARISON ANALYSIS, however, the adjustment values are not expressed in terms of dollars or percentages, but in forms of relative value (superior, inferior, or equal).*

Figure 9-14 shows a market data grid for an appraisal using relative comparison analysis. As is the case with paired data analysis, the result of relative comparison analysis is an indicated range of values for the subject property. In the example, the indicated value of the subject property is greater than the prices of comparables #1 and #3, but less than the price of comparable #2, or between $300,000 and $310,000. The appraiser must still reconcile the value indicators into a single indication of value from the sales comparison approach.

C. ANALYSIS OF PRICE PER SQUARE FOOT

In most residential appraisals, the unit of comparison is the price of the property as a whole. However, a comparison based on price per square foot can also be useful when analyzing residential properties. The procedure of selecting elements of comparison and making adjustments to account for differences is the same in both cases. The only difference is the unit price: price per total property or price per square foot.

VII. Calculation of Percentage Adjustments

Adjustments to the prices of comparables are usually calculated in terms of a dollar amount.

When an adjustment is expressed as a percentage, the percentage must be converted into dollars in order to calculate the adjustment.

In converting a percentage to a dollar figure, great care must be taken to understand exactly what the percentage is referring to. To say that Property A is worth 10% more than Property B is not the same thing as saying that Property B is worth 10% less than Property A. In the first case, the 10% is referring to the value of Property B: Property A is worth 110% (100% + 10%) of the value of Property B. In the second case, the 10% is referring to the value of Property A: Property B is worth 90% (100% - 10%) of the value of Property A. If property A is worth $100,000, the value of Property B in the first case would be $100,000 ÷ 1.1 = $90,909. In the second case, Property B's value would be $100,000 x 0.9 = $90,000.

To determine whether a percentage applies to the value of the subject property or the value of the comparable, simply state the relationship between the values of the two properties. If the relationship in value can be stated with the value of the subject first ("subject is worth X% more/less than comparable"; "subject is X% superior/inferior to

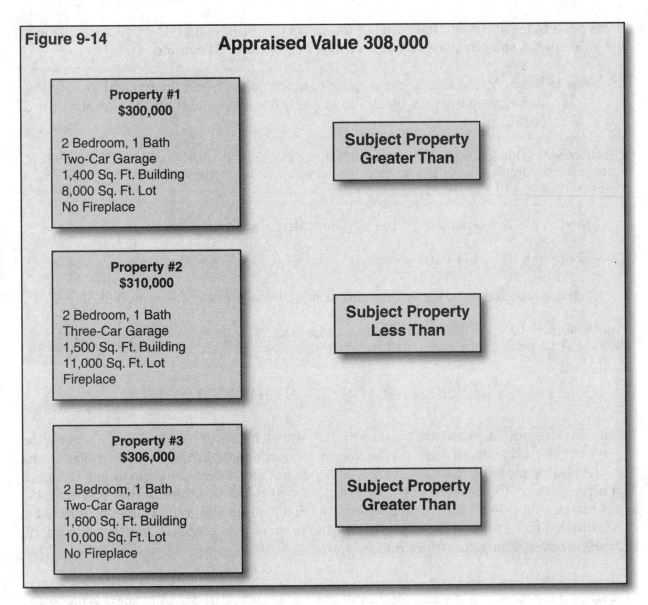

Figure 9-14   **Appraised Value 308,000**

Property #1
$300,000

2 Bedroom, 1 Bath
Two-Car Garage
1,400 Sq. Ft. Building
8,000 Sq. Ft. Lot
No Fireplace

Subject Property
Greater Than

Property #2
$310,000

2 Bedroom, 1 Bath
Three-Car Garage
1,500 Sq. Ft. Building
11,000 Sq. Ft. Lot
Fireplace

Subject Property
Less Than

Property #3
$306,000

2 Bedroom, 1 Bath
Two-Car Garage
1,600 Sq. Ft. Building
10,000 Sq. Ft. Lot
No Fireplace

Subject Property
Greater Than

comparable"), then the percentage applies to the value of the comparable. If the statement of the relationship has the comparable first ("comparable is worth X% more/less than subject"; "comparable is X% superior/inferior to subject"), then the percentage applies to the value of the subject.

If the percentage applies to the value of the comparable, the calculation of the adjustment amount is simple: just multiply the value of the comparable by the percentage amount.

Case/Example: Due to changing market conditions since the date of the comparable sale, the subject should be worth 10% more than the comparable, whose price is $80,000. The adjustment is calculated as 0.10 (10%) times $80,000 (the value of the comparable), or $8,000. Since the subject is superior to the comparable, the price of the comparable will be adjusted upward.

If the percentage applies to the value of the subject, the calculation is more difficult since the value of the subject is not known. A three-step process is required.

Step 1: If the comparable is worth more than the subject, add the percent to 1 (100%); if the comparable is worth less than the subject, subtract the percent from 1 (100%).

Case/Example: Due to a superior location, the comparable is worth 10% more than the subject. Since the comparable is worth more than the subject, add the percent (10% or 0.10) to 1.10% + 100% = 110%; or 0.10 + 1 = 1.10.

Step 2: Divide the percent by the number calculated in Step 1.

Case/Example: 0.10 ÷ 1.10 = 0.091 (rounded)

Step 3: Multiply the value of the comparable by the number calculated in Step 2.

Case/Example: 0.091 x $90,000 = $8,190 adjustment amount. Since the comparable is superior to the subject, its price will be adjusted downward.

VIII. Sequence of Adjustments

When making adjustments for a number of different elements of comparison, the sequence in which the adjustments are made does not affect the outcome of the calculation, unless one or more of the adjustments is a percentage. When an adjustment is based on a percentage, the amount of the adjustment will depend on the figure to which the percentage is applied. This figure may be the sales price of the comparable, or it may be the adjusted sales price of the comparable (the price of the comparable after adjustment for some other element of comparison).

Case/Example: The sales price of a comparable is $130,000. The appraiser determines that a + 2,000 adjustment is necessary to account for the comparable's size, and a +5% adjustment is necessary to account for changed market conditions. The amount of the adjustment for market conditions will depend on whether the percentage is applied to the sales price of $130,000, or the adjusted price of $132,000 (after adjusting the comparable sales price for size).

There are NO hard and fast rules for the sequence of adjustments in a sales comparison analysis.

It is up to the appraiser to determine the most appropriate sequence based on the appraiser's analysis of the market. In most cases, however, adjustments that concern the comparable sales transaction (such as adjustments for real property rights conveyed, financing terms, conditions of sale, and market conditions) are made first, before adjustments concerning the comparable sale property (location, physical characteristics, etc.).

IX. Reconciliation

In the final step in the sales comparison approach, the appraiser reviews all the data and the adjustments made to the comparables, and comes to a conclusion regarding the indicated value of the subject property. Normally, the adjusted sales prices of the comparables present a range of values, and the appraiser must select some value that falls within this range. This is not a mechanical process, but one that requires exercise of the appraiser's judgment and experience.

In reconciling the values indicated by the different comparables, the appraiser considers their relative reliability.

One indicator of reliability is the extent of adjustment that is required for each comparable. Comparables that require less adjustment are generally more reliable than those that require larger adjustments.

The total amount of adjustments to a comparable's sale price may be expressed as a dollar amount or a percentage, or both (see **Figure 9-15**).

Figure 9-15	
Gross Adjustment	**Net Adjustment**
- $2,000	$300,000
+$8,000	+$6,000
$10,000	$306,000

A distinction is drawn between gross adjustment and net adjustment. *GROSS ADJUSTMENT is the total dollar amount of the adjustments for the comparable, without regard to whether the adjustments are positive or negative.* Gross adjustment is the figure used to assess the reliability of a comparable. *NET ADJUSTMENT is the net sum of positive and negative adjustments.* This is the figure that is added to (or subtracted from) the sales price of the comparable, to result in the final indicator of value for the subject property.

Figure 9-16 is the sales comparison section of the Uniform Residential Appraisal Report. You will see that the report provides for three comparables and provides for adjustments (+ or -) based upon particular features. Comments can be made in the description column relating the comparable to the property being appraised.

The adjusted sale price of the comparable is based on the sale price adjusted as to the subject property. Comments as to the appraisal and applicability of comparables may be included in the comment section.

Figure 9-16

Sales Comparison Section – URAR

S A L E S There are 5 comparable properties currently offered for sale in the subject neighborhood ranging in price from $ 6 to $ 7										
There are 8 comparable sales in the subject neighborhood within the past twelve months ranging in sale price from $ 9 to $ 10										

FEATURE	SUBJECT	COMPARABLE SALE # 1		COMPARABLE SALE # 2		COMPARABLE SALE # 3	
Address 11 — 12a 12b 12c		45 — 46a 46b 46c		45 — 46a 46b 46c		45 — 46a 46b 46c	
Proximity to Subject		47		47		47	
Sale Price	$ 13		$ 48		$ 48		$ 48
Sale Price/Gross Liv. Area	$ 14 sq. ft.	$ 49 sq ft		$ 49 sq ft		$ 49 sq ft.	
Data Source(s)		e-25, e-2		e-25, e-2		e-25, e-2	
Verification Source(s)		51		51		51	
VALUE ADJUSTMENTS	DESCRIPTION	DESCRIPTION	+(-) $ Adjustment	DESCRIPTION	+(-) $ Adjustment	DESCRIPTION	+(-) $ Adjustment
Sale or Financing		52	53	52	53	52	53
Concessions		e-26, e-27, e-28	55	e-26, e-27, e-28	55	e-26, e-27, e-28	55
Date of Sale/Time		e-29, e-30, e-31	57	e-29, e-30, e-31	57	e-29, e-30, e-31	57
Location	e-14, e-15; e-16	e-14, e-15, e-16	59	e-14, e-15, e-16	59	e-14, e-15, e-16	59
Leasehold/Fee Simple	21	60	61	60	61	60	61
Site	22	62	63	62	63	62	63
View	e-5; e-6; e-7	e-5; e-6; e-7	65	e-5; e-6; e-7	65	e-5; e-6, e-7	65
Design (Style)	24	66	67	66	67	66	67
Quality of Construction	25	68	69	68	69	68	69
Actual Age	e-17; 26	e-17, 70	71	e-17; 70	71	e-17; 70	71
Condition	27	72	73	72	73	72	73
Above Grade	Total 28 / Bdrms. 29 / Baths 30	Total 75 / Bdrms 76 / Baths 77	74	Total 75 / Bdrms 76 / Baths 77	74	Total 75 / Bdrms 76 / Baths 77	74
Room Count			78		78		78
Gross Living Area	31 sq ft	79 sq. ft.	80	79 sq. ft.	80	79 sq. ft.	80
Basement & Finished	e-18; e-19; e-20	e-18; e-19; e-20	82	e-18; e-19; e-20	82	e-18; e-19; e-20	82
Rooms Below Grade	e-21; e-22; e-23; e-24	e-21; e-22; e-23; e-24	84	e-21; e-22; e-23; e-24	84	e-21; e-22; e-23; e-24	84
Functional Utility	34	85	86	85	86	85	86
Heating/Cooling	35	87	88	87	88	87	88
Energy Efficient Items	36	89	90	89	90	89	90
Garage/Carport	37	91	92	91	92	91	92
Porch/Patio/Deck	38	93	94	93	94	93	94
39	40	95	96	95	96	95	96
41	42	97	98	97	98	97	98
43	44	99	100	99	100	99	100
Net Adjustment (Total)		□101 + □102 -	$ 103	□101 + □102 -	$ 103	□101 + □102 -	$ 103
Adjusted Sale Price of Comparables		Net Adj 103a % / Gross Adj 103b %	$ 104	Net Adj 103a % / Gross Adj 103b %	$ 104	Net Adj 103a % / Gross Adj 103b %	$ 104

I □105 did □106 did not research the sale or transfer history of the subject property and comparable sales. If not, explain 107

My research □108 did □109 did not reveal any prior sales or transfers of the subject property for the three years prior to the effective date of this appraisal.
Data source(s) 110

My research □111 did □112 did not reveal any prior sales or transfers of the comparable sales for the year prior to the date of sale of the comparable sale.
Data source(s) 113

Report the results of the research and analysis of the prior sale or transfer history of the subject property and comparable sales (report additional prior sales on page 3).

ITEM	SUBJECT	COMPARABLE SALE # 1	COMPARABLE SALE # 2	COMPARABLE SALE # 3
Date of Prior Sale/Transfer	114	118	118	118
Price of Prior Sale/Transfer	115	119	119	119
Data Source(s)	116	120	120	120
Effective Date of Data Source(s)	117	121	121	121

Analysis of prior sale or transfer history of the subject property and comparable sales 122

Summary of Sales Comparison Approach 123

Indicated Value by Sales Comparison Approach $ 124

New USPAP requirements as well as secondary market rules require the appraiser to conduct research into all prior sales or transfers of the subject property for the preceding three years and to report them on the form.

In addition, all prior sales and transfers of the comparables for the year prior to the sale date of the comparables must be reported. The appraiser must disclose his/her data sources for this information.

The information for all prior sales of both subject and comparables must then be reported on the grid provided in this section. If additional space is required the appraiser is supposed to use the additional comments section on page three for this information.

Also, the appraiser must analyze all prior sales transactions of the subject and comparables for the reporting period in the space provided on the form. The reporting and analysis requirements are due to lender concerns regarding criminal property flipping.

The final portion of this section has an area to summarize and analyze the sales comparison approach, as well as record the indicated value by the sales comparison approach.

If more than three comparables are to be included for the appraisal, an additional sheet may be added (see Chapter 12).

X. CHAPTER SUMMARY

I. The sales comparison approach relies on market data to indicate the value of the subject property.

  A. Sales prices of comparable properties are adjusted to account for differences between the comparables and the subject.

  B. The appraiser analyzes sales of properties from the same market as the subject, because properties in the same market are subject to similar value influences.

II. In the sales comparison approach, the appraiser collects and verifies data, selects units of comparison, analyzes and adjusts the comparable sales prices, and reconciles the adjusted comparable prices into a single indicator of value for the subject property.

  A. Verification of data helps the appraiser form an opinion as to the reliability of the data, and may also yield additional information about the comparable sale.

  B. In order to make comparisons between properties, all prices must be stated in the same unit of comparison.

    1. Comparisons with several different units of comparison can add to the reliability of the final value indicator.

III. Comparative analysis is the most common procedure for analyzing differences in elements of comparison in residential appraisals.

  A. For each comparable property, the appraiser measures the difference between the subject and the comparable for each element of comparison.

  B. An adjustment is made to the comparable sales price for each measured difference in an element of comparison.

    1. In the case of large differences, or when market data is not available to indicate the effect of the difference on value, the comparable may have to be rejected.

  C. The appraiser must analyze each aspect of the comparable sales transaction and the comparable property that may affect the price paid.

    1. Differences or restrictions as to the real property rights conveyed in a transaction must be accounted for.

    2. If financing terms are not typical of those available in the market, the financing is not cash equivalent, and may require an adjustment based on market data.

    3. Conditions of sale (motivation of buyer and seller) should indicate an arm's length transaction.

    4. Expenditures immediately after sale are expenditures that would have to be made upon purchase of the property and that a knowledgeable buyer may negotiate into the purchase price.

5. Recent sales are preferred, because changing market conditions affect values.

6. Comparables located in the same neighborhood as the subject are the most reliable.

7. The majority of adjustments in residential appraisals are for differences in physical characteristics.

8. Economic characteristics such as income, operating expenses, lease provisions, management, and tenant mix are used to analyse income-producing properties.

9. The appraiser must be alert to any other characteristics of the subject or a comparable that could influence value, and make whatever adjustments are necessary.

D. Adjustments are made to the prices of the comparables.

1. The adjustments may be quantitative (dollar amount or percentage) or qualitative (superior, inferior, equal).

E. Paired data analysis is used to derive adjustment amounts from market data.

1. Differences in the prices paid for similar properties are attributed to the value of differences in their characteristics.

2. Analysis of large numbers of transactions is often required in order to extract reliable adjustment values.

F. Relative comparison analysis is similar to paired data analysis, except that the resulting adjustment values are qualitative instead of quantitative.

G. The formula for converting percentage adjustments into dollar amounts depends on how the percentage relationship is defined.

H. The sequence of adjustments depends on the appraiser's analysis of the market, but adjustments for transactional elements of comparison are usually made before adjustments for physical elements of comparison.

I. All the individual adjustments are totaled, then added to or subtracted from the comparable sales price to give an indicator of subject property value.

1. The net adjustment is used to calculate the adjusted price of the comparable.

2. The gross adjustment is an indicator of the reliability of the adjusted price as an indicator of subject property's value.

J. The subject property's value should fall within the range indicated by the adjusted prices of the comparables.

1. The appraiser must reconcile the various adjusted comparable sales prices, and estimate a value or range of values for the subject that is indicated by the sales comparison approach.

XI. CHAPTER QUIZ

1. For a sale to be considered comparable for purposes of the sales comparison approach to value:

    a. it must be located in the same neighborhood as the subject property.
    b. it must be competitive with the subject property.
    c. it may not include seller financing.
    d. all of the above.

2. Financing on terms that are typical of the market is called:

    a. conventional financing.
    b. cash financing.
    c. cash equivalent financing.
    d. creative financing.

3. When the subject property is superior to a comparable in some characteristic:

    a. the subject's price is adjusted upward.
    b. the subject's price is adjusted downward.
    c. the comparable's price is adjusted upward.
    d. the comparable's price is adjusted downward.

4. Which of the following adjustments would most likely be made first?

    a. Location
    b. Lot size
    c. Square footage
    d. Date of sale

5. A comparable is usually considered more reliable when it requires the least:

    a. net adjustment.
    b. percentage adjustment.
    c. gross adjustment.
    d. dollar adjustment.

Questions 6-10 are based on the following fact situation.

The subject property is a 1,700 square foot rambler, with three bedrooms, one bath, and an attached two-car garage.

    Comparable A has two baths and 1,800 square feet, and sold recently for $97,500.

    Comparable B also has 1,800 square feet, but only a one-car garage; its sales price was $92,000.

    Comparable C has a three-car garage and two baths, and sold for $95,500.

Sales Comparison Approach to Value

Market data indicates the amounts of the adjustments to be $2,000 for garage space per car, $3,500 for a bath, and $4,000 for 100 square feet of living area. Other than the differences noted here, the comparables are similar to the subject property in all respects.

6. What is the total net adjustment to the price of Comparable A?

    a. +$7,500
    b. +$3,500
    c. -$500
    d. -$7,500

7. What is the total net adjustment to the price of Comparable B?

    a. +$2,000
    b. -$2,000
    c. -$4,000
    d. -$6,000

8. What is the total net adjustment to the price of Comparable C?

    a. +$5,500
    b. +$1,500
    c. -$11,500
    d. -$5,500

9. What is the total gross adjustment to the price of Comparable B?

    a. $2,000
    b. $4,000
    c. $6,000
    d. $8,000

10. Based only on the information given, which Comparable is the most reliable indicator of the subject's value?

    a. Comparable A
    b. Comparable B
    c. Comparable C
    d. No difference

ANSWERS: 1. b; 2. c; 3. c; 4. d; 5. c; 6. d; 7. b; 8. d; 9. c; 10. c

Chapter 10
Income Approach to Value

KEY WORDS AND TERMS

Band of Investment Method
Building Residual
Cap Rate
Contract Rent
Compounding
Debt Coverage Ratio (DCR)
Direct Capitalization
Discounting
Effective Gross Income
Equity Dividend Rate
Fixed Expenses
Gross Income Multiplier
Income Capitalization
Inwood Coefficient
Land Residual
Market Rent

Net Operating Income
Operating Expenses
Operating Statement
Potential Gross Income
Pre-Tax Cash Flow
Property Residual
Recapture Rate
Reconstructed Operating Statement
Reserves for Replacement
Residual Techniques
Return of Investment
Return on Investment
Scheduled Rent
Variable Expenses
Yield Capitalization
Yield Rates

LEARNING OBJECTIVES

After completing this chapter, you should be able to:

1. explain the relationship between income and value from an investment standpoint;

2. describe the factors that determine the rate of return required by an investor;

3. list the four types of income that are used to calculate value by direct capitalization, and describe how each type of income is estimated;

4. explain the difference between market rent and scheduled rent, and their significance in the capitalization process;

CHAPTER OUTLINE

5. describe four common methods for deriving an overall capitalization rate;

6. explain the difference between a capitalization rate and an income multiplier, and their uses in appraisal practice;

7. describe the process of estimating value on the basis of residual income; and

8. calculate the present value of a future income, on the basis of specified yield requirements.

I. Use of the Income Approach

The third major approach to value is the *INCOME APPROACH, in which the appraiser utilizes an orderly approach to determine a property's value by analyzing the amount of income that the property produces.* The income approach is most commonly used when appraising investment properties, such as offices, shopping centers, or apartment buildings, but it can be used for any type of property that has an active rental market.

The Uniform Residential Appraisal Report devotes three lines to the income approach. The form states that the approach is not required by Fannie Mae. Regardless, USPAP may require it if it is necessary to properly develop the analysis of the property or if the appraiser's peers would ordinarily develop the approach. While single family residences are typically not rental property, those that are may require the application of this approach (see **Figure 10-1**).

Figure 10-1

Income Approach to Value – URAR

INCOME APPROACH TO VALUE (not required by Fannie Mae)					
Estimated Monthly Market Rent $ 38	X Gross Rent Multiplier 39	= $ 40	Indicated Value by Income Approach		
Summary of Income Approach (including support for market rent and GRM) 41					

II. Investor's Perception of Value

The income approach to value views real estate as an investment, just like stocks or bonds or savings accounts. It measures value through the eyes of an investor.

> *An investor who buys real estate is basically trading a sum of present dollars for the right to receive future dollars.*

As we saw in Chapter 2, production, the ability to create wealth by generating a return in the form of income, is a measure of value. In the income approach to value, the appraiser tries to discover the specific mathematical relationship between income and value for the subject property. Once this is done, the appraiser can then convert the income of the subject property into an indicator of its value.

To determine the relationship between income and value, the appraiser estimates the rate of return that an average investor would require in order to invest in the property. The *RATE OF RETURN is the ratio between the amount of income and the amount of the investment.* This rate is then applied to the property's income to indicate its value.

The rate of return on an investment is equal to the amount of income it produces divided by the amount the investor paid for the investment. Stated in mathematical terms:

Rate of Return = Amount of Income divided by Amount of Investment

The amount paid for the investment represents the investor's idea of its value, so the formula for rate of return can also be stated as:

Rate of Return = Amount of Income divided by Value

When this formula is rearranged, it becomes the basis for the income approach to value:

Value = Amount of Income divided by Rate of Return

Case/Example: If a property produces $10,000 of income per year, an investor who required a 10% rate of return would be willing to pay $100,000 for the property.

$10,000 income divided by 0.10 rate of return = $100,000 value

An investor expects two things:

1. repayment of the invested capital; and
2. a reward or profit as payment for the risk on making an investment.

*The repayment of capital return "of" the investment is called **RECAPTURE**, while the profit return "on" the investment is referred to as **INTEREST** or **YIELD**. The term "yield" is used to refer to the income earned by an equity investment, while "interest" refers to the income earned by a debt investment (a loan).*

A. RATE OF RETURN

An interest rate is a rate of return on capital; it is usually expressed as an annual percentage of the amount loaned or invested. An interest rate does not provide for the recovery or payment of capital (see **Figure 10-2**).

Figure 10-2   **Two Expectations of Investors**

1. **Recapture** (return **OF** the investment);

2. **Interest** or **Yield** (return **ON** the investment)

From an investor's standpoint, the rate of return is the link between value and income.

For a property that produces a given amount of income, the amount an investor would be willing to pay will depend on the rate of return the investor expects. When investors expect higher rates of return, the value of property (the amount an investor is willing to pay) is less. On the other hand, lower rates of return translate into higher property values.

Case/Example: A property produces $10,000 of annual income. An investor who required a 10% rate of return would be willing to pay $100,000 for the property.

$$\frac{\$10{,}000 \text{ annual income}}{10\% \text{ rate of return}} = \$100{,}000$$

But an investor who required a 20% rate of return would view the property as worth only $50,000.

$$\frac{\$10{,}000 \text{ annual income}}{20\% \text{ rate of return}} = \$50{,}000$$

The rate of return that an investor expects depends on two factors:

1. the risk associated with the investment; and
2. the rates of return for a risk-free investment opportunity

These two factors determine how much an investor is willing to pay for the right to receive the income from an investment.

1. Risk

The principle of anticipation (value is based on the expectation of future benefits to be derived from ownership of property) lies at the very heart of the income approach to value. The income that an investor expects to receive from an investment is future income. The amount of future income can be estimated, but it cannot be guaranteed. The element of risk, the fact that the expected income may not be realized, is a key factor in the relationship between income and value (see **Figure 10-3**).

Case/Example: If a risk free investment such as government bonds would yield a 5.5 percent return and an investor wanted an additional 4 percent return related to the risk, the investor would want a total rate of return on the investment of 9.5 percent. *(This rate is known as the CAPITALIZATION RATE or CAP RATE.)*

2. Return "of" Investment

Investors want more than just a rate of return on their investment. They want their investment returned as well over the economic life of the investment. If they did not get the investment back their effective yield would be for less than indicated.

Figure 10-3 **Graph of Relationship Between Risk and Rate of Return**

The greater the risk that the future income may not be realized, the higher the return an investor will require, and therefore the lower the value of the investment.

Case/Example: Assume an investment has an economic life expectancy of 40 years. To achieve this return of investment the investor would add 2.5 percent to the desired rate of return to see if the investment was economically viable.

100% ÷ 40 = 2.5%

In a previous example, the investor wanted a 9.5 percent rate of return to take risk into consideration. To also allow for the return of the investment, the investor would want a cap rate of 12 percent (9.5% + 2.5%).

B. COMPETING INVESTMENT OPPORTUNITIES

An investor who invests in a particular property gives up the opportunity to choose a different investment.

Throughout the global economy, investments of all sorts (stocks, bonds, savings accounts, real estate, etc.) compete with each other for capital. The amount of capital someone is willing to invest in any particular investment is influenced by the potential return (income) and the degree of risk of that investment, in relation to competing investment alternatives.

III. Income Capitalization

The process of estimating value on the basis of income is called INCOME CAPITALIZATION. (The income approach to value is sometimes called the income capitalization approach.) There are two basic forms of income capitalization: direct capitalization and yield capitalization.

In **DIRECT CAPITALIZATION**, *the income from a single period (usually a year or month) is converted directly to value*. In **YIELD CAPITALIZATION**, *the appraiser analyzes all of the anticipated cash flows over the life of the investment to determine their present value.*

A. DIRECT CAPITALIZATION

Direct capitalization is the simplest form of income capitalization. In **DIRECT CAPITALIZATION**, *the estimated income for one period (usually a year) is converted directly to an indicator of value.*

Direct capitalization is market oriented and emphasizes the analysis of market evidence and valuation by gathering the assumptions of investors. *Because of the emphasis on market rates and factors, direct capitalization is sometimes called* **MARKET CAPITALIZATION**.

The basic formula for direct capitalization is:

Value = Income divided by Rate (Cap).

In this formula, the **INCOME** *is the estimated annual or monthly income of the subject property at the time of the investment*, and the **RATE (CAPITALIZATION** or **"CAP"** rate) *is a percentage rate that is used to convert the income into value.*

Case/Example: A property has estimated annual income of $120,000. Using a capitalization rate of 12% (0.12), the value of the property would be $1 million.

$120,000 ÷ 0.12 = $1 million

Direct capitalization can also be done by multiplication, instead of division. In this case, the formula for capitalization is expressed as:

Value = Income x Multiplier (or Factor)

In the direct capitalization process, a **FACTOR** *or* **MULTIPLIER** *is simply the reciprocal of the capitalization rate*. To convert a multiplier to a rate (or vice versa), simply divide 1 by the multiplier or rate.

1 ÷ Multiplier = Rate

1 ÷ Rate = Multiplier

Case/Example: A capitalization rate of 20% (0.20) is equivalent to an income multiplier of 5.0 (1 ÷ 0.20 = 5.0). So if a property's annual income is $36,000, and the investor wanted a 20% rate of return, she would be willing to pay $180,000 for the property ($36,000 x 5.0 = **$180,000**).

To use the direct capitalization process, an appraiser must be able to determine two things:

1. the amount of income (annual or monthly) the subject property is capable of generating; and
2. the appropriate factor or rate needed to convert the income to value.

The amount of income that the subject property is capable of earning is determined by analyzing the income that is being earned by other similar properties in the market, and also by examining the terms of any existing leases on the property. The income multiplier or capitalization rate is determined by analyzing the rates of return that investors are willing to accept for investments with similar risks and returns.

B. INCOME ESTIMATION

In direct capitalization, the appraiser estimates a property's income for a single period, usually a year.

Monthly income is sometimes used to capitalize income for single-family or small multi-family residential properties. For appraisal purposes, a property's income is defined very specifically, and not necessarily in the same way that income is defined for accounting or tax purposes. Depending on the circumstances, appraisers may estimate value on the basis of:

1. potential gross income;
2. effective gross income;
3. net operating income; or
4. pre-tax cash flow.

1. Potential Gross Income (PGI)

A property's *POTENTIAL GROSS INCOME (PGI) is the total amount of revenue that the property is capable of producing at full occupancy, without any deduction for expenses.* For example, if rental rates for two-bedroom apartments are $600 per month, an apartment with ten two-bedroom units would have a potential gross income of $6,000 per month (10 x $600).

The main component of potential gross income is usually rent, the amount paid by a tenant or lessee for the right to use the property under the lease terms.

The amount of rent that is called for under an existing lease is called SCHEDULED RENT or CONTRACT RENT. In most cases, when a property is subject to an existing lease, the appraiser will determine potential gross income on the basis of the scheduled rent.

Case/Example: A certain property would rent for $20,000 per year if it were vacant and available for leasing at current market rates. However, the property is subject to an existing long-term lease with annual rent of $14,000. In this case, the appraiser would conclude that the potential gross income of the property is $14,000 per year, the amount of the scheduled rent.

For property that is not subject to an existing lease (vacant or owner-occupied property), potential gross income is determined on the basis of *MARKET RENT*, *the amount of rent the property a tenant would pay under current market conditions.* In many cases, the appraiser must determine both the scheduled rent and the market rent for a property.

Case/Example: One unit of a triplex is owner-occupied, and the other two units are leased at $750 per month. Market rent for comparable units is $800 per month. In this case, the total potential gross income of the triplex would include $1,500 scheduled rent for the two leased units, plus $800 market rent for the owner-occupied unit, for a total of $2,300.

Even when a property is subject to an existing lease, market rent may be used as the basis for calculating potential gross income. If an existing lease is due to expire in a short period of time, market rent is often a more realistic measure of the property's potential gross income.

Case/Example: A single-family residence is currently leased on a month-to-month basis at $600 per month. Market rental rates for comparable properties are $650 per month. Since the existing lease is month-to-month, a new investor (owner) could easily raise the rent to the market rate. In this case, an appraiser would conclude that market rent is a more reliable measure of potential gross income for the property.

In addition to scheduled and/or market rent, potential gross income also includes any other income that the property is capable of generating.

For example, an apartment building may have additional income from coin-operated laundry machines used by the tenants. In most small residential properties, however, the entire potential gross income will consist solely of rent.

2. Effective Gross Income (EGI)

EFFECTIVE GROSS INCOME (EGI) is defined as potential gross income, minus an allowance for vacancies and bad debt losses. This allowance is usually expressed as a percentage of potential gross income. The amount of the percentage depends on local economic conditions, supply and demand for comparable rentals, and the terms of any existing leases.

Case/Example: An apartment building has potential gross income of $15,000 per month. Vacancies and bad debts (uncollected rents) for the apartment typically amount to 5% of potential gross income. In this case, the monthly effective gross income would be calculated as follows:

Potential Gross Income $15,000.00
less Vacancies and
Bad Debts (5%) $ -750.00
Effective Gross Income $14,250.00

A deduction for vacancies and bad debt losses may NOT be necessary if the property is subject to a long-term lease with a high quality tenant.

In this case, an appraiser might conclude that the effective gross income is the same amount as the potential gross income.

3. Net Operating Income (NOI)

NET OPERATING INCOME (NOI) is the form of income that is most often used in direct capitalization. Net operating income is a more reliable indicator of value than potential or effective gross income, because it represents the amount of income that is available as a return to the investor. Properties with similar gross incomes may have widely different net operating incomes, due to differences in operating expenses.

Case/Example: Two properties each have effective gross incomes of $100,000 per year. Property A has operating expenses of $60,000 per year, while Property B has annual operating expenses of $80,000. In this case, Property A has twice as much net operating income as Property B, even though their effective gross incomes are the same.

Property A: $100,000 - $60,000 = $40,000 NOI

Property B: $100,000 - $80,000 = $20,000 NOI

To determine net operating income, all the operating expenses for the property are subtracted from the effective gross income. Payments on principal and interest are NOT deducted. Depreciation is NOT a cash expense and is NOT deducted.

OPERATING EXPENSES are any ongoing expenses that are necessary to maintain the flow of income from the property. For appraisal purposes, operating expenses fall into three categories:

1. fixed expenses;
2. variable expenses; and
3. reserves for replacement.

FIXED EXPENSES are operating expenses that do not vary depending on the occupancy of the property. They must be paid regardless of whether the property is leased or vacant. The most common examples of fixed expenses are property taxes and hazard insurance premiums.

VARIABLE EXPENSES are operating expenses that do vary depending on occupancy. They may include a wide variety of expenses, such as utility costs, property management fees, cleaning and maintenance expenses, and leasing commissions.

RESERVES FOR REPLACEMENT are funds that are set aside for replacing short-lived components of the property. A SHORT-LIVED COMPONENT is an item that has a life span that is less than the expected life of the building, such as carpeting, paint, roofing, or mechanical equipment. Normally, the amount of the reserves is calculated by dividing the replacement cost of the item by its remaining useful life.

Case/Example: The cost to replace the roofing on a building is $12,000. If the existing roof has a remaining useful life of 10 years, the annual amount to be set aside for replacement would be $1,200.

$12,000 ÷ 10 years = $1,200

Note that some items that are often listed as expenses for accounting or tax purposes are not included as operating expenses when calculating net operating income. The most notable of these are mortgage principal and interest, depreciation (book depreciation), and income taxes.

4. Pre-Tax Cash Flow

PRE-TAX CASH FLOW is also known as EQUITY DIVIDEND or BEFORE-TAX CASH FLOW. It represents the amount of income that is available to the equity investor (owner), after the debt investor (mortgage lender) has been paid its portion of the net operating income. Pre-tax cash flow is calculated by subtracting mortgage debt service from net operating income.

The amount of debt service that is deducted from net operating income includes both principal and interest payments on the mortgage loan(s).

Case/Example: A property has net operating income of $45,000 per year, and annual debt service (mortgage payments for principal and interest) of $34,000. In this case, the pre-tax cash flow is equal to $11,000 ($45,000 - $34,000).

Only cash expenses are deducted from the gross in determining cash flow. A property can be operating at a loss, because of depreciation, but still have a positive cash flow.

5. Reconstructed Operating Statements

An "operating statement" is a financial report that lists income and expenses for a property.

Owners of investment properties commonly prepare such statements for accounting and tax purposes. Although an appraiser may obtain useful information from owner-prepared operating statements, they are not used as the basis for income capitalization. *A statement of income and expenses that is used for income capitalization in appraisal is known as a RECONSTRUCTED OPERATING STATEMENT.*

There are two primary differences between a reconstructed operating statement and an owner's operating statement.

First, the reconstructed statement includes all items, but only those items, that are included in the definitions of income for appraisal purposes (as described above).

Case/Example: A reconstructed operating statement would include income in the form of market rent for an owner-occupied unit in an apartment, whereas the owner's statement would not show any income for this item. The owner's statement would probably also include an item for depreciation, which would not be found on the reconstructed operating statement.

The second major difference between reconstructed operating statements and owner's statements is that the reconstructed statement is an attempt to determine future income for the property, while the owner's statement reflects past revenues and expenses. In the income approach, it is the expected future income that is converted into value, in accordance with the principle of anticipation.

C. MULTIPLIERS AND CAPITALIZATION RATES

As mentioned above, income multipliers and capitalization rates are really just two different expressions of the same concept: the multiplier or the rate is the number that converts income into value. In the following discussion, we will refer only to capitalization rates. However, remember that any capitalization rate can be converted to a multiplier by simply dividing the number 1 by the rate.

The capitalization rate is the figure that represents the relationship between income and value.

A capitalization rate used in an appraisal of market value should reflect the rate of return that is expected by investors in the marketplace for competitive investments. Thus, capitalization rates are most reliable when they are based on an analysis of market data for comparable properties. (In an appraisal for investment value, the particular investor's required rate of return may serve as the basis for the capitalization rate.)

Appraisers use a number of techniques to estimate capitalization rates. Which technique is used depends on the availability of necessary data and the terms of the appraisal assignment. In many cases, more than one technique will be used to increase the reliability of the estimated rate. The most common techniques for estimating capitalization rates include:

1. the comparable sales method;
2. the operating expense ratio method;
3. the band of investment method; and
4. the debt coverage ratio method.

1. Comparable Sales Method (Preferred Method)

The comparable sales method is considered the most reliable means for estimating a direct capitalization rate, assuming that adequate comparable sales data are available. In the *COMPARABLE SALES METHOD, the capitalization rate is derived by analyzing the sales prices and incomes of comparable income of properties that have sold recently*. The appraiser divides the net income of the comparable by its sales price to obtain the capitalization rate.

Income Approach to Value

Case/Example: A comparable property sold recently for $120,000. The property's estimated annual income is $12,000. This comparable indicates a capitalization rate of 0.10 or 10%.

$12,000 (income) ÷ $120,000 (price) = 0.10 (Capitalization Rate)

In practice, the appraiser will analyze several comparables to determine a range of capitalization rates. The capitalization rate to be used for the subject property is then determined through reconciliation. This process is virtually identical to the process of obtaining a value indicator through the sales comparison approach to value, as described in Chapter 9.

There are three important points to remember about this method of determining a capitalization rate.

1. The sales price of the comparable may need to be adjusted to account for differences in market conditions or financing terms. (Differences in physical characteristics are normally accounted for by adjusting the calculated capitalization rate for the comparable in the reconciliation process.)

   Case/Example: A comparable property has a sales price of $250,000, and estimated annual income of $20,000. Due to changes in market conditions since the date of the comparable sale, an adjustment of minus 4% is indicated for the comparable sales price.

   $250,000 x 4% (0.04) = $10,000
   $250,000 - $10,000 = $240,000 adjusted sales price
   $20,000 (income) ÷ $240,000 (price) = 8.33% (capitalization rate)

2. The calculation of income for the comparables must be made on the same basis as the calculation of income for the subject. For example, if the income calculated for the subject is the estimated net operating income for the coming year, the income calculated for the comparables must also be their estimated net operating incomes for the coming year. (While the comparable sales method can be used to derive a capitalization rate for any of the forms of income, net operating income is generally considered the most reliable.)

3. Finally, the comparables must be similar to the subject in terms of key investment criteria, including expected resale price, expected holding period for the investment, and tax consequences of the investment.

2. Operating Expense Ratio Method

It is often difficult to obtain reliable operating expense data for comparable properties. When this is the case, the appraiser can still derive a capitalization rate for net operating income by indirect means, using the operating expense ratio (OER) method.

The first step is to calculate the capitalization rate of the comparable on the basis of effective gross income. This is done using the comparable sales method, as described above. The effective gross income of each comparable is divided by its sales price, and the results are then reconciled to get the capitalization rate for effective gross income.

Next, the appraiser must determine the average ratio of operating expenses to effective gross income (OER) for similar properties in the market. This information may be available from published sources, or determined through analysis of market data. The formula for the operating expense ratio is:

OER = Operating Expenses divided by Effective Gross Income

Finally, the appraiser calculates the capitalization rate for net operating income. To do this, the OER is subtracted from 1, and the result is multiplied by the capitalization rate for effective gross income.

Case/Example: A comparable property has effective gross income of $35,000 per year, and sold recently for $200,000. The operating expense ratio for similar properties in the market is 60%. The capitalization rate for effective gross income is calculated by dividing the income by the sales price.

$35,000 ÷ $200,000 = 0.175, or 17.5%

The result is then multiplied by 1 minus the OER, to obtain a capitalization rate for net operating income.

NOI rate = 0.175 x (1 - 0.60)
NOI rate = 0.175 x 0.40
NOI rate = 0.070, or 7.0%

3. Band of Investment Method

The band of investment method recognizes that property investments are often funded in part with borrowed money, in the form of mortgage loans. The equity investor puts up only part of the purchase price of the property, with the balance supplied by the mortgage lender. With the *BAND OF INVESTMENT METHOD, the appraiser calculates separate capitalization rates for the equity investor and for the lender(s).* The weighted average of these rates is then used as the overall capitalization rate for the property.

The capitalization rate used for the debt portion in the band of investment method is equal to the annual debt service amount (payments of principal and interest) divided by the original loan amount.

This figure can be calculated mathematically, or it can be looked up in a table of mortgage constants. A *MORTGAGE CONSTANT is simply the annual debt service divided by the loan amount.* It varies depending on the interest rate, the term of the loan, and the frequency of loan payments.

Case/Example: A loan of $70,000 has monthly principal and interest payments of $563.24, based on monthly payments at 9% interest for 30 years. The mortgage constant for this loan is the annual total of 12 monthly payments, divided by the loan amount.

$563.24 x 12 = $6,758.88 annual debt service
$6,758.88 ÷ $70,000 = 0.0966 mortgage constant

The mortgage constant could also be found in a table of mortgage constants, by looking up the constant for a 9%, 30-year loan with monthly payments.

The appraiser must also determine the capitalization rate for the equity portion of the investment. Where possible, this rate should be derived from market data, using the comparable sales approach. The rate for a comparable property can be calculated by dividing pre-tax cash flow by the amount of the equity investment. (The capitalization rate for pre-tax cash flow is sometimes referred to as the equity dividend rate, or cash-on-cash rate.)

Case/Example: A comparable sold recently for $360,000, with 25% equity and a 75% loan amount. The comparable has a pre-tax cash flow of $11,000. The amount of the equity investment is 25% of the sales price, or $90,000 ($360,000 x 25%). So the equity capitalization rate (equity dividend or cash-on-cash rate) is 12.22%.

$11,000 ÷ $90,000 = 0. 1222, or 12.22%

The equity dividend rate is usually higher than the debt capitalization rate (mortgage constant).

This is due to the fact that the equity investor has a greater degree of risk than the debt investor. The debt investor has a mortgage lien on the property, and so has first claim to the proceeds when the property is resold or foreclosed. Only the amount left over after satisfying the debt investor is available to the equity investor.

After determining the capitalization rates for debt and equity, the appraiser can calculate the overall capitalization rate to use for the subject property. This rate is the weighted average of the debt and equity rates. It is calculated by multiplying the debt and equity rates by their respective percentages of the investment, and then adding the results.

Case/Example: The subject property's sale will be financed by a 75% loan, with a loan constant of 0.0966. The appraiser has determined that 12% is an appropriate rate for equity capitalization. The debt rate is multiplied by the debt percentage, and the equity rate is multiplied by the equity percentage. The sum of the resulting figures is the overall capitalization rate.

75% x 0.0966 = 0.0725 weighted rate for debt
25% x 0.1200 = 0.0300 weighted rate for equity
0.0725 + 0.0300 = 0.1025, or 10.25% overall cap rate

The usefulness of the band of investment method depends on the availability of market data to support the estimated debt and equity capitalization rates.

In most cases, data to support the debt capitalization rate are readily available, since this rate is the mortgage constant for a loan at current market rates. Market data for equity rates can be more difficult to come by, however. When the equity rate must be derived from sources other than market data (such as published survey data), the band of investment method should only be used as a check on rates derived from another method.

4. Debt Coverage Ratio

The rationale behind the debt coverage ratio is that mortgage lenders will not loan money for an income property investment unless they are confident that the property's income can comfortably support the mortgage payment.

The **DEBT COVERAGE RATIO** *is calculated by dividing the annual net operating income by the annual debt payment.* A ratio of greater than 1.00 is typically required by most lenders, although 1.2 or 1.25 is common, with nonresidential property requiring 1.3 or 1.35.

Case/Example: A lender has determined that it is willing to make a 75% loan (75% loan to value ratio) in the amount of $150,000 secured by a property valued at $200,000 with annual net operating income of $20,000. If the annual debt payment is $15,000, then the debt coverage ratio is calculated as:

$20,000 (NOI) ÷ $15,000 (annual debt payment) = 1.33 Debt Coverage Ratio

The debt coverage ratio is a useful check, but it is NOT reliable on its own, since it is not based on market data.

D. CALCULATING VALUE BY DIRECT CAPITALIZATION

Once the appraiser has estimated the projected income for the subject property, and determined an appropriate corresponding overall capitalization rate, the calculation of value is a simple matter.

The income amount is divided by the capitalization rate, and the result is the value indicator.

Case/Example: An appraiser has estimated that a property's annual net operating income is $15,000, and that an overall capitalization rate of 10.5% is appropriate for net operating income in this case. The value of the property is then estimated as:

$15,000 ÷ 0.105 = $142,900 (rounded)

1. Gross Income Multipliers (GIM)

As noted earlier in this chapter, the conversion of income to value is sometimes accomplished by a multiplier instead of a rate. (The result is the same in either case, since multipliers and rates are simply reciprocals of each other.) When a multiplier is used to convert income, the appraiser uses multiplication, rather than division, to calculate the value.

Case/Example: The subject property has potential gross income of $9,000 per year. The appraiser has determined that the annual potential gross income multiplier for this type of property is 11. The value of the property is therefore estimated to be:

$99,000 = ($9,000 x 11)

Multipliers are most often used to convert gross income to value. The use of gross income multipliers is limited almost exclusively to appraisals of single-family residences and small multi-family residences.

Gross income multipliers may be derived for either annual or monthly income, so long as they are derived and applied consistently for all properties. In residential appraisals, a gross income multiplier is often referred to as a gross rent multiplier (GRM), since rent is usually the only form of gross income for smaller residential properties.

As discussed above, gross income is often an unreliable indicator of capitalized value, since it does not take into account operating expenses that affect the return to the investor. When using the gross income multiplier method, the appraiser simply assumes that the subject property and the comparables have similar levels of operating expenses.

2. Residual Techniques
A "residual" is something that is left over.

RESIDUAL TECHNIQUES use direct capitalization to determine the value of one component of a property, the "left over" component, when the value of the other component is known (or is estimated by some other technique). The process involves four steps.

Step 1. Determine the amount of income that is attributable to the known component of the property, by multiplying the value of the known component by an appropriate capitalization rate.

Step 2. Subtract the amount of income attributable to the known component from the total property income, to find the amount of income attributable to the unknown component.

Step 3. Convert the remaining income attributable to the unknown component to an indicator of value, by dividing by an appropriate capitalization rate.

Step 4. Add the estimated value of the unknown component to the value of the known component, to arrive at an indicator of total property value.

There are two basic residual techniques, each one following the four steps outlined above. In the *BUILDING RESIDUAL TECHNIQUE, the appraiser independently estimates the value of the land or site, and uses the residual method to find the value of the improvements.* The opposite is true of the *LAND RESIDUAL TECHNIQUE: building value is estimated independently, and the residual method is applied to determine the land or site value.*

3. Building Residual (Find Value of Improvements)

Case/Example: An appraiser has determined by the sales comparison method that the site value of the subject property is $50,000. Market data indicates that appropriate capitalization rates for land and improvements are 9.75% and 12.00%, respectively. Total annual net operating income for the property has been estimated at $17,000.

Step 1. $50,000 (land value) x 0.0975 (land capitalization rate) = $4,875 income attributable to land

Step 2. $17,000 (total income) - $4,875 (land income) = $12,125 income attributable to building

Step 3. $12,125 (building income) ÷ 0.12 (building capitalization rate) $101,000 indicated building value (rounded)

Step 4. $50,000 (land value) + $101,000 (building value) = $151,000 indicated total property value

4. Land Residual (Find Value of Land)

Case/Example: In a feasibility study, an appraiser has estimated that the cost to construct a new office building would be $120,000, and that the expected net operating income is $19,700. The appraiser has derived capitalization rates of 10% for land and 13.5% for the building.

Step 1. $120,000 (building value) x 0.135 (building capitalization rate) $16,200 income attributable to building

Step 2. $19,700 (total income) - $16,200 (building income) = $3,500 income attributable to land

Step 3. $3,500 (land income) ÷ 0.10 (land capitalization rate) = $35,000 indicated land value

Step 4. $120,000 (building value) + $35,000 (land value) = $155,000 indicated total property value

Some authorities refer to a third type of residual technique, the property residual technique. However, this is not a true residual method. In the *PROPERTY RESIDUAL TECHNIQUE, total property value is estimated by dividing total property income by the overall capitalization rate for the property.* This is nothing more than the basic direct capitalization procedure (value = income divided by capitalization rate); there is no "residual" involved.

In the above examples, we used separate rates for land and improvements. These are known as "split rates."

E. YIELD CAPITALIZATION

In direct capitalization, the appraiser estimates the value of a property on the basis of its projected income for one period, usually a year. With yield capitalization, on the other hand, property value is derived from an analysis of all the income payments that will be received over the life of the investment.

The method is profit or yield oriented; it simulates the typical investor's investment assumptions by formulas that calculate the present value of expected financial benefits according to a presumed requirement for profit or yield.

The basic process of yield capitalization has four steps.

Step 1. Select an appropriate holding period for the investment. The holding period is the life span of the investment; it is usually the length of time from the date the property is purchased by the investor until the date the property is resold.

Step 2. Estimate the amounts of all payments to the investor (cash flows) during the holding period of the investment. This includes all income from the investment, as well as the reversion, the amount received by the investor when the property is sold at the conclusion of the holding period.

Step 3. Select an appropriate yield rate (or rates) to apply to each of the cash flows.

Step 4. Using the selected yield rate(s), convert each cash flow from the property into its present value. The sum of the present values of all the cash flows is the indicated value of the investment.

IV. Discounting

The process of converting the amount of a future payment into its present value is called DISCOUNTING, or DISCOUNTED CASH FLOW ANALYSIS. This process assumes that payment of a given amount is worth less in the future than it is today, for two reasons. First of all, there is always some level of uncertainty associated with a future payment. And secondly, by waiting until sometime in the future to receive the payment, the investor loses the opportunity to use the funds for some other purpose in the meantime.

The relationship between present value and future value can be illustrated by the example of a savings account. Assume that a savings account pays 10% interest per year. If you put $100 into the account today, you will have $110 in the account after one year—the original $100 plus $10 interest. In this case, the present value of $100 is equivalent to a future value of $110.

To calculate future value from a known present value, you multiply the present amount by 1 plus the interest rate.

In the example of the savings account, we multiplied $100 by 1 plus 10%, or 1. 10, to get the future value of $110. With discounting, the calculation is simply reversed. You start with the known (or assumed) amount of the future payment, and divide by 1 plus the interest (yield) rate, to get the present value.

Case/Example: $110 (future value) ÷ 1.10 (1 plus yield rate) = $100 present value.

A. COMPOUNDING

A yield rate (or interest rate) is an amount per period, for example, 10% per year. In discounting, the yield rate must be expressed as a rate per compounding period. The **COMPOUNDING PERIOD** *is the time interval after which interest is actually paid.* (For example, compounded monthly means the accrued interest is actually paid at the end of each month.) At the end of each compounding period, the amount of the principal grows by the amount of paid interest. *The rate per compounding period is known as the* **EFFECTIVE INTEREST RATE,** *or* **EFFECTIVE YIELD RATE.**

Case/Example: An investment pays 12% per year, compounded monthly. In this case, the effective yield rate of the investment is actually 1% per month. The effect of monthly compounding is shown in the chart below.

Month	Starting Balance	Interest	Ending Balance
1	1,000.00	10.00	1,010.00
2	1,010.00	10.10	1,020.10
3	1,020.10	10.20	1,030.30
4	1,030.30	10.30	1,040.60
5	1,040.60	10.41	1,051.01
6	1,051.01	10.51	1,061.52
7	1,061.52	10.62	1,072.14
8	1,072.14	10.72	1,082.86
9	1,082.86	10.83	1,093.69
10	1,093.69	10.94	1,104.63
11	1,104.63	11.05	1,115.68
12	1,115.68	11.16	1,126.84

In this example, a present value of $1,000.00 is equal to a future value after one year of $1,126.84, at an effective yield rate of 1% per month (12% per year compounded monthly).

1. Reversion Factors

When calculating the present value of a future payment, it is customary to use financial tables or a financial calculator, rather than manually calculating the discount amount. Tables of reversion factors allow the appraiser to calculate present value by simple multiplication (see **Figure 10-4**).

Case/Example: To manually calculate the present value of a payment of $1,000 that will be made in ten years, at an effective yield rate of 10% per year, an appraiser would have to divide $1,000 by 1.10 (1 plus the yield rate) ten times, once for each year (compounding period). Using a table of reversion factors, however, the appraiser can see that the reversion factor for 10 years at 10% annual effective interest is .385543 per $1 of income. So the present value of the future $1,000 payment is $385.54 ($1,000 x .385543). The same result could be obtained by entering the payment amount, effective yield rate, and number of compounding periods into a financial calculator.

B. ANNUITIES

In discounted cash flow analysis, the term "annuity" refers to a series of regular payments, such as regular monthly rental payments under the term of a lease.

The critical characteristic of an annuity is that each payment is made at the same periodic interval. The interval can be monthly or yearly or some other regular period, but it must be the same for each payment.

*When the payments under an annuity are all the same amount (**LEVEL ANNUITY**), or when they increase or decrease at a steady rate (**INCREASING** or **DECREASING ANNUITY**),* the process of discounting the payments to their present value is simplified. The appraiser can use published financial tables or a financial calculator to determine the present value of the entire annuity.

Case/Example: An investment is projected to produce income of $1,000 per month, for a term of 5 years. *Using a yield rate of 10% per year, the appraiser can look up the corresponding present value factor (called the **INWOOD COEFFICIENT***) in a level annuity table. In this case, the factor is 47.065369 per $1 of income, so the present value of the annuity is $47,065.37 (47.065369 x $1,000). The same result could be determined by entering the term, yield rate, compounding period and periodic income amount into a financial calculator.

When the payments under an annuity vary without any regular pattern (irregular annuity), each payment must be discounted separately. The individual present values of all the payments are then added together to find the present value of the annuity.

C. YIELD RATES

As is the case with overall capitalization rates, yield rates must be selected on the basis of market data when estimating market value.

Chapter 10

Figure 10-4

Table of Reversion Factors

Years	8%	9%	10%	11%	12%
1	.9259	.9174	.9091	.9009	.8929
2	.8573	.8417	.8264	.8116	.7972
3	.7938	.7722	.7513	.7312	.7118
4	.7350	.7084	.6830	.6587	.6355
5	.6806	.6499	.6209	.5935	.5674
6	.6302	.5963	.5645	.5346	.5066
7	.5835	.5470	.5132	.4816	.4523
8	.5403	.5019	.4665	.4339	.4039
9	.5002	.4604	.4241	.3909	.3606
10	.4632	.4224	.3855	.3522	.3220
11	.4289	.3875	.3505	.3173	.2875
12	.3971	.3555	.3186	.2858	.2567
13	.3677	.3262	.2897	.2575	.2292
14	.3405	.2992	.2633	.2320	.2046
15	.3152	.2745	.2394	.2090	.1827
16	.2919	.2519	.2176	.1183	.1631
17	.2703	.2311	.1978	.1696	.1456
18	.2502	.2120	.1799	.1528	.1300
19	.2317	.1945	.1635	.1377	.1161
20	.2145	.1784	.1486	.1240	.1037
21	.1987	.1637	.1351	.1117	.0925
22	.1839	.1502	.1228	.1007	.0826
23	.1703	.1378	.1117	.0907	.0738
24	.1577	.1264	.1015	.0817	.0659
25	.1460	.1160	.0923	.0736	.0588
26	.1352	.1064	.0839	.0663	.0525
27	.1252	.0976	.0763	.0597	.0469
28	.1159	.0895	.0693	.0538	.0419
29	.1073	.0822	.0630	.0485	.0374
30	.0994	.0754	.0573	.0437	.0334

(An investor's required yield rate may be used when estimating investment value.) In some cases, different yield rates may be applied to different parts of the income stream. For example, one yield rate may be applied to calculate the present value of a property's income payments, and a separate rate in order to find the present value of the reversion payment that comes when the property is sold. In general, the yield rate is a function of the amount of risk that is associated with a particular payment.

It should be apparent that yield capitalization is much more involved than direct capitalization, since the appraiser must estimate income amounts and yield rates for each income payment that is projected to occur during the life of the investment. This approach is most appropriate when it reflects the thinking of the average investor for the type of property being appraised. For this reason, and also because of the cost involved in such detailed analysis, yield capitalization is rarely used in the appraisal of residential real estate.

Chapter 10

V. CHAPTER SUMMARY

I. The income approach views property as an investment, whose value depends on the amount of income it produces.

    A. The amount of income, in relation to the amount of the investment, is the rate of return.

        1. An investor who expects a higher rate of return will pay less for a property, in comparison to an investor who will accept a lower rate of return.

    B. The rate of return required by the average market investor depends on the degree of risk of the investment, and the rates of return available on other competing investments.

        1. According to the principle of anticipation, investors consider the potential future income from an investment. The fact that such income cannot be guaranteed is the source of risk in the investment.

        2. The higher the degree of risk, the higher the rate of return an investor will require.

        3. An investment must offer a rate of return that is comparable to rates on competing investment alternatives with similar degrees of risk.

II. Direct capitalization converts the income from a single period, usually a year, into an indicator of property value.

    A. To calculate value, the property's income is either divided by a capitalization rate, or multiplied by an income multiplier.

    B. An appraiser may capitalize potential gross income, effective gross income, net operating income, or pre-tax cash flow.

        1. Potential gross income is the total amount of income the property is capable of producing at full occupancy.

            a. For properties subject to long-term leases, potential gross income may be estimated on the basis of scheduled rent, the rent called for in the lease.

            b. For owner-occupied or vacant properties, potential gross income is based on market rent, the rent the property could produce at current market rates.

            c. Potential gross income also includes any incidental income the property may produce, in addition to the rent.

        2. Effective gross income is equal to potential gross income, minus a deduction (usually a percentage) for expected vacancies and bad debt losses.

3. Net operating income is equal to effective gross income, minus expenses of operating the property. It represents the amount of income that is available to the investor, so it is a more reliable measure of value than gross income.

    a. Fixed expenses are expenses that do not depend on the amount of income produced by the property (the level of occupancy).

    b. Variable expenses may change depending on the amount of income.

    c. Replacement reserves are amounts set aside to cover the cost of replacing short-lived components of the building. They may be calculated by dividing the replacement cost of an item by its remaining useful life.

4. Pre-tax cash flow (equity dividend) is equal to net operating income, minus debt service costs. It is the amount of income that is available to the equity investor after the debt investor has been paid.

5. The estimate of income is commonly prepared in the form of a reconstructed operating statement.

C. In direct capitalization, the capitalization rate (or income multiplier) represents the relationship between income and value.

1. In market value appraisals, the capitalization rate must be derived from analysis of market data, such as incomes and sales prices of comparable properties.

2. In the comparable sales method, the incomes of comparable properties are divided by their sales prices, to yield a range of capitalization rates for the subject property.

    a. The sales prices of the comparables must be adjusted to account for differences in market conditions or financing terms. Differences in physical characteristics are accounted for in the reconciliation phase.

    b. Income for the subject property and for the comparables must be estimated on a consistent basis.

    c. The comparables must be similar to the subject in terms of key investment criteria, such as expected resale price, holding period and tax benefits of ownership.

3. When operating expenses for comparables cannot be reliably estimated, the appraiser may use the operating expense ratio method to derive a capitalization rate for net operating income.

    a. The operating expense ratio is the average ratio of operating expenses to effective gross income for similar properties in the market.

    b. To calculate the capitalization rate for net operating income, a comparable property's capitalization rate for effective gross income is multiplied by 1 minus the operating expense ratio.

4. The band of investment technique derives the overall capitalization rate for a property by using the weighted average of separate rates for different components of the investment.

   a. The rate for the debt component is equal to the mortgage constant, which is the amount of annual debt service cost divided by the loan amount.

   b. The rate for the equity component is derived from market data for comparable sales. It is usually higher than the debt rate, due to the higher degree of risk for the equity investor.

5. The debt coverage ratio (DCR) is calculated by dividing the annual net operating income by the annual debt payment.

D. The basic formula for direct capitalization is Value = Income ÷ Rate.

1. In residential appraisals, gross income is often capitalized by means of a factor instead of a rate, using multiplication instead of division. The factor may be a potential gross income multiplier (PGIM) or an effective gross income multiplier (EGIM).

2. When the value of one component of the property (land or building) can be estimated independently, the value of the remaining component can be estimated by capitalizing the residual income attributable to it.

III. Yield capitalization involves an analysis of all cash flows that will be generated by the property during the term of the investment (holding period).

A. Each cash flow (including the expected proceeds from resale at the end of the investment) is discounted to its present value at a selected yield rate. The sum of the present values represents the indicator of subject property value.

B. Discounting calculations are simplified by use of financial tables and/or financial calculators.

C. An entire series of cash flows can be discounted in a single calculation under certain circumstances. The cash flows must occur on a regular periodic basis (annuity payments), and must be either equal (level) amounts or amounts that change (increase or decrease) in a regular pattern.

D. For appraisals of market value, the yield rate(s) used in discounting the cash flows must be derived from market data.

VI. CHAPTER QUIZ

1. The process of estimating value by capitalizing the total income from a single time period is called:

    a. direct capitalization.
    b. indirect capitalization.
    c. yield capitalization.
    d. equity capitalization.

2. A property's equity dividend is also called:

    a. potential gross income.
    b. effective gross income.
    c. net operating income.
    d. pre-tax cash flow.

3. Which of the following types of income would give the most reliable value indicator in the income approach to value?

    a. Potential gross income
    b. Effective gross income
    c. Net operating income
    d. No difference

Questions 4-6 are based on the following facts:

A property consists of 6 apartment units, with a market rent of $500 per month per unit. One of the units is occupied by the apartment manager, who receives free rent in return for managing the complex. Average bad debt and vacancies account for 10% of total rental income, and annual operating expenses are $15,000.

4. What is the property's annual potential gross income?

    a. $27,000
    b. $30,000
    c. $32,400
    d. $36,000

5. What is the property's annual net operating income?

    a. $12,000
    b. $15,000
    c. $17,400
    d. $21,000

6. If the monthly effective gross rent multiplier is 55.56, what is the indicated value of the property (rounded to the nearest $100)?

    a. $125,000

    b. $138,900

    c. $150,000

    d. $166,700

7. Using an overall capitalization rate of 8%, what is the indicated value of a property with net operating income of $35,000 per year?

    a. $280,000

    b. $437,500

    c. $560,000

    d. Cannot be determined from the information given

8. The process of converting the amount of a future payment to its present value is known as:

    a. discounting.

    b. reduction.

    c. reversion.

    d. recapture.

9. For a property that is subject to a long term lease, an appraiser would most likely estimate potential gross income on the basis of:

    a. market rent.

    b. historical rent.

    c. effective rent.

    d. scheduled rent.

10. When deriving a capitalization rate by analyzing the sales prices and incomes of comparable properties in the market, an appraiser may need to adjust the sales price of a comparable to account for differences in:

    a. market conditions.

    b. operating expenses.

    c. location.

    d. vacancy rates.

ANSWERS: 1. a; 2. d; 3. c; 4. d; 5. c; 6. c; 7. b; 8. a; 9. d; 10. a

Chapter 11
Reconciliation and Final Value Opinion

KEY WORDS AND TERMS

Appraisal Review   Relevance
Final Value Estimate   Reliability
Point Estimate   Weight
Reconciliation Judgment

LEARNING OBJECTIVES

After completing this chapter, you should be able to:

1. define the term "reconciliation" as it applies to appraisal practice;

2. describe the kinds of situations in which reconciliation is used in an appraisal;

3. describe the characteristics of a "credible" appraisal;

4. identify the factors that affect the reliability of a value indicator;

5. name the two main types of final value estimates, and list their advantages and disadvantages; and

6. explain how and why rounding is used to express value estimates.

I. Reconciliation

After applying the three approaches to value, an appraiser will end up with more than one indicator of the subject property's value. To arrive at the final value estimate, the appraiser must consider all of the evidence that supports the different value indicators, as well as the relevance of the different appraisal techniques to the particular appraisal problem at hand. This process is called reconciliation, and is the focus of this chapter.

As part of the orderly process of preparing a reconciliation, the appraiser reviews the entire appraisal to make certain that the data used, as well as the analytical techniques and the logic followed, are valid, realistic, and consistent.

Throughout the appraisal process, an appraiser develops several different indicators of the subject property's value. Those indicators may be derived by analyzing data from different comparable properties, or by using different units of comparison or different appraisal techniques.

Different value indicators serve as cross-checks against each other. Large discrepancies between different value indicators tell the appraiser that he or she has failed to consider some important value influence, or perhaps has made an error in a mathematical calculation.

The greater the number of value indicators, the greater the understanding of the market forces that affect the value of the subject property, and the more reliable the final value opinion.

But even when the value indicators all fall within a narrow range, they will rarely (if ever) be exactly the same. In the **RECONCILIATION** *step of the appraisal process, the appraiser analyzes the data and reasoning that went into the value indicators in order to arrive at a single indication of value.*

A. DEFINITION OF RECONCILIATION

In appraisal practice, the term reconciliation has two similar, but slightly different meanings. In its more limited sense, reconciliation refers to the particular step in the appraisal process when the appraiser arrives at a final value opinion.

In this step, the appraiser analyzes all the value indicators that were derived with the different approaches to value, and uses his or her judgment, based on education and experience, to provide an opinion of the subject property's value.

In a more general sense, **RECONCILIATION** *refers to the process of analyzing two or more different value indicators, and determining a single value (or range of values) that the appraiser feels is most appropriate based on all the evidence.* This process can occur whenever the appraiser needs to derive a single value from a number of alternative value indicators, not just in the case of making a final value opinion.

The word "weight" is often used by appraisers. The appraiser weighs specific data before making a judgment, gives more weight (influence) to one sale than to another, or weighs the consequence of a certain action in the market. The word weight implies that the appraiser has judged the importance, influence, or authority of the specific data being considered.

B. USE OF RECONCILIATION IN APPRAISALS

Reconciliation (in the general sense) may be required in three types of situations:

1. to reconcile values indicated by different comparable properties;
2. to reconcile values indicated by different units of comparison; and
3. to reconcile values indicated by different appraisal techniques.

1. Reconciling Values from Different Comparables

Reconciliation of values indicated by different comparable properties is very common in appraisals. The sales comparison method is considered reliable only if data from several comparable properties is available.

Consequently, reconciliation is required virtually every time comparable sales data is used in an appraisal.

Appraisers may reconcile comparable property values in order to derive:

1. an indicator of unit price (price per total property, price per square foot, etc.) for the subject property in the sales comparison approach;

2. an indicator of land or site value in the cost approach;

3. an indicator of unit cost (such as cost per square foot) in the cost approach; or

4. an income multiplier or capitalization rate for the subject property in the income approach.

Case/Example: Using the sales comparison approach to value, an appraiser analyzed three comparable sales. The resulting adjusted sales prices of the three comparables were:

Comparable #1: $85,200
Comparable #2: $81,500
Comparable #3: $87,300

To obtain a single indicator of value from the sales comparison approach, the appraiser must reconcile the three different values indicated by the comparables.

2. Reconciling Values from Different Units of Comparison

Reconciliation may also be required when different units of comparison are used. This occurs most often in the sales comparison approach.

Case/Example: In appraising an apartment building, an appraiser used the sales comparison approach to derive the following value indicators for the subject property.

Price per square foot of gross building area: $43.50
Price per dwelling unit: $52,000
Price per square foot of net leasable area: $49.00

The subject property has 11,000 square feet of gross building area, 10 units, and a net leasable area of 10,000 square feet, resulting in three different indications of value.

Value indication based on gross building area: $43.50 x 11,000 = $478,500
Value indication based on number of units: $52,000 x 10 = $520,000
Value indication based on net leasable area: $49.00 x 10,000 = $490,000

From the sales comparison approach, the appraiser must reconcile the values indicated by the three different units of comparison to reach a single indicator of subject property value.

3. Reconciling Values for Different Appraisal Techniques

The third situation that may require reconciliation occurs when different appraisal techniques generate different value indicators. An obvious example of this situation is the final value estimate, where the appraiser must reconcile the value indicators from the different approaches to value. But reconciliation of values from different techniques may occur within an approach to value as well. In the income approach, for example, an appraiser may need to reconcile values obtained by direct capitalization and yield capitalization (discounting).

II. The Reconciliation Process

Reconciliation is NOT a mathematical process.

There are no formulas involved, and appraisers should never attempt to reconcile value indicators by averaging or by using other similar mathematical techniques. Rather, reconciliation calls for judgment and experience on the part of the appraiser. The appraiser must weigh all of the evidence supporting the different value indicators, and come to a reasoned conclusion as to the meaning of that evidence, with respect to the value of the subject property.

A. REVIEWING THE APPRAISAL

There are two steps in reconciliation:

1. reviewing the processes that led to the different value indicators; and
2. making the reconciliation judgment.

To begin with, the appraiser reviews all of the data, calculations, and reasoning that led to the various value indications. One purpose of this review is to insure that no mistakes were made.

Each mathematical calculation is double-checked for accuracy, preferably by someone other than the appraiser who made the original calculations. Having a second person check the math can help turn up mistakes that would otherwise be overlooked.

The appraiser also makes sure that all appraisal techniques have been applied consistently to the subject property, and to all comparable properties, and that any assumptions were used consistently in all the various approaches and techniques. The appraiser also checks to see that:

1. all value indicators are derived on the basis of the same definition of value;

2. all properties are evaluated on the basis of the same highest and best use;

3. all properties are evaluated on the basis of the same real property interest; and

4. the characteristics of the subject property are defined consistently in the various approaches and techniques.

Case/Example: In the sales comparison approach, differences between the age and condition of the improvements of the subject property and the comparable property require an adjustment to the comparable's sales price.

In the cost approach, the effective age of the subject property's improvements is a factor in calculating straight-line depreciation. For the purposes of both appraisal methods, the age and condition of the subject property's improvements should be the same.

Another purpose of reviewing the appraisal is to assess the relative reliability of the different value indicators.

"Reliability" is a crucial factor in judging the significance of a given value indicator.

The more reliable a particular indicator, the more weight it will be given in the reconciliation process. (Assessing the reliability of value indicators is discussed in more detail below.)

The appraiser must also check to see that the information used to arrive at the value indicators is thorough and complete.

All relevant data must be considered, and all pertinent appraisal techniques must be utilized, in order to reach a credible value opinion.

Finally, the appraiser must review the appraisal to insure that the value indicators have been derived in accordance with the terms of the appraisal assignment, including the definition of value, the purpose and use of the appraisal, and any other terms that may affect the value opinion. The appraiser's job is to answer the client's specific questions concerning the value of a property.

The data selected for the appraisal, and the appraisal techniques employed should all be suited to answering the client's questions, as defined by the terms of the appraisal assignment.

Case/Example: Appraisals for mortgage loan underwriting purposes are often subject to regulations from secondary market agencies such as the Federal National Mortgage Association (Fannie Mae) or the Federal Home Loan Mortgage Corporation (Freddie Mac). In that case, the appraiser must be sure that the data and techniques used conform to the agency's regulations.

B. ASSESSING THE RELIABILITY OF VALUE INDICATORS

The reliability of a particular value indicator is a critical factor in the reconciliation process.

The reliability of a value indicator depends on three factors:

1. the amount of data that supports the indicator;
2. the level of accuracy of the indicator; and
3. the relevance of the indicator to the appraisal problem.

1. Amount of Data

All other things being equal, a value indicator is considered more reliable when it is supported by more data.

The amount of data supporting the value indicators is relevant on three levels. First, as noted in the previous paragraph, value indicators are more reliable when they are supported by data that represents a **larger sampling** of the market.

Case/Example: In the sales comparison approach to value, a value indicator supported by data from sales of 20 comparable properties is more reliable than a value that is based on only 3 comparables. In this case, the greater amount of data represents a larger slice or "sampling" of the market. According to the theory of statistics, a larger sampling results in a lower margin of error. In other words, it is more reliable.

On the second level, the reliability of a value indicator depends on the **level of detail** of the data that support it.

Case/Example: In the cost approach to value, a building cost estimate derived by the unit-in-place method is generally considered more reliable than an estimate based on cost per square foot of building area, due to the relatively higher level of detail required by the unit-in-place technique. An even more detailed cost estimate, using the quantity survey method, would be considered even more reliable still.

The third level, on which the amount of data affects the reliability of a value indicator, concerns the number of independent sources that support the indicator. A value indicator is considered more reliable when it is supported by several different sources, as compared to an indicator derived from a single source.

Case/Example: An appraiser who has estimated the value of a site by the sales comparison method may also employ allocation or extraction to obtain a second, independent indicator of site value. If the two separate value indicators are reasonably similar, the reliability of the site value estimate is enhanced.

2. Level of Accuracy

We have seen how the quantity of data supporting a value indicator can affect its reliability, but a reliable value indicator requires quality as well as quantity. The *QUALITY OF A VALUE INDICATOR is determined by its level of accuracy, and its relevance to the appraisal problem.* In assessing the level of accuracy of a value indicator, the appraiser must consider two factors:

    1. the level of accuracy of the original data; and
    2. the level of accuracy of the resulting value indicator.

The accuracy of the original data used in an appraisal is critical. If the data is inaccurate, the value conclusions drawn from it cannot possibly be reliable, regardless of the amount of data or the techniques used by the appraiser. This fundamental principle is summarized neatly by the colloquial phrase, "garbage in, garbage out."

In appraisal, the *ACCURACY OF DATA is measured by how well it has been verified.* For some types of data, such as the physical characteristics of a subject property, personal inspection by the appraiser is the most reliable form of verification. Other data, such as details of a sales transaction, are often verified by interviewing one of the parties to the transaction (the buyer or seller). The more significant the data is in terms of the value conclusion, the more important it is that the data be verified by the most reliable source possible.

Case/Example: An error in the data concerning the physical characteristics of the subject property (such as square footage of building area) could easily lead to a significant miscalculation of value. A similar error in the data concerning a comparable property is somewhat less critical, since more than one comparable will be analyzed. Any error in the comparable property data is likely to show up as a discrepancy in the adjusted sales price, in comparison to the adjusted sales prices of the other comparables. Since the subject property data is more critical to the outcome of the valuation process, it requires a higher level of verification.

In addition to confirming the accuracy of the original data, the appraiser must consider the level of accuracy of the resulting value indicator. Even if the accuracy of the original data is totally assured, the resulting value indicator may be considered more or less reliable, depending on the nature of the appraisal technique for which the data is obtained.

Case/Example: In the sales comparison approach, the sales prices of comparable properties are adjusted to account for the differences between each comparable sale and the subject property. Assuming that the comparable sales data is completely accurate, the resulting value indications (the adjusted sales prices of the comparables) may still not be 100% reliable, especially if significant adjustments were required. Each time an adjustment is made to a comparable sales price, the appraiser must determine the dollar amount of the adjustment to make. Since each adjustment amount is itself an "estimate" of value (the value of the characteristic for which the adjustment is being made), each adjustment introduces a level of uncertainty into the value indicator. The greater the number of adjustments, and the greater their dollar amounts, the greater the uncertainty in the resulting value indicator.

3. Relevance

The third factor that influences the appraiser's judgment of the reliability of a given value indicator is its relevance to the particular appraisal problem. There are two considerations when assessing the relevance of a value indicator. First, the indicator itself must be consistent with the terms of the appraisal assignment, including the definition of value used in the appraisal, and the purpose and use of the appraisal.

Case/Example: In an appraisal assignment that seeks the investment value of a property, a value indicator calculated by means of a market-derived capitalization rate would not be particularly relevant. When estimating investment value, it is the client investor's required rate of return that relates income to value, not the rate of return expected by a typical market investor.

The second consideration in assessing the relevance of a value indicator is the appropriateness of the appraisal technique used to derive the indicator. A technique is appropriate if it reflects the way the market (or the appraisal client) views the value of the subject property. Often, the relevance of an appraisal technique depends on the type of property being appraised.

Case/Example: In appraisals of single-family residences, the value indicated by the sales comparison approach is often given the most weight in the appraiser's judgment, since it is the most accurate reflection of the way that the market views the value of this type of property. Most home buyers value property on the basis of what it would cost to purchase a substitute home of comparable utility. On the other hand, an appraisal of office property might give a great deal of weight to the value indicated by the income approach, since this approach mirrors the thinking of investors who look at value in terms of the amount of income that a property is capable of producing.

C. THE RECONCILIATION JUDGMENT

After having reviewed the data, calculations and reasoning that support the different value indicators, and having corrected any errors or deficiencies that may have been discovered, the appraiser can proceed to the determination of a reconciled value.

As noted earlier, this process relies heavily on the appraiser's experience and judgment. There is no "formula" for reconciliation.

The choice of a reconciled value should be supported by the evidence in the appraisal, but the evidence should not dictate the chosen value. In the end, the appraiser's judgment must be the determining factor. As long as the appraiser has considered all the relevant evidence, and used sound logical reasoning in arriving at a value conclusion, the figure chosen by the appraiser will be a credible opinion of value.

III. Final Opinion of Value

The process of reaching a final estimate of value is essentially the same as the reconciliation process described above. The appraiser reviews all of the data, calculations and reasoning contained in the entire appraisal, and considers them in light of the terms of the specific appraisal assignment. The reliability of each value indicator is assessed, in terms of the amount of data supporting the value indicator, its level of accuracy, and its relevance to the appraisal problem. If necessary, additional data is collected and additional analysis is performed, in order to reach a defensible opinion of value.

The courts demand the appraiser testify as to one value for a particular property. Appraisal customers expect an appraiser to advise them of the value of the subject property.

In reviewing the appraisal for the final estimate of value, the appraiser must consider whether the appraisal satisfies all the requirements of a credible appraisal, as defined in the latest edition of the Uniform Standards of Professional Appraisal Practice. If it doesn't, additional data collection, verification, and/or analysis will be required before a final value estimate can be made. The answers to the following questions will indicate whether the appraisal has been completed in a credible and professional manner.

1. Has sufficient general and specific data been collected and verified in order to support the value conclusion?
2. Has any critical data (general or specific) been overlooked or omitted?
3. Has the data been described and analyzed consistently throughout the appraisal?
4. Have all relevant appraisal techniques been applied?
5. Is the derivation of all value indicators free from errors in calculation or logic?
6. Does the value conclusion reflect all the terms of the appraisal assignment, including the definition of value, the real property interest subject to the appraisal, the effective date of the appraisal, the purpose and use of the appraisal, and any other terms and limiting conditions?

A. UNIFORM RESIDENTIAL APPRAISAL REPORT (URAR)

The last section of the Uniform Residential Appraisal Report is Reconciliation. This section is shown as **Figure 11-1**.

The appraiser indicates if the appraisal was made as is or if the appraisal were subject to the property being altered, repaired or other conditions. If the construction is

Figure 11-1

Reconciliation Section – URAR

Indicated Value by: Sales Comparison Approach $ 125	Cost Approach (if developed) $ 126	Income Approach (if developed) $ 127

128

This appraisal is made 129 "as is" 130 subject to completion per plans and specifications on the basis of a hypothetical condition that the improvements have been completed, 131 subject to the following repairs or alterations on the basis of a hypothetical condition that the repairs or alterations have been completed, or 132 subject to the following required inspection based on the extraordinary assumption that the condition or deficiency does not require alteration or repair: 133

Based on a complete visual inspection of the interior and exterior areas of the subject property, defined scope of work, statement of assumptions and limiting conditions, and appraiser's certification, my (our) opinion of the market value, as defined, of the real property that is the subject of this report is
$ 134   , as of 135   , which is the date of inspection and the effective date of this appraisal.

not complete, the appraiser could indicate that the appraisal was made subject to completion in accordance with plans and specifications.

Under conditions of the appraisal, the appraiser could list any conditioning factors such as the execution of a particular lease, the issuance of a zoning variance or permits, etc.

Final reconciliation would indicate appraisal approaches used, or not used, and why. For comparables, it would indicate how they were used and why. Such as:

"Greatest weight given to Hill St. sale since it was most recent sale and only 2 doors from subject property."

The reconciliation section then reaffirms the purpose of the appraisal, which is to determine the market value, and states that the appraisal is as of the date of the inspection, which is the effective date of the report.

The opinion of market value is then set forth. The signature block which was contained in this area in the old URAR has been removed. The new report only contains a signature block located at the end of the certification. This block has space for both an appraiser and because of state licensing requirements there is also a block for a supervisory appraiser when needed.

B. POINT ESTIMATES AND RANGE VALUES

An appraisal is an opinion of value. As such, it is inherently uncertain. *Nevertheless, the majority of appraisals state the final value opinion as a single dollar amount, known as a* **POINT ESTIMATE**. In many cases, a point estimate is required by the terms of the appraisal assignment, either for legal reasons or because of client preference.

The opinion of value may be stated in an appraisal report as a single figure or range.

An alternative to a point estimate is a range value. For example, an appraiser may estimate that a property's value falls in the range of $200,000 to $220,000, and report this as the opinion of value. Range values reflect the inherent uncertainty of appraisal estimates, but they can present problems of their own. If the stated range is too broad, it can be essentially meaningless and of no use to the client. On the other hand, a narrow range may imply a level of certainty that does not exist.

Many people misinterpret a range value as a guarantee that the property's value is no lower than the bottom of the range, and no higher than the top, when in fact a *RANGE VALUE is simply the appraiser's estimate of the range in which the property's value is most likely to fall.* For this reason, many appraisers prefer to use point estimates instead of range values, even when this is not required by the terms of the appraisal assignment.

1. Rounding

As a general rule: answers should be "rounded" to reflect the input numbers that have the latest degree of precision.

Whether an opinion of value is stated as a point estimate or a range value, it is customary to round the figures to reflect the degree of certainty that the appraiser has in the value estimate.

In general the figure(s) for the opinion of value will contain no more than three significant digits (numbers other than zero), followed by the appropriate number of zeros.

A higher number of significant digits would imply a level of certainty that is unrealistic in most appraisals.

Case/Example: A value of $143,800 (four significant digits) would normally be rounded, perhaps to $144,000 (three significant digits).

The degree of rounding is a reflection of the appraiser's degree of confidence in the value opinion. Lower degrees of rounding reflect higher degrees of confidence, and vice versa.

Case/Example: In the example above, the opinion of value was rounded to the nearest $1,000, reflecting a high degree of confidence. If the appraiser had a lower degree of confidence in the opinion, the figure might have been rounded to the nearest $5,000 ($145,000), or even to the nearest $10,000 ($140,000).

C. SELF REVIEW

An appraiser should review his or her work to insure that it is easily understandable by a non-appraiser reader. Is everything documented? Can the appraiser's reasoning and logic be clearly followed and understood? Finally, the appraiser should play "devil's advocate" and pretend that he or she is a review appraiser and will be looking for any opening to discredit the appraiser's reasoning and conclusions.

Will the work pass muster in a critical review? If it won't, don't send it!

Reconciliation Section	Forms	Requirement or Instruction
This appraisal is made 'as is', subject to completion... The appraiser must select either the 'as is' or at least one of the 'subject to' checkboxes. If any of the 'subject to' checkboxes are selected, provide a description. **Reporting Format:** This appraisal is made 'as is', subject to completion... – Checkbox(es) designated with an 'x' Description (if applicable) – Text	1004/70 2055/2055 1073/465 1075/466	REQUIREMENT
My (our) opinion of the market value... The appraiser must enter the value of the subject property. The value of the subject property must match the appraised value of the subject property in the Appraiser Certification section. **Reporting Format:** My (our) opinion of the market value... – Currency, whole dollars only	1004/70 2055/2055 1073/465 1075/466	REQUIREMENT
Date of Inspection and Effective Date of Appraisal The appraiser must enter the date of the inspection, which is also the effective date of the appraisal. **Reporting Format:** Date of Inspection and Effective Date of Appraisal – mm/dd/yyyy	1004/70 2055/2055 1073/465 1075/466	REQUIREMENT

IV. CHAPTER SUMMARY

I. Reconciliation is the process of analyzing two or more different value indicators, to reach a single opinion of value.

   A. Reconciliation can also refer to the step in the appraisal process where the appraiser reaches an opinion of value.

   B. Reconciliation is used to reconcile values indicated by different comparable properties, different units of comparison, and/or different appraisal techniques.

II. Reconciliation depends on the appraiser's judgment and experience.

   A. Mathematical formulas or techniques (such as averaging) are not used in reconciliation.

   B. The process of reconciliation begins with a review of all the data, calculations and reasoning that have led to the different value indicators.

      1. All calculations must be checked for accuracy, and any mistakes corrected.

      2. The different appraisal techniques must be applied consistently to the subject property and to all comparables.

      3. The appraiser must assess the reliability of each value indicator.

      4. All pertinent data must be included and analyzed.

      5. The value indicators must be derived in accordance with the terms of the appraisal assignment.

III. The reliability of a value indicator depends on the amount of data, the level of accuracy, and the relevance to the appraisal problem.

   A. The amount of data is significant because value indicators are considered more reliable when:

      1. they are based on a larger statistical sampling of data;

      2. they are derived from more detailed data; or

      3. they are supported by several independent sources.

   B. The accuracy of a value indicator depends on the accuracy of the supporting data, and the accuracy of the technique used to derive the indicator from the data.

      1. The accuracy of data depends on how well it has been verified.

      2. The accuracy of the appraisal technique depends on the relevance of the technique to the problem.

   C. The relevance of value indicator to the particular appraisal problem influences the appraiser's judgment.

      1. The indicator itself must be consistent with the terms of the appraisal assignment.

2. The appraisal technique used to derive the indicator must be appropriate.

IV. The choice of a reconciled value should be supported by the evidence in the appraisal. The appraiser's judgment must be the determining factor.

V. The process of reaching an opinion of value is essentially the same as the reconciliation process.

A. The appraiser reviews all data, calculations and reasoning contained in the entire appraisal.

B. The reliability of each value indicator is assessed.

C. If necessary, additional data is collected and additional analysis is performed.

VI. The appraiser completes the Uniform Residential Appraisal Report's Reconciliation section.

A. The appraiser indicates if the appraisal was made as is or is subject to the property being altered.

B. Any conditioning factors are listed.

C. Any appraisal approaches used are listed.

D. The purpose of the appraisal is reaffirmed.

E. The opinion of market value is set forth and the appraiser signs and dates the appraisal report, and includes his or her appraisal license or certification number.

VII. An opinion of value of an appraised property is stated as a single dollar amount known as a "Point Estimate."

A. An alternative to the Point Estimate is the "Range Value," which is an appraiser's opinion of the range in which the property's value is most likely to fall.

B. Value opinions should be rounded.

VIII. An appraiser should review his or her work to insure that it is easily understandable to a non-appraiser reader.

V. CHAPTER QUIZ

1. The most important factor in the reconciliation process is:

    a. the amount of data.
    b. the accuracy of the value indicators.
    c. the relevance of the appraisal techniques.
    d. the appraiser's judgment and experience.

2. To reconcile different value indicators into a final estimate of value, the appraiser:

    a. calculates the average of all the different indicators.
    b. chooses the indicator that is most relevant to the appraisal problem.
    c. evaluates the reliability of the different indicators.
    d. gives the most weight to the value indicated by the sales comparison approach.

3. When reconciling value indicators, the appraiser will review the data and procedures used to derive the indicators in order to:

    a. correct any errors in computation.
    b. assess the reliability of the value indicators.
    c. insure that all appraisal techniques have been applied consistently.
    d. all of the above.

4. Which of the following is NOT a factor influencing the reliability of a value indicator?

    a. The amount of data supporting the indicator
    b. The verification of the data supporting the indicator
    c. The sophistication of the appraisal technique
    d. The relevance of the appraisal technique

5. The reliability of a value indicator derived by the sales comparison approach depends on:

    a. the number of adjustments made to the comparable sales price.
    b. the amount of the adjustments made to the comparable sales price.
    c. the manner in which the comparable sales data was verified.
    d. all of the above.

6. The amount of data supporting a value indicator is significant because:

    a. it indicates whether the appraiser has done a thorough job.
    b. a larger amount of data always leads to a more reliable value opinion.
    c. a value conclusion is more reliable when it is supported by independent sources.
    d. all of the above.

7. A value indicator derived by the income capitalization approach would be least relevant in an appraisal of:

    a. an office building.
    b. vacant land.
    c. a single-family residence.
    d. a shopping center.

8. The relevance of an appraisal technique to a particular appraisal problem would most likely depend on:

    a. the type of property being appraised.
    b. the effective date of the appraisal.
    c. the identity of the appraisal client.
    d. the size of the subject improvements.

9. A final value opinion that is stated as a single dollar amount is known as a:

    a. range value.
    b. single value.
    c. dollar estimate.
    d. point estimate.

10. In the process of reconciliation, the appraiser must choose a value that is:

    a. supported by the evidence.
    b. higher than the lowest value indicator.
    c. lower than the highest value indicator.
    d. all of the above.

ANSWERS: 1. d.; 2. c; 3. d.; 4. c; 5. d.; 6. c; 7. b; 8. a; 9. d.; 10. a

Chapter 12
The Appraisal Report

KEY WORDS AND TERMS

Appraiser's Certification
Fannie Mae Form 1004MC
Form Report
Letter of Transmittal
Narrative Report
Oral Report
PUD Addendum

Restricted Use Appraisal Report
Scope of Work
Self Contained Appraisal Report
Specific Requirements
Summary Appraisal Report
Written Report

LEARNING OBJECTIVES

After completing this chapter, you should be able to:

1. distinguish between various types of appraisal reports, and explain their uses;
2. list the essential elements that must be included in every professional appraisal report, and understand the significance of each element;
3. identify various sections of the Uniform Residential Appraisal Report (URAR), and describe how an appraisal is conveyed on this form.

CHAPTER 12 OUTLINE

I. **FUNCTION OF THE APPRAISAL REPORT (p. 379)**
II. **REPORTING REQUIREMENTS UNDER USPAP (p. 379)**
    A. Scope of Work Rule (p. 379)
    B. Oral and Written Appraisal Reports (p. 380)
    C. Narrative Reports (p. 380)
        1. Summary Information (p. 381)
        2. Definitions and Terms (p. 381)
        3. Subject Property Data (p. 383)
        4. Valuation Analysis (p. 383)
        5. Letter of Transmittal (p. 384)
    D. Form Reports (p. 384)
III. **UNIFORM RESIDENTIAL APPRAISAL REPORT (URAR) (p. 386)**
    A. Page One of the URAR (p. 393)
        1. Subject Section (p. 393)
        2. Contact Section (p. 394)
        3. Neighborhood Section (p. 395)
        4. Site Section (p. 396)
        5. Improvements Section (p. 397)
    B. Page Two of the URAR (p. 399)
        1. Sales Comparison Approach Section (p. 399)
        2. Reconciliation Section (p. 401)
    C. Page Three of the URAR (p. 402)
        1. Cost Approach Section (p. 402)
        2. Income Approach Section (p. 403)
        3. PUD Information Section (p. 403)
    D. Pages Four Through Six of the URAR (p. 404)
    E. Desktop Underwriter's Quantitative Analysis Report (p. 404)
    F. Desktop Underwriter's Property Inspection Report (p. 404)
    G. Computer and Vendor's Sotware (p. 404)
    H. Attachments to the Report (p. 411)
IV. **CHAPTER SUMMARY (p. 413)**
V. **CHAPTER QUIZ (p. 414)**

I. Function of the Appraisal Report

It is important to note that an appraisal report is not the same thing as an appraisal. An appraisal is an opinion of value, which is based on professional experience and arrived at by following recognized valuation techniques. An *APPRAISAL REPORT is the document by which the orderly process leading to the appraiser's conclusions are communicated to the intended user(s).*

The function of an appraisal report is to lead a reader from the definition of an appraisal problem to a specific conclusion through reasoning and relevant descriptive data.

The appraisal report is the final step in the appraisal process.

II. Reporting Requirements Under USPAP

Real property appraisal reports are governed by Standard 2 of the Uniform Standards of Professional Appraisal Practice which requires the appraiser to "communicate each analysis, opinion, and conclusion in a manner that is NOT misleading."

While Standard 2 of USPAP governs the content of an appraisal, it does not dictate the form, format or style of a report. These are determined by the appraiser and by the needs of the client.

The concept of the **Scope of Work** refers to the depth of necessary research and reporting required to produce a credible report that not only meets the needs of the client but that would also be considered acceptable by the appraiser's peers.

A. SCOPE OF WORK RULE

The Scope of Work Rule was developed by the Appraisal Standards Board to replace the outdated concept of departure. It was designed to provide flexibility in developing and reporting an appraisal by recognizing that the amount and depth of research varies depending upon the needs of the client and the intended use of the report. The Appraisal Board emphasizes that the amount of research and depth of reporting must not be unduly influenced by the clients desires which could result in a misleading report.

The concept of *SCOPE OF WORK refers to the depth of necessary research and reporting required to produce a credible report that not only meets the needs of the client but that would also be considered acceptable by the appraiser's peers.*

The appraiser determines the amount of work and type of report required, NOT the client.

The appraiser is the professional and has a responsibility to ensure that the report will not be misunderstood or be misleading in the marketplace. In other words, the client may not be the only user or reader of the report. The fact that a client wants something less than a complete report is not sufficient reason in itself to provide one. The appraiser has a professional responsibility to provide clients with what they actually "need," rather that what they may "want."

B. ORAL AND WRITTEN APPRAISAL REPORTS

Appraisal reports may be either oral or written.

All reports for federal loan transactions must be in writing.

Both oral and written reports may be in the form of a **Self-Contained Report** (generally a narrative), a **Summary Report** (typically a form report), or a **Restricted Use Report**.

The difference between a "Self-Contained Report" and a "Summary Report" is in the level of detail contained in the report.

Regional and local data that might take pages to report in a Self-Contained Report would typically be stated in several pages in a Summary Report.

A *RESTRICTED USE REPORT may only be used by the client alone and for one particular purpose.*

Case/Example: A report prepared to determine a partial property interest for tax purposes would hardly be relevant in obtaining a loan. Yet, an unsophisticated client might attempt to use the report for that purpose. Thus, the appraiser would probably restrict the report to the client and to that specific use.

The "Letter Opinion of Value" is NOT permitted under the rules of USPAP. This was generally a one-page letter in which the appraiser simply stated the property value.

C. NARRATIVE REPORTS

The objectives of a narrative appraisal report are to:

1. set forth in writing the answers to the questions asked by a client and
2. substantiate those answers with facts, reasons, and conclusions.

Although all written real property appraisal reports must meet minimum professional standards, the narrative report tends to be the most detailed type of written appraisal report.

A **NARRATIVE REPORT** *contains a complete description of the data relied on by the appraiser, and the reasoning that led the appraiser to the value conclusion* (see **Figure 12-1**).

The narrative report would likely be a Self-Contained report, as covered in Standards Rule 2 of USPAP.

The word "narrative" means "story." In essence, a narrative report is a story that tells the reader how and why the appraiser reached a final value conclusion. The advantage of the narrative report is that it allows the appraiser to present the material in such a way as to guide the reader through the entire appraisal process. The appraiser can explain the relevance of the selected data and the significance of the valuation techniques that were employed.

There are no hard and fast rules for organizing the material in a narrative report, other than to say that the narrative should be clearly understandable and not misleading. The structure of narrative reports may vary from appraiser to appraiser, and from one appraisal assignment to the next. Despite this variety, however, most narrative reports contain similar kinds of information, which may be grouped into several broad categories:

1. Summary Information
2. Definitions and Terms
3. Subject Property Data
4. Valuation Analysis

1. Summary Information

Summary information is often presented at the beginning of the narrative report and allows the reader to quickly identify the subject of the report and the appraisers conclusions.

Summary information includes a title page, listing the address of the subject property, the names and addresses of the appraiser and the client, and the effective date of the appraisal. The title page is followed by a table of contents which guides the reader to the different sections and subsections of the report.

A brief synopsis of important facts and conclusions is often presented near the beginning of the report as well. This summary may include such information as the appraiser's opinion of the highest and best use of the property, the estimated site value, the values derived from the three value approaches, and the final value opinion. (This information is then explained in greater detail in the data and analysis sections of the narrative report.)

2. Definitions and Terms

Several important definitions and terms that should be in the report include:

Figure 12-1

Narrative Report
Sample Narrative Report
(A Table of Contents)

I. Introduction

    1. Title page
    2. Letter of transmittal
    3. Table of contents
    4. Summary of salient facts and conclusions

II. Description, analysis, conclusions

    5. Identification of property
    6. Purpose of appraisal
    7. Description of city and neighborhood
    8. Site data
    9. Zoning
    10. Highest and best use
    11. Assessed value and taxes
    12. Description of improvements
    13. Approaches to appraisal
    14. Site valuation
    15. Cost approach
    16. Market data approach
    17. Income approach
    18. Reconciliation and final value opinion
    19. Certificate of appraisal

III. Addenda

    20. Photographs of subject property
    21. Improvements, plats, floor plan, and plot plan of subject property
    22. Sale data sheets
    23. Comparable sales map
    24. Any statistical or supporting data not included elsewhere
    25. Assumptions and limiting conditions
    26. Qualifications of appraiser

Note: Items 25 and 26 are sometimes inserted in the front of the report.

1. the definition of value used in the appraisal;
2. the definition of the property rights appraised;
3. the effective date of the appraisal;
4. the standard of value, intended use, and intended users;
5. the scope of the appraisal; and
6. assumptions and limiting conditions.

These definitions and terms may be presented in a single section of the report, or in two or more different sections. For example, the assumptions and limiting conditions are often presented in a separate section at the end of the report, while the definitions of value and property rights appraised are commonly stated in the introductory materials.

3. Subject Property Data

In narrative reports, the subject property data is often presented in a separate section, before the section containing the valuation analysis. This placement is consistent with the appraisal process itself, in which the appraiser collects and verifies the relevant data before applying the various analytical techniques.

All significant data that was relied on by the appraiser should be presented in the report, to enable the reader to understand the appraiser's reasoning.

Subject property data typically found in a narrative report includes:

1. general data relating to the region, city, and neighborhood;
2. the legal description of the subject property;
3. a description of the subject site and improvements;
4. a description of the subject property zoning, real estate taxes, and assessments; and
5. the sales history of the subject property, including the terms of any pending sale or current listing.

When data is excessively detailed, but still significant to the appraisal, it may be included as an addendum to the appraisal report, rather than in the body of the report itself. For example, if the property is subject to a commercial lease, the lease documents may be attached as an addendum to the report. In this case, the section of the report describing the subject property would contain a summary of the important lease terms, and refer the reader to the addendum for additional information.

4. Valuation Analysis

In the *VALUATION ANALYSIS SECTION of the narrative report, the appraiser describes the appraisal methods that were used in the appraisal, and the reasoning that led to the final value conclusion.* Market data that was used in the analysis (such as comparable sales data, construction cost estimates, etc.) is described as well. The valuation analysis section should include the data, techniques, and reasoning that were used to determine:

1. the highest and best use of the land as if vacant;
2. the highest and best use of the property as improved;
3. the value of the subject property site;
4. the value of the subject property under the cost approach;
5. the value of the subject property under the sales comparison approach;
6. the value of the subject property under the income approach; and
7. the final reconciled opinion of subject property value.

In addition to describing the data and processes leading up to the final value conclusion, the appraiser must certify the opinion of value.

5. Letter of Transmittal

Narrative appraisal reports are usually accompanied by a letter of transmittal. A **LETTER OF TRANSMITTAL** *is simply a brief letter addressed to the appraisal client and signed by the appraiser.* It identifies the subject property, the real property interest that was appraised, the effective date of the appraisal, and the appraiser's opinion of defined value. The letter of transmittal should also include a statement to the effect that the appraiser has performed all appropriate steps to complete the appraisal assignment (including a personal inspection of the subject property), and should identify any extraordinary assumptions or limiting conditions that apply to the value estimate.

A "Letter of Transmittal" may be a separate cover letter that accompanies the appraisal report, or it may be included as part of the report itself.

If it is included as part of the report, it is usually placed at the beginning of the report, immediately following the title page (see **Figure 12-2**).

D. FORM REPORTS

Form reports are used to communicate appraisals in a standard format.

Appraisal clients who deal with large numbers of appraisals, such as lenders, insurers, tax assessors, or relocation agencies, often require the use of form reports designed to satisfy their particular appraisal requirements.

FORM REPORTS *help to insure that all the information required by the client is included in the report, and form reports also make it easier for the client to locate and review specific items.*

Figure 12-2   **Sample Letter of Transmittal**

The letter of transmittal formally presents the appraisal report to the client. The letter may be addressed to the client, or to another person as directed, and should be prepared in compliance with standard business correspondence. The transmittal letter should contain the following elements:

1. Date of letter
2. A statement that the appraiser was requested to make the appraisal and the name of the person requesting the appraisal
3. Identification of the property appraised
4. Standard of value
5. A statement that the appraiser has made the necessary investigation and analysis to arrive at an opinion of value for the subject property
6. A reference that the letter is transmitting the report; the number of pages in the report
7. The valuation date
8. The opinion of value
9. The appraiser's signature

The letter of transmittal may contain other pertinent data the appraiser wishes to include, such as a brief description of the subject property, the certification, assumptions made in the appraisal, or limiting conditions.

When preparing an appraisal that will be communicated with a form report, the appraiser must keep in mind that the structure and contents of the particular report form are NOT a substitute for, or a guide to a competent appraisal. The appraiser must still abide by the USPAP and complete each step in the appraisal process. All relevant data must be collected and analyzed, and all appropriate appraisal techniques must be utilized, in order to make a competent value judgment.

In addition, the appraisal must be communicated in a manner that will not be misleading.

Case/Example: The space for reporting the appraiser's analysis of data is often limited on a form report. If necessary, the appraiser should attach an addendum to the form, in order to adequately communicate any analysis that are essential to understanding the value conclusions contained in the report.

Some of the most common form reports are those used in the appraisal of residential property for real estate lending purposes. These include:

1. **Uniform Residential Appraisal Report** (Fannie Mae Form 1004/Freddie Mac Form 70). Used for appraisals of single-family residences (see **Figure 12-3**).

2. **Individual Condominium Appraisal Report** (Fannie Mae Form 1073/Freddie Mac Form 465). A specialized appraisal form for individual condominium units.

3. **Small Residential Income Property Appraisal Repor**t (Fannie Mae Form 1025/ Freddie Mac Form 72). Intended for up to four residential rental units.

In March 2005, the secondary market approved new updated forms to both comply with new USPAP provisions and to address certain lender concerns regarding fraudulent property transfers. There were a total of eleven new approved forms. The most commonly used of these will be presented in this and the following chapter.

III. Uniform Residential Appraisal Report (URAR)

The Uniform Residential Appraisal Report form is one of the most commonly used form reports in the appraisal industry. This report is used in the vast majority of single-family residential appraisals made for mortgage lending purposes, and is required by most secondary market agencies, including the:

1. Federal National Mortgage Association (also called Fannie Mae);

2. Federal Home Loan Mortgage Corporation (also called Freddie Mac);

3. Government National Mortgage Association (also called Ginnie Mae), which purchases loans insured by the Federal Housing Administration and the Farmers Home Administration (FMHA), and loans insured by the Department of Veterans Affairs.

While we have previously discussed separate areas from the URAR as they applied to previous chapters we have included the entire form in this chapter in order to allow the student to acquire a more complete understanding of the form. We will also discuss the completion of the entire form in order to add emphasis to prior explanations as to the individual sections.

The URAR is a multi-page form. The first page is used to describe the subject property. The second page is devoted to an analysis of the sales comparison approach. Page three is devoted to space for additional comments, the cost approach, the income approach, and project information for planned unit developments. The last three pages are filled with the limiting conditions and the appraiser's certification. At the top of each page is a title line with a space for the appraiser's file number. The remainder of each page is divided into the sections described below.

The Appraisal Report

Figure 12-3

2

Uniform Residential Appraisal Report

File # 3   4   4a

The purpose of this summary appraisal report is to provide the lender/client with an accurate, and adequately supported, opinion of the market value of the subject property.

SUBJECT

Property Address 6		City 7	State 8	Zip Code 9
Borrower 10	Owner of Public Record 11		County 12	

Legal Description 13

Assessor's Parcel # 14   Tax Year 15   R.E. Taxes $ 16

Neighborhood Name 17   Map Reference 18   Census Tract 19

Occupant ☐20 Owner ☐21 Tenant ☐22 Vacant   Special Assessments $ 23   ☐24 PUD   HOA $ 25   ☐26 per year ☐27 per month

Property Rights Appraised ☐28 Fee Simple ☐29 Leasehold ☐30 Other (describe) 31

Assignment Type ☐32 Purchase Transaction ☐33 Refinance Transaction ☐34 Other (describe) 35

Lender/Client 36   Address 37

Is the subject property currently offered for sale or has it been offered for sale in the twelve months prior to the effective date of this appraisal? ☐38 Yes ☐39 No

Report data source(s) used, offering price(s), and date(s).   e-2; 40

CONTRACT

I ☐41 did ☐42 did not analyze the contract for sale for the subject purchase transaction. Explain the results of the analysis of the contract for sale or why the analysis was not performed.   e-3; 43

Contract Price $ 44   Date of Contract 45   Is the property seller the owner of public record? ☐46 Yes ☐47 No Data Source(s) 48

Is there any financial assistance (loan charges, sale concessions, gift or downpayment assistance, etc.) to be paid by any party on behalf of the borrower? ☐49 Yes ☐50 No
If Yes, report the total dollar amount and describe the items to be paid.   51a; e-4; 51b

NEIGHBORHOOD

Note: Race and the racial composition of the neighborhood are not appraisal factors.

Neighborhood Characteristics	One-Unit Housing Trends	One-Unit Housing		Present Land Use %	
Location ☐52 Urban ☐53 Suburban ☐54 Rural	Property Values ☐61 Increasing ☐62 Stable ☐63 Declining	PRICE	AGE	One-Unit	76 %
Built-Up ☐55 Over 75% ☐56 25–75% ☐57 Under 25%	Demand/Supply ☐64 Shortage ☐65 In Balance ☐66 Over Supply	$ (000)	(yrs)	2-4 Unit	77 %
Growth ☐58 Rapid ☐59 Stable ☐60 Slow	Marketing Time ☐67 Under 3 mths ☐68 3–6 mths ☐69 Over 6 mths	70 Low	73	Multi-Family	78 %
Neighborhood Boundaries 82		71 High	74	Commercial	79 %
		72 Pred.	75	Other	81 %

Neighborhood Description 83

Market Conditions (including support for the above conclusions) 84

SITE

Dimensions 85   Area 86   Shape 87   View e-5; e-6; e-7

Specific Zoning Classification 89   Zoning Description 90

Zoning Compliance ☐91 Legal ☐92 Legal Nonconforming (Grandfathered Use) ☐93 No Zoning ☐94 Illegal (describe) 95

Is the highest and best use of the subject property as improved (or as proposed per plans and specifications) the present use? ☐96 Yes ☐97 No If No, describe 98

Utilities	Public	Other (describe)		Public	Other (describe)	Off-site Improvements—Type	Public	Private
Electricity	☐99	☐100 101	Water	☐105	☐106 107	Street 111	☐112	☐113
Gas	☐102	☐103 104	Sanitary Sewer	☐108	☐109 110	Alley 114	☐115	☐116

FEMA Special Flood Hazard Area ☐117 Yes ☐118 No FEMA Flood Zone 119   FEMA Map # 120   FEMA Map Date 121

Are the utilities and off-site improvements typical for the market area? ☐122 Yes ☐123 No If No, describe 124

Are there any adverse site conditions or external factors (easements, encroachments, environmental conditions, land uses, etc.)? ☐125 Yes ☐126 No If Yes, describe 127

IMPROVEMENTS

General Description	Foundation	Exterior Description materials/condition	Interior materials/condition
Units ☐128 One ☐129 One with Accessory Unit	☐140 Concrete Slab ☐141 Crawl Space	Foundation Walls 152	Floors 159
# of Stories 130	☐142 Full Basement ☐143 Partial Basement	Exterior Walls 153	Walls 160
Type ☐131 Det. ☐132 Att. ☐133 S-Det./End Unit	Basement Area 144 sq. ft.	Roof Surface 154	Trim/Finish 161
☐134 Existing ☐135 Proposed ☐136 Under Const.	Basement Finish 145 %	Gutters & Downspouts 155	Bath Floor 162
Design (Style) 137	☐146 Outside Entry/Exit ☐147 Sump Pump	Window Type 156	Bath Wainscot 163
Year Built e-8; 138	Evidence of ☐148 Infestation	Storm Sash/Insulated 157	Car Storage ☐195 None
Effective Age (Yrs) 139	☐150 Dampness ☐151 Settlement	Screens 158	☐196 Driveway # of Cars 197
Attic ☐164 None	Heating ☐171 FWA ☐172 HWBB ☐173 Radiant	Amenities ☐187 Woodstove(s) # 188	Driveway Surface 198
☐165 Drop Stair ☐166 Stairs	☐174 Other 175 Fuel 176	☐181 Fireplace(s)# 182 ☐189 Fence 190	☐199 Garage # of Cars 200
☐167 Floor ☐168 Scuttle	Cooling ☐177 Central Air Conditioning	☐183 Patio/Deck 184 ☐191 Porch 192	☐201 Carport # of Cars 202
☐169 Finished ☐170 Heated	☐178 Individual ☐179 Other 180	☐185 Pool 186 ☐193 Other 194	☐203 Att. ☐204 Det. ☐205 Built-in

Appliances ☐206 Refrigerator ☐207 Range/Oven ☐208 Dishwasher ☐209 Disposal ☐210 Microwave ☐211 Washer/Dryer ☐212 Other (describe) 213

Finished area above grade contains: 214 Rooms 215 Bedrooms 216 Bath(s) 217 Square Feet of Gross Living Area Above Grade

Additional features (special energy efficient items, etc.) 218

Describe the condition of the property (including needed repairs, deterioration, renovations, remodeling, etc.).   e-9; e-10; e-11; e-12; e-13; 219

Are there any physical deficiencies or adverse conditions that affect the livability, soundness, or structural integrity of the property? ☐220 Yes ☐221 No If Yes, describe 222

Does the property generally conform to the neighborhood (functional utility, style, condition, use, construction, etc.)? ☐223 Yes ☐224 No If No, describe 225

Freddie Mac Form 70 March 2005   226   **UAD Version 9/2011** Page 1 of 6   Fannie Mae Form 1004 March 2005

URAR – Page 2

Uniform Residential Appraisal Report
File # 3 4 4a

2

There are **5** comparable properties currently offered for sale in the subject neighborhood ranging in price from $ **6** to $ **7**

There are **8** comparable sales in the subject neighborhood within the past twelve months ranging in sale price from $ **9** to $ **10**

FEATURE	SUBJECT	COMPARABLE SALE # 1	+(-) $ Adjustment	COMPARABLE SALE # 2	+(-) $ Adjustment	COMPARABLE SALE # 3	+(-) $ Adjustment
Address	11	45		45		45	
	12a 12b 12c	46a 46b 46c		46a 46b 46c		46a 46b 46c	
Proximity to Subject		47		47		47	
Sale Price	$ 13		$ 48		$ 48		$ 48
Sale Price/Gross Liv. Area	$ 14 sq. ft.	$ 49 sq. ft.		$ 49 sq ft		$ 49 sq ft.	
Data Source(s)		e-25, e-2		e-25, e-2		e-25, e-2	
Verification Source(s)		51		51		51	
VALUE ADJUSTMENTS	**DESCRIPTION**	**DESCRIPTION**	**+(-) $ Adjustment**	**DESCRIPTION**	**+(-) $ Adjustment**	**DESCRIPTION**	**+(-) $ Adjustment**
Sale or Financing		52	53	52	53	52	53
Concessions		e-26, e-27, e-28	55	e-26, e-27, e-28	55	e-26, e-27, e-29	55
Date of Sale/Time		e-29, e-30, e-31	57	e-29, e-30, e-31	57	e-29, e-30, e-31	57
Location	e-14; e-15; e-16	e-14; e-15; e-16	59	e-14; e-15; e-16	59	e-14; e-15; e-16	59
Leasehold/Fee Simple	21	60	61	60	61	60	61
Site	22	62	63	62	63	62	63
View	e-5; e-6; e-7	e-5; e-6; e-7	65	e-5; e-6; e-7	65	e-5; e-6; e-7	65
Design (Style)	24	66	67	66	67	66	67
Quality of Construction	25	68	69	68	69	68	69
Actual Age	e-17; 26	e-17; 70	71	e-17; 70	71	e-17; 70	71
Condition	27	72	73	72	73	72	73
Above Grade	Total / Bdrms / Baths	Total / Bdrms / Baths	74	Total / Bdrms / Baths	74	Total / Bdrms / Baths	74
Room Count	28 / 29 / 30	75 / 76 / 77	78	75 / 76 / 77	78	75 / 76 / 77	78
Gross Living Area	31 sq. ft.	79 sq. ft.	80	79 sq. ft.	80	79 sq ft	80
Basement & Finished	e-18, e-19, e-20	e-18, e-19, e-20	82	e-18; e-19; e-20	82	e-18; e-19; e-20	82
Rooms Below Grade	e-21, e-22, e-23, e-24	e-21, e-22, e-23, e-24	84	e-21, e-22, e-23, e-24	84	e-21, e-22, e-23, e-24	84
Functional Utility	34	85	86	85	86	85	86
Heating/Cooling	35	87	88	87	88	87	88
Energy Efficient Items	36	89	90	89	90	89	90
Garage/Carport	37	91	92	91	92	91	92
Porch/Patio/Deck	38	93	94	93	94	93	94
39	40	95	96	95	96	95	96
41	42	97	98	97	98	97	98
43	44	99	100	99	100	99	100
Net Adjustment (Total)		101 + 102 -	$ 103	101 + 102 -	$ 103	101 + 102 -	$ 103
Adjusted Sale Price of Comparables		Net Adj. 103a % Gross Adj. 103b %	$ 104	Net Adj. 103a % Gross Adj. 103b %	$ 104	Net Adj. 103a % Gross Adj. 103b %	$ 104

I **105** did **106** did not research the sale or transfer history of the subject property and comparable sales. If not, explain **107**

My research **108** did **109** did not reveal any prior sales or transfers of the subject property for the three years prior to the effective date of this appraisal.

Data source(s) **110**

My research **111** did **112** did not reveal any prior sales or transfers of the comparable sales for the year prior to the date of sale of the comparable sale.

Data source(s) **113**

Report the results of the research and analysis of the prior sale or transfer history of the subject property and comparable sales (report additional prior sales on page 3).

ITEM	SUBJECT	COMPARABLE SALE # 1	COMPARABLE SALE # 2	COMPARABLE SALE # 3
Date of Prior Sale/Transfer	114	118	118	118
Price of Prior Sale/Transfer	115	119	119	119
Data Source(s)	116	120	120	120
Effective Date of Data Source(s)	117	121	121	121

Analysis of prior sale or transfer history of the subject property and comparable sales **122**

Summary of Sales Comparison Approach **123**

Indicated Value by Sales Comparison Approach $ **124**

Indicated Value by: Sales Comparison Approach $ **125** Cost Approach (if developed) $ **126** Income Approach (if developed) $ **127**

128

This appraisal is made **129** "as is", **130** subject to completion per plans and specifications on the basis of a hypothetical condition that the improvements have been completed, **131** subject to the following repairs or alterations on the basis of a hypothetical condition that the repairs or alterations have been completed, or **132** subject to the following required inspection based on the extraordinary assumption that the condition or deficiency does not require alteration or repair: **133**

Based on a complete visual inspection of the interior and exterior areas of the subject property, defined scope of work, statement of assumptions and limiting conditions, and appraiser's certification, my (our) opinion of the market value, as defined, of the real property that is the subject of this report is $ **134** , as of **135** , which is the date of inspection and the effective date of this appraisal.

Freddie Mac Form 70 March 2005 226 **UAD Version 9/2011** Page 2 of 6 Fannie Mae Form 1004 March 2005

URAR – Page 3

Uniform Residential Appraisal Report   File # 3   4   4a

2

5

ADDITIONAL COMMENTS

COST APPROACH TO VALUE (not required by Fannie Mae)

Provide adequate information for the lender/client to replicate the below cost figures and calculations.

Support for the opinion of site value (summary of comparable land sales or other methods for estimating site value)   6

ESTIMATED ☐7 REPRODUCTION OR ☐8 REPLACEMENT COST NEW	OPINION OF SITE VALUE .... = $	14
Source of cost data 9	Dwelling 15 Sq. Ft. @ $ 16 .... =$	17
Quality rating from cost service 10 Effective date of cost data 11	18 19 Sq. Ft. @ $ 20 .... =$	21
Comments on Cost Approach (gross living area calculations, depreciation, etc.)	22	23
12	Garage/Carport 24 Sq. Ft. @ $ 25 .... =$	26
	Total Estimate of Cost-New .... = $	27

Less	Physical	Functional	External		
Depreciation	29	31	33	=$(34	)
Depreciated Cost of Improvements .... =$				35	
"As-is" Value of Site Improvements .... =$				36	

Estimated Remaining Economic Life (HUD and VA only)   13   Years   Indicated Value By Cost Approach .... =$ 37

INCOME APPROACH TO VALUE (not required by Fannie Mae)

Estimated Monthly Market Rent $ 38   X Gross Rent Multiplier   39   = $ 40   Indicated Value by Income Approach

Summary of Income Approach (including support for market rent and GRM)   41

PROJECT INFORMATION FOR PUDs (if applicable)

Is the developer/builder in control of the Homeowners' Association (HOA)? ☐42 Yes ☐43 No   Unit type(s) ☐44 Detached ☐45 Attached

Provide the following information for PUDs ONLY if the developer/builder is in control of the HOA and the subject property is an attached dwelling unit.

Legal name of project   46

Total number of phases   47   Total number of units   48   Total number of units sold   49

Total number of units rented   50   Total number of units for sale   51   Data source(s)   52

Was the project created by the conversion of an existing building(s) into a PUD? ☐53 Yes ☐54 No   If Yes, date of conversion   55

Does the project contain any multi-dwelling units? ☐56 Yes ☐57 No   Data source(s)   58

Are the units, common elements, and recreation facilities complete? ☐59 Yes ☐60 No   If No, describe the status of completion.   61

Are the common elements leased to or by the Homeowners' Association? ☐62 Yes ☐63 No   If Yes, describe the rental terms and options.   64

Describe common elements and recreational facilities   65

Freddie Mac Form 70   March 2005   226   *UAD Version 9/2011*   Page 3 of 6   Fannie Mae Form 1004   March 2005

Uniform Residential Appraisal Report

²   File # 3   4   4a

This report form is designed to report an appraisal of a one-unit property or a one-unit property with an accessory unit; including a unit in a planned unit development (PUD). This report form is not designed to report an appraisal of a manufactured home or a unit in a condominium or cooperative project.

This appraisal report is subject to the following scope of work, intended use, intended user, definition of market value, statement of assumptions and limiting conditions, and certifications. Modifications, additions, or deletions to the intended use, intended user, definition of market value, or assumptions and limiting conditions are not permitted. The appraiser may expand the scope of work to include any additional research or analysis necessary based on the complexity of this appraisal assignment. Modifications or deletions to the certifications are also not permitted. However, additional certifications that do not constitute material alterations to this appraisal report, such as those required by law or those related to the appraiser's continuing education or membership in an appraisal organization, are permitted.

SCOPE OF WORK: The scope of work for this appraisal is defined by the complexity of this appraisal assignment and the reporting requirements of this appraisal report form, including the following definition of market value, statement of assumptions and limiting conditions, and certifications. The appraiser must, at a minimum: (1) perform a complete visual inspection of the interior and exterior areas of the subject property, (2) inspect the neighborhood, (3) inspect each of the comparable sales from at least the street, (4) research, verify, and analyze data from reliable public and/or private sources, and (5) report his or her analysis, opinions, and conclusions in this appraisal report.

INTENDED USE: The intended use of this appraisal report is for the lender/client to evaluate the property that is the subject of this appraisal for a mortgage finance transaction.

INTENDED USER: The intended user of this appraisal report is the lender/client.

DEFINITION OF MARKET VALUE: The most probable price which a property should bring in a competitive and open market under all conditions requisite to a fair sale, the buyer and seller, each acting prudently, knowledgeably and assuming the price is not affected by undue stimulus. Implicit in this definition is the consummation of a sale as of a specified date and the passing of title from seller to buyer under conditions whereby: (1) buyer and seller are typically motivated; (2) both parties are well informed or well advised, and each acting in what he or she considers his or her own best interest; (3) a reasonable time is allowed for exposure in the open market; (4) payment is made in terms of cash in U. S. dollars or in terms of financial arrangements comparable thereto; and (5) the price represents the normal consideration for the property sold unaffected by special or creative financing or sales concessions* granted by anyone associated with the sale.

*Adjustments to the comparables must be made for special or creative financing or sales concessions. No adjustments are necessary for those costs which are normally paid by sellers as a result of tradition or law in a market area; these costs are readily identifiable since the seller pays these costs in virtually all sales transactions. Special or creative financing adjustments can be made to the comparable property by comparisons to financing terms offered by a third party institutional lender that is not already involved in the property or transaction. Any adjustment should not be calculated on a mechanical dollar for dollar cost of the financing or concession but the dollar amount of any adjustment should approximate the market's reaction to the financing or concessions based on the appraiser's judgment.

STATEMENT OF ASSUMPTIONS AND LIMITING CONDITIONS: The appraiser's certification in this report is subject to the following assumptions and limiting conditions:

1. The appraiser will not be responsible for matters of a legal nature that affect either the property being appraised or the title to it, except for information that he or she became aware of during the research involved in performing this appraisal. The appraiser assumes that the title is good and marketable and will not render any opinions about the title.

2. The appraiser has provided a sketch in this appraisal report to show the approximate dimensions of the improvements. The sketch is included only to assist the reader in visualizing the property and understanding the appraiser's determination of its size.

3. The appraiser has examined the available flood maps that are provided by the Federal Emergency Management Agency (or other data sources) and has noted in this appraisal report whether any portion of the subject site is located in an identified Special Flood Hazard Area. Because the appraiser is not a surveyor, he or she makes no guarantees, express or implied, regarding this determination.

4. The appraiser will not give testimony or appear in court because he or she made an appraisal of the property in question, unless specific arrangements to do so have been made beforehand, or as otherwise required by law.

5. The appraiser has noted in this appraisal report any adverse conditions (such as needed repairs, deterioration, the presence of hazardous wastes, toxic substances, etc.) observed during the inspection of the subject property or that he or she became aware of during the research involved in performing this appraisal. Unless otherwise stated in this appraisal report, the appraiser has no knowledge of any hidden or unapparent physical deficiencies or adverse conditions of the property (such as, but not limited to, needed repairs, deterioration, the presence of hazardous wastes, toxic substances, adverse environmental conditions, etc.) that would make the property less valuable, and has assumed that there are no such conditions and makes no guarantees or warranties, express or implied. The appraiser will not be responsible for any such conditions that do exist or for any engineering or testing that might be required to discover whether such conditions exist. Because the appraiser is not an expert in the field of environmental hazards, this appraisal report must not be considered as an environmental assessment of the property.

6. The appraiser has based his or her appraisal report and valuation conclusion for an appraisal that is subject to satisfactory completion, repairs, or alterations on the assumption that the completion, repairs, or alterations of the subject property will be performed in a professional manner.

URAR – Page 5

Uniform Residential Appraisal Report

2

APPRAISER'S CERTIFICATION: The Appraiser certifies and agrees that:

1. I have, at a minimum, developed and reported this appraisal in accordance with the scope of work requirements stated in this appraisal report.

2. I performed a complete visual inspection of the interior and exterior areas of the subject property. I reported the condition of the improvements in factual, specific terms. I identified and reported the physical deficiencies that could affect the livability, soundness, or structural integrity of the property.

3. I performed this appraisal in accordance with the requirements of the Uniform Standards of Professional Appraisal Practice that were adopted and promulgated by the Appraisal Standards Board of The Appraisal Foundation and that were in place at the time this appraisal report was prepared.

4. I developed my opinion of the market value of the real property that is the subject of this report based on the sales comparison approach to value. I have adequate comparable market data to develop a reliable sales comparison approach for this appraisal assignment. I further certify that I considered the cost and income approaches to value but did not develop them, unless otherwise indicated in this report.

5. I researched, verified, analyzed, and reported on any current agreement for sale for the subject property, any offering for sale of the subject property in the twelve months prior to the effective date of this appraisal, and the prior sales of the subject property for a minimum of three years prior to the effective date of this appraisal, unless otherwise indicated in this report.

6. I researched, verified, analyzed, and reported on the prior sales of the comparable sales for a minimum of one year prior to the date of sale of the comparable sale, unless otherwise indicated in this report.

7. I selected and used comparable sales that are locationally, physically, and functionally the most similar to the subject property.

8. I have not used comparable sales that were the result of combining a land sale with the contract purchase price of a home that has been built or will be built on the land.

9. I have reported adjustments to the comparable sales that reflect the market's reaction to the differences between the subject property and the comparable sales.

10. I verified, from a disinterested source, all information in this report that was provided by parties who have a financial interest in the sale or financing of the subject property.

11. I have knowledge and experience in appraising this type of property in this market area.

12. I am aware of, and have access to, the necessary and appropriate public and private data sources, such as multiple listing services, tax assessment records, public land records and other such data sources for the area in which the property is located.

13. I obtained the information, estimates, and opinions furnished by other parties and expressed in this appraisal report from reliable sources that I believe to be true and correct.

14. I have taken into consideration the factors that have an impact on value with respect to the subject neighborhood, subject property, and the proximity of the subject property to adverse influences in the development of my opinion of market value. I have noted in this appraisal report any adverse conditions (such as, but not limited to, needed repairs, deterioration, the presence of hazardous wastes, toxic substances, adverse environmental conditions, etc.) observed during the inspection of the subject property or that I became aware of during the research involved in performing this appraisal. I have considered these adverse conditions in my analysis of the property value, and have reported on the effect of the conditions on the value and marketability of the subject property.

15. I have not knowingly withheld any significant information from this appraisal report and, to the best of my knowledge, all statements and information in this appraisal report are true and correct.

16. I stated in this appraisal report my own personal, unbiased, and professional analysis, opinions, and conclusions, which are subject only to the assumptions and limiting conditions in this appraisal report.

17. I have no present or prospective interest in the property that is the subject of this report, and I have no present or prospective personal interest or bias with respect to the participants in the transaction. I did not base, either partially or completely, my analysis and/or opinion of market value in this appraisal report on the race, color, religion, sex, age, marital status, handicap, familial status, or national origin of either the prospective owners or occupants of the subject property or of the present owners or occupants of the properties in the vicinity of the subject property or on any other basis prohibited by law.

18. My employment and/or compensation for performing this appraisal or any future or anticipated appraisals was not conditioned on any agreement or understanding, written or otherwise, that I would report (or present analysis supporting) a predetermined specific value, a predetermined minimum value, a range or direction in value, a value that favors the cause of any party, or the attainment of a specific result or occurrence of a specific subsequent event (such as approval of a pending mortgage loan application).

19. I personally prepared all conclusions and opinions about the real estate that were set forth in this appraisal report. If I relied on significant real property appraisal assistance from any individual or individuals in the performance of this appraisal or the preparation of this appraisal report, I have named such individual(s) and disclosed the specific tasks performed in this appraisal report. I certify that any individual so named is qualified to perform the tasks. I have not authorized anyone to make a change to any item in this appraisal report; therefore, any change made to this appraisal is unauthorized and I will take no responsibility for it.

20. I identified the lender/client in this appraisal report who is the individual, organization, or agent for the organization that ordered and will receive this appraisal report.

2

Uniform Residential Appraisal Report

File # 3   4   4a

21. The lender/client may disclose or distribute this appraisal report to: the borrower; another lender at the request of the borrower; the mortgagee or its successors and assigns; mortgage insurers; government sponsored enterprises; other secondary market participants; data collection or reporting services; professional appraisal organizations; any department, agency, or instrumentality of the United States; and any state, the District of Columbia, or other jurisdictions; without having to obtain the appraiser's or supervisory appraiser's (if applicable) consent. Such consent must be obtained before this appraisal report may be disclosed or distributed to any other party (including, but not limited to, the public through advertising, public relations, news, sales, or other media).

22. I am aware that any disclosure or distribution of this appraisal report by me or the lender/client may be subject to certain laws and regulations. Further, I am also subject to the provisions of the Uniform Standards of Professional Appraisal Practice that pertain to disclosure or distribution by me.

23. The borrower, another lender at the request of the borrower, the mortgagee or its successors and assigns, mortgage insurers, government sponsored enterprises, and other secondary market participants may rely on this appraisal report as part of any mortgage finance transaction that involves any one or more of these parties.

24. If this appraisal report was transmitted as an "electronic record" containing my "electronic signature," as those terms are defined in applicable federal and/or state laws (excluding audio and video recordings), or a facsimile transmission of this appraisal report containing a copy or representation of my signature, the appraisal report shall be as effective, enforceable and valid as if a paper version of this appraisal report were delivered containing my original hand written signature.

25. Any intentional or negligent misrepresentation(s) contained in this appraisal report may result in civil liability and/or criminal penalties including, but not limited to, fine or imprisonment or both under the provisions of Title 18, United States Code, Section 1001, et seq., or similar state laws.

SUPERVISORY APPRAISER'S CERTIFICATION: The Supervisory Appraiser certifies and agrees that:

1. I directly supervised the appraiser for this appraisal assignment, have read the appraisal report, and agree with the appraiser's analysis, opinions, statements, conclusions, and the appraiser's certification.

2. I accept full responsibility for the contents of this appraisal report including, but not limited to, the appraiser's analysis, opinions, statements, conclusions, and the appraiser's certification.

3. The appraiser identified in this appraisal report is either a sub-contractor or an employee of the supervisory appraiser (or the appraisal firm), is qualified to perform this appraisal, and is acceptable to perform this appraisal under the applicable state law.

4. This appraisal report complies with the Uniform Standards of Professional Appraisal Practice that were adopted and promulgated by the Appraisal Standards Board of The Appraisal Foundation and that were in place at the time this appraisal report was prepared.

5. If this appraisal report was transmitted as an "electronic record" containing my "electronic signature," as those terms are defined in applicable federal and/or state laws (excluding audio and video recordings), or a facsimile transmission of this appraisal report containing a copy or representation of my signature, the appraisal report shall be as effective, enforceable and valid as if a paper version of this appraisal report were delivered containing my original hand written signature.

Signature_____

Name 5 _____

Company Name 6 _____

Company Address 7_____

        8a, 8b 8c _____

Telephone Number 9_____

Email Address 10_____

Date of Signature and Report 11 _____

Effective Date of Appraisal 12 _____

State Certification # 13_____

or State License # 14 _____

or Other (describe) 15 _____ State # 16 _____

State 17 _____

Expiration Date of Certification or License 18 _____

ADDRESS OF PROPERTY APPRAISED

19 _____

20a, 20b, 20c _____

APPRAISED VALUE OF SUBJECT PROPERTY $ 21 _____

LENDER/CLIENT

Name 22 _____

Company Name 23 _____

Company Address 24_____

        _____

Email Address 26_____

SUPERVISORY APPRAISER (ONLY IF REQUIRED)

Signature_____

Name 27_____

Company Name 28_____

Company Address 29_____

        30a, 30b 30c _____

Telephone Number 31 _____

Email Address 32_____

Date of Signature 33 _____

State Certification # 34_____

or State License # 35 _____

State 36 _____

Expiration Date of Certification or License 37 _____

SUBJECT PROPERTY

☐ 38 Did not inspect subject property

☐ 39 Did inspect exterior of subject property from street

    Date of Inspection 40 _____

☐ 41 Did inspect interior and exterior of subject property

    Date of Inspection 42 _____

COMPARABLE SALES

☐ 43 Did not inspect exterior of comparable sales from street

☐ 44 Did inspect exterior of comparable sales from street

    Date of Inspection 45 _____

A. PAGE ONE OF THE URAR
1.Subject Section

2	Uniform Residential Appraisal Report	File # 3 4 4a

The purpose of this summary appraisal report is to provide the lender/client with an accurate, and adequately supported, opinion of the market value of the subject property.

SUBJECT

| Property Address 6 | | City 7 | | State 8   Zip Code 9 |
| Borrower 10 | Owner of Public Record 11 | County 12 | | |

Legal Description 13

Assessor's Parcel # 14   Tax Year 15   R.E. Taxes $ 16

Neighborhood Name 17   Map Reference 18   Census Tract 19

Occupant [20] Owner [21] Tenant [22] Vacant   Special Assessments $ 23   [24] PUD   HOA $ 25   [26] per year [27] per month

Property Rights Appraised [28] Fee Simple [29] Leasehold [30] Other (describe) 31

Assignment Type [32] Purchase Transaction [33] Refinance Transaction [34] Other (describe) 35

Lender/Client 36   Address 37

Is the subject property currently offered for sale or has it been offered for sale in the twelve months prior to the effective date of this appraisal? [38] Yes [39] No

Report data source(s) used, offering price(s), and date(s).   e-2; 40

The first section of the URAR form, the **Subject** section, is used to identify the subject property. On the first line, the appraiser enters the property's common street address (city, state, and zip code). The address should correspond to the physical location of the property; a post office box or similar non-physical address is not acceptable.

Next, the name of the **Borrower(s)** (whose loan application is the reason for the appraisal) and the **Owner of Public Record** are requested. The next space asks for the name of the county in which the subject property is located. The next line asks for the legal description. If the legal description will not fit into the space provided, it may be attached as an addendum to the report. The appraiser then makes a reference to the addendum in the legal description blank (see Chapter 2).

Property Tax Information for the subject property is also included in the subject section. The **Assessor's Parcel Number** is the tax identification number used by the local assessor to identify the property for tax purposes. The appraiser identifies the tax year and the annual amount of ad valorem tax.

If the neighborhood has a commonly accepted name (such as "Blueberry Hill Estates" or "Marmalade Heights") this is entered as the neighborhood name along with whatever map reference will correspond to the map system most commonly used by local appraisers. Next, the appraiser should enter the number of the U.S. government census tract in which the subject is located.

The appraiser should identify if the property is **Owner Occupied, Tenant Occupied,** or **Vacant**. What, if any, is the dollar amount for Special Assessments. These are one time expenses such as for new street lighting or paving that appear on a current tax bill. Is the subject a planned unit development **(PUD)** and if so what is the amount of the homeowner's association **(HOA)** dues. Is the stated amount an annual or monthly figure?

The next two lines ask if the property rights appraised are **Fee Simple** or **Leasehold** and whether or not the property is a **Purchase Transaction** or a **Refinance Transaction**.

The next line asks the appraiser to identify the **Lender** or **Client**. This is no longer a simple one line answer. USPAP requires that the appraiser identify all **Intended Users** by name or by type. This will probably require an addendum. It is now just as important to the process to identify those persons or entities who are not intended users, along with those who are, to protect the appraiser, and prevent confusion in the marketplace.

The last two lines in the subject section ask if there is a current listing of sale or a prior listing within the past twelve months. The appraiser is asked to provide his or her data sources and the listing date and offering prices if any. If there has been no current or prior listing the appraiser should state so.

2. Contract Section

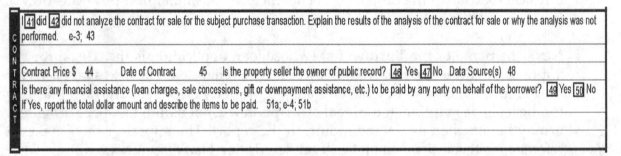

If there is a current **Contract of Sale**, the appraiser is expected to acquire a copy and to analyze the contents of the contract. If the appraiser did not obtain and analyze the contract he or she is expected to explain why they did not do so. The analysis requires the appraiser to answer a series of questions. What is the **Contract Price**? When was the **Date of Contract**? Is the seller the same as the owner? Is the property correctly described? Is any personal property included? Are there any sales concessions? Is there a gift of funds? What is the dollar amount of concessions or gift funds? What affect do they have on value?

Many of the items of comparison on the grid must be written in the manner described in the UAD (see **Appendix 5** of this book). These items would include: location, design, style, quality of construction addition, and functional utility. The former usage of descriptions such as poor, fair, average, or good and also inferior, similar, or superior have been replaced by the new numerical descriptions in the UAD, such as Q1, Q2, Q3 etc.

3. Neighborhood Section

Note: Race and the racial composition of the neighborhood are not appraisal factors.

Neighborhood Characteristics			One-Unit Housing Trends				One-Unit Housing			Present Land Use %	
Location [52] Urban	[53] Suburban	[54] Rural	Property Values [61] Increasing	[62] Stable	[63] Declining		PRICE	AGE		One-Unit	76 %
Built-Up [55] Over 75% [56] 25–75%		[57] Under 25%	Demand/Supply [64] Shortage	[65] In Balance	[66] Over Supply		$ (000)	(yrs)		2-4 Unit	77 %
Growth [58] Rapid	[59] Stable	[60] Slow	Marketing Time [67] Under 3 mths [68] 3–6 mths		[69] Over 6 mths		70 Low	73		Multi-Family	78 %
Neighborhood Boundaries 82							71 High	74		Commercial	79 %
							72 Pred.	75		Other	81 %
Neighborhood Description 83											
Market Conditions (including support for the above conclusions) 84											

In the third section of the report the appraiser describes the **Neighborhood** in which the subject property is located. The first part of this section contains a series of check boxes relating to the density and development of the neighborhood, and trends in property values and marketability. The appraiser should check one box on each line.

Next the appraiser indicates the range of prices and ages of single-family housing units in the neighborhood and the predominant (most frequently occurring) age and sales price for single-family residences. When specifying the age and price ranges, the appraiser may ignore isolated cases of properties that fall well outside the normal ranges. The UAD uses actual or chronological age stated in years. The UAD drop box does not permit the usage of effective age in this section. If the appraiser feels the effective age is a significant factor this should be reported in an addendum.

The last block in this section relates to present land use. The appraiser provides a percentage breakdown of the various land uses within the neighborhood. The total of reported percentages should equal 100%.

The bottom portion of the neighborhood section provides three spaces for the appraiser's **Comments** and **Analysis**. First, the appraiser must specify the physical boundaries of the neighborhood, and describe its defining characteristics. The boundaries should be marked or easily identifiable on an attached location map.

The second comment and analysis question asks for a **Neighborhood Description**. Are there any factors that affect marketability? Are there any significant negative value influences such as close proximity to airport flight patterns, freeway noise, chemical odors, etc.? Are there positive influences? What about parks, greenbelts, shopping, available public transportation, etc.? In general, all significant economic, governmental, social, and physical/environmental value influences should be noted.

Finally the appraiser must provide an analysis of the market conditions in the subject neighborhood. The appraiser should have relevant data to support the conclusions made in the neighborhood description area. Analysis of typical sales and financing conditions in the neighborhood is also important both as an indicator of neighborhood market trends, and for purposes of comparison between the subject property and the comparable properties in the sales comparison approach.

4. Site Section

Dimensions 85			Area 86		Shape 87		View e-5; e-6; e-7	
Specific Zoning Classification 89			Zoning Description 90					
Zoning Compliance [91] Legal [92] Legal Nonconforming (Grandfathered Use) [93] No Zoning [94] Illegal (describe) 95								
Is the highest and best use of the subject property as improved (or as proposed per plans and specifications) the present use? [96] Yes [97] No If No, describe 98								

Utilities	Public	Other (describe)		Public	Other (describe)	Off-site Improvements—Type	Public	Private
Electricity	[99]	[100] 101	Water	[105]	[106] 107	Street 111	[112]	[113]
Gas	[102]	[103] 104	Sanitary Sewer	[108]	[109] 110	Alley 114	[115]	[116]
FEMA Special Flood Hazard Area [117] Yes [118] No FEMA Flood Zone 119 FEMA Map # 120						FEMA Map Date 121		
Are the utilities and off-site improvements typical for the market area? [122] Yes [123] No If No, describe 124								
Are there any adverse site conditions or external factors (easements, encroachments, environmental conditions, land uses, etc.)?[125] Yes[126] No If Yes, describe								
127								

In the **Site Section** of the URAR form, the appraiser describes the subject property site. First the dimensions of the parcel are entered and then the area of the site is calculated. The appraiser is then asked to state the shape of the parcel and to describe any view that it may or may not have. What is the specific zoning classification and what does it allow (single-family residence, mixed usage, commercial usage, etc.) Does the zoning comply with the usage? In other words is it a legal, illegal, or nonconforming use? In some areas no zoning is required. The appraiser is asked to comment whether or not the present or proposed improvements represent the highest and best use.

There are a series of checkboxes that ask if utilities such as electricity, gas, water and the sewage system are public or private. If the utilities are private the appraiser is asked to describe them. These might consist of a private generator, solar electrical power, propane service, a private well, or a septic system. The appraiser is asked to describe the type (asphalt, concrete, dirt) of such offsite improvements as streets and alleyways and whether or not they are public or private.

The appraiser is asked to determine if the site is located in a **FEMA SPECIAL FLOOD HAZARD AREA**. Zones that are listed as "A" or "V" are so designated and the appraiser must answer yes in that case and list the specific zone, map number and date. If the answer is no, the appraiser must still list the zone type (C,D,X), map number and map date.

The appraiser must comment about whether or not the utilities and offsite improvements are typical for the surrounding market area. If the subject site's utilities and offsite improvements are dissimilar to the surrounding area there may be an adverse impact to the value of the subject site. Lastly, the appraiser is asked to note and describe any adverse conditions such as easements, encroachments, and environmental conditions.

5. Improvements Section

General Description	Foundation	Exterior Description materials/condition	Interior materials/condition
Units [128] One [129] One with Accessory Unit	[140] Concrete Slab [141] Crawl Space	Foundation Walls 152	Floors 159
# of Stories 130	[142] Full Basement [143] Partial Basement	Exterior Walls 153	Walls 160
Type [131] Det. [132] Att. [133] S-Det./End Unit	Basement Area 144 sq. ft.	Roof Surface 154	Trim/Finish 161
[134] Existing [135] Proposed [136] Under Const.	Basement Finish 145 %	Gutters & Downspouts 155	Bath Floor 162
Design (Style) 137	[146] Outside Entry/Exit [147] Sump Pump	Window Type 156	Bath Wainscot 163
Year Built e-8; 138	Evidence of [148] Infestation	Storm Sash/Insulated 157	Car Storage [195] None
Effective Age (Yrs) 139	[150] Dampness [151] Settlement	Screens 158	[196] Driveway # of Cars 197
Attic [164] None	Heating [171] FWA [172] HWBB [173] Radiant	Amenities [187] Woodstove(s) # 188	Driveway Surface 198
[165] Drop Stair [166] Stairs	[174] Other 175 Fuel 176	[181] Fireplace(s) # 182 [189] Fence 190	[199] Garage # of Cars 200
[167] Floor [168] Scuttle	Cooling [177] Central Air Conditioning	[183] Patio/Deck 184 [191] Porch 192	[201] Carport # of Cars 202
[169] Finished [170] Heated	[178] Individual [179] Other 180	[185] Pool 186 [193] Other 194	[203] Att. [204] Det. [205] Built-in

Appliances [206] Refrigerator [207] Range/Oven [208] Dishwasher [209] Disposal [210] Microwave [211] Washer/Dryer [212] Other (describe) 213

Finished area **above** grade contains: 214 Rooms 215 Bedrooms 216 Bath(s) 217 Square Feet of Gross Living Area Above Grade

Additional features (special energy efficient items, etc.) 218

Describe the condition of the property (including needed repairs, deterioration, renovations, remodeling, etc.). e-9; e-10; e-11; e-12; e-13; 219

Are there any physical deficiencies or adverse conditions that affect the livability, soundness, or structural integrity of the property? [220] Yes [221] No If Yes, describe 222

Does the property generally conform to the neighborhood (functional utility, style, condition, use, construction, etc.)? [223] Yes [224] No If No, describe 225

The description of **Improvements Section** consists of four blocks, each relating to a different aspect or characteristic of the improvements. In addition, there are four description and analysis questions.

The **General Description Section** asks the appraiser to describe the number of dwelling units (usually one for an SFR), the number of above-grade stories, and whether they are attached or detached. The appraiser is asked to check off whether or not the improvements are existing, proposed, or under construction. Next, the appraiser is asked to describe the architectural style. The year the residence was built and the appraiser's opinion of its effective age are to be noted. The *EFFECTIVE AGE reflects the appraiser's judgment as to the building's remaining economic life.* Last, there are a series of check boxes asking questions regarding the attic, if the house has one.

The **Foundation** block has entries that are basically check off boxes. If there is a basement the appraiser is asked to provide the area square footage and the degree of finish (a percent). Does the basement, if there is one, have an outside entry or a sump pump? Any evidence of dampness, infestation, or settlement must be noted and discussed in an addendum, if there is insufficient room on the form. Finally, there are a series of check boxes to note the type of heating and cooling systems.

The **Exterior Description** block has a number of spaces that ask the appraiser to state what materials are used and what condition they are in for a variety of the components of the superstructure. These include foundation walls, exterior walls, roofs, and windows. For example, exterior walls might be wood siding, brick, or stucco. Roofs might be composition shingle, or tile. Condition could be poor, fair, average, good, very good, or excellent. A series of check boxes ascertain such amenities as fireplaces, patios, pools, and fencing. Once again, an addendum might be necessary depending on the quantity and quality of the amenities.

The **Interior** block also has a series of spaces that ask for the type and quality of such items as flooring, walls, trim and finish, and bathroom appointments. The block underneath the Interior block has a series of check off boxes for parking and car storage. The Improvement section also contains check off boxes for appliances.

The form asks the appraiser to enumerate the total room count, total bedrooms, total bathrooms, and total gross square footage above grade. The appraiser is also asked to list any additional features and any special energy efficient items (such as solar heating).

The appraiser is then asked to describe the overall condition of the property listing any needed repairs, renovation, or remodeling. The appraiser is to note if there are any physical deficiencies that might affect the livability, or structural integrity of the residence.

Lastly, does the property conform to the neighborhood? Nonconforming design or style, poor functional utility, or inferior condition may cause deterioration in value. As noted in a prior chapter, nonconforming properties will possibly not be as desirable or achieve as high a value as conforming properties.

B. PAGE TWO OF THE URAR

1. Sales Comparison Approach Section

2			**Uniform Residential Appraisal Report**						File # 3	4	4a	

There are 5 comparable properties currently offered for sale in the subject neighborhood ranging in price from $ 6 to $ 7									
There are 8 comparable sales in the subject neighborhood within the past twelve months ranging in sale price from $ 9 to $ 10									

FEATURE	SUBJECT	COMPARABLE SALE # 1		COMPARABLE SALE # 2		COMPARABLE SALE # 3	
Address 11 12a 12b 12c		45 46a 46b 46c		45 46a 46b 46c		45 46a 46b 46c	
Proximity to Subject		47		47		47	
Sale Price	$ 13	$ 48		$ 48		$ 48	
Sale Price/Gross Liv. Area	$ 14 sq. ft.	$ 49 sq. ft.		$ 49 sq. ft.		$ 49 sq. ft.	
Data Source(s)		e-25, e-2		e-25, e-2		e-25, e-2	
Verification Source(s)		51		51		51	
VALUE ADJUSTMENTS	DESCRIPTION	DESCRIPTION	+(-) $ Adjustment	DESCRIPTION	+(-) $ Adjustment	DESCRIPTION	+(-) $ Adjustment
Sale or Financing Concessions		52 e-26; e-27; e-28	53 55	52 e-26; e-27; e-28	53 55	52 e-26; e-27; e-28	53 55
Date of Sale/Time		e-29; e-30; e-31	57	e-29; e-30; e-31	57	e-29; e-30; e-31	57
Location	e-14; e-15; e-16	e-14; e-15; e-16	59	e-14; e-15; e-16	59	e-14; e-15; e-16	59
Leasehold/Fee Simple	21	60	61	60	61	60	61
Site	22	62	63	62	63	62	63
View	e-5; e-6; e-7	e-5; e-6; e-7	65	e-5; e-6; e-7	65	e-5; e-6; e-7	65
Design (Style)	24	66	67	66	67	66	67
Quality of Construction	25	68	69	68	69	68	69
Actual Age	e-17; 26	e-17; 70	71	e-17; 70	71	e-17; 70	71
Condition	27	72	73	72	73	72	73
Above Grade	Total 28 Bdrms 29 Baths 30	Total 75 Bdrms 76 Baths 77	74	Total 75 Bdrms 76 Baths 77	74	Total 75 Bdrms 76 Baths 77	74
Room Count			78		78		78
Gross Living Area	31 sq. ft.	79 sq. ft.	80	79 sq. ft.	80	79 sq. ft.	80
Basement & Finished Rooms Below Grade	e-18; e-19; e-20 e-21; e-22; e-23; e-24	e-18; e-19; e-20 e-21; e-22; e-23; e-24	82 84	e-18; e-19; e-20 e-21; e-22; e-23; e-24	82 84	e-18; e-19; e-20 e-21; e-22; e-23; e-24	82 84
Functional Utility	34	85	86	85	86	85	86
Heating/Cooling	35	87	88	87	88	87	88
Energy Efficient Items	36	89	90	89	90	89	90
Garage/Carport	37	91	92	91	92	91	92
Porch/Patio/Deck	38	93	94	93	94	93	94
39	40	95	96	95	96	95	96
41	42	97	98	97	98	97	98
43	44	99	100	99	100	99	100
Net Adjustment (Total)		101 + 102 -	$ 103	101 + 102 -	$ 103	101 + 102 -	$ 103
Adjusted Sale Price of Comparables		Net Adj 103a % Gross Adj 103b %	$ 104	Net Adj 103a % Gross Adj 103b %	$ 104	Net Adj 103a % Gross Adj 103b %	$ 104

I 105 did 106 did not research the sale or transfer history of the subject property and comparable sales. If not, explain 107	
My research 108 did 109 did not reveal any prior sales or transfers of the subject property for the three years prior to the effective date of this appraisal.	
Data source(s) 110	
My research 111 did 112 did not reveal any prior sales or transfers of the comparable sales for the year prior to the date of sale of the comparable sale.	
Data source(s) 113	
Report the results of the research and analysis of the prior sale or transfer history of the subject property and comparable sales (report additional prior sales on page 3).	

ITEM	SUBJECT	COMPARABLE SALE # 1	COMPARABLE SALE # 2	COMPARABLE SALE # 3
Date of Prior Sale/Transfer	114	118	118	118
Price of Prior Sale/Transfer	115	119	119	119
Data Source(s)	116	120	120	120
Effective Date of Data Source(s)	117	121	121	121

Analysis of prior sale or transfer history of the subject property and comparable sales   122

Summary of Sales Comparison Approach   123

Indicated Value by Sales Comparison Approach $ 124

The first part of the **Sales Comparison Approach Section** of the URAR consists of a comparison grid, with spaces to list the **Basic Property Data** characteristics of the subject property and three comparables. At the top of the grid, the appraiser lists information about the locations and sales prices of the properties, and the sources of data. The street address (including the city or town) of each property is listed first, followed by the distance from the subject of each comparable (Proximity to Subject). The distances may be stated in miles, fractions of miles, or blocks. To aid the reader in locating comparables on a map, the direction (north, south, etc.) from the subject to each comparable should be given as well.

The data and/or verification sources should be clearly identified. If the source is a person (buyer, seller, broker, etc.) the identification should include the person's name and phone number. For other types of data sources, the identification should contain the specific tax stamp or document number from which the data was obtained or verified.

The lower portion of the sales comparison grid is used to show the **Value Adjustments** that were made to the prices of the comparables. The appraiser must fill in each line of the **Description Column** for the subject property and each comparable.

Sales or Financing Concessions are described for the comparables only, not for the subject, the appraiser notes the type and amount of financing, the interest rate, and any concessions that may have affected the sales price. If necessary due to limited space on the form, the description of the sales and financing concessions may be attached as an addendum.

Date of Sale/Time is also shown only for the comparables. In most cases, only the month and year of the sale are reported. Unless otherwise indicated by the appraiser, it is assumed that the date reported here is the date of settlement or closing. If another date (such as the contract date) is used, the appraiser must report this fact in a comment or addendum.

Many of the items of comparison on the grid can be described by rating each property as "poor," "fair," "average," or "good" with respect to the particular item. These items include Location, Design and Style, Quality of Construction, Condition, and Functional Utility. As an alternative, the descriptions of these items for the comparables can be stated in terms of comparison to the subject, as "inferior," "similar," or "superior." The appraiser will also include the size of the site and the type of view.

Case/Example: If the subject has a sweeping view of the mountains, this might be described on the view line as "Mountains/Good." A comparable property with a less dramatic view might be described as "Mountains/Average." A property with no view would be described as "None."

The line for **Leasehold/Fee Simple** is described as simply stating whether the real property interest is leasehold or a fee. Age is the actual or chronological age of the property, stated in years. The appraiser may also report the effective age as well, if this factor is significant. For example, the actual and effective age may be reported as A20/E15 in the space provided.

In the **Adjustment Columns** the appraiser fills in only those items where adjustments were actually made. If no adjustment is made for a particular line item, the adjustment column is simply left blank for that item. For each adjustment shown on the grid, the appraiser must indicate whether the amount of the adjustment is positive or negative (plus or minus).

The last two lines of the sales comparison grid show the net and gross total of adjustments and the resulting sales price. The appraiser indicates whether the net and gross total adjustments are positive (+) or negative (-) for each comparable. The adjusted sales price should be equal to the sales price on line 3 of the grid, plus or minus the net total adjustment.

Below the grid, are a series of lines, spaces, and boxes to list the appraiser's research of the prior sales and listing data for both the subject and the comparables. The appraiser must research and analyze all prior sales and transfers for the subject property within the preceding three years. All prior sales and transfers of the comparable properties must be researched and analyzed for the preceding one year period. The appraiser is expected to provide information on the price and date of all prior transfers, as well as the data source from which the information was obtained.

Finally, the appraiser is to provide a **Summary of Sales Comparison Approach**. Here the appraiser must explain how the values indicated by the comparables were reconciled into a single indicator of value for the sales comparison approach. Since reconciliation is not a simple averaging of the three adjusted comparable prices, the appraiser should state which comparable(s) was given the most weight in the reconciliation process and explain the reasons why. Finally, the appraiser is to provide the **Indicated Value by Sales Comparison Approach**.

2. Reconciliation Section

RECONCILIATION	
Indicated Value by: Sales Comparison Approach $ 125 Cost Approach (if developed) $ 126 Income Approach (if developed) $ 127	
128	
This appraisal is made 129 "as is" 130 subject to completion per plans and specifications on the basis of a hypothetical condition that the improvements have been completed 131 subject to the following repairs or alterations on the basis of a hypothetical condition that the repairs or alterations have been completed, or 132 subject to the following required inspection based on the extraordinary assumption that the condition or deficiency does not require alteration or repair: 133	
Based on a complete visual inspection of the interior and exterior areas of the subject property, defined scope of work, statement of assumptions and limiting conditions, and appraiser's certification, my (our) opinion of the market value, as defined, of the real property that is the subject of this report is $ 134 , as of 135 , which is the date of inspection and the effective date of this appraisal.	

In the **Reconciliation Section** of the URAR form the appraiser is asked to provide the values for the Sales Comparison Approach and the Cost and Income

Approaches, if developed. Several lines are provided for the reconciliation of these approaches. Then the appraiser is to indicate if the subject is appraised "**as is**," "**subject to repairs or alterations based on a hypothetical condition**," "**and** "**subject to inspection based on an extraordinary assumption**." When utilizing a hypothetical condition or an extraordinary assumption, the effect on value must be spelled out to the client in an addendum. Finally, the **market value and the effective date of value** must be provided.

C. PAGE THREE OF THE URAR

Page three of the URAR provides space to discuss addendum items if they are brief. This is also the page on which the **Cost Approach** and the **Income Approach** are located. The last part of the page has a section for **Project Information for PUDs (if applicable)**. The form notes that the Cost Approach and the Income Approach are not required by Fannie Mae. However, as previously discussed, these approaches may indeed be either necessary or required.

1. Cost Approach Section

COST APPROACH TO VALUE (not required by Fannie Mae)				
Provide adequate information for the lender/client to replicate the below cost figures and calculations.				
Support for the opinion of site value (summary of comparable land sales or other methods for estimating site value) 6				

ESTIMATED ☐7 REPRODUCTION OR ☐8 REPLACEMENT COST NEW	OPINION OF SITE VALUE .... = $ 14
Source of cost data 9	Dwelling 15 Sq. Ft. @ $ 16 .... =$ 17
Quality rating from cost service 10 Effective date of cost data 11	18 19 Sq. Ft. @ $ 20 .... =$ 21
Comments on Cost Approach (gross living area calculations, depreciation, etc.)	22 23
12	Garage/Carport 24 Sq. Ft. @ $ 25 .... =$ 26
	Total Estimate of Cost-New .... = $ 27
	Less Physical Functional External
	Depreciation 29 31 33 =$(34)
	Depreciated Cost of Improvements .... =$ 35
	"As-is" Value of Site Improvements .... =$ 36
Estimated Remaining Economic Life (HUD and VA only) 13 Years	Indicated Value By Cost Approach .... =$ 37

In the **Cost Approach Section** the appraiser reports his or her analysis of the property as valued by the reproduction or replacement cost of the improvements. The appraiser is to provide the sources of the cost data (generally a costing service such as Marshall & Swift, FW Dodge, etc.) The appraiser also presents commentary, on how the figures were derived, on the left side of the form. The right side of the form provides space to carry out the Cost Approach utilizing the Comparative Unit Method (Square Foot Method). The appraiser enters the figures for site value, improvement costs, and depreciation, and shows the calculations that result in the indicated value by the cost approach. The figures used here should be consistent with the figures provided in the Description of Improvements as well as the Sales Comparison Approach.

2. Income Approach Section

INCOME APPROACH TO VALUE (not required by Fannie Mae)					
Estimated Monthly Market Rent $ 38	X Gross Rent Multiplier 39	= $ 40	Indicated Value by Income Approach		
Summary of Income Approach (including support for market rent and GRM) 41					

The **Income Approach Section** consists of two lines. One line is to carry out the approach utilizing a gross income multiplier. The second line is intended to provide an explanation. This approach is generally not utilized for single-family housing unless the subject property is a rental. In that case, the appraiser will probably have to conduct a rental survey to derive the multiplier needed for the approach and complete an Owner's Operating Income Statement, if retained by the lender to do so.

3. PUD Information Section

PROJECT INFORMATION FOR PUDs (if applicable)
Is the developer/builder in control of the Homeowners' Association (HOA)? ☒ Yes ☒ No   Unit type(s) ☒ Detached ☒ Attached
Provide the following information for PUDs ONLY if the developer/builder is in control of the HOA and the subject property is an attached dwelling unit.
Legal name of project   46
Total number of phases   47   Total number of units   48   Total number of units sold   49
Total number of units rented   50   Total number of units for sale   51   Data source(s)   52
Was the project created by the conversion of an existing building(s) into a PUD?   ☒ Yes ☒ No If Yes, date of conversion   55
Does the project contain any multi-dwelling units? ☒ Yes ☒ No Data source(s) 58
Are the units, common elements, and recreation facilities complete?   ☒ Yes ☒ No If No, describe the status of completion.   61
Are the common elements leased to or by the Homeowners' Association? ☒ Yes ☒ No If Yes, describe the rental terms and options.   64
Describe common elements and recreational facilities 65

The last section of page three is **Project Information for PUDs**. The first question in this section asks if the developer/builder is in control of the Homeowner's Association. Control of an HOA by the developer has led to abusive practices in the past, and may make the property ineligible for certain financing programs. The remaining questions on the form need only to be answered if the builder or developer is indeed in control of the Association and the subject property is an attached dwelling unit. These questions are: the legal name of the project, total number of phases, total units, total units sold, total number of units rented, total number of units for sale, and the source of data for the information. Additional information to be provided asks if the units are part of a conversion (such as from apartments to SFR), or part of multi-dwelling units. Are the common elements and recreational facilities complete? Are any common elements leased by the Homeowner's Association? Finally, describe the common elements and recreational facilities.

D. PAGES FOUR THROUGH SIX OF THE URAR

The last three pages of the URAR contain the definition of **Market Value**, the **Limiting Conditions**, and the **Appraiser's Certification**.

E. DESKTOP UNDERWRITER'S QUANTITATIVE ANALYSIS APPRAISAL REPORT

This Fannie Mae report (FNMA Form 2055 – see **Figure 12-4**) may be used for drive-by appraisals. Since the appraiser need not enter the property, the dwelling, or take measurements, it contains far less detail than the URAR.

This report form is almost identical to the URAR in the amount of information required to be reported. The form notes that information provided is based on an exterior inspection from the street.

F. DESKTOP UNDERWRITER'S PROPERTY INSPECTION REPORT

This one-page Fannie Mae Report (Form 2075) is not truly an appraisal, in that the appraiser does not provide an opinion of value. The form is basically a property inspection report based on a visual inspection of the home and area.

G. COMPUTER AND VENDOR'S SOFTWARE

There are a number of software vendors (companies) that have dozens of downloadable appraisal forms including an entire UAD Dataset loan series. The computer programs significantly shorten the time required to complete appraisal reports. These programs also contain all the addendum forms that may be needed for the report.

There is also computerized data available in major markets for comparable sales data for appraisers. Today an appraiser will find that computer literacy is as important a tool as appraisal knowledge when it comes to success.

Note: For appraisal reports prepared using the Uniform Appraisal Dataset (UAD) specification, the PDF must be noted with the UAD version that was utilized in the preparation. E.g., the following notation "UAD Version 9/2011" must appear at the bottom of each page in the bottom margin with placement to the left of the page number:

Freddie Mac Form 70 March 2005   226 *UAD Version 9/2011* Page 1 of 6   Fannie Mae Form 1004 March 2005

Fannie Mae Form 2055 – Page 1

Figure 12-4

Exterior-Only Inspection Residential Appraisal Report   File # 3   4   4a

The purpose of this summary appraisal report is to provide the lender/client with an accurate, and adequately supported, opinion of the market value of the subject property.

Property Address 6	City 7	State 8 Zip Code 9

Property Address 6   City 7   State 8   Zip Code 9
Borrower   10   Owner of Public Record   11   County   12
Legal Description   13
Assessor's Parcel #   14   Tax Year   15   R.E. Taxes $ 16
Neighborhood Name   17   Map Reference   18   Census Tract   19
Occupant [20] Owner [21] Tenant [22] Vacant   Special Assessments $ 23   [24] PUD   HOA $ 25 [26] per year [27] per month
Property Rights Appraised [28] Fee Simple [29] Leasehold [30] Other (describe) 31
Assignment Type [32] Purchase Transaction [33] Refinance Transaction [34] Other (describe)   35
Lender/Client   36   Address 37
Is the subject property currently offered for sale or has it been offered for sale in the twelve months prior to the effective date of this appraisal? [38] Yes [39] No
Report data source(s) used, offering price(s), and date(s). e-2; 40

I [41] did [42] did not analyze the contract for sale for the subject purchase transaction. Explain the results of the analysis of the contract for sale or why the analysis was not performed. e-3; 43

Contract Price $ 44   Date of Contract   45   Is the property seller the owner of public record? [46] Yes [47] No Data Source(s)   48
Is there any financial assistance (loan charges, sale concessions, gift or downpayment assistance, etc.) to be paid by any party on behalf of the borrower? [49] Yes [50] No
If Yes, report the total dollar amount and describe the items to be paid. 51a; e-4; 51b

Note: Race and the racial composition of the neighborhood are not appraisal factors.

Neighborhood Characteristics	One-Unit Housing Trends	One-Unit Housing		Present Land Use %	
Location [52] Urban [53] Suburban [55] Rural	Property Values [61] Increasing [62] Stable [63] Declining	PRICE	AGE	One-Unit	76 %
Built-Up [55] Over 75% [56] 25–75% [57] Under 25%	Demand/Supply [64] Shortage [65] In Balance [66] Over Supply	$ (000)	(yrs)	2-4 Unit	77 %
Growth [58] Rapid [59] Stable [60] Slow	Marketing Time [67] Under 3 mths [68] 3–6 mths [69] Over 6 mths	70 Low	73	Multi-Family	78 %
Neighborhood Boundaries 82		71 High	74	Commercial	79 %
		72 Pred.	75	Other	81 %

Neighborhood Description   83

Market Conditions (including support for the above conclusions)   84

Dimensions   85   Area   86   Shape   87   View e-5; e-6; e-7
Specific Zoning Classification   89   Zoning Description   90
Zoning Compliance [91] Legal [92] Legal Nonconforming (Grandfathered Use) [93] No Zoning [94] Illegal (describe) 95
Is the highest and best use of the subject property as improved (or as proposed per plans and specifications) the present use? [96] Yes [97] No If No, describe 98

Utilities	Public	Other (describe)		Public	Other (describe)		Off-site Improvements—Type	Public	Private
Electricity	[99]	[100] 101	Water	[105]	[106] 107		Street 111	[112]	[113]
Gas	[102]	[103] 104	Sanitary Sewer	[108]	[109] 110		Alley 114	[115]	[116]

FEMA Special Flood Hazard Area [117] Yes [118] No FEMA Flood Zone 119   FEMA Map # 120   FEMA Map Date 121
Are the utilities and off-site improvements typical for the market area? [122] Yes [123] No If No, describe 124
Are there any adverse site conditions or external factors (easements, encroachments, environmental conditions, land uses, etc.)? [125] Yes [126] No If Yes, describe
127

Source(s) Used for Physical Characteristics of Property [128] Appraisal Files [129] MLS [130] Assessment and Tax Records [131] Prior Inspection [132] Property Owner
[133] Other (describe)   134   Data Source(s) for Gross Living Area   135

General Description	General Description	Heating / Cooling	Amenities	Car Storage
Units [136] One [137] One with Accessory Unit	[148] Concrete Slab [149] Crawl Space	[158] FWA [159] HWBB	[168] Fireplace(s) # 169	[182] None
# of Stories 138	[150] Full Basement [151] Finished	[160] Radiant	[170] Woodstove(s) # 171	[183] Driveway # of Cars 184
Type [139] Det [140] Att [141] S-Det./End Unit	[152] Partial Basement [153] Finished	[161] Other 162	[172] Patio/Deck 173	Driveway Surface 185
[142] Existing [143] Proposed [144] Under Const.	Exterior Walls 154	Fuel 163	[174] Porch 175	[186] Garage # of Cars 187
Design (Style) 145	Roof Surface 155	[164] Central Air Conditioning	[176] Pool 177	[188] Carport # of Cars 189
Year Built 146; e-8	Gutters & Downspouts 156	[165] Individual	[178] Fence 179	[190] Attached [191] Detached
Effective Age (Yrs) 147	Window Type 157	[166] Other 167	[180] Other 181	[192] Built-in

Appliances [193] Refrigerator [194] Range/Oven [195] Dishwasher [196] Disposal [197] Microwave [198] Washer/Dryer [199] Other (describe)   200
Finished area above grade contains: 201   Rooms   202   Bedrooms   203 Bath(s) 204   Square Feet of Gross Living Area Above Grade
Additional features (special energy efficient items, etc.)   205

Describe the condition of the property and data source(s) (including apparent needed repairs, deterioration, renovations, remodeling, etc.). e-9; 206

Are there any apparent physical deficiencies or adverse conditions that affect the livability, soundness, or structural integrity of the property? [207] Yes [208] No
If Yes, describe   209

Does the property generally conform to the neighborhood (functional utility, style, condition, use, construction, etc.)? [210] Yes [211] No If No, describe 212

Chapter 12

Fannie Mae Form 2055 – Page 2

COMPARISON APPROACH		12a 12b 12c	46a 46b 46c		46a 46b 46c		46a 46b 46c	
Proximity to Subject			47		47		47	
Sale Price		$ 13	$ 48		$ 48		$ 48	
Sale Price/Gross Liv. Area		$ 14 sq ft.	$ 49 sq ft.		$ 49 sq ft.		$ 49 sq ft.	
Data Source(s)			e-25; e-2		e-25; e-2		e-25; e-2	
Verification Source(s)			51		51		51	
VALUE ADJUSTMENTS		DESCRIPTION	DESCRIPTION	+(-) $ Adjustment	DESCRIPTION	+(-) $ Adjustment	DESCRIPTION	+(-) $ Adjustment
Sale or Financing			52	53	52	53	52	53
Concessions			e-26; e-27; e-28	55	e-26; e-27; e-28	55	e-26; e-27; e-28	55
Date of Sale/Time			e-29; e-30; e-31	57	e-29; e-30; e-31	57	e-29; e-30; e-31	57
Location		e-14; e-15; e-16	e-14; e-15; e-16	59	e-14; e-15; e-16	59	e-14; e-15; e-16	59
Leasehold/Fee Simple		21	60	61	60	61	60	61
Site		22	62	63	62	63	62	63
View		e-5; e-6; e-7	e-5; e-6; e-7	65	e-5; e-6; e-7	65	e-5; e-6; e-7	65
Design (Style)		24	66	67	66	67	66	67
Quality of Construction		25	68	69	68	69	68	69
Actual Age		e-17; 26	e-17; 70	71	e-17; 70	71	e-17; 70	71
Condition		27	72	73	72	73	72	73
Above Grade	Total / Bdrms. / Baths	28 / 29 / 30	Total / Bdrms. / Baths 75 / 76 / 77	74	Total / Bdrms. / Baths 75 / 76 / 77	74	Total / Bdrms. / Baths 75 / 76 / 77	74
Room Count				78		78		78
Gross Living Area		31 sq ft.	79 sq ft.	80	79 sq ft.	80	79 sq ft.	80
Basement & Finished		e-18; e-19; e-20	e-18; e-19; e-20	82	e-18; e-19; e-20	82	e-18; e-19; e-20	82
Rooms Below Grade		e-21; e-22; e-23; e-24	e-21; e-22; e-23; e-24	84	e-21; e-22; e-23; e-24	84	e-21; e-22; e-23; e-24	84
Functional Utility		34	85	86	85	86	85	86
Heating/Cooling		35	87	88	87	88	87	88
Energy Efficient Items		36	89	90	89	90	89	90
Garage/Carport		37	91	92	91	92	91	92
Porch/Patio/Deck		39	93	94	93	94	93	94
39		40	95	96	95	96	95	96
41		42	97	98	97	98	97	98
43		44	99	100	99	100	99	100
Net Adjustment (Total)			☐ 101 + ☐ 102 -	$ 103	☐ 101 + ☐ 102	$ 103	☐ 101 + ☐ 102	$ 103
Adjusted Sale Price of Comparables			Net Adj. 103a % Gross Adj. 103b %	$ 104	Net Adj. 103a % Gross Adj. 103b %	$ 104	Net Adj. 103a % Gross Adj. 103b %	$ 104

I ☐105 did ☐106 did not research the sale or transfer history of the subject property and comparable sales. If not, explain 107

My research ☐108 did ☐109 did not reveal any prior sales or transfers of the subject property for the three years prior to the effective date of this appraisal.
Data source(s) 110

My research ☐111 did ☐112 did not reveal any prior sales or transfers of the comparable sales for the year prior to the date of sale of the comparable sale.
Data source(s) 113

Report the results of the research and analysis of the prior sale or transfer history of the subject property and comparable sales (report additional prior sales on page 3).

ITEM	SUBJECT	COMPARABLE SALE # 1	COMPARABLE SALE # 2	COMPARABLE SALE # 3
Date of Prior Sale/Transfer	114	118	118	118
Price of Prior Sale/Transfer	115	119	119	119
Data Source(s)	116	120	120	120
Effective Date of Data Source(s)	117	121	121	121

Analysis of prior sale or transfer history of the subject property and comparable sales 122

Summary of Sales Comparison Approach 123

Indicated Value by Sales Comparison Approach $ 124

Indicated Value by: Sales Comparison Approach $ 125   Cost Approach (if developed) $ 126   Income Approach (if developed) $ 127
128

This appraisal is made ☐129 "as is", ☐130 subject to completion per plans and specifications on the basis of a hypothetical condition that the improvements have been completed, ☐131 subject to the following repairs or alterations on the basis of a hypothetical condition that the repairs or alterations have been completed, or ☐132 subject to the following required inspection based on the extraordinary assumption that the condition or deficiency does not require alteration or repair: 133

Based on a visual inspection of the exterior areas of the subject property from at least the street, defined scope of work, statement of assumptions and limiting conditions, and appraiser's certification, my (our) opinion of the market value, as defined, of the real property that is the subject of this report is
$ 134   , as of   135   , which is the date of the inspection and the effective date of this appraisal.

Fannie Mae Form 2055 – Page 3

Exterior-Only Inspection Residential Appraisal Report   File # 3   4   4a

ADDITIONAL COMMENTS

5

COST APPROACH TO VALUE (not required by Fannie Mae)

Provide adequate information for the lender/client to replicate the below cost figures and calculations.

Support for the opinion of site value (summary of comparable land sales or other methods for estimating site value) 6

ESTIMATED [7] REPRODUCTION OR [8] REPLACEMENT COST NEW	OPINION OF SITE VALUE				= $	14
Source of cost data 9	Dwelling 15	Sq. Ft. @ $	16		=$	17
Quality rating from cost service 10 Effective date of cost data 11	18 19	Sq. Ft. @ $	20		=$	21
Comments on Cost Approach (gross living area calculations, depreciation, etc.)	22					23
12	Garage/Carport 24	Sq. Ft. @ $	25		=$	26
	Total Estimate of Cost-New				= $	27
	Less	Physical	Functional	External		
	Depreciation 29	31	33		=$(	34)
	Depreciated Cost of Improvements				=$	35
	"As-is" Value of Site Improvements				=$	36
Estimated Remaining Economic Life (HUD and VA only) 13 Years	Indicated Value By Cost Approach				=$	37

INCOME APPROACH TO VALUE (not required by Fannie Mae)

Estimated Monthly Market Rent $ 38   X Gross Rent Multiplier 39   = $ 40   Indicated Value by Income Approach

Summary of Income Approach (including support for market rent and GRM) 41

PROJECT INFORMATION FOR PUDs (if applicable)

Is the developer/builder in control of the Homeowners' Association (HOA)? [42] Yes [43] No   Unit type(s) [44] Detached [45] Attached

Provide the following information for PUDs ONLY if the developer/builder is in control of the HOA and the subject property is an attached dwelling unit.

Legal name of project 46

Total number of phases 47   Total number of units 48   Total number of units sold 49

Total number of units rented 50   Total number of units for sale 51   Data source(s) 52

Was the project created by the conversion of an existing building(s) into a PUD? [53] Yes [54] No   If Yes, date of conversion 55

Does the project contain any multi-dwelling units? [56] Yes [57] No   Data source(s) 58

Are the units, common elements, and recreation facilities complete? [59] Yes [60] No   If No, describe the status of completion. 61

Are the common elements leased to or by the Homeowners' Association? [62] Yes [63] No   If Yes, describe the rental terms and options. 64

Describe common elements and recreational facilities 65

2 **Exterior-Only Inspection Residential Appraisal Report** File # 3 4 4a

This report form is designed to report an appraisal of a one-unit property or a one-unit property with an accessory unit; including a unit in a planned unit development (PUD). This report form is not designed to report an appraisal of a manufactured home or a unit in a condominium or cooperative project.

This appraisal report is subject to the following scope of work, intended use, intended user, definition of market value, statement of assumptions and limiting conditions, and certifications. Modifications, additions, or deletions to the intended use, intended user, definition of market value, or assumptions and limiting conditions are not permitted. The appraiser may expand the scope of work to include any additional research or analysis necessary based on the complexity of this appraisal assignment. Modifications or deletions to the certifications are also not permitted. However, additional certifications that do not constitute material alterations to this appraisal report, such as those required by law or those related to the appraiser's continuing education or membership in an appraisal organization, are permitted.

SCOPE OF WORK: The scope of work for this appraisal is defined by the complexity of this appraisal assignment and the reporting requirements of this appraisal report form, including the following definition of market value, statement of assumptions and limiting conditions, and certifications. The appraiser must, at a minimum: (1) perform a visual inspection of the exterior areas of the subject property from at least the street, (2) inspect the neighborhood, (3) inspect each of the comparable sales from at least the street, (4) research, verify, and analyze data from reliable public and/or private sources, and (5) report his or her analysis, opinions, and conclusions in this appraisal report.

The appraiser must be able to obtain adequate information about the physical characteristics (including, but not limited to, condition, room count, gross living area, etc.) of the subject property from the exterior-only inspection and reliable public and/or private sources to perform this appraisal. The appraiser should use the same type of data sources that he or she uses for comparable sales such as, but not limited to, multiple listing services, tax and assessment records, prior inspections, appraisal files, information provided by the property owner, etc.

INTENDED USE: The intended use of this appraisal report is for the lender/client to evaluate the property that is the subject of this appraisal for a mortgage finance transaction.

INTENDED USER: The intended user of this appraisal report is the lender/client.

DEFINITION MARKET VALUE: The most probable price which a property should bring in a competitive and open market under all conditions requisite to a fair sale, the buyer and seller, each acting prudently, knowledgeably and assuming the price is not affected by undue stimulus. Implicit in this definition is the consummation of a sale as of a specified date and the passing of title from seller to buyer under conditions whereby: (1) buyer and seller are typically motivated; (2) both parties are well informed or well advised, and each acting in what he or she considers his or her own best interest; (3) a reasonable time is allowed for exposure in the open market; (4) payment is made in terms of cash in U. S. dollars or in terms of financial arrangements comparable thereto; and (5) the price represents the normal consideration for the property sold unaffected by special or creative financing or sales concessions* granted by anyone associated with the sale.

*Adjustments to the comparables must be made for special or creative financing or sales concessions. No adjustments are necessary for those costs which are normally paid by sellers as a result of tradition or law in a market area; these costs are readily identifiable since the seller pays these costs in virtually all sales transactions. Special or creative financing adjustments can be made to the comparable property by comparisons to financing terms offered by a third party institutional lender that is not already involved in the property or transaction. Any adjustment should not be calculated on a mechanical dollar for dollar cost of the financing or concession but the dollar amount of any adjustment should approximate the market's reaction to the financing or concessions based on the appraiser's judgment.

STATEMENT OF ASSUMPTIONS AND LIMITING CONDITIONS: The appraiser's certification in this report is subject to the following assumptions and limiting conditions:

1. The appraiser will not be responsible for matters of a legal nature that affect either the property being appraised or the title to it, except for information that he or she became aware of during the research involved in performing this appraisal. The appraiser assumes that the title is good and marketable and will not render any opinions about the title.

2. The appraiser has examined the available flood maps that are provided by the Federal Emergency Management Agency (or other data sources) and has noted in this appraisal report whether any portion of the subject site is located in an identified Special Flood Hazard Area. Because the appraiser is not a surveyor, he or she makes no guarantees, express or implied, regarding this determination.

3. The appraiser will not give testimony or appear in court because he or she made an appraisal of the property in question, unless specific arrangements to do so have been made beforehand, or as otherwise required by law.

4. The appraiser has noted in this appraisal report any adverse conditions (such as needed repairs, deterioration, the presence of hazardous wastes, toxic substances, etc.) observed during the inspection of the subject property or that he or she became aware of during the research involved in performing this appraisal. Unless otherwise stated in this appraisal report, the appraiser has no knowledge of any hidden or unapparent physical deficiencies or adverse conditions of the property (such as, but not limited to, needed repairs, deterioration, the presence of hazardous wastes, toxic substances, adverse environmental conditions, etc.) that would make the property less valuable, and has assumed that there are no such conditions and makes no guarantees or warranties, express or implied. The appraiser will not be responsible for any such conditions that do exist or for any engineering or testing that might be required to discover whether such conditions exist. Because the appraiser is not an expert in the field of environmental hazards, this appraisal report must not be considered as an environmental assessment of the property.

5. The appraiser has based his or her appraisal report and valuation conclusion for an appraisal that is subject to satisfactory completion, repairs, or alterations on the assumption that the completion, repairs, or alterations of the subject property will be performed in a professional manner.

Fannie Mae Form 2055 – Page 5

Exterior-Only Inspection Residential Appraisal Report   File # 3   4   4a

2

APPRAISER'S CERTIFICATION: The Appraiser certifies and agrees that:

1. I have, at a minimum, developed and reported this appraisal in accordance with the scope of work requirements stated in this appraisal report.

2. I performed a visual inspection of the exterior areas of the subject property from at least the street. I reported the condition of the improvements in factual, specific terms. I identified and reported the physical deficiencies that could affect the livability, soundness, or structural integrity of the property.

3. I performed this appraisal in accordance with the requirements of the Uniform Standards of Professional Appraisal Practice that were adopted and promulgated by the Appraisal Standards Board of The Appraisal Foundation and that were in place at the time this appraisal report was prepared.

4. I developed my opinion of the market value of the real property that is the subject of this report based on the sales comparison approach to value. I have adequate comparable market data to develop a reliable sales comparison approach for this appraisal assignment. I further certify that I considered the cost and income approaches to value but did not develop them, unless otherwise indicated in this report.

5. I researched, verified, analyzed, and reported on any current agreement for sale for the subject property, any offering for sale of the subject property in the twelve months prior to the effective date of this appraisal, and the prior sales of the subject property for a minimum of three years prior to the effective date of this appraisal, unless otherwise indicated in this report.

6. I researched, verified, analyzed, and reported on the prior sales of the comparable sales for a minimum of one year prior to the date of sale of the comparable sale, unless otherwise indicated in this report.

7. I selected and used comparable sales that are locationally, physically, and functionally the most similar to the subject property.

8. I have not used comparable sales that were the result of combining a land sale with the contract purchase price of a home that has been built or will be built on the land.

9. I have reported adjustments to the comparable sales that reflect the market's reaction to the differences between the subject property and the comparable sales.

10. I verified, from a disinterested source, all information in this report that was provided by parties who have a financial interest in the sale or financing of the subject property.

11. I have knowledge and experience in appraising this type of property in this market area.

12. I am aware of, and have access to, the necessary and appropriate public and private data sources, such as multiple listing services, tax assessment records, public land records and other such data sources for the area in which the property is located.

13. I obtained the information, estimates, and opinions furnished by other parties and expressed in this appraisal report from reliable sources that I believe to be true and correct.

14. I have taken into consideration the factors that have an impact on value with respect to the subject neighborhood, subject property, and the proximity of the subject property to adverse influences in the development of my opinion of market value. I have noted in this appraisal report any adverse conditions (such as, but not limited to, needed repairs, deterioration, the presence of hazardous wastes, toxic substances, adverse environmental conditions, etc.) observed during the inspection of the subject property or that I became aware of during the research involved in performing this appraisal. I have considered these adverse conditions in my analysis of the property value, and have reported on the effect of the conditions on the value and marketability of the subject property.

15. I have not knowingly withheld any significant information from this appraisal report and, to the best of my knowledge, all statements and information in this appraisal report are true and correct.

16. I stated in this appraisal report my own personal, unbiased, and professional analysis, opinions, and conclusions, which are subject only to the assumptions and limiting conditions in this appraisal report.

17. I have no present or prospective interest in the property that is the subject of this report, and I have no present or prospective personal interest or bias with respect to the participants in the transaction. I did not base, either partially or completely, my analysis and/or opinion of market value in this appraisal report on the race, color, religion, sex, age, marital status, handicap, familial status, or national origin of either the prospective owners or occupants of the subject property or of the present owners or occupants of the properties in the vicinity of the subject property or on any other basis prohibited by law.

18. My employment and/or compensation for performing this appraisal or any future or anticipated appraisals was not conditioned on any agreement or understanding, written or otherwise, that I would report (or present analysis supporting) a predetermined specific value, a predetermined minimum value, a range or direction in value, a value that favors the cause of any party, or the attainment of a specific result or occurrence of a specific subsequent event (such as approval of a pending mortgage loan application).

19. I personally prepared all conclusions and opinions about the real estate that were set forth in this appraisal report. If I relied on significant real property appraisal assistance from any individual or individuals in the performance of this appraisal or the preparation of this appraisal report, I have named such individual(s) and disclosed the specific tasks performed in this appraisal report. I certify that any individual so named is qualified to perform the tasks. I have not authorized anyone to make a change to any item in this appraisal report; therefore, any change made to this appraisal is unauthorized and I will take no responsibility for it.

Fannie Mae Form 2055 – Page 6

2
Exterior-Only Inspection Residential Appraisal Report   File # 3   4   4a

20. I identified the lender/client in this appraisal report who is the individual, organization, or agent for the organization that ordered and will receive this appraisal report.

21. The lender/client may disclose or distribute this appraisal report to: the borrower; another lender at the request of the borrower; the mortgagee or its successors and assigns; mortgage insurers; government sponsored enterprises; other secondary market participants; data collection or reporting services; professional appraisal organizations; any department, agency, or instrumentality of the United States; and any state, the District of Columbia, or other jurisdictions; without having to obtain the appraiser's or supervisory appraiser's (if applicable) consent. Such consent must be obtained before this appraisal report may be disclosed or distributed to any other party (including, but not limited to, the public through advertising, public relations, news, sales, or other media).

22. I am aware that any disclosure or distribution of this appraisal report by me or the lender/client may be subject to certain laws and regulations. Further, I am also subject to the provisions of the Uniform Standards of Professional Appraisal Practice that pertain to disclosure or distribution by me.

23. The borrower, another lender at the request of the borrower, the mortgagee or its successors and assigns, mortgage insurers, government sponsored enterprises, and other secondary market participants may rely on this appraisal report as part of any mortgage finance transaction that involves any one or more of these parties.

24. If this appraisal report was transmitted as an "electronic record" containing my "electronic signature," as those terms are defined in applicable federal and/or state laws (excluding audio and video recordings), or a facsimile transmission of this appraisal report containing a copy or representation of my signature, the appraisal report shall be as effective, enforceable and valid as if a paper version of this appraisal report were delivered containing my original hand written signature.

25. Any intentional or negligent misrepresentation(s) contained in this appraisal report may result in civil liability and/or criminal penalties including, but not limited to, fine or imprisonment or both under the provisions of Title 18, United States Code, Section 1001, et seq., or similar state laws.

SUPERVISORY APPRAISER'S CERTIFICATION: The Supervisory Appraiser certifies and agrees that:

1. I directly supervised the appraiser for this appraisal assignment, have read the appraisal report, and agree with the appraiser's analysis, opinions, statements, conclusions, and the appraiser's certification.

2. I accept full responsibility for the contents of this appraisal report including, but not limited to, the appraiser's analysis, opinions, statements, conclusions, and the appraiser's certification.

3. The appraiser identified in this appraisal report is either a sub-contractor or an employee of the supervisory appraiser (or the appraisal firm), is qualified to perform this appraisal, and is acceptable to perform this appraisal under the applicable state law.

4. This appraisal report complies with the Uniform Standards of Professional Appraisal Practice that were adopted and promulgated by the Appraisal Standards Board of The Appraisal Foundation and that were in place at the time this appraisal report was prepared.

5. If this appraisal report was transmitted as an "electronic record" containing my "electronic signature," as those terms are defined in applicable federal and/or state laws (excluding audio and video recordings), or a facsimile transmission of this appraisal report containing a copy or representation of my signature, the appraisal report shall be as effective, enforceable and valid as if a paper version of this appraisal report were delivered containing my original hand written signature.

APPRAISER	SUPERVISORY APPRAISER (ONLY IF REQUIRED)
Signature _____	Signature _____
Name 5 _____	Name 27 _____
Company Name 6 _____	Company Name 28 _____
Company Address 7 _____	Company Address 29 _____
8a, 8b 8c _____	30a, 30b 30c _____
Telephone Number 9 _____	Telephone Number 31 _____
Email Address 10 _____	Email Address 32 _____
Date of Signature and Report 11 _____	Date of Signature 33 _____
Effective Date of Appraisal 12 _____	State Certification # 34 _____
State Certification # 13 _____	or State License # 35 _____
or State License # 14 _____	State 36 _____
or Other (describe) 15 _____ State # 16 _____	Expiration Date of Certification or License 37 _____
State 17 _____	
Expiration Date of Certification or License 18 _____	**SUBJECT PROPERTY**
	☐ Did not inspect exterior of subject property
ADDRESS OF PROPERTY APPRAISED	☐ Did inspect exterior of subject property from street
19 _____	Date of Inspection 40 _____
20a, 20b, 20c _____	
APPRAISED VALUE OF SUBJECT PROPERTY $ 21 _____	
LENDER/CLIENT	**COMPARABLE SALES**
Name 22 _____	☐ Did not inspect exterior of comparable sales from street
Company Name 23 _____	☐ Did inspect exterior of comparable sales from street
Company Address 24 _____	Date of Inspection 43 _____
Email Address 26 _____	

Appraisers are replacing their computers with notebooks, tablets, and smartphones.

H. ATTACHMENTS TO THE REPORT

A URAR typically has attachments. At a minimum, these consist of:

1. a building sketch;
2. subject photos;
3. comparable photos;
4. form 1004MC (see **Figure 12-5**)

Recently, Fannie Mae and Freddie Mac have required that subject photos include a view of the street from both directions, and photos of all major interior rooms.

Fannie Mae Form 1004MC

Figure 12-5

Market Conditions Addendum to the Appraisal Report   File No. _____

The purpose of this addendum is to provide the lender/client with a clear and accurate understanding of the market trends and conditions prevalent in the subject neighborhood. This is a required addendum for all appraisal reports with an effective date on or after April 1, 2009.

Property Address _____ City _____ State _____ ZIP Code _____

Borrower _____

Instructions: The appraiser must use the information required on this form as the basis for his/her conclusions, and must provide support for those conclusions, regarding housing trends and overall market conditions as reported in the Neighborhood section of the appraisal report form. The appraiser must fill in all the information to the extent it is available and reliable and must provide analysis as indicated below. If any required data is unavailable or is considered unreliable, the appraiser must provide an explanation. It is recognized that not all data sources will be able to provide data for the shaded areas below; if it is available, however, the appraiser must include the data in the analysis. If data sources provide the required information as an average instead of the median, the appraiser should report the available figure and identify it as an average. Sales and listings must be properties that compete with the subject property, determined by applying the criteria that would be used by a prospective buyer of the subject property. The appraiser must explain any anomalies in the data, such as seasonal markets, new construction, foreclosures, etc.

Inventory Analysis	Prior 7–12 Months	Prior 4–6 Months	Current – 3 Months	Overall Trend		
Total # of Comparable Sales (Settled)				☐ Increasing	☐ Stable	☐ Declining
Absorption Rate (Total Sales/Months)				☐ Increasing	☐ Stable	☐ Declining
Total # of Comparable Active Listings				☐ Declining	☐ Stable	☐ Increasing
Months of Housing Supply (Total Listings/Ab.Rate)				☐ Declining	☐ Stable	☐ Increasing
Median Sale & List Price, DOM, Sale/List %	**Prior 7–12 Months**	**Prior 4–6 Months**	**Current – 3 Months**	**Overall Trend**		
Median Comparable Sale Price				☐ Increasing	☐ Stable	☐ Declining
Median Comparable Sales Days on Market				☐ Declining	☐ Stable	☐ Increasing
Median Comparable List Price				☐ Increasing	☐ Stable	☐ Declining
Median Comparable Listings Days on Market				☐ Declining	☐ Stable	☐ Increasing
Median Sale Price as % of List Price				☐ Increasing	☐ Stable	☐ Declining
Seller-(developer, builder, etc.) paid financial assistance prevalent? ☐ Yes ☐ No				☐ Declining	☐ Stable	☐ Increasing

Explain in detail the seller concessions trends for the past 12 months (e.g., seller contributions increased from 3% to 5%, increasing use of buydowns, closing costs, condo fees, options, etc.).

_____
_____
_____

Are foreclosure sales (REO sales) a factor in the market? ☐ Yes ☐ No If yes, explain (including the trends in listings and sales of foreclosed properties).

_____
_____
_____
_____

Cite data sources for above information.

_____
_____

Summarize the above information as support for your conclusions in the Neighborhood section of the appraisal report form. If you used any additional information, such as an analysis of pending sales and/or expired and withdrawn listings, to formulate your conclusions, provide both an explanation and support for your conclusions.

_____
_____
_____
_____
_____
_____

If the subject is a unit in a condominium or cooperative project, complete the following: **Project Name:** _____

Subject Project Data	Prior 7-12 Months	Prior 4-6 Months	Current – 3 Months	Overall Trend		
Total # of Comparable Sales (Settled)				☐ Increasing	☐ Stable	☐ Declining
Absorption Rate (Total Sales/Months)				☐ Increasing	☐ Stable	☐ Declining
Total # of Active Comparable Listings				☐ Declining	☐ Stable	☐ Increasing
Months of Unit Supply (Total Listings/Ab. Rate)				☐ Declining	☐ Stable	☐ Increasing

Are foreclosure sales (REO sales) a factor in the project? ☐ Yes ☐ No If yes, indicate the number of REO listings and explain the trends in listings and sales of foreclosed properties.

_____
_____
_____
_____

Summarize the above trends and address the impact on the subject unit and project.

_____
_____
_____
_____
_____

Signature	Signature
Appraiser Name	Supervisory Appraiser Name
Company Name	Company Name
Company Address	Company Address
State License/Certification # State	State License/Certification # State
Email Address	Email Address

Freddie Mac Form 71   March 2009   Page 1 of 1   Fannie Mae Form 1004MC   March 2009

(Left margin vertical text: MARKET RESEARCH & ANALYSIS / CONDO/CO-OP PROJECTS / APPRAISER)

IV. CHAPTER SUMMARY

I. Real property appraisal reports are governed by Standard 2 of the Uniform Standards of Professional Appraisal Practice, and the corresponding Standards Rules.

II. An appraisal report is a means of communication. The type of report does not affect the appraisal process required to prepare a competent and credible appraisal.

III. Appraisal reports may be oral or written.

    A. Oral reports are delivered verbally, and include expert testimony given in a deposition or court of law.

    B. Narrative reports are detailed, written reports that set out all the relevant data used by the appraiser, and fully explain the appraiser's analysis and conclusions.

        1. Narrative reports are usually broken down into subsections, covering summary matters, definitions and terms, subject property data, and valuation analysis.

        2. A narrative report is usually accompanied by a letter of transmittal.

    C. Form reports are made on standardized forms, which are used by many appraisal clients such as lenders and insurers.

        1. The Uniform Residential Appraisal Report (URAR) is used in most appraisals of single-family residences that are made for lending purposes.

V. CHAPTER QUIZ

1. Standardized appraisal reports used by lenders, insurers, and similar high-volume appraisal clients are known as:

    a. uniform reports.
    b. letter reports.
    c. form reports.
    d. national reports.

2. Which type of appraisal report would be most likely to include a table of contents?

    a. Narrative report
    b. Form report
    c. Letter report
    d. Letter of transmittal

3. Use of the Uniform Residential Appraisal Report (URAR) is required for single-family residential appraisals that will be used by:

    a. Fannie Mae.
    b. Freddie Mac.
    c. the Department of Housing and Urban Development.
    d. all of the above.

4. On the URAR, the gross living area of the subject property improvements is reported in the:

    a. Subject section.
    b. Description of Improvements section.
    c. Sales Comparison Analysis section.
    d. both b and c.

5. In determining the "total" room count for a residence, the appraiser would normally include all of the following except:

    a. bedrooms.
    b. bathrooms.
    c. living rooms.
    d. dining rooms.

6. Information that will not fit in the space provided for it on a form appraisal report should be:

    a. written in the margins of the report.
    b. included in a different section of the report.
    c. omitted from the report, but kept in the appraiser's files.
    d. attached to the report as an addendum.

7. In the Sales Comparison Analysis section of the URAR form, the appraiser must report all sales of the subject property that occurred within the previous:

    a. six months.
    b. one year.
    c. two years.
    d. three years.

8. In a written appraisal report, the appraiser must certify all of the following except:

    a. that the statements of fact contained in the report are true.
    b. that the appraiser's compensation is not contingent on reporting a predetermined value.
    c. that the appraiser has (or has not) personally inspected the subject property.
    d. that the report is valid for up to 90 days from the effective date of appraisal.

9. On the URAR form, the estimated site value of the subject property is reported in the:

    a. Subject section.
    b. Site section.
    c. Comments section.
    d. Cost Approach section.

10. When requested by a client to carry out a limited appraisal, the appraiser should:

    a. inform the client that the report has lessened reliability.
    b. determine if the client's intended use will be met by such a report.
    c. determine if other intended users will understand the report.
    d. all of the above.

ANSWERS: 1. c; 2. a; 3. d; 4. d; 5. b; 6. d; 7. d; 8. d; 9. d; 10. d

Chapter 13
Appraising Special Interests

KEY WORDS AND TERMS

Community Property
Condominium Project
Cooperatives
Excess Rent
Gross Lease
Ground Lease
Joint Tenancy
Liens
Manufactured Homes

Net Lease
Planned Unit Development
Step-Down Lease
Step-Up Lease
Subdivision
Tenancy in Common
Timeshares
Triple Net Lease
Trusts

LEARNING OBJECTIVES

After completing this chapter, you should be able to:

1. describe the ways of dividing property ownership between two or more individuals or entities, including horizontal and vertical subdivisions, transfers of limited real property rights, and methods of shared ownership;

2. identify the appraisal techniques and considerations that are applicable to appraisals involving leaseholds, leased fees, easements, liens, and fractional interests in real estate; and

3. describe the characteristics of condominiums, PUDs, cooperatives, and timeshare interests, and identify the appraisal techniques that are used when appraising these types of interests.

CHAPTER 13 OUTLINE

I. Partial Interests in Real Estate

One of the fundamental factors that influence appraisals is the nature of the real property rights that are being appraised. Although appraisers usually are asked to estimate the value of fee simple estates, they are sometimes assigned the task of valuing partial interests in residential properties.

The complete ownership interest in real estate is called the **FEE SIMPLE**. The holder of a fee simple interest, or fee simple estate, has complete control over the ownership and use of the property, subject only to governmental limitations (i.e., property taxes, land use regulations, and the power of eminent domain). A fee simple interest in property can be divided between two or more individuals; when this occurs, each individual has a partial interest in the property. For example, if a husband and wife share ownership of their family home, each has a partial interest in the home. The total of all partial interests in a property may be equivalent to the fee simple interest.

A. WAYS TO DIVIDE THE FEE SIMPLE

The fee simple interest in a piece of property can be divided in three ways (see **Figure 13-1**):

1. the real property may be physically divided;
2. the bundle of rights that constitutes real property ownership may be divided; and
3. ownership of the property as a whole may be shared.

1. Physical Division of Real Property

One of the most common ways to divide the fee simple interest in a property is to divide the property itself into smaller units. This process is known as **SUBDIVISION**. The fee simple ownership of the original undivided property is divided into two or more separate fee simple interests, one for each parcel in the subdivision.

Case/Example: The owner of a five-acre tract of land may subdivide it into five one-acre parcels, each of which can then be sold separately. The original fee simple interest in the five acres is divided into five different fee simple estates, one for each of the one-acre parcels.

The familiar process of subdividing land into separate lots or parcels is called **HORIZONTAL SUBDIVISION**. But real estate can also be divided vertically. In **VERTICAL SUBDIVISION**, *the ownership of the subsurface, surface, or airspace associated with a property is separated from the ownership of the rest of the property* (see **Figure 13-2**).

Case/Example: The owner of a condominium unit has a fee simple interest in the airspace that is occupied by the unit, but does not have fee simple ownership of the land or subsurface beneath the unit.

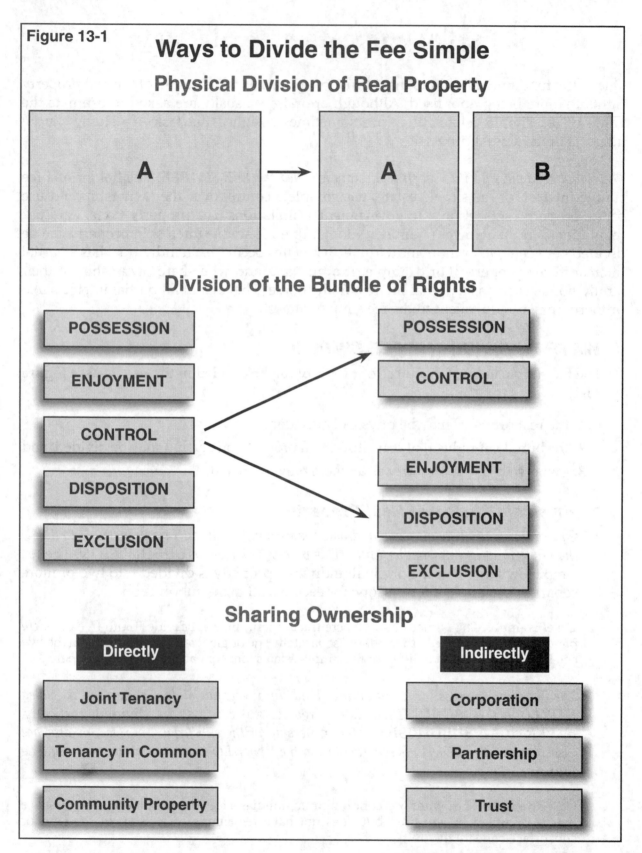

Figure 13-1

Ways to Divide the Fee Simple

Physical Division of Real Property

A → A B

Division of the Bundle of Rights

POSSESSION

ENJOYMENT

CONTROL → POSSESSION
CONTROL

ENJOYMENT

DISPOSITION → DISPOSITION

EXCLUSION

EXCLUSION

Sharing Ownership

Directly

Joint Tenancy

Tenancy in Common

Community Property

Indirectly

Corporation

Partnership

Trust

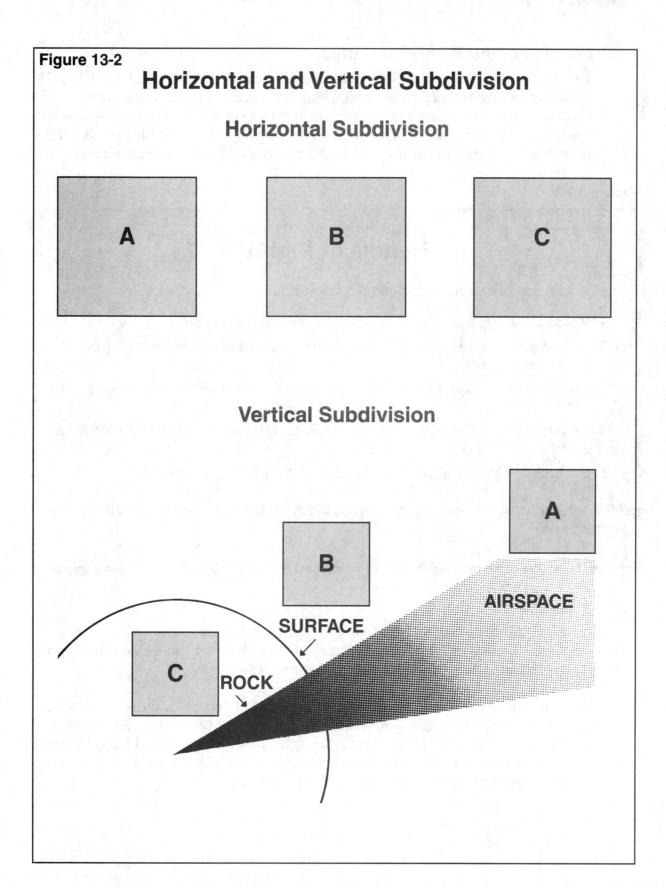

Figure 13-2

Horizontal and Vertical Subdivision

Horizontal Subdivision

A

B

C

Vertical Subdivision

A

B

AIRSPACE

SURFACE

C

ROCK

Chapter 13

2. Division of the Bundle of Rights

Fee simple ownership of real estate is often described as a *BUNDLE OF RIGHTS, including the rights to sell, will, encumber, lease, occupy, exclude, and use the property*. The second way of dividing a fee simple is to transfer some of the rights that go with the fee simple ownership. There are many different ways to divide up the bundle of ownership rights, including leases, easements, and liens (see **Figure 13-3**).

Figure 13-3

Bundle of Rights

The basic rights of ownership include the following;

1. **Possession** – is the right to occupy, rent, or keep others out.

2. **Enjoyment** – is the right to "peace and quiet" without interference from past owners and others.

3. **Control** – is the right to physically change or keep the property the way you like it.

4. **Disposition** – is the right to transfer all or part of your property to others as you see fit.

5. **Exclusion** – is the right to exclude others from use of your property.

All ownership rights are, of course, subject to governmental limitations and restrictions.

a. Leases

A *LEASE is a temporary transfer of the rights to occupy and use a property*. It divides a fee simple into a **leasehold estate**, which is held by the lessee (the tenant), and a **leased fee**, which is held by the lessor (the landlord).

The leasehold estate gives the tenant the right to occupy and use the property for the term of the lease, subject to the conditions of the lease agreement. The leased fee consists of all the remaining rights in the property, including the right to receive the rental payments and the right to recover the use and possession of the property at the expiration of the lease term.

b. Easements

An easement can be overhead or underground; for example, an electric power line easement used by a private electric company, or a pipeline easement used by a utility company. It can also be on the surface of the land; a road easement held by one person over land owned by another.

The right to use property, or a portion of a property, for a particular purpose can also be transferred for an indefinite period of time, which results in an easement. The holder of the easement has the right to use the property for a specific purpose as defined in the easement grant. The fee simple owner retains all other rights to the property, including the right to use the property in any manner, as long as that use does not interfere with the easement.

Most residential properties are subject to easements of one sort or another, such as easements for the maintenance of roadways or utilities.

Figure 13-4 illustrates a right-of-way easement that allows the owner of Parcel B to cross a portion of Parcel A. The owner of Parcel A is free to make any legal use of the land, provided that the use does not interfere with B's right of access across A's property.

Figure 13-4

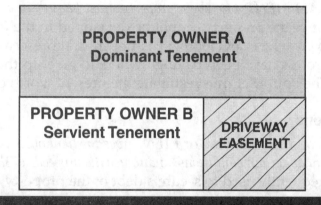

There are two basic types of easements: easements appurtenant and easements in gross. An *EASEMENT APPURTENANT benefits a parcel of land; ownership of the easement rights is attached to (or "runs" with) ownership of the benefited parcel.* In the example above, the right-of-way is an easement appurtenant to Parcel B. If the owner of Parcel B were to sell his land, the right-of-way easement would be transferred to the new owner along with the land.

In contrast to an easement appurtenant, an *EASEMENT IN GROSS benefits only a person or other legal entity, rather than a parcel of land.* Utility easements are a common example of easements in gross. These easements are granted for the benefit of the utility company, who owns the easement rights. An easement in gross does not run with the land. In other words, the ownership of an easement in gross is not transferred along with the ownership of any parcel of property. Easements can have an effect on value.

Case/Example: While underground utility easements generally would not negatively affect value, overhead utilities could have a significant effect on value as they do affect view.

Easements which present a real or perceived safety risk will have a negative effect on value.

Case/Example: A high pressure underground gas transmission pipeline or overhead high capacity electrical transmission lines, even when not physically on, over or under a property, can negatively affect the value of the property in proximity to the easement.

A *NEGATIVE EASEMENT would be an easement that prohibits the owner from a use.* It could be a height restriction for improvements in order to give another owner an easement of view. A more common negative easement is a *CONSERVATION EASEMENT whereby a property must be kept in a natural state or agricultural use.* Since the property cannot be developed in the future, it reduces present value even when development is not in the foreseeable future. Many conservancy groups have been paying owners to give up their future development rights. The appraiser must estimate the present worth of these rights.

c. Liens

A security interest, or *LIEN, gives the lienholder the right to sell the liened property under certain conditions, and to use the proceeds of the sale to satisfy a debt.* Liens are frequently used to secure a debt of the property owner.

Mortgages, deeds of trust, and real estate contracts are common examples of agreements that create liens against property.

3. Sharing Ownership of the Entire Property

The third way to divide the fee simple interest is to share it among two or more individuals or entities. Depending on the type of co-ownership, the individual rights and responsibilities of the co-owners are defined by law and/or by the terms of contractual agreements. Common forms of co-ownership include joint tenancies, tenancies in common, and community property. Co-ownership can also occur indirectly, as when property is owned by a corporation, partnership, or trust.

a. Joint Tenancy

In a *JOINT TENANCY, each of the joint tenants has an equal, undivided interest in the entire property*. A property owned by joint tenants cannot be transferred without the agreement of all of the joint tenants. Most joint tenancies include a right of survivorship, which means that if one joint tenant dies, ownership of the property automatically vests in the surviving joint tenant(s). However, one joint tenant can transfer his or her separate interest in the property. Such a transfer breaks the joint tenancy as to that tenant's share. The transferee would become a tenant in common with the other owners who, if more than one, would still remain joint tenants.

b. Tenancy in Common

A tenancy in common is similar to a joint tenancy, with a few exceptions. As is the case with joint tenants, tenants in common each own an undivided interest in the entire property. However, a *TENANT IN COMMON is free to transfer his or her interest by will*. There is no right of survivorship as there is in a joint tenancy. Another distinction between joint tenancies and tenancies in common is the fact that tenants in common do not necessarily have equal shares in the ownership. While joint tenants always have equal shares, proportionate to the number of joint tenants, tenants in common can agree to own the property in unequal shares.

Case/Example: If a property is owned by three people in joint tenancy, each of the three has an undivided one-third interest in the property. If they owned the property as tenants in common, however, the percentages of ownership would depend on the co-tenancy agreement. The co-tenants may agree that each will have a one-third share, or they may agree, for example, that one of them will have a 50% share, another 30%, and the third will have the remaining 20% share.

c. Community Property (Spanish Law)

The laws of most states provide for special forms of shared ownership between husbands and wives. A *TENANCY BY THE ENTIRETIES is one type of marital ownership; it is very similar to a joint tenancy, except the joint tenants must be husband and wife*. Real property owned "by the entireties" cannot be disposed of by either spouse without the consent of the other, and passes to the surviving spouse automatically if one of them dies (if there is no will).

Community property is another form of co-ownership between husband and wife. *COMMUNITY PROPERTY is established and defined by law in a number of states, primarily in the western part of the country (including California). The husband and wife each have an undivided one-half interest in all community property and the right of survivorship applies.*

4. Artificial Entities

Corporations, partnerships, and trusts are artificial legal entities, with characteristics, rights, and liabilities that are defined by law. These entities are capable of owning property, just as an individual person is, and they are often created for the express purpose of owning, leasing, or developing real estate.

a. Corporations

The owners of a corporation are called SHAREHOLDERS. Although the shareholders own the corporation, they do not directly own the property of the corporation. Corporate property is owned by the corporation itself, as a separate independent legal entity. Control over corporate property (such as the power to sell, lease, or mortgage the property) is vested in the officers of the corporation. The officers are appointed (and removed) by the board of directors, who are in turn subject to periodic election by the shareholders.

b. Partnerships

A PARTNERSHIP is a legal arrangement by which two or more persons or entities share rights and responsibilities with respect to a business. The rights and obligations of the partners are spelled out in the partnership agreement, which forms the basis of the partnership. In most states, real property may be owned in a partnership's name. The partnership agreement defines the percentage share of ownership of each of the partners, and also defines the extent of each partner's right to transfer, use, or encumber partnership property.

There are two types of partnerships: general and limited. Each partner in a *GENERAL PARTNERSHIP may act on behalf of the partnership, and each is also fully liable for any responsibilities of the partnership. A LIMITED PARTNERSHIP is made up of at least one general partner and at least one limited partner.* While the rights and liabilities of limited partners are restricted by individual partnership agreements and applicable state laws, limited partners are generally prohibited from any active participation in the partnership business. The rights and liabilities of the general partners are generally the same as those of a partner in a general partnership.

c. Trusts

A TRUST is a legal arrangement in which title to property is passed to a trustee, who manages the property for the benefit of a beneficiary. The beneficiary may be the original (pre-trust) owner of the property, or some other person designated to receive the income from the trust property.

B. PARTITION ACTION

A PARTITION ACTION is a court action to break up a jointly owned property (usually a joint tenancy or tenancy in common). Courts can order partition by sale or by a division of the property (where legally possible). The party who asks for a partition by sale must satisfy the court that a sale of the whole property would be economically more advantageous because the value as a single property might be greater than the total value of separate properties after a division. Parties would seek appraisals as to the value of the whole and value of the parts to reinforce their positions.

II. Appraising Partial Interests

In the previous section of this chapter, we examined the ways in which ownership of the fee simple interest can be divided among two or more persons or entities. Now we will take a look at the impact of partial ownership on value, and the appraisal techniques used to value partial interests.

A. LEASEHOLD AND LEASED FEE INTERESTS

A lease divides the ownership of property into two interests: the landlord's leased fee interest and the tenant's leasehold interest. Assuming that both interests are freely transferable, the combined values of these two estates may be equal to the total value of the fee simple.

When valuing either the leased fee interest or the leasehold interest, the appraiser must carefully consider the terms of the lease agreement itself.

The essence of appraising leasehold and leased fee interests is to compare the terms of the subject property lease agreement with the terms of similar leases that are currently available in the market. If the terms of the subject property lease are equivalent to current market terms, then the value of the leased fee is equivalent to the value of the entire fee simple, and the value of the leasehold is zero. The landlord (the owner of the leased fee) is receiving the full market rate of income from the property, so the value of her fee interest is not affected by the lease. Similarly, the tenant is obligated to pay the current market rate for the right to use the property, so his leasehold does not have any inherent value.

If the terms of the subject property lease (in comparison to market terms) favor the landlord or the tenant, then the values of both estates are affected. Terms favoring the landlord increase the value of the leased fee and decrease the value of the leasehold. If the terms favor the tenant, the value of the leasehold is enhanced, and the value of the leased fee suffers.

In valuing a leasehold or leased fee, the appraiser must consider all the terms of the subject property lease to determine whether they convey an advantage to the landlord or tenant. Terms that are most likely to have an effect on value include:

1. the amount of rent, including any scheduled changes in the rent;
2. the allocation of property expenses, such as taxes, hazard insurance premiums, and maintenance expenses;
3. the remaining unexpired term of the lease, including any renewal options; and
4. the financial stability of the tenant.

When the amount of rent is a fixed amount over the entire lease term, the lease is said to be a LEVEL PAYMENT LEASE or FLAT LEASE. However, many leases call for rent payments to be adjusted during the lease term. *When adjustments are called for at specific times and in specific amounts, the lease is called a STEP-UP LEASE or STEP-DOWN LEASE, depending on whether the adjustments are increases or decreases in the amount of rent.*

Case/Example: A five-year lease may call for payments of $1,400 per month in the first year, with annual rent increases of 5%. Since the rent increases will occur at specific times (annually) and in specific amounts (5%), the lease is a step-up lease.

Periodic rent adjustments may also be tied to market conditions, such as changes in the market value of the leased property (re-evaluation leases) or changes in the Consumer Price Index or some other economic index (index leases).

When appraising leasehold or leased fee interests, the appraiser must consider not only the current amount of contract rent, but also the effect on value of any scheduled or potential changes.

2. Other Lease Charges

A lease in which the lessee is responsible only for rent payments is called a GROSS LEASE. In a gross lease, the lessor pays for the expenses of maintaining the property, such as real estate taxes and assessments, hazard insurance premiums, and improvement maintenance expenses. *If the lessee is obligated to pay some or all of the maintenance expenses, the lease is called a NET LEASE. A lease in which the lessee pays all three categories of expenses, which include taxes, insurance, and maintenance, is sometimes called a TRIPLE NET LEASE or NET, NET, NET LEASE.*

The allocation of property expenses affects the appraiser's determination of market rent. For a given property, the amount of market rent will be higher for a gross lease, and lower if the tenant is responsible for expenses in addition to rent. For example, a property may have market rent of $1,000 per month under a gross lease, or $700 per month (plus expenses) under a triple net lease.

The allocation of expenses under a lease also allocates the risk that these expenses may increase during the term of the lease. For example, the party (the landlord or tenant) who is responsible for payment of real estate taxes bears the risk that the tax rate or assessed value will go up during the term of the lease, resulting in a higher property tax expense. The appraiser must consider the likelihood of such increases (or decreases) when estimating the effect on value of expense allocation provisions in the lease.

Case/Example: When oil prices increased drastically in the mid-1970s, long-term flat leases, where the landlord provided heating and/or cooling, resulted in a lowering of value for such properties. Expenses increased without a corresponding increase in income.

Project Information Section	Forms	Requirement or Instruction
Project Description If the project includes more than one building, the appraiser should enter the type of building in which the subject unit is located. Only one selection is permitted. If 'Other' is selected, the appraiser must enter a description. **Reporting Format:** Project Description – Checkbox designated with an 'x' Description of 'Other' (if applicable) – Text	1073/465 1075/466	INSTRUCTION
General Description - # of Stories, # of Elevators, Existing/Proposed/Under Construction, Year Built If the project includes more than one building, the appraiser should enter data for the building in which the subject unit is located. **Reporting Format:** # of Stories – See requirements in Improvements section # of Elevators – Numeric, whole numbers only Existing/Proposed/Under Construction – Checkbox designated with an 'x' Only one selection is permitted Year Built – See requirements in Improvements section Estimation of Year Built – See requirements in Improvements section	1073/465 1075/466	INSTRUCTION
Is the developer/builder in control of the Homeowners' Association (HOA)? For condominiums, the appraiser must select 'Yes' or 'No' in response to the question, "Is the developer/builder in control of the Homeowners' Association (HOA)?" located in the Project Information section. **Reporting Format:** Is the developer/builder in control of the Homeowners' Association (HOA)? – Checkbox designated with an 'x'	1073/465 1075/466	REQUIREMENT
Is there any commercial space in the project? If Yes, describe and indicate the overall percentage of the commercial space. The appraiser must select either 'Yes' or 'No' to indicate whether there is commercial space in the project. If 'Yes' is indicated, the appraiser must enter the overall percentage of commercial space in the project in which the subject property is located. **Reporting Format:** Is there any commercial space in the project? – Checkbox designated with an 'x' Percentage of Commercial Space – Numeric to 2 digits, whole numbers only	1073/465 1075/466	REQUIREMENT

3. Lease Term

The third type of lease provision that is most likely to affect the value of a leasehold or leased fee estate is the length of the remaining (unexpired) lease term. This is a major factor in the valuation of leasehold and leased fee estates because the effect on value of favorable or unfavorable lease conditions is much greater when the lease will remain in force for a longer period of time.

Case/Example: A property is currently rented for $1,000 per month in a market where similar properties rent for $2,000 per month. Ordinarily, such a large difference between contract rent and market rent would have a significant impact on the values of the leasehold and leased fee interests. However, if the lease is due to expire after one month, its effect on value will be minimal. Once the lease expires, the property can be re-rented at current market levels.

In a *PERIODIC LEASE (such as a month-to-month lease), either party can terminate the agreement with a minimum of notice*, so the effects of any favorable or unfavorable lease conditions have a minimal effect on value. Under a *TERM LEASE, however, both parties are bound for a fixed period of time—the term of the lease.*

When valuing a leasehold or leased fee, the appraiser is not concerned with the length of the lease term itself, but rather with the length of time from the effective date of the appraisal to the conclusion of the lease term.

This is the period during which any favorable or unfavorable lease conditions will affect the value of the leasehold and leased fee estates.

Case/Example: A 10-year term lease was signed in 2001. If the property (leased fee) is appraised in 2006, the appraiser will only be concerned with the remaining term (5 more years). The length of the original lease term is irrelevant to the appraisal.

4. Renewal Options

Many long-term leases include *RENEWAL OPTIONS, which allow the tenant to renew the lease on specified terms after the conclusion of the original lease term.* If the renewal terms are favorable to the tenant, the appraiser will take them into account when valuing the leasehold or leased fee. If the renewal terms favor the landlord, however, they are usually ignored by the appraiser. Since the tenant is the one who chooses whether or not to exercise the renewal option, it is unlikely that the lease will be renewed if the terms favor the landlord.

5. Financial Stability of Tenant

The financial stability of a tenant effects the likelihood of the tenant honoring the lease provisions. While an AAA rated national corporation is likely to honor its lease agreements, leases with financially shaky tenants bear a much greater risk of tenant default. This is especially important where the lease provisions are advantageous to the landlord because of an above-market rent. The appraiser, in such a situation should, consider the tenants likelihood of default and discount the above-market portion of the rent based on the tenant's financial condition.

6. Appraisal Techniques

The most effective technique for appraising leasehold and leased fee interests is usually the income capitalization approach. When appraising a leased fee, the appraiser can use residual techniques or discounting to estimate the value of the leased fee estate. To appraise a leasehold, the appraiser would capitalize or discount the difference between contract rent and market rent. In either case, the capitalized income amounts and the choice of capitalization or discount rates would be affected by such factors as the amount of contract rent, the allocation of property expenses, the length of the remaining lease term, the terms of any renewal options and the financial strength of the tenant.

B. EASEMENTS

Easements are valued in proportion to the value loss or gain sustained by the total property because of the existence of those easements.

Easements may enhance or detract from value, or they may have no effect at all. An easement that is typical of most properties in an area or neighborhood, such as a utility maintenance easement, generally has little if any effect on value. A typical easements, on the other hand, may have a substantial effect on value.

The sales comparison approach is usually the most effective way of estimating the value effects of easements.

It should be noted that an easement's effect on value is not necessarily equivalent for both the benefited and burdened properties. For example, an access or right-of-way easement may substantially enhance the value of the benefited parcel, without causing a corresponding decline in the value of the property that is crossed by the easement.

C. LIENS

Most appraisals estimate the value of property on the assumption that title is free and clear of any liens or other similar encumbrances. However, an appraiser may be called upon to estimate the value of property subject to a specific lien or liens.

Sales comparison and income capitalization techniques are the most appropriate methods for valuing such interests.

The terms of the underlying obligation (the amount, interest rate, repayment schedule, prepayment penalties, and assumability of the debt secured by the lien), are critical factors in estimating the effect on value.

Case/Example: A property with a fee simple value of $100,000 is subject to a mortgage lien in the amount of $40,000. The value of the property subject to the mortgage would depend on the terms of the mortgage note. If the note has standard-market terms and no prepayment penalty, the value of the owner's mortgaged interest may be equivalent to the value of the fee simple minus the amount of the mortgage. However, the value could be greater if, for example, the mortgage loan were freely assumable and had a below-market interest rate. In either case, the appraiser's estimate of value should be supported by adequate market evidence.

D. SHARED OWNERSHIP INTERESTS

It might seem that the valuation of a shared ownership interest, such as a 50% partnership share, would be a simple matter of applying a percentage to the total value of the property. However, this is not always the case. Shared ownership frequently entails some form of limitation on the rights of a partial owner to control the use and transfer of the property, and these limitations can in turn affect the value of the partial interest.

Case/Example: The interest of a majority shareholder in a corporation is generally worth more than his or her proportionate share of the corporate assets, since the majority interest conveys the ability to control the use and disposition of the assets.

If the value of the whole is NOT considered, the appraisal must clearly reflect that the value of the property being appraised cannot be used to estimate the value of the whole by mathematical extension.

The appraiser is required to consider those factors (such as issues of control over use and dispositions of the property) that may make a fractional interest worth more or less than its proportionate share of total property value.

III. Other Forms of Ownership

In the preceding sections of this chapter, we have examined various types of partial ownership interests in real estate, and some of the important considerations involved in appraising such interests. The remainder of this chapter will look at some more complex types of real estate interests, involving combinations of fee simple and partial interests.

A. CONDOMINIUMS AND PUDs

Condominiums and PUDs (planned unit developments) are very similar types of ownership. Each combines fee simple ownership of an individual unit with shared ownership of common areas. An owner has full title to his or her unit in a condominium or PUD, and the individual units may be sold, mortgaged, or leased.

Ownership of the common areas in the project, as well as the cost of maintaining the common areas, is shared among all the individual unit owners.

The common areas are managed by an owners' association under the terms of established bylaws, and periodic charges or dues levied on each unit in the project to cover the cost of common area maintenance.

1. Condominiums

A *CONDOMINIUM PROJECT is basically a complex where each living unit is owned separately in fee simple.* The owner of a condominium unit has fee simple title to the three-dimensional airspace (air lot) that is occupied by the unit. All of the land in the project is owned jointly, along with common elements of the building(s) such as the exterior walls, roofs, foundations, and common stairs and hallways. Jointly owned recreational facilities, such as swimming pools or tennis courts, are often present as well.

The most reliable method for appraising condominium units is the sales comparison method.

If adequate rental data is available, the income approach may also be used to support the value indicated by sales comparison. The comparables used for sales comparison must themselves be condominium properties, preferably from within the same project as the subject.

If units from other projects are used as comparables, the appraiser must make adjustments in the sales comparison to account for differences in project amenities and common area management. A significant element of comparison in this regard is the amount of charges or dues that are levied on the unit for common area maintenance. These charges can vary widely from one project to another, even when the projects offer similar amenities.

Differences between condominium projects can be very difficult to account for in terms of their effects on value. For this reason, comparables are best chosen from projects that are similar in overall layout, total number of units, and recreational facilities.

2. Planned Unit Development (PUD)

A *PLANNED UNIT DEVELOPMENT (PUD) is a kind of subdivision where the developer is allowed to exceed the normal zoning density in exchange for setting aside part of the development as open space.* The individual units or lots in a PUD, which are owned in fee simple, may be detached homes or townhouses. The open space areas are owned in common through a homeowners' association, or sometimes deeded to the local community. Like condominium projects, PUDs often include jointly-owned recreational facilities or other amenities. Appraisal considerations for PUD units are similar to those for condominiums.

The most reliable comparable sales will be found within the same development as the subject, and should be similar in type (detached or townhouse) to the subject lot.

The extent of common areas and amenities, the quality of common area management, and the level of dues or charges levied for common area maintenance, are important elements of comparison.

B. COOPERATIVES

In a *COOPERATIVE, real estate (usually an apartment building) is owned by a corporation.* Each shareholder of the corporation receives a proprietary lease of one of the apartments. (The number of required shares may vary from unit to unit within the project.) So "ownership" of a cooperative apartment unit actually consists of ownership of shares in the cooperative corporation, plus a leasehold interest in a particular unit.

The cooperative shareholder-tenants make monthly payments to the corporation to cover the costs of managing and maintaining the property and also the cost of any corporate debt service. The payment amounts are generally prorated based on the number of shares owned by each tenant. Control over the project is vested in the corporation's board of directors, who are elected by the shareholders, and who operate the project in accordance with corporate bylaws.

As is the case with condominium and PUD units, cooperative units are best appraised using the sales comparison approach, and the best comparables are units from within the same cooperative apartment building as the subject.

The appraiser may use comparables from other similar cooperatives, but must be careful to make adjustments to account for differences in corporate assets and liabilities. Many cooperative corporations carry mortgage debt which is secured by the project real estate, and the amount of such debt can have a significant impact on the value of the corporate shares.

Case/Example: A cooperative with 20 units has a mortgage debt of $400,000. Assuming each unit requires the purchase of 5% (1/20th) of the corporate shares, each shareholder would be responsible for 5% of the corporate debt, or $20,000. If a comparable unit in a different cooperative entailed only $10,000 worth of debt, an adjustment to the comparable sales price would be required to account for this difference.

If adequate rental data is available, the income approach may also be applied in the appraisal of cooperatives. However, many cooperatives prohibit their shareholder-tenants from subletting their units, in which case the income approach would not be applicable.

C. TIMESHARES

In a **TIMESHARE**, *the use rights to a property (usually a recreational property) are divided up according to the time of year*. Each timeshare interest conveys the right to use the property during a specific time period each year, such as June 1 through June 14. Ownership rights (as opposed to use rights) may or may not be included in the timeshare interest. *If the timeshare includes a proportionate share of ownership, it is called a* **TIMESHARE ESTATE**; *if not, it is a* **TIMESHARE USE**.

Some timeshares are leasehold interests for a stated number of years (timeshare use) such as 30 years, while others are fractionalized fee ownership (timeshare estate).

The sales comparison approach is usually the most reliable method for appraising timeshares, but the income and cost approaches may be applicable to particular cases as well.

Important elements of comparison for timeshares include the type of interest (estate or use) and the desirability of the time period covered by the interest in relation to the location of the property. For example, a timeshare interest in a beach property would be more valuable in May than in December, while the opposite would be true for a timeshare in a ski resort.

Timeshares are a relatively new form of ownership, and new timeshare projects are often heavily promoted by the developer. Generally, timeshare developers sell 50 weeks leaving two weeks for maintenance. Because of the sales costs and time required to make 50 sales for every unit, the total sale price of the 50 weeks is likely to be many times the value of the unit.

Very few timeshares have resales which are greater than the original purchase price. Generally, resale prices are less than 60 percent of original sale price and are frequently less than 50 percent of the sale price.

Resale prices are a more reliable indicator of value than original sale prices of timeshare units. An analysis of marketing time for re-sales will alert the appraiser to any weakness in market demand.

D. MANUFACTURED HOMES

MANUFACTURED HOMES are factory built housing that is built to the requirements of the HUD Building Code. This code is national in scope and assures sellers, buyers, and lenders that such housing meets nationally mandated standards. The HUD code unlike other building codes is mandatory for all manufactured housing and requires tested standards. Additionally, other building codes such as UBC, SBC, and BOCA for site built housing are voluntary in nature. This means that some jurisdictions may require full adherence to the building code, some only partial adherence, and others have no requirements at all! Manufactured homes enjoy a significant economic advantage over site built housing for the following reasons:

1. Because they are built in a factory there are no weather delays.
2. Factory construction eliminates site theft and vandalism.
3. Factory construction allows building to very precise tolerances due to use of jigs to precisely align walls, flooring, and interior appointments.
4. Purchasers may customize floor plans to suit their needs.
5. Material purchases are made in bulk and delivered to one factory site this reduces material costs.
6. Workers are long term employees and do not move from site to site. Since they perform the same job in an assembly line fashion they tend to become quite proficient at it.
7. A home is built in a matter of days, rather than weeks or months.
8. Manufactured homes come in all quality levels and some models are far superior in quality to the average site built home, yet cost less.

Manufactured homes have an integral steel frame that is used to transport them to a building site. When the wheels, axles, and towing bar are removed and the home is set on a permanent foundation on a building site, it is in all respects similar to a raised foundation site built home. In effect, the manufactured home is real property. As such, it should be compared to similar manufactured homes on building sites. Manufactured homes are considered to be a complex property type and require a Certified Level Appraiser for federally related transactions.

Manufactured homes located in rental parks are considered personal property. In appraising a manufactured home in a rental park, the appraiser must consider a number of factors. These include:

1. Park amenities
2. Park rules
3. Park rental fees
4. Length of lease
5. Restrictions on rent increases (rent control)
6. Blue book value

There is a blue book for manufactured homes in parks which shows wholesale and resale prices paid by or to dealers. While this is a valuable tool for the appraiser, the park where the unit is located will affect the value of the unit.

In California, some single-wide units which have a blue book value of less than $3,000 have sold for over $100,000 because they were at an ocean front park location. Premium values attach to parks having rent control compared to those not subject to rent control.

Generally, a manufactured home is classified as real property when it is placed on a permanent foundation.

The real estate status means that it is taxed as real property rather than subject to an annual license fee.

In some states, a park owner can require removal of units over a particular age. If this is the case an appraiser would attach little value to a particular park if removal could be mandated.

Some parks have poor reputations because of rules, tenant/management problems as well as fees. Conversely, some parks have an excellent reputation and re-sales of units are often significantly greater than for other parks, even though the physical plans could be very similar.

E. PREFABRICATED/MODULAR HOMES

PREFABRICATED HOMES are assembled on site in sections. Value is influenced by public perception of prefabricated homes within the community. At one time prefabricated housing was of low quality and these units sold at a discount from similar size conventionally built housing. Today, many prefabricated homes are of equal or even superior quality to conventionally built housing, and in some areas they are valued similarly. In other areas some discount would have to be considered in evaluation based on the loan market.

F. GROUND LEASES

In some areas of the country, ground leases are common. Ground leases are long-term leases. The improvements are placed on the property by the tenants. Indian land is frequently leased. Some corporate owners also lease their land rather than sell it. The federal government also owns many leaseholds.

The value of the leased premises would be based on:

1. improvements;
2. length of lease;
3. lease terms; and
4. likelihood of lease extensions at reasonable terms.

The Bureau of Indian Affairs has, in the past, influenced tribes to renew ground leases. In recent years some tribes have indicated that they will not renew leases. This has resulted in hundreds of homeowners having property which can only be marketed at a tremendous discount to the value of the improvements.

The U.S. Forest Service, at one time, leased sites for cabins. In fact, many of these cabins evolved into homes costing hundreds of thousands of dollars. The Forest Service, in many cases, has been refusing to allow extensions to these leases and requiring the owners to pay for the removal of the improvements. The effect of such action has resulted in a negative value to the property.

If the improvements revert to the fee owner at the end of the lease, the value of the fee interest would increase as the lease term decreased. Of course, the value of the improvements would be a prime factor in the value of the fee.

IV. CHAPTER SUMMARY

II. The fee simple interest in real estate may be divided to create smaller or partial interests.

  A. Subdivision splits a single fee simple interest into two or more smaller fee simple estates.

   1. Real estate may be subdivided horizontally and/or vertically.

  B. The bundle of ownership rights may be divided by means such as leases, easements, and liens.

  C. Ownership of a property may be shared by two or more individuals or entities.

   1. Ownership is shared directly in joint tenancies, tenancies in common, and marital communities.

   2. Ownership can also be shared indirectly when property is owned by an artificial entity such as a partnership, corporation, or trust.

II. The characteristics of a real property interest influence the appraiser's selection and analysis of data, and the choice of appraisal techniques.

  A. In appraisals of leaseholds and leased fee interests, the appraiser must consider the effects on value caused by the terms of the lease agreement.

   1. If contract rent is higher than market rent, the value of the leased fee is enhanced and the value of the leasehold is diminished. These value effects are reversed if market rent exceeds contract rent.

a. The amount of contract rent may be stable over the term of the lease, or it may be subject to change.

2. Allocation of property expenses affects the appraiser's estimate of market rent. Similar properties will command higher rents if the landlord pays these expenses, and lower rents if the tenant pays them.

3. The significance of the lease terms depends on the length of time that they will remain in effect: the remaining unexpired term of the lease.

a. Renewal options may increase the length of time that the lease remains in effect, but renewals are usually exercised only if the lease terms are favorable to the tenant.

4. The income approach is usually the most reliable indicator of value for leasehold and leased fee interests.

B. Easements are usually appraised by the sales comparison approach.

1. An easement may have value to the person or parcel that receives the benefit of the easement, and it may also affect the value of the burdened parcel of land. However, the effects on the values of the benefited and burdened estates are not necessarily equivalent.

C. The effect on value caused by a lien depends on the terms of the underlying obligation that is secured by the lien. This effect is most reliably determined by the sales comparison approach.

D. The value of a shared fractional interest in real estate is not necessarily equivalent to the pro rata share of ownership, due to limitations on the ability of a partial owner to control the use and transfer of the property. Sales comparison is the best method for estimating the value of fractional interests.

III. Condominiums, PUDs, cooperatives, and timeshares all have unique characteristics that may affect their values. Each of these types of properties is best appraised through sales comparison, using sales of similar properties in the same development or a similar development.

A. Condominiums and PUDs include fee simple ownership of individual lots plus shared ownership of common areas.

1. The lots in a condominium are all air lots. PUD lots may be conventional detached lots or townhouses.

2. Important elements of comparison include the types of amenities that are part of the common ownership, and the fees or dues levied on each unit to support management and maintenance of the common areas.

B. Cooperative ownership includes ownership of shares in the cooperative corporation which holds fee title to the project as well as a proprietary lease to one of the units in the project.

    1. Each owner pays a pro rata share of maintenance costs and corporate debt service. The amount of these costs is an important element of comparison for cooperative properties.

C. Timeshares allocate the use of property on the basis of the time of year. A timeshare estate also includes a share of the fee ownership, while a timeshare use does not.

    1. In making a sales comparison, the appraiser should consider the nature of the interest (estate or use), as well as the desirability of the particular time of year covered by the interest.

    2. Aggressive marketing by developers may distort original sales prices of timeshares. Resale prices are usually more reliable indicators of value.

D. Manufactured homes are built to the HUD Code. If sold with a site, a manufactured home would be valued as any other residential home. For homes sold on leased sites, the park amenities, lease terms, etc., would affect valuation.

E. Prefabricated homes are factory built in sections and site assembled. They are valued as other residential property.

F. Modular homes are factory built and transported in sections on flatbed trucks. They are generally valued at a discount compared to site-built housing.

G. Ground leases are leases where the tenant provides the improvements. The value of a ground lease to tenant and landlord would be affected by:

    1. improvements;

    2. length of the lease;

    3. terms of the lease; and

    4. likelihood of a lease extension at reasonable terms.

V. CHAPTER QUIZ

1. Which of the following interests in real estate represents the most complete form of ownership?

    a. Leasehold
    b. Leased fee
    c. Fee simple
    d. Tenancy in common

2. Which of the following interests in real estate would normally include a right of survivorship?

    a. Fee simple
    b. Joint tenancy
    c. Tenancy in common
    d. Tenancy for years

3. A real property interest that includes fee simple ownership of an air lot and a shared ownership of common areas is called a:

    a. leasehold.
    b. cooperative.
    c. tenancy in common.
    d. condominium.

4. The cost of managing and maintaining the common areas of a development is an important consideration in the appraisal of:

    a. condominiums.
    b. cooperatives.
    c. PUDs.
    d. all of the above.

5. If a lease calls for rental payments that are higher than rents for comparable properties:

    a. the value of the leased fee estate is enhanced.
    b. the value of the leasehold estate is enhanced.
    c. the effect on value depends on the original lease term.
    d. both a and c.

6. In a tenancy in common:

    a. each owner has the undivided right to use the entire property.
    b. each owner has an equal share in the ownership of the property.
    c. an owner may not transfer his or her interest without the consent of all the other co-owners.
    d. all of the above.

7. When appraising a leasehold or leased fee interest, an appraiser must:
   a. determine the value of the fee simple.
   b. consider the effect on value of the lease terms.
   c. give the most weight to the value indicated by the income approach.
   d. all of the above.

8. Ownership of a unit in a cooperative project includes:
   a. ownership of corporate shares.
   b. a leasehold interest in the cooperative unit.
   c. responsibility for a pro-rata share of corporate debt.
   d. all of the above.

9. Which of the following is NOT an important consideration in the appraisal of a leased fee estate?
   a. The amount of rent
   b. The allocation of property expenses
   c. A renewal option on terms favorable to the landlord
   d. The length of the unexpired lease term

10. When the amount of rent required by a lease is higher than rents being charged for similar properties in the market, the difference is referred to as:
    a. scheduled rent.
    b. contract rent.
    c. excess rent.
    d. market rent.

ANSWERS: *1. c; 2. b; 3. d; 4. d; 5. a; 6. a; 7. b; 8. d; 9. c; 10. c*

Chapter 14
The Appraisal Profession

KEY WORDS AND TERMS

Advisory Opinions
Appraisal Standards Board
Appraisal Qualifications Board
Competency Rule
Ethics Rule
General Certification

Jurisdictional Exception
Profession
Residential Certification
Scope of Work
Statements on Appraisal Standards
The Appraisal Foundation

LEARNING OBJECTIVES

After completing this chapter, you should be able to:

1. describe the characteristics that distinguish a profession from other types of occupations;

2. identify the major professional appraisal associations and their membership designations;

3. describe the licensing and certification requirements of the Financial Institutions Reform, Recovery, and Enforcement Act of 1989 (FIRREA);

4. explain the significance of the Uniform Standards of Professional Appraisal Practice; and

5. understand the general principles of the USPAP that are contained in its introduction section.

I. Standards

Like all professions, appraisal is governed by widely accepted standards of practice and rules of ethical conduct. Historically, these standards have been established by and enforced through various private professional associations in the form of membership standards and codes of ethics.

The creation of the Uniform Standards of Professional Appraisal Practice (USPAP), in 1987, provided another guideline for measuring the professionalism of an appraiser.

Compliance with these standards is required when either the service or the appraiser is obligated by law or regulation, or by an agreement with the client or intended users, to comply, as noted in the latest Uniform Standards of Professional Appraisal Practice (USPAP), published and maintained by the Appraisal Foundation.

In recent years, the practice of appraisal has also become subject to increasing governmental regulation, including government licensing and certification requirements.

II. Professional Associations

A *PROFESSION can be broadly defined as a calling that requires specialized knowledge.* But what really distinguishes a profession from other types of occupations is the existence of self-imposed standards of professional conduct and competence.

These standards are developed by professional associations, and enforced by the associations through their membership requirements.

Membership in a professional association usually has two basic requirements. First, prospective members must demonstrate their competence through some combination of education, experience, and/or testing. A minimum level of continuing education is often a requirement for maintaining or renewing membership as well (see **Figure 14-1**).

Many professional organizations support the education of their members (and of others in the profession) by offering seminars and courses, and also by publishing textbooks, reports and professional journals.

The second basic requirement of membership in most professional organizations is that a member must agree to be bound by the association's standards of professional conduct (standards of practice, code of ethics, etc). The association itself decides whether its members have lived up to these standards, through the process of peer review.

Membership in a professional association is indicated by a professional designation, such as IFA (NAIFA). Some organizations have more than one designation, to indicate different levels or types of professional expertise.

Case/Example: IFA and **IFAC**, designations of the National Association of Independent Fee Appraisers.

From the point of view of the general public, the significance of such designations depends on two things: the standards of competence and conduct that the association requires of its members, and the reliability of the association in enforcing those standards. The more rigorous the standards, and the more vigilant the association is in maintaining them, the more public trust is put in the professionalism of the association's members.

The names and addresses of professional appraisal organizations are included in **Figure 14-2**.

Figure 14-1

Professional Appraiser Designations

AACI - Accredited Appraiser Canadian Institute
(Appraisal Institute of Canada)

AAE - Accredited Assessment Evaluator
(International Association of Assessing Officers - IAAO)

ARA - Accredited Rural Appraisers
(American Society of Farm Managers and Rural Appraisers,Inc. - ASFMRA)

ASA - Senior Member
(American Society of Appraisers - ASA)

ASR - Senior Residential Member
(American Society of Appraisers - ASA)

CA-C - Certified Appraiser - Consultant
(National Association of Independent Fee Appraisers - NAIFA)

CAE - Certified Assessment Evaluator
(International Association of Assessing Officers - IAAO)

CAO - Certified Appraisal Organization
(National Association of Master Appraisers - NAMA)

CA-R - Certified Appraiser - Residential
(National Association of Independent Fee Appriasers - NAIFA)

CA-S - Certified Appraiser - Senior
(National Association of Independent Fee Appriasers - NAIFA)

CRA - Canadian Residential Appraiser
(Appraisal Institute of Canada)

FASA - Fellow
(American Society of Appraisers - ASA)

IFA - Independent Fee Appraiser
(National Association of Independent Fee Appriasers - NAIFA)

IFAC - Independent Fee Appraiser - Counselor
(National Association of Independent Fee Appriasers - NAIFA)

IFAS - Independent Fee Appraiser - Senior
(National Association of Independent Fee Appriasers - NAIFA)

MFLA - Master Farm and Land Appraiser
(National Association of Master Appraisers - NAMA)

MRA - Master Residential Appraiser
(National Association of Master Appraisers - NAMA)

MSA - Master Senior Appraiser
(National Association of Master Appraisers - NAMA)

RES - Residential Evaluation Specialist
(International Association of Assessing Officers - IAAO)

SR/WA - Senior - Right of Way Association
(International Right of Way Association - IRWA)

III. Standards of Professional Competence and Conduct

Prior to the 1980s, appraisers were subject to little, if any, government regulation.

Most states had no licensing or certification requirements for appraisers, and the standards of the professional associations were applied only to their own members. With the collapse of the savings and loan (S&L) industry in the 1980s, however, the appraisal profession began to undergo a profound change.

Questionable appraisal practices, and a lack of industry standards for competence and professional conduct, were viewed by many as having contributed to the S&L failures. In response to this crisis, the appraisal industry (and the federal government) began to take the first steps towards industry-wide standards for appraisers.

A. THE APPRAISAL FOUNDATION

In 1985, nine professional appraisal associations joined together to form the Ad Hoc Committee on Uniform Standards of Professional Appraisal Practice (USPAP).

The nine associations were the American Institute of Real Estate Appraisers, the American Society of Appraisers, the American Society of Farm Managers and Rural Appraisers, the Appraisal Institute of Canada, the International Association of Assessing Officers, the International Right-of-Way Association, the National Association of Independent Fee Appraisers, the National Society of Real Estate Appraisers, and the Society of Real Estate Appraisers. The original USPAP drafted by the Ad Hoc Committee took effect in 1987.

Chapter 14

Figure 14-2

Professional Appraisal Sponsors
of the Appraisal Foundation

American Society of Appraisers (ASA)
11107 Sunset Hills Rd, Suite 310
Reston, VA 20190
www.appraisers.org

American Society of Farm Managers and Rural Appraisers (ASFMRA)
950 South Cherry Street, Suite 508
Denver, CO 80246-2664
www.asfmra.org

Appraisal Institute of Canada
403-200 rue, Catherine Street
Ottawa, Ontario CANADA K2P 2K9
www.aicanada.org

International Association of Assessing Officers (IAAO)
314 West 10th Street
Kansas City, Missouri 64105
www.iaao.org

International Right of Way Association (IRWA)
19210 South Vermont Avenue, Building A, Suite 100
Gardena, CA 90248
www.irwaonline.org

National Association of Independent Fee Appraisers (NAIFA)
401 North Michigan Avenue, Suite 2200
Chicago, IL 60611
www.naifa.com

National Association of Master Appraisers (NAMA)
303 West Cypress Street
P.O. Box 12617
San Antonio, TX 78212-0617
www.masterappraisers.org

The year 1987 also saw the birth of the *APPRAISAL FOUNDATION, a non-profit corporation based in Washington, D.C., that was created by the same professional associations that made up the Ad Hoc Committee (with the exception of the Appraisal Institute of Canada).* According to the bylaws of the Appraisal Foundation, its purpose is "to foster professionalism by helping to ensure that appraisers are qualified to offer their services and by promoting the Uniform Standards of Professional Appraisal Practice."

In 1989, the USPAP were incorporated into law through the **Financial Institutions Reform, Recovery, and Enforcement Act of 1989 (FIRREA)**, commonly known as "the S&L bail-out bill." This bill also required the states to begin certifying and licensing appraisers on the basis of recognized standards of competence. (FIRREA and related federal regulations are discussed in more detail in Chapter 15.)

At about the same time that FIRREA took effect, the Appraisal Foundation set up two new boards: the Appraisal Standards Board and the Appraisal Qualifications Board. The *APPRAISAL STANDARDS BOARD (ASB) is charged with promoting the acceptance of the USPAP, and also with updating the standards on an ongoing basis to reflect new developments in appraisal practice.* The *APPRAISER QUALIFICATIONS BOARD (AQB) is concerned with the education, testing, and experience requirements for appraiser certification and licensing.*

The Appraisal Foundation has implemented a new board, the *APPRAISAL PRACTICES BOARD, which will serve to codify and implement the best practices and application for appraisers.* The Foundation has also created a publication at it's website to explain to consumers the role of the appraiser in financial transactions of all types and how the public trust is maintained by use of appraisers. The Foundation also has plans to advertize in the public media to make the general public aware of the beneficial role of appraisers in society.

appraisalfoundation.org
The Appraisal Foundation

B. CERTIFICATION AND LICENSING

As noted in the previous section, the requirement for state certification and/or licensing of appraisers originated with FIRREA. FIRREA requires that any appraisal that is made in connection with a "federally related transaction" be performed by a state-certified or state-licensed appraiser.

Complex appraisals require a state-certified appraiser, while non-complex appraisals may be performed by an appraiser who is either state-certified or state-licensed.

(The requirements of FIRREA and related federal regulations are discussed in more detail in Chapter 15.) Although certification and licensing is required by federal legislation, it is the individual states which actually manage the process.

The licensing/certification laws and regulations of each state must meet minimum standards set by federal law, but the states are free to impose their own stricter standards as well.

This is true both with respect to the standards of competence required for licensing or certification, and also with respect to the circumstances under which a license or certification is required.

Because each state has its own licensing/certification laws and regulations, the requirements vary from state to state. At a minimum, the appraiser must pass a state examination. Many states require specific education as well.

In general, the distinction between licensing and certification is based on the required level of experience, with certification requiring a certain amount of professional experience, education, and testing.

In most states, there are two types or classes of certification: residential and general. *RESIDENTIAL CERTIFICATION is the more limited of the two; as its name suggests, it qualifies the appraiser with respect to residential properties only. GENERAL CERTIFICATION places more emphasis on the income approach, and qualifies the appraiser for all types of properties.* The Appraisal Qualifications Board of The Appraisal Foundation publishes a recommended National Uniform Examination Content Outline for each type of certification, residential, and general.

Appraiser qualifications vary by state. **Figure 14-3** shows the new AQB/OREA Real Property Appraiser Qualification Criteria that went into effect as of January 1, 2008. **Figure 14-4** is a list of the various state regulatory agencies, their addresses, and Internet sites, if available.

"In the future, even Trainees/Licensed Appraisers may be required to at least have an AS Degree and have completed all AQB required courses before they can work. Certified Appraisers will be required to have a BA or higher. Colleges will have to submit appraisal coursework to AQB for approval as well." – Lev Messick

IV. The Uniform Standards of Professional Appraisal Practice

The Uniform Standards of Professional Appraisal Practice (USPAP) represent a major step towards self-regulation in the appraisal industry. These standards have been widely adopted by professional appraisal associations, and by government regulatory agencies as well. The USPAP consists of:

1. an introductory section on general ethical rules;
2. ten Standards, with associated Standards Rules; and

Figure 14-3

AQB/OREA Real Property Appraiser Qualification Criteria (Went into effect as of January 1, 2008)			
OREA License Levels	**Basic Education Requirements**	**College Level Requirements**	**Experience**
Trainee (AT)	150 Hours	N/A	N/A
Residential (AL)	150 Hours	N/A	2,000 Hours (accumulated over at least a 12-month period)
Certified Residential (AR)	200 Hours	Associate Degree*	2,500 Hours (accumulated over at least a 30-month period)
Certified General (AG)	300 Hours	Bachelors Degree**	3,000 Hours that include at least 1,500 non-residential hours (accumulated over at least a 30-month period)

* In lieu of the Associate Degree, an applicant can complete 21 college semester credits in courses covering specific subject matters: English Composition; Principles of Economics (Micro or Macro); Finance, Algebra, Geometry, or higher mathematics; Statistics, Introduction to Computers; and Business or Real Estate Law.

** In lieu of the Bachelors Degree, an applicant can complete 30 college semester credits in courses covering specific subject matters: English Composition; Micro Economics; Macro Economics; Finance, Algebra, Geometry, or higher mathematics; Statistics, Introduction to Computers; Business or Real Estate Law; and two elective courses in accounting, geography, ag-economics, business management, or real estate.

3. clarifying Statements on Appraisal Standards. In addition, the Appraisal Standards Board (ASB) has issued a number of Advisory Opinions, which give advice from the ASB on the application of the Standards to specific appraisal situations.

A. GENERAL PRINCIPLES

The first section of the USPAP consists of a preamble, four general rules (covering ethics, competency, scope of work, and jurisdictional exception), and a list of definitions.

Chapter 14

Figure 14-4

State Real Estate Appraiser Regulatory Boards

ALABAMA
Alabama Real Estate Appraiser Board
P.O. Box 304355
Montgomery, AL 36130-4355
PHONE: 334-242-8747
www.reab.state.al.us

(All information was accurate at the time of printing, yet subject to change.)

ALASKA
Board of Certified Real Estate Appraisers
333 Willoughby Avenue
P.O. Box 110806
Juneau, AK 99811-0806
PHONE: 907-465-5470
www.dced.state.ak.us/occ/papr.htm

ARIZONA
Arizona Board of Appraisal
1400 W. Washington, Suite 360
Phoenix, AZ 85007
PHONE: 602-542-1539
www.appraisal.state.az.us

ARKANSAS
Arkansas Appraiser Licensing & Certification Board
101 E. Capitol, Suite 430
Little Rock, AR 72201
PHONE: 501-296-1843
www.arkansas.gov/alcb

CALIFORNIA
Office of Real Estate Appraisers
1102 Q Street, Suite 4100
Sacramento, CA 95811
PHONE: 916-552-9000
www.orea.ca.gov

COLORADO
State of Colorado Board of Real Estate Appraisers
1560 Broadway, Suite 925
Denver, CO 80202
PHONE: 303-894-2166
www.dora.state.co.us/real-estate/appraiserlicensing.htm

CONNECTICUT
Department of Consumer Protection
165 Capitol Avenue Hartford, CT 06106
PHONE: 800-842-
www.ct.gov/dcp/site/default.asp

▼

DELAWARE
Delaware Council on Real Estate Appraisers
Cannon Building, Suite 203
861 Silver Lake Blvd.
Dover, DE 19904
PHONE: 302-744-4500
http://dpr.delaware.gov/boards/realestateappraisers/index.shtml

DISTRICT OF COLUMBIA DCRA/OPLA
1100 4th Street SW
Washington, DC 20024
PHONE: 202-442-4320
FAX: 202-442-4528
www.pearsonvue.com/dc/appraisers

FLORIDA
Division of Real Estate
400 West Robinson Street, N801
Orlando, Fl 32801
PHONE: 850-487-1395
FAX: 407-317-7245
www.myfloridalicense.com/dbpr/re/freab.html

GEORGIA
Georgia Real Estate Appraiser Board
229 Peachtree Street, NE
International Tower, Suite 1000
Atlanta, GA 30303-1605
PHONE: 404-656-3916
www.grec.state.ga.us

HAWAII
Hawaii Real Estate Appraiser Program
P.O. Box 3469
Honolulu, HI 96801
PHONE: 808-586-3000
www.hawaii.gov/dcca/areas/pvl/programs/realestateappraiser

IDAHO
Idaho Real Estate Appraiser Board
Bureau of Occupational Licenses
PO Box 83720
Boise, Idaho 83720-0063
PHONE: 208-334-3233
www.ibol.idaho.gov

ILLINOIS
Illinois Real Estate Appraisal Administration Division
James R. Thompson Center
100 West Randolph Street, Suite 9-300
Chicago, IL 60601
PHONE: 312-814-4500
www.idfpr.com/dpr/re/reabout.asp

Chapter 14

INDIANA
Real Estate Appraiser Licensure and Certification Board
Indiana Professional Licensing Agency
402 West Washington Street, Room W072
Indianapolis, IN 46204
PHONE: 317-234-3009
www.in.gov/pla/appraiser.htm

IOWA
Iowa Real Estate Appraiser Examining Board
1920 S.E. Hulsizer Road
Ankeny, IA 50021-3941
PHONE: 515-281-4126
www.state.ia.us/government/com/prof/appraiser/home.html

KANSAS
Kansas Real Estate Appraisal Board
Jayhawk Tower, Roof Garden Level
700 SW Jackson, Ste. 1102
Topeka, KS 66603
PHONE: 785-296-6736
www.accesskansas.org/kreab

KENTUCKY
Kentucky Real Estate Appraisers Board
135 W. Irvine Street, Suite 301
Richmond, KY 40475
PHONE: 859-623-1658
www.kreab.ky.gov

LOUISIANA
Louisiana Real Estate Appraisers Board
9071 Interline Avenue
Baton Rouge, LA 70809
PHONE: 225-925-1923
www.lreasbc.state.la.us

MAINE
Maine Board of Real Estate Appraisers
35 State House Station
Augusta, ME 04333-0035
PHONE: 207-624-8522
www.maine.gov/pfr/professionallicensing/professions/appraisers

MARYLAND
Maryland Deptartment of Labor, Licensing, & Regulation
Division of Occupational and Professional Licensing
Commission of Real Estate Appraisers and Home Inspectors
500 N. Calvert Street
Baltimore, MD 21202-3651
PHONE: 410-230-6165
www.dllr.state.md.us/license/reahi

▼

MASSACHUSETTS
Board of Registration of Real Estate Appraisers
990 Washington Street, Suite 302
Dedham, MA 02026
PHONE: 781-329-1996
www.mbrea.org/i4a/pages/index.cfm?pageid=3365

MICHIGAN
Dept. of Energy, Labor, & Economic Growth
Bureau of Commercial Services
P.O. Box 30004
Lansing, MI 48909
PHONE: 517-373-1820
www.michigan.gov/appraisers

MINNESOTA
Minnesota Department of Commerce
85 7th Place East, Suite 500
St. Paul, MN 55101
PHONE: 612-296-6319
www.state.mn.us/portal/mn/jsp/home.do?agency=Commerce

MISSISSIPPI
Mississippi Appraisal Board
PO Box 12685
Jackson, MS 39236
PHONE: 601-932-6770
www.mab.state.ms.us/mab/index_mab.html

MISSOURI
Missouri Real Estate Appraisers Commission
3605 Missouri Blvd.
P.O. Box 1335
Jefferson City, MO 65102-1335
PHONE: 573-751-0038
www.pr.mo.gov/appraisers.asp

MONTANA
Board of Real Estate Appraisers
301 S. Park Avenue, Suite 400
P.O. Box 200513
Helena, MT 59620-0513
PHONE: 406-841-2325
http://bsd.dli.mt.gov/license/bsd_boards/rea_board/board_page.asp

NEBRASKA
Nebraska Real Property Appraiser Board (NRPAB)
301 Centennial Mall South
Nebraska State Office Building, Lower Level
Lincoln, NE 68509
PHONE: 402-471-9015
www.appraiser.ne.gov

NEVADA
Nevada Real Estate Division
1179 Fairview Drive, Suite E
Carson City, NV 89710-5453
PHONE: 775-687-4280
www.red.state.nv.us

NEW HAMPSHIRE
New Hampshire Real Estate Appraiser Board
State House Annex, Room 426
25 Capitol Street
Concord, NH 03301-6312
PHONE: 603-271-6186
www.nh.gov/nhreab

NEW JERSEY
State Real Estate Appraiser Board
Division of Consumer Affairs
124 Halsey Street
P.O. Box 45032
Newark, NJ 07102
PHONE: 973-504-6200
www.njconsumeraffairs.gov/real

NEW MEXICO
New Mexico Real Estate Appraisers Board
Toney Anaya Building
2550 Cerrillos Road, Second Floor
Santa Fe, New Mexico 87505
PHONE: 505-476-4860
www.rld.state.nm.us/RealEstateAppraisers

NEW YORK
Department of State
Division of Licensing Services
P.O. Box 22001
Albany, NY 12201-2001
PHONE: 518-474-4429
www.dos.state.ny.us/licensing/re_appraiser/re_appboard.html

NORTH CAROLINA
5830 Six Forks Road
Raleigh, NC 27609
PHONE: 919-870-4854
www.ncappraisalboard.org

NORTH DAKOTA
North Dakota State Appraisal Board
P.O. Box 1336
Bismarck, ND 58502-1336
PHONE: 701-222-1051
www.ndreab.org

OHIO
Department of Commerce
Division of Real Estate & Professional Licensing
77 South High Street, 20th Floor
Columbus, OH 43215-6133
PHONE: 614-446-4100
www.com.ohio.gov/real/appmain.aspx

OKLAHOMA
Oklahoma Real Estate Appraiser Board
5 Corporate Plaza
3625 NW 56th, Suite 100
Oklahoma City, OK 73112
PHONE: 405-521-6636
www.ok.gov/oid/Regulated_Entities/Real_Estate_Appraiser_Board_(REAB)/

OREGON
Appraiser Certification & Licensure Board
3000 Market Street NE,Suite 541
Salem, OR 97301
PHONE: 503-485-2555
www.oregon.gov/ACLB

PENNSYLVANIA
State Board of Certified Real Estate Appraisers
P.O. Box 2649
Harrisburg, PA 17105-2649
PHONE: 717-783-4866
www.dos.state.pa.us/real

RHODE ISLAND
Rhode Island Real Estate Appraisers Board
Deptartment of Business Regulation - Appraisal Section
1511 Pontiac Avenue
Cranston, RI 02920
PHONE: 401-462-9500
www.dbr.state.ri.us/divisions/commlicensing/realestate.php

SOUTH CAROLINA
Department of Labor, Licensing, and Regulation
P.O. Box 11329
Columbia, S.C. 29211
PHONE: 803-896-4300
www.llr.state.sc.us/pol.asp

SOUTH DAKOTA
South Dakota Department of Labor and Regulation
445 East Capitol Avenue
Pierre, SD 57501-3185
PHONE: 605-773-4608
www.state.sd.us/appraisers

▼

TENNESSEE
Tennessee Real Estate Appraiser Commission
500 James Robertson Parkway
Nashville, TN 37243-1166
PHONE: 615-741-1831
http://tn.gov/commerce/boards/treac/index.shtml

TEXAS
Texas Appraiser Licensing & Certification Board
P.O. Box 12188
Austin, TX 78711-2188
PHONE: 512-459-2232
www.talcb.state.tx.us

UTAH
Department of Commerce
Utah Division of Real Estate
Box 146711
Salt Lake City, UT 84114-6711
PHONE: 801-530-6747
http://realestate.utah.gov

VERMONT
Office of Professional Regulation
Vermont Board of Real Estate Appraisers
National Life Bldg, North FL2
Montpelier, VT 05620-3402
PHONE: 802-828-1505
http://vtprofessionals.org/opr1/real_estate_appraisers

VIRGINIA
Department of Professional and Occupational Regulation
9960 Mayland Drive, Suite 400
Richmond, VA 23233-1463
PHONE: 804-367-2039
www.dpor.virginia.gov/dporweb/apr_main.cfm

WASHINGTON
Washington State Department of Licensing
405 Black Lake Blvd SW
Olympia, WA 98502
PHONE: 360-753-1062
www.dol.wa.gov

WEST VIRGINIA
Real Estate Licensing and Certification Board
2110 Kanawha Blvd., East, Suite 101
Charleston, WV 25311
PHONE: 304-558-3919
www.appraiserboard.wv.gov

▼

WISCONSIN
Wisconsin Department of Regulation and Licensing
P.O. Box 8935
Madison, WI 53708-8935
PHONE: (877) 617-1565
http://drl.wi.gov

WYOMING
Certified Real Estate Appraiser Board
First Bank Building
2020 Carey Avenue, Suite 702
Cheyenne, WY 82002
PHONE: 307-777-7141
http://realestate.state.wy.us

AMERICAN SAMOA
American Samoa Government
Pago Pago, 96799
American Samoa
PHONE: 684-633-4116

GUAM
Government of Guam
Dept. of Revenue & Taxation
Bldg 13-1, 2nd Fl. Mariner Ave, Tiyan
P.O. Box 23607
Barrigada, GU 96913
PHONE: 671-475-1844

MARIANA ISLANDS
Board of Professional Licensing
Commonwealth of Northern Mariana Islands
P.O. Box 502078
Saipan, MP 96913
PHONE: 670-234-5897

PUERTO RICO
Government of Puerto Rico
Department of State
Puerto Rico Board of Examiners
Hortencia #240, Round Hills
Trujillo Alto, PR 00976
PHONE: 787-722-2122

VIRGIN ISLANDS
Dept. of Licensing and Consumer Affairs
Government of Virgin Islands
No. 1 Sub Base, Room 205
St. Thomas, VI 00802
PHONE: 809-773-2226

B. STANDARDS AND STANDARDS RULES

There are 10 Standards in the USPAP, as shown in **Figure 14-5**. Each Standard consists of a generalized Statement (the standard itself) followed by more detailed and specific Standards Rules.

Figure 14-5

USPAP Standards

Standard 1 - Real Property Appraisal, Development

Standard 2 - Real Property Appraisal, Reporting

Standard 3 - Appraisal Review, Development, and Reporting

Standard 4 - Real Property Appraisal Consulting, Development

Standard 5 - Real Property Appraisal Consulting, Reporting

Standard 6 - Mass Appraisal, Development, and Reporting

Standard 7 - Personal Property Appraisal, Development

Standard 8 - Personal Property Appraisal, Reporting

Standard 9 - Business Appraisal, Development

Standard 10 - Business Appraisal Reporting

The Appraisal Foundation publishes new additions of USPAP annually. These contain all new changes to the document and are available directly from the Foundation by subscription service. The Appraisal Foundation may be contacted at:

The Appraisal Foundation
1155 15th Street NW, Suite 1111
Washington, DC 20005
www.appraisalfoundation.org
(202) 347-7722

C. STATEMENTS ON APPRAISAL STANDARDS

In addition to modifying existing Standards rules, the ASB has the authority (under the bylaws of The Appraisal Foundation) to issue formal *STATEMENTS ON APPRAISAL STANDARDS, which clarify, interpret, explain or elaborate on the Standards.* These Statements have the same binding force as the other provisions of the USPAP. Ten Statements have been issued to date, but expect more.

D. ADVISORY OPINIONS

ADVISORY OPINIONS illustrate the application of the USPAP in particular situations. However, Advisory Opinions do not have the binding effect of the USPAP. They neither establish new Standards nor interpret existing ones; they merely indicate the advice and opinion of the Appraisal Standards Board. Thirty-two advisory opinions have been issued through 2011.

E. MODIFICATIONS OF USPAP

The ASB has the authority to amend or modify the USPAP, as well as to issue Statements on Appraisal Standards and Advisory Opinions. Revised editions of the USPAP are issued each year, and mid-year updates may be issued as well.

Appraisers must always be aware of the latest Standards in order to insure that their actions conform to the requirements of the USPAP.

F. INTRODUCTORY PROVISIONS OF THE USPAP

The introductory provisions of the USPAP are general rules that apply to all types of appraisals. There are seven introductory provisions:

1. Preamble;
2. Ethics Rule;
3. Competency Rule;
4. Scope of Work;
5. Jurisdictional Exception Rule; and
6. Definitions
7. Glossary (Removed).

1. Preamble

The Preamble provides an overview of the USPAP. The first paragraph states the underlying rationale for the Standards, and the remainder of the Preamble explains how the USPAP documentation is organized.

The Standards include explanatory comments and begin with an **Ethics Rule**, setting forth the requirements for integrity, objectivity, independent judgment, and ethical conduct. In addition, the Standards include a **Competency Rule**, which places an immediate responsibility on the appraiser prior to acceptance of an assignment. The Standards contain a **Scope of Work Rule**. A **Definitions Rule** is also included.

The Standards deal with the procedures to be followed in performing an appraisal and the manner in which an appraisal is communicated.

A. **Standards 1 and 2** relate to the development and communication of a real property appraisal.

B. **Standard 3** establishes rules for reviewing an appraisal and reporting on that review.

C. **Standards 4 and 5** address the development and communication of various real estate or real property consulting functions by an appraiser.

D. **Standard 6** addresses the development and reporting of mass appraisals for ad valorem tax purposes.

E. **Standards 7 and 8** establish rules for personal property appraisals.

F. **Standards 9 and 10** set rules for developing and communicating business appraisals.

The Standards include Statements on Appraisal Standards issued by the Appraisal Standards Board.

Explanatory comments are an integral part of the Uniform Standards and should be viewed as extensions of the document.

2. Ethics Rule

This provision emphasizes the personal obligations and responsibilities of the individual appraiser. However, it should also be emphasized that groups and organizations engaged in appraisal practice share the same ethical obligations.

The first substantive rule of the USPAP is the *ETHICS RULE, which describes the appraiser's ethical obligations in regard to conduct, management, confidentiality, and record keeping.* The **Conduct section** requires the appraiser to take all necessary steps to avoid behavior that might be misleading or fraudulent.

The **Management section** concerns the ethics of appraisal business practices, particularly compensation arrangements and advertising. Practices specifically identified as unethical include contingent compensation arrangements, undisclosed procurement payments, and false or misleading advertising.

The third section of the Ethics Rule, the **Confidentiality section**, requires the appraiser to protect the confidentiality of information obtained from a client or results produced for a client. Disclosure of such information is limited to the client, to persons authorized by the client or by law, and to members of an authorized peer review committee.

The final section of the Ethics Rule is the **Record Keeping section**. This section sets out the record keeping requirements for all written or oral appraisals, including the types of records that must be kept, and the length of time that the records must be maintained.

3. Competency Rule

The "Competency Rule" prohibits appraisers from accepting appraisal assignments for which they are not qualified by both knowledge and experience.

An exception is allowed only if the appraiser informs the client in advance of the lack of appropriate qualifications, takes the necessary steps to insure that the appraisal is performed competently, and fully describes these facts in the appraisal report.

4. Scope of Work

The concept of the **Scope of Work** refers to the depth of necessary research and reporting required to produce a credible report that not only meets the needs of the client but that would also be considered acceptable by the appraiser's peers.

The Scope of Work Rule was developed by the Appraisal Standards Board to replace the outdated concept of departure. It was designed to provide flexibility in developing and reporting an appraisal by recognizing that the amount and depth of research varies depending upon the needs of the client and the intended use of the report. The Appraisal Board emphasizes that the amount of research and depth of reporting must not be unduly influenced by the clients desires which could result in a misleading report.

The concept of *SCOPE OF WORK refers to the depth of necessary research and reporting required to produce a credible report that not only meets the needs of the client but that would also be considered acceptable by the appraiser's peers.*

The appraiser determines the amount of work and type of report required, NOT the client.

The appraiser is the professional and has a responsibility to ensure that the report will not be misunderstood or be misleading in the marketplace. In other words, the client may not be the only user or reader of the report. The fact that a client wants something less than a complete report is not sufficient reason in itself to provide one. The appraiser has a professional responsibility to provide clients with what they actually "need," rather that what they may "want."

5. Jurisdictional Exception

The purpose of the *JURISDICTIONAL EXCEPTION is to limit the potential adverse effects of local laws in terms of the applicability of the USPAP in the local jurisdiction.* If a local law makes part of the USPAP unenforceable, the remaining parts are not affected.

6. Definitions

The definition section of USPAP defines the exact meaning of terms used in USPAP. They are an integral part of the USPAP and are not subject to any other interpretation. All users of the document are required to accept them as defined.

7. Glossary (Removed)

The **Glossary** of commonly used real estate and financial terms that used to appear in the USPAP document has been removed as it was felt that persons were confusing these terms with the official definitions that are an integral part of the standards.

The Uniform Standards of Professional Appraisal Practice is a living document that is subject to change by the Appraisal Standards Board at any time. The Board has made frequent yearly changes since the inception of the standards in 1987. Recently, the Board has announced that it plans to make changes every two years, rather than annually.

Contact Information for 2012-2013 Edition of USPAP

The ASB invites questions about USPAP, commentary on USPAP, and proposed changes to USPAP from all interested parties, including appraisers, state enforcement agencies, users of appraisal services, and the public. If you have any comments, questions, or suggestions regarding USPAP, please contact the ASB.

Appraisal Standards Board
The Appraisal Foundation
1155 15th Street, NW, Suite 1111
Washington, DC 20005
Phone: 202-347-7722
Fax: 202-347-7727
E-Mail: info@appraisalfoundation.org
appraisalfoundation.org

V. National Association of Independent Fee Appraisers Code of Ethics

8.1 Professional Conduct. A member shall conduct himself/herself at all times in a manner beneficial to the Association and to the community.

8.2 Fees. No appraisal fees may be contingent upon the valuation of an appraisal. All fees for trial testimony must be determined prior to the trial. No fees may be split without the full consent of all interested parties.

8.3 Appraisal Reports. Each appraisal must contain the following items in addition to all pertinent information known to the appraiser at the time of the appraisal:

A. A statement as to purpose and/or objectives of the appraisal, with value defined.
B. A legal description and/or adequate identification of the property appraised.
C. The date of the value estimate, the date at which the value estimate applies.
D. An adequate description of the physical characteristics of the property appraised.
E. A statement as to the known and/or observed encumbrances, if applicable.
F. A statement and analysis of the highest and best use of the property appraised, if appropriate.
G. As statement as to the property rights appraised.
H. A direct sales comparison approach and analysis, if applicable.
I. A cost approach and analysis, if applicable.
J. An income approach and analysis, if applicable.
K. A statement as to the conclusions reached in the appraisal report.
L. Documentation requirements (the appraiser must have the minimum data requirements in his/her file to property support the final estimate of value).
M. A statement as to the assumption and limiting conditions affecting the appraisal.
N. The signature of the responsible appraiser together with his/her particular designation (IFA, IFAA, IFAS, IFAC).
O. A statement concerning the maintenance of confidentiality regarding the Appraisal assignment and results thereof.
P. Designated members (IFA, IFAA, IFAS, IFAC) must disclose continuing education status clearly in every appraisal report.

8.4 Value Reports. Appraisal reports must not include:

A. Improbable and non supportable premises.
B. Vague assumptions unsupported by fact.
C. Improbable highest and best use.

8.5 Certification Statement. The certification of each appraisal must contain the statement: "This appraisal has been prepared in conformity with the code of ethics of the National Association of Independent Fee Appraisers, and the Uniform Standards of Professional Appraisal Practice as promulgated by the Appraisal Foundation." On printed forms supplied or required by client, the appraiser is bound by the above code and certification even though the statement is not contained therein.

8.6 Professional Practice. It is unethical for an appraiser to do the following:

A. Conduct himself/herself in any manner which will prejudice his/her professional status or the reputation of any appraisal organization with which he/she is connected.
B. Compete unfairly with other appraisers.
C. Injure by falsification or by malice, directly or indirectly, the professional reputation, prospects or business of any other appraiser.

D. Fail to report to the Association the actions of any member who, the option of the reporting member, has violated this code of ethics.

E. Advertise or solicit appraisal business an any manner not consonant with accepted professional practice.

F. Reveal in any way the substance of any appraisal without permission of the client or due process of law.

G. Issue a separate appraisal report when another appraiser assigned to appraise the property has had a part in the formation of the opinion of value.

H. Issue an appraisal report on only a part of a whole property without stating that it is a factional appraisal; and, as such, subject to use in a manner consistent with such limitations.

I. Accept an assignment to appraise a property of a type with which he/she has had no previous experience unless in making the appraisal, he/she associates himself/herself with an appraiser who has had experience with the type of property being appraised; or, make full disclosure of the degree of his/her experience, background and training to his/her client.

---

orea.ca.gov

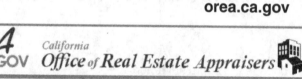

California Office of Real Estate Appraisers

Welcome to OREA

Office of Governor
Jerry Brown
Visit his Website

State of California
BUSINESS, TRANSPORTATION & HOUSING AGENCY

BOB CLARK
Director
OREA

 Forms
 Renew Online @ OREA.CA.GOV
 Search for an Appraiser
 Appraisal Management Companies
 Licensing Requirements

 File a Complaint
 Enforcement Actions
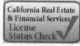 California Real Estate & Financial Services License Status Check
 Laws & Regulations
 Education

What's New	Licensees, AMC, and Education	Customer Service
Customary and Reasonable Fees OREA has no legal authority to enforce provisions of the Dodd-Frank Wall Street Reform and Consumer Protection Act of 2010 related to *Customary and Reasonable Compensation for Fee Appraisers*. The Dodd-Frank Act established the Consumer Financial Protection Bureau, and many of the pieces of the Dodd-Frank Act relating to the CFPB will go into effect on July 21, 2011. For more information, please go to: http://www.consumerfinance.gov/. Until such time as the CFPB's enforcement authority is fully implemented, violations of Customary and Reasonable Compensation	Search for an appraiser Search for an AMC Financial Services Check 2008 Basic Education Modules/Subtopics **Licensing Requirements** Please refer to pages 9-10 of OREA's Licensing Requirements Handbook for requirements to upgrade to a Certified Residential or Certified General license.	File a Complaint • AMC • Appraiser Frequently Asked Questions • Licensing FAQs • Enforcement FAQs The Fall 2009 edition of OREA's newsletter. See News and Publications for previous editions. The 2010 Edition of USPAP became effective on January 1, 2010. See also: 2010 - 2011

OREA is the regulatory agency for appraisers in the state of California. They are responsible for the licensing and disciplinary action of California appraisers. The first four pages of the latest edition of OREA's publication, "The California Appraiser," is featured starting on page 470.

on page 470.

THE CALIFORNIA

Appraiser

OREA
FALL 2009

Arnold Schwarzenegger, Governor
Dale Bonner, Secretary, Business, Transportation, & Housing Agency
Bob Clark, Director, Office of Real Estate Appraisers

Office of Real Estate Appraisers

ACTIVE LICENSES IN CALIFORNIA

As of November 30, 2009

Trainee License (AT)	2,123
Residential License (AL)	3,555
Certified Residential (AR)	6,451
Certified General (AG)	3,496
TOTAL	15,625

DIRECTOR'S MESSAGE

*OREA Director
Bob Clark*

"These are the times that try men's souls"

These words from founding father Thomas Paine's The Crisis not only describe the beginnings of the American Revolution, but also represent the attitude of many appraisal professionals during these challenging economic times. As real estate markets languish and appraisal management companies (AMCs) garner an increasingly larger share of appraisal ordering, I am frequently asked by appraisers if the end of the profession is in sight. My reply is always an emphatic "NO."

Difficult times fall on every individual and on every business at some point in time. When such times strike, we have a choice to either view the glass as half-empty or half-full. Rather than choosing to be miserable, it is provident to seek out opportunities and to move forward in a proactive manner to successfully fill available market niches.

OREA has heard from several appraisers in recent months that the Home Valuation Code of Conduct (HVCC) has destroyed their business. Conversely, some appraisers have reported that HVCC and the predominance of AMCs was the best thing that ever happened to their appraisal practice. The difference between these examples is recognition of a business model that is well established and a realization that the use of AMCs by lending institutions continues to increase. Some appraisers have actively gone after the AMC business, resulting in a high volume of appraisal assignments. While there are some AMCs that take a large portion of the appraiser's fee for their services, there are also a number that pay appraisers their full fee, separately invoicing lender clients for their administrative role in the appraisal process. While the latter is certainly a preferred model, the amount and manner of payment for appraisal costs is not an issue for government regulation.

Continued on page 2

THE CALIFORNIA
Appraiser

Official Publication of the
California Office of Real Estate
Appraisers

FALL 2009

STATE OF CALIFORNIA
Arnold Schwarzenegger,
Governor

Business, Transportation and
Housing Agency
Dale Bonner,
Secretary

Main Office:
1102 Q Street, Suite 4100
Sacramento, CA 95811

Main Phone:
(916) 552 - 9000

Administration:
Bob Clark,
    Director
Diane Westphal,
    Deputy Director
Greg Harding,
    Chief, Licensing & Enforcement
Elizabeth Seaters,
    Enforcement Supervisor
Bruce Crandall,
    Enforcement Supervisor
Shardool Doongursee,
    Licensing Supervisor

The California Appraiser:
Paul Ostrander
    Production Editor

The problem that the HVCC/AMC situation presents is that AMCs have not been accountable to any jurisdictional authority for unethical/unlawful pressure on appraisers; however, this changes with the Governor's signing of SB 237 on October 11, 2009. Effective January 2010, AMCs will be required to register with OREA in order to conduct business in California. OREA is currently engaged in promulgating the regulations that will implement this new law. There are a number of prohibited actions in SB 237 that specifically address some of the concerns and problems reported by licensed appraisers. Please refer to our website (www.orea.ca.gov) for updates on the finalization of regulations and for information on the timeframe for implementation of OREA's enforcement efforts on unlawful activity committed by AMCs.

OREA's mission is to protect public safety by ensuring the competency and integrity of licensed real estate appraisers. One of our highest priorities in endeavoring to fulfill this mission is effective enforcement of the Uniform Standards of Professional Appraisal Practice. We have experienced a significant increase in our enforcement caseload in 2009, and expect to receive close to 600 complaints by the end of the calendar year. OREA's enforcement staff has made a concentrated effort to effectively address this problem, and it is anticipated that we will close over 300 enforcement cases in 2009, a 25% increase over the past several years. As I frequently comment in presentations to appraisal professionals, our enforcement efforts are primarily complaint driven, and we greatly appreciate and rely on the willingness of individuals to submit complaints against unlawful and unethical appraisal practice. It is crucial during these tenuous economic times to consistently strive for and encourage ethical appraisal practice, but also to ensure that incompetent and unethical appraisal practitioners either change their ways, or find another line of work.

LICENSE DISTRIBUTION

The economic woes in recent years have resulted in a decline in the number of appraisers. Since reaching its maximum numbers in the beginning of 2007 with approximately 20,200 licensed appraisers, that number has continued to steadily decline at the Office of Real Estate Appraisers (OREA). In November 2009, the OREA had a total of approximately 15,700 licensed appraisers; representing a 21% decline over that period of time.

It is important to note the change in licensing distribution in the last three years after the rapid increase in licensees in the early to mid-2000s. Three years ago, the trainee and residential licenses represented approximately 60% of the licensing database, while the certified levels only encompassed 40% of the licensing database. Today, those numbers have reversed; the certified levels now represent roughly 63%. In the past two years, a great number of residential licensees have upgraded to the certified residential level. The biggest factor in this trend is residential licensees upgrading to the certified residential level.

Certified General (AG) 22%

Trainee License (AT) 14%

Residential License (AL) 23%

Certified Residential (AR) 41%

Chapter 14

LIVING WITH AMC'S

Effective May 1, 2009, the new requirements of real estate appraisers engaging with Appraisal Management Companies (AMCs) as a result of the Home Valuation Code of Conduct (HVCC) legal agreement became effective. The Office of Real Estate Appraisers (OREA) has fielded many phone calls, comments, and other communications regarding appraiser's relationships with AMCs. There is a great deal of concern and criticism regarding this new relationship. The purpose of this article is to present the appraiser's and other market participant's concerns, discuss the business model concept presented by major long term AMCs, and draw conclusions based on these findings. Real estate appraisers, agents, and appraisal management company representatives were interviewed for this article.

The purpose of the HVCC legal agreement was to ensure the independence of the appraisal process and prohibit the improper influence on appraisers by lending brokers, agents, or representatives compensated on a commission basis upon the successful completion of a loan transaction. It was agreed upon that appraisal orders would be processed by appraisal management companies, independent appraisal companies, and correspondent lenders. The response to the legal agreement has been that most appraisal orders now are being undertaken by AMCs. Under the agreement an appraiser could report to an internal function of a lender that is independent of sales or loan production. The initial reaction, however, has been that most appraisal orders are undertaken by AMCs.

During the past several months I have interviewed selected representatives of AMCs. They have presented their business practice models for their operations. The main goal of the AMC representatives interviewed is to contract for appraisal services that result in well supported valuations in a cost effective and time sensitive manner. They accomplish these goals in part by assigning appraisals according to specific geographic zip codes that appraisers specialize in. Their theory is that by utilizing appraisers in a constricted series of zip codes, they restrict the geographical coverage of appraisers and thereby enhance geographic competency. While securing geographic competency, the AMCs strive to select the most qualified and experienced appraisers within these areas according to their business models. Appraisal fees are researched thoroughly in the various geographic areas. This research is key in determining the appraisal service fees that are contracted with lenders. Many AMCs contract with lenders for their services based on a fixed fee per order that applies to their entire service areas. In the cases of appraisal assignments in diverse and unique geographical areas, the AMCs will strive to select the

most qualified and experienced appraisers and compensate them accordingly based on the business model. Most of the AMCs interviewed maintain appraisal fee panels in order to promote appraisal quality. Typically admission to the panel is based on experience, previous working relationships that demonstrated a quality work product, and the lack of published enforcement actions against an appraiser by a state regulatory enforcement agency. Appraisal assignments are reviewed internally as part of the AMC's agreement with many lenders. Changes in the fee panels occur based on these reviews. The models presented reflect AMCs in an ideal format; however, the reality is often different.

OREA receives many complaints from appraisers concerning AMCs. Many of the most experienced appraisers with reputations of quality work, have had their business greatly reduced since the HVCC agreement went into effect in May. Their primary complaint is that the AMCs are purely fee driven with little regard to the technical or geographic competency or expertise of the appraiser or the quality of the final product. There are complaints that the selection of appraisers by AMCs is based solely on fee. I have had many reported incidents where appraisers from distant geographic locations have performed assignments that have resulted in poor quality appraisals because of their lack of geographic competency. Many AMCs request that assignments be completed within a certain turnaround time that is unrealistic because of the complexity of the assignment. In one case, an experienced appraiser interviewed, said that he had been very specific about the due diligence required for a specific assignment, because it involved improvements subject to a municipality's historic register. He estimated an appraisal delivery time based on the need to contact the appropriate government agencies and research similarly impacted properties. The response from the AMC was that the property's placement on an historical register was not an issue because the assignment was only for lending. This type of interaction by an AMC is indicative, in some cases, of their lack of comprehension of appraisal issues as well as their inability to function in an independent manner. In this case, as in others, the unfortunate outcome was that the AMC selected an appraiser willing to meet their assignment guidelines. Such actions encourage appraisers to be non-complaint with the Uniform Standards of Professional Appraisal Practice.

Other complaints that I have heard concern the pressure on appraisers to appraise to predetermined values. In one recently reported incident, the appraiser was told that the opinion of value was low by a certain amount. The appraiser reviewed additional data and concluded to the same value. The AMC then withheld payment of the fee and removed the appraiser from their panel of approved appraisers.

Continued on page 4

There have also been concerns presented that some AMCs only pay appraisers at the close of escrow of the transaction which indicates an intention to only pay upon the occurrence of a subsequent event.

A common frustration, in this new AMC dominated environment, is that appraisers who had developed good clients through previous entrepreneurial business practices have now lost those clients. Some believe that they are now merely order takers and that an unnecessary intermediary has been inserted into their business resulting in lower appraisal fees. As a result many appraisers are exploring other career alternatives and planning to leave the appraisal business. A by-product of lower fees, of course, is some appraisers will attempt to complete more appraisals in a given time frame to account for the decrease in fees. During this recession, there has been great concern expressed about the role that poor quality appraisals played in the lending crisis. Appraisal compliance requirements are continually expanding and the qualifying educational requirements for appraisers are increasing. This is not the time for a new business practice that oftentimes results in a lower quality appraisal product.

Other professionals in real estate transactions have been impacted by the advent of AMCs. Two real estate brokers from a prominent real estate firm that deal in classic well-established neighborhoods in the Sacramento area were interviewed. I spoke with another broker from Southern California. They all expressed their frustration with the current AMC lender relationship. Their frustration centers around the fact that AMCs often, because they are price driven, select appraisers from distant markets for assignments. They do not take the time to become geographically competent in these markets. The neighborhoods in the Sacramento area are difficult for appraisers under normal circumstances because of the older unique custom quality residences. In one case the agent had sold a home that was on the market for less than 45 days and had several back-up offers. The appraiser selected for the assignment concluded a value significantly lower than the sales price and used comparable sales located nearby the subject property but in an inferior neighborhood. The appraiser did not understand the neighborhood boundaries, and was not at all accountable for the quality of the appraisal. The real estate agent attempted to contact the appraiser to provide relevant sales comparables that were not considered in the appraisal. The AMC informed the agent that they were not permitted to talk with the appraiser. That was not the intent of HVCC, nor is it prohibited. An agent can often be a source of the most relevant market data. It is important that

appraisers be willing to benefit from the research developed by knowledgeable brokers or agents for a specific market area or property type.

At the present time AMCs are not regulated. On October 11, 2009, Senate Bill 237 was signed which will require that AMCs register with the Office of Real Estate Appraisers effective January 1, 2010. OREA is currently developing the regulations that the AMCs must be in compliance with. The regulations will state the requirements for registration with OREA. Registrant applications will be reviewed, and there will be an issuance fee which is yet to be determined. The backgrounds of registrants will be reviewed. For example, an applicant who has been recently convicted of a felony will not be eligible for registration. Also, appraisers who have had significant licensing disciplinary actions imposed by a state regulatory organization would not be eligible for registration as a principal of an AMC. Such disciplinary actions include revocation and surrender of license. The regulations will codify a series of prohibitions that AMCs must adhere to. The pressuring of appraisers to conclude at specified values, the withholding of appraisal fees because of the failure of the appraiser to conclude at a set value, and the payment of fees based on a stipulated event, i.e. close of escrow, will be prohibited based on the draft regulations. There must be valid cause to remove an appraiser from an approved panel. Valid cause must be based on appraisal quality issues. The draft regulations should be available for public comment in the very near future.

The lending and appraisal professions are in the initial implementation phase of the HVCC legal agreement. There are AMCs with positive business plans that should ensure appraiser independence. Unfortunately there are numerous AMCs in operation now that, according to feedback received by OREA, are abusive of the appraisal process. With registration it is likely that many AMCs will initially shut down because of the fees necessary in all states. The remaining AMCs will be large companies with the ability to operate nationally or smaller AMCs that specialize on a regional basis. Upcoming AMC regulations will enhance the overall competency and reliability of AMCs. Continue to view the OREA website for information on the registration of AMCs.

Greg Harding

VI. CHAPTER SUMMARY

I. Professional appraisal associations set standards for conduct and competence through their membership requirements.

A. Many professional associations contribute to the level of competence in the appraisal industry by sponsoring educational programs and publications.

B. Standards of conduct are enforced through a process of peer review.

C. The significance of membership in a professional association is related to the quality of the standards that the association maintains for its members.

II. The development of uniform standards of professional practice for appraisers began in the 1980s, at the time of the crisis in the savings and loan industry.

A. Major appraisal associations formed the Ad Hoc Committee on Uniform Standards of Professional Appraisal Practice (USPAP) in 1985, and later established the non-profit Appraisal Foundation to oversee the standards.

1. The Appraisal Foundation includes the Appraisal Standards Board (ASB), which is responsible for the ongoing development of uniform standards of professional practice, and the Appraisal Qualifications Board (AQB), which develops and promotes standards of professional training and competency. The Appraisal Practices Board serves to codify and implement the best practices and application for appraisers.

B. The Uniform Standards of Professional Appraisal Practice (USPAP), originally issued in 1987, represent the first attempt to create industry-wide standards of practice for appraisers.

C. The USPAP was incorporated into law by the Financial Institutions Reform, Recovery, and Enforcement Act of 1989 (FIRREA), which also requires licensing and certification of appraisers.

1. Licensing or certification is required for appraisals made in connection with "federally related" transactions.

2. Certification requires a higher level of competence than licensing. State-certified appraisers may perform complex appraisals, while state-licensed appraisers may only perform non-complex appraisals.

3. Many states have two types of certification: residential certification for residential appraisals only, and general certification for all types of appraisals.

D. The USPAP consist of several General Rules, ten Standards with associated Standards Rules, and a number of Statements on Appraisal Standards, Guide Notes, and non-binding Advisory Opinions issued by the Appraisal Standards Board.

   1. The Ethics Rule of USPAP governs conduct, management, confidentiality, and record keeping.

   2. The Competency Rule requires the appraiser to verify that he or she has the necessary knowledge or experience prior to accepting an appraisal assignment.

   3. The concept of the Scope of Work refers to the depth of necessary research and reporting required to produce a credible report that not only meets the needs of the client but that would also be considered acceptable by the appraiser's peers.

VII. CHAPTER QUIZ

1. The licensing and certification requirements of FIRREA are administered by:

 a. the Appraisal Foundation.
 b. the federal government.
 c. the individual states.
 d. the Appraisal Qualifications Board.

2. In order to perform a complex appraisal in connection with a federally related transaction, an appraiser must:

 a. be state-licensed.
 b. be state-certified.
 c. have a minimum of 5 years experience.
 d. all of the above.

3. The USPAP Standard that governs real property appraisal reports is:

 a. Standard 1.
 b. Standard 2.
 c. Standard 3.
 d. Standard 4.

4. Which of the following does NOT have the same binding effect as the USPAP?

 a. Statements on Appraisal Standards
 b. Standards Rules
 c. Advisory Opinions
 d. Comments

5. USPAP rules governing business practices such as advertising and compensation arrangements are found in the:

 a. Ethics Provision.
 b. Competency Provision.
 c. Departure Provision.
 d. Preamble.

6. Which of the following practices would always be considered unethical under the terms of the USPAP?

 a. Payment of an undisclosed commission in connection with an appraisal assignment.
 b. Acceptance of compensation that is based on reporting a direction in value that favors the cause of a client in an appraisal or consulting assignment.
 c. The reporting of a predetermined result (Opinion of Value).
 d. All the above.

7. As defined by USPAP, "appraisal practice" includes:

    a. appraisal only.
    b. appraisal, review, and consulting.
    c. all work performed by an appraiser.
    d. appraisal and review.

8. The Competency Rule:

    a. allows lenders to determine an appraiser's qualifications.
    b. requires appraisers to take Continuing Education classes.
    c prohibits accepting assignments for which they are not qualified by knowledge and experience.
    d. all of the above.

9. An appraiser who lacks the knowledge and experience to perform an assignment competently may remedy this situation by means of:

    a. personal study.
    b. association with an appraiser who has the necessary knowledge or experience.
    c. retaining others who have the necessary knowledge or experience.
    d. any of the above.

10. The organization that is responsible for updating the USPAP to reflect changes in the appraisal profession is the:

    a. Appraisal Standards Board.
    b. Appraisal Qualifications Board.
    c. Appraisal Practices Board.
    d. Uniform Standards Board.

ANSWERS: 1. c; 2. b; 3. b; 4. c; 5. a; 6. d; 7. c; 8. c; 9. d; 10. a

Chapter 15
Financial Institutions and Regulations

KEY WORDS AND TERMS

Appraiser Qualification Board
De Minimus Value
Depository Institutions
Fannie Mae
Federal Financial Institutions
  Examinations Council
Federal Reserve System
Financial Institutions Reforms, Recovery
  and Enforcement Act of 1989 (FIRREA)

Freddie Mac
Ginnie Mae
Housing Finance Board
National Credit Union Administration
Office of the Comptroller of the Currency
Office of Thrift Supervision
Primary Market
Secondary Market
Title XI

LEARNING OBJECTIVES

After completing this chapter, you should be able to:

1. identify the different types of depository financial institutions;

2. understand the roles of the primary and secondary markets in real estate finance;

3. describe the basic features of the Financial Institutions Reform, Recovery, and Enforcement Act of 1989 (FIRREA);

4. identify the five federal financial institutions regulatory agencies;

5. define the term "federally related transaction" as it applies to appraisals under Title XI of FIRREA and describe its significance;

Chapter 15

CHAPTER OUTLINE

6. list the basic requirements for appraisals under Title XI;
7. describe the role of the Appraisal Subcommittee of the Federal Financial Institutions Examinations Council;
8. list the types of federally related transactions that require the services of a state-certified (as opposed to a state-licensed) appraiser;
9. understand the minimum appraisal standards established by the five federal financial institutions regulatory agencies; and
10. understand the appraisal requirements of the major secondary market organizations (Fannie Mae and Freddie Mac).

I. Financial Institutions

One of the most common uses for an appraisal is to help evaluate property that is offered as collateral for a loan. This is especially true in the case of appraisals of smaller (1-4 unit) residential properties. The vast majority of such appraisals are made in the context of financing or refinancing the property. Consequently, the policies and regulations of financial institutions are of great importance to residential appraisers.

A. DEPOSITORY INSTITUTIONS

Before we examine the role of financial institutions and their regulators, we need to take a brief look at the real estate financing industry. There are several different categories of real estate lenders, but for the purposes of this chapter we will be concerned primarily with depository financial institutions. A *DEPOSITORY INSTITUTION is one that accepts deposits from its account holders.* In most cases, the institution then uses the money from those deposits to make loans to borrowers.

Depository institutions include savings institutions (also known as savings and loan institutions or thrifts), commercial banks and credit unions.

Whether a financial institution is a commercial bank, savings institution, or credit union depends on its charter. A *CHARTER is essentially a license to operate a depository financial institution, granted by either the federal government or a state government.* The type of charter determines which state or federal agencies has regulatory authority over the institution, and which rules apply to its operations.

Case/Example: A financial institution may be a federally chartered savings and loan association or a state chartered credit union.

Insurance companies are also considered institutional lenders. They are state licensed and controlled.

B. NONINSTITUTIONAL LENDERS

Noninstitutional lenders play a significant role in real estate financing. *NONINSTITUTIONAL LENDERS are lenders that are not depositories of account holders.* They include pension funds, trusts and individual investors. Real Estate Investment Trusts (Mortgage REITs) also invest in larger commercial mortgages.

Noninstitutional investors generally are not direct lenders. They generally buy loans originated by others.

II. Primary and Secondary Finance Markets

Financial institutions operate in the primary market for real estate loans, which are made up of individual borrowers and lenders.

When a financial institution (or other real estate lender) makes a real estate loan to a home buyer, the transaction takes place in the PRIMARY MARKET.

Financial institutions also operate in the *SECONDARY MARKET, where real estate loans are treated as investments, just like stocks or bonds.* A financial institution (or other primary market lender) can sell its loans to secondary market investors and then use the proceeds from the sales to make new loans in the primary market (see **Figure 15-1**).

Since the secondary market operates on a national scale, it serves to smooth out local imbalances in the supply and demand for real estate financing.

In practice, loans are usually not sold directly from lenders to investors in the secondary market. The primary lenders sell the loans to a "middle man," who then "packages" the loans into investments called mortgage backed securities. It is these securities that are then sold to investors on the open market.

The three largest "middle men" in the secondary market are the Federal National Mortgage Association (FNMA or "Fannie Mae"), the Government National Mortgage Association (GNMA or "Ginnie Mae"), and the Federal Home Loan Mortgage Corporation (FHLMC or "Freddie Mac").

III. FIRREA

The Financial Institutions Reform, Recovery, and Enforcement Act of 1989 (FIRREA) has had an enormous impact on both financial institutions and the appraisal industry. This law was enacted in response to the crisis in the savings and loan industry in the 1980s, when

Figure 15-1

Secondary Mortgage Markets

The financing of real estate has been facilitated greatly by the development of the secondary mortgage market. Many lending institutions formerly made home loans and held them; now they are able to sell loans in the secondary market and thus secure additional funds for home financing. A number of private investors and institutions purchase home mortgages.

A major influence on the secondary mortgage market is the activity of the Federal National Mortgage Association (FNMA). "Fannie Mae" purchases mortgages from primary mortgage markets, thus increasing liquidity among primary mortgage lenders. It issues long-term debentures and short-term discount notes to raise most of its funds. FNMA programs emphasize insured and guaranteed mortgages.

 fanniemae.com

The Federal Home Loan Mortgage Corporation (FHLMC) known as The Mortgage Corporation or "Freddie Mac" conducts both mortgage purchase and sales programs. Its main emphasis is on conventional mortgages.

 freddiemac.com

The Government National Mortgage Association (GNMA or "Ginnie Mae") is a government organization that gets its funds from the U.S. Treasury. It specializes in the purchase of mortgages which require government support.

 ginniemae.gov

questionable real estate lending practices and other factors led to widespread failures among savings institutions. FIRREA was designed to provide for the orderly liquidation of the failed S&Ls, and to impose regulations that would prevent a similar crisis from repeating itself in the future. It established the Resolution Trust Corporation (RTC).

A. RESOLUTION: FAILED SAVINGS INSTITUTIONS

One of the major purposes of FIRREA (RTC) was to handle the resolution (closing down) of insolvent savings institutions.

FIRREA established a new government agency called the **RESOLUTION TRUST CORPORATION (RTC)**, *which was responsible for resolving savings institutions that failed between January 1, 1989 and August 9, 1992.* The RTC acted as the conservator and receiver of the assets of these failed S&Ls, and arranged for the disposition of those assets, either by liquidation or by negotiating mergers, with more healthy financial institutions.

While the Resolution Trust Corporation has completed its tasks, other provisions of FIRREA live on.

B. REORGANIZATION OF FEDERAL FINANCIAL REGULATORS

A second major feature of FIRREA was the reorganization of the federal agencies responsible for regulating the savings and loan industry. Prior to FIRREA, S&Ls were regulated by the Federal Home Loan Bank Board (FHLBB), which also oversaw the system of twelve regional Federal Home Loan Banks. **FIRREA eliminated the FHLBB**, and replaced it with two new agencies. The **OFFICE OF THRIFT SUPERVISION (OTS)** *is the new agency responsible for regulation of savings institutions, and oversight of the regional Federal Home Loan Banks is now handled by the* **HOUSING FINANCE BOARD (HFB)**.

OTS is a division of the Treasury Department, while HFB falls under the Department of Housing and Urban Development (HUD).

The second agency eliminated by FIRREA was the **Federal Savings and Loan Insurance Corporation (FSLIC)**. The FSLIC had been responsible for insuring the accounts of depositors in participating savings and loan institutions, just as the **FEDERAL DEPOSIT INSURANCE CORPORATION (FDIC)** *insured accounts in participating commercial banks.* FDIC now handles the deposit insurance for both banks and thrifts, through two separate insurance funds. The **SAVINGS ASSOCIATION INSURANCE FUND (SAIF)** *covers deposits in savings banks, while bank deposits are covered by the* **BANK INSURANCE FUND (BIF)**.

C. FEDERAL FINANCIAL INSTITUTIONS REGULATORY AGENCIES (FFIRA)

In order to understand the effect of FIRREA on the appraisal industry, it is important to know what is meant by the term federal financial institutions regulatory agencies (FFIRA). For the purposes of FIRREA, FFIRA refers to five government agencies that have various regulatory powers over financial institutions such as banks, savings and loan institutions, and credit unions.

These five agencies that FIRREA has control over are:

1. the Federal Reserve System,
2. the Federal Deposit Insurance Corporation,
3. the Office of the Comptroller of the Currency,

4. the Office of Thrift Supervision, and
5. the National Credit Union Administration.

1. Federal Reserve System ("The Fed")

The *FEDERAL RESERVE SYSTEM, commonly referred to as "the Fed," is the central banking system for the United States.* It is an independent agency that is responsible for national monetary policy. It also has regulatory authority over commercial banks who are members of the Federal Reserve System. The Fed is controlled by a seven-member Board of Governors.

frb.fed.us
Federal Reserve System

2. Federal Deposit Insurance Corporation (FDIC)

As noted earlier in this chapter, the FDIC manages the system of national deposit insurance for participating banks and savings institutions. It also has conservator and receiver powers with respect to insolvent commercial banks and with respect to thrifts that become insolvent after August 9, 1992. The FDIC is an independent agency, whose chairman is also the chairman of the RTC.

fdic.gov
Federal Deposit Insurance Corporation

3. Office of the Comptroller of the Currency (OCC)

The *OFFICE OF THE COMPTROLLER OF THE CURRENCY (OCC) is a division of the Treasury Department. It regulates federally chartered commercial banks.*

occ.treas.gov
Office of the Comptroller of the Currency

4. Office of Thrift Supervision (OTS)

The *OFFICE OF THRIFT SUPERVISION (OTS) was created by FIRREA to take over the responsibilities of the disbanded Federal Home Loan Bank Board, with respect to regulating savings and loan institutions.* Like the OCC, it is part of the Treasury Department.

ots.treas.gov
Office of Thrift Supervision

5. National Credit Union Administration (NCUA)

This independent agency, commonly known as *NCUA, has regulatory authority over nationally chartered credit unions.*

ncua.gov
National Credit Union Administration

D. REAL ESTATE APPRAISAL REFORM AMENDMENTS: TITLE XI

From the standpoint of the appraisal industry, the most significant part of FIRREA is Title XI also known as the Real Estate Appraisal Reform Amendments. The purpose of TITLE XI is to:

"provide that federal financial and public policy interests in real estate related transactions will be protected by requiring that real estate appraisals utilized in connection with federally related transactions are performed in writing in accordance with uniform standards by individuals whose competency has been demonstrated and whose professional conduct will be subject to effective supervision" (see **Figure 15-2**).

Figure 15-2

Title XI: Real Estate Reform Amendments

1 – Appraiser Licensing/Certification
2 – Uniform Standards of Practice
3 – Uniform Qualification Standards
4 – Supervision (Regulation) of Appraisers

In other words, *TITLE XI is designed to promote uniform standards for appraisal practice and appraiser qualifications, and to establish regulatory power over the appraisal industry.*

Every appraisal that falls within the scope of Title XI must satisfy three basic requirements:

1. it must be performed by a state-certified or state-licensed appraiser;
2. it must be performed in accordance with specified appraisal standards; and
3. it must be a written appraisal.

1. Appraiser Licensing and Certification

The first basic requirement of Title XI is that all covered appraisals must be performed by state-licensed or state-certified appraisers.

The distinction between state-certification and state-licensing involves the nature of the qualifying standards imposed by the appraiser certification and licensing agencies. To be state-certified, an appraiser must satisfy requirements that measure up to the minimum qualifications established by the **Appraiser Qualifications Board (AQB) of the Appraisal Foundation**, and must also pass an examination that is equivalent to the Uniform State Certification Examination approved by the AQB.

Individual states may impose stricter requirements for state-certifications; so long as the minimum AQB standards are met.

In contrast, the qualifications for a state-licensed appraiser are established by the individual states. The AQB has issued recommended qualification standards for state-licensing, but these are not strictly mandatory. Although there are no minimum qualification standards for state-licensing, the standards established by a state must be consistent with the purpose of Title XI. The *APPRAISAL SUBCOMMITTEE of FFIEC has the authority to decide whether state-licensing criteria are adequate or not.* The Appraisal Subcommittee of the Federal Financial Institutions Examinations Council (FFIEC) is described in more detail below.

asc.gov
Appraisal Subcommittee of the Federal Financial Institutions Examination Council

2. Appraisal Standards

The second basic requirement of Title XI is that appraisals must be performed in accordance with specified standards of appraisal practice.

Title XI specifically recognizes the Uniform Standards of Professional Appraisal Practice (USPAP) as the minimum standards for appraisals covered by FIRREA. It also directs the Federal Financial Institutions Regulatory Agencies (FFIRA) to establish minimum standards for appraisals that fall under their jurisdiction. FFIRA appraisal standards include the USPAP plus additional standards issued by each agency.

Law and Regulations

The Supplemental Standards Rule was deleted because changes to USPAP have eliminated the need for the rule. Appraisers are required to follow all laws and regulations. Laws are developed by legislatures and courts both federal and state. Regulations are developed by federal and state regulatory agencies. No private entity may make laws and regulations. Please see the Scope of Work Rule, the Competency Rule, and the Jurisdictional Rule of USPAP. Further, instructions from a client or an attorney do not establish jurisdictional exceptions.

– The Uniform Standards of Professional Appraisal Practice are published and maintained by the Appraisal Foundation.

The *APPRAISAL STANDARDS BOARD (ASB) develops, interprets, and amends the Uniform Standards of Professional Appraisal Practice (USPAP).* The ASB is composed of six appraisers who are appointed for three year terms by the Board of Trustees of The Appraisal Foundation. Members of the ASB may serve two consecutive three year terms. Activities of the Board are directed by the Chair, who is appointed by the Board of Trustees for a one year term.

3. Written Appraisals

The third requirement of Title XI is that all appraisals under FIRREA must be written appraisals.

The term **WRITTEN APPRAISAL** *is defined to mean an appraisal "that is independently and impartially prepared by a licensed or certified appraiser, setting forth an opinion of defined value of an adequately described property, as of a specific date, supported by presentation and analysis of relevant market information."*

4. Appraisal Subcommittee of FFIEC

In addition to setting up requirements for appraiser licensing/certification and for appraisal standards, Title XI established the Appraisal Subcommittee of the Federal Financial Institutions Examinations Council. The *FEDERAL FINANCIAL INSTITUTIONS EXAMINATIONS COUNCIL (FFIEC) is an agency that was created in 1978 for the purpose of promoting greater uniformity among federal financial regulations issued by different government agencies.* Its members include representatives from the five Federal Financial Institutions Regulatory Agencies, as well as from the Department of Housing and Urban Development.

The Appraisal Subcommittee of FFIEC consists of five members who must have demonstrated appraisal knowledge and competence. One member is appointed by each of the five FFIRAs. The Appraisal Subcommittee is required to:

1. monitor state requirements for licensing and certifying persons qualified to perform appraisals;
2. determine which federally related transactions shall require a state certified or licensed appraiser;
3. maintain a national register of state certified and licensed appraisers;

   Each state licensing and certifying agency must submit to the appraisal subcommittee, a roster of persons licensed and/or certified. State certifying agencies can charge appraisers an annual registry fee. The annual fee is in addition to any state licensing fees.

4. monitor and review practices, procedure and structure of the Appraisal Foundation; and
5. report annually to Congress.

E. APPRAISALS COVERED BY FIRREA

Whether or not an appraisal is subject to the requirements of Title XI depends on whether it is made in connection with a federally related transaction. A federally related transaction is defined as:

"any real estate-related financial transaction which

(a) a Federal Financial Institutions Regulatory Agency or the Resolution Trust Corporation engages in, contracts for, or regulates; and

(b) requires the services of an appraiser."

For purposes of this definition, real estate-related financial transactions include any transaction involving:

"(a) the sale, lease, purchase, investment in or exchange of real property, including interests in real property, or the financing thereof;

(b) the refinancing of real property or interests in real property; and

(c) the use of real property or interests in property as security for a loan or investment, including mortgage-backed securities."

The concept of a "federally related transaction" is significant because it defines the scope of the application of Title XI.

The appraisal regulations of Title XI apply to all federally related transactions, which means they apply to almost all appraisals that are performed for almost any financial institution in connection with the transfer or financing of real estate.

In addition to appraisals in connection with federally related transactions, any appraisal that is made in connection with a loan that is sold to Fannie Mae or Freddie Mac must be made by a state-certified or state-licensed appraiser. This requirement applies regardless of whether the loan itself is a federally related transaction.

1. De Minimus Value

One of the characteristics of a federally related transaction is that it "requires the services of an appraiser." According to regulations issued by the Federal Financial Institutions Regulatory Agencies, transactions *with a value that is less than a certain minimum amount (DE MINIMUS VALUE)* do not require the services of an appraiser. By definition, such transactions are not federally related transactions, so they do not require state-certified or state-licensed appraisers.

The de minimus value currently set by each FFIRA is $250,000.

2. Appraisals Requiring a State-Certified Appraiser

As noted in Chapter 14, state-licensed appraisers may perform relatively simple appraisals, while more complex appraisals require a state-certified appraiser.

Title XI requires the use of state-certified appraisers in all federally related transactions with a value of $1 million or more.

Each FFIRA has issued additional regulations specifying the types of transactions that require a state-certified appraiser. These regulations focus on three factors:

1. the value of the transaction;
2. whether or not the subject property is "residential" (i.e., one-to four-unit residential property); and
3. whether or not the subject property is "complex" (i.e., the property, the form of ownership, or market conditions are not typical).

Current FFIRA regulations require state-certified appraisers in the following types of federally related transactions:

1. all transactions with a value of $1 million or more;
2. all non-residential transactions with a value of $250,000 or more; and
3. all complex residential transactions with a value of $250,000 or more.

If a transaction does not require a state-certified appraiser, then the appraisal may be performed by either a state-certified or a state-licensed appraiser.

F. FFIRA APPRAISAL STANDARDS

Title XI of FIRREA requires the five FFIRAs to establish standards for appraisals in connection with federally related transactions. Most of the agencies have issued regulations adopting the following 14 minimum standards, which apply to all appraisals in connection with federally related transactions.

Appraisals of one-to-four unit residential property may be exempted from Standards 2-14, provided that they satisfy the requirements of Standard 1 and also conform to the appraisal standards of Fannie Mae and Freddie Mac. (Fannie Mae and Freddie Mac appraisal standards are discussed later in this chapter.)

---

14 Minimum Appraisal Standards

1. The appraisal must conform to the Uniform Standards of Professional Appraisal Practice (USPAP).
2. The appraisal must disclose any steps that the appraiser needed to take in order to comply with the Competency Provision of the USPAP. (This requirement has not been adopted by NCUA.)

▼

---

3. The appraisal must be based upon the following definition of market value:

The most probable price which a property should bring in a competitive and open market, under all conditions requisite to a fair sale, the buyer and seller each acting prudently and knowledgeably, and assuming the price is not affected by undue stimulus. Implicit in this definition is the consummation of a sale as of a specified date and the passing of title from seller to buyer under conditions whereby:

   (a) buyer and seller are typically motivated;

   (b) both parties are well informed or well advised, and acting in what they consider their own best interests;

   (c) a reasonable time is allowed for exposure in the open market;

   (d) payment is made in terms of cash in US dollars or in terms of financial arrangements comparable thereto; and

   (e) the price represents the normal consideration for the property sold, unaffected by special or creative financing or sales concessions granted by anyone associated with the sale.

4. The appraisal must:

   (a) be written and presented in a narrative format, or on an approved form with all necessary addenda;

   (b) be sufficiently descriptive to enable the reader to ascertain the estimated market value and the rational for the estimate; and

   (c) provide detail and depth of analysis that reflect the complexity of the real estate appraised.

5. The appraiser must analyze and report in reasonable detail any prior sales of the property being appraised that occurred within the following time periods:

   (a) for one-to four-family residential property, three years preceding the date when the appraisal was prepared; and

   (b) for all other property, three years preceding the date when the appraisal was prepared.

6. If the subject property is income-producing, the appraiser must analyze and report data on current revenues, expenses, and vacancies for the property.

7. The appraiser must analyze and report a reasonable marketing period for the subject property.

8. The appraiser must analyze and report on current market conditions and trends that will:

   (a) affect projected income if the subject property is income-producing; or

   (b) affect the absorption period if the subject property is newly developed; to the extent that such conditions and trends affect the value of the subject property.

▼

9. The appraiser must analyze and report appropriate deductions and discounts for:

   (a) any proposed construction;
   (b) any completed properties that are partially leased or leased at other than market rents as of the date of the appraisal; or
   (c) any tract developments with unsold units.

10. The appraiser must certify (in addition to the certifications required by USPAP) that the appraisal assignment was not based on a requested minimum valuation, a specific valuation, or the approval of a loan.

11. The appraisal must be reported in sufficient detail to allow the reader to evaluate the reasonableness of the appraiser's analysis and value conclusions.

12. The appraisal must include a legal description of the subject property.

13. The appraiser must identify any personal property, fixtures, or intangible items that are not real property but are included in the appraisal. These items must be valued separately from the real property, and the appraiser must discuss the impact of their inclusion or exclusion on the estimate of market value for the real property.

14. The appraiser must reasonably consider each of the three approaches to value (sales comparison, cost, and income approaches), must explain the reasons for choosing not to use any approach that was not used, and must reconcile the value indicators from the approaches that were used.

In addition to these 14 minimum standards, if any information that is necessary or relevant to the appraisal is not available, the appraiser must disclose this fact and give an explanation in the appraisal.

IV. Secondary Market Appraisal Regulations

Primary lenders such as banks and savings institutions operate in local markets. Their loan officers are familiar with the local trends that may affect the value of the real estate that is the collateral for their loans. Investors in the secondary market, however, do not have this advantage. They may be purchasing securities that are backed by mortgages from all over the country.

In essence, the secondary market investors must rely on the primary market lenders to properly qualify their loans; that is, to properly investigate the creditworthiness of their borrowers and to verify that there is sufficient value in the real estate collateral to insure recovery of the loan funds in the event of borrower default. Because of this reliance, the secondary market organizations that purchase and package loans demand that those loans meet specific criteria.

Loans that meet all of the standards of the secondary market are called **CONFORMING LOANS**, and they are eligible to be sold to organizations such as Fannie Mae and Freddie Mac. These organizations will not purchase nonconforming loans that do not meet their standards.

Secondary market loan standards include specific requirements for appraisals that are made in connection with the loans, and these standards are adhered to by most primary lenders.

The following sections describe the appraisal requirements of Fannie Mae and Freddie Mac, the two most important secondary market organizations with respect to residential real estate. These regulations pertain to all appraisals of one- to four-unit residential properties in connection with loans that will be sold to Fannie Mae or Freddie Mac.

A. APPRAISER QUALIFICATIONS

Fannie Mae and Freddie Mac require that all appraisals be performed by appraisers who are state-licensed or state-certified in accordance with the procedures established in Title XI of FIRREA.

To insure the objectivity of appraisals, the appraiser must be selected and hired directly by the lender, not by one of the parties to the real estate transaction. Lenders are required to verify that the appraiser has the knowledge and experience required for the type of property being appraised, and that the appraiser is actively engaged in appraisal work on a regular basis.

Appraisers can be corporations, partnerships or individuals, but the individual who signs the appraisal must be licensed or certified as required.

If a financial institution hires or pays for an appraisal from a person who is not licensed or certified for an appraisal requiring a licensed or certified appraiser, Title XI provides that the financial institution shall be subject to civil penalties.

1. Recognition of Other State Licensing/Certification

A state appraiser licensing agency is required to recognize, on a temporary basis, a person licensed or certified in another state for a federally related transaction if the appraiser registers with the state for temporary practice.

This would allow an out-of-state appraiser to perform a particular assignment within a state. It does not mean that an out-of-state appraiser can set up practice and solicit assignments within a state where the appraiser is not licensed or certified.

2. Unlicensed Assistants

An unlicensed assistant may assist in the preparation of an appraisal if:

1. the assistant is under the direct supervision of a licensed or certified individual, and
2. the appraisal is signed by a licensed or certified individual.

3. Restrictions Against Discrimination

A qualified licensed or certified appraiser shall not be excluded from assignments because of membership or lack of membership in a particular professional appraisal organization.

4. Non-Federal Related Loans

Most noninstitutional lenders that are not required to even have appraisals, nevertheless require appraisals for their own protection. A great many of these lenders require appraisals that conform to federal requirements as if they were federally related.

B. UNACCEPTABLE APPRAISAL PRACTICES

The following practices are prohibited by Fannie Mae and Freddie Mac requirements:

Unacceptable Practices

1. Use of inaccurate data regarding the subject property, the neighborhood or a comparable property.
2. Failure to report and comment on any factor that may have a negative value influence on the subject property.
3. Use of a comparable property (in the sales comparison approach) that has not been personally inspected by the appraiser by, at a minimum, driving by and inspecting the exterior.
4. Use of comparables that are not as similar as possible to the subject property, or use of inappropriate comparables.
5. Use of comparable sales data that is provided by a party to the transaction (such as the buyer, seller or real estate broker) without independent verification of the data.
6. Making sales comparison adjustments that do not reflect market reactions, or failing to make adjustments that do reflect market reactions.
7. Consideration of discriminatory factors (race, color, sex, religion, handicap, national origin, family status) in the valuation analysis.
8. Developing a conclusion that is not supported by market data.

V. Reporting Requirements

A. REPORT FORMS
Appraisals must be made on approved forms.

The forms for one-to-four unit residential properties include the Uniform Residential Report Form, the Small Residential Income Property Appraisal Report, Desktop Underwriter Quantitative Analysis Appraisal Report, and the Appraisal Report Individual Condominium or PUD Unit.

B. AGE OF APPRAISAL REPORT
Appraisals must be dated within one year prior to the date of the loan made by the primary lender.

In addition, if the appraisal is dated more than four months prior to the loan date, the appraiser must certify that the property has not declined in value since the date of the report.

C. REQUIRED ATTACHMENTS
Because Fannie Mae and Freddie Mac appraisals are reported on form reports, additional information must be provided in the form of attachments or addenda. Each appraisal report must be accompanied by the following:

1. at least three clear original photographs of the subject property, showing front and rear views of the subject, and a view of the street;

2. photographs showing the front view of each comparable sale used in the sales comparison approach (clear copies may be acceptable if original photographs of the comparables are not available);

3. a map showing the location of the subject property and all comparables; and

4. a sketch of the subject property improvements showing dimensions and the appraiser's calculations of gross living area (exterior dimensions are used for detached residences, interior dimensions for condominiums and interior PUD units).

In addition to these mandatory attachments, other addenda may be required for certain types of properties. For example, special addenda or additional forms are required for income properties, PUDs and properties whose values are affected by energy efficiency features.

D. COMPLETION CERTIFICATES

When an appraisal has been made subject to the completion of repairs or improvements to the subject property, the appraiser must issue a certificate of completion once the repairs or improvements have been completed.

This certificate verifies that the conditions stated in the original appraisal have been complied with. If necessary (as, for example, in the case of new construction that was appraised on the basis of plans and specifications) new photographs of the completed improvements must accompany the certification.

In general, property must be appraised subject to completion of repairs or improvements if conditions exist that affect the livability of the property.

Property with structural defects that do not affect livability may be appraised on an "as is" basis, in which case a completion certificate is not necessary.

E. SELECTION OF COMPARABLE PROPERTIES

A valuation based on the sales comparison approach must be included in the appraisal report.

The sales comparison analysis must be based on at LEAST THREE COMPLETED (CLOSED OR SETTLED) COMPARABLE SALES, although the appraiser may use additional comparable sales (including prior sales of the subject property), contacts, or listings, if appropriate, to support the sales comparison analysis.

Comparable sales should be no older than one year prior to the appraisal date, and the appraiser must comment on the reasons for using any comparables that are older than six months.

In the case of properties in established neighborhoods or projects, the best comparables are those in the same neighborhood or project as the subject. However, in the case of new developments (new subdivisions, condominiums, or PUD projects), at **least one comparable should be outside the control of the developer/builder**. This could be a comparable from a similar neighborhood or project outside the new development, or a resale within the development that did not involve the developer/builder.

Financial Institutions and Regulations

VI. Other Appraisal-Related Internet Sites

Forms and Worms, Inc.
realestategraphics.com

Foundation of Real Estate Appraisers
frea.com

Association of Appraiser Regulatory Officials
aaro.net

Institute of Business Appraisers
go-iba.org/default.asp

International Real Estate Digest
ired.com

Inman News Features
inman.com

The Real Estate Educators Association
reea.org

Association of Real Estate License Law Officials
arello.org

Urban Land Institute
uli.org

National Association of REALTORS®
realtor.com

Appraisal Directory (State Boards, Find an Appraiser, Education and Training)
appraisaldirectory.com

B. Title XI established the Appraisal Subcommittee of the Federal Financial Institutions Examination Council (FFIEC).

  1. The FFIEC promotes uniformity in the regulations issued by the different FFIRAs and by the Department of Housing and Urban Development (HUD).

  2. The Appraisal Subcommittee is responsible for monitoring appraiser licensing and certification programs and for overseeing the Appraisal Foundation.

C. Appraisals covered by Title XI must be performed by state-certified or state-licensed appraisers.

  1. State-certified appraisers must meet the standards of the Appraisal Qualification Board of the Appraisal Institute.

  2. State-licensed appraisers must meet the standards set by the individual state in which they are licensed.

  3. State-certified appraisers are required for all transactions with a value of $1 million or more, for all non-residential transactions with a value of $250,000 or more, and for residential transactions with a value of $250,000 or more where the property to be appraised, the form of ownership, or the market conditions are not typical.

      a. All other appraisals for federally related transactions may be performed by either a state-certified or a state-licensed appraiser.

D. Appraisals covered by Title XI must be performed in accordance with specified appraisal standards and must be in writing.

  1. The FFIRAs have issued regulations listing 14 Standards for appraisals.

  2. Appraisals of one-to-four unit residential properties that conform to Fannie Mae/Freddie Mac standards are exempt from most of the FFIRA Appraisal Standards.

IV. In order to be able to sell their loans in the secondary market, most lenders require their appraisals to conform to secondary market (Fannie Mae/Freddie Mac) standards.

  A. Fannie Mae/Freddie Mac appraisals must be performed by state-licensed or state-certified appraisers.

  1. The appraiser must be selected directly by the lender.

  2. Lenders must verify appraiser qualifications.

B. Certain appraisal practices are not acceptable to Fannie Mae/Freddie Mac.

1. Appraisers must use accurate data, and report on any negative value influences.

2. Comparables must be personally inspected by the appraiser. They should be as similar to the subject as possible, and comparable data must be validated by someone other than a party to the transaction.

3. Sales comparison adjustments must reflect market reactions and conclusions must be supported by market data.

4. The appraisal may not consider discriminatory factors.

C. Fannie Mae/Freddie Mac appraisals must be reported on approved forms.

1. Appraisals must be dated within one year prior to the loan date. Appraisals dated more than 4 months prior to the loan date require the appraiser's certification that the property has not declined in value.

2. Required addenda include photos of the subject and comparables, a location map, and a sketch of the subject improvements showing dimensions and calculations of gross living area.

3. Completion certificates are required when an appraisal is made subject to completion of repairs or improvements.

4. Use of the sales comparison approach, based on at least three completed sales, is mandatory. Comparable sales should be no older than one year, preferably no older than six months.

VIII. CHAPTER QUIZ

1. The agency designated by FIRREA to oversee the operations of the Appraisal Foundation is the:

    a. Appraisal Subcommittee of the Federal Financial Institutions Examinations Council.
    b. Board of Governors of the Federal Reserve System.
    c. RTC Oversight Board.
    d. Appraiser Qualification Board.

2. If an appraisal is subject to the requirements of FIRREA, but does not require the services of a state-certified appraiser, it may be performed by:

    a. a state-licensed appraiser.
    b. a state-certified appraiser.
    c. any appraiser.
    d. either a or b.

3. A state-certified appraiser must meet standards of competence that are defined by:

    a. the Appraisal Subcommittee.
    b. the Appraisal Standards Board.
    c. the Appraisal Qualification Board.
    d. the Appraisal Institute.

4. The primary market for real estate loans includes all of the following, EXCEPT:

    a. Fannie Mae.
    b. commercial banks.
    c. savings institutions.
    d. credit unions.

5. The agency responsible for monitoring the appraiser licensing systems of the individual states is the:

    a. Appraisal Foundation.
    b. Appraiser Licensing Board.
    c. Appraisal Oversight Committee.
    d. Appraisal Subcommittee FFIEC.

6. Fannie Mae/Freddie Mac regulations require appraisals to be performed:

    a. within 3 months prior to the loan date.
    b. within 4 months prior to the loan date.
    c. within 6 months prior to the loan date.
    d. within 1 year prior to the loan date.

7. The appraiser's sketch of subject property improvements attached to a Fannie Mae/Freddie Mac appraisal should show:

    a. the location of the improvements on the lot.
    b. the appraiser's calculations of gross living area.
    c. the interior dimensions of all rooms.
    d. the exterior dimensions of condominium units.

8. When an appraisal is made subject to the completion of repairs or improvements to the subject property, Fannie Mae/Freddie regulations require the appraiser to:

    a. issue a certificate of completion when the construction is finished.
    b. prepare a new appraisal if construction takes longer than six months.
    c. review the appraisal to determine whether market conditions have changed during the construction period.
    d. all of the above.

9. In a Fannie Mae/Freddie Mac appraisal, the appraiser may use comparable sales data provided by the real estate broker in the transaction, provided that:

    a. the appraiser independently verifies the data.
    b. the broker has already received a commission.
    c. the appraiser reasonably believes the data is reliable.
    d. the appraiser was not selected for the assignment by the broker.

10. In a Fannie Mae/Freddie Mac appraisal of a property in a new development, the appraiser must use at least one comparable sale that:

    a. was completed within three months prior to the appraisal date.
    b. is located in a different development than the subject.
    c. is located in a different neighborhood than the subject.
    d. is outside the control of the developer/builder.

ANSWERS: 1. a; 2. d; 3. c; 4. a; 5. d; 6. b; 7. b; 8. a; 9. a; 10. d

Appendix
Information

The goal of this book is to announce the new Federal appraisal loan standards called "Datasets." More specifically, the Uniform Appraisal Dataset Specification (UAD) is found in **Appendix 5**. The first four appendices include forms that use those standards, i.e., standardized language established by Fannie Mae and Freddie Mac for definitions, numbers, and typed-in text boxes by using information from the Dataset. Our Appendices are:

> **Appendix 1:** Uniform Residential Appraisal Report (URAR)
> **Appendix 2:** Individual Condominium Unit Appraisal Report
> **Appendix 3:** Exterior-Only Inspection Individual Condominium Unit
>   Appraisal Report
> **Appendix 4:** Exterior-Only Inspection Residential Appraisal Report
> **Appendix 5:** Uniform Appraisal Dataset Specification (UAD)

The most commonly used of all residential appraisal reports required by Fannie Mae and Freddie Mac is the URAR Single Family Appraisal Report Form. This form is reproduced in the book in its entirety. It is also broken down section by section with instructions as to how to fill it out properly.

However, there are several other commonly used forms that also warrant close attention. They comprise the first four appendixes that follow.

Typically, the **Uniform Residential Appraisal Report (URAR) (Appendix 1)** and the **Individual Condominium Unit Appraisal Report (Appendix 2)** are generally carried out by both Licensed and Certified Appraisers. Generally, there is no particular complexity of property type or of the financing involved in these. However, if there is such complexity or the property value exceeds one million dollars, a certified appraiser must be engaged. The **Exterior-Only Inspection Individual Condominium Unit Appraisal Report (Appendix 3)** and the **Exterior-Only Inspection Residential Appraisal Report (Appendix 4)**, which are often referred to in the business as "drive-by" appraisals, are UAD-ready with fill in boxes and drop down choices.

Authors Note: Typically, Appendix 3 and 4 forms are used to remove Private Mortgage Insurance (PMI) on Fannie Mae and Freddie Mac loans that exceed 80% LTV. For this purpose the appraiser who completed the first appraisal must also fill out these forms.

Although not reproduced in these appendices, appraisers should know that Manufactured Homes and Cooperatives are both "off limits" to the Licensed Appraiser in a federally related transaction. Appraisals of manufactured homes and cooperatives are complex appraisals. Licensed Appraisers are not allowed to carry out complex appraisals. Having said that, the appraisal of both of these property types may be "off limits" to some Certified Appraisers as well. Both manufactured homes and cooperatives require specialized knowledge and training of property type and financing over and above the normal course of studies provided to most appraisers. The appraiser is required, by the new Fannie Mae form, to certify that he/she has the specialized knowledge and training for these property types. Thus, you should not appraise these property types as a Certified Appraiser unless you are really competent to do so.

Manufactured homes may be real estate, condominiums, or personal property! The manufactured home report requires the appraiser to be conversant with manufactured home foundation types, differences in costing, as well as marketability issues of manufactured homes verses site built housing. The appraiser must also be conversant with the real estate laws in his/her state that permit the conversion of personal property manufactured housing to real estate or condominium formats. The appraiser must also be conversant with manufacturing and construction differences between site built and manufactured homes. Since many such residences are located in outlying areas, the appraiser must also be familiar with wells, septic systems, and private electrical and gas facilities. Finally, a manufactured home in a "mobile home park" is generally personal property (which introduces even more complex valuation issues for the average real estate appraiser) and the appraiser is governed by Standards 7 and 8 of the USPAP, in that instance.

Appraising a Cooperative also requires specialized knowledge and training on the part of the appraiser. In general, as the form shows, the appraiser is asked to comment on and analyze leases, stock transfer fees, ground rents, tax abatements, and the project blanket financing. All of this is obviously more financially complex and specialized than the information required by the URAR.

The **Fannie Mae and Freddie Mac Uniform Appraisal Dataset Specifications: Field – Specific Standardization Requirements (Appendix 5)**, is the most revolutionary change in the appraisal and lending industry in decades as mandated by those organizations in order for an appraisal to fulfill lender qualifications. The inclusion of this Appendix is an attempt to comply with the UAD Dataset Regulations set forth by Fannie Mae and Freddie Mac as of September 2011. In spite of the controversy regarding the future of Fannie Mae and Freddie Mac as government sponsored entities, the regulations promulgated in the Dataset Regulations are expected to survive even their originators demise. Loan applications presented to the VA and the FHA are expected to comply with the regulations set forth in the UAD, which we include as Appendix 5.

Visit eFanniemae.com for updated versions of the UAD Specifications as they are always in a state of flux and can be expected to change.

Appendix 1
Uniform Residential Appraisal Report (URAR)

Uniform Residential Appraisal Report   File # 3   4   4a

2

The purpose of this summary appraisal report is to provide the lender/client with an accurate, and adequately supported, opinion of the market value of the subject property.

SUBJECT

Property Address 6	City 7 State 8 Zip Code 9
Borrower 10	Owner of Public Record 11 County 12
Legal Description 13	
Assessor's Parcel # 14	Tax Year 15 R.E. Taxes $ 16
Neighborhood Name 17	Map Reference 18 Census Tract 19

Occupant [20] Owner [21] Tenant [22] Vacant   Special Assessments $ 23   [24] PUD   HOA $ 25   [26] per year [27] per month
Property Rights Appraised [28] Fee Simple [29] Leasehold [30] Other (describe) 31
Assignment Type [32] Purchase Transaction [33] Refinance Transaction [34] Other (describe) 35
Lender/Client 36   Address 37
Is the subject property currently offered for sale or has it been offered for sale in the twelve months prior to the effective date of this appraisal? [38] Yes [39] No
Report data source(s) used, offering price(s), and date(s).   e-2; 40

CONTRACT

I [41] did [42] did not analyze the contract for sale for the subject purchase transaction. Explain the results of the analysis of the contract for sale or why the analysis was not performed.   e-3; 43

Contract Price $ 44   Date of Contract 45   Is the property seller the owner of public record? [46] Yes [47] No   Data Source(s) 48
Is there any financial assistance (loan charges, sale concessions, gift or downpayment assistance, etc.) to be paid by any party on behalf of the borrower? [49] Yes [50] No
If Yes, report the total dollar amount and describe the items to be paid.   51a; e-4; 51b

NEIGHBORHOOD

Note: Race and the racial composition of the neighborhood are not appraisal factors.

Neighborhood Characteristics			One-Unit Housing Trends			One-Unit Housing		Present Land Use %	
Location [52] Urban	[53] Suburban	[54] Rural	Property Values [61] Increasing	[62] Stable	[63] Declining	PRICE	AGE	One-Unit	76 %
Built-Up [55] Over 75% [56] 25–75%	[57] Under 25%		Demand/Supply [64] Shortage	[65] In Balance	[66] Over Supply	$ (000)	(yrs)	2-4 Unit	77 %
Growth [58] Rapid	[59] Stable	[60] Slow	Marketing Time [67] Under 3 mths	[68] 3–6 mths	[69] Over 6 mths	70 Low 73		Multi-Family	78 %
						71 High 74		Commercial	79 %
						72 Pred. 75		Other	81 %

Neighborhood Boundaries 82

Neighborhood Description 83

Market Conditions (including support for the above conclusions) 84

SITE

Dimensions 85   Area 86   Shape 87   View e-5; e-6; e-7
Specific Zoning Classification 89   Zoning Description 90
Zoning Compliance [91] Legal [92] Legal Nonconforming (Grandfathered Use) [93] No Zoning [94] Illegal (describe) 95
Is the highest and best use of the subject property as improved (or as proposed per plans and specifications) the present use? [96] Yes [97] No   If No, describe 98

Utilities	Public	Other (describe)		Public	Other (describe)	Off-site Improvements—Type	Public	Private
Electricity	[99]	[100] 101	Water	[105]	[106] 107	Street 111	[112]	[113]
Gas	[102]	[103] 104	Sanitary Sewer	[108]	[109] 110	Alley 114	[115]	[116]

FEMA Special Flood Hazard Area [117] Yes [118] No   FEMA Flood Zone 119   FEMA Map # 120   FEMA Map Date 121
Are the utilities and off-site improvements typical for the market area? [122] Yes [123] No   If No, describe 124
Are there any adverse site conditions or external factors (easements, encroachments, environmental conditions, land uses, etc.)? [125] Yes [126] No   If Yes, describe
127

IMPROVEMENTS

General Description	Foundation	Exterior Description materials/condition	Interior materials/condition
Units [128] One [129] One with Accessory Unit	[140] Concrete Slab [141] Crawl Space	Foundation Walls 152	Floors 159
# of Stories 130	[142] Full Basement [143] Partial Basement	Exterior Walls 153	Walls 160
Type [131] Det. [132] Att. [133] S-Det./End Unit	Basement Area 144 sq. ft.	Roof Surface 154	Trim/Finish 161
[134] Existing [135] Proposed [136] Under Const.	Basement Finish 145 %	Gutters & Downspouts 155	Bath Floor 162
Design (Style) 137	[146] Outside Entry/Exit [147] Sump Pump	Window Type 156	Bath Wainscot 163
Year Built e-8; 138	Evidence of [148] Infestation	Storm Sash/Insulated 157	Car Storage [195] None
Effective Age (Yrs) 139	[150] Dampness [151] Settlement	Screens 158	[196] Driveway # of Cars 197
Attic [164] None	Heating [171] FWA [172] HWBB [173] Radiant	Amenities [187] Woodstove(s) # 188	Driveway Surface 198
[165] Drop Stair [166] Stairs	[174] Other 175 Fuel 176	[181] Fireplace(s) # 182 [189] Fence 190	[199] Garage # of Cars 200
[167] Floor [168] Scuttle	Cooling [177] Central Air Conditioning	[183] Patio/Deck 184 [191] Porch 192	[201] Carport # of Cars 202
[169] Finished [170] Heated	[178] Individual [179] Other 180	[185] Pool 186 [193] Other 194	[203] Att. [204] Det. [205] Built-in

Appliances [206] Refrigerator [207] Range/Oven [208] Dishwasher [209] Disposal [210] Microwave [211] Washer/Dryer [212] Other (describe) 213
Finished area **above grade** contains: 214   Rooms 215   Bedrooms 216   Bath(s) 217   Square Feet of Gross Living Area Above Grade
Additional features (special energy efficient items, etc.) 218

Describe the condition of the property (including needed repairs, deterioration, renovations, remodeling, etc.).   e-9; e-10; e-11; e-12; e-13; 219

Are there any physical deficiencies or adverse conditions that affect the livability, soundness, or structural integrity of the property? [220] Yes [221] No   If Yes, describe 222

Does the property generally conform to the neighborhood (functional utility, style, condition, use, construction, etc.)? [223] Yes [224] No   If No, describe 225

Freddie Mac Form 70 March 2005   226   **UAD Version 9/2011**   Page 1 of 6   Fannie Mae Form 1004 March 2005

Uniform Residential Appraisal Report

File # 3   4   4a

2		

There are   5   comparable properties currently offered for sale in the subject neighborhood ranging in price from $ 6   to $ 7

There are   8   comparable sales in the subject neighborhood within the past twelve months ranging in sale price from $ 9   to $ 10

FEATURE	SUBJECT	COMPARABLE SALE # 1		COMPARABLE SALE # 2		COMPARABLE SALE # 3	
Address	11 / 12a 12b 12c	45 / 46a 46b 46c		45 / 46a 46b 46c		45 / 46a 46b 46c	
Proximity to Subject		47		47		47	
Sale Price	$ 13		$ 48		$ 48		$ 48
Sale Price/Gross Liv. Area	$ 14 sq. ft.	$ 49 sq. ft.		$ 49 sq. ft.		$ 49 sq. ft.	
Data Source(s)		e-25, e-2		e-25, e-2		e-25, e-2	
Verification Source(s)		51		51		51	
VALUE ADJUSTMENTS	DESCRIPTION	DESCRIPTION	+(-) $ Adjustment	DESCRIPTION	+(-) $ Adjustment	DESCRIPTION	+(-) $ Adjustment
Sale or Financing		52	53	52	53	52	53
Concessions		e-26, e-27, e-28	55	e-26, e-27, e-28	55	e-26, e-27, e-28	55
Date of Sale/Time		e-29, e-30, e-31	57	e-29, e-30, e-31	57	e-29, e-30, e-31	57
Location	e-14, e-15, e-16	e-14, e-15, e-16	59	e-14, e-15, e-16	59	e-14, e-15, e-16	59
Leasehold/Fee Simple	21	60	61	60	61	60	61
Site	22	62	63	62	63	62	63
View	e-5, e-6, e-7	e-5, e-6, e-7	65	e-5, e-6, e-7	65	e-5, e-6, e-7	65
Design (Style)	24	66	67	66	67	66	67
Quality of Construction	25	68	69	68	69	68	69
Actual Age	e-17; 26	e-17; 70	71	e-17; 70	71	e-17; 70	71
Condition	27	72	73	72	73	72	73
Above Grade	Total / Bdrms / Baths	Total / Bdrms / Baths	74	Total / Bdrms / Baths	74	Total / Bdrms / Baths	74
Room Count	28 / 29 / 30	75 / 76 / 77	78	75 / 76 / 77	78	75 / 76 / 77	78
Gross Living Area	31 sq ft	79 sq ft	80	79 sq ft	80	79 sq ft	80
Basement & Finished	e-18, e-19, e-20	e-18, e-19, e-20	82	e-18, e-19, e-20	82	e-18, e-19, e-20	82
Rooms Below Grade	e-21; e-22; e-23; e-24	e-21; e-22; e-23; e-24	84	e-21; e-22; e-23; e-24	84	e-21; e-22; e-23; e-24	84
Functional Utility	34	85	86	85	86	85	86
Heating/Cooling	35	87	88	87	88	87	88
Energy Efficient Items	36	89	90	89	90	89	90
Garage/Carport	37	91	92	91	92	91	92
Porch/Patio/Deck	38	93	94	93	94	93	94
39	40	95	96	95	96	95	96
41	42	97	98	97	98	97	98
43	44	99	100	99	100	99	100
Net Adjustment (Total)		101 + 102 -	$ 103	101 + 102 -	$ 103	101 + 102 -	$ 103
Adjusted Sale Price of Comparables		Net Adj. 103a % Gross Adj. 103b %	$ 104	Net Adj. 103a % Gross Adj. 103b %	$ 104	Net Adj. 103a % Gross Adj. 103b %	$ 104

I [105] did [106] did not research the sale or transfer history of the subject property and comparable sales. If not, explain   107

My research [108] did [109] did not reveal any prior sales or transfers of the subject property for the three years prior to the effective date of this appraisal.
Data source(s)   110

My research [111] did [112] did not reveal any prior sales or transfers of the comparable sales for the year prior to the date of sale of the comparable sale.
Data source(s)   113

Report the results of the research and analysis of the prior sale or transfer history of the subject property and comparable sales (report additional prior sales on page 3).

ITEM	SUBJECT	COMPARABLE SALE # 1	COMPARABLE SALE # 2	COMPARABLE SALE # 3
Date of Prior Sale/Transfer	114	118	118	118
Price of Prior Sale/Transfer	115	119	119	119
Data Source(s)	116	120	120	120
Effective Date of Data Source(s)	117	121	121	121

Analysis of prior sale or transfer history of the subject property and comparable sales   122

Summary of Sales Comparison Approach   123

Indicated Value by Sales Comparison Approach $ 124

Indicated Value by: Sales Comparison Approach $ 125   Cost Approach (if developed) $ 126   Income Approach (if developed) $ 127

128

This appraisal is made [129] "as is" [130] subject to completion per plans and specifications on the basis of a hypothetical condition that the improvements have been completed, [131] subject to the following repairs or alterations on the basis of a hypothetical condition that the repairs or alterations have been completed, or [132] subject to the following required inspection based on the extraordinary assumption that the condition or deficiency does not require alteration or repair: 133

Based on a complete visual inspection of the interior and exterior areas of the subject property, defined scope of work, statement of assumptions and limiting conditions, and appraiser's certification, my (our) opinion of the market value, as defined, of the real property that is the subject of this report is
$ 134   , as of   135   , which is the date of inspection and the effective date of this appraisal.

Uniform Residential Appraisal Report

File # 3   4   4a

2

5

ADDITIONAL COMMENTS

COST APPROACH TO VALUE (not required by Fannie Mae)

Provide adequate information for the lender/client to replicate the below cost figures and calculations.

Support for the opinion of site value (summary of comparable land sales or other methods for estimating site value)   6

ESTIMATED [7] REPRODUCTION OR [8] REPLACEMENT COST NEW		OPINION OF SITE VALUE		= $	14
Source of cost data 9		Dwelling 15	Sq. Ft. @ $ 16	= $	17
Quality rating from cost service 10 Effective date of cost data 11		18 19	Sq. Ft. @ $ 20	= $	21
Comments on Cost Approach (gross living area calculations, depreciation, etc.)		22			23
12		Garage/Carport 24	Sq. Ft. @ $ 25	= $	26
		Total Estimate of Cost-New		= $	27
		Less Physical Functional External			
		Depreciation 29 31 33		=$(34	)
		Depreciated Cost of Improvements........................		= $	35
		"As-is" Value of Site Improvements.......................		= $	36
Estimated Remaining Economic Life (HUD and VA only) 13 Years		Indicated Value By Cost Approach		= $	37

INCOME APPROACH TO VALUE (not required by Fannie Mae)

Estimated Monthly Market Rent $ 38   X Gross Rent Multiplier   39   = $ 40   Indicated Value by Income Approach

Summary of Income Approach (including support for market rent and GRM)   41

PROJECT INFORMATION FOR PUDs (if applicable)

Is the developer/builder in control of the Homeowners' Association (HOA)? [42] Yes [43] No   Unit type(s) [44] Detached [45] Attached

Provide the following information for PUDs ONLY if the developer/builder is in control of the HOA and the subject property is an attached dwelling unit.

Legal name of project   46

Total number of phases   47   Total number of units   48   Total number of units sold   49

Total number of units rented   50   Total number of units for sale   51   Data source(s)   52

Was the project created by the conversion of an existing building(s) into a PUD? [53] Yes [54] No   If Yes, date of conversion   55

Does the project contain any multi-dwelling units? [56] Yes [57] No   Data source(s)   58

Are the units, common elements, and recreation facilities complete? [59] Yes [60] No   If No, describe the status of completion.   61

Are the common elements leased to or by the Homeowners' Association? [62] Yes [63] No   If Yes, describe the rental terms and options.   64

Describe common elements and recreational facilities   65

Appendix 1

2   **Uniform Residential Appraisal Report**   File # 3   4   4a

This report form is designed to report an appraisal of a one-unit property or a one-unit property with an accessory unit; including a unit in a planned unit development (PUD). This report form is not designed to report an appraisal of a manufactured home or a unit in a condominium or cooperative project.

This appraisal report is subject to the following scope of work, intended use, intended user, definition of market value, statement of assumptions and limiting conditions, and certifications. Modifications, additions, or deletions to the intended use, intended user, definition of market value, or assumptions and limiting conditions are not permitted. The appraiser may expand the scope of work to include any additional research or analysis necessary based on the complexity of this appraisal assignment. Modifications or deletions to the certifications are also not permitted. However, additional certifications that do not constitute material alterations to this appraisal report, such as those required by law or those related to the appraiser's continuing education or membership in an appraisal organization, are permitted.

SCOPE OF WORK: The scope of work for this appraisal is defined by the complexity of this appraisal assignment and the reporting requirements of this appraisal report form, including the following definition of market value, statement of assumptions and limiting conditions, and certifications. The appraiser must, at a minimum: (1) perform a complete visual inspection of the interior and exterior areas of the subject property, (2) inspect the neighborhood, (3) inspect each of the comparable sales from at least the street, (4) research, verify, and analyze data from reliable public and/or private sources, and (5) report his or her analysis, opinions, and conclusions in this appraisal report.

INTENDED USE: The intended use of this appraisal report is for the lender/client to evaluate the property that is the subject of this appraisal for a mortgage finance transaction.

INTENDED USER: The intended user of this appraisal report is the lender/client.

DEFINITION OF MARKET VALUE: The most probable price which a property should bring in a competitive and open market under all conditions requisite to a fair sale, the buyer and seller, each acting prudently, knowledgeably and assuming the price is not affected by undue stimulus. Implicit in this definition is the consummation of a sale as of a specified date and the passing of title from seller to buyer under conditions whereby: (1) buyer and seller are typically motivated; (2) both parties are well informed or well advised, and each acting in what he or she considers his or her own best interest; (3) a reasonable time is allowed for exposure in the open market; (4) payment is made in terms of cash in U. S. dollars or in terms of financial arrangements comparable thereto; and (5) the price represents the normal consideration for the property sold unaffected by special or creative financing or sales concessions* granted by anyone associated with the sale.

*Adjustments to the comparables must be made for special or creative financing or sales concessions. No adjustments are necessary for those costs which are normally paid by sellers as a result of tradition or law in a market area; these costs are readily identifiable since the seller pays these costs in virtually all sales transactions. Special or creative financing adjustments can be made to the comparable property by comparisons to financing terms offered by a third party institutional lender that is not already involved in the property or transaction. Any adjustment should not be calculated on a mechanical dollar for dollar cost of the financing or concession but the dollar amount of any adjustment should approximate the market's reaction to the financing or concessions based on the appraiser's judgment.

STATEMENT OF ASSUMPTIONS AND LIMITING CONDITIONS: The appraiser's certification in this report is subject to the following assumptions and limiting conditions:

1. The appraiser will not be responsible for matters of a legal nature that affect either the property being appraised or the title to it, except for information that he or she became aware of during the research involved in performing this appraisal. The appraiser assumes that the title is good and marketable and will not render any opinions about the title.

2. The appraiser has provided a sketch in this appraisal report to show the approximate dimensions of the improvements. The sketch is included only to assist the reader in visualizing the property and understanding the appraiser's determination of its size.

3. The appraiser has examined the available flood maps that are provided by the Federal Emergency Management Agency (or other data sources) and has noted in this appraisal report whether any portion of the subject site is located in an identified Special Flood Hazard Area. Because the appraiser is not a surveyor, he or she makes no guarantees, express or implied, regarding this determination.

4. The appraiser will not give testimony or appear in court because he or she made an appraisal of the property in question, unless specific arrangements to do so have been made beforehand, or as otherwise required by law.

5. The appraiser has noted in this appraisal report any adverse conditions (such as needed repairs, deterioration, the presence of hazardous wastes, toxic substances, etc.) observed during the inspection of the subject property or that he or she became aware of during the research involved in performing this appraisal. Unless otherwise stated in this appraisal report, the appraiser has no knowledge of any hidden or unapparent physical deficiencies or adverse conditions of the property (such as, but not limited to, needed repairs, deterioration, the presence of hazardous wastes, toxic substances, adverse environmental conditions, etc.) that would make the property less valuable, and has assumed that there are no such conditions and makes no guarantees or warranties, express or implied. The appraiser will not be responsible for any such conditions that do exist or for any engineering or testing that might be required to discover whether such conditions exist. Because the appraiser is not an expert in the field of environmental hazards, this appraisal report must not be considered as an environmental assessment of the property.

6. The appraiser has based his or her appraisal report and valuation conclusion for an appraisal that is subject to satisfactory completion, repairs, or alterations on the assumption that the completion, repairs, or alterations of the subject property will be performed in a professional manner.

Freddie Mac Form 70   March 2005   226   **UAD Version 9/2011**   Page 4 of 6   Fannie Mae Form 1004   March 2005

2 **Uniform Residential Appraisal Report** File # 3 4 4a

APPRAISER'S CERTIFICATION: The Appraiser certifies and agrees that:

1. I have, at a minimum, developed and reported this appraisal in accordance with the scope of work requirements stated in this appraisal report.

2. I performed a complete visual inspection of the interior and exterior areas of the subject property. I reported the condition of the improvements in factual, specific terms. I identified and reported the physical deficiencies that could affect the livability, soundness, or structural integrity of the property.

3. I performed this appraisal in accordance with the requirements of the Uniform Standards of Professional Appraisal Practice that were adopted and promulgated by the Appraisal Standards Board of The Appraisal Foundation and that were in place at the time this appraisal report was prepared.

4. I developed my opinion of the market value of the real property that is the subject of this report based on the sales comparison approach to value. I have adequate comparable market data to develop a reliable sales comparison approach for this appraisal assignment. I further certify that I considered the cost and income approaches to value but did not develop them, unless otherwise indicated in this report.

5. I researched, verified, analyzed, and reported on any current agreement for sale for the subject property, any offering for sale of the subject property in the twelve months prior to the effective date of this appraisal, and the prior sales of the subject property for a minimum of three years prior to the effective date of this appraisal, unless otherwise indicated in this report.

6. I researched, verified, analyzed, and reported on the prior sales of the comparable sales for a minimum of one year prior to the date of sale of the comparable sale, unless otherwise indicated in this report.

7. I selected and used comparable sales that are locationally, physically, and functionally the most similar to the subject property.

8. I have not used comparable sales that were the result of combining a land sale with the contract purchase price of a home that has been built or will be built on the land.

9. I have reported adjustments to the comparable sales that reflect the market's reaction to the differences between the subject property and the comparable sales.

10. I verified, from a disinterested source, all information in this report that was provided by parties who have a financial interest in the sale or financing of the subject property.

11. I have knowledge and experience in appraising this type of property in this market area.

12. I am aware of, and have access to, the necessary and appropriate public and private data sources, such as multiple listing services, tax assessment records, public land records and other such data sources for the area in which the property is located.

13. I obtained the information, estimates, and opinions furnished by other parties and expressed in this appraisal report from reliable sources that I believe to be true and correct.

14. I have taken into consideration the factors that have an impact on value with respect to the subject neighborhood, subject property, and the proximity of the subject property to adverse influences in the development of my opinion of market value. I have noted in this appraisal report any adverse conditions (such as, but not limited to, needed repairs, deterioration, the presence of hazardous wastes, toxic substances, adverse environmental conditions, etc.) observed during the inspection of the subject property or that I became aware of during the research involved in performing this appraisal. I have considered these adverse conditions in my analysis of the property value, and have reported on the effect of the conditions on the value and marketability of the subject property.

15. I have not knowingly withheld any significant information from this appraisal report and, to the best of my knowledge, all statements and information in this appraisal report are true and correct.

16. I stated in this appraisal report my own personal, unbiased, and professional analysis, opinions, and conclusions, which are subject only to the assumptions and limiting conditions in this appraisal report.

17. I have no present or prospective interest in the property that is the subject of this report, and I have no present or prospective personal interest or bias with respect to the participants in the transaction. I did not base, either partially or completely, my analysis and/or opinion of market value in this appraisal report on the race, color, religion, sex, age, marital status, handicap, familial status, or national origin of either the prospective owners or occupants of the subject property or of the present owners or occupants of the properties in the vicinity of the subject property or on any other basis prohibited by law.

18. My employment and/or compensation for performing this appraisal or any future or anticipated appraisals was not conditioned on any agreement or understanding, written or otherwise, that I would report (or present analysis supporting) a predetermined specific value, a predetermined minimum value, a range or direction in value, a value that favors the cause of any party, or the attainment of a specific result or occurrence of a specific subsequent event (such as approval of a pending mortgage loan application).

19. I personally prepared all conclusions and opinions about the real estate that were set forth in this appraisal report. If I relied on significant real property appraisal assistance from any individual or individuals in the performance of this appraisal or the preparation of this appraisal report, I have named such individual(s) and disclosed the specific tasks performed in this appraisal report. I certify that any individual so named is qualified to perform the tasks. I have not authorized anyone to make a change to any item in this appraisal report; therefore, any change made to this appraisal is unauthorized and I will take no responsibility for it.

20. I identified the lender/client in this appraisal report who is the individual, organization, or agent for the organization that ordered and will receive this appraisal report.

Uniform Residential Appraisal Report   File # 3   4   4a

21. The lender/client may disclose or distribute this appraisal report to: the borrower; another lender at the request of the borrower; the mortgagee or its successors and assigns; mortgage insurers; government sponsored enterprises; other secondary market participants; data collection or reporting services; professional appraisal organizations; any department, agency, or instrumentality of the United States; and any state, the District of Columbia, or other jurisdictions; without having to obtain the appraiser's or supervisory appraiser's (if applicable) consent. Such consent must be obtained before this appraisal report may be disclosed or distributed to any other party (including, but not limited to, the public through advertising, public relations, news, sales, or other media).

22. I am aware that any disclosure or distribution of this appraisal report by me or the lender/client may be subject to certain laws and regulations. Further, I am also subject to the provisions of the Uniform Standards of Professional Appraisal Practice that pertain to disclosure or distribution by me.

23. The borrower, another lender at the request of the borrower, the mortgagee or its successors and assigns, mortgage insurers, government sponsored enterprises, and other secondary market participants may rely on this appraisal report as part of any mortgage finance transaction that involves any one or more of these parties.

24. If this appraisal report was transmitted as an "electronic record" containing my "electronic signature," as those terms are defined in applicable federal and/or state laws (excluding audio and video recordings), or a facsimile transmission of this appraisal report containing a copy or representation of my signature, the appraisal report shall be as effective, enforceable and valid as if a paper version of this appraisal report were delivered containing my original hand written signature.

25. Any intentional or negligent misrepresentation(s) contained in this appraisal report may result in civil liability and/or criminal penalties including, but not limited to, fine or imprisonment or both under the provisions of Title 18, United States Code, Section 1001, et seq., or similar state laws.

SUPERVISORY APPRAISER'S CERTIFICATION: The Supervisory Appraiser certifies and agrees that:

1. I directly supervised the appraiser for this appraisal assignment, have read the appraisal report, and agree with the appraiser's analysis, opinions, statements, conclusions, and the appraiser's certification.

2. I accept full responsibility for the contents of this appraisal report including, but not limited to, the appraiser's analysis, opinions, statements, conclusions, and the appraiser's certification.

3. The appraiser identified in this appraisal report is either a sub-contractor or an employee of the supervisory appraiser (or the appraisal firm), is qualified to perform this appraisal, and is acceptable to perform this appraisal under the applicable state law.

4. This appraisal report complies with the Uniform Standards of Professional Appraisal Practice that were adopted and promulgated by the Appraisal Standards Board of The Appraisal Foundation and that were in place at the time this appraisal report was prepared.

5. If this appraisal report was transmitted as an "electronic record" containing my "electronic signature," as those terms are defined in applicable federal and/or state laws (excluding audio and video recordings), or a facsimile transmission of this appraisal report containing a copy or representation of my signature, the appraisal report shall be as effective, enforceable and valid as if a paper version of this appraisal report were delivered containing my original hand written signature.

Signature_____	**SUPERVISORY APPRAISER (ONLY IF REQUIRED)**
Name 5 _____	
Company Name 6 _____	Signature _____
Company Address 7_____	Name 27 _____
8a, 8b 8c _____	Company Name 28 _____
Telephone Number 9_____	Company Address 29_____
Email Address 10_____	30a, 30b 30c _____
Date of Signature and Report 11 _____	Telephone Number 31 _____
Effective Date of Appraisal 12 _____	Email Address 32 _____
State Certification # 13_____	Date of Signature 33 _____
or State License # 14_____	State Certification # 34 _____
or Other (describe) 15 _____ State # 16 _____	or State License # 35 _____
State 17 _____	State 36 _____
Expiration Date of Certification or License 18 _____	Expiration Date of Certification or License 37 _____
ADDRESS OF PROPERTY APPRAISED	**SUBJECT PROPERTY**
19 _____	
20a, 20b, 20c _____	☐ 38 Did not inspect subject property
APPRAISED VALUE OF SUBJECT PROPERTY $ 21 _____	☐ 39 Did inspect exterior of subject property from street
LENDER/CLIENT	Date of Inspection 40 _____
Name 22 _____	☐ 41 Did inspect interior and exterior of subject property
Company Name 23 _____	Date of Inspection 42 _____
Company Address 24_____	
_____	**COMPARABLE SALES**
Email Address 26_____	☐ 43 Did not inspect exterior of comparable sales from street
	☐ 44 Did inspect exterior of comparable sales from street
	Date of Inspection 45 _____

Appendix 2
Individual Condominium Unit Appraisal Report

Individual Condominium Unit Appraisal Report File # 3 4 4a

2

The purpose of this summary appraisal report is to provide the lender/client with an accurate, and adequately supported, opinion of the market value of the subject property.

SUBJECT

Property Address 6	Unit # 7 City 8 State 9 Zip Code 10
Borrower 11	Owner of Public Record 12 County 13

Legal Description 14

Assessor's Parcel # 15 Tax Year 16 R.E. Taxes $ 17

Project Name 18 Phase # 19 Map Reference 20 Census Tract 21

Occupant ▢22 Owner ▢23 Tenant ▢24 Vacant Special Assessments $ 25 HOA $ 26 ▢27 per year ▢28 per month

Property Rights Appraised ▢29 Fee Simple ▢30 Leasehold ▢31 Other (describe) 32

Assignment Type ▢33 Purchase Transaction ▢34 Refinance Transaction ▢35 Other (describe) 36

Lender/Client 37 Address 38

Is the subject property currently offered for sale or has it been offered for sale in the twelve months prior to the effective date of this appraisal? ▢39 Yes ▢40 No

Report data source(s) used, offering price(s), and date(s). e-2; 41

CONTRACT

I ▢42 did ▢43 did not analyze the contract for sale for the subject purchase transaction. Explain the results of the analysis of the contract for sale or why the analysis was not performed. e-3; 44

Contract Price $ 45 Date of Contract 46 Is the property seller the owner of public record? ▢47 Yes ▢48 No Data Source(s) 49

Is there any financial assistance (loan charges, sale concessions, gift or downpayment assistance, etc.) to be paid by any party on behalf of the borrower? ▢50 Yes ▢51 No
If Yes, report the total dollar amount and describe the items to be paid. 52a; e-4; 52b

NEIGHBORHOOD

Note: Race and the racial composition of the neighborhood are not appraisal factors.

Neighborhood Characteristics		Condominium Unit Housing Trends			Condominium Housing			Present Land Use %		
Location ▢53 Urban ▢54 Suburban ▢55 Rural		Property Values ▢62 Increasing ▢63 Stable ▢64 Declining			PRICE	AGE		One-Unit	77	%
Built-Up ▢56 Over 75% ▢57 25–75% ▢58 Under 25%		Demand/Supply ▢65 Shortage ▢66 In Balance ▢67 Over Supply			$ (000)	(yrs)		2-4 Unit	78	%
Growth ▢59 Rapid ▢60 Stable ▢61 Slow		Marketing Time ▢68 Under 3 mths ▢69 3–6 mths ▢70 Over 6 mths			71 Low 74			Multi-Family	79	%
Neighborhood Boundaries 83					72 High 75			Commercial	80	%
					73 Pred. 76			Other	82	%

Neighborhood Description 84

Market Conditions (including support for the above conclusions) 85

PROJECT SITE

Topography 86 Size 87 Density 88 View e-5; e-6; e-7

Specific Zoning Classification 90 Zoning Description 91

Zoning Compliance ▢92 Legal ▢93 Legal Nonconforming – Do the zoning regulations permit rebuilding to current density? ▢94 Yes ▢95 No
▢96 No Zoning ▢97 Illegal (describe) 98

Is the highest and best use of the subject property as improved (or as proposed per plans and specifications) the present use? ▢99 Yes ▢100 No If No, describe 101

Utilities	Public	Other (describe)		Public	Other (describe)	Off-site Improvements—Type	Public	Private
Electricity	▢102	▢103 104	Water	▢108	▢109 110	Street 114	▢115	▢116
Gas	▢105	▢106 107	Sanitary Sewer	▢111	▢112 113	Alley 117	▢118	▢119

FEMA Special Flood Hazard Area ▢120 Yes ▢121 No FEMA Flood Zone 122 FEMA Map # 123 FEMA Map Date 124

Are the utilities and off-site improvements typical for the market area? ▢125 Yes ▢126 No If No, describe 127

Are there any adverse site conditions or external factors (easements, encroachments, environmental conditions, land uses, etc.)? ▢128 Yes ▢129 No If Yes, describe
130

PROJECT INFORMATION

Data source(s) for project information 131

Project Description ▢132 Detached ▢133 Row or Townhouse ▢134 Garden ▢135 Mid-Rise ▢136 High-Rise ▢137 Other (describe) 138

General Description	General Description	Subject Phase		If Project Completed		If Project Incomplete	
# of Stories 139	Exterior Walls 146	# of Units	152	# of Phases	158	# of Planned Phases	164
# of Elevators 140	Roof Surface 147	# of Units Completed	153	# of Units	159	# of Planned Units	165
▢141 Existing ▢142 Proposed	Total # Parking 148	# of Units For Sale	154	# of Units for Sale	160	# of Units for Sale	166
▢143 Under Construction	Ratio (spaces/units) 149	# of Units Sold	155	# of Units Sold	161	# of Units Sold	167
Year Built e-8; 144	Type 150	# of Units Rented	156	# of Units Rented	162	# of Units Rented	168
Effective Age 145	Guest Parking 151	# of Owner Occupied Units	157	# of Owner Occupied Units	163	# of Owner Occupied Units	169

Project Primary Occupancy ▢170 Principle Residence ▢171 Second Home or Recreational ▢172 Tenant

Is the developer/builder in control of the Homeowners' Association (HOA)? ▢173 Yes ▢174 No

Management Group – ▢175 Homeowners' Association ▢176 Developer ▢177 Management Agent – Provide name of management company. 178

Does any single entity (the same individual, investor group, corporation, etc.) own more than 10% of the total units in the project? ▢179 Yes ▢180 No If Yes, describe 181

Was the project created by the conversion of an existing building(s) into a condominium? ▢182 Yes ▢183 No If Yes, describe the original use and the date of conversion.
184

Are the units, common elements, and recreation facilities complete (including any planned rehabilitation for a condominium conversion)? ▢185 Yes ▢186 No If No, describe
187

Is there any commercial space in the project? ▢188 Yes ▢189 No If Yes, describe and indicate the overall percentage of the commercial space.
e-32; 190

Freddie Mac Form 465 March 2005 226 **UAD Version 9/2011** Page 1 of 6 Fannie Mae Form 1073 March 2005

2   **Individual Condominium Unit Appraisal Report**   File # 3   4   4a

Describe the condition of the project and quality of construction. 5

Describe the common elements and recreational facilities. 6

Are any common elements leased to or by the Homeowners' Association? ⬛7 Yes ⬛8 No If Yes, describe the rental terms and options. 9

Is the project subject to ground rent? ⬛10 Yes ⬛11 No If Yes, $ 12 per year (describe terms and conditions) 13

Are the parking facilities adequate for the project size and type? ⬛14 Yes ⬛15 No If No, describe and comment on the effect on value and marketability. 16

I ⬛17 did ⬛18 did not analyze the condominium project budget for the current year. Explain the results of the analysis of the budget (adequacy of fees, reserves, etc.), or why the analysis was not performed. 19

Are there any other fees (other than regular HOA charges) for the use of the project facilities? ⬛20 Yes ⬛21 No If Yes, report the charges and describe. 22

Compared to other competitive projects of similar quality and design, the subject unit charge appears ⬛23 High ⬛24 Average ⬛25 Low If High or Low, describe 26

Are there any special or unusual characteristics of the project (based on the condominium documents, HOA meetings, or other information) known to the appraiser? ⬛27 Yes ⬛28 No If Yes, describe and explain the effect on value and marketability. 29

Unit Charge $ 30 per month X 12 = $ 31 per year   Annual assessment charge per year per square feet of gross living area = $ 32

Utilities included in the unit monthly assessment ⬛33 None ⬛34 Heat ⬛35 Air Conditioning ⬛36 Electricity ⬛37 Gas ⬛38 Water ⬛39 Sewer ⬛40 Cable ⬛41 Other (describe) 42

General Description	Interior materials/condition	Amenities	Appliances	Car Storage
Floor # 43	Floors 51	⬛56 Fireplace(s) # 57	⬛66 Refrigerator	⬛72 None
# of Levels 44	Walls 52	⬛58 Woodstove(s) # 59	⬛67 Range/Oven	⬛73 Garage ⬛74 Covered ⬛75 Open
Heating Type 45 Fuel 46	Trim/Finish 53	⬛60 Deck/Patio 61	⬛68 Disp ⬛69 Microwave	# of Cars 76
⬛47 Central AC ⬛48 Individual AC	Bath Wainscot 54	⬛62 Porch/Balcony 63	⬛70 Dishwasher	⬛77 Assigned ⬛78 Owned
⬛49 Other (describe) 50	Doors 55	⬛64 Other 65	⬛71 Washer/Dryer	Parking Space # 79

Finished area **above grade** contains: 80 Rooms 81 Bedrooms 82 Bath(s) 83 Square Feet of Gross Living Area Above Grade

Are the heating and cooling for the individual units separately metered? ⬛84 Yes ⬛85 No If No, describe and comment on compatibility to other projects in the market area. 86

Additional features (special energy efficient items, etc.) 87

Describe the condition of the property (including needed repairs, deterioration, renovations, remodeling, etc.). e-9; e-10; e-11; e-12; e-13; 88

Are there any physical deficiencies or adverse conditions that affect the livability, soundness, or structural integrity of the property? ⬛89 Yes ⬛90 No If Yes, describe 91

Does the property generally conform to the neighborhood (functional utility, style, condition, use, construction, etc.)? ⬛92 Yes ⬛93 No If No, describe 94

I ⬛95 did ⬛96 did not research the sale or transfer history of the subject property and comparable sales. If not, explain 97

My research ⬛98 did ⬛99 did not reveal any prior sales or transfers of the subject property for the three years prior to the effective date of this appraisal.
Data source(s) 100

My research ⬛101 did ⬛102 did not reveal any prior sales or transfers of the comparable sales for the year prior to the date of sale of the comparable sale.
Data source(s) 103

Report the results of the research and analysis of the prior sale or transfer history of the subject property and comparable sales (report additional prior sales on page 3).

ITEM	SUBJECT	COMPARABLE SALE # 1	COMPARABLE SALE # 2	COMPARABLE SALE # 3
Date of Prior Sale/Transfer	104	108	108	108
Price of Prior Sale/Transfer	105	109	109	109
Data Source(s)	106	110	110	110
Effective Date of Data Source(s)	107	111	111	111

Analysis of prior sale or transfer history of the subject property and comparable sales. 112

Freddie Mac Form 465 March 2005   226   **UAD Version 9/2011**   Page 2 of 6   Fannie Mae Form 1073 March 2005

Fannie Mae Form 1073/Freddie Mac Form 465

Individual Condominium Unit Appraisal Report

2

File # 3   4   4a

There are 5 comparable properties currently offered for sale in the subject neighborhood ranging in price from $ 6 to $ 7 .

There are 8 comparable sales in the subject neighborhood within the past twelve months ranging in sale price from $ 9 to $ 10 .

FEATURE	SUBJECT	COMPARABLE SALE # 1		COMPARABLE SALE # 2		COMPARABLE SALE # 3	
Address and Unit #	11 12a 12b 12c12d	50 51a 51b 51c 51d		50 51a 51b 51c 51d		50 51a 51b 51c 51d	
Project Name and Phase	13 14	52 53		52 53		52 53	
Proximity to Subject		54		54		54	
Sale Price	$ 15		$ 55		$ 55		$ 55
Sale Price/Gross Liv. Area	$ 16 sq. ft.	$ 56 sq. ft.		$ 56 sq. ft.		$ 56 sq. ft.	
Data Source(s)		e-25; e-2		e-25; e-2		e-25; e-2	
Verification Source(s)		58		58		58	
VALUE ADJUSTMENTS	DESCRIPTION	DESCRIPTION	+(-) $ Adjustment	DESCRIPTION	+(-) $ Adjustment	DESCRIPTION	+(-) $ Adjustment
Sale or Financing Concessions		59 e-26; e-27; e-28	60 62	59 e-26; e-27; e-28	60 62	59 e-26; e-27; e-28	60 62
Date of Sale/Time		e-29; e-30; e-31	64	e-29; e-30; e-31	64	e-29; e-30; e-31	64
Location	e-14; e-15; e-16	e-14; e-15; e-16	66	e-14; e-15; e-16	66	e-14; e-15; e-16	66
Leasehold/Fee Simple	23	67	68	67	68	67	68
HOA Mo. Assessment	24	69	70	69	70	69	70
Common Elements and Rec. Facilities	25 26	71 73	72 74	71 73	72 74	71 73	72 74
Floor Location	27	75	76	75	76	75	76
View	e-5; e-6; e-7	e-5; e-6; e-7	78	e-5; e-6; e-7	78	e-5; e-6; e-7	78
Design (Style)	29	79	80	79	80	79	80
Quality of Construction	30	81	82	81	82	81	82
Actual Age	e-17; 31	e-17; 83	84	e-17; 83	84	e-17; 83	84
Condition	32	85	86	85	86	85	86
Above Grade Room Count	Total 33 | Bdrms. 34 | Baths 35	Total 88 | Bdrms. 89 | Baths 90	87 91	Total 88 | Bdrms. 89 | Baths 90	87 91	Total 88 | Bdrms. 89 | Baths 90	87 91
Gross Living Area	36 sq. ft.	92 sq. ft.	93	92 sq. ft.	93	92 sq. ft.	93
Basement & Finished Rooms Below Grade	e-18; e-19; e-20 e-21; e-22; e-23; e-24	e-18; e-19; e-20 e-21; e-22; e-23; e-24	95 97	e-18; e-19; e-20 e-21; e-22; e-23; e-24	95 97	e-18; e-19; e-20 e-21; e-22; e-23; e-24	95 97
Functional Utility	39	98	99	98	99	98	99
Heating/Cooling	40	100	101	100	101	100	101
Energy Efficient Items	41	102	103	102	103	102	103
Garage/Carport	42	104	105	104	105	104	105
Porch/Patio/Deck	43	106	107	106	107	106	107
44	45	108	109	108	109	108	109
46	47	110	111	110	111	110	111
48	49	112	113	112	113	112	113
Net Adjustment (Total)		114 + 115 -	$ 116	114 + 115	$ 116	114 + 115	$ 116
Adjusted Sale Price of Comparables		Net Adj. 116a % Gross Adj. 116b %	$ 117	Net Adj. 116a % Gross Adj. 116b %	$ 117	Net Adj. 116a % Gross Adj. 116b %	$ 117

Summary of Sales Comparison Approach 118

Indicated Value by Sales Comparison Approach $ 119

INCOME APPROACH TO VALUE (not required by Fannie Mae)

Estimated Monthly Market Rent $ 120   X Gross Rent Multiplier 121 = $ 122   Indicated Value by Income Approach

Summary of Income Approach (including support for market rent and GRM) 123

Indicated Value by: Sales Comparison Approach $ 124   Income Approach (if developed) $ 125

126

This appraisal is made 127 "as is" 128 subject to completion per plans and specifications on the basis of a hypothetical condition that the improvements have been completed, 129 subject to the following repairs or alterations on the basis of a hypothetical condition that the repairs or alterations have been completed, or 130 subject to the following required inspection based on the extraordinary assumption that the condition or deficiency does not require alteration or repair: 131

Based on a complete visual inspection of the interior and exterior areas of the subject property, defined scope of work, statement of assumptions and limiting conditions, and appraiser's certification, my (our) opinion of the market value, as defined, of the real property that is the subject of this report is $ 132 , as of 133 , which is the date of inspection and the effective date of this appraisal.

2   **Individual Condominium Unit Appraisal Report**   File #   3   4   4a

This report form is designed to report an appraisal of a unit in a condominium project or a condominium unit in a planned unit development (PUD). This report form is not designed to report an appraisal of a manufactured home or a unit in a cooperative project.

This appraisal report is subject to the following scope of work, intended use, intended user, definition of market value, statement of assumptions and limiting conditions, and certifications. Modifications, additions, or deletions to the intended use, intended user, definition of market value, or assumptions and limiting conditions are not permitted. The appraiser may expand the scope of work to include any additional research or analysis necessary based on the complexity of this appraisal assignment. Modifications or deletions to the certifications are also not permitted. However, additional certifications that do not constitute material alterations to this appraisal report, such as those required by law or those related to the appraiser's continuing education or membership in an appraisal organization, are permitted.

SCOPE OF WORK: The scope of work for this appraisal is defined by the complexity of this appraisal assignment and the reporting requirements of this appraisal report form, including the following definition of market value, statement of assumptions and limiting conditions, and certifications. The appraiser must, at a minimum: (1) perform a complete visual inspection of the interior and exterior areas of the subject unit, (2) inspect and analyze the condominium project, (3) inspect the neighborhood, (4) inspect each of the comparable sales from at least the street, (5) research, verify, and analyze data from reliable public and/or private sources, and (6) report his or her analysis, opinions, and conclusions in this appraisal report.

INTENDED USE: The intended use of this appraisal report is for the lender/client to evaluate the property that is the subject of this appraisal for a mortgage finance transaction.

INTENDED USER: The intended user of this appraisal report is the lender/client.

MARKET VALUE: The most probable price which a property should bring in a competitive and open market under all conditions requisite to a fair sale, the buyer and seller, each acting prudently, knowledgeably and assuming the price is not affected by undue stimulus. Implicit in this definition is the consummation of a sale as of a specified date and the passing of title from seller to buyer under conditions whereby: (1) buyer and seller are typically motivated; (2) both parties are well informed or well advised, and each acting in what he or she considers his or her own best interest; (3) a reasonable time is allowed for exposure in the open market; (4) payment is made in terms of cash in U. S. dollars or in terms of financial arrangements comparable thereto; and (5) the price represents the normal consideration for the property sold unaffected by special or creative financing or sales concessions* granted by anyone associated with the sale.

*Adjustments to the comparables must be made for special or creative financing or sales concessions. No adjustments are necessary for those costs which are normally paid by sellers as a result of tradition or law in a market area; these costs are readily identifiable since the seller pays these costs in virtually all sales transactions. Special or creative financing adjustments can be made to the comparable property by comparisons to financing terms offered by a third party institutional lender that is not already involved in the property or transaction. Any adjustment should not be calculated on a mechanical dollar for dollar cost of the financing or concession but the dollar amount of any adjustment should approximate the market's reaction to the financing or concessions based on the appraiser's judgment.

STATEMENT OF ASSUMPTIONS AND LIMITING CONDITIONS: The appraiser's certification in this report is subject to the following assumptions and limiting conditions:

1. The appraiser will not be responsible for matters of a legal nature that affect either the property being appraised or the title to it, except for information that he or she became aware of during the research involved in performing this appraisal. The appraiser assumes that the title is good and marketable and will not render any opinions about the title.

2. The appraiser has provided a sketch in this appraisal report to show the approximate dimensions of the improvements. The sketch is included only to assist the reader in visualizing the property and understanding the appraiser's determination of its size.

3. The appraiser has examined the available flood maps that are provided by the Federal Emergency Management Agency (or other data sources) and has noted in this appraisal report whether any portion of the subject site is located in an identified Special Flood Hazard Area. Because the appraiser is not a surveyor, he or she makes no guarantees, express or implied, regarding this determination.

4. The appraiser will not give testimony or appear in court because he or she made an appraisal of the property in question, unless specific arrangements to do so have been made beforehand, or as otherwise required by law.

5. The appraiser has noted in this appraisal report any adverse conditions (such as needed repairs, deterioration, the presence of hazardous wastes, toxic substances, etc.) observed during the inspection of the subject property or that he or she became aware of during the research involved in performing this appraisal. Unless otherwise stated in this appraisal report, the appraiser has no knowledge of any hidden or unapparent physical deficiencies or adverse conditions of the property (such as, but not limited to, needed repairs, deterioration, the presence of hazardous wastes, toxic substances, adverse environmental conditions, etc.) that would make the property less valuable, and has assumed that there are no such conditions and makes no guarantees or warranties, express or implied. The appraiser will not be responsible for any such conditions that do exist or for any engineering or testing that might be required to discover whether such conditions exist. Because the appraiser is not an expert in the field of environmental hazards, this appraisal report must not be considered as an environmental assessment of the property.

6. The appraiser has based his or her appraisal report and valuation conclusion for an appraisal that is subject to satisfactory completion, repairs, or alterations on the assumption that the completion, repairs, or alterations of the subject property will be performed in a professional manner.

Fannie Mae Form 1073/Freddie Mac Form 465

APPRAISER'S CERTIFICATION: The Appraiser certifies and agrees that:

1. I have, at a minimum, developed and reported this appraisal in accordance with the scope of work requirements stated in this appraisal report.

2. I performed a complete visual inspection of the interior and exterior areas of the subject property. I reported the condition of the improvements in factual, specific terms. I identified and reported the physical deficiencies that could affect the livability, soundness, or structural integrity of the property.

3. I performed this appraisal in accordance with the requirements of the Uniform Standards of Professional Appraisal Practice that were adopted and promulgated by the Appraisal Standards Board of The Appraisal Foundation and that were in place at the time this appraisal report was prepared.

4. I developed my opinion of the market value of the real property that is the subject of this report based on the sales comparison approach to value. I have adequate comparable market data to develop a reliable sales comparison approach for this appraisal assignment. I further certify that I considered the cost and income approaches to value but did not develop them, unless otherwise indicated in this report.

5. I researched, verified, analyzed, and reported on any current agreement for sale for the subject property, any offering for sale of the subject property in the twelve months prior to the effective date of this appraisal, and the prior sales of the subject property for a minimum of three years prior to the effective date of this appraisal, unless otherwise indicated in this report.

6. I researched, verified, analyzed, and reported on the prior sales of the comparable sales for a minimum of one year prior to the date of sale of the comparable sale, unless otherwise indicated in this report.

7. I selected and used comparable sales that are locationally, physically, and functionally the most similar to the subject property.

8. I have not used comparable sales that were the result of combining a land sale with the contract purchase price of a home that has been built or will be built on the land.

9. I have reported adjustments to the comparable sales that reflect the market's reaction to the differences between the subject property and the comparable sales.

10. I verified, from a disinterested source, all information in this report that was provided by parties who have a financial interest in the sale or financing of the subject property.

11. I have knowledge and experience in appraising this type of property in this market area.

12. I am aware of, and have access to, the necessary and appropriate public and private data sources, such as multiple listing services, tax assessment records, public land records and other such data sources for the area in which the property is located.

13. I obtained the information, estimates, and opinions furnished by other parties and expressed in this appraisal report from reliable sources that I believe to be true and correct.

14. I have taken into consideration the factors that have an impact on value with respect to the subject neighborhood, subject property, and the proximity of the subject property to adverse influences in the development of my opinion of market value. I have noted in this appraisal report any adverse conditions (such as, but not limited to, needed repairs, deterioration, the presence of hazardous wastes, toxic substances, adverse environmental conditions, etc.) observed during the inspection of the subject property or that I became aware of during the research involved in performing this appraisal. I have considered these adverse conditions in my analysis of the property value, and have reported on the effect of the conditions on the value and marketability of the subject property.

15. I have not knowingly withheld any significant information from this appraisal report and, to the best of my knowledge, all statements and information in this appraisal report are true and correct.

16. I stated in this appraisal report my own personal, unbiased, and professional analysis, opinions, and conclusions, which are subject only to the assumptions and limiting conditions in this appraisal report.

17. I have no present or prospective interest in the property that is the subject of this report, and I have no present or prospective personal interest or bias with respect to the participants in the transaction. I did not base, either partially or completely, my analysis and/or opinion of market value in this appraisal report on the race, color, religion, sex, age, marital status, handicap, familial status, or national origin of either the prospective owners or occupants of the subject property or of the present owners or occupants of the properties in the vicinity of the subject property or on any other basis prohibited by law.

18. My employment and/or compensation for performing this appraisal or any future or anticipated appraisals was not conditioned on any agreement or understanding, written or otherwise, that I would report (or present analysis supporting) a predetermined specific value, a predetermined minimum value, a range or direction in value, a value that favors the cause of any party, or the attainment of a specific result or occurrence of a specific subsequent event (such as approval of a pending mortgage loan application).

19. I personally prepared all conclusions and opinions about the real estate that were set forth in this appraisal report. If I relied on significant real property appraisal assistance from any individual or individuals in the performance of this appraisal or the preparation of this appraisal report, I have named such individual(s) and disclosed the specific tasks performed in this appraisal report. I certify that any individual so named is qualified to perform the tasks. I have not authorized anyone to make a change to any item in this appraisal report; therefore, any change made to this appraisal is unauthorized and I will take no responsibility for it.

20. I identified the lender/client in this appraisal report who is the individual, organization, or agent for the organization that ordered and will receive this appraisal report.

2   **Individual Condominium Unit Appraisal Report**   File # 3   4   4a

21. The lender/client may disclose or distribute this appraisal report to: the borrower; another lender at the request of the borrower; the mortgagee or its successors and assigns; mortgage insurers; government sponsored enterprises; other secondary market participants; data collection or reporting services; professional appraisal organizations; any department, agency, or instrumentality of the United States; and any state, the District of Columbia, or other jurisdictions; without having to obtain the appraiser's or supervisory appraiser's (if applicable) consent. Such consent must be obtained before this appraisal report may be disclosed or distributed to any other party (including, but not limited to, the public through advertising, public relations, news, sales, or other media).

22. I am aware that any disclosure or distribution of this appraisal report by me or the lender/client may be subject to certain laws and regulations. Further, I am also subject to the provisions of the Uniform Standards of Professional Appraisal Practice that pertain to disclosure or distribution by me.

23. The borrower, another lender at the request of the borrower, the mortgagee or its successors and assigns, mortgage insurers, government sponsored enterprises, and other secondary market participants may rely on this appraisal report as part of any mortgage finance transaction that involves any one or more of these parties.

24. If this appraisal report was transmitted as an "electronic record" containing my "electronic signature," as those terms are defined in applicable federal and/or state laws (excluding audio and video recordings), or a facsimile transmission of this appraisal report containing a copy or representation of my signature, the appraisal report shall be as effective, enforceable and valid as if a paper version of this appraisal report were delivered containing my original hand written signature.

25. Any intentional or negligent misrepresentation(s) contained in this appraisal report may result in civil liability and/or criminal penalties including, but not limited to, fine or imprisonment or both under the provisions of Title 18, United States Code, Section 1001, et seq., or similar state laws.

SUPERVISORY APPRAISER'S CERTIFICATION: The Supervisory Appraiser certifies and agrees that:

1. I directly supervised the appraiser for this appraisal assignment, have read the appraisal report, and agree with the appraiser's analysis, opinions, statements, conclusions, and the appraiser's certification.

2. I accept full responsibility for the contents of this appraisal report including, but not limited to, the appraiser's analysis, opinions, statements, conclusions, and the appraiser's certification.

3. The appraiser identified in this appraisal report is either a sub-contractor or an employee of the supervisory appraiser (or the appraisal firm), is qualified to perform this appraisal, and is acceptable to perform this appraisal under the applicable state law.

4. This appraisal report complies with the Uniform Standards of Professional Appraisal Practice that were adopted and promulgated by the Appraisal Standards Board of The Appraisal Foundation and that were in place at the time this appraisal report was prepared.

5. If this appraisal report was transmitted as an "electronic record" containing my "electronic signature," as those terms are defined in applicable federal and/or state laws (excluding audio and video recordings), or a facsimile transmission of this appraisal report containing a copy or representation of my signature, the appraisal report shall be as effective, enforceable and valid as if a paper version of this appraisal report were delivered containing my original hand written signature.

APPRAISER

Signature _____
Name 5_____
Company Name 6 _____
Company Address 7 _____
         8a, 8b 8c _____
Telephone Number 9_____
Email Address 10 _____
Date of Signature and Report 11_____
Effective Date of Appraisal 12 _____
State Certification # 13 _____
or State License # 14_____
or Other 15 _____ State # 16 _____
State 17_____
Expiration Date of Certification or License 18_____

ADDRESS OF PROPERTY APPRAISED
  19 _____
  20a, 20b, 20c, 20d _____
APPRAISED VALUE OF SUBJECT PROPERTY $ 21_____
LENDER/CLIENT
Name 22 _____
Company Name 23_____
Company Address 24 _____
Email Address 26 _____

SUPERVISORY APPRAISER (ONLY IF REQUIRED)

Signature_____
Name 27_____
Company Name 28 _____
Company Address 29_____
         30a, 30b 30c _____
Telephone Number 31 _____
Email Address 32 _____
Date of Signature 33 _____
State Certification # 34_____
or State License # 35 _____
State 36 _____
Expiration Date of Certification or License 37 _____

SUBJECT PROPERTY
☐38 Did not inspect subject property
☐39 Did inspect exterior of subject property from street
     Date of Inspection 40 _____
☐41 Did inspect interior and exterior of subject property
     Date of Inspection 42 _____

COMPARABLE SALES
☐43 Did not inspect exterior of comparable sales from street
☐44 Did inspect exterior of comparable sales from street
     Date of Inspection 45 _____

Appendix 3
Exterior-Only Inspection
Individual Condominium Unit Appraisal Report

Exterior-Only Inspection Individual Condominium Unit Appraisal Report File # 3   4   4a

The purpose of this summary appraisal report is to provide the lender/client with an accurate, and adequately supported, opinion of the market value of the subject property.

Property Address 6	Unit # 7	City 8	State 9	Zip Code 10

Borrower 11   Owner of Public Record 12   County 13

Legal Description 14

Assessor's Parcel # 15   Tax Year 16   R.E. Taxes $ 17

Project Name 18   Phase # 19   Map Reference 20   Census Tract 21

Occupant [22] Owner [23] Tenant [24] Vacant   Special Assessments $ 25   HOA $ 26   [27] per year [28] per month

Property Rights Appraised [29] Fee Simple [30] Leasehold [31] Other (describe) 32

Assignment Type [33] Purchase Transaction [34] Refinance Transaction [35] Other (describe) 36

Lender/Client 37   Address 38

Is the subject property currently offered for sale or has it been offered for sale in the twelve months prior to the effective date of this appraisal? [39] Yes [40] No

Report data source(s) used, offering price(s), and date(s). e-2; 41

I [42] did [43] did not analyze the contract for sale for the subject purchase transaction. Explain the results of the analysis of the contract for sale or why the analysis was not performed. e-3; 44

Contract Price $ 45   Date of Contract 46   Is the property seller the owner of public record? [47] Yes [48] No Data Source(s) 49

Is there any financial assistance (loan charges, sale concessions, gift or downpayment assistance, etc.) to be paid by any party on behalf of the borrower? [50] Yes [51] No
If Yes, report the total dollar amount and describe the items to be paid. 52a; e-4; 52b

Note: Race and the racial composition of the neighborhood are not appraisal factors.

Neighborhood Characteristics	Condominium Unit Housing Trends	Condominium Housing	Present Land Use %
Location [53] Urban [54] Suburban [55] Rural	Property Values [62] Increasing [63] Stable [64] Declining	PRICE AGE	One-Unit 77 %
Built-Up [56] Over 75% [57] 25–75% [58] Under 25%	Demand/Supply [65] Shortage [66] In Balance [67] Over Supply	$ (000) (yrs)	2-4 Unit 78 %
Growth [59] Rapid [60] Stable [61] Slow	Marketing Time [68] Under 3 mths [69] 3–6 mths [70] Over 6 mths	71 Low 74	Multi-Family 79 %
Neighborhood Boundaries 83		72 High 75	Commercial 81 %
		73 Pred. 76	Other 82 %

Neighborhood Description 84

Market Conditions (including support for the above conclusions) 85

Topography 86   Size 87   Density 88   View e-5; e-6; e-7

Specific Zoning Classification 90   Zoning Description 91

Zoning Compliance [92] Legal [93] Legal Nonconforming – Do the zoning regulations permit rebuilding to current density? [94] Yes [95] No

[96] No Zoning [97] Illegal (describe) 98

Is the highest and best use of the subject property as improved (or as proposed per plans and specifications) the present use? [99] Yes [100] No If No, describe 101

Utilities	Public	Other (describe)		Public	Other (describe)	Off-site Improvements—Type	Public	Private
Electricity	[102]	[103] 104	Water	[108]	[109] 110	Street 114	[115]	[116]
Gas	[105]	[106] 107	Sanitary Sewer	[111]	[112] 113	Alley 117	[118]	[119]

FEMA Special Flood Hazard Area [120] Yes [121] No FEMA Flood Zone 122   FEMA Map # 123   FEMA Map Date 124

Are the utilities and off-site improvements typical for the market area? [125] Yes [126] No If No, describe 127

Are there any adverse site conditions or external factors (easements, encroachments, environmental conditions, land uses, etc.)? [128] Yes [129] No If Yes, describe
130

Data source(s) for project information 131

Project Description [132] Detached [133] Row or Townhouse [134] Garden [135] Mid-Rise [136] High-Rise [137] Other (describe) 138

General Description	General Description	Subject Phase	If Project Completed	If Project Incomplete
# of Stories 139	Exterior Walls 146	# of Units 152	# of Phases 158	# of Planned Phases 164
# of Elevators 140	Roof Surface 147	# of Units Completed 153	# of Units 159	# of Planned Units 165
[141] Existing [142] Proposed	Total # Parking 148	# of Units For Sale 154	# of Units for Sale 160	# of Units for Sale 166
[143] Under Construction	Ratio (spaces/units) 149	# of Units Sold 155	# of Units Sold 161	# of Units Sold 167
Year Built e-8; 144	Type 150	# of Units Rented 156	# of Units Rented 162	# of Units Rented 168
Effective Age 145	Guest Parking 151	# of Owner Occupied Units 157	# of Owner Occupied Units 163	# of Owner Occupied Units 169

Project Primary Occupancy [170] Principle Residence [171] Second Home or Recreational [172] Tenant

Is the developer/builder in control of the Homeowners' Association (HOA)? [173] Yes [174] No

Management Group – [175] Homeowners' Association [176] Developer [177] Management Agent – Provide name of management company. 178

Does any single entity (the same individual, investor group, corporation, etc.) own more than 10% of the total units in the project? [179] Yes [180] No If Yes, describe 181

Was the project created by the conversion of an existing building(s) into a condominium? [182] Yes [183] No If Yes, describe the original use and the date of conversion.
184

Are the units, common elements, and recreation facilities complete (including any planned rehabilitation for a condominium conversion)? [185] Yes [186] No If No, describe
187

Is there any commercial space in the project? [188] Yes [189] No If Yes, describe and indicate the overall percentage of the commercial space.
e-32; 190

2 **Exterior-Only Inspection Individual Condominium Unit Appraisal Report** File # 3   4   4a

Describe the condition of the project and quality of construction 5

Describe the common elements and recreational facilities. 6

Are any common elements leased to or by the Homeowners' Association? ☐ 7 Yes ☐ 8 No If Yes, describe the rental terms and options. 9

Is the project subject to ground rent? ☐ 10 Yes ☐ 11 No If Yes, $ 12   per year (describe terms and conditions) 13

Are the parking facilities adequate for the project size and type? ☐ 14 Yes ☐ 15 No If No, describe and comment on the effect on value and marketability. 16

I ☐ 17 did ☐ 18 did not analyze the condominium project budget for the current year. Explain the results of the analysis of the budget (adequacy of fees, reserves, etc.), or why the analysis was not performed. 19

Are there any other fees (other than regular HOA charges) for the use of the project facilities? ☐ 20 Yes ☐ 21 No If Yes, report the charges and describe. 22

Compared to other competitive projects of similar quality and design, the subject unit charge appears ☐ 23 High ☐ 24 Average ☐ 25 Low If High or Low, describe 26

Are there any special or unusual characteristics of the project (based on the condominium documents, HOA meetings, or other information) known to the appraiser? ☐ 27 Yes ☐ 28 No If Yes, describe and explain the effect on value and marketability. 29

Unit Charge $ 30   per month X 12 = $ 31   per year   Annual assessment charge per year per square feet of gross living area = $ 32

Utilities included in the unit monthly assessment ☐ 33 None ☐ 34 Heat ☐ 35 Air Conditioning ☐ 36 Electricity ☐ 37 Gas ☐ 38 Water ☐ 39 Sewer ☐ 40 Cable ☐ 41 Other

Source(s) Used for Physical Characteristics of Property ☐ 42 Appraisal Files ☐ 43 MLS ☐ 44 Assessment and Tax Records ☐ 45 Prior Inspection ☐ 46 Property Owner

☐ 47 Other (describe) 48   Data Source(s) for Gross Living Area 49

General Description	Amenities	Appliances	Car Storage
Floor # 50	☐ 58 Fireplace(s) # 59	☐ 68 Refrigerator	☐ 74 None
# of Levels 51	☐ 60 Woodstove(s) # 61	☐ 69 Range/Oven	☐ 75 Garage ☐ 76 Covered ☐ 77 Open
Heating Type 52 Fuel 53	☐ 62 Deck/Patio 63	☐ 70 Disp ☐ 71 Microwave	# of Cars 78
☐ 54 Central AC ☐ 55 Individual AC	☐ 64 Porch/Balcony 65	☐ 72 Dishwasher	☐ 79 Assigned ☐ 80 Owned
☐ 56 Other (describe) 57	☐ 66 Other 67	☐ 73 Washer/Dryer	Parking Space # 81

Finished area **above** grade contains: 82   Rooms 83   Bedrooms 84   Bath(s) 85   Square Feet of Gross Living Area Above Grade

Are the heating and cooling for the individual units separately metered? ☐ 86 Yes ☐ 87 No If No, describe and comment on compatibility to other projects in the market area. 88

Additional features (special energy efficient items, etc.) 89

Describe the condition of the property (including apparent needed repairs, deterioration, renovations, remodeling, etc.). e-9; 90

Are there any physical deficiencies or adverse conditions that affect the livability, soundness, or structural integrity of the property? ☐ 91 Yes ☐ 92 No If Yes, describe 93

Does the property generally conform to the neighborhood (functional utility, style, condition, use, construction, etc.)? ☐ 94 Yes ☐ 95 No If No, describe 96

I ☐ 97 did ☐ 98 did not research the sale or transfer history of the subject property and comparable sales. If not, explain 99

My research ☐ 100 did ☐ 101 did not reveal any prior sales or transfers of the subject property for the three years prior to the effective date of this appraisal.

Data source(s) 102

My research ☐ 103 did ☐ 104 did not reveal any prior sales or transfers of the comparable sales for the year prior to the date of sale of the comparable sale.

Data source(s) 105

Report the results of the research and analysis of the prior sale or transfer history of the subject property and comparable sales (report additional prior sales on page 3).

ITEM	SUBJECT	COMPARABLE SALE # 1	COMPARABLE SALE # 2	COMPARABLE SALE # 3
Date of Prior Sale/Transfer	106	110	110	110
Price of Prior Sale/Transfer	107	111	111	111
Data Source(s)	108	112	112	112
Effective Date of Data Source(s)	109	113	113	113

Analysis of prior sale or transfer history of the subject property and comparable sales. 114

2   **Exterior-Only Inspection Individual Condominium Unit Appraisal Report** File # 3   4   4a

There are	5	comparable properties currently offered for sale in the subject neighborhood ranging in price from $	6	to $	7

There are	8	comparable sales in the subject neighborhood within the past twelve months ranging in sale price from $	9	to $	10

FEATURE	SUBJECT	COMPARABLE SALE # 1		COMPARABLE SALE # 2		COMPARABLE SALE # 3	
Address and Unit #	11 12a12b12c12d	50 51a51b51c51d		50 51a51b51c51d		50 51a51b51c51d	
Project Name and	13	52		52		52	
Phase	14	53		53		53	
Proximity to Subject		54		54		54	
Sale Price	$ 15		$ 55		$ 55		$ 55
Sale Price/Gross Liv. Area	$ 16 sq. ft.	$ 56 sq. ft.		$ 56 sq. ft.		$ 56 sq. ft.	
Data Source(s)		e-25; e-2		e-25; e-2		e-25; e-2	
Verification Source(s)		58		58		58	
VALUE ADJUSTMENTS	DESCRIPTION	DESCRIPTION	+(-) $ Adjustment	DESCRIPTION	+(-) $ Adjustment	DESCRIPTION	+(-) $ Adjustment
Sale or Financing Concessions		59 e-26; e-27; e-28	60 62	59 e-26; e-27; e-28	60 62	59 e-26; e-27; e-28	60 62
Date of Sale/Time		e-29; e-30; e-31	64	e-29; e-30; e-31	64	e-29; e-30; e-31	64
Location	e-14; e-15; e-16	e-14; e-15; e-16	66	e-14; e-15; e-16	66	e-14; e-15; e-16	66
Leasehold/Fee Simple	23	67	68	67	68	67	68
HOA Mo. Assessment	24	69	70	69	70	69	70
Common Elements And Rec. Facilities	25 26	71 73	72 74	71 73	72 74	71 73	72 74
Floor Location	27	75	76	75	76	75	76
View	e-5; e-6; e-7	e-5; e-6; e-7	78	e-5; e-6; e-7	78	e-5; e-6; e-7	78
Design (Style)	29	79	80	79	80	79	80
Quality of Construction	30	81	82	81	82	81	82
Actual Age	e-17; 31	e-17; 83	84	e-17; 83	84	e-17; 83	84
Condition	32	85	86	85	86	85	86
Above Grade	Total / Bdrms. / Baths	Total / Bdrms. / Baths	87	Total / Bdrms. / Baths	87	Total / Bdrms. / Baths	87
Room Count	33 / 34 / 35	88 / 89 / 90	91	88 / 89 / 90	91	88 / 89 / 90	91
Gross Living Area	36 sq. ft.	92 sq. ft.	93	92 sq. ft.	93	92 sq. ft.	93
Basement & Finished Rooms Below Grade	e-18; e-19; e-20 e-21; e-22; e-23; e-24	e-18; e-19; e-20 e-21; e-22; e-23; e-24	95 97	e-18; e-19; e-20 e-21; e-22; e-23; e-24	95 97	e-18; e-19; e-20 e-21; e-22; e-23; e-24	95 97
Functional Utility	39	98	99	98	99	98	99
Heating/Cooling	40	100	101	100	101	100	101
Energy Efficient Items	41	102	103	102	103	102	103
Garage/Carport	42	104	105	104	105	104	105
Porch/Patio/Deck	43	106	107	106	107	106	107
44	45	108	109	108	109	108	109
46	47	110	111	110	111	110	111
48	49	112	113	112	113	112	113
Net Adjustment (Total)		114 + 115 -	$ 116	114 + 115 -	$ 116	114 + 115 -	$ 116
Adjusted Sale Price of Comparables		Net Adj. 116a % Gross Adj. 116b %	$ 117	Net Adj. 116a % Gross Adj. 116b %	$ 117	Net Adj. 116a % Gross Adj. 116b %	$ 117

Summary of Sales Comparison Approach   118

Indicated Value by Sales Comparison Approach $ 119

INCOME APPROACH TO VALUE (not required by Fannie Mae)

Estimated Monthly Market Rent $ 120   X Gross Rent Multiplier   121   = $ 122   **Indicated Value by Income Approach**

Summary of Income Approach (including support for market rent and GRM).   123

Indicated Value by: Sales Comparison Approach $ 124   Income Approach (if developed) $ 125

126

This appraisal is made 127 "as is" 128 subject to completion per plans and specifications on the basis of a hypothetical condition that the improvements have been completed 129 subject to the following repairs or alterations on the basis of a hypothetical condition that the repairs or alterations have been completed, or 130 subject to the following required inspection based on the extraordinary assumption that the condition or deficiency does not require alteration or repair: 131

Based on a visual inspection of the exterior areas of the subject property from at least the street, defined scope of work, statement of assumptions and limiting conditions, and appraiser's certification, my (our) opinion of the market value, as defined, of the real property that is the subject of this report is $ 132 , as of 133 , which is the date of the exterior inspection and the effective date of this appraisal.

This report form is designed to report an appraisal of a unit in a condominium project or a condominium unit in a planned unit development (PUD). This report form is not designed to report an appraisal of a manufactured home or a unit in a cooperative project.

This appraisal report is subject to the following scope of work, intended use, intended user, definition of market value, statement of assumptions and limiting conditions, and certifications. Modifications, additions, or deletions to the intended use, intended user, definition of market value, or assumptions and limiting conditions are not permitted. The appraiser may expand the scope of work to include any additional research or analysis necessary based on the complexity of this appraisal assignment. Modifications or deletions to the certifications are also not permitted. However, additional certifications that do not constitute material alterations to this appraisal report, such as those required by law or those related to the appraiser's continuing education or membership in an appraisal organization, are permitted.

SCOPE OF WORK: The scope of work for this appraisal is defined by the complexity of this appraisal assignment and the reporting requirements of this appraisal report form, including the following definition of market value, statement of assumptions and limiting conditions, and certifications. The appraiser must, at a minimum: (1) perform a visual inspection of the exterior areas of the subject property from at least the street, (2) inspect and analyze the condominium project, (3) inspect the neighborhood, (4) inspect each of the comparable sales from at least the street, (5) research, verify, and analyze data from reliable public and/or private sources, and (6) report his or her analysis, opinions, and conclusions in this appraisal report.

The appraiser must be able to obtain adequate information about the physical characteristics (including, but not limited to, condition, room count, gross living area, etc.) of the subject property from the exterior-only inspection and reliable public and/or private sources to perform this appraisal. The appraiser should use the same type of data sources that he or she uses for comparable sales such as, but not limited to, multiple listing services, tax and assessment records, prior inspections, appraisal files, information provided by the property owner, etc.

INTENDED USE: The intended use of this appraisal report is for the lender/client to evaluate the property that is the subject of this appraisal for a mortgage finance transaction.

INTENDED USER: The intended user of this appraisal report is the lender/client.

DEFINITION OF MARKET VALUE: The most probable price which a property should bring in a competitive and open market under all conditions requisite to a fair sale, the buyer and seller, each acting prudently, knowledgeably and assuming the price is not affected by undue stimulus. Implicit in this definition is the consummation of a sale as of a specified date and the passing of title from seller to buyer under conditions whereby: (1) buyer and seller are typically motivated; (2) both parties are well informed or well advised, and each acting in what he or she considers his or her own best interest; (3) a reasonable time is allowed for exposure in the open market; (4) payment is made in terms of cash in U. S. dollars or in terms of financial arrangements comparable thereto; and (5) the price represents the normal consideration for the property sold unaffected by special or creative financing or sales concessions* granted by anyone associated with the sale.

*Adjustments to the comparables must be made for special or creative financing or sales concessions. No adjustments are necessary for those costs which are normally paid by sellers as a result of tradition or law in a market area; these costs are readily identifiable since the seller pays these costs in virtually all sales transactions. Special or creative financing adjustments can be made to the comparable property by comparisons to financing terms offered by a third party institutional lender that is not already involved in the property or transaction. Any adjustment should not be calculated on a mechanical dollar for dollar cost of the financing or concession but the dollar amount of any adjustment should approximate the market's reaction to the financing or concessions based on the appraiser's judgment.

STATEMENT OF ASSUMPTIONS AND LIMITING CONDITIONS: The appraiser's certification in this report is subject to the following assumptions and limiting conditions:

1. The appraiser will not be responsible for matters of a legal nature that affect either the property being appraised or the title to it, except for information that he or she became aware of during the research involved in performing this appraisal. The appraiser assumes that the title is good and marketable and will not render any opinions about the title.

2. The appraiser has examined the available flood maps that are provided by the Federal Emergency Management Agency (or other data sources) and has noted in this appraisal report whether any portion of the subject site is located in an identified Special Flood Hazard Area. Because the appraiser is not a surveyor, he or she makes no guarantees, express or implied, regarding this determination.

3. The appraiser will not give testimony or appear in court because he or she made an appraisal of the property in question, unless specific arrangements to do so have been made beforehand, or as otherwise required by law.

4. The appraiser has noted in this appraisal report any adverse conditions (such as needed repairs, deterioration, the presence of hazardous wastes, toxic substances, etc.) observed during the inspection of the subject property or that he or she became aware of during the research involved in performing this appraisal. Unless otherwise stated in this appraisal report, the appraiser has no knowledge of any hidden or unapparent physical deficiencies or adverse conditions of the property (such as, but not limited to, needed repairs, deterioration, the presence of hazardous wastes, toxic substances, adverse environmental conditions, etc.) that would make the property less valuable, and has assumed that there are no such conditions and makes no guarantees or warranties, express or implied. The appraiser will not be responsible for any such conditions that do exist or for any engineering or testing that might be required to discover whether such conditions exist. Because the appraiser is not an expert in the field of environmental hazards, this appraisal report must not be considered as an environmental assessment of the property.

5. The appraiser has based his or her appraisal report and valuation conclusion for an appraisal that is subject to satisfactory completion, repairs, or alterations on the assumption that the completion, repairs, or alterations of the subject property will be performed in a professional manner.

2   **Exterior-Only Inspection Individual Condominium Unit Appraisal Report** File # 3   4   4a

APPRAISER'S CERTIFICATION: The Appraiser certifies and agrees that:

1. I have, at a minimum, developed and reported this appraisal in accordance with the scope of work requirements stated in this appraisal report.

2. I have performed a visual inspection of the exterior areas of the subject property from at least the street. I have reported the condition of the improvements in factual, specific terms. I have identified and reported the physical deficiencies that could affect the livability, soundness, or structural integrity of the property.

3. I performed this appraisal in accordance with the requirements of the Uniform Standards of Professional Appraisal Practice that were adopted and promulgated by the Appraisal Standards Board of The Appraisal Foundation and that were in place at the time this appraisal report was prepared.

4. I developed my opinion of the market value of the real property that is the subject of this report based on the sales comparison approach to value. I have adequate comparable market data to develop a reliable sales comparison approach for this appraisal assignment. I further certify that I considered the cost and income approaches to value but did not develop them, unless otherwise indicated in this report.

5. I researched, verified, analyzed, and reported on any current agreement for sale for the subject property, any offering for sale of the subject property in the twelve months prior to the effective date of this appraisal, and the prior sales of the subject property for a minimum of three years prior to the effective date of this appraisal, unless otherwise indicated in this report.

6. I researched, verified, analyzed, and reported on the prior sales of the comparable sales for a minimum of one year prior to the date of sale of the comparable sale, unless otherwise indicated in this report.

7. I selected and used comparable sales that are locationally, physically, and functionally the most similar to the subject property.

8. I have not used comparable sales that were the result of combining a land sale with the contract purchase price of a home that has been built or will be built on the land.

9. I have reported adjustments to the comparable sales that reflect the market's reaction to the differences between the subject property and the comparable sales.

10. I verified, from a disinterested source, all information in this report that was provided by parties who have a financial interest in the sale or financing of the subject property.

11. I have knowledge and experience in appraising this type of property in this market area.

12. I am aware of, and have access to, the necessary and appropriate public and private data sources, such as multiple listing services, tax assessment records, public land records and other such data sources for the area in which the property is located.

13. I obtained the information, estimates, and opinions furnished by other parties and expressed in this appraisal report from reliable sources that I believe to be true and correct.

14. I have taken into consideration the factors that have an impact on value with respect to the subject neighborhood, subject property, and the proximity of the subject property to adverse influences in the development of my opinion of market value. I have noted in this appraisal report any adverse conditions (such as, but not limited to, needed repairs, deterioration, the presence of hazardous wastes, toxic substances, adverse environmental conditions, etc.) observed during the inspection of the subject property or that I became aware of during the research involved in performing this appraisal. I have considered these adverse conditions in my analysis of the property value, and have reported on the effect of the conditions on the value and marketability of the subject property.

15. I have not knowingly withheld any significant information from this appraisal report and, to the best of my knowledge, all statements and information in this appraisal report are true and correct.

16. I stated in this appraisal report my own personal, unbiased, and professional analysis, opinions, and conclusions, which are subject only to the assumptions and limiting conditions in this appraisal report.

17. I have no present or prospective interest in the property that is the subject of this report, and I have no present or prospective personal interest or bias with respect to the participants in the transaction. I did not base, either partially or completely, my analysis and/or opinion of market value in this appraisal report on the race, color, religion, sex, age, marital status, handicap, familial status, or national origin of either the prospective owners or occupants of the subject property or of the present owners or occupants of the properties in the vicinity of the subject property or on any other basis prohibited by law.

8. My employment and/or compensation for performing this appraisal or any future or anticipated appraisals was not conditioned on any agreement or understanding, written or otherwise, that I would report (or present analysis supporting) a predetermined specific value, a predetermined minimum value, a range or direction in value, a value that favors the cause of any party, or the attainment of a specific result or occurrence of a specific subsequent event (such as approval of a pending mortgage loan application).

19. I personally prepared all conclusions and opinions about the real estate that were set forth in this appraisal report. If I relied on significant real property appraisal assistance from any individual or individuals in the performance of this appraisal or the preparation of this appraisal report, I have named such individual(s) and disclosed the specific tasks performed in this appraisal report. I certify that any individual so named is qualified to perform the tasks. I have not authorized anyone to make a change to any item in this appraisal report; therefore, any change made to this appraisal is unauthorized and I will take no responsibility for it.

20. I identified the lender/client in this appraisal report who is the individual, organization, or agent for the organization that ordered and will receive this appraisal report.

Exterior-Only Inspection Individual Condominium Unit Appraisal Report File # 3 4 4a

21. The lender/client may disclose or distribute this appraisal report to: the borrower; another lender at the request of the borrower; the mortgagee or its successors and assigns; mortgage insurers; government sponsored enterprises; other secondary market participants; data collection or reporting services; professional appraisal organizations; any department, agency, or instrumentality of the United States; and any state, the District of Columbia, or other jurisdictions; without having to obtain the appraiser's or supervisory appraiser's (if applicable) consent. Such consent must be obtained before this appraisal report may be disclosed or distributed to any other party (including, but not limited to, the public through advertising, public relations, news, sales, or other media).

22. I am aware that any disclosure or distribution of this appraisal report by me or the lender/client may be subject to certain laws and regulations. Further, I am also subject to the provisions of the Uniform Standards of Professional Appraisal Practice that pertain to disclosure or distribution by me.

23. The borrower, another lender at the request of the borrower, the mortgagee or its successors and assigns, mortgage insurers, government sponsored enterprises, and other secondary market participants may rely on this appraisal report as part of any mortgage finance transaction that involves any one or more of these parties.

24. If this appraisal report was transmitted as an "electronic record" containing my "electronic signature," as those terms are defined in applicable federal and/or state laws (excluding audio and video recordings), or a facsimile transmission of this appraisal report containing a copy or representation of my signature, the appraisal report shall be as effective, enforceable and valid as if a paper version of this appraisal report were delivered containing my original hand written signature.

25. Any intentional or negligent misrepresentation(s) contained in this appraisal report may result in civil liability and/or criminal penalties including, but not limited to, fine or imprisonment or both under the provisions of Title 18, United States Code, Section 1001, et seq., or similar state laws.

SUPERVISORY APPRAISER'S CERTIFICATION: The Supervisory Appraiser certifies and agrees that:

1. I directly supervised the appraiser for this appraisal assignment, have read the appraisal report, and agree with the appraiser's analysis, opinions, statements, conclusions, and the appraiser's certification.

2. I accept full responsibility for the contents of this appraisal report including, but not limited to, the appraiser's analysis, opinions, statements, conclusions, and the appraiser's certification.

3. The appraiser identified in this appraisal report is either a sub-contractor or an employee of the supervisory appraiser (or the appraisal firm), is qualified to perform this appraisal, and is acceptable to perform this appraisal under the applicable state law.

4. This appraisal report complies with the Uniform Standards of Professional Appraisal Practice that were adopted and promulgated by the Appraisal Standards Board of The Appraisal Foundation and that were in place at the time this appraisal report was prepared.

5. If this appraisal report was transmitted as an "electronic record" containing my "electronic signature," as those terms are defined in applicable federal and/or state laws (excluding audio and video recordings), or a facsimile transmission of this appraisal report containing a copy or representation of my signature, the appraisal report shall be as effective, enforceable and valid as if a paper version of this appraisal report were delivered containing my original hand written signature.

APPRAISER

Signature _____
Name 5 _____
Company Name 6_____
Company Address 7_____
        8a, 8b, 8c _____
Telephone Number 9 _____
Email Address 10_____
Date of Signature and Report 11 _____
Effective Date of Appraisal 12 _____
State Certification # 13_____
or State License #14 _____
or Other 15_____
State 17 _____
Expiration Date of Certification or License 18 _____

ADDRESS OF PROPERTY APPRAISED
19_____
20a, 20b, 20c, 20d _____

APPRAISED VALUE OF SUBJECT PROPERTY $ 21 _____
LENDER/CLIENT
Name 22 _____
Company Name 23 _____
Company Address 24 _____
Email Address 26_____

SUPERVISORY APPRAISER (ONLY IF REQUIRED)

Signature_____
Name 27 _____
Company Name 28_____
Company Address 29 _____
        30a, 30b, 30c _____
Telephone Number 31_____
Email Address 32 _____
Date of Signature 33_____
State Certification # 34 _____
or State License # 35 _____
State 36_____
Expiration Date of Certification or License 37_____

SUBJECT PROPERTY
☐ 38 Did not inspect exterior of subject property
☐ 39 Did inspect exterior of subject property from street
Date of Inspection 40 _____

COMPARABLE SALES
☐ 41 Did not inspect exterior of comparable sales from street
☐ 42 Did inspect exterior of comparable sales from street
Date of Inspection 43 _____

Appendix 4
Exterior-Only Inspection
Residential Appraisal Report

Exterior-Only Inspection Residential Appraisal Report   File # 3   4   4a

| The purpose of this summary appraisal report is to provide the lender/client with an accurate, and adequately supported, opinion of the market value of the subject property. |

SUBJECT

| Property Address 6 | | City 7 | State 8 | Zip Code 9 |

Borrower 10   Owner of Public Record 11   County 12

Legal Description 13

Assessor's Parcel # 14   Tax Year 15   R.E. Taxes $ 16

Neighborhood Name 17   Map Reference 18   Census Tract 19

Occupant [20] Owner [21] Tenant [22] Vacant   Special Assessments $ 23   [24] PUD   HOA $ 25 [26] per year [27] per month

Property Rights Appraised [28] Fee Simple [29] Leasehold [30] Other (describe) 31

Assignment Type [32] Purchase Transaction [33] Refinance Transaction [34] Other (describe) 35

Lender/Client 36   Address 37

Is the subject property currently offered for sale or has it been offered for sale in the twelve months prior to the effective date of this appraisal? [38] Yes [39] No

Report data source(s) used, offering price(s), and date(s). e-2; 40

CONTRACT

I [41] did [42] did not analyze the contract for sale for the subject purchase transaction. Explain the results of the analysis of the contract for sale or why the analysis was not performed. e-3; 43

Contract Price $ 44   Date of Contract 45   Is the property seller the owner of public record? [46] Yes [47] No   Data Source(s) 48

Is there any financial assistance (loan charges, sale concessions, gift or downpayment assistance, etc.) to be paid by any party on behalf of the borrower? [49] Yes [50] No
If Yes, report the total dollar amount and describe the items to be paid. 51a; e-4; 51b

NEIGHBORHOOD

Note: Race and the racial composition of the neighborhood are not appraisal factors.

Neighborhood Characteristics	One-Unit Housing Trends	One-Unit Housing	Present Land Use %
Location [52] Urban [53] Suburban [55] Rural	Property Values [61] Increasing [62] Stable [63] Declining	PRICE AGE	One-Unit 76 %
Built-Up [55] Over 75% [56] 25–75% [57] Under 25%	Demand/Supply [64] Shortage [65] In Balance [66] Over Supply	$ (000) (yrs)	2-4 Unit 77 %
Growth [58] Rapid [59] Stable [60] Slow	Marketing Time [67] Under 3 mths [68] 3–6 mths [69] Over 6 mths	70 Low 73	Multi-Family 78 %
Neighborhood Boundaries 82		71 High 74	Commercial 79 %
		72 Pred. 75	Other 81 %

Neighborhood Description 83

Market Conditions (including support for the above conclusions) 84

SITE

Dimensions 85   Area 86   Shape 87   View e-5; e-6; e-7

Specific Zoning Classification 89   Zoning Description 90

Zoning Compliance [91] Legal [92] Legal Nonconforming (Grandfathered Use) [93] No Zoning [94] Illegal (describe) 95

Is the highest and best use of the subject property as improved (or as proposed per plans and specifications) the present use? [96] Yes [97] No If No, describe 98

Utilities	Public	Other (describe)		Public	Other (describe)	Off-site Improvements—Type	Public	Private
Electricity	[99]	[100] 101	Water	[105]	[106] 107	Street 111	[112]	[113]
Gas	[102]	[103] 104	Sanitary Sewer	[108]	[109] 110	Alley 114	[115]	[116]

FEMA Special Flood Hazard Area [117] Yes [118] No   FEMA Flood Zone 119   FEMA Map # 120   FEMA Map Date 121

Are the utilities and off-site improvements typical for the market area? [122] Yes [123] No If No, describe 124

Are there any adverse site conditions or external factors (easements, encroachments, environmental conditions, land uses, etc.)? [125] Yes [126] No If Yes, describe 127

IMPROVEMENTS

Source(s) Used for Physical Characteristics of Property [128] Appraisal Files [129] MLS [130] Assessment and Tax Records [131] Prior Inspection [132] Property Owner
[133] Other (describe) 134   Data Source(s) for Gross Living Area 135

General Description	General Description	Heating / Cooling	Amenities	Car Storage
Units [136] One [137] One with Accessory Unit	[148] Concrete Slab [149] Crawl Space	[158] FWA [159] HWBB	[168] Fireplace(s) # 169	[182] None
# of Stories 138	[150] Full Basement [151] Finished	[160] Radiant	[170] Woodstove(s) # 171	[183] Driveway # of Cars 184
Type [139] Det. [140] Att. [141] S-Det./End Unit	[152] Partial Basement [153] Finished	[161] Other 162	[172] Patio/Deck 173	Driveway Surface 185
[142] Existing [143] Proposed [144] Under Const.	Exterior Walls 154	Fuel 163	[174] Porch 175	[186] Garage # of Cars 187
Design (Style) 145	Roof Surface 155	[164] Central Air Conditioning	[176] Pool 177	[188] Carport # of Cars 189
Year Built 146; e-8	Gutters & Downspouts 156	[165] Individual	[178] Fence 179	[190] Attached [191] Detached
Effective Age (Yrs) 147	Window Type 157	[166] Other 167	[180] Other 181	[192] Built-in

Appliances [193] Refrigerator [194] Range/Oven [195] Dishwasher [196] Disposal [197] Microwave [198] Washer/Dryer [199] Other (describe) 200

Finished area **above** grade contains: 201   Rooms 202   Bedrooms 203   Bath(s) 204   Square Feet of Gross Living Area Above Grade

Additional features (special energy efficient items, etc.) 205

Describe the condition of the property and data source(s) (including apparent needed repairs, deterioration, renovations, remodeling, etc.). e-9; 206

Are there any apparent physical deficiencies or adverse conditions that affect the livability, soundness, or structural integrity of the property? [207] Yes [208] No
If Yes, describe 209

Does the property generally conform to the neighborhood (functional utility, style, condition, use, construction, etc.)? [210] Yes [211] No If No, describe 212

Exterior-Only Inspection Residential Appraisal Report   File # 3   4   4a

SALES COMPARISON APPROACH

There are   5   comparable properties currently offered for sale in the subject neighborhood ranging in price from $ 6   to $ 7

There are   8   comparable sales in the subject neighborhood within the past twelve months ranging in sale price from $ 9   to $ 10

FEATURE	SUBJECT	COMPARABLE SALE # 1		COMPARABLE SALE # 2		COMPARABLE SALE # 3	
Address 11	12a 12b 12c	45	46a 46b 46c	45	46a 46b 46c	45	46a 46b 46c
Proximity to Subject		47		47		47	
Sale Price	$ 13		$ 48		$ 48		$ 48
Sale Price/Gross Liv. Area	$ 14 sq. ft.	$ 49 sq. ft.		$ 49 sq. ft.		$ 49 sq. ft.	
Data Source(s)		e-25, e-2		e-25, e-2		e-25, e-2	
Verification Source(s)		51		51		51	
VALUE ADJUSTMENTS	DESCRIPTION	DESCRIPTION	+(-) $ Adjustment	DESCRIPTION	+(-) $ Adjustment	DESCRIPTION	+(-) $ Adjustment
Sale or Financing		52	53	52	53	52	53
Concessions		e-26; e-27; e-28	55	e-26; e-27; e-28	55	e-26; e-27; e-28	55
Date of Sale/Time		e-29; e-30; e-31	57	e-29; e-30; e-31	57	e-29; e-30; e-31	57
Location	e-14; e-15; e-16	e-14; e-15; e-16	59	e-14; e-15; e-16	59	e-14; e-15; e-16	59
Leasehold/Fee Simple	21	60	61	60	61	60	61
Site	22	62	63	62	63	62	63
View	e-5; e-6; e-7	e-5; e-6; e-7	65	e-5; e-6; e-7	65	e-5; e-6; e-7	65
Design (Style)	24	66	67	66	67	66	67
Quality of Construction	25	68	69	68	69	68	69
Actual Age	e-17; 26	e-17; 70	71	e-17; 70	71	e-17; 70	71
Condition	27	72	73	72	73	72	73
Above Grade	Total 28 / Bdrms 29 / Baths 30	Total 75 / Bdrms 76 / Baths 77	74	Total 75 / Bdrms 76 / Baths 77	74	Total 75 / Bdrms 76 / Baths 77	74
Room Count			78		78		78
Gross Living Area	31 sq. ft.	79 sq. ft.	80	79 sq. ft.	80	79 sq. ft.	80
Basement & Finished	e-18; e-19; e-20	e-18; e-19; e-20	82	e-18; e-19; e-20	82	e-18; e-19; e-20	82
Rooms Below Grade	e-21; e-22; e-23; e-24	e-21; e-22; e-23; e-24	84	e-21; e-22; e-23; e-24	84	e-21; e-22; e-23; e-24	84
Functional Utility	34	85	86	85	86	85	86
Heating/Cooling	35	87	88	87	88	87	88
Energy Efficient Items	36	89	90	89	90	89	90
Garage/Carport	37	91	92	91	92	91	92
Porch/Patio/Deck	38	93	94	93	94	93	94
39	40	95	96	95	96	95	96
41	42	97	98	97	98	97	98
43	44	99	100	99	100	99	100
Net Adjustment (Total)		101 + 102	$ 103	101 + 102	$ 103	101 + 102	$ 103
Adjusted Sale Price of Comparables		Net Adj. 103a % / Gross Adj. 103b %	$ 104	Net Adj. 103a % / Gross Adj. 103b %	$ 104	Net Adj. 103a % / Gross Adj. 103b %	$ 104

I 105 did 106 did not research the sale or transfer history of the subject property and comparable sales. If not, explain   107

My research 108 did 109 did not reveal any prior sales or transfers of the subject property for the three years prior to the effective date of this appraisal.
Data source(s) 110

My research 111 did 112 did not reveal any prior sales or transfers of the comparable sales for the year prior to the date of sale of the comparable sale.
Data source(s) 113

Report the results of the research and analysis of the prior sale or transfer history of the subject property and comparable sales (report additional prior sales on page 3).

ITEM	SUBJECT	COMPARABLE SALE # 1	COMPARABLE SALE # 2	COMPARABLE SALE # 3
Date of Prior Sale/Transfer	114	118	118	118
Price of Prior Sale/Transfer	115	119	119	119
Data Source(s)	116	120	120	120
Effective Date of Data Source(s)	117	121	121	121

Analysis of prior sale or transfer history of the subject property and comparable sales 122

Summary of Sales Comparison Approach 123

Indicated Value by Sales Comparison Approach $ 124

RECONCILIATION

Indicated Value by: Sales Comparison Approach $ 125   Cost Approach (if developed) $ 126   Income Approach (if developed) $ 127
128

This appraisal is made 129 "as is", 130 subject to completion per plans and specifications on the basis of a hypothetical condition that the improvements have been completed, 131 subject to the following repairs or alterations on the basis of a hypothetical condition that the repairs or alterations have been completed, or 132 subject to the following required inspection based on the extraordinary assumption that the condition or deficiency does not require alteration or repair: 133

Based on a visual inspection of the exterior areas of the subject property from at least the street, defined scope of work, statement of assumptions and limiting conditions, and appraiser's certification, my (our) opinion of the market value, as defined, of the real property that is the subject of this report is
$ 134   , as of   135   , which is the date of the inspection and the effective date of this appraisal.

Freddie Mac Form 2055 March 2005   226 *UAD Version 9/2011*   Page 2 of 6   Fannie Mae Form 2055 March 2005

Fannie Mae Form 2055/Freddie Mac Form 2055

ADDITIONAL COMMENTS

5

COST APPROACH TO VALUE (not required by Fannie Mae)

Provide adequate information for the lender/client to replicate the below cost figures and calculations.

Support for the opinion of site value (summary of comparable land sales or other methods for estimating site value) 6

COST APPROACH

ESTIMATED [7] REPRODUCTION OR [8] REPLACEMENT COST NEW	OPINION OF SITE VALUE				= $	14
Source of cost data 9	Dwelling 15		Sq. Ft. @ $	16	=$	17
Quality rating from cost service 10 Effective date of cost data 11	18 19		Sq. Ft. @ $	20	=$	21
Comments on Cost Approach (gross living area calculations, depreciation, etc.)	22					23
12	Garage/Carport 24		Sq. Ft. @ $	25	=$	26
	Total Estimate of Cost-New				= $	27
	Less	Physical	Functional	External		
	Depreciation	29	31	33	=$(34	)
	Depreciated Cost of Improvements				=$	35
	"As-is" Value of Site Improvements				=$	36
Estimated Remaining Economic Life (HUD and VA only) 13 Years	Indicated Value By Cost Approach				=$	37

INCOME APPROACH TO VALUE (not required by Fannie Mae)

INCOME

Estimated Monthly Market Rent $ 38 X Gross Rent Multiplier 39 = $ 40 Indicated Value by Income Approach

Summary of Income Approach (including support for market rent and GRM) 41

PROJECT INFORMATION FOR PUDs (if applicable)

PUD INFORMATION

Is the developer/builder in control of the Homeowners' Association (HOA)? [42] Yes [43] No Unit type(s) [44] Detached [45] Attached

Provide the following information for PUDs ONLY if the developer/builder is in control of the HOA and the subject property is an attached dwelling unit.

Legal name of project 46

Total number of phases 47 Total number of units 48 Total number of units sold 49

Total number of units rented 50 Total number of units for sale 51 Data source(s) 52

Was the project created by the conversion of an existing building(s) into a PUD? [53] Yes [54] No If Yes, date of conversion 55

Does the project contain any multi-dwelling units? [56] Yes [57] No Data source(s) 58

Are the units, common elements, and recreation facilities complete? [59] Yes [60] No If No, describe the status of completion. 61

Are the common elements leased to or by the Homeowners' Association? [62] Yes [63] No If Yes, describe the rental terms and options. 64

Describe common elements and recreational facilities 65

2   **Exterior-Only Inspection Residential Appraisal Report**   File # 3   4   4a

This report form is designed to report an appraisal of a one-unit property or a one-unit property with an accessory unit; including a unit in a planned unit development (PUD). This report form is not designed to report an appraisal of a manufactured home or a unit in a condominium or cooperative project.

This appraisal report is subject to the following scope of work, intended use, intended user, definition of market value, statement of assumptions and limiting conditions, and certifications. Modifications, additions, or deletions to the intended use, intended user, definition of market value, or assumptions and limiting conditions are not permitted. The appraiser may expand the scope of work to include any additional research or analysis necessary based on the complexity of this appraisal assignment. Modifications or deletions to the certifications are also not permitted. However, additional certifications that do not constitute material alterations to this appraisal report, such as those required by law or those related to the appraiser's continuing education or membership in an appraisal organization, are permitted.

SCOPE OF WORK: The scope of work for this appraisal is defined by the complexity of this appraisal assignment and the reporting requirements of this appraisal report form, including the following definition of market value, statement of assumptions and limiting conditions, and certifications. The appraiser must, at a minimum: (1) perform a visual inspection of the exterior areas of the subject property from at least the street, (2) inspect the neighborhood, (3) inspect each of the comparable sales from at least the street, (4) research, verify, and analyze data from reliable public and/or private sources, and (5) report his or her analysis, opinions, and conclusions in this appraisal report.

The appraiser must be able to obtain adequate information about the physical characteristics (including, but not limited to, condition, room count, gross living area, etc.) of the subject property from the exterior-only inspection and reliable public and/or private sources to perform this appraisal. The appraiser should use the same type of data sources that he or she uses for comparable sales such as, but not limited to, multiple listing services, tax and assessment records, prior inspections, appraisal files, information provided by the property owner, etc.

INTENDED USE: The intended use of this appraisal report is for the lender/client to evaluate the property that is the subject of this appraisal for a mortgage finance transaction.

INTENDED USER: The intended user of this appraisal report is the lender/client.

DEFINITION MARKET VALUE: The most probable price which a property should bring in a competitive and open market under all conditions requisite to a fair sale, the buyer and seller, each acting prudently, knowledgeably and assuming the price is not affected by undue stimulus. Implicit in this definition is the consummation of a sale as of a specified date and the passing of title from seller to buyer under conditions whereby: (1) buyer and seller are typically motivated; (2) both parties are well informed or well advised, and each acting in what he or she considers his or her own best interest; (3) a reasonable time is allowed for exposure in the open market; (4) payment is made in terms of cash in U. S. dollars or in terms of financial arrangements comparable thereto; and (5) the price represents the normal consideration for the property sold unaffected by special or creative financing or sales concessions* granted by anyone associated with the sale.

*Adjustments to the comparables must be made for special or creative financing or sales concessions. No adjustments are necessary for those costs which are normally paid by sellers as a result of tradition or law in a market area; these costs are readily identifiable since the seller pays these costs in virtually all sales transactions. Special or creative financing adjustments can be made to the comparable property by comparisons to financing terms offered by a third party institutional lender that is not already involved in the property or transaction. Any adjustment should not be calculated on a mechanical dollar for dollar cost of the financing or concession but the dollar amount of any adjustment should approximate the market's reaction to the financing or concessions based on the appraiser's judgment.

STATEMENT OF ASSUMPTIONS AND LIMITING CONDITIONS: The appraiser's certification in this report is subject to the following assumptions and limiting conditions:

1. The appraiser will not be responsible for matters of a legal nature that affect either the property being appraised or the title to it, except for information that he or she became aware of during the research involved in performing this appraisal. The appraiser assumes that the title is good and marketable and will not render any opinions about the title.

2. The appraiser has examined the available flood maps that are provided by the Federal Emergency Management Agency (or other data sources) and has noted in this appraisal report whether any portion of the subject site is located in an identified Special Flood Hazard Area. Because the appraiser is not a surveyor, he or she makes no guarantees, express or implied, regarding this determination.

3. The appraiser will not give testimony or appear in court because he or she made an appraisal of the property in question, unless specific arrangements to do so have been made beforehand, or as otherwise required by law.

4. The appraiser has noted in this appraisal report any adverse conditions (such as needed repairs, deterioration, the presence of hazardous wastes, toxic substances, etc.) observed during the inspection of the subject property or that he or she became aware of during the research involved in performing this appraisal. Unless otherwise stated in this appraisal report, the appraiser has no knowledge of any hidden or unapparent physical deficiencies or adverse conditions of the property (such as, but not limited to, needed repairs, deterioration, the presence of hazardous wastes, toxic substances, adverse environmental conditions, etc.) that would make the property less valuable, and has assumed that there are no such conditions and makes no guarantees or warranties, express or implied. The appraiser will not be responsible for any such conditions that do exist or for any engineering or testing that might be required to discover whether such conditions exist. Because the appraiser is not an expert in the field of environmental hazards, this appraisal report must not be considered as an environmental assessment of the property.

5. The appraiser has based his or her appraisal report and valuation conclusion for an appraisal that is subject to satisfactory completion, repairs, or alterations on the assumption that the completion, repairs, or alterations of the subject property will be performed in a professional manner.

Fannie Mae Form 2055/Freddie Mac Form 2055

APPRAISER'S CERTIFICATION: The Appraiser certifies and agrees that:

1. I have, at a minimum, developed and reported this appraisal in accordance with the scope of work requirements stated in this appraisal report.

2. I performed a visual inspection of the exterior areas of the subject property from at least the street. I reported the condition of the improvements in factual, specific terms. I identified and reported the physical deficiencies that could affect the livability, soundness, or structural integrity of the property.

3. I performed this appraisal in accordance with the requirements of the Uniform Standards of Professional Appraisal Practice that were adopted and promulgated by the Appraisal Standards Board of The Appraisal Foundation and that were in place at the time this appraisal report was prepared.

4. I developed my opinion of the market value of the real property that is the subject of this report based on the sales comparison approach to value. I have adequate comparable market data to develop a reliable sales comparison approach for this appraisal assignment. I further certify that I considered the cost and income approaches to value but did not develop them, unless otherwise indicated in this report.

5. I researched, verified, analyzed, and reported on any current agreement for sale for the subject property, any offering for sale of the subject property in the twelve months prior to the effective date of this appraisal, and the prior sales of the subject property for a minimum of three years prior to the effective date of this appraisal, unless otherwise indicated in this report.

6. I researched, verified, analyzed, and reported on the prior sales of the comparable sales for a minimum of one year prior to the date of sale of the comparable sale, unless otherwise indicated in this report.

7. I selected and used comparable sales that are locationally, physically, and functionally the most similar to the subject property.

8. I have not used comparable sales that were the result of combining a land sale with the contract purchase price of a home that has been built or will be built on the land.

9. I have reported adjustments to the comparable sales that reflect the market's reaction to the differences between the subject property and the comparable sales.

10. I verified, from a disinterested source, all information in this report that was provided by parties who have a financial interest in the sale or financing of the subject property.

11. I have knowledge and experience in appraising this type of property in this market area.

12. I am aware of, and have access to, the necessary and appropriate public and private data sources, such as multiple listing services, tax assessment records, public land records and other such data sources for the area in which the property is located.

13. I obtained the information, estimates, and opinions furnished by other parties and expressed in this appraisal report from reliable sources that I believe to be true and correct.

14. I have taken into consideration the factors that have an impact on value with respect to the subject neighborhood, subject property, and the proximity of the subject property to adverse influences in the development of my opinion of market value. I have noted in this appraisal report any adverse conditions (such as, but not limited to, needed repairs, deterioration, the presence of hazardous wastes, toxic substances, adverse environmental conditions, etc.) observed during the inspection of the subject property or that I became aware of during the research involved in performing this appraisal. I have considered these adverse conditions in my analysis of the property value, and have reported on the effect of the conditions on the value and marketability of the subject property.

15. I have not knowingly withheld any significant information from this appraisal report and, to the best of my knowledge, all statements and information in this appraisal report are true and correct.

16. I stated in this appraisal report my own personal, unbiased, and professional analysis, opinions, and conclusions, which are subject only to the assumptions and limiting conditions in this appraisal report.

17. I have no present or prospective interest in the property that is the subject of this report, and I have no present or prospective personal interest or bias with respect to the participants in the transaction. I did not base, either partially or completely, my analysis and/or opinion of market value in this appraisal report on the race, color, religion, sex, age, marital status, handicap, familial status, or national origin of either the prospective owners or occupants of the subject property or of the present owners or occupants of the properties in the vicinity of the subject property or on any other basis prohibited by law.

18. My employment and/or compensation for performing this appraisal or any future or anticipated appraisals was not conditioned on any agreement or understanding, written or otherwise, that I would report (or present analysis supporting) a predetermined specific value, a predetermined minimum value, a range or direction in value, a value that favors the cause of any party, or the attainment of a specific result or occurrence of a specific subsequent event (such as approval of a pending mortgage loan application).

19. I personally prepared all conclusions and opinions about the real estate that were set forth in this appraisal report. If I relied on significant real property appraisal assistance from any individual or individuals in the performance of this appraisal or the preparation of this appraisal report, I have named such individual(s) and disclosed the specific tasks performed in this appraisal report. I certify that any individual so named is qualified to perform the tasks. I have not authorized anyone to make a change to any item in this appraisal report; therefore, any change made to this appraisal is unauthorized and I will take no responsibility for it.

Exterior-Only Inspection Residential Appraisal Report   File # 3 4   4a

2

20. I identified the lender/client in this appraisal report who is the individual, organization, or agent for the organization that ordered and will receive this appraisal report.

21. The lender/client may disclose or distribute this appraisal report to: the borrower; another lender at the request of the borrower; the mortgagee or its successors and assigns; mortgage insurers; government sponsored enterprises; other secondary market participants; data collection or reporting services; professional appraisal organizations; any department, agency, or instrumentality of the United States; and any state, the District of Columbia, or other jurisdictions; without having to obtain the appraiser's or supervisory appraiser's (if applicable) consent. Such consent must be obtained before this appraisal report may be disclosed or distributed to any other party (including, but not limited to, the public through advertising, public relations, news, sales, or other media).

22. I am aware that any disclosure or distribution of this appraisal report by me or the lender/client may be subject to certain laws and regulations. Further, I am also subject to the provisions of the Uniform Standards of Professional Appraisal Practice that pertain to disclosure or distribution by me.

23. The borrower, another lender at the request of the borrower, the mortgagee or its successors and assigns, mortgage insurers, government sponsored enterprises, and other secondary market participants may rely on this appraisal report as part of any mortgage finance transaction that involves any one or more of these parties.

24. If this appraisal report was transmitted as an "electronic record" containing my "electronic signature," as those terms are defined in applicable federal and/or state laws (excluding audio and video recordings), or a facsimile transmission of this appraisal report containing a copy or representation of my signature, the appraisal report shall be as effective, enforceable and valid as if a paper version of this appraisal report were delivered containing my original hand written signature.

25. Any intentional or negligent misrepresentation(s) contained in this appraisal report may result in civil liability and/or criminal penalties including, but not limited to, fine or imprisonment or both under the provisions of Title 18, United States Code, Section 1001, et seq., or similar state laws.

SUPERVISORY APPRAISER'S CERTIFICATION: The Supervisory Appraiser certifies and agrees that:

1. I directly supervised the appraiser for this appraisal assignment, have read the appraisal report, and agree with the appraiser's analysis, opinions, statements, conclusions, and the appraiser's certification.

2. I accept full responsibility for the contents of this appraisal report including, but not limited to, the appraiser's analysis, opinions, statements, conclusions, and the appraiser's certification.

3. The appraiser identified in this appraisal report is either a sub-contractor or an employee of the supervisory appraiser (or the appraisal firm), is qualified to perform this appraisal, and is acceptable to perform this appraisal under the applicable state law.

4. This appraisal report complies with the Uniform Standards of Professional Appraisal Practice that were adopted and promulgated by the Appraisal Standards Board of The Appraisal Foundation and that were in place at the time this appraisal report was prepared.

5. If this appraisal report was transmitted as an "electronic record" containing my "electronic signature," as those terms are defined in applicable federal and/or state laws (excluding audio and video recordings), or a facsimile transmission of this appraisal report containing a copy or representation of my signature, the appraisal report shall be as effective, enforceable and valid as if a paper version of this appraisal report were delivered containing my original hand written signature.

APPRAISER

Signature _____
Name 5 _____
Company Name 6 _____
Company Address 7 _____
8a, 8b 8c _____
Telephone Number 9 _____
Email Address 10 _____
Date of Signature and Report 11_____
Effective Date of Appraisal 12_____
State Certification # 13 _____
or State License # 14_____
or Other (describe) 15_____State # 16_____
State 17 _____
Expiration Date of Certification or License 18_____

ADDRESS OF PROPERTY APPRAISED
19 _____
20a, 20b, 20c _____
APPRAISED VALUE OF SUBJECT PROPERTY $ 21 _____
LENDER/CLIENT
Name 22 _____
Company Name 23_____
Company Address 24 _____

Email Address 26 _____

SUPERVISORY APPRAISER (ONLY IF REQUIRED)

Signature _____
Name 27_____
Company Name 28 _____
Company Address 29_____
30a, 30b 30c_____
Telephone Number 31 _____
Email Address 32 _____
Date of Signature 33 _____
State Certification # 34_____
or State License # 35 _____
State 36 _____
Expiration Date of Certification or License 37 _____

SUBJECT PROPERTY
☐38 Did not inspect exterior of subject property
☐39 Did inspect exterior of subject property from street
Date of Inspection 40_____

COMPARABLE SALES
☐41 Did not inspect exterior of comparable sales from street
☐42 Did inspect exterior of comparable sales from street
Date of Inspection 43_____

UNIFORM MORTGAGE DATA PROGRAM

Fannie Mae and Freddie Mac
Uniform Appraisal Dataset Specification

Appendix D:
Field-Specific
Standardization Requirements

Document Version 1.1

Version Date: February 18, 2011

Document Version and Revision History

Date	Version #	Description
12/16/2010	1.0	Initial version
2/18/2011	1.1	Minor formatting changes.

Uniform Appraisal Dataset Specification

Table of Contents

Introduction

To improve the quality and consistency of appraisal data on loans delivered to the GSEs, Freddie Mac, and Fannie Mae, at the direction of the Federal Housing Finance Agency, have developed the Uniform Appraisal Dataset (UAD), which defines all fields required for an appraisal submission for specific appraisal forms and standardizes definitions and responses for a key subset of fields.

For conventional loans delivered to the GSEs on or after March 19, 2012, (and with application dates on or after December 1, 2011), Fannie Mae and Freddie Mac will require lenders to deliver electronic appraisal data prior to the loan delivery date. The appraisal data must conform to UAD and be delivered through the Uniform Collateral Data Portal (UCDP). The UAD and UCDP will help lenders, the GSEs, and other industry participants manage collateral risk through efficient collection and use of high-quality appraisal data.

The UAD supports improved quality and accuracy of the appraisal data while preserving each GSE's ability to determine what the data means to loan performance and loan quality. The GSEs will each continue to exercise independent business judgment in evaluating and maintaining business terms, credit policies, and analytics. Differences in the assessment and use of the appraisal data will remain due to unique and separate business policies, mortgage products, and processes.

Purpose and Overview

This document provides requirements for completing the GSEs' uniform residential appraisal report forms listed in the table below (the appraisal forms) and covers many but not all of the fields on the appraisal forms. These requirements are in addition to either or both GSEs' appraisal-related policies and guidelines, which are subject to change. Conforming to the UAD is in addition to, and does not replace, appraisers' development and reporting responsibilities as required by the Uniform Standards of Professional Appraisal Practice (USPAP).

Appraisal Form Name	Fannie Mae Form Number	Freddie Mac Form Number
Uniform Residential Appraisal Report	1004 **(Appendix 1)**	70
Individual Condominium Unit Appraisal Report	1073 **(Appendix 2)**	465
Exterior-Only Inspection Individual Condominium Appraisal Report	1075 **(Appendix 3)**	466
Exterior-Only Inspection Residential Appraisal Report	2055 **(Appendix 4)**	2055

The requirements are organized in the order in which they appear on the appraisal form. Information is organized in a table format and contains the form field label(s), a description of the requirement, the corresponding appraisal forms to which it applies, and a reporting format. "Reporting format" defines the standardized format for entering data on the appraisal forms.

Each form field is labeled as either a requirement or an instruction. For form fields labeled as a requirement, UCDP will validate the data and will return an error message if the data does not conform to the defined reporting format. For form fields labeled as an instruction, the UCDP will not validate the reporting format but the data must be transmitted if populated by the appraiser. All fields that are listed as Requirements in Appendix D: Field Specific Standardization Requirements are labeled as either Required (R) or Conditionally Required (CR) in Appendix B: GSE Appraisal Forms Mapping. All other fields are labeled as Transmit (T) in Appendix B.

Uniform Appraisal Dataset Specification

Field-Specific Standardization Requirements		
Subject Section	**Forms**	**Requirement or Instruction**
Property Address, City, State, ZIP Code The appraiser must enter an address that conforms to the United States Postal Service (USPS) address standards in Publication 28 – Postal Addressing Standards (pub28) for complete addresses. Address standards can be found at USPS.gov. The subject address must be populated consistently throughout the form. The following address elements must be included in these fields: • Street number • Street name (including pre-directional indicator, suffix, post-directional indicator, and unit number when applicable) • City • USPS two-letter state or territory representation • 5-digit ZIP Code or ZIP+4 code (either with or without the dash) **Reporting Format:** Property Address – Text City – Text State – 2-letter USPS abbreviation ZIP Code – 5-digit ZIP Code or ZIP+4 code (either with or without the dash)	1004/70 2055/2055 1073/465 1075/466	REQUIREMENT
Unit # The appraiser must enter the address unit number/designator. **Reporting Format:** Unit # – Text	1073/465 1075/466	REQUIREMENT
County The appraiser should enter the name of the county in which the subject property is located. If the subject property is not located in any county (e.g., the subject property is located in an independent city), enter the name of the local municipality or district in which the property is located. **Reporting Format:** County – Text	1004/70 2055/2055 1073/465 1075/466	INSTRUCTION
Assessor's Parcel # The appraiser should enter any available assessor's parcel number(s) that would further identify the subject parcel/property. The parcel number(s) should be in the same format used by the taxing agency, including all spaces and dashes as applicable. If no parcel number is available, enter 'None'. **Reporting Format:** Assessor's Parcel Number – Text The appraiser should separate multiple parcel numbers with a semicolon.	1004/70 2055/2055 1073/465 1075/466	INSTRUCTION

Appendix 5

Field-Specific Standardization Requirements		
Subject Section	**Forms**	**Requirement or Instruction**
Tax Year, Real Estate Taxes $ The appraiser should enter the tax year. If the tax year spans two calendar years, the appraiser should enter the first year only. The appraiser should report the amount of taxes payable on the subject property, expressed as an annual or annualized amount. If real estate taxes are payable to more than one entity, the appraiser should enter the annualized sum of all real estate taxes (not including special assessments). **Reporting Format:** Tax Year – 4 digit year, yyyy Real Estate Taxes – Currency, whole dollars only	1004/70 2055/2055 1073/465 1075/466	INSTRUCTION
Neighborhood Name The appraiser should enter a neighborhood name. It may be a name recognized by the municipality in which the property is sited, such as a subdivision name. If there is not a neighborhood name recognized by the municipality, enter the common name by which residents refer to the location. **Reporting Format:** Neighborhood Name – Text	1004/70 2055/2055	INSTRUCTION
Project Name The appraiser must enter the legal name of the project for the subject property and each comparable property. **Reporting Format:** Project Name – Text	1073/465 1075/466	REQUIREMENT
Occupant The appraiser must indicate whether the subject property is occupied by the owner or a tenant, or is vacant as of the effective date of the appraisal. Only one selection is permitted. For properties that are comprised of one unit with an accessory unit, the selection must reflect the occupancy status of the main unit. **Reporting Format:** Occupant – Checkbox designated with an 'x'	1004/70 2055/2055 1073/465 1075/466	REQUIREMENT
Special Assessments $ The appraiser should enter any special assessment applicable to the subject property. It must be expressed as an annual or annualized amount. If there is more than one special assessment, enter the annualized sum of all special assessments. If there are no special assessments applicable to the subject property, enter the numeral zero (0). **Reporting Format:** Special Assessments $ – Currency, whole dollars only	1004/70 2055/2055 1073/465 1075/466	INSTRUCTION

UAD Appendix D: UAD Field-Specific Standardization Requirements   Page 6 of 36   Document Version 1.1

Uniform Appraisal Dataset Specification

PUD (Indicator) The appraiser must indicate if the property is located in a Planned Unit Development (PUD). If the checkbox is indicated, the appraiser must select 'Yes' or 'No' in response to the question, "Is the developer/builder in control of the Homeowners' Association (HOA)?" located in the PUD Information section. **Reporting Format:** PUD (Indicator) – Checkbox designated with an 'x'	1004/70 2055/2055	REQUIREMENT
HOA $, Per Year, Per Month The appraiser must enter all applicable homeowners' association (HOA) fees associated with the subject property. Additionally, the appraiser must select the appropriate checkbox to indicate if the amount is payable per year or per month. Only one selection is permitted. If the amount is paid on a different frequency (e.g., bi-monthly or semi-annually), it must be normalized as either per year or per month for reporting. If there are multiple fees assessed, such as for a HOA and a master association, the appraiser must first convert the fees to the appropriate frequency (if necessary) and then report the total of all fees in this data field. For instance, if the property is subject to a monthly HOA fee and a quarterly master association fee, the quarterly fee must be converted to a monthly fee and added to the monthly HOA fee. If there are no HOA fees applicable to the subject property, enter the numeral zero (0). *Note: For appraisals of condominium units, the amount of any applicable condominium association fees must be included in the HOA fees section.* **Reporting Format:** HOA $ – Currency, whole dollars only Per Year, Per Month – Checkbox designated with an 'x'	1004/70 2055/2055 1073/465 1075/466	REQUIREMENT
Assignment Type The appraiser must indicate the transaction type for the assignment – Purchase, Refinance, or Other. Only one selection is permitted. If 'Other' is selected, a description must be provided. **Reporting Format:** Assignment Type – Checkbox designated with an 'x' Description of 'Other' (if applicable) – Text	1004/70 2055/2055 1073/465 1075/466	REQUIREMENT
Lender/Client The appraiser must enter the name of the lender. Any applicable AMC name should only be entered in the Appraiser Certification Section. **Reporting Format:** Lender/Client – Text	1004/70 2055/2055 1073/465 1075/466	REQUIREMENT

Field-Specific Standardization Requirements		
Is the subject property currently offered for sale or has it been offered for sale in the 12 months prior to the effective date of this appraisal? Report data source(s) used, offering price(s), and date(s).	1004/70 2055/2055 1073/465 1075/466	REQUIREMENT

The appraiser must identify whether the subject property is currently offered for sale or has been offered for sale in the twelve months prior to the date of the appraisal by selecting either the 'Yes' or the 'No' checkbox.

Reporting Format:
Is the subject property currently offered for sale or has it been offered for sale in the 12 months prior to the effective date of this appraisal? – Checkbox designated with an 'x'

If the answer is 'No,' the data source(s) used must be provided. If the answer is 'Yes,' the following information is required:
- Days on Market (DOM) – The appraiser must enter the DOM for the subject property. DOM is defined as the total number of continuous days from the date that a property is listed or advertised for sale through the date that it is taken off the market or contracted for sale. DOM applies not only to properties that are listed in a Multiple Listing Service (MLS), but also applies to properties marketed for sale outside MLS. If the subject property was not individually listed or advertised for sale, enter the numeral zero (0). If the DOM is unknown, enter 'Unk'.
- Offering Price(s) – The appraiser must report the original offering price and a history of price changes, if any.
- Offering Date(s) – The appraiser must report the date(s) that the property was offered for sale.
- Data Source(s) Used – The appraiser must report the data source(s) used to obtain the offering information. If the data source is MLS, the appraiser must enter the abbreviated MLS organization name, followed by a pound sign (#), and the specific listing identifier.

If the subject property was offered For Sale by Owner (FSBO) or otherwise marketed for sale outside of MLS, the appraiser must report the original offering price, history of price changes, if any, and the date(s) the property was offered for sale, etc., to the extent that this information is known or available to the appraiser in the normal course of business.

Reporting Format:
DOM – Numeric to 4 digits, whole numbers only or 'Unk'
Text – Include the following three items:
Offering Price(s) – Currency, whole dollars only
Offering Date(s) – mm/dd/yyyy
Data Source(s) Used – Abbreviated MLS#Listing Identifier or Text
The PDF creator (the software that creates the PDF) will automatically insert a semicolon to separate DOM from other data values. The PDF creator will also insert "DOM".

Examples (if Yes):
DOM150;Subject property was offered for sale on 03/01/2010 for $200,000. The data source is MRIS#12345AB.

DOMUnk;Subject property was listed for sale by owner for $200,000. The data source is a public source.

Example (if No):
MRIS MLS

Field-Specific Standardization Requirements		
Contract Section	**Forms**	**Requirement or Instruction**
I did/did not analyze the contract for sale for the subject purchase transaction. The appraiser must indicate whether analysis was performed on the contract for sale. **Reporting Format:** I did/did not analyze the contract for sale for the subject purchase transaction. – Checkbox designated with an 'x' The appraiser must also indicate the type of sale for this transaction from the list of available choices. The appraiser must start at the top of the list and select the first sale type that applies. Only one selection is permitted. The valid sale types are as follows: **SALE TYPE** REO sale Short sale Court ordered sale Estate sale Relocation sale Non-arms length sale Arms length sale After selecting a valid sale type, enter an explanation of the results of the analysis of the contract or why the analysis was not performed. **Reporting Format:** Sale Type – Appraiser must select one value from the specified list Description of Analysis – Text The PDF creator will automatically insert a semicolon to separate the data values. **Example:** Arms length sale;Text of the appraiser analysis of the sales contract	1004/70 2055/2055 1073/465 1075/466	REQUIREMENT
Contract Price $ The appraiser must enter an amount in this field if the "Assignment Type" is a purchase transaction. Contract price must be the same as the sales price for the subject property in the Sales Comparison Approach section. **Reporting Format:** Contract Price $ – Currency, whole dollars only	1004/70 2055/2055 1073/465 1075/466	REQUIREMENT
Date of Contract The appraiser must enter a contract date if the "Assignment Type" is a purchase transaction. **Reporting Format:** Date of Contract – mm/dd/yyyy	1004/70 2055/2055 1073/465 1075/466	REQUIREMENT

Field-Specific Standardization Requirements		
Contract Section	**Forms**	**Requirement or Instruction**
Is the property seller the owner of public record? The appraiser must indicate 'Yes' or 'No' if the "Assignment Type" is a purchase transaction. **Reporting Format:** Is the property seller the owner of public record? – Checkbox designated with an 'x'	1004/70 2055/2055 1073/465 1075/466	REQUIREMENT
Is there any financial assistance (loan charges, sale concessions, gift or down payment assistance, etc.) to be paid by any party on behalf of the borrower? The appraiser must indicate 'Yes' or 'No' if the "Assignment Type" is a purchase transaction. If 'No' is selected, enter the numeral zero (0) in the dollar amount field. **Reporting Format:** Is there any financial assistance (loan charges, sale concessions, gift or down payment assistance, etc.) to be paid by any party on behalf of the borrower? – Checkbox designated with an 'x' If 'Yes' is selected, enter the total dollar amount of all financial assistance (loan charges, sale concessions, gift or down payment assistance, etc.) paid by any party on behalf of the borrower, including any closing costs or other payments from the seller or other third party. If the appraiser is not able to determine a dollar amount for all or part of the financial assistance, the number must reflect the total known dollar amount. Leave this field blank if the entire financial assistance amount is unknown. If there is any unknown financial assistance amount, the text 'There is a financial assistance amount that is unknown' will appear in this field. Next, the appraiser must provide a description of the items being paid. **Reporting Format:** Total Financial Assistance – Currency, whole dollars only (if applicable) Description of Analysis of Financial Assistance – Text The PDF creator will automatically insert a semicolon to separate the data values. **Examples:** $5000;There is a financial assistance amount that is unknown.;Down payment assistance, plus furniture of unknown value. $5000;;Down payment assistance. *Note: Financial assistance or concessions paid by any party on behalf of the borrower include both monetary and non-monetary items, including below-market-rate mortgage financing, gifts of personal property, payment of property taxes and/or HOA dues for a period of time, etc.*	1004/70 2055/2055 1073/465 1075/466	REQUIREMENT

Uniform Appraisal Dataset Specification

Field-Specific Standardization Requirements

Neighborhood Section	Forms	Requirement or Instruction
One-Unit Housing Trends **Property Values** The appraiser must indicate whether property values for one-unit housing in the subject's neighborhood are increasing, stable, or declining. Only one selection is permitted. **Demand/Supply** The appraiser must indicate whether the demand/supply of one-unit housing in the subject property's neighborhood is in shortage, in balance, or over supply. Only one selection is permitted. **Marketing Time** The appraiser must indicate whether the marketing time for one-unit housing is under 3 mths, 3–6 mths, or over 6 mths. Only one selection is permitted. **Reporting Format:** Property Values – Checkbox designated with an 'x' Demand/Supply – Checkbox designated with an 'x' Marketing Time – Checkbox designated with an 'x'	1004/70 2055/2055	REQUIREMENT
Condominium Unit Housing Trends **Property Values** The appraiser must indicate whether property values for condominium unit housing in the subject's neighborhood are increasing, stable, or declining. Only one selection is permitted. **Demand/Supply** The appraiser must indicate whether the demand/supply of condominium unit housing in the subject property's neighborhood is in shortage, in balance, or over supply. Only one selection is permitted. **Marketing Time** The appraiser must indicate whether the marketing time for condominium unit housing is under 3 mths, 3–6 mths, or over 6 mths. Only one selection is permitted. **Reporting Format:** Property Values – Checkbox designated with an 'x' Demand/Supply – Checkbox designated with an 'x' Marketing Time – Checkbox designated with an 'x'	1073/465 1075/466	REQUIREMENT
Neighborhood Boundaries The appraiser should provide an outline of the neighborhood boundaries, which should be clearly delineated using 'North', 'South', 'East', and 'West'. These boundaries may include but are not limited to streets, legally recognized neighborhood boundaries, waterways, or other natural boundaries that define the separation of one neighborhood from another. Appraisers should not reference a map or other addendum as the only example of the neighborhood boundaries. **Reporting Format:** Description of Neighborhood Boundaries – Text	1004/70 2055/2055 1073/465 1075/466	INSTRUCTION

Field-Specific Standardization Requirements

Site Section	Forms	Requirement or Instruction
Area For sites/parcels that have an area of less than one acre, the size must be reported in square feet. For sites/parcels that have an area of one acre or greater, the size must be reported in acreage to two decimal places. The unit of measure must be indicated as either 'sf' for square feet or 'ac' for acres. A numeric value must be entered followed by the appropriate unit of measure. The total size of the entire site/parcel must be entered. No other data is permitted. **Reporting Format:** Area less than one acre – whole numbers only + unit of measure Area equal to one acre or more – numeric to 2 decimals + unit of measure **Examples:** 27840 sf 3.40 ac	1004/70 2055/2055	REQUIREMENT
View The appraiser must provide one of the ratings from the list below to describe the overall effect on value and marketability of the view factors associated with the subject property.	1004/70 2055/2055 1073/465 1075/466	REQUIREMENT

ABBREVIATED ENTRY	OVERALL VIEW RATING
N	Neutral
B	Beneficial
A	Adverse

The appraiser must also provide at least one, but not more than two, view factor(s) from the list below to provide details about the overall view rating selected above.

ABBREVIATED ENTRY	VIEW FACTOR
Wtr	Water View
Pstrl	Pastoral View
Woods	Woods View
Prk	Park View
Glfvw	Golf Course View
CtySky	City View Skyline View
Mtn	Mountain View
Res	Residential View
CtyStr	City Street View
Ind	Industrial View
PwrLn	Power Lines
LtdSght	Limited Sight
See Instruction Below	Other – Appraiser to enter a description of the view*

*Other: If a view factor not on this list materially affects the value of the subject property, the appraiser must enter a description of the view associated with the property (see second example below). The description entered must allow a reader of the appraisal report to understand what the view associated with the property actually is. Descriptors such as 'None', 'N/A', 'Typical', 'Average', etc., are unacceptable. Descriptions should be entered carefully because the same text will be represented in both the Site section and the comparable sales grid for the subject property. The text must fit in the allowable space.

Uniform Appraisal Dataset Specification

Site Section	Forms	Requirement or Instruction
Reporting Format: View Rating – Appraiser must select one value from the specified list View Factors – Appraiser must select one or two factors from the specified list Description of 'Other'(if applicable) – Text The PDF creator will automatically insert a semicolon to separate the data values. **Examples:** B;Mtn;Wtr A;RRtracks [example of appraiser-entered 'Other' description] Refer to the complete list of acceptable abbreviations provided at the end of this document in Exhibit 3: Requirements – Abbreviations Used in Data Standardization Text.		
Utilities The appraiser must indicate for each utility whether it is 'Public' and/or 'Other'. Utilities include electricity, gas, water, and sanitary sewer. The appraiser must also enter a description if 'Other' is indicated. If the utility is not present, enter 'None' in the description field. **Reporting Format:** Electricity – Checkbox(es) designated with an 'x' Gas – Checkbox(es) designated with an 'x' Water – Checkbox(es) designated with an 'x' Sanitary Sewer – Checkbox(es) designated with an 'x' Description of 'Other' (if applicable) – Text	1004/70 2055/2055 1073/465 1075/466	REQUIREMENT
Street/Alley The appraiser should indicate whether the street or alley type is 'Public' and/or 'Private'. Enter 'None' in the appropriate description field if there is no street or alley. **Reporting Format:** Street – Checkbox(es) designated with an 'x' Alley – Checkbox(es) designated with an 'x' Description of Street/Alley – Text	1004/70 2055/2055 1073/465 1075/466	INSTRUCTION

Field-Specific Standardization Requirements		

Project Information Section	Forms	Requirement or Instruction
Project Description If the project includes more than one building, the appraiser should enter the type of building in which the subject unit is located. Only one selection is permitted. If 'Other' is selected, the appraiser must enter a description. **Reporting Format:** Project Description – Checkbox designated with an 'x' Description of 'Other' (if applicable) – Text	1073/465 1075/466	INSTRUCTION
General Description - # of Stories, # of Elevators, Existing/Proposed/Under Construction, Year Built If the project includes more than one building, the appraiser should enter data for the building in which the subject unit is located. **Reporting Format:** # of Stories – See requirements in Improvements section # of Elevators – Numeric, whole numbers only Existing/Proposed/Under Construction – Checkbox designated with an 'x' Only one selection is permitted Year Built – See requirements in Improvements section Estimation of Year Built – See requirements in Improvements section	1073/465 1075/466	INSTRUCTION
Is the developer/builder in control of the Homeowners' Association (HOA)? For condominiums, the appraiser must select 'Yes' or 'No' in response to the question, "Is the developer/builder in control of the Homeowners' Association (HOA)?" located in the Project Information section. **Reporting Format:** Is the developer/builder in control of the Homeowners' Association (HOA)? – Checkbox designated with an 'x'	1073/465 1075/466	REQUIREMENT
Is there any commercial space in the project? If Yes, describe and indicate the overall percentage of the commercial space. The appraiser must select either 'Yes' or 'No' to indicate whether there is commercial space in the project. If 'Yes' is indicated, the appraiser must enter the overall percentage of commercial space in the project in which the subject property is located. **Reporting Format:** Is there any commercial space in the project? – Checkbox designated with an 'x' Percentage of Commercial Space – Numeric to 2 digits, whole numbers only	1073/465 1075/466	REQUIREMENT

UAD Appendix D: UAD Field-Specific Standardization Requirements   Page 14 of 36   Document Version 1.1

542

Uniform Appraisal Dataset Specification

Improvements Section	Forms	Requirement or Instruction
# of Stories The appraiser must indicate the number of stories for the subject property. Do not use any designators or descriptors, such as '1 story' or 'one story and a half.' For condominiums, the appraiser must enter the number of stories for the building in which the subject unit is located. **Reporting Format**: # of Stories – Numeric to 2 decimal places	1004/70 2055/2055 1073*/465* 1075*/466* *FIELD IS LOCATED IN PROJECT INFORMATION SECTION	REQUIREMENT
# of Levels The appraiser must indicate the number of levels for the subject unit. Do not use any designators or descriptors, such as '1 level'. **Reporting Format**: # of Levels – Numeric, whole numbers only	1073*/465* 1075*/466* *FIELD IS LOCATED IN UNIT DESCRIPTION SECTION	REQUIREMENT
Design (Style) The appraiser should enter an appropriate architectural design (style) type descriptor that best describes the subject property. Valid descriptions include, but are not limited to, 'Colonial,' 'Rambler,' 'Georgian,' 'Farmhouse'. Do not use descriptors such as 'brick,' '2 stories,' 'average,' 'conventional,' or 'typical' as these are not architectural styles. Design style names may vary by locality. The appraiser should report the name of the design style that is applicable within the local market area. **Reporting Format**: Design (Style) – Text	1004/70 2055/2055	INSTRUCTION
Year Built The appraiser must indicate the year the subject property was built. If it is unknown or unavailable to the appraiser within the normal course of business, the appraiser must estimate the year the subject property was built. **Reporting Format:** Year Built – 4-digit number, yyyy Estimation of Year Built – A tilde (~) must precede the year built **Examples:** 1978 ~1950 (The PDF creator will insert the tilde)	1004/70 2055/2055 1073*/465* 1075*/466* *FIELD IS LOCATED IN PROJECT INFORMATION SECTION	REQUIREMENT

543

Field-Specific Standardization Requirements

Improvements Section	Forms	Requirement or Instruction
Basement Area, Basement Finish If a basement exists, the appraiser must indicate the basement size in square feet and the percentage of the basement that is finished. If there is no basement, enter the numeral zero (0) in both fields. **Reporting Format:** Basement Area – Numeric to 5 digits, whole numbers only Basement Finish – Numeric to 3 digits, whole numbers only	1004/70 2055/2055	REQUIREMENT
Heating, Cooling The appraiser should select the heating and/or cooling types. If there is no heating or cooling source, the appraiser should indicate 'Other' and enter 'None'. **Reporting Format:** Heating Types (for 1004 and 2055) – Checkbox(es) designated with an 'x' Cooling Types – Checkbox(es) designated with an 'x' Description of 'Other' (if applicable) – Text	1004/70 2055/2055	INSTRUCTION
Heating, Cooling -- *(for Condominiums)* The appraiser should indicate the heating and cooling types. If there is no heating source, the appraiser should indicate 'None'. If there is no cooling source, the appraiser should indicate 'Other' and enter 'None'. **Reporting Format:** Heating Types (for 1073 and 1075) – Text Cooling Types – Checkbox(es) designated with an 'x' Description of 'Other' (if applicable) – Text	1073*/465* 1075**/466** *FIELD IS LOCATED IN THE UNIT DESCRIPTION SECTION **FIELD IS LOCATED IN THE UNIT IMPROVEMENTS SECTION	INSTRUCTION
Amenities The appraiser should select the appropriate checkbox(es) to indicate the amenities available. The appraiser should enter the numeral zero (0) in the appropriate space if there are no fireplaces or woodstoves. The appraiser should enter 'None' in the appropriate space if there is no patio/deck, pool, fence, porch, or other amenity. **Reporting Format:** Amenity Types – Checkbox(es) designated with an 'x' Description of Amenity – Text	1004/70 2055/2055 1073*/465* 1075**/466** *FIELD IS LOCATED IN THE UNIT DESCRIPTION SECTION **FIELD IS LOCATED IN THE UNIT IMPROVEMENTS SECTION	INSTRUCTION

Uniform Appraisal Dataset Specification

Improvements Section	Forms	Requirement or Instruction
Car Storage, Driveway, Garage, Carport The appraiser must indicate whether the subject property has a driveway, garage, and/or carport, or has no car storage. If the subject property has a driveway, garage, and/or carport, the appraiser must enter the number of spaces for each type of car storage; if none, enter the numeral zero (0). **Reporting Format:** Car Storage Types – Checkbox(es) designated with an 'x' # of Cars - Numeric to 2 digits, whole numbers only	1004/70 2055/2055 1073*/465* 1075*/466* *CAR STORAGE AND # CARS FIELDS ARE LOCATED IN UNIT DESCRIPTION SECTION	REQUIREMENT
Finished Area Above Grade Contains _____Rooms The appraiser must enter the total number of finished rooms above grade. **Reporting Format:** # of Rooms – Numeric to 2 digits, whole numbers only	1004/70 2055/2055 1073*/465* 1075*/466* *FIELD IS LOCATED IN UNIT DESCRIPTION SECTION	REQUIREMENT
Finished Area Above Grade Contains _____Bedrooms This appraiser must enter the total number of bedrooms above grade. **Reporting Format:** # of Bedrooms – Numeric to 2 digits, whole numbers only	1004/70 2055/2055 1073*/465* 1075*/466* *FIELD IS LOCATED IN UNIT DESCRIPTION SECTION	REQUIREMENT
Finished Area Above Grade Contains _____Bath(s) The appraiser must enter the total number of full baths and partial baths above grade. A three-quarter bath is to be counted as a full bath in all cases. Quarter baths (baths that feature only a toilet) are not to be included in the bathroom count. The number of full and half baths must be entered, separated by a period. The full bath count is represented to the left of the period. The half bath count is represented to the right of the period. **Reporting Format:** # of Bath(s) – Numeric to 2 decimal places Separate full bath count from half bath count with a period (.), nn.nn **Example:** 3.2 indicates three full baths and two half baths above grade.	1004/70 2055/2055 1073*/465* 1075*/466* *FIELD IS LOCATED IN UNIT DESCRIPTION SECTION	REQUIREMENT
Square Feet of Gross Living Area Above Grade The appraiser must enter the total square footage of the above grade living area. **Reporting Format:** Square Feet of GLA – Numeric to 5 digits, whole numbers only	1004/70 2055/2055 1073*/465* 1075*/466* *FIELD IS LOCATED IN UNIT DESCRIPTION SECTION	REQUIREMENT

Field-Specific Standardization Requirements		
Improvements Section	**Forms**	**Requirement or Instruction**
Describe the condition of the property (including needed repairs, deterioration, renovations, remodeling, etc.)	1004/70 1073*/465*	REQUIREMENT

Interior/Exterior Complete Inspection Reports:
The appraiser must provide the following information:

*FIELD IS LOCATED IN UNIT DESCRIPTION SECTION

  Overall Condition Rating – The appraiser must select one of the following ratings that best describes the overall condition of the subject property or unit. For condominium properties, the rating must reflect the overall condition for the individual unit being appraised. Only one selection is permitted. The rating for the subject property must match the overall condition rating that is reported in the Sales Comparison Approach section.

- C1
- C2
- C3
- C4
- C5
- C6

  The definitions for the ratings listed above are provided in Exhibit 1: Requirements – Condition and Quality Ratings Usage.

  The appraiser must indicate 'Yes' or 'No' if there has been any material work done to the kitchen(s) or bathroom(s) in the prior 15 years. If 'No', the text 'No updates in the prior 15 years' must be provided. If 'Yes', additional information for kitchens and bathrooms must be provided.

  Kitchen(s) and Bathroom(s) – Level of Work Completed and Timeframes – The appraiser must identify any work completed in the kitchen(s) and bathroom(s) along with the timeframes in which the work was completed. The appraiser must select one of the values from the lists below for both the kitchen(s) and the bathroom(s).

    Level of Work Completed:
- not updated
- updated
- remodeled

  Definitions for the Level of Work Completed are provided in Exhibit 2: Requirements – Definitions of Not Updated, Updated, and Remodeled.

    Timeframes:
- less than one year ago
- one to five years ago
- six to ten years ago
- eleven to fifteen years ago
- timeframe unknown

  Timeframes represent the time period in which the majority of the improvements were completed.

  Descriptions or Comments – The appraiser must provide a description of the condition of the improvements to the subject property.

UAD Appendix D: UAD Field-Specific Standardization Requirements   Page 18 of 36   Document Version 1.1

546

Uniform Appraisal Dataset Specification

Field-Specific Standardization Requirements		
Improvements Section	**Forms**	**Requirement or Instruction**
Reporting Format: Condition Rating – Appraiser must select one value from the specified list Indicator of Work Completed in Prior 15 Years – 'Yes' or 'No' response Level of Work Completed for Kitchen(s) and Bathroom(s) – Appraiser must select one value from the specified list Timeframes for Work Completed for the Kitchen(s) and Bathroom(s) – Appraiser must select one value from the specified list Description of Condition of Improvements – Text The PDF creator will populate the selected text from the specified lists for 'Overall Condition Rating' (Improvement Area), 'Level of Work Completed,' and 'Timeframe for Work Completed.' A semicolon will be used to separate the overall condition rating from the kitchen and bathroom improvements. **Examples:** C4;No updates in the prior 15 years;[enter description of property condition] C3;Kitchen-updated-less than one year ago;Bathrooms-remodeled-one to five years ago;[enter description of property condition] C2;Kitchen-not updated;Bathrooms-remodeled-less than one year ago;[enter description of property condition]		
Exterior-Only Inspection Residential Appraisal Report Forms: The appraiser must report the overall condition of the property or unit using one of the overall condition ratings. **Reporting Format:** Condition Rating – Appraiser must select one value from the specified list Description of Condition of Improvements – Text	2055/2055 1075*/ 466* *FIELD IS LOCATED IN UNIT DESCRIPTION SECTION	REQUIREMENT

Field-Specific Standardization Requirements

Sales Comparison Approach Section	Forms	Requirement or Instruction
Address The appraiser must enter the subject property address and the address for each comparable sale. Refer to "Property Address" and "Unit#" (if applicable) data fields in the Subject section for the requirements on completing this field. **Reporting Format:** Property Address – Text Unit # (if applicable) – Text City – Text State – 2-letter USPS abbreviation ZIP Code – 5-digit ZIP Code or ZIP+4 code (either with or without the dash)	1004/70 2055/2055 1073/465 1075/466	REQUIREMENT
Proximity to Subject The appraiser must enter the proximity of the comparable sales to the subject property, expressed as a distance in miles. The distance between the subject property and each comparable property is to be measured using a straight line between the properties. The direction of the comparable property in relation to the subject property must be expressed. If the address for a comparable property is not found by the appraiser's mapping program, the appraiser must choose a location on the map as close as possible to the address of the comparable property to derive an accurate distance calculation. **Reporting Format:** Proximity to Subject – Numeric to 2 decimal places + 'miles' + Directional **Example:** 1.75 miles NW	1004/70 2055/2055 1073/465 1075/466	REQUIREMENT
Sale Price The appraiser must enter the sale price of the subject property (if applicable) and each comparable property. The sale price for the subject property must match the contract price reported in the Contract section. If any of the comparable properties sold for a price that was not in whole dollars, the appraiser must round the sales price to the nearest dollar. If any of the comparable properties is a listing or pending sale, the appraiser must enter the offering price or contract price as applicable. **Reporting Format:** Sale Price – Currency, whole dollars only	1004/70 2055/2055 1073/465 1075/466	REQUIREMENT

Uniform Appraisal Dataset Specification

Sales Comparison Approach Section	Forms	Requirement or Instruction
Data Source(s) The appraiser must provide the data source(s) utilized to obtain the data for each comparable sale. When using MLS as the data source, the MLS organization acronym or abbreviation followed by '#' and the listing identifier (numbers and letters) must be reported. If the appraiser utilizes additional data sources that do not fit into this data field, they must be provided in the comments section or addenda in the appraisal report. Additionally, the appraiser must provide the DOM for each comparable sale for the latest time period that the property was listed or advertised for sale. DOM is defined as the total number of continuous days from the date that a property is listed or advertised for sale until the date that it is taken off the market or sold. DOM applies not only to properties that are listed in the MLS, but also applies to properties marketed for sale outside MLS. If the comparable property was not individually listed or advertised for sale, enter the numeral zero (0). If the DOM is unknown, enter 'Unk'. **Reporting Format:** Data Source(s) – Abbreviated MLS#Listing Identifier or Text DOM – Numeric to 4 digits, whole numbers only The PDF creator will automatically insert a semicolon to separate the data values and print the letters 'DOM' prior to the response. **Examples:** MRIS#AA123456789;DOM 220 MRIS#BB123456789;DOM Unk	1004/70 2055/2055 1073/465 1075/466	REQUIREMENT
Sale or Financing Concessions *Note: This field, comprised of two lines, is used to capture sale type, financing type, and any concessions. The information must be entered on line 1 and line 2 as indicated.* **Line 1** The appraiser must indicate the sale type for each comparable property. If more than one sale type applies to the comparable property, the appraiser must start at the top of the list and identify the first sale type that applies. The valid values are:	1004/70 2055/2055 1073/465 1075/466	REQUIREMENT

ABBREVIATED ENTRY	SALE TYPE
REO	REO sale
Short	Short sale
CrtOrd	Court ordered sale
Estate	Estate sale
Relo	Relocation sale
NonArm	Non-arms length sale
ArmLth	Arms length sale
Listing	Listing

Field-Specific Standardization Requirements		
Sales Comparison Approach Section	**Forms**	**Requirement or Instruction**

Line 2
The appraiser must enter the financing type from the list below and the total amount of concessions, if any, for each settled sale. If there are no sales or financing concessions, enter the numeral zero (0).

ABBREVIATED ENTRY	FINANCING TYPE
FHA	FHA
VA	VA
Conv	Conventional
Seller	Seller
Cash	Cash
RH	USDA – Rural housing
See Instruction Below	Other – Appraiser to enter a description of the financing type*

*Other: If the financing type is not on this list, the appraiser must enter a description of the financing type. The text must fit in the allowable space.

Note: Below-market financing can have an impact on market values and therefore is of particular importance. A variety of government programs, such as state and local bond programs, provide below-market financing. The appraiser must indicate if sales transactions with below-market financing are used for comparable sales.

Reporting Format:
Line 1: Sale Type – Appraiser must select one value from the specified list

Line 2: Financing Type – Appraiser must select one value from the specified list
Description of 'Other Financing Type' (if applicable) – Text
Concession Amount – Numeric, whole numbers only
The PDF creator will automatically insert a semicolon to separate the data values.

Example:
Line 1: ArmLth
Line 2: FHA;5000

Date of Sale/Time For each comparable property, the appraiser must first identify the status type from the list of options below.	1004/70 2055/2055 1073/465 1075/466	REQUIREMENT

Status Type
Active
Contract
Expired
Withdrawn
Settled sale

- If the comparable property is an active listing, the appraiser must specify 'Active'.
- If the comparable property is under contract, or an expired or withdrawn listing, the appraiser must first indicate the date status type using the abbreviations below followed by the corresponding contract, expiration, or withdrawal date in mm/yy format. Use 'c' for contract, 'w' for withdrawn listings, and 'e' for expired listings.

Uniform Appraisal Dataset Specification

Sales Comparison Approach Section	Forms	Requirement or Instruction

Abbreviated Entry	Date Status Type
c	Contract Date
s	Settlement Date
w	Withdrawn Date
e	Expiration Date

- If the comparable property is a settled sale and the contract date is known, the appraiser must first indicate the date status type 's' followed by the settlement date (mm/yy), and then the date status type 'c' followed by the contract date (mm/yy). For settled sales for which the contract date is unavailable to the appraiser in the normal course of business, the appraiser must enter the abbreviation 'Unk', for unknown, in place of the contract date.

Reporting Format:
Status Type – Appraiser must select one value from the specified list
Date – mm/yy
Contract Date Unknown Indicator (for Settled Sales only) – Select 'Yes' or 'No'
The PDF creator will automatically insert the abbreviated Date Status type and a semicolon to separate the data values (for settled sales only). If the appraiser indicates the contract date is unknown, the PDF creator will populate 'Unk' after the semicolon.

Examples:
Active listing: Active
Contract: c04/10
Expired listing: e04/10
Withdrawn listing: w04/10
Settled sale (contract date known): s04/10;c02/10
Settled sale (contract date unknown): s04/10;Unk

551

Field-Specific Standardization Requirements

Sales Comparison Approach Section	Forms	Requirement or Instruction
Location The appraiser must select one of the following ratings to describe the overall effect on value and marketability of the location factor(s) associated with the subject property and each comparable property. The abbreviation for the rating must be entered.	1004/70 2055/2055 1073/465 1075/466	REQUIREMENT

ABBREVIATED ENTRY	OVERALL LOCATION RATING
N	Neutral
B	Beneficial
A	Adverse

The appraiser must also select at least one, but not more than two, location factor(s) from the list below. If two factors are entered, separate them with a semicolon. The abbreviation for the factor must be entered, with the exception of 'Other'.

ABBREVIATED ENTRY	LOCATION FACTOR
Res	Residential
Ind	Industrial
Comm	Commercial
BsyRd	Busy Road
WtrFr	Water Front
GlfCse	Golf Course
AdjPrk	Adjacent to Park
AdjPwr	Adjacent to Power Lines
Lndfl	Landfill
PubTrn	Public Transportation
See Instruction Below	Other – Appraiser to enter a description of the location*

*Other: If a location factor not on this list materially affects the value of the property, the appraiser must enter a description of the location associated with the property. The description entered must allow a reader of the appraisal report to understand the location factor(s) that is associated with the property. Descriptors such as 'None', 'N/A', 'Typical', 'Average', etc., are unacceptable. The text must fit in the allowable space.

A list of acceptable abbreviations and definitions is also provided at the end of this document in Exhibit 3: Requirements – Abbreviations.

Reporting Format:
Location Rating – Appraiser must select one value from the specified list
Location Factors – Appraiser must select one or two factors from the specified list
Description of 'Other' (if applicable) – Text
The PDF creator will automatically insert a semicolon to separate the data values.

Example:
B;AdjPrk;WtrFr

Uniform Appraisal Dataset Specification

Sales Comparison Approach Section	Forms	Requirement or Instruction

Site

For sites/parcels that have an area of less than one acre, the size must be reported in square feet. For sites/parcels that have an area of one acre or greater, the size must be reported in acreage to two decimal places. The unit of measure must be indicated as either 'sf' for square feet or 'ac' for acres. A numeric value must be entered followed by the appropriate unit of measure. The total size of the entire site/parcel must be entered. No other data is permitted in this field.

Reporting Format:
Area less than one acre – whole numbers only
Area equal to one acre or more – numeric to 2 decimals
Indicate the unit of measure as either 'sf' for square feet or 'ac' for acres as appropriate.

Examples:
6400 sf
3.40 ac

Forms: 1004/70 2055/2055 — *REQUIREMENT*

View

The appraiser must provide one of the ratings from the list below to describe the overall effect on value and marketability of the view factor(s) associated with the subject property and each comparable property.

Forms: 1004/70 2055/2055 1073/465 1075/466 — *REQUIREMENT*

ABBREVIATED ENTRY	OVERALL VIEW RATING
N	Neutral
B	Beneficial
A	Adverse

The appraiser must also provide at least one, but not more than two, view factor(s) from the list below to provide details about the overall view rating selected above.

ABBREVIATED ENTRY	VIEW FACTOR
Wtr	Water View
Pstrl	Pastoral View
Woods	Woods View
Prk	Park View
Glfvw	Golf Course View
CtySky	City View Skyline View
Mtn	Mountain View
Res	Residential View
CtyStr	City Street View
Ind	Industrial View
PwrLn	Power Lines
LtdSght	Limited Sight
See Instruction Below	Other – Appraiser to enter a description of the view*

*Other: If a view factor not on this list materially affects the value of the property, the appraiser must enter a description of the view associated with the property (see second example below). Descriptions should be entered carefully because the text will be represented in both the Site Section and the Sales Comparison Approach section for the subject property. The description entered must allow a reader of the appraisal report to understand what the view is that is associated with the property. Descriptors such as 'None', 'N/A', 'Typical', 'Average', etc., are unacceptable. The text must fit in the allowable space.

Reporting Format:
View Rating – Appraiser must select one value from the specified list
View Factors – Appraiser must select one or two factors from the specified list
Description of 'Other' (if applicable) – Text
The PDF creator will automatically insert a semicolon to separate the data values.

Example:
B;Mtn;Wtr
A;RRtracks [example of appraiser-entered 'Other' description]

Refer to the complete list of acceptable abbreviations provided at the end of this document in
Exhibit 3: Requirements – Abbreviations Used in Data Standardization Text.

Uniform Appraisal Dataset Specification

Sales Comparison Approach Section	Forms	Requirement or Instruction

Condition
 	
The appraiser must select one overall condition rating for the subject property and each comparable property from the list below. The overall condition rating selected for the subject property must match the overall condition rating that was reported in the Improvements section so that it is consistent throughout the appraisal report. Multiple choices are not permitted.
 	
    • C1
    • C2
    • C3
    • C4
    • C5
    • C6
 	
The definitions for these condition ratings are provided in Exhibit 1: Requirements – Condition and Quality Ratings Usage.
 	
Reporting Format:
Condition Rating – Appraiser must select one value from the specified list
	1004/70
	2055/2055
	1073/465
	1075/466
		REQUIREMENT

Above Grade Room Count, Gross Living Area The appraiser must enter the total number of rooms as well as the number of bedrooms and bathrooms for the subject property and each comparable property. The appraiser must also enter the gross living area for the subject property and each comparable property. The appraiser must follow the same standards outlined in the Improvements section under "Finished Area Above Grade" and "Square Feet of Gross Living Area Above Grade." **Reporting Format:** # of Rooms – Numeric to 2 digits, whole numbers only # of Bedrooms – Numeric to 2 digits, whole numbers only # of Bath(s) – Numeric to 2 decimal places Separate full bath count from half bath count with a period (.), nn.nn Gross Living Area – Numeric to 5 digits, whole numbers only **Example:** 3.2 indicates three full baths and two half baths above grade.	1004/70 2055/2055 1073/465 1075/466	REQUIREMENT

Field-Specific Standardization Requirements		
Sales Comparison Approach Section	**Forms**	**Requirement or Instruction**

Basement & Finished Rooms Below Grade
 	
Line 1
The appraiser must report:
   ▪ Total square footage of the property improvements below grade – If there is no basement, enter the numeral zero (0). No other information may be entered.
   ▪ Finished square footage of the property improvements below grade, if applicable. Do not indicate a percent finished.
   ▪ The type of access to the basement, if applicable. The allowable values are 'Walk-out' (wo), 'Walk-up' (wu), or 'Interior only' (in), which must be abbreviated on the appraisal report form to fit in the available space.
 	
Line 2
The appraiser must report the number of each type of finished rooms in the basement on Line 2 of this data field. The room type descriptors are:
	1004/70
	2055/2055
	1073/465
	1075/466
		REQUIREMENT

ABBREVIATED ENTRY	ROOM TYPE
rr	Recreation Room
br	Bedroom
ba	Bathroom
o	Other

The appraiser must enter the numeral zero (0) if there are no rooms of a particular type.

Reporting Format:
Line 1: Total Square Footage – Numeric to 5 digits, whole numbers only
Line 1: Finished Square Footage – Numeric to 5 digits, whole numbers only
Line 1: Basement Access – Appraiser must select one value from the specified list (values wo, wu, or in)
The PDF creator will automatically insert the text 'sf' to separate the data values.

Line 2: Room Count/Type – Numeric to 1 digit*
*For bathrooms, the format is n.n – full baths separated from half baths with a period (.). The PDF creator will automatically insert the room type abbreviations to separate the data values.

Examples:
Line 1: 1000sf750sfwu
Line 2: 1rr1br1.0ba2o

| **Energy Efficient Items**

The appraiser must enter any energy efficient items for the subject property and each comparable property. If there are no energy efficient items, enter 'None'.

Reporting Format:
Energy Efficient Items – Text | 1004/70
2055/2055
1073/465
1075/466 | REQUIREMENT |

Uniform Appraisal Dataset Specification

Field-Specific Standardization Requirements		
Sales Comparison Approach Section	**Forms**	**Requirement or Instruction**
Garage/Carport The appraiser must indicate the total number and type of off-street parking spaces associated with the subject property and each comparable property. If there is no off-street parking, enter 'None'. **Reporting Format:** Garage/Carport – Text	1004/70 2055/2055 1073/465 1075/466	REQUIREMENT
+(-) $ Adjustment If a feature or aspect of the subject property differs from a feature or aspect of a comparable property and the appraiser determines that no adjustment is warranted, the appraiser must enter a zero (0) in the adjustment line. The zero (0) will indicate to the reader/user of the report that the appraiser considered the difference and determined that no adjustment should be made. When the features for the subject and comparable sale(s) are the same and no adjustment is warranted, leave the field blank - do not enter or default to zero. Net Adjustment is the sum of all adjustments. If there are no adjustments, the net adjustment value must be zero (0). **Reporting Format:** +/- $ Adjustment – Currency, whole dollars only	1004/70 2055/2055 1073/465 1075/466	REQUIREMENT
My research did/did not reveal any prior sales or transfers… The appraiser must select the appropriate checkbox to indicate either 'did' or 'did not' for this statement. Only one response is permitted for each statement. **Reporting Format:** My research did/did not reveal any prior sales or transfers of the subject property… – Checkbox designated with an 'x' My research did/did not reveal any prior sales or transfers of the comparable sales… – Checkbox designated with an 'x'	1004/70 2055/2055 1073*/465* 1075*/466* *FIELDS ARE LOCATED IN PRIOR SALE HISTORY SECTION	REQUIREMENT
Date of Prior Sale/Transfer The appraiser must report the date(s) of prior sale(s) or transfer(s) of the subject property for the three years prior to the effective date of the appraisal. The appraiser must report the date(s) of the prior sale(s) or transfer(s) of any comparable property during the twelve months prior to its date of sale. If more than one prior transfer of the subject property or any of the comparable sale(s) occurred within the applicable time period, the additional transfer(s) must be listed and reported in the "Analysis of Prior Sale or Transfer History of the Subject Property and Comparable Sales" field. **Reporting Format:** Date of Prior Sale/Transfer – mm/dd/yyyy	1004/70 2055/2055 1073*/465* 1075*/466* *FIELD IS LOCATED IN PRIOR SALE HISTORY SECTION	REQUIREMENT

Appendix 5

Field-Specific Standardization Requirements		
Sales Comparison Approach Section	**Forms**	**Requirement or Instruction**
Price of Prior Sale/Transfer The appraiser must report the price(s) of prior sale(s) or transfer(s) of the subject property for the three years prior to the effective date of the appraisal. The appraiser must report the price(s) of the prior sale(s) or transfer(s) of any comparable property during the twelve months prior to its date of sale. If more than one prior transfer of the subject property or any of the comparable sales occurred within the applicable time period, the additional transfer(s) must be listed and reported in the "Analysis of Prior Sale or Transfer History of the Subject Property and Comparable Sales" field. **Reporting Format:** Price of Prior Sale/Transfer – Currency (include a dollar sign), whole dollars only	1004/70 2055/2055 1073*/465* 1075* 466* *FIELD IS LOCATED IN PRIOR SALE HISTORY SECTION	REQUIREMENT
Data Source(s), Effective Date of Data Source(s) – *Prior Sales* The appraiser must enter the data source(s) and effective date(s) of the data source(s) associated with the prior transfer(s) of each property. If the data source is MLS, the appraiser must enter the abbreviated MLS organization name, followed by a pound sign (#) and the specific listing identifier. **Reporting Format:** Data Source(s) – Text Effective Date of Data Source(s) – mm/dd/yyyy	1004/70 2055/2055 1073*/465* 1075* 466* *FIELDS ARE LOCATED IN PRIOR SALE HISTORY SECTION	REQUIREMENT
Indicated Value by Sales Comparison Approach $ The appraiser must enter the reconciled value of the Sales Comparison Approach. **Reporting Format:** Indicated Value by Sales Comparison Approach $ – Currency, whole dollars only	1004/70 2055/2055 1073/465 1075/466	REQUIREMENT

Uniform Appraisal Dataset Specification

Reconciliation Section	Forms	Requirement or Instruction
This appraisal is made 'as is', subject to completion... The appraiser must select either the 'as is' or at least one of the 'subject to' checkboxes. If any of the 'subject to' checkboxes are selected, provide a description. **Reporting Format:** This appraisal is made 'as is', subject to completion... – Checkbox(es) designated with an 'x' Description (if applicable) – Text	1004/70 2055/2055 1073/465 1075/466	REQUIREMENT
My (our) opinion of the market value... The appraiser must enter the value of the subject property. The value of the subject property must match the appraised value of the subject property in the Appraiser Certification section. **Reporting Format:** My (our) opinion of the market value... – Currency, whole dollars only	1004/70 2055/2055 1073/465 1075/466	REQUIREMENT
Date of Inspection and Effective Date of Appraisal The appraiser must enter the date of the inspection, which is also the effective date of the appraisal. **Reporting Format:** Date of Inspection and Effective Date of Appraisal – mm/dd/yyyy	1004/70 2055/2055 1073/465 1075/466	REQUIREMENT

Field-Specific Standardization Requirements

Appraiser Certification Section	Forms	Requirement or Instruction
State Certification # or State License # – *(Appraiser and Supervisory Appraiser if required)* The appraiser and supervisory appraiser (if applicable) must enter their license or certification number(s) as they appear on the Appraisal Subcommittee (ASC) website, http://www.asc.gov, unless otherwise mandated by state law or regulation. If the jurisdiction does not provide license numbers for trainees and a trainee performs the appraisal, the term "trainee" must be entered in the (Appraiser Certification Section) "or Other (describe)" field. If there is no supervisory appraiser, leave the field blank; do not make any entry (such as N/A or none). **Reporting Format:** State Certification or License Number – Text	1004/70 2055/2055 1073/465 1075/466	REQUIREMENT
Expiration Date of Certification or License – *(Appraiser and Supervisory Appraiser if required)* The appraiser and supervisory appraiser (if applicable) must enter the expiration date of their license or certification number(s). If there is no supervisory appraiser, leave the field blank; do not make any entry (such as N/A or none). **Reporting Format:** Expiration Date – mm/dd/yyyy	1004/70 2055/2055 1073/465 1075/466	REQUIREMENT
LENDER/CLIENT **Name** The appraiser must enter the name of the appraisal management company (AMC) in this field if the appraisal is ordered through an AMC. If no AMC is involved, 'No AMC' must be entered. **Reporting Format:** Name (AMC Name) – Text	1004/70 2055/2055 1073/465 1075/466	REQUIREMENT

Uniform Appraisal Dataset Specification

EXHIBITS

Exhibit 1: Requirements – Condition and Quality Ratings Usage

Appraisers must utilize the following standardized condition and quality ratings within the appraisal report.

Condition Ratings and Definitions

C1

The improvements have been very recently constructed and have not previously been occupied. The entire structure and all components are new and the dwelling features no physical depreciation.*

*Note: Newly constructed improvements that feature recycled materials and/or components can be considered new dwellings provided that the dwelling is placed on a 100% new foundation and the recycled materials and the recycled components have been rehabilitated/re-manufactured into like-new condition. Recently constructed improvements that have not been previously occupied are not considered "new" if they have any significant physical depreciation (i.e., newly constructed dwellings that have been vacant for an extended period of time without adequate maintenance or upkeep).

C2

The improvements feature no deferred maintenance, little or no physical depreciation, and require no repairs. Virtually all building components are new or have been recently repaired, refinished, or rehabilitated. All outdated components and finishes have been updated and/or replaced with components that meet current standards. Dwellings in this category either are almost new or have been recently completely renovated and are similar in condition to new construction.

C3

The improvements are well maintained and feature limited physical depreciation due to normal wear and tear. Some components, but not every major building component, may be updated or recently rehabilitated. The structure has been well maintained.

C4

The improvements feature some minor deferred maintenance and physical deterioration due to normal wear and tear. The dwelling has been adequately maintained and requires only minimal repairs to building components/mechanical systems and cosmetic repairs. All major building components have been adequately maintained and are functionally adequate.

C5

The improvements feature obvious deferred maintenance and are in need of some significant repairs. Some building components need repairs, rehabilitation, or updating. The functional utility and overall livability is somewhat diminished due to condition, but the dwelling remains useable and functional as a residence.

C6

The improvements have substantial damage or deferred maintenance with deficiencies or defects that are severe enough to affect the safety, soundness, or structural integrity of the improvements. The improvements are in need of substantial repairs and rehabilitation, including many or most major components.

EXHIBITS

Quality Ratings and Definitions

Q1

Dwellings with this quality rating are usually unique structures that are individually designed by an architect for a specified user. Such residences typically are constructed from detailed architectural plans and specifications and feature an exceptionally high level of workmanship and exceptionally high-grade materials throughout the interior and exterior of the structure. The design features exceptionally high-quality exterior refinements and ornamentation, and exceptionally high-quality interior refinements. The workmanship, materials, and finishes throughout the dwelling are of exceptionally high quality.

Q2

Dwellings with this quality rating are often custom designed for construction on an individual property owner's site. However, dwellings in this quality grade are also found in high-quality tract developments featuring residences constructed from individual plans or from highly modified or upgraded plans. The design features detailed, high-quality exterior ornamentation, high-quality interior refinements, and detail. The workmanship, materials, and finishes throughout the dwelling are generally of high or very high quality.

Q3

Dwellings with this quality rating are residences of higher quality built from individual or readily available designer plans in above-standard residential tract developments or on an individual property owner's site. The design includes significant exterior ornamentation and interiors that are well finished. The workmanship exceeds acceptable standards and many materials and finishes throughout the dwelling have been upgraded from "stock" standards.

Q4

Dwellings with this quality rating meet or exceed the requirements of applicable building codes. Standard or modified standard building plans are utilized and the design includes adequate fenestration and some exterior ornamentation and interior refinements. Materials, workmanship, finish, and equipment are of stock or builder grade and may feature some upgrades.

Q5

Dwellings with this quality rating feature economy of construction and basic functionality as main considerations. Such dwellings feature a plain design using readily available or basic floor plans featuring minimal fenestration and basic finishes with minimal exterior ornamentation and limited interior detail. These dwellings meet minimum building codes and are constructed with inexpensive, stock materials with limited refinements and upgrades.

Q6

Dwellings with this quality rating are of basic quality and lower cost; some may not be suitable for year-round occupancy. Such dwellings are often built with simple plans or without plans, often utilizing the lowest quality building materials. Such dwellings are often built or expanded by persons who are professionally unskilled or possess only minimal construction skills. Electrical, plumbing, and other mechanical systems and equipment may be minimal or non-existent. Older dwellings may feature one or more substandard or non-conforming additions to the original structure.

EXHIBITS

Exhibit 2: Requirements – Definitions of Not Updated, Updated, and Remodeled

Not Updated

Little or no updating or modernization. This description includes, but is not limited to, new homes.

Residential properties of fifteen years of age or less often reflect an original condition with no updating, if no major components have been replaced or updated. Those over fifteen years of age are also considered not updated if the appliances, fixtures, and finishes are predominantly dated. An area that is 'Not Updated' may still be well maintained and fully functional, and this rating does not necessarily imply deferred maintenance or physical/functional deterioration.

Updated

The area of the home has been modified to meet current market expectations. These modifications are limited in terms of both scope and cost.

An updated area of the home should have an improved look and feel, or functional utility. Changes that constitute updates include refurbishment and/or replacing components to meet existing market expectations. Updates do *not* include significant alterations to the existing structure.

Remodeled

Significant finish and/or structural changes have been made that increase utility and appeal through complete replacement and/or expansion.

A remodeled area reflects fundamental changes that include multiple alterations. These alterations may include some or all of the following: replacement of a major component (cabinet(s), bathtub, or bathroom tile), relocation of plumbing/gas fixtures/appliances, significant structural alterations (relocating walls, and/or the addition of square footage). This would include a complete gutting and rebuild.

EXHIBITS

Exhibit 3: Requirements – Abbreviations Used in Data Standardization Text

Abbreviation	Full Name	Appropriate Fields
ac	Acres	Area, Site
AdjPrk	Adjacent to Park	Location
AdjPwr	Adjacent to Power Lines	Location
A	Adverse	Location & View
ArmLth	Arms Length Sale	Sale or Financing Concessions
ba	Bathroom(s)	Basement & Finished Rooms Below Grade
br	Bedroom	Basement & Finished Rooms Below Grade
B	Beneficial	Location & View
Cash	Cash	Sale or Financing Concessions
CtySky	City View Skyline View	View
CtyStr	City Street View	View
Comm	Commercial Influence	Location
c	Contracted Date	Date of Sale/Time
Conv	Conventional	Sale or Financing Concessions
CrtOrd	Court Ordered Sale	Sale or Financing Concessions
DOM	Days On Market	Data Sources
e	Expiration Date	Date of Sale/Time
Estate	Estate Sale	Sale or Financing Concessions
FHA	Federal Housing Authority	Sale or Financing Concessions
GlfCse	Golf Course	Location
Glfvw	Golf Course View	View
Ind	Industrial	Location & View
in	Interior Only Stairs	Basement & Finished Rooms Below Grade
Lndfl	Landfill	Location
LtdSght	Limited Sight	View
Listing	Listing	Sale or Financing Concessions
Mtn	Mountain View	View
N	Neutral	Location & View
NonArm	Non-Arms Length Sale	Sale or Financing Concessions
BsyRd	Busy Road	Location
o	Other	Basement & Finished Rooms Below Grade
Prk	Park View	View
Pstrl	Pastoral View	View
PwrLn	Power Lines	View
PubTrn	Public Transportation	Location
rr	Recreational (Rec) Room	Basement & Finished Rooms Below Grade
Relo	Relocation Sale	Sale or Financing Concessions
REO	REO Sale	Sale or Financing Concessions
Res	Residential	Location & View
RH	USDA – Rural Housing	Sale or Financing Concessions
s	Settlement Date	Date of Sale/Time
Short	Short Sale	Sale or Financing Concessions
sf	Square Feet	Area, Site, Basement
Unk	Unknown	Date of Sale/Time
VA	Veterans Administration	Sale or Financing Concessions
w	Withdrawn Date	Date of Sale/Time
wo	Walk Out Basement	Basement & Finished Rooms Below Grade
wu	Walk Up Basement	Basement & Finished Rooms Below Grade
WtrFr	Water Frontage	Location
Wtr	Water View	View
Woods	Woods View	View

Glossary

A

Actual Age - Chronological age.

Ad Valorem Taxes - Taxation based on property value.

Age-Life Tables - Tables showing estimated economic life for various types of structures.

Allocation Method - An evaluation based on the assumption that a certain percent of the value is attributable to land and the balance to improvements.

Annuity - A series of payments made at regular periods.

Appraisal - An opinion of value.

Appraisal Foundation - Chartered by Congress to develop education and ethical standards for appraisers. It oversees the activities of the ASB, AQB, and APB.

Appraisal Practices Board (APB) - The APB (2010) identifies and issues opinions on recognized valuation methods and techniques for the purpose of voluntary appraisal guidance.

Appraisal Qualifications Board (AQB) - The AQB is concerned with education, testing, and experience requirements for appraiser certification and licensing.

Appraisal Report - The means that appraisers' value conclusions are communicated to the client.

Appraisal Standards Board (ASB) - The ASB promotes acceptance of the USPAP, and updates standards to reflect new developments in appraisal practice. The Appraisal Standards Board is responsible for developing USPAP.

Appurtenance - Something that transfers with real property ownership.

Assessed Value - Value placed by tax assessing official.

Assumptions - Facts an appraiser assumes to be true but has not verified.

B

Band of Investment Method - A method to determine capitalization rate by determining interest rates on liens and desired return for investor's equity.

Baseline - East-West line used to measure property by rectangular survey.

Building Residual - A method of determining building value by determining property value (capitalization method) and then subtracting site value (sales comparison method).

Bundle of Rights - All the beneficial rights of ownership.

C

Cash Flow - Actual cash remaining after deducting cash expenses from cash received.

Certification - A Requirement of the Uniform Standards of Professional Appraisal Practice (USPAP).

Community Property - Property that is jointly owned by husband and wife as defined by law.

Comparables - Property selected because of similarity using the Sales Comparison Approach.

Comparative Unit Method - Cost estimation based on square footage or cubic footage of a structure.

Compatibility - A building in harmony with its use and environment.

Condominium - An apartment-like complex where each unit is separately owned.

Consulting - The process of providing information, analysis of real estate data and recommendations and/ or conclusions.

Cooperative - Ownership by a corporation where owners own a share in the corporation plus a lease from the corporation.

Corner Influence - The effect a corner location has on value.

Cost Approach - The value determination based on cost to build less deprecation, plus value of the land.

Cost - The expenditures to acquire or develop.

Cost-to-Cure Method - Determining the amount of depreciation by the cost to cure the deficiencies.

Cost Trend Indexing - Estimating reproduction cost by applying the construction index to the cost when the structure was built and the current index.

D

De Minimus Value - Minimum value for federally related loans requiring an appraisal.

Depreciation - A loss in value.

Depth Table - An appraisal table showing value of each portion of a property's depth.

Desktop Underwriter's Property Inspection Report - A drive-by inspection (no value estimate).

Desktop Underwriter's Quantitative Appraisal Report - A drive-by appraisal report.

Development Cost - Cost to create a project.

Development Method - A method for land evaluation that deducts cost of improvements (for highest and best use) from total value property would have if developed.

Development State - First stage of real estate cycle.

Direct Costs - Cost of labor and material for an improvement.

Discounting - The process of converting future income into present value.

Disintegration - Final stage of real estate cycle caused by age.

E

Easement in Gross - An easement benefitting a person rather than a property.

Easement - Nonexclusive right to use property of another.

Economic Life - Period a structure is estimated to provide value.

Economic Obsolescence - Depreciation caused by forces exterior to the property.

Effective Age - Functional age based on actual condition.

Effective Demand - Demand coupled with purchasing power.

Effective Gross Income (EGI) - Gross income less a factor for vacancy and collection loss.

Eminent Domain - Government power to take private property for public use upon payment of consideration.

Encumbrance - An interest in real estate that does not include possessory rights.

Energy Efficiency Ratio (EER) - A measure of energy efficiency usually associated with heating and cooling systems.

Escheat - The right of government to title when an owner dies without a will or heirs.

Estate - A possessory right to occupy and use real estate.

Estate in Remainder - The party (other than the grantor) who is to receive the estate upon the termination of a life estate.

Estate in Reversion - The estate of the grantor who receives the life property upon the death of a party designated under a life estate.

Excess Rent - Rent in excess of market rent.

Extraction Method - An evaluation method for land where the value of the improvements is deducted from total value (may also be used for improvement value where land value is known).

Extraordinary Assumption - An assumption, directly related to a specific assignment, which if found to be false, could alter the appraiser's opinions or conclusions.

F

Federal Deposit Insurance Corporation (FDIC) - Federal insurer for banks and savings and loans.

Federal Reserve System - The central banking system for the U.S.

Financial Institutions Reform, Recovery and Enforcement Act (FIRREA) - An act requiring appraisal licensing or certifications for designated federally related lending as well as appraisal standards.

Fixed Expenses - Expenses that do not depend on occupancy and do not vary.

Fixture - A former item of personal property which has become part of the realty.

Footing - Concrete poured on the ground that bears the weight of the structure.

Form Report - A standardized appraisal form used by lenders.

Foundation - Wall (usually concrete) resting on a footing which supports the floor system.

Freehold Estate - An estate that includes title (fee simple and life estates).

Full Bath - Toilet, washbasin and tub.

Functional Obsolescence - Depreciation that was built into a structure by design.

G

Gable Roof - Roof where two sides slope from the ridgeboard to the eaves.

Garn-St. Germain Depository Institutions Act - A 1982 act which removed lending restraints from the savings and loan industry.

General Certification - An appraiser certification for all types of property.

General Data - Data as to real estate values in general.

General Lien - Lien which covers all property of debtor.

Going Concern Value - The value of an ongoing business or project.

Gross Lease - Lease with flat rent payments.

Gross Rent Multiplier (GRM) - An evaluation method whereby the income is multiplied by a factor (based on sales in relationship to gross for other properties).

Ground Lease - Lease where tenant leases land and provides the improvements.

Ground Rent - Rent received under a ground lease.

Ground Rent Capitalization - The rent under a ground lease is capitalized to determine land value.

H

Half-Bath - Toilet and washbasin.

Highest and Best Use - That legal and probable use that results in maximizing the value of the land.

Hip Roof - Roof where sloping surfaces rise from the eaves on all sides.

Hypothetical Condition - That which is contrary to what exists but is supposed for the purpose of analysis.

I

Income Approach - Value determination based on income generated by a property.

Independent Fee Appraiser - An appraiser who is self-employed or an employee of an appraisal firm.

Indirect Costs - Costs other than labor or material such as overhead, financing, design costs, permit fees, etc.

Infrastructure - Public improvements which support a property.

Intended Use - The use or uses of an appraiser's reported appraisal, appraisal review, or appraisal consulting assignment opinions and conclusions, as identified by the appraiser on the basis of communication with the client at the time of the assignment.

Intended User - The client and any other party as identified by name or type, as users of the appraisal, appraisal review, or appraisal consulting report by the appraiser on the basis of communication with the client at the time of the assignment.

Institutional Lender - A depository institution.

Insurable Value - Value an insurance company is willing to reimburse.

Interior Function Zone - Relationship of interior sleeping, living and working areas.

Investment Value - Value to a particular investor having a specific goal.

Involuntary Lien - Liens which arise through operation of law.

J-L

Joint Tenancy - An undivided interest in property with the right of survivorship.

Joists - Horizontal beams supporting floor and ceiling.

Land Residual Method - The land evaluation method which capitalizes the value of the improvements to find the income attributable to the improvements. The remaining income would be attributable to the land.

Land Residual Value - A method of determining land value where the property value is determined and the building value (cost approach is deducted to obtain residual land value).

Legal Description - One accepted by the courts as providing the exact boundaries of a property.

Letter of Transmittal - Cover letter for appraisal report.

Life Estate - An estate that ends upon the death of a designated party.

Limiting Conditions - A statement or explanation which limits the application of an appraisal report.

Liquidation Value - Value based on a sale within a relatively short period of time.

Lot and Block System - Legal method of describing property by recorded subdivision designation.

M

Manufactured Home - A home that is built to the HUD Code.

Market Rent - Rent that market conditions would allow.

Market Value - The probable price a willing, informed buyer will pay to a willing, informed seller given a reasonable marketing time.

Maturity - Equilibrium stage of real estate cycle.

Mean - An arithmetic average.

Median - The middle value in a sample of values.

Meridian - North-South line used to measure property by rectangular survey.

Metes and Bounds - A legal description identifying property by its boundaries using distances and directions from boundary points.

Mode - The most frequently occurring value in a sample of values.

Modular Home - A factory-built home which is manufactured to meet local building codes.

Monument - A point on a metes and bounds description from which distances and angles are measured. Can be man-made (cement marker) or natural (rocks or trees).

N

Narrative Report - The most detailed appraisal report.

Net Lease - Lease where tenant pays taxes, insurance and maintenance. Landlord receives a net amount.

Net Operating Income - Gross income less expenses (depreciation, principal and interest payments are not deducted).

Non-Conforming Use - A use in violation of current codes.

Non-Freehold Estate - A leasehold.

Noninstitutional Lender - A lender that is not a depository institution.

Non-Possessory Interests - Encumbrances.

O-P

Observed Condition Method - Appraiser estimates the amount of each type of deprecation separately.

Operating Expense Ratio Method - Estimating operating expenses are determined as a percentage of effective gross income for similar properties and applied to subject property.

Oral Report - A verbal appraisal report.

Orderly Process - A logical series of steps that are taken in order to insure a reliable result.

Paired Data Analysis - Using comparables to determine the effect on value of a single element.

Partition Action - A court order to break up joint ownership.

Periodic Tenancy - A leasehold tenancy that renews itself automatically in the absence of notice to terminate.

Physical Deterioration - Loss in value because of wear and tear factors dealing with age.

Plottage - An increase in value resulting from combining several contiguous properties for a single use.

Point Estimate - Appraisal value as a set dollar amount.

Point of Beginning - The starting point for a metes and bounds description.

Point of Diminishing Return - At some point, benefits from increased production will start to decline.

Police Power - Right to regulate for protection of health, safety, morals and public welfare.

Possessory Interests - An estate in real property.

Potential Gross Income - Income based on 100 percent occupancy.

Prefabricated Home - Home that is site assembled of factory built components.

Price - The amount actually paid.

Principle of Anticipation - Value is affected by perceived future benefits.

Principle of Balance - The benefits are maximized when the elements of production are in balance.

Principle of Change - Values are not constant because supply and demand are in constant flux.

Principle of Competition - When extraordinary profits are made, competition will enter the marketplace and profits will be reduced.

Principle of Conformity - Values are enhanced when surrounding properties conform in use to subject property.

Principle of Consistent Use - Both the land and improvements must be valued based on the same use.

Principle of Contribution - The value of an improvement is equal to the increase of value added to the property.

Principle of Substitution - A person will not pay more for a property than the cost of another property having equal function and desirability.

Principle of Surplus Productivity - The cost that exceeds the cost of labor, capital and management (coordination) is attributable to the land.

Profit a Prendre - Right to take something from property (crops, timber, minerals, etc.).

Planned Unit Development (PUD) - A development where lots are owned by unit owners but there are areas in common ownership.

Purpose of Appraisal - See Standard of Value.

Q-R

Quantity Survey Method - A detailed cost estimation based on the cost of every element in the construction.

R-Value - A measurement of insulation.

Rafters - Diagonal boards supporting the roof.

Range - The spread between the lowest and highest numbers in a sample of values.

Ranges - Vertical rows of townships.

Range Value - A value expressed by an appraiser as a price range that a sale is likely to fall within.

Rate of Return - The percentage return on capital.

Recapture - Return of investment through depreciation.

Reconciliation - Value ascertained by evaluating values obtained by various methods.

Rectangular Survey - Government survey system of describing property.

Reference Point - A monument on a metes and bounds description.

Relative Comparison Analysis - Comparison based on quality difference rather than dollars.

Replacement Cost - The cost to build a building having the same utility and desirability.

Reproduction Cost - Cost to build a replica of a structure.

Reserves for Replacement - Funds set aside to replace a short-lived component of a property.

Residential Certification - An appraiser certification for residential property only.

Restricted Appraisal Report - A report that restricts the use and reliance of the report.

Review - The process of critically studying a report prepared by another.

S

Sales Comparison Approach - Value determination based on sales of similar properties.

Scheduled Rent - Rent based on existing leases.

Secondary Mortgage Market - Market where existing loans are sold.

Section - A one mile square parcel of land created by government survey.

Self-Contained Report - Appraisal report which contains all material necessary to fulfill the requirements of the Uniform Standards of Professional Appraisal Practice for an appraisal report.

Siting - The placement of a structure on the lot.

Slab - Concrete floor poured directly on the ground.

Special Assessments - Taxes levied for improvements that benefit a property.

Specific Data - Data pertaining to a particular property.

Specific Lien - Lien that applies only to designated property.

Square Footage - A measurement of area based on exterior dimensions of a structure excluding garage.

Staff Appraisers - Appraisers employed by a business or agency on a salaried basis.

Standard Deviation - A mathematical formula that measures how far prices vary from the mean.

Standard of Value - The type of value that the client is seeking (i.e. market value, investment value, etc.)

Straight-Line Depreciation - Depreciating the same amount from value each year over the economic life of a structure.

Studs - Vertical framing boards in a wall.

Subdivision - A division of a parcel into separate smaller parcels.

Summary Appraisal Report - A report which differs from the self-contained report in that the explanations are deleted.

Supply and Demand - An economic valuation principle that states market value is determined by the interrelationship of these two factors in the appropriate market as of the date of the appraisal.

T

Tenancy For Years - A leasehold that has a definite termination date.

Tenancy In Common - An undivided right in property without the right of survivorship.

Three-Quarter Bath - Toilet, washbasin and shower unit.

Time Share - A fractionalized ownership of a unit where owner has exclusive occupancy for a designated time period.

Township - A 6 x 6 mile area created by government survey.

Township Tiers - Horizontal rows of townships.

Trade Fixture - A fixture installed by a business or trade that remains personal property.

U-V

Uniform Residential Appraisal Report (URAR) - Appraisal form required by Fannie Mae and Freddie Mac.

Uniform Standards of Professional Appraisal Practice (USPAP) - Ethical and performance standards developed by the Appraisal Standards Board and promulgated by the Appraisal Foundation.

Unit-In-Place Method - Quantities of building components are measured and priced based on cost manuals to determine replacement cost.

Value in Use - Value based on a particular use.

Value - The present worth of future benefits; the worth of an item expressed in monetary terms.

Variable Expenses - Expenses which vary with occupancy.

Voluntary Lien - Lien created voluntarily by debtor.

Index

Index

G

Gable Roof: 239
Garn-St. Germain Depository Institutions Act: 7
General Certification: 452
General Data: 93, 145
General Lien: 18
General Partnership: 426
Geodetic Survey System: 119
Going Concern Value: 56
Government National Mortgage Association (GNMA): 482
Government Restrictions of Property Rights: 20
  Eminent Domain: 20
  Escheat: 21
  Police Power: 21
  Special Assessments: 21
  Taxation: 21
Green Machines: 248
Gross Adjustment: 319
Gross Income Multipliers (GIM): 345
Gross Lease: 429
Gross Rent Multiplier: 99
Ground Lease: 204, 438
  Ground Rent: 204
Ground Rent Capitalization Method: 204
Guide Meridian: 118

H

Half Bath: 233
Header: 238
Heating and Air Conditioning: 248
  Energy Efficiency Ratio (EER): 249
Highest and Best Use: 96, 161, 163, 183, 189, 196, 307
  Four Characteristics of Highest and Best Use: 186
    Economically Feasible Use: 186
    Legally Permitted Use: 185
    Maximally Productive Use: 187
    Physically Possible Use: 186
  Interim Uses: 188
  Principle of Anticipation: 187
  Purpose of Highest and Best Use Analysis: 184
  Vacant and Improved Land: 188
Highest and Best Use Analysis: 96
Highest and Best Use Principle: 47
Hip Roof: 239
Horizontal Subdivision: 419
Hoskold Method: 135
Houses, Classification of: 215
  Apartment Building: 215
  Attached House: 215
  Detached House: 215

  Number of Units: 215
  Party Wall Agreement: 215
  Row House: 215
  Single-Family Residence: 215
Houses, Types of: 215
  Bi-Level House: 218
  One-Story House: 217
  One and One-Half Story House: 217
  Split-Level House: 218
  Two-Story House: 218
House Design, Elements of: 222
  Interior Functional Zone: 223
  Room Characteristics: 225
    Bathrooms: 227
    Bedrooms: 227
    Dining Rooms: 227
    Family Rooms: 226
    Kitchens: 225
    Laundry/Utility Rooms: 226
    Living Rooms: 226
  Siting: 222
Housing Finance Board (HFB): 484
Hypothetical Condition: 80

I

IFA: 447
Improvement: 12
Income: 335
Income Approach: 98, 331, 403
  Discounting: 347
  Gross Rent Multiplier: 99
  Income Approach Section of the URAR: 403
  Income Capitalization: 334
    Calculating Value by Direct Capitalization: 344
      Gross Income Multipliers (GIM): 345
      Residual Techniques: 345
    Direct Capitalization: 335
    Income Estimation: 336
      Effective Gross Income (EGI): 337
      Net Operating Income (NOI): 338
      Potential Gross Income (PGI): 336
      Pre-Tax Cash Flow: 339
      Reconstructed Operating Statement: 339
    Market Capitalization: 335
    Multipliers and Capitalization Rates: 340
      Band of Investment Method: 342
      Comparable Sales Method: 340
      Debt Coverage Method: 344
      Operating Expense Ratio Method: 341
    Yield Capitalization: 347
  Interest: 332

Full Definitions from USPAP

From: *Uniform Standards of Professional Appraisal Practice, 2012-2013 Edition*
   www.uspap.org
   Appraisal Standars Board, The Appraisal Foundation

Page 3

APPRAISAL: (noun) the act or process of developing an opinion of value; an opinion of value. (adjective) of or pretaining to appraising and related functions such as appraisal practice or appraisal services.

> **Comment:** An appraisal must be numerically expressed as a specific amount, as a range of numbers, or as a relationship (e.g., not more than, not less than) to a previous value opinion or numerical benchmark (e.g., assessed value, collateral value).

Page 4

VALUE: the monetary relationship between properties and those who buy, sell, or use those properties.

> **Comment:** *Value* expresses an economic concept. As such, it is never a fact but always an opinion of the worth of a property at a given time in accordance with a specific definition of value. In appraisal practice, value must always be qualified — for example, market value, liquidation value, or investment value.

Page 5

APPRAISAL PRACTICE: valuation services performed by an individual acting as an appraiser, including but not limited to appraisal, appraisal review, or appraisal consulting.

> **Comment:** *Appraisal practice* is provided only by appraisers, while *valuation services* are provided by a variety of professionals and others. The terms *appraisal*, *appraisal review*, and *appraisal consulting* are intentionally generic and are not mutually exclusive. For example, an opinion of value may be required as part of an appraisal review and is required as a component of the analysis in an appraisal consulting assignment. The use of other nomenclature for an appraisal, appraisal review, or appraisal consulting assignment (e.g., analysis, counseling, evaluation, study, submission, or valuation) does not exempt an appraiser from adherence to the *Uniform Standards of Appraisal Practice*. ▼

APPRAISAL CONSULTING: the act or process of developing an analysis, recommendation, or opinion to solve a problem, where an opinion of value is a component of the analysis leading to the assignment results.

Comment: An appraisal consulting assignment involves an opinion of value but does not have an appraisal or an appraisal review as its primary purpose.

Page 6

APPRAISAL REVIEW: the act or process of developing and communicating an opinion about the quality of another appraiser's work that was performed as part of an appraisal, appraisal review, or appraisal consulting assignment.

Comment: The subject of an appraisal review assignment may be all or part of a report, workfile, or a combination of these.

Textbooks From
Educational Textbook Company

etctextbooks.com

*Sometimes our textbooks
are hard to find!*

*If your bookstore does not carry our
textbooks, please send us a check or
money order and we'll mail them to you
with our 30-day money back guarantee.*

Other Great Books from Educational Textbook Company:*

California Real Estate Principles, 13th ed., by Huber.	$100.00 ____
California Real Estate Practice, 6th ed., by Huber & Lyons.	$100.00 ____
How To Pass The Real Estate Exam, 7th ed. - e-book (850 Exam Questions), by Huber. . .	$99.00 ____
California Real Estate Law, 7th ed., by Huber & Tyler.	$100.00 ____
Real Estate Finance, 7th ed., by Huber & Messick.	$100.00 ____
Real Estate Finance: Appraiser's Edition, 6th ed., by Huber & Messick.	$100.00 ____
Real Estate Economics, 5th ed., by Huber, Messick, & Pivar.	$100.00 ____
Real Estate Appraisal – Principles and Procedures, 4th ed., by Huber, Messick, & Pivar. .	$100.00 ____
Residential Real Estate Appraisal, by Huber & Messick.	$100.00 ____
Mortgage Loan Brokering, 5th ed., by Huber, Pivar, Zozula.	$100.00 ____
Property Management, 5th ed., by Huber, Lyons, & Pivar.	$100.00 ____
Escrow I: An Introduction, 3rd ed., by Huber & Newton.	$100.00 ____
Real Estate Computer Applications, by Grogan & Huber.	$100.00 ____
Homeowner's Association Management, by Huber & Tyler.	$100.00 ____
California Business Law, 3rd ed., by Huber, McGrath, & Tyler	$100.00 ____
Hubie's Power Prep 700 CD – 700 Questions, by Huber.	$100.00 ____

---

* PRICES EXPIRE 1/1/2013

Subtotal _____

Add shipping and handling @ $10.00 per book _____

Add California sales tax @ 9.75% _____

TOTAL _____

Allow 2-3 weeks for delivery

Name: _____

Address: _____

City, State, Zip: _____

Phone: _____

Check or money order: Educational Textbook Company, P.O. Box 3597, Covina, CA 91722